# 2Stoned

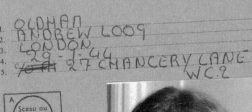

1. OLDHAM
2. ANDREW LOOG
3. LONDON
4. 29-1-44
5. 27 CHANCERY LANE WC.2

A Sceau ou cachet de l'autorité
B Sceau ou cachet de l'autorité
C Sceau ou cachet de l'autorité

UNITED KINGDOM OF GREAT BRITAIN
AND NORTHERN IRELAND

INTERNATIONAL MOTOR TRAFFIC

INTERNATIONAL DRIVING PERMIT

Convention on Road Traffic of 19 September 1949

Issued at LONDON

VALID FOR ONE YEAR FROM

Date.................

ROYAL
AUTOMOBILE
CLUB
13 MAY 1974
91-4-0365
PALL MALL

SECRETARY OF STATE FOR THE ENVIRONMENT

THE ROYAL AUTOMOBILE CLUB

† Signature or Seal of the
Association empowered
by the Authority.

N. Miller Bardwin

SECRETARY GENERAL

# 2Stoned

*Written and Produced by*
Andrew Loog Oldham

Interviews and Research by Simon Spence

Edited by Christine Ohlman

Secker & Warburg
LONDON

Published by Secker & Warburg 2002

2 4 6 8 10 9 7 5 3 1

First published in Great Britain in 2002 by
Secker & Warburg
Random House, 20 Vauxhall Bridge Road,
London SW1V 2SA

Random House Australia (Pty) Limited
20 Alfred Street, Milsons Point, Sydney,
New South Wales 2061, Australia

Random House New Zealand Limited
18 Poland Road, Glenfield
Auckland 10, New Zealand

Random House (Pty) Limited
Endulini, 5a Jubilee Road, Parktown 2193, South Africa

The Random House Group Limited Reg. No. 954009
www.randomhouse.co.uk

A CIP catalogue record for this book is available
from the British Library

ISBN 0 436 28015 9

Papers used by The Random House Group are natural, recyclable products made
from wood grown in sustainable forests; the manufacturing processes conform to the
environmental regulations of the country of origin

Typeset by SX Composing DTP, Rayleigh, Essex
Printed and bound in Great Britain by
Biddles Ltd, Guildford & Kings Lynn

For the hope, dignity and example . . .

Celia Oldham Ferluga
11 February 1920 – 28 January 2002

Ruby Oldham
Sometime in 1989 – 15 February 2002

**Roberta Goldstein**, friend and muse: There's a whole generation out there that doesn't go a day in their life without the Rolling Stones in it. When the Stones came here for that first tour they were poor, they were brilliant. We had a lot of parties – we *were* a party. One of the best took place the night the lights went out in New York. That was in 65. The Stones were in a hotel on the West Side. Brian was there playing his harp when the lights went out.

You could see America through their eyes. The Stones loved the attitude and energy of New York; we'd walk it and we'd talk it. Andrew loved New York, too. It was a movie come true for him – the Brill Building and 1650 Broadway, running around from office to office listening to that Jewish rock 'n' roll coming out of New York. It all had that sweet sound, the Carole King sound, the music of Bob Crewe. It wasn't 'I see a red door and I want it painted black.' It was more up; it was pop.

**Al Kooper**, musician/writer/producer: I was weaned at 1650 Broadway in NYC from 1958 to 1965. I started in the offices of Leo Rogers, an underhanded personal manager with a great deal of charisma. 1650 was the 'real' Brill Building. 1619 Broadway was the 'actual' Brill Building, but two hundred times more action and success took place in 1650. The 'actual' Brill Building was the last bastion of Tin Pan Alley and was widely regarded as an old man's building. Other than Leiber, Stoller, Bacharach, Barry and Greenwich, everything else took place at 1650 Broadway. The problem was 1650 was just 1650; it had no title to hang any memorabilia on. So the Brill Building gets all the credit, but that's completely false. In the offices of 1650: Paul Simon, Tony Orlando, Carole King, Gerry Goffin, Barry Mann, Cynthia Weil, Neil Sedaka, Lenny Bruce, Dionne Warwick, the Shirelles, Chuck Jackson, Aldon Music, Roosevelt Music, Allegro Recording Studios, Artie Ripp, Bobby Lewis, the Jive Five, the Cadillacs, the Isley Brothers, Aaron Schroeder, Gene Pitney, Luther Dixon, the Strangeloves, Bob Gaudio, End Records, Gone Records, Bell Records, Amy-Mala Records, Scepter

Records, BelTone Records, Dimension Records, and yours truly. The education I received in that building for seven years far outweighs any university matriculation. The adjoining coffee shop, B/G, had the greatest pancakes in the United States. I commuted from Queens. Also from my neighbourhood were the Temptations (the white version, with Artie Ripp) and Paul Simon and Artie Garfunkel. Nearby neighbours were bassist Harvey Brooks and pianist Paul Harris.

Dylan and the Beatles began the destruction of 1650. The new hip area became Greenwich Village in downtown Manhattan. But from 1958 to 1965, all the great music that came out of New York City was primarily conceived at 1650 Broadway.

**Roberta Goldstein**: It was magic as soon as the Stones opened their mouths. We'd never heard anything like that accent. When they were singing you couldn't really tell what country they were from. When they started giving interviews, they had such incredible style. Mick was very bright, as was Charlie. The rest were very quiet. Keith was very shy; I loved Keith for his shyness.

They'd saved a lot of money to get over to the States and every day and every minute counted. Then there was Alan Stroh, what a darling. He worked with Bob Crewe, came from a very rich family in the meat business, and lived for show business. Alan was the manager of Mitch Ryder – this was during the period when Mitch and Bob were having all those hits. Everybody was broke, running hard, living well and helping each other out. I went out with Alan and Bob every night. Andy Warhol would be drooling in the corner – oh, anything to get to our table.

The English were just blowing me away, me and a billion others. We'd first met them all on that first Stones tour of America. Then I went to London. On the first day I arrived, Andrew had just bought this brand new Rolls-Royce. We went to the Scotch of St James and Paul McCartney was there. We all went to Andrew's house afterwards. I'd brought over Beach Boys records and we sat around listening to the Beach Boys. We were so young and innocent and everybody thought we were wild.

Andrew was like a little giant, but he had so many people pulling on him. When you manage a group it's like having five kids – one wants vanilla, one wants raspberry, one wants chocolate. This is when the 60s began for me. There was just so much talent and fun around, just so many people doing great things, like Dion, another genius who never got his due. On that first tour I saw the Stones do some TV show in an NY studio, something like

2

*Saturday Night Dance Fever* or *Clay Cole*. There were like four hundred screaming little women. Mick would be sitting on the side of the stage looking like he was going to sleep, so relaxed. But as soon as it was time to go to work, that man started to move. He gave himself a hell of a workout; he was working out before people knew what a workout was.

At this point they weren't into hard drugs at all. I'm talking marijuana here and a few pills there. One time the Stones were on a concert out of town and Keith's girlfriend Linda Keith and I took an acid trip. The group flew back every night to New York, so they were out in North Carolina on that particular day. I don't know where Andrew was. He only liked to go to towns that had Bonwit Teller stores; Macy's didn't cut it for him. Anyway, Linda says, 'I don't want Keith to know that I took a trip.' So Keith gets back late to the hotel in Manhattan and he's like pumped from working and flying and he sees us staring at the walls. He goes, 'What did you girls do tonight?' 'Wow!' we said, 'we smoked this really strong thing.' We did have some, actually – it was strong pot. We gave it to him, and the poor guy threw up.

They used to play cards on the flight, and Keith would complain that he was always losing. So we gave him a bi-phetamine and the next night Keith went out again on another gig. He got back and said he'd won $300, so he was very happy.

The Stones were really fresh and innocent and hoping to make it big. Then everything came at once; it was like a snowball that just became an avalanche, with the clothes and the talking and the movies – all at the same time James Bond came out. Everything just mushroomed. It was like Englandmania. The English won that war; even crappy acts became successful.

Bob Crewe lived wonderfully at the Dakota; it was fantasyland. That's where I met Andrew. Bob threw a beautiful party for the Stones, very posh, catered by one of the finest people in the city and then, of course, Mick sat on a table and broke everything . . . class act. Andrew enjoyed it because he got to meet all the moguls and mogulettes. Ahmet Ertegun was there, and Harry Cohn, whose father started Columbia Pictures. That impressed Andrew. Liza Minnelli was there. That was a damn good party.

Bob's home was a gathering place. I met Lionel Bart there, Brian Epstein, Leonard Bernstein (who also lived in the Dakota). Bob's was one of the most fabulous apartments you'd ever lay eyes on. And it wasn't even his best apartment, just his Dakota pad. The really good apartment was on the East Side on Fifth Avenue. I called it Glitter House. You could fall asleep and hear the animals in the Central Park Zoo; it was three storeys of heaven.

Set designer Sean Kenny would be there with Lionel or Andrew; he did a lot of work with Anthony Newley as well. He invited us to a preview of *Stop The World (I Want To Get Off)*. It was just incredible. We didn't have to go to London for the swingin' 60s – it came to us. It was like the Beatles and . . . *voilà!* Suddenly the 60s had moved to New York. You gotta understand that at this point very few people knew what the hell they were doing.

**ALO:** Young men grow, innocence goes, and the kids, albeit all right, start to become street fighting men. We had this almost molecular affinity with America. Its music fed the soul of the Stones – it *was* the soul. American music was life-giving plasma; it was our future, the great escape as we flamed into being with fashion and rhythm. It was the explanation, the clue, the glue and the door to the room at the top to which absolute beginners and definite winners found the key.

When one is young, summer records define your life. Later they explain it. In June of 1964 the US charts were topped by the Dixie Cups' rendition of the Phil Spector, Jeff Barry and Ellie Greenwich ditty 'Chapel Of Love' on the Red Bird label. The Beach Boys' 'I Get Around' and the Four Seasons' 'Rag Doll' completed this trio of great Popness while Herman's Hermits, Gerry & the Pacemakers, Peter and Gordon, Billy J. Kramer and the Dave Clark Five nipped at their heels with the best and worst of the British Invasion. Even the Bachelors got to no. 12. Throughout this magical spring and summer, the Beatles always had some half a dozen singles in the US Top 20.

The Rolling Stones were running late. In Britain we were running within our breath; in America we would soon be running ahead and out of it. One single, 'I Wanna Be Your Man', had been released and withdrawn. The side had then been coupled with 'Not Fade Away' and rereleased, and apart from a few idyllic plays in the Midwest, would do just that. The Stones' first LP outing, dressed and sold to no. 1 in the UK – via its urgent accuracy and my immaculate no-name imagery – had been repackaged behind my back by London Records and given a title, *England's Newest Hitmakers*, putting the event lower on the graphics pole than a Freddie & the Dreamers cover. We were pissed off.

In Rockin' Britain (and somewhat in Europe) the Stones already had a track record from their two Top 10 singles, a Top 10 EP and a no. 1 album – plus an avalanche of good cop/bad cop press, adulation and scorn (the good cops being the Mop Tops). I screamed inches of ink while my erstwhile partner from the vaudeville machine, Eric Easton, booked the hoopla. The

4

hoopla, the Rolling Stones, played and delivered. Game, set, match. Now Eric handed over the North American booking to a crew named GAC, who could have been CIA if appearances and attitude were anything to go on. These ten per centers lived in a conservative Barnum-less world of staggered vents, brogued battleship shoes, broadcloth button-down shirts and Washington power haircuts and were more at home with Jackie Mason than Nanker Phelge. To get as many newspaper inches for the Stones in the States as I'd been able to get at home, they'd have had to heist an atomic bomb.

America! Where presidents were knocked off, the widow in the pink pillbox hat and bloodstained Chanel mini passed as royalty, and the British Invasion was looked upon with the same disdain as the Twist, hula hoops and surfin'. I suspected my British box of tricks was not going to work here. We desperately needed a vocal following, and to get that we needed real plastic bullets, real hits, and lotsa, lotsa radio play.

On 1 June 1964 at New York's formerly-Idlewild-recently-renamed-Kennedy Airport, the Stones were welcomed by a few hundred girls that London Records had managed to round up. If the Beatles' landing four months earlier had been directed by Cecil B. DeMille, our arrival was helmed by Mel Brooks. All those Yank cars that had seemed so exotic and out of reach back in Blighty were a dime a dozen in the States. In the drizzle of the Manhattan drabness, they looked strangely cumbersome and lacklustre. Once we left the airport we were invisible; not a soul knew who we were. The movie was out of sync with life as I'd known it, jump-cutting between black and white and colour. The voices didn't match the picture. Putting reality together with the movie was a strain, and, as for the soundtrack, it had become a hollow-reverbed nightmare – the audio was wrong, all wrong. I don't recall being excited; all I remember is being scared.

The Stones stayed at the Astor Hotel on Times Square. I saved some money and went looking to get myself recharged and to cadge a sleep on Phil Spector's ground-floor office couch on the East River somewhere in the sixties. Phil's office was a dull, couched and plywooded affair – his taste was reserved for vinyl. I was not invited upstairs to the penthouse residence, where, I believe, a marriage was on the rocks.

The Stones were a small cult, a collector's item, i.e. we didn't mean shit. They did *The Les Crane Show*, hosted by some stagger-brained, lacquered pimp with a smile and demeanour so cut out and fake we felt like we'd stopped off on the wrong set and were in *Hogan's Heroes* meets *The Twilight Zone*. God, suddenly old Auntie Beeb seemed great and far-seeing in comparison and we missed her so! It's okay to have your home kind question

5

and ridicule you, but I took this vulturistic gnawing and nit-picking at the Stones' very soul as a personal violation of all that was dear to me. Brian Jones looked like he'd been turned inside out, his heart and soul flayed and scalped before his very own eyes. He hurt and we hurt for him, though nowt was said except a curse on those stillborn Yanks. If we'd anything to declare at Ellis Island, perhaps it was that our skins were not as thick as we'd thought (the Stones' collective leathery eye had not yet formed).

But that was all about to change and did, with Charlie in the lead, as we were stalked up Seventh Avenue by some creature from the Manhattan radio lagoon named Clay Cole. Cole looked like an electro-shock Anthony Perkins on steroids. His questions never got past 'Why did you grow your hair?' What a dolt! Didn't he know this kind of banter was reserved for the Mop Tops and Herman's Hermits? The movie snapped back into focus when the dapper Watts told this inane prick to fuck off. He did, and we moved on up to 57th suddenly feeling whole again. You might say we were spoilt brats who didn't much care for this new bashing we were getting abroad. It was the old Christians and lions game. It was the original *Planet of the Apes,* and I was feeling more like Roddy McDowell than Mr NRA.

From the papier-mâché *The Day of the Locust* New York reception we winged to Los Angeles, hovered over it, and arrived as LA's surviving movieola barracudas were shit-deep in make-up and cliché. Just another day in the celluloid killing fields. Yes, I was pissed off. The plane had bad lighting, most of the colours and fabric were tired and inspired by vomit, façade and disease, and the stewardesses looked best in long shots, evoking Sandra Dee and all of Alfred Hitchcock's best blonde apparitions.

The image on the West Coast screen momentarily moved from B-movie to VistaVision as Phil Spector's right-hand promo man Sonny Bono greeted us at the airport with an open heart and hand to La-La Land. There was hope yet. Thirtysomething Salvatore Bono looked as whacked as the Stones – and he worked for a living! Bono was all Sicilian LA heart. Clad in barber-pole striped trousers, an Italian sweater of the sort thus far only dared by Carnaby poofters, sole- and heelless calf-length Indian moccasins, and paisley neckscarf, he was a sight to see. In his car boot were boxes of Caesar and Cleo 45s because, in those pre-'I Got You, Babe' days, he was part of a duo called Caesar and Cleopatra with his then-girlfriend, Cher.

The next day the movie went back to black and white as we started rehearsals for *The Dean Martin Hollywood Palace Show* – the first surprise being that there was no Dean to be seen. Two days of rehearsals with a Dean stand-in followed. Meanwhile, Deano was out on the links, touching up his tan. He turned up for the filming, immaculate and decadent (which equalled rich), and proceeded to insult the Stones as his way of getting in and out of a commercial break and into the bowels of America's suburban heartland. The insults one could handle, and the goodfella laconicism — just. It was not having thought of a stand-in for Mick that hurt to the management core.

**James Phelge**, *Phelge's Stones*: Not much news was getting back to the office regarding the Stones' progress on the tour. I rang Keith and spoke to him at one of the hotels where they were staying. He was generally 'knocked out' with America, saying they might be going to the Chess studios and that

The Rolling Stones and ALO, Hollywood 1964

the tour was going great. We only spoke briefly as he was busy with a press conference and I was running out of change for the pay phone, so I didn't find out much more. I had to wait until they arrived back in England, when we met up again at the office for a full debriefing. The boys had spent a small fortune on clothes while they were away and were determined to show them off back home. Most of the clothing was lightweight American summer wear and Charlie looked particularly cool in a finely striped blue and white jacket that Andy Wickham, Andrew's PR guy, described as 'surf wear'. Some of it certainly looked as if it belonged on a beach.

I asked Keith about the television show when the band had met Dean Martin. Keith turned up his nose, describing Martin as a 'right fuckin' offer'. Apparently he had given the band a hard time, making them the butt of sarcastic jokes at every opportunity. Mick had tried to be sarcastic in return by saying it was 'so nice to have Mr Martin on our show', but that sounded somewhat tame, if not childish.

**ALO**: Apart from the Dean Martin experience everybody enjoyed Los Angeles. You could see a lot more of the girls in such a climate and, LA being LA, the Summer of Love was already here. Most of the girls didn't need to undress; they already had. We got good news from England – the album was still no. 1. On the 5th the Stones played their first US concert at the Swing Auditorium in San Bernadino. A lot of enthusiastic fans showed and placed (even if the promoter didn't). The Stones felt better for it; they were back doing what they did best.

Sonny Bono took us for a ride to the RCA studios on Sunset. That afternoon I met three important elements in the Stones recording future: Jack Nitzsche, Dave Hassinger and the RCA studio itself. Thank you, Sonny, for being an angel in your own time and helping us find our breath.

We next flew south-west to San Antonio, Texas on propellers. Here in God's country our East Coast education in buttoning our lips served us well. In San Antonio we weren't just freaks, we were rodents. The Stones were to play two days at a State Fair. Wood-panelled station wagons manned by off-duty good ol' boys greeted us with surly what-the-heel-kinda-freaks-we-got-here? disdain. Some mellowed out when they realised we weren't 'contagious or queer', but we didn't when we realised that we were due to play directly after a *grand mer* troop of performing seals. The menfolk chewed gum, cud or baccy. While scuffing their heels in the sand, they eyed us like bulls in heat at the idea of some pansy-quiffed matador for dinner. The more enthusiastic girls, well . . . Whereas in LA, girls just wanted to touch and be touched, down near the border they were a little more hands-on. They wanted to poke, squeal, and see if we were real.

The mood was tense. This was not turning out to be the America of anybody's dreams. For once the Stones and I didn't have much to say to each other. Something was awry and it wasn't us. We had a crisis on our hands and I needed a serious diversion – quickly – that would save the moment and allow the band to get their druthers. We weren't scoring except for the sex, which wasn't going to put us high on the charts, either, except in a doctor's office on a 'my dick stings when I piss, doctor, and I'm due home in a week' basis.

How to keep the dream alive? Keep it moving!

While the Stones Barnum 'n' Bailey'd and freaked 'n' geeked at the State Fair, I worked the phone in the downtown two-storey San Antonio motel. The bookings were lacklustre, with far too many days off for a three-week tour. New York and Detroit were somewhat promising, but the idea of Minneapolis, Omaha and Harrisburg without a hit record did not bode well. We'd left our status behind in our faraway homeland. After one year of solid slogging through and finding our recording legs and then beating down the Beatles' braveheart wall by winning fans north of St Albans via performance, we'd jumped on to our first 505 transatlantic flight and kaleidoscoped into this crazy, half-baked, mid-60s, partially Beatle-ised USA playland without the benefit of even Tom Wolfe. We'd made it through two dislocated American wonderlands – the Brill-funky-Broadway of New York and the surreal beach-party mind-bend of LA – and now we'd been unceremoniously plunked down into this sawdust fiasco in San Antonio. In a normal life, one should have enjoyed the rest, the dust, the breeze and the change, and given thanks for the opportunity to break bread and visit a piece of America in all its very own life-affirming, cattle-prodding, queer-baiting glory.

But I was up for, and we had time for, no such thing. Brian made some effort to be at one with the locals, but with him it was hard to tell what was real and what was an ongoing, insatiable cry for attention. Bill and Charlie put bullets in their respective guns, with Bill firing blanks at every Miss Motel America in sight and Charlie trying out some genuine six-shooters on the outskirts of town. Keith, I hoped, was writing about it, while Mick rested his self in the arms of Texas, writing about *that* (I also hoped). I starred in my own version of *The Parallax View*, gnawing my quicks nigh to the bone, wondering how to stop this reel from slipping the spool as I turned for assist to my old pal, the phone.

So I called Phil Spector and asked him to get us booked just as soon as was possible into Chess studios. Phil called back and said he'd set up two days of recording time, two days hence. So I was all beam and sheen when our driver, a *Cool Hand Luke* type, stationwagoned me out to the State Fair grounds for the last day of the Stones troll. I wondered if somewhere behind the glare of his prison-guard reflectors he'd heard of the late Lt. Andrew Loog. If I told him that my father was from Texas, would that change anything? I doubted it. I bit my tongue, now as sore as my nails, and resisted. There wasn't any point in engaging in small talk or trying to explain what we were doing there.

To them we were stone freaks – or worse – but compared with what was to come in the Brit export line, we were more akin to Herman's Hermits. If they wanted to see themselves reflected in a distorted mirror they'd have to wait for the Sex Pistols, who would launch themselves at Randy's Road House down the road some thirteen unlucky years later.

As I wondered whether I'd dressed down enough for the locale, I pondered why Texans seemed to dress only in denim and beige. Was it so they'd match up with the upholstery, with earth, ergot, barley and sage? And why was it that these beer-pawed Texans always drove one-handed, leaving their right arm curled around the passenger seat as if it were their goddamn God-given right to have someone curled up next to them? I felt too thin, wimpy and wiry to have my potential Texan fatherhood taken seriously by these big bad johns. After the long dust-filled ride over I happily greeted the lads. We now had something really exciting to talk about – the mythical Chess studios.

All of them saw me beaming and knew something was up. 'Pack your bags,' I said. 'There's a change in the itinerary; we're going to Chicago to record.' From their all-at-once heartfelt smiles of wonder I knew that it was still worth playing God.

**James Phelge**, *Phelge's Stones*: If the Martin show had been the low point, it would soon be overshadowed by the trip to Chicago and Chess recording studios. Brian would be incredulous at the fact that he'd discovered one of his musical heroes at the studio painting the ceiling. Muddy Waters was up a ladder when they arrived and had climbed down to welcome the Stones and help carry their guitars into the building. Keith revealed that some of the 'live' recordings issued by Chess were not recorded that way at all. In the Chess archives were reels of tapes with nothing but audience noise recorded upon them. Chess used these to dub the 'live' effect on to whatever tracks they chose. When I asked Keith what the likelihood was of getting the same taped audience on two different records he replied, 'Not much chance. They've got fuckin' miles of it.'

**ALO**: Playing God was just my sideline, actually. Getting records cut and thy hustle done was my principal business. Chicago was a piece of heaven on earth for the Stones, for the earth was scorched on most of our mid-American concert stopovers. We hadn't set any records; we didn't have the goods. 2120 South Michigan Avenue housed Chess Records and Studios and in two days the group put down some thirteen tracks – their most relaxed and inspired session to date – moved, no doubt, by our newfound ability to sell coals to Newcastle. Who would have thought a bunch of English kids could produce black R 'n' B in the States? And here they were in the *sanctum sanctorum* of Chicago blues, playing in the lap of their gods. The ground-floor room was a gem, as was Chess engineer Ron Malo. He treated them just like . . . musicians. The derision, jibes and plain stupidity of the American deejay goblins were left out in the gutter. The Stones were to South Michigan Avenue born, and the session was a joy to record.

**Keith Richards**, *In Their Own Words*: Back (in the old *Five By Five* days) when we were recording in Chicago and Los Angeles, we used to go down to the local record stores, buy up a whole bunch of soul singles, sit down by the record player and learn 'em – things like the 'Oh, Baby (We Got A Good Thing Going)' and the old Otis Redding stuff. Then we'd record 'em as quickly as possible.

**ALO**: Nothing sensational happened at Chess except the music. For those two days, the Stones were finally true blues artists and legend has it that true blues artists didn't have producers – they just came in and got it done. I was producing the sessions in the greatest sense of the word: I had provided the environment in which the work could get done. The Stones' job was to fill up the available space correctly and this they did. This was not the session for pop suggestions; this was the place to let them be. Oh, I may have insisted on a sordid amount of echo on the under-belly figure to 'It's All Over Now', but that was only ear candy to a part that was already there. I remember being impressed with the order of things and how quietness and calm got things done. I remember meeting Leonard and/or perhaps Phil Chess, and being cognisant of the fact that there was no suppressive limey stymieing from the head office to the factory floor.

Truth was, the Jews and blacks were equal on the Yankee nigger parade and the shared affinity showed and glowed in the music. There was no knighted vinyl baron, pin-striped and up in the clouds, no war-pensioned doorman with orders to separate the wheat from the chaff, no scum line below which the artist could sing, swim, tour and sink. There was just a factory floor and a very relaxed combo of artists, musicians, engineers and salesmen all at one with each other and getting their jobs done and royalty Cadillacs royally driven. I think it's called a democracy, for all its warts and whores. It was all inspired, but one track, 'It's All Over Now', would bring the Stones a little bit closer to our devoutly-wished-for consummation, the real deal – a genuine American hit.

Back in that first week of June 1964, as the Stones stomped the less-than-sweet, successless streets of New York radiolandia, one bright beacon of good faith had emerged in the form of Murray the K (as in Kaufman, as in the Fifth Beatle). We were doing the radio stations and they were doing us with their relentless shards of glass and barbed witless jibes when Murray decided to adopt us, take us in tow, claim us for his very own by becoming the Sixth Stone (he hadn't been introduced to Stu, obviously). It was still the same lame game as we smiled all over Murray's WINS radio station. 'Whadja think of the Beatles, guys – are you pals or rivals?' 'How long since you had a haircut? Just kiddin', Murray luuuuvvves you.' 'I can assure my listeners, they are clean, the Stones are clean. They do wash – don't you, guys?'

Oh, just play the fuckin' record and announce the concert date so we can piss off. Murray was a shard above the rest. He'd decided that if we were good enough for the Beatles, we were good enough for Murray. We were getting there the hard way. These first American tours would be the Rolling Stones' Hamburg. For me there'd be no more time for the Soho sweetness of *Expresso Bongo*, or the Shetland social games of the French New Wave and *Les Cousins* and *Le Beau Serge*. The Stones and I were working in the coal mine. The Brill Building didn't house J.J. Hunsecker in its penthouse. Columbus found America by mistake; we'd find it through songs.

Murray the K done for the day, Keith and I headed for a shopping foray into the upper seventies on Madison Avenue. Most of the clobber was not for us (in dollars or sense), just an American attempt to copy the look we'd left behind, but where, it had to be said, it was done better. New York's Upper East Side version of that English look was bland and expensive. The waists on the tweed jackets hinted at a cut and flair that didn't deliver. The stitching screamed 'machined in Michigan' and the brogues were pure day-off Dixon of Dock Green. But the walk was swell and we enjoyed our peek at the vanities on money'd Mad Avenue.

Tucked into the 68th Street corner, where in years to come Jackie Rogers would give good fashion, was an austere gold-leaf painted jewellers that discreetly allowed – via hand-written window cards – that they dealt in estate jewellery.

'Ah, dead people's stuff,' said Keith as I ogled a huge crested beauty of a ring with my name all over it.

With Keith my worthy henchman I hastily attempted to enter the premises, to no avail. The door was locked. I'd started politely knuckling the windowed portion of the door when a chinless vino-vein'd troll in his fifties shoved his pink bulldog features though t'other side of pane and with *faux hauteur* pointed towards the bell to be used to request entry. I rang the bell and pointed to the ring on the velvet tray on the left. The frail bulldog pursed his leprous lips and gestured 'no'. He was a creature out of E.C. Comics, a crazed bone-yard dog cursed from fondling the jewellery of the deceased.

'No, what?' I wondered, 'No, we're closed? No, it's not for sale? No, we just put it in the window to frustrate punters the likes of you?' Then we got the true meaning of the no. 'No, we're not letting you in our shop. We are not used to high boot-heeled, jean'd and drainpiped, button-down striped shirt'd, waistcoated topped with British Railways peaked caps and happy-gait urchins asking to come in. And there's two of you . . . you might kill us.' Welcome to the swingin' 60s, baby!

I wanted that ring; I wanted it badly. In a state of aroused telepathy I could read the thoughts leaking out of his filigreed mind. Little sepulchral mummies were lip-synching, 'How do we know you have any money?' I pulled out about one hundred bucks and flashed it. I kept pointing at the ring while attempting to shovel the cash through the knee-high mailbox as a show of intent. The runt on the other side went down on his knees in an attempt to stop my cash from soiling his shop, tut-tutting, getting more flustered, more veined and pink, and with his free or drinking hand attempted to wave Keith and me away.

'Fuck him,' said Keith. I agreed, but I still wanted the crested royal knuckle-duster. I let the lower half of the door have it with an instep-propelled smack of my Anello & Davide boot. Had I been Jimmy Greaves I'd have definitely scored a goal on that one. The pin-striped leech jumped back aghast, visibly shocked by this quick turn to violence and pantomimed picking up the phone as if to call the police.

'You fuckin' marzipan poof reject,' I offered, or something of the sort.

Keith rebel yelled, gave the world the finger, laughed, took me by the arm and guided me away. As we giggled and crossed Madison arm in arm in the direction of the park, Keith yelled over our shoulders to the few onlookers that had gathered to view the kick-in (and had been joined on the pavement by the newly brave, still tut-tutting salesman). 'Cunts!'

I felt better and, buoyed by Keith, less like one.

Keith Richards and ALO, New York, 1965

We grabbed some hasty victuals from the hot dog stand on the corner of Fifth, then cabbed west across the park and back into our own Holly Golightly world to attend a Bob Crewe party in our honour. The yellow stretch cab wheeled out of the park at 72nd across Central Park West and let us out at the austere and majestic granite entrance to the Dakota. Three short 60s-filled years later, the building would become infamous for housing Roman Polanski's *Rosemary's Baby*. Sixteen years on, it would be the site of the killing of John Lennon. Keith and I asked for 'Bob Crewe, please.' The rest of the Stones were already there. Bob's apartment was a film set, all ornate mod-Roman gay splendour over the park – marbled floors, bronzed Ma Bell's, African-motif zebra and leopard throw rugs, and enough brocade, tassel and gilt to assure you that you weren't visiting John Huston. The living room sunk down to a waist-high setting with an aqua-Nero motif, complete with statues of nubile youth that gushed water. Bob Crewe was Doris Day, if Doris Day had been all man and stayed gorgeous. Leonard Bernstein chatted with actor/neighbour Robert Ryan who asked Mick if he knew Terence Stamp whom he'd worked with two years before on *Billy Budd*. Mick didn't or wouldn't. Lenny B and Ryan turned away from Jagger and resumed discussing elevator problems at the Dakota. Bob Crewe was above it all and flying. Ahmet Ertegun looked diplomatically dapper. He didn't make a play for the Stones, but it did look as if he'd made one for Liza Minnelli. She wondered if we'd met her mother. I had.

One of Bob's guest rooms (named Africa) housed our old mate Lionel Bart, who had introduced me to Liza's mum Judy Garland a month before in London. The living room filled with more famous Yanks and friendly English faces. My host's ability to spin such a night in such sumptuous surroundings summoned none too flattering comparisons between Bob's situation and my own. Bob Crewe produced the Four Seasons; I produced and co-managed the Rolling Stones. While I was living in a one-bedroom rented furnished flatlet opposite the Regent's Park Zoo and Primrose Hill, he was lording it up in a six-room complete with sunken living room overlooking Central Park. He had his offices on the sixth floor of a slate peninsula on West 60th that overlooked Columbus Circle and Central Park South. Atlantic Records had its digs in the same building and next door was Morris Levy and his rumoured Mafia-driven Roulette Records. Meanwhile, over the ocean, my partner Tony Calder and I made an otherwise drab block of Baker Street flats our office, graced by visits from various Stones. Things were livened up by the presence of the quietly mad Roy Moseley on the floor above and the quite mad Kit Lambert and Chris Stamp, managers of the Who, etc., who had taken over a flat on a lower floor. I mulled over the discrepancies between *chez* Crewe and *chez* yours truly, my envy well concealed on my sleeve so as not to invade my wellbeing.

Sometime during the evening, Murray the K pulled me to one side and put a 45 single between my hand and his. Murray stood out in these svelte surroundings, grey-blue straw titfer atop his hair replacement and ghastly tangerine skin. He was wearing a Cadillac upholstery coloured Teflon sweater with winkle pickers that set off fuchsia-flamed trews that wouldn't even pass for wallpaper in Slough. Murray had no shame but was master of his game . . . pop kingmaker.

He backed me against the wall, both of us still holding the 45, his free hand gripping my beige suede-jacketed elbow. 'Andy, I love the guys; I think they are fabulous. I know the Beatles love 'em too – George told me so. I don't go out of my way for many people, y'know, but I'm promoting the hell out of them – you're gonna sell tickets. The Stones are special. I really like them.'

This rotund puck of pop caught his breath and allowed me time to acknowledge this outpouring. 'Murray, they like you too,' was all I could muster.

'They *do*?' He came back at me, smiling vices. 'Great. I could feel it, especially Brian, real straight guy, sweetheart, really genuine, Mick too. Listen, Andy, I don't often do this and I promise you, forget whatever you've heard – I don't want anything for it, I just love this business we're in and that's the truth of it. Don't want no freebies, no B-sides.'

He paused and grinned –  this was pure pop oxymoronic air we were breathing. 'All I want,' he continued, 'is to know that whenever the guys play New York – and you will, often, I promise – you have ol' Murray the K behind you now, you're gonna be big . . .' (The wonderful thing about America, I somehow found time to think, is you have nothing to do with getting there. Other people do it for you and you are merely beholding, beholding – left holding the bag.) Murray, meanwhile, droned on, 'Anyway, all I want is that Murray here is the only disc jockey who MC's your New York shows and—' Murray pushed me further against the Africa-motif'd wall – 'and you and the guys remember Murray when those cocksuckers put me down . . . and they will, just you remember.'

America was turning into beads of sweat trickling from questionable hairlines and Paul Simon was still Tom of Tom & Jerry. I felt the vinyl; now it was all in mine. 'Feel what's in your hand, Andy. It's yours; it's for you and the boys. Just take it home and record it. I guarantee it. Murray guarantees it, babe. I just gave you your very first American hit.' He had, and God Bless

America, land of a thousand dances. I'd just gone to the perfect party and got laid by the perfect partner, Murray the K. Bob Crewe beamed knowingly from the other side of the room and raised his glass in a welcome-to-the-good-ship-lollipop salute while musical guest Tiny Tim entertained guests with that and other ditties from another room. The 45 that Murray the K left in my hand was the Bobby Womack-composed, Sam Cooke SAR-labelled, breaking-out-black-but-not-white-in-the-Midwest-and-South

smasharoonie, 'It's All Over Now'. As recorded ten days later at Chess in Chicago, it would take the Stones into the American Top 30 a couple of months hence for the very first time.

Two weeks earlier on the West Coast while the Stones tackled San Bernadino, I'd tackled music publishers' row south of Sunset Boulevard, searching for that perfect piece of song that would put a parachute in our recording plane. I listened to a lot of airbag vomit-inducing ditties. America was in the throes of Beatle recovery and nine out of ten songs emoted variations on feeling fine, pleasing everybody from me to you, and hey-hey-hey. Sonny Bono and I cruised into the parking lot of a one-storey 30s hacienda on the south side of Sunset in his Caesar & Cleo trunk-filled maroon convertible. We breezed and smiled our way through a reception full of friendly faces and into the offices of Liberty and Imperial Records and its publishing arm, Metric Music, which had handled the breathtaking Bono-and-Jack Nitzsche-penned 'Needles And Pins' (as sanctified by Jackie DeShannon on the Liberty label). Oh Lord, don't let me be misunderstood. Film sets merged with real life and I was home.

Please recall that up to a month earlier my experience of record companies had been via surly, uniformed doormen and wish-thee-nothing resentful drip-dry average-clad civil servants umbrella'd by a couple of ingenious well-clad vinyl barons, Sir Edward Lewis and Sir Joseph Lockwood, respectively of Decca and EMI. But the Liberty/Imperial/Metric machine was all beige, stucco and tanned – it purred and relaxed in true Johnny Stompanato/West Coast mode. The late Mr Stompanato, an alleged womanising low-life gangster, had impressed me from the UK newspapers at the tender age of thirteen, clutching Lana Turner at London Airport. Michael Madsen should play him and does often. Johnny had an open silk shirt that in black and white matched his skin and neck chain. He threatened to kill Lana's co-star Sean Connery, was deported from England as an undesirable and deported to the next life by Lana's daughter when Johnny fell onto the kitchen knife she was weaving. At the time, my kind of guy.

The Liberty company had been started in the late 50s when Al Bennett left his gig at Randy Wood's Dot label and, together with the Skaff brothers (Bob and Phil) and Sy Waronker, formed Liberty. They were a smash out of the box with their first release, 'Witch Doctor' by David Seville, who later gifted Liberty and a lot of the world's children, mine included, with Alvin & the Chipmunks. Once they had thrust and parried with pressing, selling and getting paid, Liberty settled into becoming one of the major independents. Eddie Cochran, Johnny Burnette, Timi Yuro, Martin Denny, Julie London, Jackie DeShannon, Sandy Nelson, Gene McDaniels, the Olympics, Johnny Rivers, the Ventures, Fats Domino, Ricky Nelson, Bobby Vee, the Teddy Bears, the Fleetwoods and the Chipmunks were some of the Liberty/Imperial acts that helped seal the deal for a successful and diverse independent record company. A&R was headed by the impeccable Snuff Garrett, whose marriage of Bobby Vee with Goffin and King and other Aldon Music/Lou Adler West Coast-helmed writers gave Liberty a rousing run of pop anthems in the first three years of the 60s.

It was a great big world becoming miraculously smaller and more accessible. The ease with which I was welcomed at Liberty amazed me. It was a far cry from East Coast rudeness masquerading as style and flare. No one was scared, everybody shared. (I am leaving Phil Spector out of this analogy, it having become apparent on spending time with him in the States that he was already heading for the hills. In addition to releasing the Teddy Bears via Imperial, Spector produced and mixed quite a few Liberty/Imperial darlings like Timi Yuro, although uncredited for doing so before he headed east.)

In a side room I met Tommy La Puma, who worked with the writers signed to Metric Music. Tommy, a short, jovial man whom a circa *Taxi* Danny De Vito would have had no problem portraying, played me some appalling results of Beatlemania on West Coast songwriters – even the likes of Randy Newman wanted to hold your hand. We fast-forwarded through more well-meaning drivel. Then, up came a white-labelled Imperial 45 bearing the artist's name, Irma Thomas, and her devastating recording via Jerry Ragavoy of 'Time Is On My Side'. Yes, it was my good fortune to hear God two times on this first tour. Once, when the Valentinos literally jumped out of the grooves and into our path with 'It's All Over Now', and a second time when Irma beamed 'Time Is On My Side' my way. All that was needed in the case of those two songs was devoted apostles to pick up the mantle. White boys' will be done, as it is on radio and in America.

That languid LA afternoon, Sonny Bono had some Cher-ing to do and so Tommy La Puma took me to meet Bob Krasnow. Bob was and always would be a great record man. At the time he worked for Syd Nathan's King Records, home of James Brown. Bob would run Blue Thumb Records with La Puma and, later, Elecktra Records on his tod, where I would pick up with him again in the 80s on my last New York run. Tommy drove me to somewhere in some valley to meet Bob, talk more about 'Time Is On My Side', and get stoned . . . very stoned. Thus far my no. 1 smoking pleasure had been opiated hash, very mellow and very much a body, as opposed to a mind, high. At Krasnow's we talked and talked and suddenly I got legless and could barely walk, tell the time, or listen to 'Time Is On My Side' without sliding into delta-9 time. I became paranoid for the first time in my life and for no other reason but the jane playing with my brain. A second unwanted movie was running in my mind. I had no control over the screenplay and the improvisations were getting out of control.

Around seven I left the jovial Krasnow and La Puma, Bob waving goodbye like a beaming Buddha, wishing me luck on the drive back to our motel on the Strip. My last thought as I tried to follow the widening chasm in my mind's road was, 'I think I've got it . . . "Time Is On My Side" is the answer, if I ever get back to the Sunset Strip alive.' I arrived at the Landmark Motel dazed but in one piece, my mind slowly gathering itself. A little bud called Flo, who looked more like Chris Rock than Pam Grier, had been waiting poolside for my return. Halter-topped, she slipped that off and slipped me inside her before I could say a word. The attraction was, apparently, not so much my looks as my accent; when I spoke she got excited. She was sweet and young fun that summer of 64, but by the next tour when I fell into her again she was stoned and dazed and caught in the waste of dying. She remains a sweet memory, doth Flo. I got off the plane at London Airport mid-morning and stopped off in Harley Street before going to the flat to make sure my dick wouldn't sting Sheila when I got it home.

*

It was the winter of 1970. We'd rung out our own versions of the 60s and a lot of things had changed. It was as if some malign curse had been put upon that once-unstoppable decade. Ghosts, famous long ago, now haunted the streets. Walking south on Seventh Avenue down from Carnegie Hall in front of a most bizarre handbag shop, I passed two bums, two carrier bags apiece, in old and matching sneakers, twenty-dollar 50s tweed raglan-shouldered overcoats, mottled and frayed wool caps and scarves and not a smile between them. They both had that faraway look that frequently comes with the shattering collision of looks-like-meth dreams and reality. As we walked along, my companion caught me studying their aura for signs of story, of a life. He asked me if I knew who the two were. I didn't. They were Jerome Rado and James Ragni, he said, the creators of *Hair*, a musical once considered revolutionary and innovative but, to my taste, recycled theatrical air with hair and nudity. The two 'bums' looked frazzled and shattered. Their eyes told of a thousand losses as they trudged along clutching their paper carrier bags the way they had once clasped hope to their bosoms. I mindfilmed that forlorn Age of Aquarius moment with Messrs Rado and Ragni and walked on.

Sometimes it was I who was the ghost. On that Aquarian-haunted corner as I strode my block on a perfectly cast fall day in the early 80s, outside the Russian Tea Room I spied a well-fed, primefine looking Michael Caine. We had met a couple of times in the 60s – hadn't we all – but mindful of Caine's busier and more people-filled itinerary the past twenty years and to save the fellow from searching through his mind to locate my mug, I was happy to reintroduce myself with a 'Hello, Michael, Andrew Oldham, how are you?' Given the cue Mr Caine did a perfect take. He pulled himself up an unneeded extra inch by clutching the collar of his dapper double-breasted navy blue overcoat, sucked in the air, rosied up his face for the close-up and hit his mark. 'Andrew!' he chimed, 'so good to see you – keeping well?' His eyes blinkrated to zero as he realised there was no need for an answer. 'Just fine, Michael,' I said anyway. 'Living here now.' 'Jolly good,' Caine soldiered on. 'How are the lads?' The lads, I thought, how are the fuckin' lads? My hackles bristled. Climb down, laddie, I told myself. He's just put your mug together with its reference and hasn't updated his mind's Filofax yet. There's no offence here, you twit, he's just trying to be polite. 'How are the lads?' 'Oh, just great, Michael. Everybody's just fine.' My reading of the line must have been perfect, because Caine breathed a sigh of relief. This could be a take, after all. 'Oh, great, good to hear that. Say hello to Mick for me. Good to see ya, Andrew.' Michael slapped my arm in camaraderie, braced himself up the unneeded inch again, locked eyes for a reverse angle shot, turned left and strode on up 57th. I recovered – kind of.

Those days a chance encounter with a friendly acquaintance could be most disturbing, leaving my body screaming for relief and my mind diving for the grinder, without which one could say goodbye to the rest of the day. If I hadn't been in the nick I was in, I'd have learnt a valuable, time-saving lesson that day at the school of Caine, instead of later. 'How Are The Lads?' Hmmmm . . . point made, taken later. Much later.

*

On a brisk autumn day in London of 74 I found myself dodging taxis with a good pal, the late Ron Kass. In the early 70s Ron left Apple Records and was living a wonderful world in London, married to the actress Joan Collins and running the UK Warner Brothers discery. It was somewhat to Ron and less than is thought to Colombia that I owe my entry into the long year's night of the marching powders. Oh, I'd said hello to the lady before, but I'd never slept over.

We were striding across the Strand heading for the Savoy for a meet with Shep Gordon, Alice Cooper's manager. Ron handed me a small brown vial with the words, 'You bring it out, Andrew, it'll look better coming from you.' 'It', we established, was cocaine. I did indeed bring it out and later thought what a nice way this was to do business. Ron and I became drug buddies – having our toast buttered at the Connaught seemed to compensate the sweat on my brow, his lips and our shared fall from grace. This toot'n'tryst continued in the hills of Beverly where Joan and Ron had moved after striking *Dynasty* gold. During that *Dynasty* run I'd taken two Colombian gentlemen to the Century City pad shared by her and Ron. None of us ate; we all had the snivels, sweated in coke rote munchies and eyed the bathroom as if it were going to disappear. I had visited Ron and Joan on an earlier occasion for an English Sunday roast. This was long before Joan's *Dynasty* success had her leave Blighty, and before her sexy potboilers, *The Bitch* and *The Stud*, based on her sister Jackie's books, allowed the grand dame to rise forever against England's mudraking view of her. She was not at all worried about us going AWOL in the loo, Joan being the champion at loo décor. Both their Century City pad of the 80s and the 70s 'purple belt' Surrey cottage were stocked with every one of Joan's magazine covers since her 1951 début in *Lady Godiva Rides Again*. Back at Century City the Colombians and I continued to admire Miss Collins as we all cut across each other's sentences, grinding funky to the bone with the coca-plus of laughing at jokes before we'd got to the punchline. The T-bone was served but just got cold as we looked at it. The salad kept it company. Joan must have thought we were all dieting.

At this 1970s time Ron was attempting to restore some financial dignity to the life of chum Lionel Bart, who'd been staying at Cap d'Antibes with friends, had broken his arm and was in need of a pal. It was a long way from the late 50s/early 60s pop-hit-a-week via Tommy Steele, Cliff Richard, *Fings Ain't Wot They Used To Be* and Lionel's jewel in the crown, *Oliver!* This Lionel, who had made Marianne Faithfull possible for me by financing the session, had bet the farm (as in his *Oliver!* royalties) on a new show, *Maggie May*, and lost. With Sean Kenny there had been many attempts to catch the wind – *Quasimodo*, *Gulliver's Travels* – but fame was a daft mistress to Lionel. He was down in the dumps and was probably getting the message that the body would only take so much more abuse in search of its owner's next national anthem. So at Ron's behest I'd headed, kind of gladly, for my old stomping ground, the Côte d'Azur, perhaps to recharge my own batteries in the land where so much had begun for me, where Lionel had once been pearly king and queen of the Croisette catwalk in Larry Parnes and *Oliver!* days gone by. The drive from Nice Airport was breezy and balmy. I felt invigorated by the soothing evening air, my very being ecstatic as I looked back through the rear window of the taxi at the same view Cary Grant had Grace Kelly'd all those VistaVision turns ago in Hitchcock's *To Catch a Thief*, the route where so much had started me up into go.

How had I managed to turn it all into this sour stench of success? Still clad with verve I managed to pull it off on occasion, but had it not been for my eternal optimism I would surely have been as worn out as the Lionel Bart I was about to meet. It was no longer about fashion. It was about fading fables, the inability to participate and produce. I say 'sour stench of success', but I was still managing to stay just above the fray. 'The smell of opium was more agreeable than the smell of success,' Graham Greene had written on the same Antibes patch for his *A Sort of Life*.

I was very lucky to have left England in 1970 for the calm and anonymity of Connecticut, where I was able to find some respite before the self-induced storm. I had left behind two failed marriages, the first (as I saw it then) to the Stones, and the second to Sheila – a double marriage that had been borderline bigamy. I had remained a child and fled my very own, whom I could not even remember holding. The scarecrow of my soul, Dr Luke McLoughlin, did his best to calm my beasts with a hamperful of drug mixtures, electric shock treatment and truth serums designed to drive out the demons and stop me from stepping on any more mental landmines. In sum total all this did was allow me a reasonable tan. Underneath I was very pale, wan and alone. I'd forgotten what an intimate hug felt like, but was too chemically blocked and cold to realise it. I made do with the comfort of pals, a joint, a brilliant idea never worked on in the morning and a drink or four. Moving to Connecticut had been good and had soothed my well-tempered madness for a while. Until, that is, I attempted to re-enter the fray.

**Sheila Klein**: I remember Andrew getting a card in the post from the Tax Office. It said 'please send by return of post £600,000'. Soon after that we'd left England and were living in Connecticut. We were all so in it, we didn't know how to get out of it. There was no map, there was nobody we knew who'd been on this route before. There was no community in Connecticut; we had no good friends there and he'd lost his identity. He didn't know who he was. What he was, was deeply wounded. He couldn't get his teeth into anything. It was really miserable. Ever since we'd got married we'd split up every year without fail and then get back together again, the reason being I needed a period to recharge. I'd just get so drained by the whole thing. After three months away I'd be back to myself, grounded and strong and knowing what everything was about. Then within a month of moving back in with him and all the chaos, I wouldn't know whether I was coming or going. We fell out a long time before we arrived in Connecticut but I was still trying to make it work. It was hell in Connecticut. I was smoking a lot of cigarettes and drinking too much and I realised I had to start taking care of my health. I think some of that must have worn off on Andrew. He got incredibly bored living there; it was just so deadly dull. If you didn't play bridge or tennis, forget it. He would go off somewhere and I would live there for about a month without speaking to anybody. There was no coherence to anything, no synchronicity, because everything and Andrew was so fractured. I wouldn't say it was that he used people. He just used them up. And now they'd used him up. It took me ten years to recover from our relationship. At the end of it I couldn't speak.

**ALO**: In 1974 I was still getting over leaving the Stones and attempting to deal with the thought that at thirty I might have shot my load. I had bought into and was living in my own well-heeled abyss. I spent the early 70s recording 4-F Crosby, Stills wannabes I'd swept off East Coast village greens and had convinced the white guys running Motown were the next Nash, Young and Joni Mitchell combined. I was drinking and detained enough to be able to give you the floor plans of Connecticut's best jails. I had just started taking coke daily and still thought it wasn't taking me. I'd left England in 1970, after the taxman had told me to pay up or set sail. I settled in the rolling hills of Connecticut, existed on Stouffer's stew, pot and vodka and caught every *Mod Squad*, *Columbo* and *Harry-O* for nigh on four years. I also partied in the hills of Beverly. I looned in a somebody's garden, lined up marching powder on a sundial in the night for Ringo and Peter Sellers. I complained about the 60s and Ringo called me a twat and told me off. All the grinning Goon could say was, 'Oh, I do love doing drugs with you rock people!'

Back east, I sat on my tod in my 450 Merc looking down on my land, and I cried. Fuck Hey Jude, I thought, I have to make this better. So I packed and flew to London, my time in tax exile up. I hustled a glam cry-bi guy, Brett

Smiley, to Ian Ralfini's Anchor Records and sold a talented Duncan Browne to Ron Kass. Duncan I had first recorded in 1968. The result, 'Give Me, Take You', is well remembered but did not sell well at the time. He'd garner some singles success with Mickie Most before we took another crack at it in 74. Duncan, who died very prematurely of cancer in 1993, remains one of the artists I was proudest to stand in a room with and watch evolve. Brett Smiley was a fine writer with a multi-destructive lifestyle to write about, which he did well. I had come across Brett after a Detroit trip that had me meet Russ Gibb, entrepreneurial educator extraordinaire. Russ pointed me in the direction of Brett, who was not far from his arm. I recalled pal Jerry Brandt's adventures with Elektra/Asylum Records over Jobriath in 1970, and figured, 'my fag's not real, I've got the real deal, I can do this better'. That was pure 70s-speak and finally not true for either Herr Brandt or myself, although we'd both had fun getting it done. Jerry's problem may have been dealing with David Geffen, who'd once worked under him in the mail room at William Morris. My problem may have been I'd never worked in the mail room.

I hired a suite in the Hotel Pierre and had the walls adorned with large cool Gered Mankowitz blow-ups of Brett (in person he was getting on my nerves). I sat there for four days on room service, hope and blow waiting for Ian Ralfini to call and say I'd got a deal. He did and I was free at last to hustle London once again.

I'd met Russ Gibb at LB's. I'd met LB (an American known to all simply by his initials) because John Lennon had told me in New York, 'Andrew, when you're in Detroit, stop off for some free sushi and coke at LB's. He's this great old queen dealer who'll give you anything you want; all ya gotta do is have your picture taken with him.' I did call and stop by, got high, and sure 'nuff, a snapped and beaming John was up there on the wall of *fua* and fame. I made a friendship with LB that continued long after they shipped him off to jail. He'd been shopped by one of his musclebound young drivers named Charles, who chauffeured the coke north from Texas in a one-headlighted Rolls with a little old grandma in *Beverly Hillbillies* dressed-up mode sitting aback as decoy. Charles decided to take over the farm and retire LB to jail and pasture. I communicated with LB at his new Terre Haute, Indiana, digs and attempted to be conciliatory and Zen about his fate. 'No need, Andrew,' LB wrote back, 'I go bareback riding on horses and boys at least three times a week. It's heaven. I'm in a great retirement home where finally the drugs and the boys are free.'

**Ken Mewis**, friend: After Andrew left the UK for Connecticut I joined him and became his personal assistant at doing nothing. The days would start with

Bloody Marys at a local bar and end up with vodka, Stouffer's beef stew and *The Mod Squad* on TV. We watched a lot of TV. Irwin Schiff was a very large American whom Andrew had met through either Doc Cavalier or the bunch of gangsters at Hemdale. Irwin weighed 400 pounds and had to sit sideways in order to drive a very big Cadillac. He had been an interrogator for the US Army; he'd take two Vietcong up in a helicopter and throw the first one out in the expectation of getting something out of the remaining one. Irwin became friendly with Andrew and he'd speak about this a lot. He got killed at the beginning of the 90s in an East Side Italian place over a plate of pasta.

Andrew 'used' Irwin to represent him in his legal separation from Sheila. It took place at Doc Cavalier's studio in Wallingford. Sheila's boyfriend was this lawyer/banker named Sam Clapp who worked for IOS and Bernie Kornfeld. I remember Irwin getting his 400 pounds into the Caddy and chasing this guy Sam waving a pistol and yelling back at Andrew, 'Shall I shoot?'

Andrew had decided to get out of the rut he was living in and into the 70s. He got rid of the Volvo and Camero and bought a 450 Mercedes. One day he took me up Route 7 from the house in Wilton into northern Connecticut, off the highway and up some dirt roads to the top of a mountain. He pointed at the valley and said, 'I own all of that, but it's not doing me much good, is it?'

**Gered Mankowitz**, photographer: The thing was that, in a way, Andrew was an old dog already and he just had to lick his wounds and re-establish himself. He did it with great style, but with a completely different set of trappings. When I saw him in Connecticut he was okay. He looked like a wild man with very long hair and long beard. He was full of bounce, humour and looniness. Andrew had his health problems and his need for medication was eccentric. He was drinking a lot and taking an awful lot of prescription pills. It was now a recognised type of lifestyle; nobody knew it had its origin in severe depression. Lots of people had had psychiatric treatment and it had all reached ridiculous levels. You could now see the ECT in him. That was scary; it had to have been sophisticated torture. He was only about twenty-seven but on most days he looked fifty. I accepted these things not as being normal but as being part of the man. He'd bought a second-hand car, a white two-door Volvo. 'It's Simon Templar, my dear,' he told me. 'Got to have a bit of an image, even in Connecticut.'

**ALO**: So I turned up on the Cap d'Antibes doorstep of Lionel Bart's hosts and hugged the man. I didn't much like what I saw. Li's hosts, his 'English

Pals', were treating him like the village invalid, the Jew of Pooh Corner. They were enjoying that game of 'giving a helping hand to poor ol' needy Li' far too much. They were treating him as a pet, a curious mascot, which is what they saw him as. It was obvious his spirits were in need of a lift and a move. 'Enough of this, Lionel,' I rallied and prescribed a change of scenery. 'Pack yer bag but rest the arm. What you need is some room service and a friendly hotel.' Perhaps I was speaking for us both. I drove us into Cannes, the Croissette and the Hotel Martinez. An hour or two later things were much improved. Lionel was buoyed by the 'good to see you, Meester Bart' chorus that greeted him from the older attending farts and the eager-to-serve display of hotel trainees brimming with youth and promise.

Once ensconced, Lionel and I stood on the balcony of our double Med-facing suite, enjoying the calm and nursing two *jus de framboise*, looking down at the strolling early evening Croisette tourist fair. With my chameleon nature I found myself drifting into Lionel's play, early Jewish drawing room Noël Coward. 'Here, Ang, that's not bad,' sighed Lionel. 'What's not bad, Li?' I enquired, enjoying the *jus de framboise* cut-glass container reflecting the evening light through the empty half – a light show of night blues sharding against a fierce Mediterranean maroon. 'Them,' replied Lionel, pointing downwards towards a group of boisterous and tanned, short-trousered Aryan lads. This was all I needed – a one-armed Hebe hot to trot for Nazi fare attempting to requisition yours truly as his pimp. 'No, they're not bad looking at all, Ang. While I fix my arm a bit why don't you go down and suss 'em out? See if they want some of my raspberry juice.' I looked over at Lionel to see if he was serious or pulling my leg. 'You gotta be kidding, Lionel, look at the size of those butch fucks. And besides, I don't even speak German.' I protested, Lionel sulked, his fine black devil's peak hairdo crouched over the forehead, a still-spoilt kid who'd had it all and wanted seconds. His expressive eyes winked and resumed play. 'Go on, Ang – if Terry Stamp was here he'd do it for me,' he challenged. Well, I thought, Tel wasn't here and I wasn't about to, so Lionel just brooded in his raspberry juice.

\*

By July 1964, the first Rolling Stones tour of America was over. I'd checked out my errant member, post-Flo, and was about to make the huge mistake with Sheila of apologising for not being there for her by marrying her. Back at the manor of the heart, my mother Celia remained both aloof from my early rumblings of success, first as a publicist, then manager, and unconvinced about my ability to make my way and be happy with my good lot. She accepted my enthusiasm about the Rolling Stones and my excitement about Marianne Faithfull's potential but hoped I would not get 'stars in my eyes and end up disappointed'. Unavoidable, mother dear, but I would come out the other end.

Back in the mum fighting days of 63 Celia had no doubts about what my life should be. Her idea of what happened when you didn't stick to the straight and narrow was the fate of our upstairs neighbour at 19 Netherhall Gardens, Frank Norman, the East End con and gadabout who had breezed into showbiz, cracked open the safe to the la-de-dahs, the flush 'n' flash punters and gained his freedom with his book *Bang to Rights* and the Lionel Bart-tuned, Norman-written, Sean Kenny-designed, Joan Littlewood-assembled triumph, *Fings Ain't Wot They Used To Be*. Frank had moved up to the dry side of Hampstead Heath. It was the other side, north of Sheila's, where the real villains lived and wet their beaks.

My mother did not have much time for Frank's nightly bird-pulling esprit. I, however, greatly admired the man, his leer at life, and the fact that he didn't attempt to drink, drive and the rest. My ground-floor bedroom faced the street and I'd lain there many times with a smile to the ceiling listening to the familiar sequence of sounds of the night. Taxi chugs up the hill, stops or stalls on the corner. Frank falls out and bird comes tumbling after. Frank picks himself up and puts on the charm, bird laughs – sometimes it's a cackle – that is picked up in the evening echo. Frank chuckles, high heels climb the steps, key finds its way into lock, there's a thumpety-thump over my head as Frank and dolly climb to his room at the top. I'd often hear one last long-distance laugh or leer that would let me know Frank was home. 'What's he really got?' my mother would harp on. 'Every night he comes home drunk in a taxi. He's very pleasant, mind you, always civil. Alone or with a different girl each night; it's not a life, Andy.' Oh, how she willed it so, and bit her tongue perhaps as she thought back to when she was young and footloose in her pre-Andy days as a World War II hope and glory wild child and it might have been her I heard outside my bedroom wall, laughing and giddy as the Frank Norman of her day tried to fit his key into her front door.

Of the Rolling Stones, Keith was her favourite. Once when I asked her and pressed for a reason she explained, 'Well, you can see that Keith has a good heart . . . and he likes dogs.' So does Bill, Mother, I wanted to say, but didn't. What had endeared Keith to my mother, apart from his honesty, was my recounting how Keith and I had bypassed the UK quarantine laws by smuggling a puppy into England via Heathrow from Los Angeles in a hatbox with holes punched into it for breathing space. The puppy stayed docile throughout the long flight as we'd shared our Valium with it. I left out the details of how Keith and I had come across the dog, saying simply, 'And a fan gave it to us', leaving out the fact that the fan, Flo, was the haltered, poolside, heaving young Negrita that Keith and I had both bedded. Alas, she had a screw loose and suddenly turned on us, flaying at us with a kitchen knife, catching and nicking me before Keith disarmed her. Later, after she calmed down, she felt bad about the knife-wielding, good about the heaving, and just before we were to leave LA she stopped off at our motel and gifted Keith with the puppy.

My mother had been telling me Keith was her favourite ever since she'd come for tea at the temporary office I'd set up at the Mayfair Hotel in mid-1966. A lot went on at the Mayfair. It was there Mick and Marianne first settled on each other and the Rolling Stones furthered their rep as the great unwashed. The Mayfair staff confused the constant reek of hashish emanating from the three suites as our own special brand of body odour. 'What about the others?' I asked my mother. 'Well,' she said, inspecting her hands once more for wear and tear, pursing her lips to ensure the same while calling to mind the others. 'Brian is an odd lot. I don't think he likes you, Andrew. There's something not quite right about him. Charlie and Bill are the only normal ones amongst you so I suppose that's why you've got no time for them. And as for you three, I think you are all a little touched. I don't know what you find so funny all the time.' Well, *life* was (and I wasn't smoking in front of Celia yet).

She kept away from Jagger as a solo subject. He was something she'd rather forget since he'd stayed over one night in late December back in 63. Mick and I had spent a lot of time together – as did Mick, Keith and I from the time I followed them to 33 Mapesbury Road in early 1964. Mick was developing nicely; he already had a grab-on instinct. Now he was about study, spit and polish as I pressed him into the responsibilities to come, both as front man to the world and the Rolling Stones. Off the road he was as busy as on, doing phone and solo in-person interviews, calling folk to thank them for the interviews done, all to the extent that we both had one major thought and action in mind – to propel the Stones juggernaut. One of his major roles was simply that of being seen around, checking how effectively my image-beaming of the Stones was penetrating the clubs. I would use Mick, on his social nights out, while he was at his most seemingly innocent and coy, to find out how their image and myth garden was growing – as in, were people treating him any differently as a result of what had been in the papers, and what, generally, was the Stones buzz of the moment? Mick was a poll-taker working under the guise of being one of the chaps. Mick as Best Pal – an endearing sight. He'd be out with Chrissie Shrimpton, would affect surprise about any new Stones gossip that came his way and, if questioned about any of our more outrageous plants, would pass the buck, saying, 'Oh, that Andrew!' then gleefully report back to me that the ploy had hit its mark. Our days started and ended on one subject: the Rolling Stones.

On the night in question, he had come back from some ballroom show, was more than a little blitzed and not up to much social contact, having shagged himself out on the road. Shortly after 2 a.m. we ended up at my mother's flat in Netherhall Gardens, taking tea and talking life through as earnest young things are born to do, though quietly, so as not to wake mother. I'd already mastered the holding and placing of cup and saucer in sink in silence and could mime 'another cuppa' clearly. We would talk ourselves into the bravura of protective armour we'd need to wear to confront those in our way. 'We Can Change The World' was the mantra of the day; the universal law and order would come later. After that other cuppa and an hour or so of gabbing over tomorrows, Mick was in no mood to get off the chair, get himself together and go anywhere. I told him to forget about leaving and to come and sleep in my room. 'You're right,' Mick's Shetland-clad puma frame sighed, accepted my offer and followed me to my room. 'Just a few hours; I've really had it,' Mick rationalised to the shadows on the wall and the floor creaked in agreement. We'd both really had it; we overslept and more. My mother went to work shortly before 8.30 without bothering to check on me, leaving me to sleep. I had been in need of kip more than I knew and soon Mick and I were dead to the world.

My mother came back from work just on 4.30 in the afternoon and, not knowing whether I was there or not, she came into my room – during the day my door was usually open. I came to with a start, my mother at the head of the bed focused not on me but the sleeping Mick on the other side of the bed. 'Mummy,' I said in the shock of seeing her there. 'We worked late . . . what time is it?' It being deep winter, it was now as dark outside as it had been nearly light when we got to sleep. The verbals brought a little life to Mick, who semi-stirred, one eye open focusing up at mum. 'Hello, Mrs Oldham,' Sir Mick yawned but got no further, turned over and refastened himself to my bed. 'Mrs Oldham' hadn't said a word; she never would. She gave us both one last stern look that showed she did not like the order of her life being disturbed, backed out of the room and shut the door.

'Will she be—'

'All right?' I finished Mick's question and answered same. 'Yes, she will be.' Mick eased and dozed; I semi-snoozed until I heard the front door close.

So Mick and I got up and started the day. By that time it seemed all very funny. Before we left the flat we had coffee and Mick called Chrissie. To shatter the tense atmosphere of Celia's catching us in a perceptive position of compromise, Mick went into one of his Goons-meet-Percy-Thrower imitations. 'Now, listeners, what will happen in next week's episode? What will happen now that Celia has found her Andy with *that* singer in flagrant whatever you call it? Has her Andy been led astray by those nasty rock 'n' roll boys?' I let the shock of shocking my mother go and we both laughed ourselves silly. It must have been a funny sight, but not for my mother, who could never embrace my life or the Rolling Stones.

**Sheila Klein**: Andrew used to get hysterical from being at Mick's beck and call all the time. He said he felt like a nursemaid and that's when he went to doctor's and was getting stuff prescribed for him. Then he started mixing the prescribed with the non-prescribed and he'd manufacture what mood he wanted to be in by what he was taking, thinking that would give him some kind of control, I suppose. It was very intense at that time and I suppose for him to have the courage he needed. Mick could be absolutely ghastly. If you think about the sound of the name Jagger it's very pointy edges. Mick would whinge a lot. You know the scene in *Spinal Tap* with the sandwich? That's what he was like. I don't think he said one pleasant word to me ever, not one word. He was very jealous and wanted Andrew's attention all the time. If I wanted attention from Andrew I had to jump up and down louder than Mick. It was very hard work. Chrissie would make every molehill into a mountain. Having been to boarding school Andrew liked being one of the boys; it wasn't a big deal. To my mind, Chrissie made more of Andrew and Mick than was actually going on. They may have slept together but I would say that Andrew and Mick never actually made love or had sex, even though they were closer than Andrew and I for quite a while.

**ALO**: I knew I'd have to leave home soon. The Mick incident was, in a way, the end of my first marriage – the one to my mum. Underneath the veneer, there's instinct. As it is, mere couples have a hard enough time of it – father–mother–child structures have to have the will to work, since three into two don't go. In many ways I had been married to my mum, even flirting with the taboo of finding her attractive. Mick, Sheila and the Rolling Stones proved just too much for that 'us' to endure.

'Look,' I said, '*Les Cousins* is on for another week. Let's go and see it together', meaning just Sheila and I. Last Saturday had been a nightmare for this boy attempting to feel his way into a first date. We were pretty drunk already when Peter Meaden, his girlfriend Gina and I arrived at the party at Marc Geubard's flat at 45 Maresfield Gardens. We parked Peter's motorbike and sidecar in the hedge and started talking to it. Two hours later we were drunker, cheaper, trying to sort out our lives and prevent another Saturday night fiasco. There were two late arrivals at the party, a stocky butch-dirt-blond Aryan mod and a girl quite his opposite in the best possible way – great body, great aura, and shiny, sexy and happy with and about herself. Her eyes went through you, her smile lingered forever and took you into the next day. Though just seventeen, she had that earthy motherlode. She was so at one with herself she'da made a devastating terrorist – you wouldn't have minded when her bullets ripped through you. At least you'd have been inside her and at home. And that's roughly what happened to me the second time I laid eyes on Sheila Klein. Face of a smiling zen-yid angel promising quicksand of the flesh, dangerous bliss, virtual captivity, and everything you can possibly imagine or desire. Neither of us at that moment could have foreseen the fate that would find us and rip us apart as I courted the demons of consuming fame. As blue turned to grey, sorrow would replace trust with deception and the fucking over of the other one's mind. And that's only what I did to her. What she did is hers.

The first time I'd seen her was a week earlier at the Everyman when I'd performed my vaudeville troll for her amusement, and there were the two times I'd bitten the bullet that Saturday night. I got her telephone number from Marc and now, on the phone, had only just got past the shrink detective, Papa Doc Hyman Sydney Klein. 'Are you a friend of Sheila's?' he'd prodded. 'Not yet,' I feyed, pursing my lips as my mother used to do. It was hard for Sheila to talk with shrinkstalker nearby, but she agreed to call me back later on Swiss Cottage 2017 and did, the next Saturday afternoon. Celia handed the phone to me as if it were contagious. When Sheila whispered that she could get out on Sunday night and would meet me in front of the Hampstead tube station at 8.15, in time to catch the 8.45 showing of *Les Cousins*, her 'yes' put me in a total state. Twice my mother asked me what was wrong; why was I rushing around the flat, talking non-stop, ironing a selection of trousers and shirts? 'Andrew, haven't you already ironed the blue gingham twice?' She did offer the occasional, 'Here, let me do it, the back is all creased.' Sunday came and I couldn't concentrate on anything except the sound of Sheila's breath and her shadow-dancing face. By the time 7.30 arrived, I'd already had two baths and tried on all my clothes twice. I settled on the black trousers, French New Wave rollneck, and my faded beige Clark's ankle lace-up booties. My Adams of Piccadilly beige camel-hair peaked-lapelled driving coat topped me off.

Celia was towelling dry her hair in her bedroom above one bar of electric fire. I quietly opened the living room bar, coughed through the squeak, and quickly grabbed a shot of Maneshevitz. I listened for mother but all was mum in her room, so I slugged at the decantered sherry just to be sweet and sure. I cleaned my teeth again, cursed a zit, tried to lower my voice from the ceiling, bade mother goodnight and eleven minutes later was saying hello to Sheila Klein.

I lost my nervousness when together we let in the Everyman screen. I could easily slip and sink myself into Jean-Claude Brialy and did. I'd retrieved me again and I was back ahead of the pack, laconic and flippant, no longer afraid of the dark. I reached out for her hand; it was already there. After the film we had a change of reels and ten minutes later we were standing outside her house. 'Come in,' Sheila whis-purred. 'My parents are asleep, so we can talk in the kitchen.' This we did, drinking tea, talking and starting that slight dance into each other's ways. She shone in the harsh kitchen lighting and her mod freckles endeared her to me.

She told me that her parents had more or less 'grounded' her, having taken no joy in the most recent young man she had been seeing. (I hoped it was the blond frogman I'd seen her with.) Sheila had it that her parents felt dating was taking her away from her art and upcoming exams. I put the teacups silently into the kitchen sink, shivered and let her walk me to the door. The next Wednesday Sheila again invited me to her home. On entering I first got the once over by her redheaded brother (I'd checked him out before you could say 'referral') before being greeted by her mother, Eileen, and her father. They were all smiles, overcurious and nervously welcoming. Eileen was a mid-forties strained Scots beauty as adrift as Hope Lange in *Death Wish*. After this charade of hollow hello's Sheila told them we were going up to her bedroom and took me by the hand. I found this a bit surprising, in light of her parents' qualms about the effect of boys on their daughter's education. As we sat on the bed in her first-floor room, Sheila showed me photos, old and new, followed by some of her sketches and paintings. 'I thought your parents weren't happy 'bout you having, um . . . boys around,' I ventured. 'Yes,' she smiled, 'it was funny; they were all curious to meet you, my brother, too.' 'Well,' I blushed, 'they were very friendly, considering.' 'They were curious, all right,' she giggled. Now she really had my interest. 'I told them they had nothing to worry about. I told them you were gay.' Suddenly I felt not very gay at all, but bitten by the hand that had fed me, confused, and just a bit betrayed. I looked out of the window as the sun and I sunk down over the horizon.

*

After the first US tour we were welcomed back to England by close to a thousand die-hard fans, and yours truly by the exuberant Reg King. Reg, ever tacky and immaculate, had the powder-blue Chevrolet Impala illegally parked outside Arrivals with that incurable twinkle in his eye that dared any rozzer to move him on. His smile could launch a thousand straight chickens and his hug was warm and welcome. I was exhausted from the long flight home and the energy expended by 'nothing-to-declare-ing' my way through Customs. As Reg pinky-ringed the wheel on his way around and out of the airport and headed on to the Great West Road for London town, I reclined into the midnight-blue mock-leather Chevy passenger seat. While I had been in the States Reg had fallen in love and got himself in a state. It was good to sit back and listen to the perils attached to Reg's penchant for heterosexual young men, betting the course of his race on the hope that they might stray from their straight and, as some would have it, narrow path. It was an attractive, engaging bunch that gathered around Reg, and he was a devoted master of the chase. Hearing of his latest adventures gave me the ten minutes' space I needed to shiv the myth into being as to how the Rolling Stones had conquered the States and were returning to their homeland triumphant. The next episode, I hoped, would be customised for the media by the simultaneous Stateside and UK release of the major coup of our Chess recording sessions, 'It's All Over Now' backed with 'Good Times, Bad Times' (what better title to describe our first North American tour?). This last-minute triumph would fudge the truth of our minor-league Stateside status and I reasoned that its success could be helped, in part, by a press that was not yet on the lookout for failure. Time was still on our side.

The ride into London remains a drag to this day – the usual depressing, grey-overcast welcome mat. The architectural suburban mundaneness that borders the ride into my old hometown was, and is, as predictable as a Manfred Mann ditty. The bleak vista is only broken, shortly before Hammersmith, by a couple of interesting sandcastle-art industrial turreted complexes sprayed in a radiant green/grey puke, housing either a paint or chocolate factory – perhaps both. But I had no time to be tired of London or life. I was fired by the Yank unhappening and consumed by the notion of what *could* happen for the Stones. We were going to have to go back and back, until we got it right. Meantime, I had this unreal holiday on ice to overcome. My mission was to convey, via some well-designed mediaspeak, how groundbreaking our US tour had been. My partner Tony Calder immediately spotted the snarling cocky resilience emanating from us all. Regardless of our lacklustre Stateside showing, the land had left its rub on us. While America broke new musical ground weekly, Britain still accepted what little it could, and tried to sweep the rest under the rug. There were a few bright sparks, deejays Alan Freeman and Jimmy Savile, the *Ready Steady Go!* crew – even David Jacobs was a fully paid up non-groveller – but there was none of the flame we'd warmed to in America.

All in all, being back in Britain was a rude awakening, a Magna-Carta-stuck-in-my-throat that served to remind me that the fair isles into which I had been born were gated and padlocked, an unwelcoming playground for an entrepreneur. I chewed on this fat, spat it out and shuddered at my melancholy welcome home all the way down from my dove-brown suede hunting jacket to my deep-brown Chelsea boots. I did feel tired, if only for a long moment. Black clouds hovered over my patch of Dover and I knew what it was to be in England and depressed again.

I didn't like it that the home fires were not burning, and I was fed up being a bad British boy. In America it was a given that bad boys moved up to and between Park and Fifth and Long Island Sound daily. The machine fed on Gatsbys and mavericks, and the economy, wellbeing and humour of a nation depended on it. I came back to England feeling more of a mad boy, and with Reg at the wheel I had the right to be one. I'd come back to England with a different edge, a new mission and calling. The Stones had the edge, too. It became very apparent on their first homecoming weekend – when they played the Alexandra Palace and did *Ready Steady Go!* and *Juke Box Jury* all in one two-day chop – that something forceful, wimp-deleting, empowering and American had taken over. The defining movement travelled north from the hips and the wrists to the shoulders and hands and child-bearing lips, and Mother Jagger started to think and resist like a man.

## · CHAPTER 2 ·

**ALO**: It was July of 1964 and London was soon to become pungent with the Stones. From their clubs, the city's masons and elders huffed at our good fortune and cursed the cut of our cloth and mouth. We had raised the ante in matters of acceptance and rejection. You better sit down kids. Those of you back from America had better not act above your pre-ordained station. The Stones as one would dismiss these warnings and grind them under a well-heeled Chelsea boot, not knowing that within three years they'd be the ones under society's brogue.

On stage the Stones could now turn on a dime. America had invaded their very being and – *voilà!* – they were now rhythm kings, champions of stress and groove who knew what it was all about. No more limey phantasmagoria for them. They'd been knighted out of serfdom and had returned as little big men; they strutted their hour upon the stage, duelling guitars soaring and buoyed by their coming of age at Chess unto America. Keith and Brian got glued as one for a little while longer before the latter reverted to cuntdom. Mick never missed an opportunity to dance his persona into the very souls agog before him. You could see the transference as he sculpted them, invaded them, converted them. Charlie and Bill provided the grounding, the mooring upon which the front-line could skip, bop and weave, secure that the real on the dough-re-mi's, Messrs. Wyman & Watts, would follow their every move like rhythm piranhas at a flesh meet. The Stones began to finesse that muscle, the one that, when expertly flexed, turns an audience into a faithful flock.

The Stones on *Juke Box Jury* turned out to be excellent press fodder. The show, hosted by David Jacobs, featured guests casting their votes on the week's vinyl offerings. The Stones, with no prompting from me, proceeded to behave as complete and utter yobbos and in twenty-five minutes managed to confirm the nation's worst opinion of them once and for all. They grunted, they laughed amongst themselves, were merciless towards the drivel that was played and hostile towards the normally unflappable Mr Jacobs. This was no planned press move. Brian and Bill made some effort to be polite but Mick, Keith and Charlie would have none of it. Eventually the two Bs had to join in, put up and go with the flow.

The *Daily Mail* had it that they had 'scandalised millions of parents'. Even the *New Musical Express*, supposedly an on-our-side young musical rag, screamed that the Stones were 'an utter disgrace'. Not bad for a Saturday afternoon's work. Then they went off on holiday. My holiday came when 'It's All Over Now' went to no. 1 the very next week. It was telegrams and 'fuck the world I wanna rock on' all round.

The group came back holiday'd out – ready, willing and stable. And from the second week of July through to the second week of October, on an extended ballroom and cinema marathon, they gigged non-stop the length and breadth of Britain before stopping off in Paris. The Stones would be playing Bruno Coquatrix's famed L'Olympia; slumming, slouching and building up a following of frogs was not exactly on the agenda. It was straight to the top, ma! Top of the Tour d'Eiffel! L'Olympia was no slouch gig. The Stones would seize the hour on a stage that had held, once, Edith Piaf, and now the likes of Johnny Halliday, Eddy Mitchell and Dick Rivers. They rocked it, headed home, turned around and headed out again for two appearances in New York at the Academy of Music to kick off the second North American tour.

Mick Jagger, Charlie Watts and ALO, Paris 1964

**Seymour Stein**, promotion man, co-founder Sire Records: At twenty-two, I was working at Red Bird Records on the ninth floor in the Brill Building with George Goldner who, with Jerry Leiber and Mike Stoller, had formed the Red Bird label. Andrew came in with Keith. He said he wanted to see Jerry Leiber; he wanted some songs for the Stones. Jerry Leiber didn't want to see them, but as they were leaving I jumped up, chased them to the elevators, and brought them back to my office. I gave them 'Down Home Girl', a record we had with Alvin Robinson, and the Stones later recorded it.

This was 1964. Leiber and Stoller had started writing as teenagers; their first hits, like the original 'Hound Dog' with Big Mama Thornton, were in the early 50s. They moved on to Atlantic as writers/producers and had a great run with the Coasters, Ben E. King and the Drifters. They took Phil Spector under their care; one result was 'Spanish Harlem'. They developed a great stable of writers: Neil Diamond, Jeff Barry and Ellie Greenwich and others were all signed to the Leiber–Stoller publishing company. The Brill had two fabulous restaurants on the ground floor, the Turf and Jack Dempsey's. The Turf had great cheesecake and you could hang out for hours at Dempsey's over one cup of coffee.

**ALO**: London Records (Decca's American subsidiary) had reputedly invested $85,000 in the Stones. But what on? They were wasting it on double-page adverts in *Billboard* proclaiming: 'They're Great! They're Outrageous! They're Rebels! They Sell! They're England's Hottest! . . . But Hottest Group!' I hated the ad equally as much as the tacky title London Records had put over the top of the Stones' debut UK LP (rush-released in the US for the tour) – *England's Newest Hitmakers*. I was angry, but what could I do? I couldn't even get through to London Records on the telephone. Their HQ in New York was just an address. Well, I did have one get-together; Keith and I met label-topper Walt Maguire in a bar off Tenth Avenue and he basically pleaded with us to give them a chance. He was a nice Irish guy mildly in his cups and Keith and I decided to leave the guy be. We were both aware we hadn't delivered the vinyl. Decca's US division existed by milking maximum American profit out of middle-of-the-road English recorded orchestras like Mantovani and Frank Chacksfield, although its curious partnership with Willie Mitchell's Hi label would later blossom into Al Green. London Records did not even pretend to be a major contender in America; it was just a very profitable sideline for Decca *jefe* Sir Edward Lewis. The Stones and I were probably lucky that London was not a major in the States. They operated out of the docks on West 23rd and Tenth, not a good address, but they were a company where we could at least remain a priority until the hits came along.

**Seymour Stein**: Originally it was called American Decca, started by British Decca in 1933 and owned by them until the start of World War II. Sir Edward sold it because he needed the money for radar research. When he tried to buy it back after the war they wouldn't sell it to him. So he started London Records and in the beginning only released British music. There were people in America who wished that rock 'n' roll would disappear. Our equivalent of Mantovani was Mitch Miller, who was the head of Columbia Records. He hated rock 'n' roll.

Capitol, the Beatles' label, was originally started in the 40s and sold to EMI in 1955 for about $8 million of steel. But Capitol was still run independently and they didn't put out much EMI product. They turned the Beatles down twice. The early Beatles recordings came out on Vee Jay and Swan. Vee Jay didn't pay royalties and that's how EMI/Capitol were able to get the Beatles records back.

The big difference between the American and English record businesses was that in England there were no independents. EMI was at least half the business, Decca was about a third, then you had Pye and Philips. The independents in America at that same point probably controlled 75 per cent of the singles business and 40 per cent of the business on LPs. What gave rise to the independents in America was the rise of R 'n' B and country music. You had these labels springing up all over the country – King, Atlantic, Chess, Vee Jay, Imperial, Specialty, Duke, Peacock, Old Town. In Philadelphia you had Cameo Parkway and Chancellor; these labels came out of the success of Dick Clark's *American Bandstand*.

I introduced Andrew to Roberta Goldstein, an upper-middle-class girl whose parents ran a hotel business in upstate New York and whose cousin had married Neil Sedaka. She came to New York with a vengeance and became a major celebrity within the music business – an early groupie, but in the classiest sense. She had a great apartment on 63rd Street. She was twenty-two and in those days you didn't have that; you lived at home with your family in Brooklyn or Queens. Roberta was friendly with Al Nevins and Don Kirshner, who had Gerry Goffin and Carole King, Barry Mann and Cynthia Weil – all the writers. Between the two of us we knew a lot of people and we loved Andrew. She knew Bob Crewe. Bob was a big liver; he had a triplex and an apartment at the Dakota. Hovering in the background was Bob's brother, Dan. Bob was one of the great talents, a great songwriter.

Carole King and Gerry Goffin, New York, 1962

**Bob Crewe**, songwriter/producer: I got started in 1950, writing and what have you. There was never such a thing as an independent record producer back then; that did not exist until Frank Slay and I invented it. I got partnered up with Frank in New York in early 1950 at a social event. He was playing piano and I started singing, writing and producing with him. We got to know Jerry Wexler at Atlantic Records very well. Jerry produced many of the great early R 'n' B soul artistes – Joe Turner, Ray Charles, T-Bone Walker, the Drifters, Solomon Burke, Wilson Pickett, Aretha Franklin. He was a great teacher; Jerry was my mentor. We made four sides with a wonderful black group, the Rays – among them 'Silhouettes' and 'Daddy Cool'. The records were financed by Gene Goodman, Benny Goodman's brother, and released on our own label, XYZ Records, with a custom pressing deal from Columbia. 'Silhouettes' became a hit in Philadelphia and 'Daddy Cool' hit two days later in Washington and Baltimore. And that's how we began our string of hits with Freddie Cannon, Billy and Lilly and Danny and the Juniors. I met Frankie Valli and Bob Gaudio wandering the halls of 1650 Broadway. In 1961 we had our first chart record, 'Bermuda', with the Four Seasons and then busted really big at the end of 62 with 'Sherry'.

**Seymour Stein**: Another building just as important as the Brill was 1650 Broadway, a block and a half away. It didn't have a name, it wasn't as glamorous and it had cheaper rent. That was where Kama Sutra had their offices. Artie Ripp idolised George Goldner, who was a great innovator but could not hold on to anything he had. George was a tremendous gambler; he would lose his record companies over a game or a bet. He was a great lover of the mambo and started a label called Tico Records, which was a big influence in bringing around people like Tito Puente; George championed that. Then he had Frankie Lymon & the Teenagers and drifted into rock 'n' roll. He became very successful but it was short-lived. Frankie Lymon died of an overdose. After Tico, George started the Rama and Gee labels. Gee had the Crows record in 1954, 'Gee', which was for me the first rock 'n' roll record.

Artie Ripp thought of himself as a young George Goldner. He started Kama Sutra with two partners, Phil Steinberg and Hy Mizrahi. They had the Lovin' Spoonful, Melanie, the 1910 Fruitgum Company, and the whole bubblegum thing. For a while they were a hot little company.

**ALO**: Artie Ripp and Phil Steinberg were the epitome of this newfound Manhattan celebration, Jewish cowboys who had ridden in from the plains of the Bronx and Brooklyn to feast on this half-mile radius of melody, diming and hustle. They reigned over it as their own Dodge City via Kama Sutra, their indie production company. Ripp was blessed by his name, merely having to add an 'off' to it to get misunderstood and blessed into the game. Artie was a taller, speedy, rock 'n' poppin' version of 50s actor Richard Conte, and I liked him. His passion, his balls and his smoke could get you transfixed to whatever piece of vinyl he was promoting or rehearsing on you and make you a believer faster than Neil Diamond. Phil Steinberg had a heart and physique to equal at least five of the Magnificent Seven. He minded Artie's front, mouth, mind and sidewalk in the same way Chris Stamp minded the creativity of Lambert and Townshend. Third partner Mizrahi was not seen around and rumoured to spend most of his time at the racetrack with TV's Ben Casey, actor Vince Edwards. Phil Steinberg's tight Hebrew curls locked into his Victor McLaglenesque skull, encasing the warmest eyes and smile you'd wish to behold while a true Cisco Kid black and silver studded cowboy suit gloved his massive frame. Phil and I would get even closer later in 68 when he visited me at the London nursing home in which I was attempting to wring and dry out my drug-addled famepain when he was facing some parallel monsters. Meanwhile, back at the pharmacological patio, drugs reigned while we thought it was us. Artie Ripp would later be the coil that sprung Billy Joel on the world, even if the first outing was released at Rippspeed – Joel's pitch on this faultily mastered single came nearer Alvin and the Chipmunks than the Brooklyn Pavarotti tone he'd warbled and intended.

So in the world of late 1964 the jury was out, but the results thus far were good. I bid adieu to Kama Sutra, left Seymour Stein to decide who'd make the *Billboard* charts the next week, and walked the fifteen blocks up Broadway to Columbus Circle and the north-west corner building on Broadway and 61st, now home to Starbucks, then home to Atlantic Records and the Bob Crewe companies, operating under a name with Bob's normal flair for understatement – Genius Inc.

Bob's digs were a far cry from the garish Rupert Pupkin/Acid-À-Go-Go-meets-Miami-Fountainbleu vomit green décor that templed the Kama Sutra gang. Bob had a style and sense of art and equation reflected in hues of orange, raw brown and ochre that were up-to-the-minute and flattering to all. The feel of his offices was generous and devoid of panic and that mood would inspire my decorating schemes later on.

The Stones, holiday done, kicked off their three-month 'Secure The Homeland' tour on 24 July 1964 at the Empress Ballroom on as-good-as-real Beatles home turf, Blackpool. The seaside holiday resort was invaded by drunken braveheart laddies who'd stormed south of the border looking for a real good-bad time, your prototype football hooligans.

The Stones started into a tight show, acting oblivious to the bawl of 'think yer as good as the Beatles' rebel yells, gobs and scowls that latreened, hooted'n'hollered from the swaying front rows of inbred factory fodder. Mick played it close to the chest and smothered his valence into the band so as not to escalate the goading into pitchforks. Brian Jones went for the opposite. He took the moment as his to upstage the sensibly reticent Mick and started off on a preening, affected dance taunting the drunken butch frontliners. From the semaphoric pit all flags signalled danger and rage as the occupants began a contest to see which of them could gob on a Stone. Had Brian made it to Altamont, nobody would have gotten out alive.

**Bill Wyman**, *Stone Alone*: Keith was livid. He moved over to where Brian was being abused and gave the ringleader a warning between songs. Minutes later, Keith was spat on. Outraged, he retaliated by jamming the heel of his boot down on the knuckles of the spitting troublemaker who had been leaning with his hands and chin resting on the lip of the stage. Nor did he end it there; after taking one step backwards, he plunged the toe of his boot into the lout's nose. In the ensuing riot we would have been slaughtered if the stage hadn't been six foot high.

**Ian Stewart**, in *Stone Alone*: It was very nearly the date on my gravestone. There were no cops, no bouncers, just a couple of old retainers in uniform at each corner of the stage. Then one guy in the front spat at Keith, and Keith kicked him in the head. And that was it. Good night. The whole place erupted. Keith thought he was God and that he could kick one of these guys and get away with it.

**ALO**: A thirsty evil was starting to permeate our proceedings. The wild west of America had rubbed its leg against us and had given us a licence to be louts. We were beginning to abuse our altitude. Violence and anger would become permanent fixtures.

Mick would laugh it off with a condescending or nervous shrug. With a flick of his wrist, as if tossing the ash off the end of a cigarette, he would feign the irritation of a tired housewife – 'Oh, you lot! At it again!' He'd moan, 'Go back to the Alamo', while Keith and I practised our fast draws with flick knives, stilettos and bravado. On some occasions Mick would butch up, snarl and join the gang. The newspapers enjoyed these ballroom showdowns, putting the group on the nation's breakfast tables the following morning, extolling the bravado of Jagger and Co. I would put my two cents' worth in, explaining the meaning of Mick: 'He stirs up some incredibly intense feelings in many males. Sex, rage and rebellion – he brings it all to the surface.' This only served to further fan the flames.

A few weeks later I managed to create my own mayhem on *Juke Box Jury*, albeit behind the scenes. I was in London and actress Judy Huxtable, Sean Kenny's wife at the time, had been booked to appear on the panel. Sean, who was away, asked if I'd mind escorting her there and playing manager. 'Not at all,' I told Sean. 'My pleasure. I'd much rather a busman's holiday than another Saturday-À-Go-Go domestic.'

I hugged the last of the afternoon joint and Reg hugged the curb as we said goodbye to Holland Park and zoomed into the Bush. Two blocks west, the Chevy Impala made a right and screeched into a parking spot a few paces from the BBC studio entrance. Judy H was on the first show. The BBC covered two shows fortnightly; the first one went out live at 5.25 p.m. and the other was taped immediately after and was aired the following Saturday. The live show went smoothly, happily back on its track after the Stones had derailed it a couple of weeks earlier. Judy, yours truly and the effervescent Reg repaired to the empty Green Room.

On the box was the taping of the second show (it being a few minutes past 5.55 p.m.). On the 'other side', the commercial ITV channel's *Thank Your Lucky Stars* would be booming out. I changed the channel to *Lucky Stars*; we poured ourselves a drink and sat down to watch the popular rival. The door was flung open and in stepped a burly, curly beetroot-faced BBC commissionaire. He looked at us, looked at the telly, back at us and snapped, 'You are not allowed to have *that* on in here. It's against BBC policy.'

With that he marched over to the set and turned it back to the BBC channel, which for some reason wasn't even showing the *Juke Box Jury* then being taped, but some regular BBC programming.

'Hold on!' said Reg. 'Switch it back, dear, we was watching the other side.'

'I don't care,' blustered burly curly. 'You can't watch it in here!'

'That's ridiculous,' Judy chimed in. 'I've just been a guest on—'

'That doesn't make any difference,' slobbered the uniformed beetroot with disdain. I stood up, happy that I now had a new show to attend to and a fresh mark to hit.

'Do you have to be so fuckin' rude?' I enquired, engine running.

'And we don't allow that language in here, mister,' the commissionaire honked back as Reg headed for the TV and switched it back to ITV. The commish switched it back. By now a few people had gathered in the room, either as a result of the raised voices or the end of the *JBJ* taping. Having an audience to our regrettable behaviour was like adding fuel to the fire.

'Right. You lot will all have to vacate the premises,' the commish snapped. 'Now!'

'Oh, fuck off, you worn out bit of useless shrapnel . . . fuckin' leave us alone,' I suggested. I knew where this take was going, understood my role and was warming to it. Burly huffed and puffed, turned on his heels and marched out with an 'I'll be back'. He returned, followed in short order by a half-dozen played-out burlies.

'Right, then,' crowed burly number one, buoyed by the numbers. 'You are hereby ordered to leave the premises. This way out,' he beckoned in his best *Dixon of Dock Green*. 'Mr Cotton's orders. He's the head of Light Entertainment here.'

I hadn't got 'Yeah, very fuckin' light' out of my mouth before little Billy Cotton Jr entered the room. His father had been a band-leading icon of the airwaves from World War II on, much-loved for his opening signature cry of

'Wakey, Wakey! Hello all!' What Lawrence Welk was to the immigrant American viewer, Billy Cotton was to the UK.

'I think you had all better leave. Miss Huxtable, you were an invited guest of the show, but your friends . . .' he tutted in our direction. Bill Cotton Jr was a penpusher, a dribbler, a bed wetter and wimp. This was my possibly addled point of view at the time – so there need be no cause for alarm amongst the next batch of Cottonettes.

'You're Andrew Oldham, aren't you? You are one of the managers of the Rolling Stones, aren't you?' Junior said, accusingly.

Guilty as charged, I nodded.

'He swore at me, Mr Cotton, sir.' Burly got hotter and bolshier.

'I think we may as well leave, Judy,' I suggested. 'Just as well,' sneered Burly. It was that or the police. 'Troops over the Chinese line,' I thought. Reg didn't bother to think and shoved Burly out into the corridor. 'You and whose fuckin' army? You lame creased piece of shit,' Reg roared theatrically. I could see he was getting into his part, too. 'Eyes front,' he screamed and winked in my direction. 'If you do not leave this instant, I'll call the police!' barked Cotton Jr. Down the corridor we went, through the ground floor reception and out on to the street. Following us was a semi-battalion of commissionaires and, at a safe distance, the diminutive scowling head of Light Entertainment whom I thought I heard say, 'Just because he's with the Rolling Stones he thinks he can—'

The Chevy was three cars to our left. We walked to it and started to get in, Judy first, while the madding crowd spilled out on to the evening pavement and gawked at our expulsion. Standing out front was Bill Cotton Jr who now had more than a few punters to play to. David Jacobs, fellow deejay Pete Murray and a dozen others had also come out to see what was happening.

David Jacobs was explaining in faultless announcer tones what had just transpired to the equally dapper, taller, blue-blazered Pete Murray. 'That's pretty silly, David,' said Murray.

'People like him give the business a bad name. He won't be around long,' I heard Cotton leer as I opened the passenger door to let myself in. I got pissed, reached down into the glove compartment for the black, leather-bound steel-tipped cosh and started in towards Little Big Man Bill.

'Wakey, Wakey, you wanker. Wait till you feel this in the side of your fuckin' head.'

A sixth or theatrical sense had me keep the cosh partially hidden from view as I headed for the man. I was all out of sync, moving forward into busy traffic when I should have been on the exit ramp, fading on a fast and lasting remark. Instead, I was moving in a direction *fatale*.

'No, Andrew . . .'

I was a yard away from whacking the git when a tall bugger grabbed me from behind in a body hold. It was yer BBC Radio 2 deejay, Pete Murray. His customary laid-back RAF eloquence evaporated as Pete Murray snarled in my ear in flawless cockney, 'Don't be a cunt, Andrew, there's witnesses! It's not worth it . . . bugger off.'

I relaxed and allowed myself to look around and see the set clearly, a little bit of noir *Chinatown* finale in Shepherd's Bush. It was a crane shot – the whirly a good twenty feet up, looking down on Pete pinning my cosh-bearing arm to my side. I'm on the wrong set, I thought to myself. My script told me to cut and run for cover.

Mr Murray felt me relax and let me go. I walked back to the car, got in and allowed Reg to screech us away. It was another day of the locusts, the establishment holding its line, the tea-leaf gangsters marking time, all rolled into one. I did not, however, need a reading of those tea leaves to know that 2Stoned I might already be, but it was still way too early in this boy's tale for him to be charged with possession of pot and GBH.

*

In November 1989 I was in Manhattan, as was Marianne Faithfull. It was one of those razor-sharp Kojak sunny late fall days. My eldest son Sean, now twenty-four, and I set off to see Marianne at the Church of St Anne and the Holy Trinity in Brooklyn in what was to be a recorded performance dedicated to the works of Kurt Weill. Not my cup of tea, or lederhosen either. I was raised on the ultimate 'look out, ol' Mackie's back', with which Bobby 'Mack The Knife' Darin had stylishly made the leap from the 'Splish Splash/Dream Lover' teen crooner into the Sinatra stakes, and, in doing so, had set the standard for future pop interpretations of Weill. (The other Weil in pop was, of course, Cynthia Weil of Mann and Weil, collaborators on such classics as 'You've Lost That Lovin' Feelin' and 'We Gotta Get Out Of This Place.')

Every other decade, it seems, a bunch of air-rarefied muso exiles from mainstream revive Weill's Weimar forebodings. This newfound lust for Kurt's dark melodies and intricate arrangements by ex-junkies and vegetarians is as inviting as a summer season stuck on a pier with Matt Monro crooning 'Monday, Monday'. I'd rather they opted for 'Twenty Flight Rock', or my idea of Kurt Weill – the real deal, Mr Gene Vincent.

Nevertheless, it remained a glorious fall Brooklyn day, and my son and I were enjoying stellar syntony. Faithfull, the occasion, plus the plonk and

Bobby Darin, ALO and Bob Crewe, Manhattan, 1973

the day's freedom combined to will us together and we liked it. We walked past Norman'd Mailerville cobblestoned redbricked mews with views of the murky East River. Sean and I kicked up the leaves and passed many a tree as I wondered aloud 'which one of ye grew for Brooklyn'. Then it was time to hush up and say hello to Marianne.

I was pleased to see her rise to the occasion. Her audience seemed to consist of Mariannettes, ash-grey faces who'd bypassed life and jumped directly from youth into rehab and spinsterville. Marianne gave them hope and soothed their despair as they rubbed their souls together within the warmth of their black-velveted angel on tits. She looked like a deliciously poisonous gift of chocolates, all paint-boxed and absolut.

God bless her for living through hell, but at some stage of the game you should really stop going back there. I shuddered at the metaphorical whimsy of it all, guided Sean and myself out of the still of St Mary's and into the still of the night.

This was the first time I'd seen her since we'd neighboured in the early 80s, she above Canal on-off Greenwich, me below on Tribeca's Beach Street. Marianne was living with some physically abusive monster who'd have failed the audition for a Kiss tribute band. My pal Tony Russo set up a formal dinner expressly so that we could beat up the little shit and I packed a cosh and one of those dual-purpose knuckle-duster switchblades for the occasion. Tony was back-up and Magnum'd, as in Eastwood. My wife Esther, sons

Sean and pram 'n' bottled one-year-old Maximillian came, too. When we got there the boyfriend was not to be seen – either he'd made himself scarce or was out for the count.

Tony and I decided on a line of down in the bathroom, forgot about our planned vigilantism and settled down to Marianne's brave but nervous roast beef, mash and gravy dinner, served up with reflective laughs braised in a sauce of selective memory. Sean was told what style his father once had (just what neither of us needed to hear) and Marianne asked once too often how Esther was able to deal with such a handful as myself.

Fuck this charade of broken English, I thought, as all of us – Russo, Faithfull and me – pretended for the night that we were all so Manhattan'd and well. Take me home to Hall & Oates and 'Out Of Touch', my insides screamed. The night was saved by Russo, whose take on us Brits and his adventures researching the pleasures of Her Majesty's prisondom were fresh meat for us prisoners of Greenwich Avenue – and as funny as a move out of jail.

But any leftover joy started to run out for me when I heard Marianne say, 'Did I tell you, I asked Chris [as in Blackwell, owner of Island Records, who had guided Marianne on the successful second run of her career] if I could record "As Tears Go By" again?' It felt as if she were offering me a nightmare for dessert.

'What would you want to do that for?' I muttered, passing my silver cigarette box towards Tony, motioning him away from the Davidoff's and towards the joints at the left-hand end.

'Would you be interested in doing it with me?' she asked. I shuddered visibly at the thought. Don't get me wrong. I still loved the song; it would always have a special place in my heart. But my bottle was almost empty and I had dedicated its remainder to building my lot with Esther. I didn't have enough left for another go-round in the world of vinyl.

'Chris doesn't think we could do it,' she went on. 'Bully for fuckin' Chris,' I thought. 'Glorified wheelbarrow merchant, let him go remake "My Boy Lollipop" if he's so damn keen on cover versions.'

By now I couldn't wait to get wasted, Hall & Oates and home.

'Of course,' Marianne continued, 'when I mentioned doing it with you, he said, "Just what I need, Oldham and Faithfull, two burnt-out people working together".'

Ouch! Chris & Blackwell, but well canned and very spot on.

A few months later, Tony Russo and I had cause to wish we had ferreted out Marianne's live-in motherfucker and done him in. I got a call from Tony on the scrambled line from his Bleecker Street loft. He told me to meet him in the lobby of the Gramercy Park Hotel as soon as possible. Marianne was there with him and not well.

I cabbed from Beach Street with a mad Russian. I alighted, thanked and tipped my man in line with the eight-minute ride. Boris Somethingorotherivitch, my huggie-bear of a cabbie, had been very accommodating. He'd even slowed down for one corner just so I could 'get my things in order', which in 80s-speak meant 'fuckin' slow down so I can do a line'.

Tony stood in the lobby, trusty replica Magnum .357 ever ready and tucked into his Levi'd belt. Russo was deceptively bespectacled, ponytailed, impatient and solicitous, a walking ad for the Paragon Sporting Store in fur-lined silver/beige anorak and a couple of layers of woollen sweaters, his tight five-foot-seven frame cuffed in mountain brown Dexter's – though Tony's treks were not exactly the kind Paragon had in mind.

After a glass of wine, cup of espresso, or bagel, Tony, a video editing star who was going through a little burning out (which is probably why Creature One, the photographer Mick Rock, had introduced us in the first place), would become very British, metamorphing out of his Sicilian New Yorkese roots to regale us all with brilliant, comic Brit-speak. With den mother cocaine as our surrogate mum, Tony and I became instant family speedpals. There were less than six degrees of separation between us and more than six grams in common. That's why we were converging on the Gramercy that brittle November fateful faithfull night.

'She nearly fucking did it this time, Andrew,' Tony spoke of Marianne in drip-drop-*Get-Carter* rapid fire as he wound me past the bar and towards a room on the dark lower ground floor.

'That fucking little cunt whacked her so hard her jaw had to be wired up.' Tony referred to the little live-in runt we should have trampled back on the eve of our dinner. He took out a room key and let us both in on another episode of nearly so-long-Marianne.

I've entered a lot of dark rooms in my time. Hotel rooms, cold and expensively dreary or faded and repainted by the overdosing of drugs, take on that look of a room with a view of the already dead. To check in and check out on living scours the colour from even the brightest room. The curtains, the couches, the bedspread get sheened over with a deadly pallor.

Marianne lay in bed, her upper torso twisted in pain. Her jaw was wired up. The metal holding it together blended into her steel-grey complexion, which matched the yellow/white dead fluff of the blanket on her breasts. The lights in the room somehow only served to make the room murkier. I had to think fast to stop myself being sucked into this madness. Here was this whacked-out hopeless fawn hit and run over by her life, she who had cried wolf once too often and now lay twittering between life and death. I can't remember what we said; all I know is I reached into my every last reserve. We talked about talent, joy and fun – the very topics I'd found so painful at that recent dinner. I now turned them into visions to be cherished, embraced and reached for, consummations devoutly to be wished. Russo had assured me we weren't there to fill the stalls; we had to give the performances of our lives.

I shocked on. I chastised her for waste, praised her for being, looked for signs of my words gripping her very soul. She insisted on coughing and smoking. I still had my Johnny Carson phobia about smoking in bed; in her state she could easily drop a cigarette and set fire to everything. But Marianne, wire-jawed, smacked and/or morphined up as she was, could hardly be expected to follow my Carson-learnt one-foot-on-the-floor smoking-in-bed rule. I insisted on placing plastic room service buckets filled to the brim with ice all over the bed. I instructed a half-asleep Marianne that these were fucking ashtrays, and she was to use them – and don't you dare fucking nod out now. I was in the white heat of my holy rolling and she'd better not spoil one of Russo's and my finest hours.

It was the blind leading the blind. Tony and I, lecturing, rallied Marianne between bouts of lines in the bathroom. We emerged, fortified, to pounce on Marianne for rounds three, four and five of 'pep talk' to keep her awake and coax her back into some spark of a breathing life.

It was not ten years later that another sweetheart of rock rage, Steve Marriott, met the end of his turn on this earth. He had got 2Stoned and had smoked in bed. He nodded out, both he and the bed caught fire, the bed slipped into gear and carried Stevie away to his maker.

Marianne checked out of the Gramercy Park Hotel and into the Hazleton clinic. I'm not sure if it all clicked on that round or the next – I was 2Stoned and not counting – but for sure Marianne turned the corner and reclaimed her life.

I think this Marianne-doth-Kurt-Weill-in-Brooklyn outing was the first time I'd ever seen her perform live. But I would not really see her fully *a-live* until the following Friday when Marianne played New York's Bottom Line.

She was tremendous. On stage alone save bass and guitar, she did not need saving, she was sailing. Here she would have to be better than good. She wasn't torching Berlin retreads but throwing open the pages to herself and her screenplay. She got and gave more than good; she winged, arrowed and rose above the trinity she had lived and died for these twenty-five years: 'As Tears Go By', drugs & fur & Mars bars, and Michael Phillip Jagger. She referred to 'em all, sung 'em and triumphed over the lot. She rose above any critique of her vocal style. In the miracle of the night, she suddenly was.

After a polite interlude I went through to see her backstage. It was the opposite of our Brooklyn backstage hello which had been more like 'fuck you for being here'. Marianne glowed from the night's success. I glowed from seeing a performance that could play anywhere in the world and win, a world in which you didn't have to know 'As Tears Go By' to place her, neither did you have to have followed her tabloid'd life. You just had to be able to experience this woman at one with her life's journey and let her explain it to you in song, let her be there just for you, but finally, thank God, there for herself.

Our eyes smiled that smile. She saw how moved I was.

'Marianne,' I said, 'finally I can admit to you.'

It was not taken as rudeness, as dismissive, or as high-handed as it may sound. She got my heartfelt shorthand and knew exactly what I meant.

She smiled and just said, 'I was good, wasn't I?'

Yes, she was.

*

**Tim Rice**, lyricist: In 1966 I entered the music business full-time as a 'management trainee' at EMI Records. This was a nebulous term and trade for promising young men in suits whose future would probably include being dispatched to a top position in EMI's operations in Mexico City or Auckland five years down the road after shuffling around the various departments becoming 'well-rounded' in all things EMI. My first duties were vague in the extreme; I was assigned to half a desk and put by a phone that seemed to be the line for disgruntled fans. My first call came from the president of the official Dean Martin Appreciation Society. My second call came from Andrew Lloyd Webber, who wanted to know if I'd managed yet to place any of our songs with EMI artists. My first weeks proved that this was not to be a non-stop riot of glamour and hobnobbing with the stars, although in week two I did manage to pee alongside Peter Noone of Herman's Hermits.

Management trainees were all boys, no woman allowed, and we all seemed to be the product of public schools. We wore suits and ties and clocked in by 9 a.m. whether or not we had been out late the night before, allegedly working and talent spotting (and this was year six of the swinging 60s!). After a short while I was moved into A&R. This was tantamount to winning the pools – I could have been sent to the classical department or ended up in the mail room, but I lucked out in Artistes and Repertoire, where the hit records were conceived, the stars came by to discuss their next waxing, and Norrie Paramor was king. In a strange way it was rather organised, but it was organised in the wrong way for the changing music business. It was the end of the era when the record companies were able to boss the artists around, but they were still doing so and hanging on to the pecking order of earlier days. The vast majority of the records of the day were produced by in-house record producers who were all on salary, with no royalties. The whole thing was run like a perfectly ordinary business in which 'flair' wasn't really encouraged. You wore your suit and tie, you clocked in by 9 o'clock and you clocked out at 5.30. It was all run in a very un-showbiz way, although one saw changes as the 60s wore on, especially as artists started to compose their own material and demand a say in how they sounded. A lot of the people at the top of the music empire weren't really music men and didn't know quite what they'd got with groups like the Beatles. The artists and managers were still fairly deferential to the record companies and didn't really worry or think too much about the deals they perhaps could get.

I know that Andrew was an exception with the Stones because he produced them outside of Decca; they weren't done by an in-house producer. This was a big change; he was way ahead of his time there, working in this way that was normal to Americans but only practised by a few in England. You had Joe Meek with the Tornados at Decca and EMI; Dennis Preston leasing Lonnie Donegan and Chris Barber to Pye/Nixa; Robert Stigwood in a direct deal with Roland Rennie and Sir Joseph Lockwood; and Michael Barclay and Phillip Waddilove with Eden Kane at Decca. That was about it and that's pretty much the way it stayed until the new movers and shakers like Denny Cordell, Tony Secunda, Kit Lambert and Chris Stamp moved in later in the 60s and demanded a bigger cut and a bigger say and started getting their own labels.

The Beatles, at least until the end of 65, were still very much just an act who were summoned to the studio by their record company to do their sessions. George Martin was on a salary; most of the EMI producers were. EMI was very strict about filling in forms twenty-four hours ahead of every job. Junior A&R men like me spent a lot of time filling in forms. You had to state exactly what was wanted in the studio, what microphones were needed, what instruments were going to be played. Everything had to be fixed up for every session well in advance, with hundreds of forms. I remember getting into trouble more than once, for either being a minute late or for not filling in a form exactly. You had to turn up at a quarter to ten, fifteen minutes before the session, to make sure everything was plugged in right. The sessions were run very much like school, 10–1, an hour off for lunch, 2–5, an hour off, and evening sessions, 6–9 or 7–10.

Even Cliff Richard, a very big star, was expected to do three sides in a one three-hour session. I was very impressed with Cliff; he just knew his stuff. He would have always worked out exactly what he was doing. When I joined, things were just starting to change. I worked a lot from Norrie's house and had to walk his Boxer dogs, no doubt the same way Andrew used to walk the models' dogs at Mary Quant's – all part of the training.

**ALO:** 'What do you think?' the early A&R man would ask.

This was a set-up in which basically nobody stepped up to the plate and claimed the mantle of 'producer'. The A&R fella, A as in Artist, R as in repertoire, would select the material and match it to the artist and in that order, unless an artist had already scored a hit or two. The arranger would select the key and arrange the song or cop the already existing American arrangement. The engineer would record the singer vocalising to the arrangement. The A&R man would generally nod approval. If the take had some magic, it could make it, but jumping in and grappling with a song in an attempt to secure that magic was not part of the A&R job description; that sort of enthusiasm would cost too much time and money. No, the general malaise was to follow the formula – pick the song, record in a three-hour haze, bung the ingredients on a conveyor belt and hope for a hit.

In America the guvnor of pre-Beat boom A&R was Mitch Miller, arguably the most successful A&R man in the history of the record business. He broke his musical legs playing oboe and cor anglais on many a renowned recording. He toured with George Gershwin and accompanied him on piano. In the late 40s he started working for record companies as a recording executive, concentrating on classical and children's records. Eventually, he was producing Vic Damone, Frankie Laine, Guy Mitchell, Johnny Mathis, Rosemary Clooney, Percy Faith, Johnny Horton, Mahalia Jackson and Johnnie Ray. It was during his CBS tenure that the meaning of 'country division' actually came into its own with the early recordings of Ray Price, Lefty Frizell and Marty Robbins. He was also an instigator in the marriage of screen and vinyl, notably with the recordings he commissioned for *High Noon* and *The Bridge on the River Kwai*.

In 1985 Mr Miller told Ted Fox, 'The same rules always apply . . . taste, musicianship, getting the best out of the artist. Many times the artist doesn't know what his best characteristics are, and you're there to remind them. You can't put in what isn't there, but you can remind them of what they have and what they're not using.'

'So what do you think?' the A&R man still asked.

'Oh, twelve, eight, four (violins, violas and cellos). Three trumpets, three 'bones (trombones), two altos (saxophones) and a bari. Three girls, piano, drums, bass, percussion and guitar. That should do it,' would be an arranger's response with a line-up suited to an already successful star. Otherwise, divide it all in two and that would be the budget for an absolute beginner.

'Sounds good,' imagined the A&R man, before putting down the phone and getting back to the paperwork on his desk. 'Could you call the Musicians' Union and I'll see you on the session.'

'Okay. We've got that charity dinner at Bruce Forsyth's house on Friday, the one Lionel and Joyce Blair are organising for Dr Barnardo's.'

'Okay, I'll see you there.'

**Tim Rice**: At the start of 1963 the four top-selling artists in the UK were Elvis Presley, Cliff Richard, the Shadows and Frank Ifield. Norrie Paramor produced all of them except Elvis. He stayed at EMI and I worked for him. The other producers went off to form Air London. George Martin had the Beatles, of course, and all of Brian Epstein's major acts. He was joined by Ron Richards, who did the Hollies, and John Burgess, who had done Adam Faith, Manfred Mann, Peter & Gordon and Freddie & the Dreamers. The fourth partner in Air was Peter Sullivan, an in-house A&R man for Decca, who produced Englebert Humperdinck and Tom Jones under Dick Rowe's supervision. All these guys went off and formed their own company so they could get royalties. Norrie was not involved with that, perhaps because he was a little bit older than the rest. He was the generation before George Martin, 'a generation' then being a short period of time.

By late 66 and 67 it was becoming a struggle in Manchester Square. A lot of the hits had started to come from outside. The Move, Joe Cocker and Procol Harum all came from the David Platz Essex Music set-up and were produced by Denny Cordell. The Beatles, the Hollies and Manfred Mann were all technically coming in from Air London, even though they were EMI acts. I think the only house-grown hits were from Vince Hill with that lovely but desperately corny 'Edelweiss' and 'Thank U Very Much' by the Scaffold. My job was to listen to all these tapes that came in, most of them just awful. I managed to make one record out of that process with a group called the

Shell. But you could tell what was okay and what was awful. Nowadays with home studios and CDs, people can record themselves so well that it's harder to separate the junk from a finished record.

**ALO:** There remain three elements that make up a hit record: a hit song, a hit song and a hit song. Quincy Jones was quoted in his Michael Jackson run as saying, 'You can't shine shit', but with all due respect to some recent accomplished recordings, I'm not sure if that's true today.

**Tim Rice**: Even as far as the Beatles were concerned, the attitude was that if the records stopped working there was always panto. But there was a lot to be said for the time and the process. Careers got built and artists had a chance to develop, foul up, pick themselves up, dust themselves off and move on. It's very hard today for an act to develop and stick with their own thing. You are the result of a big record company marketing meeting where they decide whether you are worth sticking a million pounds into to get you known. It should be easier to make a record, but it's not. The record companies have all the control again and are only interested in you if they can market the hell out of you and hit no. 1 first week out. All the executives are on points and incentives and in most cases have better deals than the acts. Building careers would seem to be out of the window.

**ALO**: Back in the day of building careers or cleaning windows, you never approached Regent Sound from the east, always from the west. You'd have bounded up or down Charing Cross Road, or bounded out of Soho underneath the arches that bridged Foyle's Book Shop and officed the workshop of Sean Kenny on the second floor between a one and three where the likes of Hélène offered French lessons to the discerning business gent, who, if nabbed, could claim he was en route to Foyle's.

As I sprinted over the Charing Cross Road and headed towards the no. 4 with Regent Sound on its ground floor, the wooden hanging signs that denoted the five or six music publishers per square foot swayed in the afternoon breeze, eerily reminding one of Shylocks and pawnbrokers, while the storefront windows were flooded with the sheet music of the day. The piano copies were fronted by $8 \times 10$ glossy shots of young, tousled men with eight-quid guitars and crucifixes, worried thirtyish crooners in cardigans and sucking on pipes *à la* Bing Crosby, and/or wasp-waisted, flair-skirted, peroxide-topped smiling damsels of song, one of whom could have been Hélène, but was actually, the caption assured us, the pre-'Downtown' Petula

Charlie Watts, Denmark Street, 1964

Clark, who'd had seven Top 20 hits pre-1962, including her versions of 'Alone', 'Ya Ya Twist', 'The Little Shoemaker', 'My Friend The Sea', and 'Majorca'.

That corner, and that run, for some unbeknownst reason amongst all the could-be's, reminds me of Kim Fowley, Paul Simon and Dick James. Dick looked out from a first-floor window on the north corner of Charing Cross Road and Denmark Street, counting his blessings and royalties, happy to have hung up his wig along with his days as the voice on the theme song to TV's *Robin Hood*. One day, two years earlier, a music biz miracle had befallen him when a northern manager named Brian Epstein had walked in off the street and said, 'Please take my Beatles!' and Dick did.

Here I want to bring on stage a wonderful transatlantic character. Enter Mr Love & A Percentage, Peter Kameron, a princeling on the LA Hebe-wisdom circuit. Pete nobbed and chipped away at life high in the Hollywood Hills above Mount Zeus. He'd come up through the Bronx and Brooklyn, the original white boy on hope. He Lindy'd and jitterbugged his way through the 40s keeping his priorities in his sights: good babes, good music, good company, a little wisdom and good dope. In another life he could have been retired in Boca Raton playing mah-jongg; in this life he was a deli-baron with a palette for talent.

Pete managed and/or published the likes of Pete Seeger, Odetta and the Modern Jazz Quartet. The early 50s found him bringing *West Side Story* to Europe. He was point man for the setting up of Essex Music in the UK. He was music consultant to Harry Saltzman and Cubby Broccoli for the James Bond films and he was Terence Stamp's manager for a while in the 60s when James Woolf passed on. He then became 'the manager of the managers of the Who' – meaning that he attempted to manage the Who's managers, Kit Lambert and Chris Stamp.

**Pete Kameron**, entrepreneur, music publisher: In 1952 I went over to London to look into the publishing business. At that time I was there with Howie Richmond, who had set up Folkways Music, to meet the foreign affiliates – our sub-publishers. When I arrived there was a man in striped trousers and top hat and a limo waiting to take me to a press conference. I was the manager of the Weavers; we had a big hit at the time with 'Goodnight, Irene'. Anyway, that was my introduction to London.

What started out as a three-week trip turned into four months. I was trying to understand how things worked in Europe, because at the time the whole record and publishing business was in America, and the European thing was ancillary. After about a week, I went to see the person who was representing our catalogue in Paris. I was starting to get some strange feelings about the European end of the business. When I got back to New York, I said, 'You know what? I think we're being screwed. I think we should set up a European performing rights society.' And that's what Howie did in 1954. This is how David Platz came on the scene. He'd been working for Southern Music, and over the years he received stock and eventually a full partnership. That's how Essex Music came about. I left Howie in 1955 and went into business with Monte Kay as Kameron & Kay, managing a roster of jazz artists including the Modern Jazz Quartet, Chris Conner, Charlie Mingus and J.J. Winding. Monte and I then set up a publishing company from London. At this point, I was going to be vertical, and I was no longer going to be dependent on management. The only reason I went into management was to build up these other assets, and they made me quite wealthy in the coming years. That was the beginning of my understanding of the business, especially going over to Europe on tours with the Modern Jazz Quartet through 56 and 57, and getting that first-hand knowledge.

We changed the whole thing in America. We broke the thing down and the big companies started to pay off. We had sixty-eight disc jockeys set up throughout the country and we made up acetates and sent them to these key guys. It changed the face of the business – later it was called payola. And later the same thing started to happen in Europe. In Europe they're so charming. You gotta lift up your pants or something; you had a standard 10/50/50 count and by the time it got siphoned through France or Italy back to England you got paid in sauce. With the growth of the jazz thing in Europe we were in a good position to negotiate and I was able to push the horizons as to what we could demand and make.

**ALO**: Paul Simon, with his short-order cuteness, was getting laid by London, strumming his guitar on the coffee bar circuit. He and Art Garfunkel – the former Tom & Jerry – were waiting for CBS to get excited over their first LP, which they did when producer Bob Johnson overdubbed drums, guitar and bass, after which 'The Sounds Of Silence' went to no. 1 and CBS called the little boy home. While strumming and bumming in London Paul hung out on the right street to learn that there were fifty ways to sign a writer (and not too many of them good for the writer). He formed Charing Cross Music, signed himself to himself and published happily ever after, thus becoming one of the rare examples of writing thoroughbreds who didn't get skinned alive the first time round the course.

Andy Wickham may have insisted that I meet Kim Fowley because he was very tall and American. Mr Fowley, I would guess, came to London with P.J. Proby, maybe with Bobby Jameson, whom Keith Richards and I would produce. The important thing is he came, got laid and carried on about 'Nut Rocker' but it was the man himself that impressed. One did not know his background but one could sense it. Kim came to Regent Sound one bright afternoon when I was making my first LP with the Andrew Oldham Orchestra and we created a devastating remake of 'The House Of The Rising Sun', which we renamed 'The Rise Of The Brighton Surf' in homage to the recent Easter punch-up in Brighton between the raving Mods and charismatic Rockers, thereby giving England its own *West Side Story* – real on-the-seafront street theatre. Kim stayed while Mick crooned 'Da Doo Ron Ron'. Quite sexy it was, too, with Mick doing a laconic slo-mo hurt reading. A couple of proleptic members of Procol Harum helped out on 'My Boy Lollipop' and 'I Want To Hold Your Hand'. That's where I met the long and the short of it, when he and Paul Simon were two Yanks, not in Oxford, but at the right time in London Town.

57

**Kim Fowley**, entrepreneur, producer: Paul Simon was one of the people that I spoke to, because when you're under twenty-five and you're standing on Tin Pan Alley, you talk with anybody Jewish or in the Mafia or that's gay, flamboyant or magical – not necessarily in that order. Of course, back then any woman who was beautiful, magnificent or perverse, or any guy who looked like a moron who had money to invest was also fair game, or any kid who knew another kid who was a Beatle, knew a Beatle, or might be a future Beatle. I always used to categorise everybody, like, 'What can I get out of this man or woman?' Sometimes I got money, sometimes I got information. It certainly wasn't money with Paul Simon.

I came to England in 1964 because I'd produced the record 'Popsicles And Icicles' by the Murmaids on Chattahoochie Records. We were no. 1 for a week and we were knocked out by 'I Want To Hold Your Hand' by the Beatles. Suddenly I realised that everything I'd been doing was going to be made redundant by the Beatles. It was just like when Elvis came out. If you were making Eddie Fisher records, nobody needed you or Eddie Fisher anymore. So, suddenly, nobody needed garage, doo-wop, girl group, any of that Spector stuff. Nobody needed anything; they had the Beatles.

I brought a suitcase full of money so that I could buy my way into Swinging London and I brought records along, so that I could show engineers and say, 'Can you get a sound like that?' I only had two addresses: one was for P.J. Proby and the other was for Ardmore & Beechwood, EMI's publishing division, where there was the guy, Syd Coleman, who'd told Brian Epstein to call George Martin to listen to a few of the Beatles' songs. Syd was publishing some of my things. I got to London on a Saturday and couldn't see him, so I called my other friend, James Marcus Smith, alias P.J. Proby. He appointed me his publicist. He knew I'd done PR for Doris Day's husband Marty Melcher at Arwin Records and that I knew how to go on stage and introduce people. Proby says, 'You're my James Brown-type announcer and PR guy' and he got me a room and a discount.

P.J. Proby got to England before me because he had been hitchhiking through Laurel Canyon and Portland Mason, the daughter of Pamela Mason and the actor James Mason, picked him up and took him home to play for her friends. One of the guys who was there was Jack Good, who did the TV shows *Oh, Boy!* and *Boy Meets Girl*, and when Jack Good sees Proby looking like God, like John Derek meets John Barrymore Sr, singing that Johnny Cash song, 'Bad News Travels Like Wildfire', he jumps up and says, 'You are going to be the American star in *Around The Beatles*!' Just like that. 'You look like Elvis. Nobody in England has seen Elvis. I'll give you a couple of hundred dollars, a round-trip ticket and I'll put you on this Beatles TV show and produce your records. Can you handle that?' Proby says, 'Sure.' It was a different time; you didn't have lawyers and committees then. I asked Proby if he'd had sex with the mother and daughter and he said 'Yes'. So, Proby meets Jack Good a few days later and they fly to London and go straight to Rediffusion, walk up to John and Paul, and Good says, 'Here's your star.' Proby was the only guy that Lennon and McCartney ever introduced on television or on stage.

I worked for Proby from May to November doing his PR and compère work. I had a wonderful time; I got to live Elvis-style. We moved into this Knightsbridge mews house which Shirley Bassey had lived in. Proby had the master bedroom, I had the second bedroom, and downstairs this guy James Phelge – who'd been the Phelge in Nanker Phelge – and the drummer for the Pretty Things, Viv Prince, used to fight over the floor or the couch. I never got to spend my money; everything was free. It was odd; from 1959 I'd had seven chart records in the States up to February of 1964 and then we all got totally replaced by Beatlemania, and by May, at age twenty-four, I was a publicist in England. I'd been no. 1 in England as a writer with 'Nut Rocker' by B. Bumble & the Stingers and I co-produced 'Alley Oop' with Gary Paxton, which made the Top 20, and now I was a press agent. Oh, I got around. I did some experimental recordings with Jimmy Page and Ritchie Blackmore, did some early things for Chris Blackwell, met Dick Rowe, met Joe Meek.

Kim Fowley and ALO, Denmark Street, 1964

By the time I got to Regent Sound and Denmark Street, I didn't care who it was – old or young, rich or poor, gay or straight, famous or non-famous, girl-boy or junkie guitar player – as long as he or she looked rock 'n' roll and I could benefit, have an orgasm, get information, fame or money. I just burst into flame. I wasn't that introspective. I didn't know all the Michael Caine issues about class. I hustled everybody. Paul Simon was just a guy who was standing there. He had Brill Building vibrations, so I just worked him. I probably told him I'd run his catalogue; I probably told him how to have a career for the next forty years. I had sex with either Susan George or Susannah York. I remember that, but I can't remember the difference between them. One of them I dated and one of them I slept with.

I was sought out by Andrew Loog Oldham's genius, Andy Wickham, because I was doing PR for Proby. Remember, I was an Army/National Guard/Air Force guy, which meant I did hand-to-hand combat. I was good with weapons. I knew all about the Kray Twins. I was a Reg King for Proby. I could fight, I could dance, I could fuck, I could get things done.

I turned up at Regent Sound and Andrew said, 'Get in there and sing, make something up.' That's how 'The Rise Of The Brighton Surf' came about. Jimmy Page and John Paul Jones were playing on the tape. I was in the studio because I was one of the in-crowd. You show up because it's somewhere you know you are supposed to be. If Proby had been there, Andrew would have got him to sing. Every night of the week there was pussy, there was touring, there were records, there was money. It was a wonderful time. If you were rejected by one person, there'd be fifty others waiting to fuck with you.

\*

**ALO**: It was in the spring of 1970 that I'd first met Nigel Thomas when producer Denny Cordell brought him by my Wilton, Connecticut, home. I don't know what it was that drew Nigel into our game. It certainly never seemed to be a love of music, but it served very well as bed and board to Nigel's love of life. Positively jaded, challenging, witty, a smooth, lovable, villainous black sheep, Nigel was all this and more, a totally wonderful pirate – tall, dark-haired and moustached, pale with black-coaled eyes, seemingly blackhearted until he let you in. He deigned to be in the music business. We became very good friends and when in 1977 Esther and I were married, Nigel made a very best man. On the one occasion I got him to ante up on his showbiz beginnings, he alluded to 'doing' nightclub bookings on the London West End cabaret circuit for the Simon Sisters, who later split, became vain and begat Carly. At the time of our Connecticut meeting, Nigel was managing and Denny Cordell producing, the Joe Cocker–Leon Russell 'Mad Dogs and Englishmen' tour and recordings. (One evening Joe Cocker sat in front of my living room fire. Outside, it was snowing heavily and northern cold. He sipped his hot toddy, looked into the fire, silent and miles away, but seemingly at ease and happy. He looked up, smiled and said, 'I'd been wondering what was between New York and Boston. So this is it, eh? Not bad, is it? Not bad at all.')

Denny Cordell was always his own man. He produced a good life, along with Procol Harum, Joe Cocker, Freddie King and the Move. He also uncovered Tom Petty and, with Leon Russell, formed the Shelter Record Company.

Early on, after some UK successes, he was rewarded by the powers that be and allowed to travel to the States to record Georgie Fame with New York's finest.

Essex Music, headed in London by Dr Jekyll and Mr Platz and TRO-Essex, its US owner, had more than a fair chunk of Denny (and the Stones, it would turn out) and were doing more than well from being in the right place, right time, when Cordell scored his first national anthem with Procol Harum's 'A Whiter Shade Of Pale' and exploded Joe Cocker into our lives with the classic reworking of Lennon and McCartney's 'With A Little Help From My Friends'.

The TRO-Essex New York house arranger was Tony Visconti, who helped the office look young. Tony was eventually shuttled to the UK where he produced David Bowie, Iggy Pop and T-Rex.

Arrangements for the Fame sessions – as in size and type of studio, number of musicians, time and day – were made by transatlantic phone before Denny and Clive (Georgie Fame) flew off to New York. In a business loath to splurge on expensive instant communication, this was a rarity in and of itself. Airmail, cables and telexes were the norm in a world where 45 rpm records spoke louder than phones.

The session was set for 2 p.m. A sharp rhythm section and New York's best brass were on hand, instruments set up and chops ready, at two sharp. At 2.30 Tony Visconti was going a little spare, with no Denny, no Georgie, and New York's finest happily sitting about kibitzing while being paid by the hour.

About ten of three Denny and Georgie strolled into the studio and beamed a huge hello all around the room, both looking as though they'd just smoked a very nice lunch.

Visconti had a lot of questions. 'Where have you been, why are you late, these guys, the studio, it's all a lot of money. . .'

Denny looked Visconti over, sat down, crossed his legs, tweed coat falling as it should. 'Hold on, Tony,' he began. 'Cool it, man, we're here. Tell everybody we'll begin in a minute. You could have asked us how was lunch.' The relaxed producer removed his coat and Georgie tried to remove or at least contain his grin.

Visconti sighed. 'Just give me the parts and I'll give them out to the musicians.'

'What parts?' enquired Cordell.

'The arrangements for the musicians to read from.' Visconti modulated up into stress.

'We don't have any parts, do we, Clive?' Denny shrugged.

Clive agreed – no parts.

Tony was at a loss to know how fifteen musicians were going to function without written arrangements to read and play from. 'So what do we do with no parts? How does anybody know what to play? How are we going to record three sides with no parts in under two hours?' Then he stabbed angrily, 'Is this how you do it in England?'

Visconti didn't get it. He'd have to go to England to get it.

'Exactly, Tony, you've got it, dear boy,' smiled laconic Cordell. 'How we do it, is . . . first we put the kettle on for a cup of tea. While it's boiling we roll a good joint. Then we put on the record we're going to copy and then we get down to work . . .'

I don't recall a lot of time spent with Denny Cordell in the London of the 60s. We were all very busy working and we can all remember the hits. But further on, in 1977, I was watching the night move by with Lou Adler at the Upper West Side Manhattan club Trax when across the room my eyes locked with the beaming Cordell – hair now grey immaculate blanco, setting off his double-breasted grey flannel suit, all portly and settled in. No more the lithe on-the-road black curls, black smile, jeans and cowboy bandana; he was at the beginning of his Squire Cordell run. He oozed over to where Lou and I sat. Glued to his side was an Anglo-gaunt, intense and quiet fairheaded young gent introduced to us as Tom Petty. Petty was pleased, to meet us. He liked my Stones period, so I was pleased and had he been pressed on it, probably also liked Johnny Rivers, which would have pleased Lou.

But it was more than a courtesy call – Denny was enjoying having us say hello to his star. He'd moved out from behind the studio control room, unshackled himself from Essex Music and England, and moved up front and on to Los Angeles. Both Lou and I enjoyed the real sub-text of what he was saying: 'Hey guys, it's my turn to shine in the street, say hello to *my* star.'

Always a pleasure and thank you, Denny – and well done, Mr Petty, for having the savvy to jumpstart your own good lot with the life-enhancing Denny Cordell. There are only a few 'firsts', Denny, and I hope your children know that you were one of that noble band.

These 'firsts' in life not only succeed and, often enough, give balance to the madness, but their work manages to rise above the medium and define it for that moment in time. 'Firsts' also know when to leave the room. Denny, as you sit down to eat upstairs with Tony Secunda and Nigel Thomas, give them my love and make sure David Platz gets the bill. In our industry of human happiness, many pushed, tricked and stumbled to the front pews, but only a few became 'firsts'. I recall our very last chat in my Tribeca loft in the 80s when our words belonged to each other. We'd eaten with Seymour and Linda Stein in Chinatown, and later you came back to my place. We felt the need once more for a solid chat, some hash and a cup of tea. We both wondered through the night at what was going on, agreeing that New York now belonged to someone else.

Somewhere in the night one of us recalled that duty was ours and events were God's. I walked you down the five flights to Beach Street, you bundled up and I pointed you towards Greenwich and a morning cab north to your hotel, Kennedy Airport and back home to Ireland. I cheer your grin and loved your shine, Cordell, you who left nothing for the cutting room floor.

*

It's still July 1964 as 'It's All Over Now' becomes the Stones' first British no. 1. I rented the higher floored flat, 147, of Ivor Court. A number one group needed their own office, so Tony Calder, Andy Wickham and the girls kept Image on track from the black-and-white, *Modesty Blaise*-ish 138, while our letter heading could now boast 138/147 Ivor Court and look like a real business. Image now handled Marianne Faithfull for management and its main PR base was the northern agency Kennedy Street Enterprises, which gave us Herman's Hermits, Freddie & the Dreamers, Wayne Fontana & the Mindbenders, Dave Berry and food on the table. 'The more the merrier' being Tony's and my calling card, we also somehow repped those three nice bland tubs of lard known as the Bachelors. We suffered through lunch at a showbiz Soho eatery with their manager Philip Solomon telling how things were done *à la* Arthur Askey and Lew Grade. One of the Bachelors, Dec, joined us and we gained a new respect for them when we saw him drive off in a Merc.

Later in the year we would suffer in the London Hilton breakfast room with another expert, Murry Wilson, father and manager to the Beach Boys, and would walk out repping their European press interests and, for a while, their UK music publishing. Calder and myself still enjoyed calling the old farts in the record companies and booking agencies who'd all dismissed us in one way or another on our early tails and now had to take our calls, as we repped their bread and butter.

Hashish was becoming part of the daily menu as was, on extremely busy weeks, speed. I had not yet hit rotation city but that wouldn't be a long time coming. Hash was a wonderful creative tool. After a hard Sidney Falco–J.J. Hunsecker split-screen schizoid *Sweet Smell of Success* day manning the phones, injecting our hustle into every moving thing, it was the perfect segue. As Reg put his foot down, I put my head back and we flew across town to an evening studio date, business date or supper. It seemed a perc of the way of life – the Percodan would come later.

I enjoyed flaunting my new best friend, Mafalda (Mrs Tony) Hall, an effervescent interior decorator by whim and trade, who gadded about London plying her taste while hubby rocked on attempting to London/Americanise the taste buds of disposable income as far as the airwaves could get him. For my quarters in 138 I had Mafalda work from my sketches and make a one-off roll of wallpaper with a marijuana-leaf motif. Now not only the carpets were thick, but the walls too. The Stones and I tittered away on more than one occasion as I suggested to some well-meaning photographer that the 'light was good against that wall and perhaps he should snap the fellas against it', and there remain a few good shots of the Stones posed mischievously against my special wall.

Peter Noone with Herman's Hermits would soon be Top 5 with the Mickie Most production of the Goffin and King gem, 'I'm Into Something Good'. Peter came down from Manchester to London and Ivor Court to do some press as the disc was about to be released in August. I took him up on to the Ivor Court rooftop to take a breather with me and admire the view. We made an odd couple looking over Regent's Park, Peter wiry, young and fresh meat, pea-coat-clad in cynical city. Young lad up in smoke, away from home and mum and dad, you could sell him, devour him and protect him all at the same time. After this chat I introduced him to my new best friend, hashish, and had him smoke a huge joint all on his ownsome. I asked him if he'd enjoyed it, whether anything in the land of his perception had changed. He said 'Yes' and swayed. 'Right,' I said, metamorphosing myself into northern bluff, 'now that you've done it, it had better be the very last time. If I ever hear of you doing drugs I'll kill ya.' And with that we found our way back downstairs.

The second Rolling Stones EP, *Five By Five* – somewhat of a racing certainty – would be released on the same day as Marianne Faithfull's 'As Tears Go By'. The first Stones long player had stayed in the album charts for nineteen weeks and reached no. 19 in the singles charts, not bad for an outing with no title.

*Five By Five* was culled from the Chess sessions. By way of saying 'thank you to you, their friends and fans', I wrote in the sleeve notes, ' we have included an extra track on this latest disc outing'. I should have added a thank you to Elvis Presley for being as pretty as Natalie Wood and giving me the 'bonus' idea via his five-pronged 1957 *Jailhouse Rock* soundtrack EP.

Image's PR clients were also well repped and stacking up the charts. The Beach Boys surfed into the Top 10 for the first of many times with 'I Get Around' and were soon joined by Bob Crewe's Four Season'd 'Rag Doll', the Bachelors' harmless bit of old blarney 'I Wouldn't Trade You For The World', Mr Noone's 'I'm Into Something Good', and our very own Buddhist, Dave Berry, with 'The Crying Game'.

**Kim Fowley**: So Andy Wickham invites me to this party that had Marianne Faithfull being unveiled by Andrew and his cronies, Lionel Bart and all that East End/West End theatre crowd. By then I was going to the Ad Lib Club every night. The place would be full of all the people with titles and inheritances who were trying to be in the pop world with all the rock 'n' roll slime, and we'd all hang out together. There was a bunch of them standing around this Faithfull get-together, and in comes Andrew. He's dressed in a white suit in Tom Wolfe mode and he's pretending that he's older than he is, and I'm pretending that I'm older than I am. So it was like a meeting of two thirty-year-olds, except that one was nineteen and the other was twenty-four. And there was Marianne Faithfull, the whole big-titted Aryan goddess; the peak of wet-pussy goddess. I came on hard and hit on her immediately. She was impressed enough that later she asked me to marry her to take the rap for her pregnancy.

Andrew controlled the room with her. We were both there with our pieces of meat. Mine was Proby, his was Faithfull. Andrew was a great hustler. He was old-school Broadway–Beverly Hills. He had his 'I'll kill you, I'll charm you, I'll leave you for dead' act. No wonder we didn't really talk to each other at any length, because we were both doing it. I didn't try to work Andrew and, much to my surprise, he never tried to hustle me, because I had more money than he did. I might have had more money than Eric Easton.

**ALO**: Outside of the studio, life was again on edge. I could feel that old whore depression shading every thought; I could feel the dark lady of angst invading every pore. The sensation is so all-consuming it seems to grab a vein in your head, tie itself around yer nerves and hold on. Every time you think, the noose around that thought squeezes the vein until you're in excruciating pain. Your eyelids are sandbagged; it hurts just to focus on anything or have anybody focus on you. The pain in your temples is boiling quicksand but you say 'fuck that dame of genetic swill' and manage to hide it and work. The days are once again clipped and frayed. Even your speech registers pain; it must be apparent to everyone you talk to. You are crawling across the desert on your hands and knees, the mirage recedes, even the solace of solitude is no longer available. Sometimes a joint of hash, a cuppa tea or strong whisky drink will calm you, but it could just as easily go the other way, and find you once again gripped in the bedlam of kill.

I know it's only a fuckin' hit record, not the cure for cancer, but I'm young, privileged and invaded. I think the success of Marianne and 'As Tears Go By' is overwhelming me. I'd had a similar self-questioning episode over 'I Wanna Be Your Man'. Instead of patting myself on the back and saying, 'Only you, you lucky bugger, would have the luck to run into John and Paul and have them hand you a potential hit', I get only mad internal chatter in my head about the what and why of it all. What if I hadn't left the Rolling Stones rehearsal at that particular moment? Why had I turned right? What if I'd turned left towards Covent Garden? What if I hadn't run into John and Paul?

To a depressive and busy lad, just recalling how 'As Tears Go By' got made was exhausting. I'd remember the musicians' sigh of relief at not having to play the B-side, Lionel's fart-stopper, anymore (it was originally to be the A-side). That feeling of release can be heard in the very playing of 'As Tears Go By', making it so magical and un-B-side-ish. The mere idea of trying to repeat that sequence was draining. And for what? For the 2,000, 3,000 quid a hit record made you? The girl was not going to be big on stage, and at that time she did nothing except, of course, all the essentials after the fact.

Marianne was hailed as Britain's latest pop sensation. 'As Tears Go By' would enter the Top 10 in Britain and snuggle into the Top 20 in the States, where *Billboard* magazine would name her 'the greatest discovery of the year'. Now that I'd sold her and had my way in the world with her, depression caused me to scorn the success itself. What had I done, after all? I'd taken an attractive, educated girl, 'possibly a virgin, with big tits, sings and thinks with acoustic guitar, has hit, will probably fuck – you could be the lucky one! – please buy record at a store near you or send an sae and recent photo to 138/147 Ivor Court'. I'd moved her out of the Baez/Greco Gauloise bohemian coffee bar circuit and on to my revered and sacred pop charts. I was a regular fucking Siegfried and Roy. I would make one lame effort at a follow-up with Marianne, but my heart wasn't in it, girl. I'd then call it a day and allow her to move on to Tony Calder.

This was no way to handle a hit, but once you're on the up-the-down staircase, you start looking around for the 'if-nots', rent space and live there.

Nobody knew how to help, and if help was offered I rejected it out of hand. I wanted something that worked now. I'd drink it off, sex it off, smoke it off and if I woke up the next day and it was not spent and gone, I'd repeat myself again until it was.

The Rolling Stones didn't help. I wished them away on a permanent tour. Having achieved some modicum of success, they now seemed to have something to lose – or was this just something I perceived? They seemed to think I was there to unburden themselves and moan to. I was getting very short-tempered, and my personal life with Sheila was shot. I looked into the hearts and minds of older soldiers like Lionel Bart and Sean Kenny; a drink with them would temporarily assuage my horrors. After a warm night out with the boys I'd glow a little, lighten up and be on the mend again.

In 1964 Sheila and I were much too young to get married, and had my mother and her parents not been so against the legalised union I might not have forced the issue and we might not have eloped. Or perhaps Sheila had told me she would leave me and this was the cure – marriage as a bouquet for bad behaviour. Aside from giving some title and stability to having children, I don't know why she wanted to be married to me. I could be gracious and say she loved me, which she did, and I thought I did. But she didn't know me, and neither did I.

The honeymoon took place before, not after, the marriage, and while Sheila was the only thing in my life we had a very good time. I was happy, my ambition at the time achieved. I was with her. I met the Rolling Stones and they became my passion and ambition, and I worked at that and stopped working at being with Sheila. We were children – I was, at least. I didn't know enough at nineteen about life to realise how I was hurting her, and I certainly had no business making her my wife.

Sheila had had enough of my overwound clock. She was fed up with the numb, spent friend she had on her hands and headed for the South of France to 'cool out'. I followed her, but not before I'd done more damage that I'd later have to extricate myself from. Out of my mind – what else? – I had supplied some inexcusable, embarrassingly lame tripe to the *Melody Maker*.

The headline ran, 'Andy Won't Be Handy For The Stones'. The article stated, 'The sixth Rolling Stone is retiring from show business', and went on and on in that vein.

'I don't enjoy it anymore,' I told them. 'There are a lot of talented people of my age in this country, but there's no room for them to move. You start out wanting to earn loot and when you get it there's nothing left.' The article concluded: 'Oldham has been mainly instrumental in building the Rolling Stones image. We wonder if they'll let him go?' The Rolling Stones had no say in the matter; that would come later. I was off again to the South of France, only confirming Eric Easton's self-satisfied tut-tut opinion of my instability and unbusiness-like demeanour. The next week, the second week of September, *Melody Maker* ran the full interview under the banner, 'Stones Man Says "I Quit!"'

The Rolling Stones should have fired or disowned me, but they knew this was just a stray mangled bullet. They knew that I still had quite a few live chambers to fire on their behalf.

Even in the madness I was still copping the great moves I'd witnessed when I was in school. I traced my bizarre behaviour back to *Look Back In Anger* playwright John Osborne's famous 'I quit Britain' drama of 1959. Combine that with Yves Saint Laurent's nervous breakdown on being forced into the frog army that same year, and you've got the weight and shape of every pained and plaintive move I made.

**Sheila Klein**: Andrew would complain he was now like a nursemaid to the whole band, that it was all beneath him. I remember him breaking down and saying he felt like a prostitute; that was around the time he did that interview in the *Melody Maker*. His sense of morals, or lack of them, was amazing; somewhere in there he had an incredibly strong puritanical streak. He didn't realise that the fact that he was being of service was a positive thing. Anyway, I ran away to France. I'd about had it up to here competing for attention with Mick and his whims. It was my way of taking things up a bit. You know, if I'm not around for him to lean on let's see what happens. Because I was carrying a pretty heavy load even then, so I was looking for a fair exchange of energy back. With Andrew I was pretty much jumping in the deep end myself, and then came the Stones, but I'd made a decision to go for it. I suppose I knew he'd come and get me, that it was just a matter of time. I mean there are some things that Mick couldn't quite give him.

The South of France was the most interesting groovy place to be, very hip. It was just at the point when I'd really begun to enjoy myself there, and wasn't bothered whether he came for me or didn't, that he showed up. Andrew was like that, psychic. He always got the timing just right on the edge.

**ALO:** The *Melody Maker* informed all its readers I was retiring the next week with a lot of money and an ulcer. In the article I was hailed by some as a genius and by more as an exhibitionist idiot.

But I was not suffering from an ulcer; that was a stand-in for what was ailing me. I just refused to mention the word depression. My black moods were still unfathomable to me, all the more so because the trigger of depression seemed to be success.

I had done the *Melody Maker* piece while at an all-time low. When I returned from the South of France with Sheila I was back on track, my effervescent sparkle intact and apparent. I'd left one matter unsorted, the matter of getting wed.

While in Juan-les-Pins, I'd had Sheila call her parents from a call box and advise them that we wished to get married. She didn't get as far as asking for their blessing. From London to Juan came a resounding parental 'No!' We decided to return to London and work on both of them and my mum as well. I was lining up Celia as a public relations ally – although I didn't need her consent. Her only words on the matter were, 'I think you are both being very stupid and I hope you change your mind before you do something you will both regret.' Sheila's parents' consent *was* needed; their daughter was underage.

Back in London I looked around me and saw the commotion I had caused via the *Melody Maker* piece. I hope I mumbled an apology to Keith, Mick, Bill and Charlie about letting the side down and having spoken out of turn in public. I also hoped Brian Jones would not sense an ally and invite me to hang. I then basically rolled over the whole event, went to sleep, got up, and went to work.

It was back in Regent Sound with engineer Bill Farley to cut some more Stones sides. The standout was the group's rendition of Willie Dixon's 'Little Red Rooster'. They played it with so much love and flair that you could hear the passion and ease in every groove. There was nothing to balance once they settled into it; they balanced themselves and sunk into the deep blues.

Brian really shone on this back-to-the-roots occasion of joy. Mick squirrelled his tab-collared frame against the wall. It was cold and he rubbed his bum on the wall in warm up, then summoned up his boy-coy blues in a masterful, relaxed, on-the-edge vocal display. Charlie slapped the rest of the sound into place and magic oozed into the room and stuck to the tape.

The group thought it would make an ideal single. I was caught between agreeing and seeing it from a different point of view. I vacillated about it daily. Some days I felt it was too uncommercial, totally the wrong can of goods to propel the Stones' UK ascent. The next day I'd hear it and think it was just what the good doctor ordered. It was time to hold back the momentum, to avoid having to top this, top that. Why not use the occasion to enable us to set our own pace? The idea of a comfortable Top 5 record that reminded the Stones fans of their Delta chops and played to the bottom-line R 'n' B faithful, instead of another booming no. 1, was very attractive. With that idea in mind 'Little Red Rooster' b/w 'Off The Hook' was scheduled for a first week of November release.

The whole process had been an audio dream. Tony Calder and I went up to Decca's West Hampstead studio to master the tape on to disc, and the audio brilliance was so apparent that the thing basically mastered itself.

**Tony Calder**: We really worked 'Little Red Rooster' – today it would be called a career move. The only person who wanted to put it out was Andrew. What he wanted was a record that he could claim was a piece of art and wasn't an out-and-out attempt at further commercial success. I was against it. I said, 'This'll never be a fuckin' hit; this'll kill them.' He said, 'No, you don't understand how big they are. This is where we can manipulate the charts and have a career record.' We boosted the pre-orders, got a lot of the fans who bought for us in the key chart shops ordering before the fucker came out. It came out and went straight into the charts at no. 1. I'd just thought it was the greatest mistake ever – you couldn't dance to it, Decca hated it and Eric Easton thought Andrew was nuts. It *made* the Stones. That they were able to take a blues thing to no. 1 took the game to a whole new level. Andrew was able to show the business the band's popularity and translate it into record success. I was staggered; I hated the record.

We used the fan club to go and buy heavy the first week once we'd bumped up the pre-orders. Then we had John and Mick, our carpetbaggers, our Afghan hash dealers, out there monitoring the girls and the shops. It was all very primitive. We only had to do about forty-five shops to get results. Shirley Arnold would organise the autographs and the thank you letters from the Stones to the fans for getting out there for us. We were amongst the very few who took that first step. Today you've got strike forces that service seven hundred shops that return to the charts, and there are buying teams that are going out and buying the product. The public isn't supposed to know that; basically it's still a criminal act, conspiracy to defraud. Today it's a regular sandcastle, house of lawyers. At least we put our hands in our pocket and went out and bought the records into the charts. Those records were counted as sold and the artist got paid.

**ALO**: While the Stones were away in the north of England Sheila and I lay in each other's arms, checked each other's smiles, let things get physical and did a lot of walking and talking on Hampstead Heath and Primrose Hill.

'We could get married in Scotland, Andrew.' Sheila held my hand as we looked down on the zoo. She then told me she thought she was pregnant. The fact that she was with child only sealed the deal, so getting married in Scotland was what we decided to do. I wanted to be wed anyway, muted by love, good intent and the chorus of parental no's.

We'd decided then and there on Primrose Hill. We both felt very good, very nervous, excited and shy with pride. The sky was white above Primrose Hill and grey beyond the zoo. As we looked the other way towards Chalk Farm, the sky also made up its mind – it was both white and grey above the railway lines that ran along and around the foot of Haverstock Hill. I asked for Sheila's hand towards the evening of the day. She put her hand in mine and we started to walk back down the lane. I squeezed that last-felt drop of innocence and held on to it as if my very life depended on it; and on that day it did, with the thought of a new life on both our minds as we held each other home. I really felt that hope of innocence, though it would be mostly gone by the day she'd say 'I do'. The next day would be our last in London.

'My parents think I'm going to be staying at Linda Keith's. We'll be in Glasgow before they think something's wrong,' Sheila smiled as she packed her suitcase, and for the first time something felt very wrong. But I was raised on my word and without one we drove to the airport, two hearts, one confused, beating as one.

**James Phelge**, *Phelge's Stones*: Mick and Keith had moved into a new flat – 10a Holly Hill, in upmarket Hampstead. Finally they had moved on from the messy living conditions that had prevailed at Edith Grove and Mapesbury Road. The flat was a chalet-styled apartment with an extended lounge decorated with pine-wood panelling. A few steps took you down to a sub-level bedroom complete with fitted wardrobes and an adjoining shower. A young girl came in a few times a week to keep the place looking immaculate. Even the clothes now lived in the wardrobes instead of their usual places on the nearest floor. Keith had a Gibson twelve-string acoustic guitar and matching six-string on one of the walls. The record player was in its usual home down in the bedroom. Mick was away and I was in the brand-new kitchen boiling a saucepan of water upon the stove. Knowing full well there was no food in the house, Keith came in to see what I was cooking.

'I'm just boiling my watch, man,' I said, prodding it with a spoon. 'It's stopped and I'm teaching it a lesson.'

'Why don't you just wind it up?' he asked.

We went back to the bedroom for a smoke. Keith had his Epiphone guitar out and kept playing the chords of 'Rag Doll', the Four Seasons' song that had recently charted. He was quite taken with the song and knew all the words to it. When the cigarette ran out I went back to the kitchen and Keith wandered behind, still playing 'Rag Doll'.

**Kim Fowley**: Bobby Jameson showed up in my office in 1964 in Hollywood before I became the P.J. Proby PR genius. He was a Buddy Holly imitator and an imitator of Tommy Roe. Later, Keith and Andrew recorded him with some garage-type Four Seasons' bit with a Keith and Andrew song that sounded like 'Rag Doll' on meth. I heard that a little girl came up to him on a break and asked for his autograph, and he hit her in the face because he was afraid to be touched by strangers. And that's what got Bobby banned in England, or that's where it spread that he hit little kids, which is real eerie.

One day in 1964 we're sitting in the Knightsbridge mews house, me and Proby and Viv Prince, and in comes a group of partygoers. We were like the Four Horsemen of the Apocalypse sitting there. The rule was if the light wasn't on, you could come by and bring pussy for us or food or beer or whatever, and we'd all sit around. In the door comes Lulu, pimples between her tits, with none other than Graham Nash; they were a couple that night. And in walks Spike. Spike was introduced as a roadie for the Rolling Stones; he set up equipment for them, and he looked like a rock star kind of a guy. And in comes Brian Jones. That's where I met Brian for the first time, that night. We're all sitting there and chatting away, and then it's time to go home. Proby and I look at each other and say, 'Where's the cat?' We had a kitten that one of the fans had given Proby. 'Wait a minute, Brian Jones had his coat buttoned. I think he stole the cat.' All four of us go thundering out into the street and chase him, and there's Brian with P.J. Proby's kitten under his shirt and coat. We didn't want to fight him. 'We agree with you, it's a nice cat, but it's *our* fucking cat; don't *steal* it.' Brian says, 'Well, you guys are bastards – how could you *possibly* be nice to this cat?' Proby says, 'I don't mistreat little animals, only people in the record business! I love my cat, give me my fucking cat back!' That was the least amount of perversion I'd ever seen from two weird rock 'n' roll guys. About a week or two later, the doorbell rings and it's Spike, alone, but with a crew cut. 'What happened to you?' 'I've come here for guidance,' he says, and he starts crying. 'I was getting more applause than Mick or Keith or the rest of the boys when I would go on stage to set up the equipment. Mick and Keith held me down and shorn me, like a sheep, to teach me a lesson that there are five Rolling Stones and I'm not one of the five.' We cheered him up and said, 'Hair grows, you'll be okay, go to work somewhere else. Don't kill yourself; it's not worth it. Form your own band.' We never saw him again. The reason I mention it is because Spike wasn't mentioned by Andrew in *Stoned* – Andrew tells me he doesn't remember Spike, but I do. I thought the whole thing with the cat and Spike's haircut may have contributed to Proby believing that his cock was bigger than Mick Jagger's. He had no way of knowing, but apparently Chrissie Shrimpton knew.

**James Phelge**, *Phelge's Stones*: In September Andrew surprised everybody by disappearing for a few days and announcing on his return that he had been to Scotland to get married. I had met him over a year before and had seen no indication that he even had a girlfriend. Though he worked as a seeker of publicity, Andrew was able to keep his private life secret if he wanted. I never did meet his wife.

ALO and Sheila Klein Oldham, Glasgow Registry Office, 1964

As the band basked in the success of having achieved no. 1 with 'It's All Over Now' and 'Little Red Rooster', news of Charlie's marriage somehow leaked out. When Mick, Keith and Andrew were confronted with it they stood stunned in near-disbelief. The band was going from strength to strength and news of the marriage could jeopardise this success for everyone involved. There was still a considerable stigma attached to pop stars who were married – many people thought this heralded the beginning of the end. Keith saw Charlie's marriage, to begin with at least, as a treasonable act. After the initial shock, the final verdict was that the deed was done and that the only sensible course of action was to live with it. Andrew hoped that having two married Stones (Bill having previously tied the knot) would not adversely affect the group's fortunes.

**Tony Calder**: The relationship between Andrew and Sheila was over before they were married really. I think it fell apart when he was commuting between London and Glasgow every day. He'd get the plane out of Glasgow in the morning, do some work, fly back to Glasgow knackered on the last flight up. What's she going to do all day? You're meant to have this romantic thing going, running away to get married, three weeks residency in Glasgow so that he can get married to a girl who is underage. I was the best man at the wedding. He didn't want a family; that was too much responsibility. He just wanted to go back on the road.

**George Gallacher**, lead singer/writer, the Poets: Glasgow in the early 60s was a dangerous place for young men. The gangs were back – the Tongs, the Fleet, the Shamrock, the Cumbie, the San Toi and other murderous groupings. Inspector Silletoe's purges of the 1930s were meant to have cleansed the city of the notorious razor gangs but this cleansing had only been temporary. This time around the violence was less inter-gang and more gratuitous, with innocent outsiders now more likely to be victims than gang members.

The Poets were formed in 1963 after I'd been stabbed in a fracas at a dance hall when our bass player John Dawson and myself were set about by members of the Cumbie mob for playing for the wrong promoter. These dance halls and the big swing bands that played them pre-rock had been central to working-class, music-mad Glasgow's pre-war and post-war social life – a weekend escape.

The first time I met Andrew was bizarre. I'd just got into bed at six o'clock in the morning after playing a double gig, only to be wakened by an apoplectic mother telling me the Stones' manager is in the fucking living room wanting to speak with me. I didn't know whether this was a dream or my dear mother had found the acid tabs. And there he was sharing a bottle of Whyte & McKays with my old man, in a council house in Hagill, one of the most fucked up areas of Glasgow. My father, a fanatical Stalinist with that strange contradictory Calvanistic morality the Glaswegian communists seemed to carry, was breaking bread with the urban, capitalist sonofabitch manager of the notorious Rolling Stones, despoilers of the nation's daughters, corruptors of youth. And there's me looking at these two anti-Christs and my good Catholic mum searching for a crucifix to shut them up while I'm trying to make sense of the whole scene.

Andrew was sitting there as if it were the most natural thing in the world; it was the nearest I ever got to a social situation with Andrew. Andrew had come to Scotland to marry Sheila and had stumbled across an article on us in a Scots pop magazine. He then contacted our management, arranged to hear us and signed us. We were recording in London two weeks later and our first recording came out the next month.

**ALO**: We got back married from Glasgow and Sheila and I had to do our bit for the press, which I found as uncomfortable as being married. I hugged our Cairn terrier, Genius, for support. Earlier, Sheila had brought over this young boy named Andy who'd lived in Antrim Grove around the corner from me when I'd lived on Haverstock Hill. She seemed to be offering young Andy to me as a branched olive to make up for a fight we'd just had. I refused, thinking, but not saying, that if I were going to visit this anomalous attraction I'd rather pick my own. Sheila left, taking, I gathered, young Andy for her own.

During the first two weeks of October the Rolling Stones arrived in New York for an afternoon and evening show at the Academy of Music to kick off their second North American tour.

These two sold-out shows were followed on Sunday by the Stones' début on the Yank equivalent of our own *Sunday Night at the London Palladium – The Ed Sullivan Show*, a make or break Sunday night eight o'clock national event. The Stones mimed 'Around And Around' and 'Time Is On My Side'. The latter, released as a US-only single in September, was hovering around the Top 30, imitating our first near-hit. Much later it would emerge as one of the first signposts of the time and prove a perennial favourite amongst North American fans, especially as they got older. The chorus would become less a well-remembered refrain and more a statement of stop-clocking and hope.

Once again Phil Spector kindly lent me his couch in the ground floor office of the same building where he maintained his East sixties penthouse. I came back there shortly after eleven on the Sunday night following the Sullivan performance, the show done and discussed over a Broadway deli dinner with a few of the Stones and Stu. Much to my surprise Phil was in the office, all diminutive, huddled and black, hovering over his chipper promotion man Danny Davis. The office was small and unspectacular, the type of ground floor space now tenanted by dentists and chiropractors. Spread open across the desk was a Sony-type suitcase record player and speakers, built like a huge Samsonite – a mighty machine with a mighty sound.

Phil didn't pay much attention to me. I sat down on the couch as he just managed a barely audible, 'Great Sullivan show, the guys were terrific.'

Then he went back to what he'd been doing. He had a white-labelled 45 rpm test pressing on the turntable and he put it into play. The room was filled with this amazing sound. I had no idea what it was, but it was the most incredible thing I'd ever heard. I slowly and numbly felt my way through the aural maze and discerned what I thought were two black guys singing a very sad, tortured, oh so laboured and stated regret about things 'she' didn't do anymore when they kissed, of eyes no longer closing when they called her name . . . or was it kissed her lips?

Underneath lay a bed of sustained everything – drones of echo'd majestic hurt that lasted forever, the only movement provided by a La Bamba-thick bass on quinalbarbitone. Come the chorus, the track, as one, started a stop-start tymphflayed, ricochet'd beat as voices, angels and strings strained in Wagnerian, classical ache, followed by another verse of higher pain. On the altar of middle eight the rhythm got down on its knees, pulling the symphonic sustain along to the next corner – and just 'babys' and 'please'. The two voices' gospel shrieks and wails were then propelled by a bass-end Latin suggestion of rhythm and hope through the last heaven's gate to the final, telling chorus.

That last chorus was as if Jesus had risen, as if Moses had come down with the Ten Commandments of sound.

I had no idea what the record was and nobody was telling me. Phil grunted, scratched his goatee and sighed. Danny Davis studied his hands, Phil and the wall. The record, player on auto, started again.

Was this Phil's work? I wasn't sure. It was certainly nothing like his usual up-tempo avalanches of fulfilled and celebrated love, heavy with percussion, pianos, guitars, keyboards, stabbing horns and wailing black nubile songbirds, as in the Crystals' epic 'He's A Rebel', or the Ronettes' transcendent 'Be My Baby'.

Yet it *had* to be Phil, unless we were all dreaming (and we could be). I'd never heard a recorded track so emotionally giving or empowering. There was so much sound that I would not have been surprised if I'd just heard three different recordings playing different parts of the whole. The audio fidelity was that awe-inspiring.

The record was the Righteous Brothers' 'You've Lost That Lovin' Feeling'.

# · CHAPTER 3 ·

**ALO**: Keith Richards and I shared a great moment together in the Los Angeles of 1965. The shared moment was Frank Sinatra.

The kicks had moved from Route 66 to Sunset Strip. The Stones and I were on a productive run ensconced, when touring and travelling allowed, at the RCA recording studios on the corner of Sunset and Iver. We were in the middle of a nearly two-year roll, and it seemed we could do no wrong. 'Satisfaction', 'The Last Time', 'Play With Fire', 'Under My Thumb', 'Get Off Of My Cloud', 'Lady Jane', 'Out Of Time', 'Mother's Little Helper', '19th Nervous Breakdown', 'Have You Seen Your Mother, Baby?', 'Paint It, Black'. Mick and Keith's songs just kept getting stronger – on the money and of the moment.

One mid-afternoon I sidled up to Keith in the centre of studio A. As usual, he was jeaned and slightly scarved, on stool, guitar in hand, fag in mouth, plastic cups around.

'Let's take a break around five,' I said.

'Okay,' said Keith, not giving me much thought, not wishing to leave the moment.

Mo Ostin and Joe Smith, the two number ones at Warner/Reprise, had invited me to attend a Frank Sinatra session at 5.30 at Universal (a recording studio, nothing to do with the Universal entertainment conglomerate), a few blocks along on the south side of Sunset.

Mo and Joe built Warner/Reprise from the early 60s into the Warner–Elektra–Atlantic/WEA giant it became by the mid-70s. Ostin soldiered up through the Sinatra admin. ranks and came into the Warner's pack when Frank's Reprise Company merged with Warner Brothers Records. Joe Smith began as a deejay at Yale spinning Nat 'King' Cole platters in the 50s. Under their astute professional care, WEA represented the true artists' home. They remain remarkable record men whose ease with themselves, the music and the artists was a pleasure to be around. They were never desperate.

As regards the Sinatra invite, I couldn't bring the whole group – they weren't invited. Anyway, I didn't want to. Mick, as a vocalist and true star, would have had to make light of the occasion, 'Oh, shall I bring a spare toupee?'

'Can I bring Keith?' I asked Joe Smith on the phone from the RCA reception. 'We may as well have two musicians there.'

'Sure,' said a relieved Joe, for Keith was still thought of as 'the quiet one'.

Keith and I whipped out smartly at five. We stood on the sidewalk outside RCA for a minute watching the Sunset Strip evening rush hour crawl begin. Then a honk from a black Caddy on the other side of the street beckoned us over to Joe Smith's car.

'So where are we going, Andrew?' asked Keith as we rolled on to Sunset.

'Joe's taking us to meet Frank Sinatra,' I grinned.

'Oh, nice one', said Keith, surprised but not amazed.

Fifteen Warhols later we sat in the quiet control room of the Universal studio, the engineer fiddling with dials on the consul and me, Joe Smith and Sagittarian Keith sitting behind him on the couch waiting for Sinatra to arrive.

A few minutes later arrive he did, though to our surprise he didn't come into the control room. The man walked straight into the studio and headed for the stool in the centre of the room, surrounded by bafflers inside which stood a mike, cans and speakers.

He sat down, adjusted himself into the stool, put a headphone on one ear, indicated he wanted the playback via the headphones and speakers, which were positioned so as not to bleed into the microphone when played at a reasonable level. He snapped his fingers to feel the air in the room, agreed with the shine on his shoes, and signalled to the booth to roll the tape. Frank was ready to go.

We were not many years down the road from direct to disc, the original mode of recording that had replaced cylinders, or 'rolls'. After direct to the mono-lathe came monaural tape, then two-track, thus enabling us to hear duplications in stereo. Now in these mid-60s the biz had teched up and graduated to four-track, meaning recordings could be made utilising four separate channels, which upon being filled would be paired down to stereo or mono.

The musical tracks were already in place and ol' blue eyes was crooning into the warmth of the studio. Keith and I sat a wee bit gobsmacked at the pro-ease we were seeing and hearing. In the next forty-five minutes Frank Sinatra recorded two or three takes each on three songs. When satisfied with his handling of a song after two or three takes he didn't stop, or come into the control room, or ask to listen to what he had just done. He knew what he had done and just said, 'Next one', and perhaps, 'please'.

This was high style. We were used to listening and analysing vocal performances on studio monitors, headphones and even car speakers before saying yes or no. The consummate Mr Sinatra knew, at the moment of doing, what was right or wrong.

The three songs recorded, he eased off the chair, put the headphones back into their place cradling the neck of the microphone stand, then walked through the studio and into the control room.

On entering the booth, ignoring us, he slapped the back of the engineer and asked, 'Everything okay?'

The engineer said, 'Yes, sir.' The 'sir' was both mock Bilko and of total respect.

'Okay, you know which ones to use,' came back Frank.

Now that's the tall order. Keith and I looked at each other on that one. Frank expected the engineer to be as tuned to Sinatra as he was to himself. No drama, no questions. You're here because you are a pro and this is how the consummate Frank gets it done. Sinatra turned towards the couched and carpeted visitors' section and Joe Smith got up. They smiled and greeted each other, arms clasped around the other's arm and shoulder, one dignified notch away from a hug.

'Hello, Frank,' said Joe. 'You sounded just great.'

Frank gave out a ring-a-ding smile and said nothing. He knew, but didn't know, who we were, and now that the work was done he checked the state of his French cuffs, approved, and wondered – two, three, four – wondered – dropped the smile in all save the eyes and wondered about us with a flick towards Joe.

Joe got the flick. 'Frank,' Joe's left arm allowed towards Keith and me, his right still clasping Sinatra's elbow as we both rose for the occasion. 'I'd like you to meet Keith Richards and Andrew Oldham from the Rolling Stones. They're in from England. I just wanted them to be able to meet you.'

Joe, too, was a pro's pro. No unnecessary detail, as in 'guitarist/writer/manager/producer'. Just the facts for the ring-a-ding man – don't confuse the attention span granted.

Sinatra politely – and he did have searing great ol' blue eyes when he put them to you – shook hands with Keith and me, thanked us for coming to see him and hoped we were having a good time here in his realm.

'You guys know Harold Davison?' he asked as he tugged his hand back.

'Yes, we do,' I spoke for us both in reference to Frank's UK promoter.

'Say hello to him for me. And to Marion.' He ref'd the late singer Marion Ryan, Mrs Harold Davison. Sinatra then said goodbye to one and all and left us alone in the control room.

We were both pretty knocked aback. Keith and I knew we'd just seen an amazing example of the *modus operandi* of a master, and Joe Smith was delighted to see the pleasure on our faces as we thanked him for bringing us to this memorable occasion. We ambled into the hall and were chatting about life in general, or slagging other acts, when I turned and looked down the long hall, through the glass studio doors out on to Sunset. There, black-straw-hatted, black silk or mohair slub-suited, in a black open Lincoln Continental, waiting for the lights to be green, sat Sinatra at the wheel. There was no entourage, bodyguards, Rat Pack or clan. Just a man, content, alone, the day's work done, joining the rest of the early LA evening traffic, going home.

It was just one of those things, just one of those fabulous things – Mr Frank Sinatra.

Few people have the happy experience of being able to sit and realise they have become who they truly are, to confront the worth of the work. I have, and it is a loud encounter with a clear sound.

The Stones records could not have been done in New York in that particular time because, like London, New York has seasons. That's why we went to LA to record. LA placed a tone on the records we made there. Walking outside a studio any time of the year (and this was a year when everybody was well and everything was going well) into the LA sunshine was a trip.

And with us on that trip, faithfully, always the consummate pro, was Jack Nitzsche. Jack ended up playing on the whole RCA Stones run – all their records from that time. After I was introduced to him by Sonny Bono he just appeared at the sessions. I didn't ask him what he was doing there in case he asked me for money. There are three keyboard players on those mid-60s Stones RCA sessions. If it's a blues figure, it's Ian Stewart on piano. On a few occasions when it's slightly strange it might be Brian, but the rest – all the piano, organ, harpsichord playing – the denseness, the body, the glue – is Jack Nitzsche.

There are some tracks you can definitely hear him on; for example, the harpsichord on 'Play With Fire' is Jack. His overall contribution is a little harder to pinpoint. If I were to try and define it, I'd say he provided the melodic bond, the undercurrent to Keith and Brian's layers of guitar brainwash.

He didn't arrange – that was the Stones' job – he led, he sat in the pit, he was the metronome in groove time. On some of the tracks, like 'Satisfaction' – depending on the system you're hearing it on – you might not hear Jack's piano, but it's fucking there and if it weren't there, you'd miss it. Whereas on 'Let's Spend The Night Together', of course you can hear it.

And then there was that mythical instrument, the Nitzschephone. I made that up for the credits on those Stones albums. It was just a regular piano (or maybe an organ) miked differently. The idea was meant to be: 'My God, they've had to invent new instruments to capture this new sound they hear in their brains!' And they *were* inventing fresh sounds with old toys – therefore it deserved to be highlighted. It was the read-up of creation, of imagination – getting credit for a job well done. You wouldn't, for instance, have found a 'nitzschephone' on a Freddie & the Dreamers record.

Jack Nitzsche and Keith Richards, RCA Hollywood, 1965

Jack gave us an understanding of tone. Which tone fits the universe? Which thing was hummable in the street? It was never a tone or a key that would embarrass a member of the public and dissuade him or her from singing along. On the up-tempo things, that's the key he provided. Tone was key in those days, because we were, in a way, only one step away from direct-to-disc recording. Everything was down to placement and miking. Where somebody sat and what leaked into what was critical. We were pre-separation. Jack had that knowledge of instrument levels, of placement. The other thing Jack had was a grasp of, and interest in, sex. How to inject sex into the sound is a gift of understanding between you and your third ear. That's a huge component. And I suppose after a while it can become a little frustrating if you know how to make perfectly recorded sex. Could leave you with frustrations in the other world.

He would go on to be a producer himself – already was, as a matter of fact. There were no rules then – just *be* it and get on with it. With Nick Venet he produced 'Love Her', the first Walker Brothers record. It was made at that same RCA studio where the Stones recorded. That was the Barry Mann/Cynthia Weil song that became the Walkers' first single when they arrived in England.

Jack continued to work on Stones albums up through *Let It Bleed* and *Sticky Fingers.* And of course he was in Neil Young's band, Crazy Horse. He played keyboards on and wrote arrangements for all those Crazy Horse albums. Boy, could he sit a track down. Jack never developed a 'style' as a producer; I don't think he had one. Basically, he chased, caught and defined the style of the artist, which, for many, is what a producer is supposed to do.

Back in 64 when we first met him, Jack was robust. If he took drugs he didn't take them in front of me. He was sweet, shy, polite, cooperative and fucking talented. What else do you want, you know? Then he went home. He was boring on other people's time. I remember him fondly as a married man who should have stayed happily married. We don't know what goes on once somebody closes his own oak door, but where he was at the time was in a place that was very warm and attractive. I know Charlie and Shirley Watts were very attracted to that side of him – they spent a lot of time with him and Gracia Nitzsche while everybody else was out chasing pussy and buying clothes. You can only wish that kind of thing would go on forever for people like Jack, but, for whatever reasons, he wanted to change his life, and unfortunately, he was one of those people who could only do that with dire consequences to themselves.

Jack's musician-idolising-fetishising thing was a treacherous area.

You're supposed to make the public fall in love with the act – if you do, too, it's fatal and Jack was sometimes guilty. It's the same thing as in the 80s when the whole of America in radioland fell in love with Emmylou Harris's hair. I find it a little gross what some programme directors wanted to do with her hair. That business where Jack is supposed to have shoved a gun in Carrie Snodgrass's cunt is an example of that madness and drug-driven entitlement.

We all go through a period where we're good at one thing and we think that qualifies us to be good at other things. And that's probably where Jack got his dick cut off. He couldn't play producer. In a way Jack was almost too sensitive and he played with some pretty fucking hard people. I mean I'm sure Mink DeVille is probably a sweetheart, but when I met him, his opening line was: 'I don't trust anybody who doesn't do opiates.' I ran into Jack on the staircase of the Speakeasy in 1974 when I was producing Donovan. I hadn't seen him since 66 and Jack's opening words to me were: 'Andrew! How are you? Do I have to be bisexual to make it?' And I went, 'Uh oh – you've been hanging around with Mick too long, honey.' Mick has this habit of playing with people who haven't actually got the head for it, like Mick Taylor. Mick and Keith assisted him into Humpty Dumpty land inside two years.

Aside from the odd gig, mainly from the 70s Jack was doing film scores: *The Exorcist*, *9½ Weeks*, *Stand By Me*, *An Officer and a Gentleman*, *Performance*, *Cutter's Way*, *The Crossing Guard* and *One Flew Over the Cuckoo's Nest*, for which he was nominated for an Academy Award. He did *Hardcore* – that was a great soundtrack – and *The Hot Spot*, the Dennis Hopper movie – great use of Miles Davis and all that blues stuff. But Hollywood is also a very gothic place. Jack had to mix with a lot of sick fucks in quicksand.

The last time I saw him it was a gorgeous occasion. Phil Spector flew Jack to his Rock and Roll Hall of Fame induction ceremony, and all of us were managing to behave for the evening. Jack looked just like Jack of old and it was wonderful. He was all apple pie, you know, American apple pie around the waist. I had a sweet time, but what's not to have a sweet time on the night Phil was being honoured? For once he wasn't behaving like a Manichevitz/Prozac-driven pig – which he had on other occasions, though not of late. Phil was very sweet that night. We went over to Mick Jones of Foreigner's apartment on Central Park and Phil was telling me off about taking drugs – the pot calling the kettle beige.

The final curtain must have come very fast for Jack – it does; I know from personal experience. I was only three weeks away from my own last act when

I decided I wanted to live. Jack was robust at the Rock and Roll Hall of Fame and then he decided to crash and burn.

He became a kind of maniac towards the end. I saw a picture of him taken in the Mayflower Hotel in New York the August of his demise and he looked absolutely terrifying. He looked like he hadn't recovered from Neil Young. Do you remember that wonderful cover of Willie Nelson with the cowboy hat? Like the old Gringo Indian, but with every fucking disease under the sun. That sounds harsh, I know. I'm not trying to be tough on Jack. I'm trying to give people storm warnings, which we know they won't take, 'cause everybody's invincible till the final curtain comes down or fluffs you on the shoulder.

But through it all, Jack Nitzsche had the ability to sit and to figure it out, to get to the square root of the sound.

I only remember two other fellas getting in the inner sanctum at the RCA sessions, Lou Adler and J.W. Alexander. Everybody else, from assorted would-be's, chicks and thunder, had to cool their heels in the RCA lobby guarded by two off-duty cops (we had to watch our backs, keep all strays and the union away). Inside the studio there was no booze, some pot, no girls and a lot of work. Work was still play.

Where the boys are, wherever ever are the Stones. It was the usual tight ship at RCA – just the nine of us: five Stones, Stu, engineer Dave Hassinger, keyboarding Jack Nitzsche and *moi*.

\*

Twenty-five years later the brown tape box holding the three recorded takes of 'Everybody Needs Somebody to Love' (one of Atlantic Records' soul gems written by Bert Berns, Solomon Burke and Jerry Wexler) and two more of another Bert Berns Atlantic classic, 'Cry To Me', is in my hands. It's early 1989 and all does not toll well in my head. Allen Klein has asked me to stop into his office to look over some old tapes they are attempting to clarify. I'm out of sorts trying to clarify mere life. Last night I'd done a cable TV interview and was in such a bad mood that when I was asked, in all fairness, 'What did I do?' referring back to the Stones, I snapped, 'What did I do? I took credit for other people's work . . .' I'm still into finding new versions of what constitutes bottom; I need a fucking life before I run out of mine. Around twelve I leave the Iroquois Hotel. God, I know that walk. I'm past the rewards of drinking; my shyness is not lifted, it's deepened by the Italian moonshine that is my new preference and by the lines that pitter patter in its wake. Already part of the now pathetic loop, I've got the depression I brought to life's party, that black-hearted son of a gun that still joins me on every celebratory occasion and reminds me to shoot myself. And I've added the chemical brother and aunt, alcohol, to boot the last man inside me down. It's a gallowed walk on which I'll forever see the pavement; I'm not into looking up anymore. I downwalk the 44th Street block west across Sixth Avenue, pick up my stride, hit my marks for a bravado puffed entrance into a bistro called One, Two, Three. I hail a morning espresso and grappa, run to the john for my second morning line, and then make sure I'm not sweating too much with a second grappa – though the burning in my liver would light a fire. I head towards Broadway and north ten blocks in an attempt to walk the morning's boozefest into a façade of good health, gargle in the rest room, wipe off the last rim of sweat, do a toot for longevity and sway into Allen's office around one. The tape boxes are put in front of me and the tapes racked up for me to listen to – another fucking chore of duty in the twilight zone. It's not a good year for me to be listening to Stones outtakes; it just makes me feel like one.

My attention is drawn to words written on the tape box in a different hand and ink than the take-by-take data. The two words are 'Brian Wilson'. Does this mean anything to me, I'm asked. Well, the work of Brian Wilson has done a lot for me, while doing a lot to himself. *Pet Sounds* was a land of hope and glory to me, but in this moment I cannot fathom the what and why of his name scrawled there in red.

Meanwhile, inside my head I can keep secrets, and I'm grinning and recalling as the tape is slowly rewound, for I certainly remember Brian Wilson coming to the Stones sessions. He sat in the neoned RCA reception, maybe next to a Buffalo Springfield. He didn't come into the studio; nobody 'came in' when we were in. I left the control room to clear my head and ears. It had been another eighteen-hour stretch on a four-day watch, and the tracks for the album were more or less down. After that much time in front of the console, you are merely guessing, but fortunately it was the year of guessing it right. I stretched into the hall and whacked on my two ears with a tweak of my forefinger and thumb, one crack each. The sky opened up inside and I was back in the land of heard. (I was not familiar with my third ear yet. Well, I knew him, but I didn't always go along with him.)

Five minutes later my ears were more than clear as a result of a Hawaiian joint that rushed me back to work. As I got up from the not-even-nearly-leather studio reception couch I heard Brian Wilson say, 'One day I will write songs that people will pray to.' Dear Brian nearly had it right, God only knows. He should have said, 'One day I will write songs that will move people to pray for *me*.' He already had.

Back in the studio a take was completed on 'Everybody Needs Somebody To Love'. It had been a good day. The music ended and I heard myself speak from the console, directing my voice at Mick. Keith had already spoken with himself.

'It's fine. If we use take two, there's something to be fixed. The piano . . . you know?'

Mick replied curtly, 'Yeah, fine. Yooou knowww, this isn't a fuckin' Brian Wilson record you knooow.'

'I know that', I replied, 'I've been with you long enough to know the difference, dear.'

A snigger or twitter south-west in the studio – Stu or Bill Wyman.

'Well, what do you wanna do about it?' I said into the void.

'Nothing,' said Mick.

'Nothing?' I asked him.

'Keep two and fix it?' came the pouted reply.

The answer's 'yes', I said to myself, got up and left. It was still so in January of 89.

I recalled, too, a second time the California Boy had graced us with his presence some months later, on the day that we nailed the tracks for 'My Obsession' and 'All Sold Out'.

**Brian Wilson**, songwriter/producer/Beach Boy, *Wouldn't It Be Nice? My Own Story*: One day in late January or early February Lou Adler, who'd left Jan and Dean to become manager of the Mamas and the Papas, invited me to attend a Rolling Stones recording session. Things were at a standstill when I showed up at the RCA Victor studio, but there seemed to be a hell of a party in progress. Tables overflowed with booze, drugs and food. Girls were everywhere. Adler introduced me to Keith Richards and Mick Jagger. They seemed nice, not like the hell raisers I'd read about. But I told them I could never work in such a crazed atmosphere. To me, the studio was like a church.

'It works for us,' said Mick, who told me he was a fan of the Beach Boys. 'You want a drink?'

'No, thanks,' I said. 'I heard that you throw acid in people's Cokes.' I wasn't joking.

Rather than take offence, Mick had a good laugh. He said they did get high and then pulled out a huge, fragrant joint from his shirt pocket. 'You want a hit?' he asked.

'Sure,' I said, taking a puff.

Mick told me to keep it, as he had to go back to work. Then he rounded up the rest of his band, taking charge almost as I did with the Beach Boys, except that it took the Stones upwards of half an hour before everyone finished his drinks or did whatever and moseyed back into the studio. In the meantime, I'd settled back in the corner of a sofa and puffed at the joint Mick'd given me. It was potent stuff. Pretty soon I didn't know what the heck was going on. 'Where am I?' I asked a girl standing nearby.

'At a recording studio,' she smiled.

'What am I doing?' I asked.

'You're listening to the Rolling Stones,' she said, dancing.

'Oh, yeah,' I said. 'What are they recording?'

'It's called "My Obsession",' she said. 'Are you Brian Wilson?'

'Yes,' I said.

'I love you,' she said, kissing me on the cheek and dancing off into another part of the room.

Influenced by the pot, I thought 'My Obsession' was the best fucking rock 'n' roll song I'd ever heard in my life, and by the time I managed to make it home, a good several hours after spacing at the studio, I felt as if the Stones had knocked me on my ass and just didn't see how the Beach Boys were going to compete. I cancelled my writing session with Tony Asher and stayed in bed for two straight days, smoking pot and licking my wounds.

*

**ALO**: Back to the subject of keyboards, and of the faithful. It seemed light years ago, that day in 1963 that I'd sat in my back office *chez* Eric Easton and decreed to Mick and Brian that Rollin' had to have a 'g', and that the Rolling Stones could only be five – ergo, Ian Stewart would have to go. A lot would then happen to all of us on this good ship rock 'n' pop. Ten years down the pike and into the 70s all the rules would have changed. In 1963 there were, for all outward appearances, just five Rolling Stones. But in the end, Stu would stay with the Stones a lifetime longer than I did.

A while back in the midst of my madness I'd have liked to have had it that it was one of my brilliant moves, and give you every twist and turn with callous delight. I'd have told you that such a cold correct move could only have been made by a cold astute fucker and I was never uncomfortable about what I caused to go down in front of Stu. Some years ago I might have, but not now.

Brian had to add insult to injury by following up on my 'Stu must go' dictum with a fake assurance to Ian that he would be taken care of financially and would always be a part of the band. I didn't see the other Stones giving lip service to this charade but none of them blocked my move, either.

There were some fundamental things I know Ian Stewart and I agreed on. Like, the more the Stones rolled on, as the hits got bigger and better, Brian Jones would deliver some of his finest music in his second burst of inspiration. He surprised us with his adept picking up of an instrument hitherto unknown to him and coming up with that polished gem that made recordings like 'Lady Jane', 'Out Of Time', 'Paint It Black', and so many more.

But while Brian got off on the dulcimer, the sitar, marimbas, recorders and more, he stopped getting down on the guitar and Keith found himself doing double duty, not only on call as himself but subbing for Brian. Sometimes on the road Brian would shine and summon up all the power and glory of his bottleneck anthems, 'I Wanna Be Your Man' and 'Little Red Rooster', while scaling the twin guitar peaks of the first three Stones LPs with Keith. But all this was slipping away, as was Brian. Midway through March of 1966 at RCA studios came a night I couldn't leave the room (as opposed to knowing when to and being able to). Brian had finally arrived at the studio, after days of who-knew-where-or-when, in absolutely no condition to clock in and work.

He managed to plug his guitar into his amp, but that was as far as it got. He was bulbous and bloated; no colour was right for him that day. Everything he wore, an absurd combo of velvet, stripes and squares, reeked of disregard of the very fabric of clothing into life, of untoward disarray. He collapsed on the not-too-comfortable, cold wood studio floor. He didn't notice; he was beyond feeling shame or hurt. Grey to the gills, ready to explode in mind and body, he clutched his guitar like a life preserver, though life was hard to find. He just lay in a pathetic fetal position on the floor, draining the life out of the room.

Mick got paler. It was catching. I noticed with regret I was wearing maroon. Mick folded his arms and pursed his oracular gob. He would have been much more at home in an apron and slippers tizzying around the kitchen tutting at the spuds for not coming to the boil. But we were in the studio, where time was never on our side and we had work to do.

For nearly an hour we all walked on eggshells, overdubbing on already recorded basic tracks, working around the sad centrepiece of Pisces pain that lay in the middle of the studio, oblivious to being in the centre of the very world he had dreamed of and where he was now self-destructing centre stage. After nearly two hours of stepping around and over Brian, Dave Hassinger – following the night's unspoken flight plan of 'ignore him, we don't need to talk about it, we need to work' – set up microphones for percussion and organ, with baffles surrounding the set-up to keep any Brian sound out, as we now needed optimum quiet for the overdub.

Our engineer then let us know he could no longer ignore the hum coming from the amp in response to Brian's constantly rearranging his crashed form nearer it and the mikes.

We had been working on 'What To Do', which was fitting as we all waited on each other to sort out Dave Hassinger's immediate problem of Brian zonked out on the studio floor. We all looked around the room, the floors, the walls and each other for a volunteer to deal with the man overboard.

I looked at Charlie, who just looked back and dared me. I looked over at Dave Hassinger, sitting there chewing the cud, his arms around his neck, feet resting on the recording console. He'd clocked out and his body language quite clearly said, 'I've told you the problem. One of you has to tell me how to deal with it.'

I looked at the still-sullen pissed-off Mick. He wasn't going anywhere and his look back at me was in anger and said, 'Produce your way out of this one, then let me know. I've had it.' Charlie surveyed his kit domain and stayed in it. Bill managed to ignore the proceedings and find something to smile on for at least five of every hour.

I locked into Keith's eyes. He took them on a trip around the room and dropped me off on top of the Jones heap – the Brian unseen – then brought us both back and squared off at me. Fuck him, I thought. Mick had picked up on Keith's call and sent out the same message to management.

This was not part of the job description I thought I'd signed on for. I could do Sidney Falco, but not Monroe Stahr. I got up off the control room chair, walked into the studio towards Brian and the humming amp. I found the on/off switch, put it in off, yanked the guitar lead out of the amp and walked back into the control room. Nothing needed to be said. It was all part of the gig, the beginning of the last rites, my day would come. We all went back to work, knowing what to do and doing it, even though one of our aircraft was missing in action.

Back in the control room Dave Hassinger stirred, Jack Nitzsche eased his heart back out to the Hammond and Glock, and the Stones started rolling again.

'That's what happens when you fly without radar,' were Keith's last words on the night.

*

In the first few days of December 1989 I saw Charlie Watts in heaven, an appropriate pre-Christmas vision in keeping with my times. The Charlie

Watts Orchestra and more than twenty jazz musicians from England, Scotland, Wales and Ireland descended upon the States for a short tour. They kicked off in Boston, then headed for the perfect venue, the Jerry Brandt-created Ritz on West 13th Street off Lower Third Avenue in the hub of New York.

I sat in the balcony feeling a total glow, watching Charlie beaming behind his drums, enjoying every moment of being exactly where he wanted to be. My beam was moved along by my companion for the night, Pete Kameron. I didn't even need to drink, life was in such order. When you are on that end of the drug run you fight for the night when it's all smooth. That night I was lucky. It was totally perfect as Charlie, sky grisly blue, all clear, cottoned, linened, canvas-brogued and silk-bowed, took over the whole room and let us into a very special musical place in his life, and we loved it. The band turned and swayed on a dime and took us back to the swing we were weaned on. Show done, I went backstage alone, Pete K having decided to go uptown. I knew I was backstage at the Ritz and not on a nod, but I could have been rushing past effervescent Isobel on the door of the Rediffusion *Ready Steady Go!* Holborn Green Room. Charlie Watts stood by the other very special place in his life, Shirley Watts, and Tony King, seeing I was on and probably into behaving, graced me a 'here we are again' happy beam and willed me into the room. Tony looked great and not a day older than Decca. Keith Richards and Patti Hansen rounded out the circle. Tony King wanted to continue looking as good tomorrow, so he limo'd us to Keith and Patti's Lower Broadway loft. Keith said come up; Tony smiled goodnight and happily left us tucked into the evening.

Keith opened my first visit to one of his homes in twenty-six years with a blast on his number one topic that fall, Mick. It was that year, the year of the thirty-year itch for Mick and Keith, and Keith showed no mercy. 'Cunt of the month', 'She should join Aerosmith', a slew of Joan Rivers one-liners dedicated to the one we love – Michael Phillip. It was fast and funny – his outburst, recorded, could have been the comedy album of the year – then, just as suddenly, it was over. We switched channels, moved from E! to A & E as I listened to Keith's joy and pleasure at his recent production outing for Aretha Franklin on the Stones' classic, 'Jumpin' Jack Flash', the title song of the Whoopie Goldberg comedic flick of the same name.

Keith was proud of his work and deservedly so. I loved the video, the shots of Keith ruling over the control room, totally in his element and in charge. The fact that I'd stopped off at the Colony and bought the single told him more than any of my words.

'It was great, man,' Keith chimed. 'We just went in and cut it. Three days,' he continued proudly. 'We did the whole fucking thing in three days, start to finish, video as well. She was great, ol' Aretha. I sat the bitch down at the piano and told her if she moved or got up, I'd fucking kill her. That's how I got it done; she didn't stand up once in three days. In and out, job done.'

Minutes later we'd moved to another room, switched channels again, and Keith was playing tracks. I don't know how the subject of Ian Stewart came up, but he had to have been on Keith's mind a lot following his recent sudden death in England.

'Stu hated you, Andrew,' Keith informed me. He paused, allowed the dime to drop and continued, 'but not as much as he hated Brian; he wanted to kill Brian.' Keith let us both mull on that one, and I thought I heard him add, 'Maybe he did.'

As said, Stu and I had been of like mind on a few things. Much to my surprise, 'Satisfaction' was one of them. While Mick and Keith were having entitled qualms and debating the value of their national anthem, Stu didn't give it a second thought and joined the ranks of those who loved it from the giddy-up. We also agreed, no vote needed, that I knew nothing about 'their blues', and Stu would probably have added 'rhythm' as well. Looking at the big picture I'd add that my very lack of inclination for the blues, especially that version purveyed by little rich-miss white boys, actually helped me appreciate those Rollin' Stones more clearly in the beginning. It helped me to see what *might* be. I'm remembering that first time I saw the sextet in April of 63 at the Station Hotel, Richmond, and how I'd been overwhelmed by this power and force and my life being over as I knew it. I had happily said hello to the rest of that life, felt the hit of totality, not blinded by an opinion of 'dem dere blues'.

'He never forgave you for kicking him out of the group, Andrew,' was what I heard Keith say instead.

'Yeah, maybe, but I couldn't have done it without help,' was how I answered, wondering what revisionist journey this trip was all about. 'Well,' I sighed, trying to move it further in to close the cycle, 'I'm just glad Stu captured my essence so eloquently before he died. He's gone and he did me a favour. I'll never have to wonder what he really thought of me.'

'What did he say?' asked Keith.

'He said he wouldn't piss on me if I was on fire,' I replied. We both laughed; Stu tied the knot and grinned.

Keith's *Murder She Wrote* scenario was way north-west of any of my realities. All of this was water under the bridge, but Stu's passing was bringing it all back for Keith.

There were now three sides out and about on the 'Sixth Stone'. I knew what I'd been cause to and Keith could account for his own behaviour, and slipping around in there was the truth. Neither Keith nor I was lying. We were both the masters of convenience, the art there to serve and protect.

A few months later I'd stopped off in England on my way to no good in Oslo and was catching up with Cynthia Stewart on the phone.

'So how was Keith towards you when you met?' Cyn had asked, cutting straight to the point in a way that reminded me of what a wonderful minder and ally she had been.

'He was fine, really nice,' I said.

'Good,' said Cyn, waiting for more.

I made her wait, but not long. I told her about the Charlie show, seeing Tony King, my visit to Keith's and how Joan Rivers would have applauded his timing and dissing of Mick.

'There was only one weird moment,' I remembered, piquing Cyn's interest.

'What weird moment?' she asked.

'It was about Stu. We were off at a tangent, first what Stu thought of me, then how he loathed Brian. Then I realised I was listening to Keith speculate on how maybe Stu hated Brian enough to kill him. Fucking blew me away, I can tell you. I'd never heard that one before.'

'Oh, I have.' Cyn flatlined. 'Back at the time Brian died I thought about it too, and, in fact, Andrew, I went through Stu's diary just to see if he could have, but he couldn't have. He just couldn't have been there when thingumajig, I mean Brian, of course, just couldn't have been there when Brian died. Anyway, what did Keith say Stu thought of you?'

Cynthia had opened the door I'd left ajar, so I could tell her. 'He said Stu hated me and never forgave me for kicking him out of the Stones.'

'Hmmm.' Even Cyn had to mark time on that one. 'He was a strange man, Andrew, was our Stu. He didn't show it, but he was always terribly hurt by what happened.'

'He had to be, Cyn.' I was followed by silence.

'What did Keith say about the others?'

'Nothing.'

'It's so sad', said Cynthia. 'You know, I never thought that Stu ever felt that it was you he should hate.'

'I didn't either, but it was never spoken about.'

'Couldn't be,' agreed Cyn. 'And what did our Keith have to say about himself?'

'Nothing,' I said. 'I'm not even sure if Keith thinks he was there, you know, when it got done. When I did it, he just carried on about Brian.'

'Yes', sighed Cyn. We'd played this one into sadness and it was time to move on. 'I think, in the end, that's what hurt Stu the most. He thought Brian was disgusting. He despised him, the little dwarf.'

'Yeah, well, Keith sounded still cut up about Stu's death.'

'He would be. Stu loved him a great deal.'

'I know', I heaved – now we were both drained by the whole exchange. I'd rather have been teasing the lovely Cyn, not torturing her or me. The laughs were too long ago. 'I don't know, darlin', I just wanted everybody to stay the way I made them. I didn't want any—'

'Disappointments?' Cynthia finished my thought.

'Yeah.'    ·

'Oh, you can be sure of one thing, Andrew, Stu knew . . .'

I thought it was all pretty clear and understood what and why he thought of me. Again, no words were spoken – big boys don't cry. First, I knew nothing about music as *he* knew music. He saw me in there in the thick of it with his Stones, and he could not quite understand why the Stones were letting me happen. He saw where Mick was going and didn't like what I was leading him to, or what was being allowed to happen to his idea of the group. Stu also saw the handwriting on the wall for the eventual end of me and the Stones, so perhaps that knowledge removed the need to hate. He didn't gloat; he never used his position to move that ship into port, and he never made one move of payback for what had happened.

One day in the early 70s I was staying with Cynthia at the Ealing house she shared with Stu for a day and a half between flights. Cynthia was out. I was in their kitchen brewing coffee when in walked Stu, back from a morning of golf with Glyn Johns.

We'd never been alone in a room and we both attempted to warm above the cutting edge. I nursed my coffee, and we small-talked. I kept thinking, Christ, if Stu ever wanted to beat the shit out of me, here was his big moment. No Reg the Butcher, no weapon, no sturdy steel-tipped shoes. My elegant monogrammed suede slippers left me less than the tea leaf gangster Chris Stamp had so fondly labelled me, and my paisley morning jacket probably invited a bashing from the likes of the golf-clad Stu.

Nothing happened. We chatted on and I noticed for the first time the wonderful warmth and soul that smiled through his eyes. That morning in his and Cynthia's kitchen I stood and talked with a good-looking man named Ian Stewart. We closed the cycle and we knew where we stood with each other. My later flippancy with Keith was protective, stoned and not needed.

I realised that day, and forgot until I cleared up my mind, that Stu knew all along what I was about and what I had done; and finally he knew, better than anyone, and took to his grave, what everybody else had not done about it. Now, Cynthia has told me that this exchange I've recalled as taking place between us never happened, and that I've dreamt it up. So be it; I've just given you the truth of my recall.

Ian Stewart, the sixth Stone, US, 1965

· **CHAPTER 4** ·

**Nik Cohn**, writer: Towards the end of 1964, when I was working for the *Observer*, Andrew had a group called the Poets. He had already got a reputation as the English Phil Spector. I was quite interested in the Poets so I went to one of their recording sessions and I quite liked the cut of Andrew's jib. I liked his outrageousness. I was younger than him and had never hung out with the bands. I got close with Kit Lambert and Chris Stamp. I found the managers more interesting because they were more articulate. I'd got off the bus from Newcastle at the beginning of 1964 with no possible prospect of employment and within twelve months I was wealthier than my parents had ever been. Before 1964, it was unheard of for anyone in Fleet Street to be under the age of twenty-five. But then the world changed.

**George Gallacher**: Andrew had come to Glasgow because the age of consent was lower than that of England so that he could marry Sheila without all that legal crap. He'd been over to Edinburgh and while lingering in the airport he'd come across a Scottish music magazine called *Beat News* which had a picture of the Poets on the cover. He came back up to Glasgow and tracked us down.

The trouble with old pop stars of the 60s, even minor ones, is that the line between apocrypha and truth is somewhat blurred, a combination of the effects of sulphate and age. But I do recall being wakened in the early hours of a Sunday morning by my mother to be told that the Stones' manager was in my living room drinking whisky with my father and offering to audition us. One hour later we were in the Flamingo Ballroom letting him hear our material; a week later we were in London recording 'Now We're Thru'.

**ALO**: You've heard the magic dadaist simplicity that is Ennio Morricone, his soundtracks to *Frantic* and *The Mission*. That suspense that gives musical life its tug and tension pulled me to the Poets and their Scottish drone-mod sensibility. It's the drone that gets you; the English just don't know how to drone. The Poets had started out as a songwriting acoustic threesome fronted by George Gallacher; then they strapped on bass and drums and hit the dance hall chains. I liked the fact that the Glasgow street toughs were all for the Poets, would protect them. The band had street cred where it counted, and I wanted the cause and feel of that cred down on tape.

Their managers were another story. Alan Singleton was the other witness at my wedding. He and a well-intentioned fellow named Joe Stirling were part of the new disease that had erupted as a result of Brian Epstein. Loads of middle-class well-to-do businessmen, most of them in their late twenties and working for dad, saw this beat revolution as a chance to gather up the frayed corners of an uneventful youth and take one more stab at the game before circumstances had them settle down. Dance halls and town halls were invaded by briefcase-clinging, scarved and overcoated eager youngish men with a daddy-given Humber Hawk in the car park, all figuring there was nowt much to this Beatle game. A lot were gay, and thought that management skills required no more than a hardening of the arteries with wishful thinking when the sultry lead guitarist plugged in. Others drank too much, hated being in dad's employ, or merely wanted to get hetero-laid by reflection. Some had honest music ambitions, but all of them underestimated what had made Epstein tick. As a result, most of this motley crew had their five-minute local dance and faded back into the suburbs whence they came.

The very day Sheila and I were wed, we arrived back in London with Tony Calder. I was happy to be done with Glasgow. Tony headed for the office while Sheila and I posed for photographers.

Some time later the woman's page of the *Sunday Express* ran an article by Anne Edwards headlined, 'When Your Little Girl Says: "I'm engaged".' Under the sub-heading 'Too Young', we read:

What is more natural than the disappointment of another set of parents whose nineteen-year-old daughter Sheila Klein married a while ago, without their consent, a pop group manager of twenty who had long, golden hair and used make-up, and claimed he met her when he was drunk in a Hampstead street.

'He's not the kind of man,' said the daughter, 'you would look at and say he would make the perfect kind of husband, is he?'

'We thought she was too young to marry,' said the mother mildly.

Somewhat less than mildly, I agreed. I also determined and probably decreed that neither Sheila nor mum should be opening their traps to the Sunday newspapers.

**Sheila Klein Oldham**: My parents thought I was in France while we were in Scotland. Andrew was commuting down to London to produce Marianne Faithfull. Tony Calder was around all the time. Andrew was a very good producer; he had all the hand movements off. He really knew how to get someone to sing. He'd torture them until they really came up with some heartfelt thing. He wanted a whole real performance, and he knew how to wind someone up and get a top-calibre performance. Judy Garland was interested in him producing something for her. When we met her she was wearing shorts; she had great legs but they were very white. Lionel Bart tried to put them together; he was always matching.

Andrew was not into business; he was into killing himself for the Stones. Marianne he got tired of. He gave the business and financial power to Tony Calder. Andrew much preferred to be in the studio conducting a big orchestra, preferably his own. Tony was a workaholic, incredible perseverance, practical; if he said he'd do it, he'd do it. They had an ideal partnership. If they'd worked on their personal stuff they could have been incredibly successful.

The day we got married we flew back to London and went to the Hilton to stay with Bob Crewe. In Bob's suite we had another ceremony in order to add him to the list of best men. Alan Stroh was there, too, and served as a postal-order priest; he had a mail order certificate from Philadelphia that allowed him to perform marriages. Alan and Bob were really bitchy about our getting married. I went into the bathroom and had a good cry. Andrew got on with all the gays. They were like the Mafia. If you weren't in with them you weren't in.

**Bob Crewe**: Andrew and I would have incredible times together, whether it was in New York or Knightsbridge, where you could get the fish and chips and all that stuff. Then we would go to these dance clubs together with some of the Stones. I met Ringo and Dusty Springfield when I was with Andrew, because he knew everybody.

It wasn't party all the time, although Andrew was very serious about having fun. He was also very serious about the music. He was very curious about things and he had and still has a great sense of the classics coming into pop. He just had that sensibility of refinement interwoven with the raunchiest combination, and it worked!

**ALO**: Bob gave me a wonderful wedding present, the backing track of his Four Seasons' masterpiece, 'Rag Doll'. Listening to the four-track was an epiphany. Compared to the audio clarity and brilliance I heard on this four-track recording, I'd just been fumbling my way through. The separation, sonic level and placement were masterful. I'd only had the opportunity to see Phil Spector perform in airports and on headwaiters, never in the studio. He kept that part all to himself. Bob Crewe was more sharing, and his 'Rag Doll' four-track gave me a technical standard to aspire to. Bob wanted to record an orchestral album of his Four Seasons successes. I recommended Pye studios as the best place to go. Bob flew arranger Charlie Calello into town from New York and got down to it. I followed the Bob Crewe Orchestra into the studio with the Poets.

**George Gallacher**: It was fantastic, the centre of the universe – London 1964 and the Poets in the charts. We're down in London, 'new to the charts', and Andrew's minder Reg King is doing his best to ruin it. I had been doing an interview for some pop magazine and had to meet the rest of the group down at the TV studio. It was a grand sunny day and I was engrossed in Budd Schulberg's *What Makes Sammy Run?*, a novel that Andrew had given me claiming it was his bible, a tale of sleazy Hollywood politics of the 40s whose super-slug anti-hero Sammy Glick apparently provided Andrew with the ethical model needed for survival in the 60s pop jungle. Andrew's Chevy Impala convertible was something else on a day like this, roof down, state-of-the-art sound system blasting Lou Johnson's 'Message To Martha' on the Philips turntable that had a slot into which you just pushed your fave piece of vinyl.

Reg was Andrew's driver and minder. We were always very polite and he was always very friendly towards us. He was a courteous man. Reg's gayness was never evident, but on this day the opposite image was going to be reinforced. We were cruising down Great Cumberland Place and into Marble Arch, me reading, Reg saying nothing, Lou Johnson in the background. I was only half-aware of the shouting at first and paid little attention; to me it was just part of the general Marble Arch melee, horns blaring, nothing unusual. Then I felt something hit me on the side of the head. As I turned towards the source, a builder's van sped away and someone yelled, 'Fuckin' poofter!' Of course I might have expected it; I was reeling in the back of this powder-blue machine in velvet suit and matching frilly shirt and jabot. Reg gave chase and within a minute we were alongside the van, he with one hand on the wheel and the other reaching for the glove compartment. It was over in an oh, so deliberate minute. So beautiful, almost frozen in time; Reg still looking ahead, motionless except for his right arm moving in a perfect arc and the sun glinting on something, then the windscreen of the van shattering. Reg swung left on to Sussex Gardens and asked for Lou Johnson again.

It has often been suggested that Andrew's relationship to the artists he worked with was somewhat peripheral. In reality, he was there for us every minute of every session, even the seminal ones, completely focused, integral to the art. How the fuck else could that magical sound have emerged?

Our main contact would be in the studio. That was the time when I was most comfortable with him. It was great; we seemed to have as much time as we liked. The studios then were sterile affairs, but with the use of screens and lighting Andrew made them more intimate. We always worked from night into the early morning. A lot of the things we produced were written in the studio, and here Andrew was infinitely patient and encouraging. Whatever magic he had was at its best in the studio. I think the stark simplicity of our material allowed Andrew to indulge in his Phil Spector doppelgänger, with pre-eminent reverb and percussion. We weren't the Stones or the Beatles but our stuff was completely original, distilled minimalism. I remember Andrew playing 'Now We're Thru' to John Lennon and the word coming back that Lennon thought it was 'fuckin' weird'. That was great . . . what a compliment!

Brian Jones, Mick Jagger and ALO, London Airport, December 1965

**ALO**: Years later, nearer now than then, I was beating a hasty retreat from London, heading for Heathrow, British Airways and Bogotá. I was no doubt at the end of a drug-rope after another attempt to pull it together. Safe in the back of the cab and on the way home, I breathed a sigh of relief and allowed myself some one-on-one with my cabbie. After a warm-up off-tossing of a few pleasantries through the glass that protects carrier from carried, it was clear who I was, had been, and where I was going. Once it was established that I was a decent fella, the cabbie, a chap about my age with leather collar'd coat pulled up to meet a tweed scarf that clashed, as it should, with his Andy Capp, got down to some basic chat about South America, 'The Great Train Robber' Ronnie Biggs, and life in the sun.

'Ever met up with Ronnie Biggs, then?'

'No, South America is a very big place, y'know, it's anuvver six fuckin' hours from Bogotá to Rio de Janeiro, anyway they speak Portuguese, don't they . . . at 'ome in Colombia we speak Spanish and that's enough.'

As we took in the Hammersmith flyover and belted for the M4 I'd reverted to the accent my mother had not paid for, the one that Mick Jagger gets away with on stage and at press conferences but would probably not try within a mile of Bow Bells or the brothers Stamp.

'Ever miss it, then?'

'Miss what?' I yelled.

'England! Ever miss England?' he exclaimed in a tone that nearly had me as fucking dumb for not sussing there could only be one 'it', our England – not Great Britain, just the great always-be-an England.

'Not really. Bogotá's been my home for fifteen years. The climate's kinda spring and autumn all the year. We're 8,000 feet up so we don't have to put up with air conditioning and heaters and it doesn't get dark at a quarter to four about five months a year.'

'Well, then, that says it all, don't it? No point in coming back, mate, you've got it made.'

I actually had. It's always the same in the back of a cab or slinging lame arrows dipped in untruths to a fellow airplane passenger as both of you lift glasses of cheer to that life that really only exists on journeys and ceases when you get to the end of the ride or the cloud.

'Ever see the lads?' The cabbie flew my way now that we were all equal.

I knew who the lads were.

Oh, God, that one. I had enough cocaine to smooth the ride back to Bogotá. You're not likely to get searched for blow on a flight to the mother nation; the traffic goes the other way, and on those occasions I didn't feel lucky, I'd just miss the flight. I gauged the cabbie's take on me and selected a secure angle from which it would seem more as if I had a cold than as if I were whoofing a line in the back of a cab.

'You mean the Stones?' I cleared my throat and nasals to make sure every last iota of the marching powder had the op to jump-start my brain into fielding the question, because truth was I hadn't seen the lads in years and hadn't got around to handling it.

'Yeah, the Stones. Mick 'n 'em, do you still see 'em or what?'

I'd got Ronnie Biggs, had got 'it', so why was I being so slow with the Stones, was the tone from the pure heart of the real at the wheel.

'Not really,' I began. 'What happens is whatever the relationship you had when you left is the one you pick up on whenever you see each other, whether it's twelve minutes later or twelve years . . .' I waited for that premise to land on the front seat, then curled on, 'so if I haven't seen Charlie or Keith you basically pick up on the level you left off.'

This was not going over.

'What about Mick then?'

'No, we don't really have much to say to each other.'

'What, stuck up is he?'

'No, kinda like a first wife.'

'Oh dear,' Andy Capp gave a veritable chuckle of one who'd been there before. 'Nuff said then'.

The rain began to greet us as we started to whiz past the Feltham turn-off.

'When I sussed who you were when I picked you up, I'd actually been meaning to tell you, I like the Stones, 'course I do, but do you know what it is you did that really impressed me?'

I would bet a five that it wasn't Marianne Faithfull. Humble Pie? No . . . Small Faces, maybe. Amen Corner, never. Maybe he'd seen me do the line.

'It was the Poets.' He nearly cackled at the thought of that one – he knew I was nowhere near. 'Gotcha on that, didn't I?' he chuckled.

'You certainly did,' I replied and allowed him to carry on. He went into a description of how he thought 'Now We're Thru' was a smashing record and how it was a real shame it hadn't gone further up the charts. By the time we said our goodbyes on the pavement outside Terminal 3, Andy Capp had given me one of those moments that made the whole nine yards very worthwhile, worth all the madness. I beamed at the pleasure of having given him such pleasure. Time stood still, wrapped around the loose ends and edits, and for a moment life was all in a very good day's work.

**Tony Calder**: Marianne had caused a real sensation, just the pictures alone. David Bailey fell in love with her and he did those famous pictures with the ankle sox on . . . everybody wanted to fuck her. Decca was crying out for more Marianne. It all got a bit big and Andrew decided he was the star. He said, 'I'm not going to record her anymore', like it was the end of the world as we'd known it. I said, 'Don't be a cunt.' He was going off on drugs, pills, liquid speed. He didn't want to know about Marianne; he'd had it with her. Things might have been different if he'd wanted to fuck her like the rest of the world. She bored him. He said, 'She's not cred; I can't work with her anymore.' He just didn't want things that were acceptable. He couldn't make her anti-establishment. He preferred John Lennon's reaction to the Poets.

**Marianne Faithfull**, *Faithfull*: The follow-up to 'As Tears Go By' was 'Blowin' In The Wind'. A total disaster. All I remember about that session was how dreary I sounded; I had just come off the road and I was exhausted. I was overwhelmed, too, by the very idea of doing a follow-up. When I did 'As Tears Go By' I'd seen it as a way of getting out of my A levels, but now I had to face the possibility that this was not going to be just a break in my old life, it was something that was going to go on and on, a real nightmare.

I did my best to blame Andrew and Decca for 'Blowin' In The Wind' but it was my own doing entirely. Poor Andrew, it wasn't his fault at all. He was trying to please me; he knew I didn't understand at all the game being played with art and control. And, of course, I worshipped Bob Dylan. So Andrew went against his better judgement and it was a fiasco. Despite the fact that he was inevitably right about everything, I was having problems with Sir Andrew. It was the fog-and-amphetamine factor that bothered me. He was really out there at the time. I was intimidated by the cool, mystifying jivespeak of his that passed for chat. I had no idea what he was talking about most of the time. He was too hip for me, and on top of everything else to have a mad hatter as your manager – it was all too much.

After 'Blowin' In The Wind' I jumped ship. I left Andrew for his partner, Tony Calder. Tony was not a bad guy, a bit sleazy in the nicest possible way. Tony split away from Andrew to take care of me, and we made a couple of very good records, 'Come And Stay With Me' and 'This Little Bird'. They are my personal favourites from that period.

After 'This Little Bird' I dumped Tony Calder too. By then I'd had enough of all these exotic people. I wanted a little fat old man, preferably bald and wearing glasses – an agent from Hollywood movies about Tin Pan Alley. What had unnerved me about Andrew and Tony and that whole crew was that they were so young. Andrew was barely older than I was. I wanted someone more adult.

**Nik Cohn**, *Awopbopaloobop Awopbamboom*: Marianne Faithfull epitomised everything that had changed in pop. Her mother was a baroness, true class, and herself, she'd been to a convent school. When she got out, Andrew Loog Oldham saw her at a party and employed her on the spot. You could see his point – she was the perfect face. She looked incredibly virginal, incredibly sexual and she had the strangest sad smile you ever saw. When she sang, she sighed and she drooped her eyelids in poses of infinite lustful purity. She didn't naturally belong in pop; she was high above it.

Marianne Faithfull, London, 1964

**ALO:** Marianne embarrassed me and for that I left her. From the moment I had caught sight of her I'd recognised my next adventure. In another century you'd have set sail for her – in 1964 you recorded her. And this I did, and was able to enjoy the totality of it, the egg and the shell. On vinyl Marianne was my audiofile Grace Kelly, a siren slut from the top drawer to undermine a nation's hard-on. But away from my vinyl screen, on stage and alone, Marianne was not very good; she was no longer truehearted Kelly and I was no longer Bing. 'True Love' flew out of the window, and that was too much to bear. I found it too painful to contemplate Marianne alone on the stage with an acoustic Jimmy Page in some pop fodder treadmill. And so the eggshell broke, and I abandoned her. I lived in my world where I expected my stars to be stars 24/7, *la vida loca total*. I expected it like the truculent Flo Zitfelt schoolboy pimpressario I was. My stars had to remain stars in my eyes, or be gone.

I should have paid her not to work or put up the dough for an orchestra. But I didn't, ma; I was still learning on the job. In 1997 in the magazine *Marie Claire* Marianne would describe 'As Tears Go By' as having been 'a weight around my neck for thirty-two years'. She should have learnt to swim.

Life in the UK was ceasing to be interesting. In America I could breathe, while at home I felt alien. Life was more clinical as I fought to control everything, unaware that I had hit a rotation of loops where my drug-taking was starting to control me. With the Stones I bit my tongue and just hoped they could not hear the scream inside on those occasions when a veritable pneumatic drill rearranged my brain and veins.

On 18 October 1964, I joined the Rolling Stones on their first European concert, squeezed in between the UK Charlie and Inez Foxx tour and flying to the US for the second bout with North America. I regarded the Stones' European début at the legendary L'Olympia as a triumphant return for yours truly to what, thus far, had been my second homeland and street alma mater. At the Paris press conference I was already trez tipsy and gay as I toasted Vince Taylor, Charles de Gaulle and Johnny Halliday. To a local gendarme about to nick Keith and I for having our cab park too long in an illegal zone I announced 'Je suis James Bond.' Without missing a beat the cop hit me with, 'Move on, 007, move on.'

We did – to the Pierre Cardin boutique on the rue St Honoré de Fauberg. While Christian Dior had dressed the drawing rooms of the world, Courrèges would edify outer planetary, pre-Sputnik mathematical beauty. As Chanel had inspired and anointed him as her spiritual heir, Yves Saint Laurent stuttered on the rue Spontini, broke down at the thought of de-designed service apparel, marched on and found his stride, line and glory by instigating ready-to-wear. Through it all, there was always Pierre Cardin. Stable, spacy, spatial and smart Cardin, aware of the world but not at war with it, whereas Yves, according to partner/lover Pierre Berge, 'was born with a nervous breakdown'. The Stones took Paris, Paris took us shopping, and I arrived home in stylish breakdown clobber in time to appear as myself on the BBC TV Saturday night extoller of what was new and available in vinyl, *Juke Box Jury*.

I did the show a little tipsy but all smiles and good manners, enjoying my fellow panellists, *Carry On* comedian Sid James and the crass and lovely Diana Dors. Miss Dors was indeed a legend; she was as famous off-screen as Marianne Faithfull would later become off-vinyl. Whereas Marianne's scandals would have a hippy-dippy love and free sex all-around aroma to them, Diana Dors was rumoured to take on battalions and football teams with ease. The British showbiz 50s whence Diana had sprung were rife with rumour and recall of mad drunken orgies, secret two-way mirrors and cameras filming the UK big screen stars and little screen stars at their biggest and barest.

Sitting next to Miss Dors on the *Juke Box Jury* panel, I would become so taken (and panicked) by that sexy know-it-all gaze that, while going into raptures or slaggery over some new piece of vinyl, I gesticulated and my glass of water spilt straight into the divine Diana's lap. Neither the rest of the panel, David Jacobs nor Great Britain's viewers heard her hit me with the quick aside, 'My, my, couldn't you wait—' The camera cut to host Jacobs with BBC efficiency and the show rolled on.

Half an hour later I was rolling with laughter in the Green Room at Miss Dors' contagious wit. She had that art of tailoring herself just for you that I'd witness a few years later when I met Tony Curtis, that instinct for knowing which side of themselves to play to forever endear them to you after that first giddy meet. I don't know what held Diana's talent back; perhaps it was her rep for having spent that much time on her back. The woman I met was a sizzling star, a warm, full-blooded, all-knowing swell raw-diamond talent.

Diana and I took over the room, entertaining each other and all present. Like had met like, was attracted and challenged, and sparks, wit and affection flew. Our dance was cut into by a BBC steward who informed I was required in reception by Bill Cotton, the head of Light Entertainment, and old Pete Murray, the don't-be-a-cunt-there-are-witnesses co-star from my earlier backstage *JBJ* stand. I wondered if I'd got on the show by mistake and 'Wakey, Wakey' Jr had just discovered the gaff and wanted another op at a shout-out. I said adieu, but it was a long goodbye, to my new best friend Diana; alas, we would never really meet again.

Mick Jagger and Eric Easton, Tettenhall Magistrates Court, 1964

I got to the reception determined to keep my cool. Mr Cotton was almost a cuppa niceness. The problem, I was informed, was not me at all; in fact he'd enjoyed me on the show. The problem was this gentleman in the foyer, my partner and Rolling Stones co-manager Eric Easton, all northern and fit to boil.

Eric had sat in his home in Acton or Ealing – I could never tell the diff – with his pal and business associate Sean O'Mahony and, for some strange poperatic reason, taped the audio portion of the just-televised broadcast of *Juke Box Jury*. This was no mean feat. Taping a programme was nowhere near as easy as it is today – you had to be a man with a mission to mike up and record the audio off your telly back then. But Eric knew what he was about and had made up his mind to get angry and now, some forty minutes after show time, was waving his pathetic little reel of tape in the face of anyone who'd pay him any attention, demanding the BBC immediately put out a retraction for David Jacobs' having referred to me in his introduction as, 'Ladies and gentlemen, please welcome the manager of the Rolling Stones, Mr Andrew Oldham.'

Bill Cotton refused the request. He knew perfectly well that Eric was the Rolling Stones co-manager and agent – hadn't he booked the group on to the very same *Juke Box Jury* and made the booking through Eric? Whatever this nonsense was about it would be better settled backstage. No retraction would be forthcoming and Eric, at a loss of ash 'n' dash and armed with O'Mahony, left in a 'you'll be sorry' huff. I'd been getting laid in the brain by Britain's reigning blonde bombshell till Mr Lacklustre showed up.

**Sean O'Mahony**, publisher, *Beatles Monthly* and *Rolling Stones Monthly*: Eric was furious. Wouldn't you be if you were the co-manager and Andrew had told the producer he was sole manager? He'd helped this young bloke and then watched as he grew in importance. Now Eric was being pushed sideways. It was all disorganised, and Eric wasn't used to this total lack of discipline. Most people in show business would have been annoyed if their partner walked around stoned; it could do you a lot of damage. Inevitably, because Andrew was younger and more in tune with the Stones, particularly with Mick Jagger's views, Eric started to become sidelined. Eric was a great man for a deal; he believed in never paying more than he had to. I remember when Mick rang from the US and told Eric to get Chrissie Shrimpton a car for her birthday. Eric organised a great deal on a Mini, but when Mick heard he'd saved some money on the full price he was furious. As far as he was concerned he didn't want a discounted car for his girlfriend. The problem was that the Stones didn't appreciate Eric's attitude, except when that attitude got them more money for a booking.

**ALO**: The day after my *JBJ* appearance, the Stones, Stu and I – minus Easton – flew out for the group's next North American tour.

Mick Jagger, Keith Richard, ALO, Sheila Klein Oldham and Bill Wyman,
London Airport, October 1964

**Al Kooper**: In 1964, the British Invasion began to erode the office I worked
in as a songwriter in New York City. The Beatles and the Stones stepped off
their planes and influenced us all. I remember going to see the Stones in New
York. I was so mesmerised that I walked out covered in sweat and promptly
fainted! I had cut out pictures of them from magazines and pasted them in
my notebooks. I wanted to look like that and play music like that for a living.

Within a year, I had put a B3 organ stamp on Dylan's 'Like A Rolling
Stone' and joined a Greenwich Village band, the Blues Project, a New York
approximation of the Stones. I met Jagger and Jones with Dylan and was
quite impressed, especially with their wardrobes.

**Cynthia Plaster Caster**, groupie: I couldn't meet the Beatles because they
were too popular by the time they got to Chicago, but the Stones were pretty
unknown. They came to Chicago to record *12 × 5* at Chess Records. I was
just eighteen. I called up the likely hotels, asked to be put through to them

and waited to see how the hotels responded. The second hotel I call up connected me to Brian Jones's room and as soon as I heard the phone ringing I knew I'd hit the jackpot and hung up.

Barbara and I and a few friends taxi'd over fast to the hotel. We flipped out when we saw in the lobby this bunch of long-haired, foreign, tight-crotched boys. I approached the first one I saw, Andrew Loog Oldham, their manager, and asked him, 'Are you a Stone?' His breath reeked of Scotch as he replied, 'Yeah, baby!' and thrust his tongue into my ear. I went into true shock. Everything around me was like a whirling haze and my girlfriend's voice was like an echo chamber. It left me cross-eyed, staggering towards the elevator after the other Stones.

I stayed in the lobby – my mother had told me never to go to a man's hotel room – but Barbara followed Mick and Keith to their room for a chat, whereupon Oldham attempted entry. Mick and Keith wouldn't let him in because he was drunk and armed with a gun. He got in anyway and, brandishing the gun, chased Barbara around the room, too strong to be subdued by Mick and Keith. They yelled to Charlie Watts to come and help them, but he couldn't be bothered because it had happened so many times. Finally Charlie did get tired of all the commotion, walked in, bopped Oldham on the head and knocked him out cold, walked on back to the next room and carried on watching television. They dragged Oldham's unconscious body into the bathroom, and then Brian Jones sauntered along, patted my girlfriend on the wrist and offered her a cup of tea.

I was bitten by the bug. I wanted to see more longhairs and I loved the music. There was a problem though; we were still virgins. We were getting interested in sex, finding out bits and pieces about the facts of life. My fascination with what dicks looked like was growing all the time. We were pretty silly; I mean, to me, it was more comfortable to talk to a pop star if I could make myself and them laugh.

**ALO**: The sex was great. Thank you, Brian. Somehow we had twenty-four hours to kill in New York, and I accepted Brian's offer to spend some time together and let him guide me, play host, take me into his form of escape and freedom which was yer basic sex-and-drugs with a gorgeous bevy of lithe black and pink dames in a hotel suite overlooking Central Park. The leer of happiness on his face was a pleasant disgrace as he watched me dive into his world of sex games, sex roles and oblivion.

Some twelve or fifteen hours later I woke up and knew I still hadn't landed.

I'd been taken everywhere, been everything, welcomed the sexual freedom so much so that I didn't feel the need to have my own thoughts. I was a red door and she sang paint it black. I lay in bed with D and S on either side of me – so many of me – arms, heads, neck and sex entwined. Brian stayed on the sofa, but woke when the two black pearls and one thin pink blonde got up. I shared a bath with the two Negritas. As Brian sat on the tiled marble bathroom floor, tired but happy, the pink blonde had her head on his. There were five of us – and, despite what you may have been taught, three into two will go. Five became one, a sexual androgyny mystified in one popper-driven phallic rush, chomping at the sexual food chain while worshipping and devouring yourself.

That night Brian had once again been the leader of the pack; he'd been my manager for the night and decided what would be best for me. The darkness of the carnal pleasure was nevertheless lit so bright it made it hard to go outside.

Again in New York, some nine months, a year – I'm not sure – later, following the sexfest . . . and in 66 to be sure, there was another scene with Brian, an eerie and gothic one that would leave a mark forever and would mould a huge chunk of my future into a dead-end street.

It was past 2.30 in the morning at the Drake Hotel where, for some bizarre reason, Brian and I had ended up with adjoining suites. I heard him on a muffled call from his bedroom. He then re-entered the central living room and said to a wasted me, 'Andrew, I have to see this doctor. I don't want to go alone . . . would you go with me?'

These were the days before you could channel-switch with your cable TV – back then, you could only do it in your mind. A year earlier Abkco gofers had happily delivered or collected prescriptions to and from my suite. I was the young genius having his every crazed whim catered to. Now I was being asked to help Brian, dying twit, to hammer another nail in his coffin!

And mine, perhaps. Suddenly managing the Stones was neither mine nor fun.

'What kind of doctor, Brian?' I asked in a tone that carried the weight of, 'What kind of fuckin' doctor can it be you've found who sees patients at three in the morning?' I must admit I was curious.

'Well, it's hard to describe what he does, but he's good . . .'

Little Brian was anxious, in no mood to discourse. He wanted to get going but still needed Andy to hold his hand. 'So are you ready? Are you coming?' He smiled.

We both laughed at the coming fiasco of God-knows-what and elevator'd down to the lobby and the waiting limo.

We limo'd uptown on Park Avenue (we limo'd around the clock now) and crossed over to Lexington near 72nd, Brian giving the directions on a first-name basis to the driver. 'Frank, it's here. We'll be back, just stay and wait, okay?'

'Sure thing, Brian,' said Frank.

'Nice guy,' Brian informed me as we hit the pavement. Perhaps he was Stu-ing Frank.

We ambled to the left of an apartment's ground-floor entrance, through a door and down a hall. At the first door on the right Brian pressed a call button and yelled, 'Lewis Jones to see the doctor.' The door buzzed, we hit the click and entered a small reception.

Doctors' receptions can be grim reminders and reapers of one's potential lot at the best of times. But through an eerie 3 a.m. neon haze nobody beats the scenery. The magazines were as grubby and unkempt as their readers who looked up with a collective hostile gaze that said, 'We were here first and don't forget it.' Brian knew what he was about; this was his beat. He crossed the reception and a glass partition opened slightly. He leant inside the opening and spoke to the other side.

'Hello, dear, how are you?' Brian gushed. 'The doctor's expecting me. I've brought my manager. I told the doctor I would.'

'Yes, Mr Jones,' said a quiet tired female voice, 'I'll buzz you through. You're to go right in, both of you.'

We were buzzed through, Mr Jones leading the way. The man with no neck and no future turned to give me a good luck smile that told me that he was just as buzzed with the proceedings as the door. We marched drug left into the general area where on one side there was a long line of occupied Formica/linoleum, curtained cubicles, confirming the adage that the city never sleeps. Opposite the cubicle drapes was an open door leading into a dark office, impossible to detail in the bad light. Behind an oak tank of a desk and its backdraught of papers, samples and medical journals sat a man of medium height, age fifty to sixty. What was left of his hair was dishevelled, greying to black and curly. He had a sweaty, pale face with eyes orbiting behind specs and was attired in a day-old button-down shirt, old striped tie limp and dead, and off-white doctor's trust-me overall with fading blood marks over the pockets where the good doc had perhaps wiped his hands instead of washing them.

'Hello, doc, how are you?' scraped Brian.

'Fine.' The doctor didn't sound sure. He looked my way. 'This is your . . . sit here and you come on in'.

I sat and Brian followed the doc. I looked around. After my eyes adjusted to the dimness I could discern a row of medical jars filled with scissors of all shapes and sizes standing up in disinfectant water. Alongside in another jar was what seemed to be, at first sight, some strange human part, but on closer examination was revealed as – again standing in water – either a trio of frankfurters or perfectly-cloned pricks. The next jar was waterless and half-filled with soggy sauerkraut, and the last jar held about half a dozen pickled cucumbers. Below this shelved valley of the jars was a large steel fridge-like sterilisation container and above the shelf an array of framed diplomas, citations and individually signed photos. I started to scan the photos. The first one I recognised was that of the other LBJ – Lyndon Baines Johnson, President of the United States. The photo was signed but on a quick scan impossible to decipher beyond the 'To' and 'Your Good Friend'. Next to that was a citation from the office of the President, same Lyndon B, recognising the good works and giving thanks for and on behalf of his country to . . . Dr Max Jacobson.

Another photo was a long shot of three or four serious-looking suited men and Jackie Kennedy. One of the men was JFK and half-hidden behind him in the photo was the doctor I had just met. The wall was clad with droves of more citations, diplomas, thank yous from the JFK administration and the Attorney General, RFK. The last photo to the right of the wall was of Jackie K in that famous Dallas Chanel and Roy Halston pillbox hat, looking sad and noble. There were several sombre suits of power around her, and there, again in the upper right background, was the ominous Dr Max.

The same Dr Max exited his office with Brian, walked past me and down the cubicled hall, opened a curtain halfway down and gestured to Brian to follow him in. Five or so minutes later the doctor came out, leaving Brian behind the curtain, and popped into the next cubicle. I heard conversation exchanged. Then the doc came out and came my way, went behind his desk, wiped his hands over his blood-stained overalls and from jar no. 1 took a frankfurter, dunked it in the sauerkraut of jar no. 2, took a bite, chewed, looked at me, took another bite, chewed, swallowed. Frank gone.

'So tell me what is wrong with you,' Dr Jacobson prompted, smiling as he little-fingered some sauerkraut and frank out of his uneven teeth.

'Nothing, I just came to keep . . . him . . . Mr Jones company. I'm his manager and—'

'Yes, I know, but Lewis told me I should see you, said I should help you, so please tell me what is wrong.'

I seized on the good old on-the-road standby. 'I do have herpes on my penis. It's not from sex, it's nerves.'

113

'That's nothing. I'll give you some ointment before you go. Lewis tells me you lead a stressful life, you have to keep going constantly, keep on the ball, people rely on you all of the time, need your decisions, that sort of thing.' Dr Max inspected a speck of frank on the end of his finger and flicked it with his thumbnail on to the floor. 'I know what it's like, a lot of people need you . . .' He indicated the wall behind him. 'Like the President. It's the same sort of thing, just a different war.'

He took on a George C. Scott, *Dr Strangelove* stillness while he let that one drop in on me. He was good – getting his bearings with me and enjoying himself. He wrapped himself around a thought and carried on. 'I used to go down to the White House two or three times a week when he was there; he needed me a lot. I travelled to Florida, went to the conventions, spent a lot of time with him on the road before he got elected. Do you know what I did for him . . . for them?'

His hand surveyed the photo'd wall again. I thought about the poor fuckers in the reception chomping that bit of insanity that must accompany syntony for these office hours and habits. It was all right if you were on the road, but not on the street where you live.

'No, I don't know what you did for them, doctor.'

He was going to tell me anyway. He zeroed in on me as if making that decision, his eyes smiled, and he continued. 'I give everyone a specific shot designed for their individual needs, but it's mainly, the essence is a shot of concentrated highly potent vitamins that rejuvenate along with certain combined extracts from the glands of . . . a monkey.'

He shuffled some papers on his desk and studied me. I was solid as a rock, giving nothing up. I was the audience and Dr Max was the show. 'Do you have anything against injections?'

'No,' I lied. I was terrified of them.

Later I'd know that he lied, too. His injections were nothing but speed.

'By the time the President is at the podium, he's believable, he believes in what he's saying with a passion and power and awareness. The audience has confidence in their President's confidence. That's what I did for him. You could almost say I helped get him elected. All of them.' His hand acknowledged the photo'd wall. 'I help them all.'

Then we're all one big fuckin' happy family, aren't we, I thought. Dr Max Jacobson gestured to the wall again.

'I took care of Mrs Kennedy at her husband's funeral.' He grew quieter, circumspect, as if remembering the time. 'The nation needed to see their former First Lady strong, with dignity, showing courage in the face of loss, an example to the grieving country in its very time of need. I helped with that.'

Christ, I thought, how does he know – or does he even care – that I'm not from the *News of the World*. He got my thought, the canny old fuck, shrugged his shoulders, sighed and gestured a 'whatever' into the air.

'I've been studying you while I have been talking'. The accent occasionally gave off a *mittel*-European burr. For the most part it was no-coastal bland American flat. 'I'd like to give you a treatment, an injection. I know what you need, I can tell. See how it feels, how you feel over the next few days. It's not drugs. It's vitamins and an extract, a compound of monkey glands – your body will love it. I think you'll feel better, function better, you'll find things easier and you'll feel more assured with people and at work.'

Dr Max had rung enough bells and all of them hit home. Feel better, find things easier to do, function better, more assured, better with people . . . just like a president.

'Follow me.' He got up and led the way to hell.

The cubicle opposite the office had its curtain half-open. A woman was sitting with her back to me, red hair pulled up in a blue velvet bun, legs crossed under a grey tweed pleated skirt. She sat alert by a bed, pad on lap, pen in hand. She was taking dictation from an elegant, slight, late forties man, abed. His eyes were raised in thought. He had grey-silver hair swept back off a working forehead. His hands were entwined in a choreography that rhymed with his mind. He was wearing an open-necked blue silk shirt and cashmere cardigan of a blue/powder grey that eased into the grey of his cuffed flannels over darker grey socks. A pair of brown suede tasselled slip-ons sat neatly on the floor. It took only a second, but I got it. His eyes caught mine as I passed and took him in. He then said something about the sets not moving fast enough.

Alan Jay Lerner continued dictating in his room, spent needles in the bedpan beside him, secretary asking was that stage left a second time.

'Yes, lie down, roll up your sleeve.' I was abed next door, wondering who was there. I looked behind me for blood on the walls.

'That's right, that was Alan Jay Lerner. He's written a lot of his new show here. People like you have to keep working. That's where I come in . . . make a fist.'

Like a gunslinger's fast draw he was suddenly at the ready, syringe in hand, syringe to my vein. Some of my blood spat at the wall and over Dr Max's jacket as my balls swallowed themselves and my gills flexed in fear.

The last thing I remember was my *cojones* saying goodbye and driving up my arse as the needle plunged into my arm.

Brian was waiting with a smile for me as I re-entered the reception, herpes cream on my dick, bottle in the palm of my hand. He smiled at our little secret. Conspiracy, that's what the smile said. He was feeling that good already; he didn't want to spend any time on how bad he'd felt before. We limo'd down to the Village, to the Electric Circus on St Mark's Place. It was way past four, nearer to five, and the Circus was closed. Brian banged on the door and asked for the owner, Jerry Brandt, ex-William Morris agent, now trend-making host to Manhattan. Jerry came to the door, hugs passed all round and he welcomed us in.

Jerry left us alone. The 60s were nearly over as we made our way to the floor. There in the middle of this psychedelic arena, lying on his back on the floor, guitar in hand, plugged into the house sound system, oblivious to us, oblivious to all, lost in his sound coming back at him from a 360-degree soundaround blast, was the purple haze himself, Jimi Hendrix.

After fifteen minutes of this, my watch said five and I left Brian huddling with Jimi. I caught a cab outside and headed uptown to the hotel. I got up the next day feeling like a president, and over the next three days made some of the worst decisions of my life.

· **CHAPTER 5** ·

**ALO**: The merry-go-round of 1964 continued with the release of the Andrew Loog Oldham Orchestra's homage to Lionel Bart's new musical, *Maggie May*, produced after Lionel's plans to have me record an LP of tunes from the show with Judy Garland went nowhere. The legendary, fatal Miss Garland was in London tasting the end of her career while residing in the well-heeled American-occupied zone of Belgravia's Chester Square. She would soon astound London by apologising to her audience for her condition and then attempt to sing her entire act prostrate from the floor of the Talk of the Town.

I was up for the possible recording of Judy Garland and *Maggie May*, in the main to give Lionel pal-support. I was scheduled to tea off with her and Lionel at four o'clock one afternoon, but the diva made us wait until dark, only making it downstairs in time for hubby no. 4 or 5 to pour us into the night. She reminded me of a bottle-opener; shame was, she doubled as the cork. She was past being able to meet new people and the new hubby's endearing gift seemed to be making her feel forever on stage, even when at home. The living room was hardly that, and when our star decided we hadn't suffered enough to be funny or at one with her, she gave us a look that killed for wasting her time and took herself back upstairs.

The rehearsals for *Maggie May* had become bloody murder, due in some large part to the bloody antics of Rachel Roberts, out of the kitchen sink, up from Llanelly, fresh from *Saturday Night and Sunday Morning* and *This Sporting Life* and now a grande panicked dame – Mrs Rex Harrison at the time, and no fair lady.

The collapse of the Judy Garland project should have been an omen to me, but I was yet buoyed by my youth and outward armour of invincibility. In truth, I found Miss Garland a pathetic old bag still able to field the odd *bon mot*, but hardly worth a whole innings – at least that's what I told Mick when he enquired after the state of Judy. I should have noted that she'd already had ECT and that – along with the possibility of an Everly Brother and the definitely of Alan Jay Lerner, Eddie Fisher, Van Cliburn, Tennessee Williams and a Kennedy brother – she had flirted with Dr Max Jacobson. Judy was just north of forty but was wearing out rapidly and had notched up attempted ODs at all the best locations. She would later be thrown off the flic that fabric'd the very life of her, Jacqueline Susann's *Valley of the Dolls*, and two years later, after another gay London wedding with Johnnie Ray as best man, she would pull the plug and throw herself off the lot of life. Needless to say, my plans to immortalise the tail end of Judy on vinyl came to naught, and neither did I take any warning from her life of my own peaks and valleys to come.

In America the Stones and I were on the threshold of big-time vinyl reality. 'Time Is On My Side' was knocking on the Top 30 Stateside door in our best showing yet while also, unbeknownst to us, breaking out regionally in Vietnam. Back in England we were cock of the walk as 'Little Red Rooster' crowed its way to no. 1. I got home from my new home, America, and Sheila told me she was pregnant with Sean.

**Sheila Klein Oldham:** Andrew was not interested in anything lower than the Stones; he had an overview that was much more objective than the band's. He always knew the women would have the power. The Stones understood what Andrew meant about banning the women. When Anita Pallenberg came on the scene Andrew was impressed that her son was supposed to have been fathered by Marlon Brando. That was the plus in Andrew's eyes. She was really good looking, the most powerful Stones woman. It was when the drugs took over that the real control went out of the window. That is when Andrew lost his bottle. Drugs and women, a serious combination. To have Sean was a conscious choice. I was quite independent, not pinning everything on Andrew. He'd made me understand that if he was able to achieve some of his dreams then he'd be happier inside himself. He took me out to the Scotch Club when I was pregnant. He was an outrageous dancer; he could clear the dance floor. It was a blissful time and everything was magic. It was life on the way up. The Stones hadn't got to the top and the press hadn't caught on to what was really going on, the huge cultural change, all the pieces coming together, the pill . . .

**ALO:** 'Conscious choice' implies an informed decision; I was merely informed. I accepted the news of Sheila's pregnancy, examined my feelings and kept them to myself. I really had no idea of how to react – the idea of being a father held no reality for me. I had no experience by which to quantify it. I had no favourite movie on the subject into which I could immerse myself and role-play the news into reality. I was confused. The roles I was playing daily as I went about my business on behalf of the Stones bordered on schizo-frenetic. It was too much of a stretch to contemplate finishing the work day as a doting father-to-be. I sighed and let Sheila get on with it.

One definition of insanity, especially as it relates to alcoholism and addiction, is that one repeats the same action expecting a different result. I started to add new combos to my self-medication, upped the level of my daily pot inhalation, imbibed with more frequency in a futile effort to keep myself spirited and drugged above the malaise that was slowly invading and entrenching my ability to be. Some would say that the malaise was the drugupmanship, but remembering the pain of those icicled moments (and the warmth once I'd bandaged and distilled them), I'd beg to disagree. I was unaware I was approaching heavy rotation.

Life for Sheila on the social stratum was barren enough due to my schedule and chosen agenda. I severely limited my forays into sociarama to events at which I could control the room and the players. I thus suppressed Sheila's ability to enjoy the life and windfall I'd begotten us, and encouraged her in a way that would just add another nail to the coffin of our no-hope of a future together. I as much as told her to carry on going out with others and that I'd look the other way, although I never could.

For many, Mick and I were the subject of wishful thinking. This is understandable, as for that while we were as close as two young men could be. But we were close over a cause – and that cause remained the Rolling Stones, or Mick Jagger, and whatever that difference may be. We were all experiencing an exciting awaking in a world the reality of which, just five years earlier, would have been an excommunicable hallucination. Imagine you are just twenty years old and dreams have come true . . . well, some days might be overwhelming, and you might look for shelter with a fellow dream-weaver. The effect this closeness had on our friends and lovers didn't really bother us – we knew it for what it wasn't.

I was as close with Keith, but the tone was more boisterous. It was also more acceptable to bash around with Keith than with the perceived more attractive and ambiguous Mr Jagger. In any case, wishful thinkers didn't dream of going to bed with Keith; they dreamt of staying up with him.

This business I had chosen (or become addicted to, might be a better way of putting it) had somewhere along the line begun to consume the majority of my waking moments. I looked around the well-intentioned guests spending their nights off in songbird Alma Cogan's drawing room and viewed a prophetic babbling madness. It would only take Ralph Bellamy, neck-cravated, fingers jewelled, with grey locks devilishly combed forward unto youth, and Ruth Gordon, all motherly and caringly intrusive, to have popped from next door as neighbours to have had me become John Cassavetes in *Rosemary's Baby*. Suddenly I wanted no part of London showbiz desperation. I'm reminded of writer Keith Altham's recall of jazz scribe George Melly meeting Mick Jagger backstage sometime late in the 80s and remarking on how Mick had more facial lines than he. Mick is supposed to have retorted that they were laugh lines, whereupon the portly Melly remarked that surely nothing was that funny.

Only in America could I freefall and feel at home and not mind when the workday had ended. Perhaps it had something to do with the fact that the race was still young for us in America and the stakes not nearly as high. But America had loads to offer, and I wanted it all. The rules of play were vinyl and airplay, and I liked the isolation amongst the sweep and grandeur of the land. The movies that had screened my youth had not let me down once I'd been allowed to follow the same steps on the same streets as my heroes. I have no idea whether I could sense the danger that would follow the fame at home – but I could feel the dangerous trait of boredom. I knew I'd have to find a part that equipped me for life in better Texas order than the emptiness of James Dean as Jett Rink in *Giant*.

In contrast, the malaise of having made it in England was starting to wear my ambition thin. You could say I was starting to lose my grip. Something was around the corner and it was not a new boutique. Within two years, by age twenty-two, I would get my perceived comeuppance – and, to quote Leonard Cohen, 'they sentenced me to twenty years of boredom, for trying to change the system from within'.

On the social side, Paul McCartney, John Lennon and myself (as opposed to Mick, Keith and myself) liked the occasional tea-time get-together with Alma Cogan and sometimes her mum and Ad Lib owner boyfriend Brian Morris. Alma, the UK's most-loved singing bird of the 50s, gracefully allowed her old-school pro showbiz demeanour to carry her into the 60s, guesting on TV and starring in the occasional summer season in Blackpool. When at home in London, Alma played grand hostess and den mother to all of us upstarts, hosting soirees attended willingly by Beatles, a couple of Stones, Epstein and *moi*. Lionel's Bart and Blair, Sean Kenny, Stanley Baker and Sean Connery, Tommy Steele, Chris Hutchins, Maurice Kinn, Alan Freeman and Vidal Sassoon brought up the rearguard. Alma treated us one and all as equally blessed runts of the same showbiz litter.

I'm told it's at one such afternoon occasion that Paul McCartney, seated at the Cogan tiny grand, twiddled and diddled his way into 'Yesterday' while it was still called 'Scrambled Eggs', as a result of Alma's mum asking if he wanted any. At another of her quieter afternoon tea and scones get-togethers Alma played John Lennon and me a song she and her arranger Stan Foster had composed called 'Now That I Found You'. John gave her an 'Alma, do it with fuckin' Andrew. It's more than an LP filler; he'll make you sound like the fuckin' Ronettes, won't you, Andrew?' (Her A&R man had told her that it was filler, and she did, later, record it with me.)

Earlier in the afternoon the debonair actor Cary Grant strolled in as if we were on the set of *To Catch a Thief*. Mr Grant said he was contemplating *Father Goose* and felt like it. In fact, he'd draw anchor two years later, and his next film, 1966's *Walk Don't Run*, would be his last. Perhaps he autosuggested to John the optimum movement of being able to move on.

On this trip Mr Grant stopped long enough for tea and an immaculate display of charmed charisma that transported itself from the very screen into the living room of life with no need of lighting and pancake. God had given him a permanent starzen. His ease was so deliberate that I had to quash my desire to applaud. I still recall the texture of the man; he veritably Monroe Stahr'd into the room. The light cuffed flannels, open-necked shirt and blazer blended incestuously with the perfect tan. I wish some pages of time had been a little bit more read on that day I sat with Messrs Leach & Lennon – we could have discussed their propensity towards LSD and had them compare notes between tabs of shortbread and cups of tea. Instead, we discussed the merits of Palm Springs as a good weekend and required behaviour at royal premieres.

In October and November of 1964 the Beatles were engaged on their last full-blown British concert tour, although there would be a mini Christmas run at the end of 1965. There was no doubt that the crown was still theirs to wear. Paul McCartney found time to attend the latest James Bond *Goldfinger* premiere and play tambourine on an Alma Cogan EMI session.

Other freeze-frames from 1964: the Beatles, Mick Jagger, Cilla Black and the Ronettes spend some time at the Brian Morris-run Ad Lib. Ex-21s rocker Vince Taylor stands on the steps of the Ad Lib and tells everybody who will listen to fuck off and to come to France where he is God. 'I Feel Fine' goes to no. 1 on the UK charts making space for 'Little Red Rooster' to crow in the same space a fortnight later. Brian Epstein exchanges contracts on 24 Chapel Street on the tip of Belgravia, the house in which, just short of three years later, he will decide he's had enough of this life and move on to the next.

That autumn, the musical charts were a curious mixture of the old and the new – the old hanging on with sleight-of-new-hand and aplomb. Holland, Dozier and Holland; Gerry Goffin and Carole King; Bob's Crewe and Gaudio; Jackie DeShannon; Barry Mann and Cynthia Weil plus Burt Bacharach and Hal David songmonopolied the rest of the November 64 proceedings via the latest waxings from the Supremes, Herman's Hermits, the Four Seasons, the Searchers, Gene Pitney, Sandie Shaw and Adam Faith. The old guard were repped by Henry Mancini, Jim Reeves, Matt Monro and the Bachelors; the indifferent and the desperate by Julie Rogers and Manfred Mann; the perennials by the ever-penumbral Cliff Richard and an operatic Roy Orbison.

Shock 'n' freak was represented by the Anglodefiled P.J. Proby, who took no song chances by hitching his pipes to *West Side Story*'s 'Somewhere' while his velvet trousers performed scandalous twice-nightly splits on stage for the national tabloids. Hope and opportunity were represented by the assault of the Kinks with the relentless anthem 'All Day And All Of The Night'. Percolating in the lower reaches of the charts with George 'Shadow' Morton's declassic production were the Shangri-Las with 'Remember (Walking In The Sand)'. Overall, the top 20 was a mixed happy bag with a chorus and verse for a whole nation to bleat to and plenty of rhythm to dance to.

*Maggie May* had its opening night on 22 September at the primo West End Adelphi Theatre. The night before I'd sat bewitched and gobsmacked as Sean Kenny and writer/critic/National Theatre gadfly Kenneth Tynan joined our table at the Terrazza and the two of them debated the future of cartoon as the true cinematic hope. I nursed an Irish coffee and mummed the word as these two duelled. Tynan and Kenny argued as one that, Walt Disney's cartoon clerical hold notwithstanding, the future of film lay in full-length cartoons – which, in theory, could deliver a level above the range any mere actor could bring to the proceedings. Although the duo used the power of painting as the example of image over reality, Sean Kenny was already thinking in terms of the digital manipulation that enhances today's movies. Ken Tynan, for all his bravado and skill, seemed a man of the 50s who would be downed by the 60s and what lay beyond. Tynan was more than pale – he was grey in palette and grey in pallor. He could not bring himself to embrace what me and the Stones or the Beatles were about. He thought us unqualified to duel in the field of art and said so. Sean Kenny brushed him away with enthusiasm and a good call. 'You're just scared, Ken. Why don't you just give in and join them?'

To Sean, with his engineer- and draughtsman-like mind, the shock of the new was never a shock. Here was a man who revolutionised the working possibility of a stage with his bare hands. Sadly and so too-soon, Sean suffered a brain haemorrhage in 1974 and died while at a meeting in the offices of Bernard Miles at the Mermaid Theatre. I was beside myself and could only take his death personally. I felt lost without this very great friend and will forever miss the sense of ordered madness and worldly wear-thee-well that he brushed into the lives of all those lucky enough to have been touched by him.

Tynan would, in fact, 'give in and join them' with *Oh, Calcutta!* and the primed BBC Radio 3 moment when he became the first man to say 'fuck' over the national airwaves – an early sex pistol to be sure – no doubt blessed with Lenny Bruce recall of how a *bon mot* expletive will get attention to your cause.

But in this *bon* moment he just crossed his legs, pursed his lips and flicked his fag ash somewhat in my direction. His eyes spoke of countless aberrations and perceived betrayals that I would not be privy to until I'd scarred my own future. We hadn't yet read his diaries – his kinky habits, mild sado and get-away whipping weekends, and all the oxymoronic behaviour the so-called straight Englishman gets up to when cricket no longer does it for him. I always think it's a pity when one cannot somehow apply one's aberrations to one's work.

The Stones and I would run into a lot of that as we contemplated sleeping with the enemy in our attempt to enter the film world. Besides Tynan, writers Keith Waterhouse and Willis Hall and directors Nicholas Ray and Bryan Forbes would all fix us with a disdain based on fear that their moment was over. The exceptions and 'their own men' in this exchange were Lionel Bart, Sean Kenny and director Michael Winner.

Opening night found Sheila and I dressing up for the musical whore, which was nervous fun and took longer than the night itself. I gave Reg the Butcher the evening off, as his presence always seemed to unnerve Sheila. I wore a silk and mohair six-button double-breasted evening suit, elastic-sided pump-in boots, crisp white shirt with covered braided buttons and links, and black braided bow tie. You'll forgive me for forgetting what Sheila wore. It may have been Portobello, it may have been Mary Quant or even early Ossie Clark, but all you need know is that my bride of two weeks looked beautiful. We arrived at the Adelphi Theatre and glowed under the strange changing light of the mid-60s where the old guard and values held court but allowed us in to play, due to their need of our fresh young mugs to deliver them unto the next day's morning papers.

We mingled with Lionel and his 'fiancée'/mate Alma Cogan. Peter Sellers and Britt Ekland were there, as were Roy Moseley with Anthony Perkins; Noël Coward and Binkie Beaumont; and Rex Harrison and Sybil Burton, bringing up their rear. Sybil was married to the Welsh B-actor/mountain-of-fame climber, Richard Burton, who'd just been propelled into the lap of the gods and a cool million per flick assisted by his on screen/off screen bedding of Elizabeth Taylor. Sybil would move later that year to New York and open the best-known East Coast disco, Arthur's, where a good time was had by all Brits who drank and danced in Sybil's booth and, as Brits will do when gathered together, earnestly laugh down and up at their host – the great New York City. This list of Brits did not include the Stones who, after a half-hour at Arthur's, would beat a healthy musical retreat uptown to the Apollo in Harlem.

Far from Harlem, Rex Harrison looked embalmed and embarrassed. He had the expression of a man who wished he'd never crossed the Strand and left the safety of his quarters in the Savoy. Rachel Roberts – wife number four in a tally of six – was *Maggie May*'s not-so-lady-like leading lady, a boisterous boozy diva who had been carrying on so much backstage over the past few weeks' rehearsal that leading man Kenneth Haigh looked at her with a murderous glint in his eye. Rachel had turned her actress insecurity into a twister of a Welsh tornado and had the production, cast and crew by the balls, which she squeezed and twisted. She so darkened any light left in the show that there was good reason to wonder whether it would go on. Lionel and Alma – dressed in matching winter furs of Russian Jewish pop nobility – went from mate to mate sparking the opening-night crowd to quell the night's doomy vulnerability.

Judy Garland was swaying in the wheeze with her latest gay betrothal on one arm and the ghost of prescriptions past on the other. Kenny Lynch, with manager Jean Lincoln on a rare night out, wondered why so many whores would spend good money to see another one gone bad. Smiling in the same stalls was one of Lionel's former Artful Dodgers from better *Oliver!* days, child star Gregory Phillips, whom I'd record in a few months. Gregory, managed by Roy Moseley, had played Dirk Bogarde and Judy Garland's child in *I Could Go On Singing*. Judy looked upstage and saw Gregory, remembered the klieg lights and the call to action, and waved a brave but wan hello. It was an evening not unlike the Brady Bunch meets *The Wicker Man* in which we were *The Mod Squad*.

Gregory Phillips had studied at the Italia Conti Acting School with pre-Faces Steve Marriott. They were both renowned brothers of the big song and schlong as they played in the same band at the Italia Conti and raved their way through 'Peggy Sue' and 'Cut Across Shorty'. They maybebabied their way into any young things that would let them with the occasional wink of hope at the odd old gay thing who wished they could. The world was getting taller and smaller as it came together in the final push towards the downsizing of whatever 60s you call your own. Steve, Greg and I would find a lot of time together to laugh at the prismed world through rolling papers.

My life, to all intents and purposes, probably began with the opening guitar figure of 'That'll Be The Day'. There may have been songs in the big band or nightclub crooner days that took a similar stance towards the *femme fatale*, but I hadn't heard them. For my school pals and me, Buddy Holly's 'So if we ever part, then I'll leave you, de-dum-de-dum' spoke of an alternative. We lived in a screenplay in which it looked like all our mates were slowly going down to a quicksand of pussy, but those lyrics gave me hope. It was that dividing time in youth when you get to see which of your friends are still standing after that first close encounter with the other. Friendship was taking on a different weight. My professional time with both Greg and Steve – short with Greg, long with Steve – had added value because this thing between us precluded any professional lie. We didn't have to translate, edit or exchange any thought between us – all was understood. At the age when I'd been discovering Buddy, these two scamps were already out in the trenches of 'yerz paid yer money, now yerz gets your laugh'. That was additional glue.

**Roy Moseley**, writer/manager: Brian Epstein was working in a store called Ashcroft & Dorr on Charing Cross Road, which was the first paperback book shop. In the basement was this boy called John Kitching, who was a friend of mine. John looked after the record department and Brian was his assistant. At that time you had listening booths – like telephone boxes where you put on headphones. Brian spent most of his time listening to classical music. This was after he'd left RADA and before he moved back to Liverpool, went to work in his father's business and took the path that led him to the Beatles. At that time 'Mr Wonderful' by Sammy Davis Jr was out on Brunswick. John and I played it all the time. Brian had no interest in popular music. He did appreciate Judy Garland, but then we all did.

Later I was a song plugger. I was a dresser, too – I did a bit of everything. That's when I first worked for Vivien Leigh. Then I went to work for the Bernard Delfont Agency. I went for my interview with Keith Devon, and Bernard Delfont walked into the room. Keith Devon said, 'Tell him who you know.' I said, 'Laurence Olivier.' Delfont sniffed and left the room and that's how I got the job. The Delfonts wanted young blood; they knew what was going on. My job was to seduce young talent. They sent me to America for three weeks, to MGM Records and Liberty Records. I had to get Dory Previn and Jackie DeShannon, that awful bitch who was with Eddie Cochran, and that other one, Sharon Sheeley. Dreadful woman. I knew Elvis; he was absolutely wonderful. I used to go to his house and watch television. I met Fabian; I'm still very close with him. Then I came back to England and worked in the front office and then things started to happen for me when I got Jet Harris because I'd known Cliff Richard.

Jet was touring with Sam Cooke and Little Richard. He had that boy with him, Billy Preston. Jet called me over some problem the show was having at the Liverpool Empire. I called Brian Epstein – not because I wanted his help, but because I wanted to sign the Beatles to the Delfont Agency. Jean Lincoln – she worked for Michael Sullivan who booked Shirley Bassey and Shani Wallis – was handling Kenny Lynch. She was a very pretty dark-haired girl with the most wonderful light sky blue eyes. Andrew was in love with her – he and Mick used to spend a lot of time with her. She was soft, gentle and bawdy. She and I became professional lovers immediately. I wasn't fond of the opposite sex, but I fell in love with Jean on the spot. Jean was very important. Anyway, she and I were the young ones at the agency and she'd shown me this photo of the Beatles. I didn't know if they were any good, but they looked pretty in the photograph. Of course I knew Brian Epstein, and he said, fine, he'd take a meeting at the Delfonts. The next time he was in London – I think Andrew was doing their publicity by this time – Brian came up to the office at no. 1 Jermyn Street. He left John Lennon in the café downstairs next to the tube station. Brian told Keith Devon how much he thought the Beatles were worth a week and asked Keith Devon if he agreed. Devon just said, 'If you think the Beatles are worth £600, you're mad!' Brian was an educated man; he went quite pink in the cheeks when he got annoyed. He got up and left, but he was polite enough to keep his lunch date with me. So John Lennon, Brian and I went to lunch and that's how the Delfont Agency *didn't* get the Beatles.

The Grades and the Delfont Agency really were the schvelvet mafiosa. They controlled everything: Lew Grade ran the commercial TV stations, Leslie Grade ran the theatre chains and Bernie Delfont ran the agency that booked the artists on to the telly and the stage. All of the American acts wanted to appear on the TV show *Sunday Night at the London Palladium*. The whole nation watched it. Some act would want to do the show, and we'd say, 'Okay, phone Leslie Grade, he'll handle the booking.' The act would say, 'But I'm with MCA.' We'd say, 'I said if you want to do the show, phone Leslie Grade.' And the act would end up with two agents. We put all our acts with the BBC – you never saw one of our acts receive a gold disc on anything but *The Billy Cotton Band Show*. It was such a monopoly. I mean, Billy's son was the BBC head of Light Entertainment; he used to book his own dad! So we'd put all our acts with the BBC – Morecambe & Wise, everybody. We'd let the BBC make them big for us, then we'd take them away and put them on our own ATV.

There was a whole buzz of people like me and Andrew, people who had choices they didn't even know they had. Andrew walked in one day while I was managing Jet Harris. He was doing publicity at this time; this was before the Stones. He didn't ask me if he could actually represent Jet; he just wanted to be able to *say* he did! I thought this was amazing. I said yes. Andrew was very grateful. Later I gave him the job for real and suddenly he had two clients at the Delfont Agency, Jet Harris and Kenny Lynch. I think maybe I took advantage of him. I'd send him on the road ahead of me. You see, I only went out on tour to collect the money. I'd get sent out every Friday to collect the week's take, so I'd send Andrew up mid-week, just to schmooze the act. He had such perspicacity for one so young. He had these marvellous brown eyes on this long face and he looked so good in a suit.

I think it was John Lennon who told Andrew to go and look at this group in Richmond, which turned out to be the Rolling Stones. Andrew asked me if I wanted to go – it was on a Sunday night. I couldn't; I had to be in Blackpool. Andrew idolised Jimmy Woolf, who was famous as the manager of Laurence Harvey and Terence Stamp – that's what he wanted to be. So Andrew saw the Stones and the rest was history. He went to Dick Rowe at Decca. Dick was supposed to be the man who had turned down the Beatles, when in fact it was Tony Meehan. Anyway, Andrew was right on the money, with just pure instinct. He was bright, just like a CinemaScope screen; he took it all in. What he didn't know was that Sir Edward Lewis, after the Beatles fiasco, had turned around to Dick Rowe and said, 'If you don't get me a decent group in four weeks, you're out of here.' Dick Rowe told me once, 'You know, Roy, I'm a happily married man, I've got about ten children, but I'd love to fuck Mick Jagger.'

When Loog first crashed into my office at the Delfont 'Org' it was a great shock because I found him immediately attractive. But, damn it, Delfont's father-in-law was in the same room, so I could not, did not, and never even had the opportunity to have Loooooooooog – or should I say, try to have. And that, of course, is the first lucky impression that I believe Loog gave to all men. Andrew was tall, as I remember, skinny, and his hair was the colour of my beloved golden retriever, Ralph. In fact, he looked rather like a retriever in a very smart 60s suit which I do not believe Loooog had purchased from the awful Carnaby Street. But Brian Epstein, Loog and myself (in the skirt-length leather coat that John Lennon gave me) always looked good. The others all looked horrible. God, what a rotten, uneducated lot they were. The millions certainly were not made from looks, personality or talent – just strumming 'gee-tars!'

Loog really was very attractive. He knew it and he used it. But at the same time, he should be credited with creating a new wave of man. He was the original androgynous innovator, and it's lasted to this very day – except that the male today is more careless about his make-up and the clothes are gone completely.

Sadly, sooner than I would have liked, Looooog flew high. So high, in fact, that although we lived in the same apartment house, he only *showed* me his Phantom V but never invited me to partake of its pleasures.

What Loog wanted from me that day was to allow him to take credit for publicity for the pop artists I had brought to the 'Org'. It was amusing that he was asking this great favour of this slightly older office boy. But after he'd fluttered those long and luscious eyelashes just the right number of times, I was putty in his hands. For all I cared, he could have represented Sir Norman Wisdom and Dame Shirley. In fact, I would have given him the whole office, including Bernie – and for a roll in the hay I would have thrown in the Grades.

**ALO**: In early 1963 I'd decided that a couple of Delfont acts would be good for my PR business. They worked regular, therefore they might be able to pay me regular. I met the young office Turks – Jean Lincoln and Roy Moseley – the upstarts hired to deal with the young talent and keep them out in the reception. Jean was one of the loves of my life who took me in and showed me what's what. Roy was a decanter full of the intoxicating fumes of show business. He gravitated towards star turns and made that energy the source of his life. I was smitten with his enthusiasm for the game – he didn't close up shop and get away from the madness for a real life in some suburban trough. He lived it, dreamt it and worked it – in my book he had it made. Roy was practical and romantic, a great combination.

**Roy Moseley**: The next thing I know, he's asking me for money to rent this office from Eric Easton. I was used to Eric Easton coming into the office because he used to book the Clacton Pier that we owned. As regards ending up with the Rolling Stones, I mean, talk about luck. I was surprised that Eric Easton had an office on Regent Street, let alone room to spare. I went round there with Andrew and paid his first four weeks' rent for him. Sixteen quid it was, and he still owes me. Eric Easton had not yet been hit by the tornado. He was a very third-rate, straight little businessman. He always wore one of those suits, grey and white weave, sort of wool and mohair. He was a grey man, grey altogether. He wasn't a bad looking man, dark hair, balding in front, everything very neat, except no personality. When Andrew walked in on Eric Easton that day God walked in, too. I wondered how Eric was going to cope with Andrew and, of course, he didn't.

I was very close to Brian Jones at the very beginning while he was still living at home. Later when I lived in 152 Ivor Court where Andrew had his offices, Brian and I kept knowing each other quiet. I was somebody he could come and talk to.

Andrew can honestly claim something which Epstein and others could not: he was the ultimate poncie, live-wire, high-profile manager, and I believe that the Rolling Stones were initially built on their manager's personality.

I saw them on a *Thank Your Lucky Stars* TV recording. I was there with Gregory Phillips. I remember asking the nurse at the studio to clean the Stones up because they were so filthy and I didn't want my young boy mixing with them. Mick came up to me and said, 'What do you expect, Roy, we've been living in the back of a van the past ten days.' And I said, 'Yes and it looks like it, go and have a shower.' I seem to remember one of them had lice in his hair.

Years later, after it was all over with Andrew, Mick cornered me in a book shop in Charing Cross Road and we talked between the shelves of the biography section. He begged me to find him a movie. This was around 1970. He said he had to do something apart from the Stones. 'I want to be a movie star, please Roy, find me a movie.' He was very unhappy after Andrew left; I don't care what anybody says. I thought Mick was a lovely guy when I knew him, but most unfortunate with Marianne Faithfull. She was always lying there half-naked or showing something, but that's not against her, so was Bette Davis. These women just held all the boys to ransom with their bodies. The girls must take the blame, after all. They were enticing and a man's only as strong as the end of his dick.

Nureyev told me Mick and Andrew were lovers; he told me that because

Nureyev and I were lovers. I was friendly with him to the end. Anyway, Nureyev used to hang out with Mick and Peter O'Toole and sundry others. Nureyev once asked me about Andrew. I said I had no idea.

**Gregory Phillips**, actor/singer: When I first met Andrew Loog Oldham I was fifteen years old. Steve Marriott was my best friend and we were always strumming guitars and singing stuff. At fourteen, I'd got a leading role in *I Could Go On Singing* with Dirk Bogarde and Judy Garland and my life had changed forever. Incidentally, Kit Lambert, later co-manager of the Who, was an assistant director on that film. Steve got the part of the Artful Dodger in the first production of Lionel Bart's *Oliver!* But more of them later.

I became very friendly with Judy and more or less lived in her house. Her daughter Liza Minnelli introduced me to sex, not to mention vodka and fags. Judy was already a huge star, which meant that my career started on the highest possible note for the time. The film was a hit and, because of that and Judy's protection, my career could go any way and anywhere I wanted. What I wanted was to make music and sing rock 'n' roll. I moved agencies and wound up with the Bernard Delfont Agency and a three-record deal with Pye Records. I had a staff producer, Ray Horrocks from Pye, who was basically a novelty/comedy record specialist. He had several hits with Anthony Newley. Delfont secured for me a personal manager, Roy Moseley. Roy was one of the few people I dealt with in the music business who didn't try to take advantage of me or rip me off. Roy believed in my talent.

Roy also believed that I was a clean-cut, clean-living pretty young man/boy in suits with clean fingernails, clean hair, clean everything, *à la* Pat Boone and Ricky Nelson. That was how he wanted to promote me. There would be no smoking, swearing and above all no sex with girls. My rivals were to be acts like Tommy Quickly and Herman's Hermits. Although there was nothing sexual in our relationship, Roy was gay. His best mate was Barry Burnett. Barry's dad was Al Burnett, owner of the Stork Club, a well-known, slightly naughty nightclub patronised by movie stars, visiting musicians and gangsters like the Krays. So Roy thought he was connected and tough. I don't think he had any idea that I was even better connected.

Through Judy Garland and Liza and our friend Katie Manning, I was hanging out with anyone and everyone who came into town – people like Sammy Davis Jr and Shirley Bassey. I had some good nights out with Sammy Davis. In my professional persona, I was supposed to be a fresh-faced innocent. I went along with it, of course, because I wanted to get into the music business and make records. But I was not innocent at all. I had become an experienced and precocious child-star. I was used to wearing handmade mohair three-piece suits with covered buttons, carrying a gold Dunhill lighter in my pocket, hanging out with the big names, Judy's friends. They viewed me as some kind of good-time Arthur Rimbaud – a wild child. Best of all, I had a career. In fact I led a double life under Roy Moseley's management.

I cut three singles with Pye Records. I had the best available backing musicians and songwriters, because Delfont was a top agent. 'Angie', written by Tom Springfield, was a brilliant song. I sang and double-tracked it in about an hour. 'Everybody Knows' was written by the great Mitch Murray. 'Don't Bother Me' was the first George Harrison song to be released. I co-wrote the B-sides of 'Everybody Knows' and 'Don't Bother Me' with Peter Bellote, later a producer of massive hits with Donna Summer. I appeared on all the then-current TV music shows like *Thank Your Lucky Stars* and *Ready Steady Go!* in my sharp suits. One of the Delfont acts at the time was the singer John Leyton. I was on a bill with him when his sister Sarah turned up. Liza knew her. I was very green at that stage but I was intrigued by Sarah's talk of 'blowjobs' and 'groupies'. She had been living with P.J. Proby for a while, who was said to be sex-crazed and having a high old time. Later, Sarah revealed to me what she had learnt with Proby. All that was very different from how Roy Moseley wanted his stars to behave. Somewhere around the time of 'Angie', through an acting job I was doing I met up with a gay singer called Nicky Scott, who would later be managed by Simon Napier-Bell and produced by Mick Jagger. Nicky took me down to Brighton and introduced me to the circle of theatricals, mostly gay, who lived down there. Terence Rattigan, Robin Maugham and Lionel Bart were the luminaries of this compound. The gorgeous Sarah Miles was also a fixture, as I remember. The first time I ever smoked dope was in Nicky Scott's flat. I crashed out cold on a sofa and there was a candle burning above me, spilling wax. My hair was full of it when I woke up. I just thought it was very funny and took to the weed like a duck to water.

So here I was, leading my double life and wearing my handmade suits. One day I had lunch with Tony Meehan and Jet Harris, who had both worked on my records. Jet had been sacked by the Cliff Richard people for being too wild, and Tony Meehan was brilliant *and* wild. They were going back after lunch to Delfont's office and I went with them. After a while this pink spotty-faced person, who looked my age, came in. He caught my attention straight away. He wore dark glasses, a white silk shirt with fancy cuffs, tight pin-striped trousers with cross pockets which he kept his thumbs in, a light grey herringbone jacket, a gold chain bracelet and an expensive watch. This was Andrew. He appeared to be very shy. But the way he spoke, the way he talked about the business – tough, streetwise and funny – was the opposite of shy. He looked like a sort of camp merchant banker with his Beatles haircut. I think he was working for Brian Epstein at the time. I could see that he had some sort of extra rapport with Meehan and Harris. When Moseley left the room for a minute they sent him up, hilariously – 'What's *she* got on today', that kind of thing. He left after about five minutes. I was impressed. I thought I was well dressed, but actually he made me realise instantly that I was just dressed as a rich version of my dad. He had style, and it was all of his own making and all of our generation. I asked Roy Moseley and Delfont who he was. They said, 'Oh, he does some of our publicity and is always trying to flog us this bunch of dirty drug fiends. He's great, but the band is awful. He's called Andrew Oldham. His band is called the Rolling Stones.' They didn't get the point at all.

Roy Moseley was a diamond – a good man and a prime mover. He was the catalyst for a lot of open doors, got me to Pye Records and Andrew. He was connected and he was powerful management. He had Jet and Tony Meehan; they were no. 1. The last time I saw Roy was at Hermione Gingold's. I was with Moony, Keith Moon. We stuck a popper up each of his ample nostrils and split.

From the very beginning, the first contact, I sensed that Andrew was interested in me. It was something to do with the fact that I already had a career – as he did. I was certainly knocked out by him.

**ALO**: Decca would release the first two Andrew Loog Oldham Orchestra albums within a month of each other. The first, *16 Hip Hits*, was released on their budget label Ace of Clubs with sleeve notes by Kim 'Nut Rocker' Fowley. I had submitted a cover photo of myself taken by Crispian Woodgate in which I had a huge pussy zit on my chin. I informed the Decca art department that I wanted the buying public to be able to squeeze the zit and get the puss out. Decca was not impressed with this suggestion.

Kim Fowley introduced me to another young American, Bobby Jameson, and within days Keith Richards and I were recording him at Decca's West Hampstead studios. Keith and I composed a low-life sleeze 'n' dumpster sort of homage to George 'Shadow' Morton's Shangri-Las recordings crossed with Bob Crewe's 'Rag Doll' titled 'All I Want Is My Baby'. I was fascinated with the structure of 'Rag Doll' and Keith was tolerant of my love of the Shangri-Las. Armed with the track of the Mick and Keith ballad 'Each And Every

Day Of The Year' for the B-side, we stalked Mr Jameson into the studio. Keith handled the A-side arrangements and Jimmy Page played lead guitar. Jameson had arrived in the UK as part of the P.J. Proby flock. He wore one black glove and was Walker Brother pretty head to foot – he could have been a Walker Brother. All of that and being American was enough of a calling card in those days to get you recorded.

**George Gallacher**: Tony Calder was the one the Poets dealt with day to day. We viewed him as a crook, a wide boy, a trickster. He was supposed to take care of the business side while Andrew took care of the art. From where I sat, what Tony did for Andrew was help him spend his money. On the other hand, Tony was also the bastard that doled out that pittance of £8 a week subsistence which barely kept us alive. There was no planned itinerary for gigs. Fuck knows who his geography teacher was, but he must have had ocular leprosy or some fucking sight pathology of some sort – or maybe Tony just took a pin and stuck it in the map. We had to call the office each day to find out where we were playing that fucking night. Now it all seems ridiculous, but back then Tony would take anything and everything that came his way from these wanky fly-by-night agents and promoters who made small fortunes on the back of 60s bands. We would play Aberdeen one night, then phone the office to be told we were in Bath the next night, then phone the next day to be told of a gig in Perth. It was fucking murder and all accomplished in a 15 cwt van loaded with six group members, all the gear and the myriad human flotsam we picked up on our way. We got all those groupies who fucked in transit along with tramps and others of society's losers. This berserk journey continued daily for about eight months after the first single hit the charts. It was only sustainable for me with the aid of those wonderful pharmaceuticals; so fucked was I at the end that I turned up at my mother's house to be told by her that I wasn't home.

The Poets were doing *Ready Steady Go!* We were pretty nervous about it and were looking for some reassurance from fellow Scot Jack Bruce, who was playing with Graham Bond and Ginger Baker in the Graham Bond Organisation. Anyway, courteous as always, we attempted to introduce ourselves only to be met with aloofness and a dismissive 'Oh no, not another pop band!' from the great leader, who then went on to berate us, the Beatles, the Stones, the Who and the whole panoply of pop. He lectured us on 'the novelty value of pop and its superficiality' as opposed to 'the intrinsic poetry and spirituality of jazz, blues, rock, fusion' which he claimed to have originated (and, talented innovator that he was, he probably did). The hectoring continued until the tirade eventually drove us back to our dressing room thoroughly dejected. As we sat there demoralised and pondering our obvious inadequacies, desperate to get the hell out of the place, there came a knock on the door. I opened it to be confronted by an electric-blue mohair suit occupied by a six-foot-three black god. 'Hi guys, I'm Marvin. Just thought I'd look in to wish you well' – he shook our hands – 'Maybe won't see you after the show, but some other time, huh? Hope your disc goes all the way!' Marvin Gaye . . . *Jesus!*

**ALO**: John Paul Jones was still going under his real name, John Baldwin. I gave him his new name for the solo recording of 'Baja' we'd made and sold to Pye. I got the name from a 1959 poster I recalled from Swiss Cottage for a Warner Brothers flick that died starring Robert Stack, *John Paul Jones*. I had no idea he was a real live controversial American hero; I just knew that John looked the part and could do the charts, and that I didn't want my arranger to be named after a piano.

**John Paul Jones**, arranger, bass player/Led Zeppelin: I had started to arrange for Andrew more or less full time. Andrew established me as an arranger, which is what I wanted to do rather than just be a session musician. I remember Kim Fowley from the *16 Hip Hits* sessions at Regent Sound. It was just after the big fight with the Mods and Rockers in Brighton, and we came up with a thing called 'The Rise Of The Brighton Surf' to the tune of 'The House Of The Rising Sun'. Mick Jagger came in to do the vocals on 'Da Doo Ron Ron'. We were pretty drunk by that time. Andrew was running around doing vocals on 'I Wanna Be Your Man' – I think Mick had bet him he didn't dare do it. Reg King was there – a really nice bloke. I used to like Reg the Butcher; I used to get along with him. As neither Andrew nor I had passed our driving tests, Reg used to pick me up in the Chevy. Andrew had acquired a gun from somewhere and I'd get in the Chevy and Reg would laugh when I found it under the seat.

I'd got into session work playing for Jet Harris and Tony Meehan. I wanted to make a solo record; I wanted to be the new Jet Harris. Somehow I met up with Andrew and we made a single at Regent Sound called 'Baja', a Jack Nitzsche surf-type sound. I'd already played bass on some of Andrew's sessions. I did some Marianne Faithfull recordings and then I played and arranged some of an album we did of Lionel Bart's *Maggie May* show at IBC studio. I also auditioned Nico for Andrew. Andrew had some sort of thing going with Dick Rowe at Decca that was beyond the Rolling

Stones – Andrew recorded night and day. Work was all party and the party was all work. Jimmy Page and I did the Gregory Phillips record at Regent Sound.

Roy Moseley, Jet Harris and Tony Meehan, London, 1962

**Roy Moseley:** The first group Jet Harris had was the Jet Blacks. We advertised for musicians, but that put me in a quandary. I couldn't bring them up to the office, so I hired a room in a pub close to Warren Street tube station, behind that wonderful furniture store, Heal's. I picked 'em all. There was Glen Hughes; he died in a fire. Then there was John McLaughlin; he went on to play with Miles Davis. On bass I hired John Baldwin. I gave him his name, John Paul Jones. I know Andrew says he did and John probably says his mum came up with it, but it was me. I'd entered into a long relationship with the actress Bette Davis; we weren't married but we lived together for a long time. I'd met her when she started to work in England. In 1959 she'd done a cameo in *John Paul Jones*. I was not up on American history, but I had such a crush on Bette. I saw the film and I thought it was a nice name, so I gave it to John.

I'd met Cliff Richard when I worked at the Hackney Empire. I'd worked for Jack Good and Rita Gillespee when they were producing *Oh, Boy!* That's how I knew Jet Harris. The first two things Jet did in 1962 were 'Some People' and 'Main Title Theme From *The Man with the Golden Arm*'. Jet was a sweetheart. It was his idea to get Tony Meehan as arranger and producer. Tony was one of the most obnoxious people I'd ever met. Then came 'Diamonds', written by Jerry Lordan; it went to no. 1 in February 63. That was followed in June by 'Scarlett O'Hara' which also went no. 1, depending upon which chart you were following. That was named for Vivien Leigh. I asked Jerry to do it, very proudly and foolishly. I was very young and she and Sir Larry had been an enormous influence on me. She hated it. I gave her the 45 and she threw it in the trash can. It's awful how Andrew, Jet, Hank B. Marvin and Jerry Lordan all ended up with that terrible doctor who gave Andrew all that shock treatment. Luke McLoughlin, that was his name. Awful man, said he could cure Jet of drinking, just had him on hundreds of pills. The widow of comedian Tony Hancock took him to court when Tony committed suicide in Sydney. Andrew was very lucky to have come out of that alive, let alone with any brain. Anyway, the beginning of 1963 was when it all started to change. It was an amazing time to be in the business. You had the old guard fighting it out with the new for the top chart placings. The Beatles were no. 1, Jet and Tony were no. 2. The rest of the Top 10 was Andy Williams, Gerry & the Pacemakers, Roy Orbison, Cliff Richard, Frank Ifield, Billy J. Kramer & the Dakotas and Del Shannon. It was a wonderful time for pop music. We were the ones, people like me, Jean Lincoln, Brian Epstein and Andrew, who helped turn it all around and make it British.

## · CHAPTER 6 ·

**Sid Maurer**, artist/entrepreneur: I worked for both Columbia and Decca in New York City during the 40s, starting at age seventeen as an assistant art director and working my way up. I was living on Riverside Drive in one room and I started my own studio right there. I got work from RCA, then MGM, and then it went along until I had a big studio. That was MPI Graphics. Little by little, I got known as the guy in New York who did album covers.

In about 1958, the record business began to explode. Before that, if you wanted to buy an album, you had to have a cart to take it home, because it was all shellac. You would take maybe five or six shellac records in thick sleeves and they weighed about six pounds. Then in the mid-50s vinyl began to take over and everybody – from the Four Aces to Buddy Holly and the Hi-Lo's – started making records.

A funny thing happened a year later. I was living on Long Island. A couple of these label guys were living out there and we used to drive out to Long Island together after work. They pulled over one day and told me that now it was going to cost me 10 per cent back to them. I was paying these guys every month in green, a kickback. Of course, what I did was I double billed, so I could cover my kickbacks! Lo and behold, about a year later, there's an investigation that started with Alan Freed, the big payola scandal. I was called to testify in front of the Grand Jury. Really, I was on a small scale next to the big guys upstairs in the music department. I got lucky, though, because the morning I was going to go to court under immunity, the District Attorney had a heart attack and he was out for about seven months. By that time my case was so backlogged that I never heard from them again.

At the time the vinyl LP came along, RCA hadn't yet geared up their own art department. They hired two freelance artists: me and Andy Warhol. When I met Andy, he was doing shoe drawings for advertisements. He and I got to know each other, and then he made a right turn and got to paint. I made a left turn and worked in my studio in New York and got pretty big doing

137

album covers. Then I opened another studio in Los Angeles to handle Capitol, United Artists, etc., so I was going back and forth.

The guys who ran Decca, Jubilee, Roulette all of these labels that started in the mid-to-late 40s and on through the 50s, all of these guys came out of the garment district. They weren't record men – they were schmata guys! They didn't know a fuckin' thing about music; they could care less. What they did do was to hire good producers, guys like Bob Thiele.

In about 1968 Epic hired me to do all of their LP covers exclusively, and that's where I met Donovan. I eventually became his manager. One of the reasons that Don and I became friends was that I didn't wear a suit. When I first met Don, he looked like Jesus Christ. He was wearing a long white robe that went down to the ground, with bare feet. Which is why they said, 'You've gotta come over right away and meet this guy.' We went back to my suite, smoked a couple of joints and got comfortable. We spent about three days together, just working on his album cover.

Meanwhile, Freddie Frank noticed me and we became pals. Freddie was a promotion man at Epic and he was one of the few guys who knew how to reach the deejays quietly. Freddie and I finally hooked up and went into the record business together with a company called Roadshow. We went into the R 'n' B business, the black business. See, Freddie grew up in South Philadelphia, and he knew all the brothers anyway, and Freddie could take care of the brothers. They wouldn't take money from a white man. Freddie was almost black. He drove a lot of records, Freddie.

**Fred Frank**, promotion man: I came up through the ranks, through the independents during the payola period in Philadelphia, which was the focal point of all the investigations. When I was fifteen and a half I was in the service, and when I came home from Korea I was eighteen, nineteen years old, and I worked for Chips Distributing. Harry Chipitz was one of the founders of independent distribution. I came up via the streets, and he wanted somebody that could communicate with these guys who also came up via the streets. Every week on a certain day, I would deliver envelopes. I never looked in the envelopes, thank God. I would deliver envelopes to all of the key people all over the Philadelphia area. This was during the payola period. I would run to Dick Clark's office, I would go by WIBG, where Tom Donohue, Joe Niagara and Bob Mitchell were. They were the hottest jocks in town – I was just the kid who delivered the 'playlists', ha, ha, ha.

One night they were having a meeting about a record called 'The Twist', and they came out and said, 'Go over to this place and pick up this guy

Checker. You may have to wait for him, because he works in a chicken plucking factory.' I went over there and the stink almost drove me out of my mind. I meet him, and he says, 'Gimme a minute; I gotta go and shower first before we can go.' So, he came out and he looked really good. I brought him to this meeting that was very 'hush-hush' about covering Hank Ballard's record of 'The Twist' with Chubby as the artist. I wasn't there at the meeting, but we know what took place afterwards: Hank didn't get shit, and Chubby got a major record because Dick Clark started playing it. I started taking Chubby all over the place. I was sort of his promotion man, taking him all over the place to record hops, etc., and it began to springboard all over the United States, because Dick Clark was *the man*. And I was Chipitz's man and Chipitz and Dick and some other people were this little combine. This was a couple of years before Parkway Records, but it was the same cast of characters, and this was the first play that they called as a group, this conglomerate that I was a part of. It was just so obvious. Here's Chubby Checker, a chicken plucker one day, and on the national charts three weeks later.

All of a sudden the word got out that investigations were going on and Harry told me one day, 'They wanna talk to you.' So they called me down, swore me in, and said, 'Why were you delivering all this money?' and I said, 'I beg your pardon. What money?' All I did was deliver the playlist to Georgie Woods and so forth. I also delivered the acts to Dick Clark. I delivered Ike & Tina Turner; I delivered everybody. I'm nineteen years old, I'm a kid; what am I supposed to say? I never opened the envelopes. I figured it was none of my business, and I think that's why they used me and I got as far as I did in the music business.

Then I went to work for Epic. This was 1961. I was in the South; they hired me to promote eighteen states. I came back to New York around 1963 and became head of all promotion. This was just before the Dave Clark Five came over, and for that while Dave was the hottest thing after the Beatles.

We had Jeff Beck at the time, and Beck was just about to score, but nobody in the company at the time understood Jeff or the Yardbirds. I was getting airplay, but we were doing campaigns that nobody else was doing because we were still involved in the above-ground acts, and the Yardbirds were just under. We did have a pretty good album with them, and then there was Jeff Beck's 'Truth'. I actually directed the video for that, and I did the Yardbirds video for 'Shapes Of Things' at the Fillmore East. We couldn't use lights. We sat up on the fourth row; we had one take and we did the best thing we could. There was so much marijuana in that place that if you took two

139

breaths you were totally fucked up. Of course, at the beginning of the concert, they announced, 'No smoking anything', but as soon as the lights went out you saw joints as long as a baseball bats. It was incredible. Rod Stewart sitting up there and it's 104 degrees and he's wearing a muffler. The camera guys were saying that they didn't want to shoot him sweating, but I said, 'Screw it, let him rock.' It was fabulous.

**Harvey Kubernik**, writer: I met Andrew in 2000 at Brian Wilson's *Pet Sounds* concert in a box at the Hollywood Bowl.

I'm from the border of Los Angeles and Hollywood. Echo Park. Queen of Angels Hospital, right off Sunset and Alvarado. Jack Nitzsche died there, Dustin Hoffman was born there. After living in downtown LA and the Crenshaw Village area in the mid-50s, I moved as a tyke with my family to Culver City in 1957, on the fringe of the beach community in West LA. I was a mile from the MGM studios, Tito's Tacos, Airport Village, a greasy and delicious collection of fast food stands, the Selznick studios, Desilu studios, and Johnnie's Pastrami, with jukeboxes on the counter. Tarzan Lake was up the block, and TV writer Rod Serling did some filming for his *The Twilight Zone* in the neighbourhood. La Ballona Creek was our back yard. Now you can't swim in it.

I was just starting junior high in the Wilshire District in 1964 when the Rolling Stones first appeared on our shores. At the Wilshire Theater, I saw the closed-circuit showing of the Beatles' début Washington, DC, concert, live with the Beach Boys and Lesley Gore.

Born in LA, a by-product of the multi-racial Los Angeles City Public School System, graduating college at San Diego State University, makes me a bio regional and geographical child of Hollywood. My father Marshall is a stockbroker, had Lou Adler and Elmer Valentine as clients for a while. Johnny Rivers took my parents and myself to the Whisky À Go-Go when it was on La Cienega. My parents grooved behind Johnny's Southern rock 'n' roll, but were big Frank Sinatra fans.

HUAC [House Un-American Activities Committee] and the Hollywood blacklist were subjects they never taught us in any school, and MGM and many of the studios were right in front of our noses. Luckily, this topic was never hidden at our dinner table. The whole family worked to elect John F. Kennedy in 1960. Never once did any teacher I had even in college ever discuss HUAC and the Hollywood blacklist. And I went to schools with kids whose parents were ruined by this senseless witchhunt. As cinematographer Haskell Wexler once said in the *Los Angeles Times* about fellow lensman

James Wong Howe, 'You'll notice that most of the people he worked with were what we used to call progressives. People talk about the blacklist, but there was an atmosphere of suspicion and hostility against people who were socially aware.'

Thank God we've always had mavericks in the cinema and music world. Andrew was someone who gave something back from the corner of Sunset and Ivar. He'd already studied James Wong Howe's camera techniques. Andrew set foot in a Hollywood period when the contract player was still working and the star system was being revamped.

Perhaps only Charlie Watts in the Rolling Stones had the knowledge or a sense of history about Hollywood and Los Angeles gleaned from his own extensive jazz collection. He used a Gretsch drum kit like the one his hero Shelley Manne played. He dug Stan Kenton. Watts was into drummer Louie Bellson and mad for stickmen Chico Hamilton and Billy Higgins. He knew that Charlie 'Bird' Parker lived and gigged around this city years before.

Watts, Bill Wyman, Keith Richards, Brian Jones and especially Mick Jagger were aware of the potent 40s and 50s/early 60s super hot R 'n' B, seminal rock 'n' roll record labels that thrived in Los Angeles.

I hate to be the person who tells the world that Chess Records and Vee Jay weren't the only fantastic record labels that nurtured the Stones. A lot of the labels the Stones were attracted to were based in Los Angeles – Specialty, Capitol, Dootone. Modern, where Elmore James, John Lee Hooker, Howlin' Wolf, Richard Berry and Johnny 'Guitar' Watson did records, was actually in Culver City. B.B. King was on Kent. Aladdin Records was located in Beverly Hills; they put out discs by Amos Milburn, Louis Jordan, Floyd Dixon, Lowell Fulson, Lester Young, Charles Brown, Helen Humes and Maxwell Davis, a mentor to Leiber and Stoller.

LA always had mind-blowing R 'n' B radio stations. In Crenshaw Village and Culver City in the late 50s and early 60s I heard deejays Hunter Hancock and Joe Adams, 'The Mayor of Melody'. I was filing the soul sounds of KDAY and Wolfman Jack's broadcasts out of Del Rio, Texas, on XERB. These were all AM stations. Motown and Stax were blaring. Muddy Waters, Chuck Berry, Bo Diddley, Rufus Thomas doing 'Walking The Dog', the Impressions, Ike & Tina Turner, and Mick's mainman, Jimmy Reed, on all dials. Thee Midniters of 'Whittier Blvd' and Bob and Earl of 'Harlem Shuffle' came out of LA. There were others: the Hollywood Flames, Jesse Belvin, the Flamingos, the Olympics, the Rivingtons, the Larks, Jackie Lee of 'Do The Duck', with Barry White on drums, and the Premiers with 'Farmer John'. Hey folks, Alan Freed in 1960 was on KDAY for a year.

New Orleans jazz legends like Kid Ory or Barney Bigard and R 'n' B/rocker heroes Earl Palmer and Little Richard had moved to LA in the 40s and 50s and influenced the sound of the Stones. The dude who wrote 'Down The Road A Piece', Don Raye, also co-wrote 'Cow Cow Boogie' that pianist/big band leader Freddy Slack did.

The Stones and Andrew Loog Oldham entered Hollywood and Los Angeles at a subject-specific time when the city's complexion was radically changing. Twenty years earlier, the post-World War II Los Angeles and Hollywood area was frantic, loud and hectic. Jump blues and jazz helped define the new hue sound cues of an expanding environment. In the early 60s the old WASP money of downtown LA was being challenged by Jewish money from the Westside, Beverly Hills, Century City, the beach and the valleys.

White flight, which we used to call 'white fright', drove the scared people away from the city into the suburbs. That was a good thing. I was happy.

Then, a lot of the real people couldn't afford to split, so the real rock 'n' roll children stayed in the LA and Hollywood loop and the Stones' music and way of life reflected this culture. I dug knowing the Rolling Stones made their music in my city. I'd ride my skateboard or walk by RCA and smile.

The Rolling Stones visited NYC – they stayed in LA. Making records. And don't tell me Keith Richards was above listening to Ricky Nelson's singles, especially with James Burton supplying the licks. Ricky Nelson went to Hollywood High. Keith inducted Burton and Johnnie Johnson in 2001 into the Rock and Roll Hall of Fame. Burton also played on Dale Hawkins' record of 'Suzie Q' that the Stones took a swing at in 1965.

Can you imagine how different the Andrew Loog Oldham and Rolling Stones Hollywood-birthed records would be if they had been waxed in New York? I shudder at the thought.

Sonny Bono co-wrote 'She Said Yeah' on *December's Children*. Bono had great R 'n' B and bitchin' rock 'n' roll credentials. Sonny had scripted 'She Said Yeah' under a pseudonym, 'S. Christy', with Larry Williams. Christy was the name of his first daughter. Sonny used to be in the meat business and would scribble songs while driving a meat truck to butcher shops. He was from Inglewood High.

Bobby Troup composed 'Route 66', the song that kicked off the Stones' first LP. Troup was married to one of Liberty Records' ladies, Julie London, who charted with 'Cry Me A River', arranged by guitarist Barney Kessel.

Radio station KFWB, a 1964–6 supporter of the Rolling Stones, was actually on Hollywood Boulevard. B. Mitchel Reed was there, spinning some

Byrds, Bob Dylan, Beach Boys, Stones and Who rare B-sides on acetates. BMR wasn't chained to a playlist and was later involved with Tom Donahue in LA's early FM rock radio trip on KMET in the late 60s.

I also went to summer school at University High after the 10th grade. I felt the connective tissue to Jan & Arnie & Dean, Liz Taylor, Sandra Dee, Henry Vestine of Canned Heat, Bruce Johnston, Jack Jones, Dick and Dee Dee, Nancy Sinatra, Randy Newman, James Brolin, Ryan O'Neal, Kim Fowley, Love's Bryan Maclean, my cousin Sheila Kubernik, John Densmore and Robby Krieger of the Doors.

Phil Harris, a big band singer married to actress Alice Faye, had a big record store on Hollywood Boulevard. I never felt like he loved rock and roll, but he loved the blues. I had never seen a Jewish person from the southern states. His nickname in showbiz was 'the mouth from the South'. Harris was very friendly. I thought it was more of a cultural breakthrough when someone at Capitol Records got a Beatles display in the Phil Harris window. He liked to play golf. I used to watch juiceheads with their original wives buy their Jackie Gleason albums from the Phil Harris store.

Walter E. Hurst had his law offices on Hollywood Boulevard. He started the first music law class at UCLA and in 1964 Kim Fowley spoke at the lecture series followed by Sam Cooke, J.W. Alexander behind the wheel as usual. I didn't really know Walter until the late 60s. He was a humanitarian, not really a lawyer. He had fled from Auschwitz as a child.

Walter was Kim Fowley's lawyer for over thirty years. Did legal work for Jack Nitzsche. Bobby Womack kept his pet bulldog in one of the rooms; that freaked Jack out. Earl Palmer; Eden Abez, writer of 'Nature Boy', a hit for Nat 'King' Cole; producer Roger Corman; Eddie Cochran and Jerry Capeheart; Plas Johnson; Ernie Freeman; Rene Hall; J.W. Alexander; songwriter Sharon Sheeley; Iron Eyes Cody were all clients. So were Baker Knight, who wrote 'Lonesome Town'; the Burnett Brothers, Johnny and Dorsey; and Mickey Jones, a drummer with Johnny Rivers who would tour with Bob Dylan in 1966.

Hollywood still had magic in the 60s. That's why the music of the period was on fire. That's why the Stones' albums of the 1964–7 era still smoke.

You could see everyone walking on Hollywood or Sunset Boulevard. I sold daily newspapers to a bunch of actors. It was really easy to go and view a film at the Pix, the Oriental, the Egyptian and the World on Hollywood Boulevard. Hollywood was not the tourist trap it's become the last thirty-five years. On any given night or day, I could catch Nick Adams, Phil Silvers, James Garner (always at Musso and Frank's), Sterling Hayden, Ralph

Meeker, Dennis O'Keefe. Sal Mineo would be walking on the street. Gloria Grahame, who went to LA High, was on the pavement. Dennis Hopper and Jack Nicholson were everywhere.

I was on the soundstage for the Monkees' *Head*. I went to see *Shindig* being done at the ABC studios on Prospect Avenue off Sunset. The Four Tops were awesome. Their clothes were awesome, too. Green iridescent suits and alligator shoes with silky shirts. Their singer Levi Stubbs wore his hair in a cool process.

I had seen the Beatles on NBC's *Jack Parr*, before Ed Sullivan took a bow with the lads. In 1964 *The Red Skelton Show* on CBS showed a clip of the Stones lip-synching 'Down the Road A Piece' and 'Little Red Rooster'. 'Mom! The Rolling Stones are doing Sam Cooke's song!' Brian Jones was very impressive on the tube. Maybe the first time I had seen anyone play slide guitar.

The 1964–7 new LA music and dance shows were fabulous. I didn't have to watch a bunch of kids from Philadelphia wiggle on *American Bandstand*.

When I met Andrew at the Brian Wilson concert in 2000 he was with Lou Adler.

**Lou Adler**: In the beginning of 1959 I was partners with Herb Alpert, and the first production deal we made was for Jan & Dean at Lou Bedel's Dore Records. We just went to Hollywood and Vine, walked into Dore and peddled the master. When we started with Jan & Dean at Dore, they were still attending University High School with Nancy Sinatra, Kim Fowley and Ryan O'Neal. They were both seventeen, and 'Baby Talk' was the first hit Herb and I produced with them. We made that record in Jan's garage.

**Herb Alpert**: I found the song from Lee Silvers. He played me a bunch of demos and I picked that one out of the stack. After we had the track, which was on a 7½ quarter inch tape, we got some musicians together for the overdubs. They had a helluva time trying to follow the thing; the timing was all over the place, even with a metronome. The intonation was horrendous. The musicians were just scrambling, trying to make sense of it all. There's one spot on 'Baby Talk' that I have to cough over if I'm ever listening to it on the radio and somebody's listening with me, because the record just comes unhinged. But it had a 'sound'. To me, that's one of the most important ingredients. We never recorded in Gary Paxton's garage, although some hit records like 'Monster Mash' and 'Alley Oop' came out of there.

Lou and I had started with Sam Cooke right after 'You Send Me' in 1957, and 'I Love You (For Sentimental Reasons)'. We didn't work on that but we watched the session. We graded the song on one of our critiques for Bumps Blackwell. There was a contest about how many times Sam said 'I Love You'. It was fifty-seven or fifty-eight times. I think Jan Berry won. The engineers were great with razor blades. There was an edit every two inches with the Jan & Dean stuff.

Herb Alpert, Bumps Blackwell, Sam Cooke and Lou Adler,
Hollywood, 1957

**Lou Adler:** There were independents in LA like Challenge, Liberty and Dot, and then there were those early little companies like Aladdin who had a lot of the black doo-wop groups and hits like 'Earth Angel' by the Penguins. All these labels had street corner groups who moved around and recorded under different names. Jesse Belvin must have been the lead singer for five different groups, each with their own hit. There were six or seven of these companies, and they made a lot of money and paid the artists off with cars and clothes instead of accounting for royalties. This was how it all worked until Randy Wood of Dot came along and started handing out gold records to Pat Boone. Everybody looked up and said, 'Wait a minute, are they really making that much money?' Pretty soon everybody, including the majors, jumped in. West Coast rock 'n' roll!!!

Most of the rock 'n' roll action came from independent producers. People like Herb and I did not have access to the majors like RCA, Columbia or Capitol; we just didn't know how to get in. So we looked through the phone book and found a name that had 'Records' behind it. That's how we started working with Keen Records and Sam Cooke.

**Herb Alpert**: Towards the beginning of the 60s, people started getting into the colours and feeling that are in a room. If it makes you feel good, it's going to enhance the quality of whatever you're sending out. That was an ingredient that I never saw in London, especially the times I went over there with the Tijuana Brass. The recording in LA was much, much different. First there was Hal Blaine's Wrecking Crew, the guys that played on all the big dates. We couldn't afford them when we started out. Those guys were mercenaries, a travelling squad of the very best. Then there were the engineers; they were very tuned in. Bones Howe was one – he was at Radio Recorders for a while, and then he moved to Western Recorders, which is where I worked with him.

**Lou Adler**: The first time we ran into Bones at Radio Recorders, he would have nothing to do with rock 'n' roll; he was very down on that kind of music. I produced three Everly Brothers songs at Radio Recorders. It was at a crazy time when Don and Phil were really not getting along. I remember on one song, when we got to the bridge – which Don was supposed to sing – we didn't hear him and were wondering why. Phil had knocked Don out.

In LA, there were a lot of record hops at roller rinks, halls etc. They were run by the local deejays. Three or four artists would come by and lip-synch their records for maybe a hundred and fifty kids, sometimes less – most times less. You just had to keep trying to build up a local following. Then you had to try and get to Philadelphia to try and catch the eye or ear of Dick Clark, because if you could get on *American Bandstand* your record would break nationally. Dick Clark nationalised the music; he helped the regional hits break out.

The first identifiable LA sound was the surf sound; it was the first nationally recognised sound that came out of the West Coast in 1962–3. The look was also very West Coast. When I took Jan & Dean to Philadelphia, everybody there was Italian and five foot seven, and my guys were six foot one, tanned and definitely West Coast.

By the time I met Andrew, I had been in the record business since 1957. I don't know if I found him or he found me. We never did any business; we just exchanged roles and duties. Andrew was innovative and he was also a student. He studied everything, all the deals going on around him, and took what he learnt back to the UK. He had incredibly good instincts. The bond between Andrew and me was established very quickly. Our ways of thinking were very close and you never know what causes that because we did have very different upbringings.

ALO and Lou Adler, New York, 1965

**ALO**: I'd met Lou in the autumn of 64 – theta had it be and still does. We'd said hello at the recording of *The T.A.M.I. Show*, where his act, Jan & Dean, were hosting and mine were following James Brown. Gospel and gossip has it that Mick Jagger nearly threw up at the prospect of following James Brown on to the stage at *The T.A.M.I. Show*. This is nonsense. Mick just applied himself that night, pulled out all the stops he knew (and some he didn't) and worked harder than the hardest working man in show business. By doing so Mick started the first real Stones American roll.

**Toni Basil**, dancer, choreographer, singer, actress: I met the Rolling Stones through Jack Nitzsche, after Jack cast them in *The T.A.M.I. Show*. Jack was the music director and put the band together. I was doing choreography for *Shindig* around that time. *The T.A.M.I. Show* was a two-day event held at the Santa Monica Civic Auditorium. It was filmed for general release to theatres. I remember watching the monitor in the Green Room and seeing James Brown do a run of his performance for the audience. I ran to the bathroom and tried to do his steps while looking in the mirror, trying to figure out his moves, his cadences.

Then I recall seeing Brian Jones, who was very elusive, and Mick, Keith and the other Stones hovering around, close to the TV monitor. They were freaking out over James Brown, digging him so much that they actually backed away from the TV screen. Then I saw the look on their faces as the realisation kicked in that they would have to follow him on stage. And just so, this change came over them.

James Brown had this huge orchestra with back-up singers, and James was the greatest dancer I had ever seen in my life. I'd never heard any squeals like this, enhancing his repetition, the phrases like the repeats in 'Please, Please, Please' as he fell to his knees and came back up. One of the greatest theatrical televised whatever-you-want-to-call-it screen performances ever. Forget live performance, this was going on screen to movie houses. It was going to go down in history. As a dancer and a choreographer I understood it on another level, and I said to David Winter, the choreographer, 'The Stones gotta follow him . . . Jesus Christ, how is that possible?'

Anyway, Jack Nitzsche told me that Andrew Oldham was so smart that he staged a massive equipment breakdown as well as suggesting some camera angles just to hold things up so time would pass after James Brown's performance. That was the buzz. It was Andrew – he was smart, he was buying time. Well, I'm sorry, I don't care how much time was gonna go by. I just thought these guys were dead in the water. The Santa Monica Civic Auditorium's stage was very wide. Since we were the choreographers, David and I decided to go out and sit on the side of the stage off camera; I wanted to see what the hell was going to happen. I wanted to see the audience's reaction to them. I wanted to see how they were going to get out of this one. Anyway, a lot of time went by, a lot of time. It seemed longer than a half-hour to me. So finally, maybe the tune was 'Around And Around', where there is this big cymbal crash in the opening of the song and Mick had a tambourine in his hand and simultaneously with the crash in the music Mick jumped up in the air, and, as he jumped up in the air, Brian Jones turned his back to the audience, which was the first rebellious piece of theatre I had ever seen in my entire life. I come from vaudeville. My parents were in vaudeville, and on stage you never turned your back to the audience. So Mick was jumping in the air, Brian had his back to the audience and Mick hit the ground in a crouch. And not one person, including me, ever remembered James Brown again.

Mick Jagger, Vancouver, 1965

It was fantastic – Mick's moves. What is this? This kind of paraplegic funky chicken. What is he doing? As a trained dancer and even as a go-go dancer and a street dancer, I had never seen such moves in my life. I mean, what they really were was post-modern and right on the beat. It doesn't matter what you're doing as long as you're grabbing the beat. But Mick was doing physicalities that no one had ever seen before, in the same way James Brown was doing physicalities that no one had ever seen before. Elvis Presley, James Brown and Mick Jagger had some similarities regarding dancing. They moved exactly to the beat. They understood the backbeat. James, of course, understood it from a gospel sense. But Mick – even though his moves were very abstract, they were almost like what white boys do who can't dance – Mick always danced to the beat. Elvis, James and Mick *nailed* the beat.

And Brian had his back to the audience for a lot of the set. He was a rebellious comet and hardly turned around, which made it extremely powerful, gave it a theatrical ambience.

When it was over, the Stones didn't take a bow, which I thought was shocking. I mean, even James Brown came on and took a bow.

**Lou Adler**: At *The T.A.M.I. Show*, the Stones stood out compared with the very choreographed black acts. For one, they were playing their own instruments. In the US from 1961 to 1964, there weren't any bands; we had a vocalist or vocalists and we used a studio rhythm section. So, the sound and also the look of the Stones were unique. I forget now exactly how the Stones looked. But, I remember that you got the feeling that they were tough street kids – I don't know if we were all just imagining it. It was all very different from the West Coast acts like Jan & Dean and the Beach Boys, who were very clean-cut. It was America's first look at scruffy. Dion & the Belmonts were tough guys from the Bronx, and if they didn't like what was going on, they'd leap off the stage and fight with the audience. But they would still be dressed neatly.

**ALO**: 321 South Beverly Drive sat down on the scrubbed 'n shrubbed Warren Beatty side of LA's Wilshire, and floor two housed Dunhill Records, about to get hot with 'Eve Of Destruction'. Dunhill had been formed on the heat of Adler's run of hits with Johnny Rivers, for which it served as the production company. Now it was an independent record company distributed by ABC. Dunhill was eared by Adler, flanked by Andy Wickham (who'd left ALO Image, choosing LA sun over London gloom), and hawked by a cigar-chomping sales suit named Jay Lasker. An agent named Hal Landers and a former tap dancer named Bobby Roberts made up the rest of the company's roster. These latter two went on to give the world the Charles Bronson life-enhancing Michael Winner-directed *Death Wish*.

One early spring day in 65, Lou said please find the time to come on down to Dunhill and be surprised. I did. I was silver bracelet clad and Lou was gold; he smoked Luckys while I Salem'd my lot, though sooner or later we ended up smoking the same leaf. He wore red and I didn't know I could. *Le bon* clobber was still by Sy Devore; deVoss had yet to come on the map. We paid neat homage to Dino, Joe Di Carlo and hi-rolled button-down shirts. Our trousers were either cords, jeans or benchmark *Ocean's Eleven* and we could pass for well-meaning casual doo-wop pimps. When I got to the second-floor Dunhill abode, I greeted Lou and stopped to say hello to Andy Wickham. He knew he'd met the beginning of the new world, as did I. Then Lou popped his head around the door and said 'Andrew, come say hello to the Mamas and the Papas.' We walked down the hall into a room and saw them standing there. John Phillips wore a darker red and wanted to know what you thought before you thought it; Cass gushed that motherlode and wondered how well you knew the Beatles; Denny cleared his majestic throat of debris; and Michelle knew what she had as she kinda invited you in.

That afternoon all the leaves modulated as John sat atop the oak exec desk and acoustic'd the four of them through all the hits. I was privileged to hear a medley of their life thus far, and, as their national anthems rounded the room, I got to hear some of their future, too. Later Michelle would come up with 'Dedicated To The One I Love', Cass would call John's name with 'Words Of Love', and Lou would get them somewhat 'Dancing In The Street'. But for the most part John Boy had already written the ticket stubs, entry to the royal circle of pop given to the golden few who manage to define the moment in the right rhythm, time and attitude of the day.

I heard 'em all that day, 'California Dreamin'', 'Monday, Monday', 'Go Where You Wanna Go', and more. I fell in love with the choral camaraderie, the full-blown bravado leads, the insolent oh-so-coherent trade-offs and with Papa John Phillips, our own 60s Cole Porter/Irving Berlin, whose marvellously structured, sophisticated and witty ditties popped under your skin and into your heart. He would stir and scribe again with 'San Francisco (Be Sure To Wear Some Flowers In Your Hair)', 'Creeque Alley', and my own favourite, 'Twelve Thirty'. But basically, privileged *moi* had heard the lot. Not bad for an afternoon off on a busman's holiday . . .

Thus far, America's pop chart firefight against us Brits had been the Beach Boys and Four Seasons. The Beach Boys had the sound and they had a genius in Brian Wilson, but alas – save Dennis – all looked like their dad, Murry. And despite the Four Seasons' matinee-idol personas in photos by Bruno of Hollywood, the group looked like they would be just as happy breaking your legs as hugging your pillow.

I left very pleased. Lou was Billy Rose, and I'd just heard the Golden Horseshoe. The Mamas and the Papas would unite world-pop traffic from Haight-Ashbury to Park Avenue. My mate had the real thing. And with a heart full of smiles all round, I headed happily north-east back up to Sunset and mine.

ALO, Sheila Klein Oldham, Michelle and John Phillips, Cass Elliott and Lou Adler, Los Angeles, 1966

## CHAPTER 7

**ALO**: The music industry was winding down for Christmas and I was winding up my *A Clockwork Orange* schemes – dreams for transporting the Stones to the silver screen via Anthony Burgess's 1962 book that had so fuelled my life and helped me feel normal. Christmas for me was a down time. Growing up, it had been something other people did and my mother and I only pretended to do. I looked for ways to fan the flames of January rather than stoke the fires at home.

**David Bailey**, photographer: I wanted to make a film of *A Clockwork Orange* with Mick and the Stones. This was before Stanley Kubrick. Nobody really knew who the Stones were in America at the time. I was going to do it with Andy Warhol, but their manager, or whatever of the Stones, Andrew, wanted more money for the group than had been budgeted for the whole film.

**ALO**: I remember finding out in short order that the cinematic rights to *A Clockwork Orange* were not available, but this did not stop me getting press for the Stones on the intention and the idea. United Artists had just released the Beatles' first film *A Hard Day's Night* to hearty press, popular acclaim and even more Mop Top mania, if such a thing were possible. The lead act was pulling even further ahead and I did not want the Stones to be left out in the celluloid cold.

The first mentions of a forthcoming Rolling Stones feature film had appeared in the UK press shortly before the first American tour in June of 64. The film, provisionally titled *Rolling Stones*, was scheduled to go into production upon the group's return to the UK in July. All that remained to be decided was where to shoot it. Peter Sellers and Lionel Bart were to be the co-producers and the script was being co-written by Bart and myself. The executive producer was going to be Peter O'Toole's manager, Jules Buck, hence the quote Keith Richards wafted on the possibility of Mr O'Toole's making a cameo as 'the group's manager'. Penny Valentine reported in *Disc* and Chris Hutchins in the *NME* that the film would deal 'with a group of drifters'. All of this was waffle that, boosted by the marquee value of Sellers and O'Toole, I managed to get into the press as part of my effort to not straggle too far behind the Beatles and their filmic progress.

The next piece of celluloid fiction on which I gained press ink for the Stones was a piece of nonsense called *Back, Behind and In Front*. I didn't even bother to gild this lily with marquee value, relying on Keith's quote that he 'was already working on the recording of the soundtrack' and my promise to Chris Hutchins that if he printed my latest film story I'd give him an exclusive on the tracks of the next Stones LP.

Around that time I met the endearing UK movie maverick Michael Winner when John Sandiland included us as a duo in a series he was writing for *Queen* magazine in which two celebrities, well-known backroom boys, got together to discuss having 'made it' in their respective diverse but similar careers. Michael had already made his mark and reputation with Brit noir outings *The System* (1963) and *West Eleven* (1964), after starting out with the Billy Fury popalong *Play It Cool* in 1962 and a poorly received version of *The Mikado* starring Frankie Howerd a year later. With the daunting *Death Wish* and, later, *The Mechanic*, Winner would move on to the company of Charles Bronson in the early 70s and define the art of rape and mayhem in a way that had not been possible for Mr Burgess and *A Clockwork Orange* less than a decade before. The times they seemed to be changing, and mighty fast.

Michael Winner lived in Bryanston or Montagu Square, a short walk north of Great Cumberland Place and Seymour Street. An appointment was set for our meet and chat one 6 p.m. on a midweek spring-of-1965 evening. I'm not sure what I was up to, but, to be sure, it was all work and no good.

I was on a showboat roller coaster, crashing here and whenever, working myself and my crew everywhere. As a result I turned up for the dual-celeb interview at Michael Winner's a good day late. Winner opened the door to his flat with the sureness of somebody advertising the advantages of 'making it' in his early thirties as perhaps being preferable to doing so when barely nineteen. He beamed me into his sumptuous ground-floor living room and offered me a drink, which I declined. 'John Sandilands couldn't wait, dear boy,' smiled Michael. 'He left a little ratty about a quarter to eight.' . . . '*Last night*,' he added to be sure I got it. I did and though steeped in fatigue made an effort to rise above a tired mumble and informed my host that I was jolly well aware of what day it was – and the fact that I'd turned up twenty-four hours late. But, surely, I brazenly insisted, that was better than not having turned up at all. Mr Winner huffed and took that one in, leaning against the marble fireplace opposite me as I reclined (nigh on slumbering) on his comfortable, svelte settee.

I allowed myself the same look around his abode that I'd allowed myself on my first visit to Bob Crewe's Dakota grandeur and decided again, *vis-à-vis* Sheila's and my shabby Primrose Hill quarters, that I must be doing something wrong, regardless of how well my cars were appointed. 'Quite, dear boy,' sighed Winner. 'If you don't mind my saying, I think you look as if what you need is a bowl of cornflakes and a good night's sleep.' Whereupon one of England's rudest men took himself off to his kitchen and came back with a bowl of Kellogg's. I ate up gratefully and then followed the second part of his recommendation and fell into a nice deep slumber on his couch, waking refreshed the following day. A cup of tea, not much banter, just a smile and I was away, well rested and back at work.

Michael Winner remained generous and pragmatic with his advice to me over the years whenever I was considering cutting loose into a film project. At the time he pointed out how little the Beatles had actually been paid for the privilege of entering the film arena and warned me that this was the sort of remuneration the Stones should expect from the film industry. I think he was advising us to stay on the road and follow the money. It was not for nowt that he later reminded me that Ringo Starr had probably received more money for his roles in *The Magic Christian* and *That'll Be The Day* than the Beatles had received fourfold for *A Hard Day's Night* and *Help!*

In the same square W1–Winner mile a year later, Mick Jagger and I would meet the veteran director Nicholas Ray. *A Clockwork Orange* having dissolved into a fade out, Allen Klein put forward a book that had originally come his way via the Dave Clark Five, whom he represented in the US. The book was *Only Lovers Left Alive* by a north of England schoolteacher, Dave Wallis. The plot, passable and an attention-getter, was thus: our island's grown-ups are committing suicide and its teenagers are turning Britain into a fascist jungle. The *Daily Mirror* reported I'd told them, 'The book could have been written for the Stones.'

Allen Klein had pulled off a coup in his negotiations on behalf of the Stones and myself with the Decca Record Company. Decca would only get the rights to a film soundtrack if they coughed up an extra million and a half. That million and a half additional dollars alone should have shamed us into doing a film. It was during our quest for film that we met a lot of old farts . . . and Bryan Forbes. Writers Keith Waterhouse and Willis Hall may have been hired to write a draft screenplay and, if so, their ideas felt duller than the words already on the pages of Wallis's book. It wasn't *A Clockwork Orange* but it would have to do, even though its plot was less than credible when one actually read it all the way through. Unfortunately, Waterhouse and Hall's screenplay would prove even less believable or exciting. The generation gap appears quickly and defines itself even faster in matters of art and workissimo, especially when that work is cast unto a generation removed to whom the very staying power of the Beatles, Stones and the rest was a matter of some discomfort and not much joy. If I appear to get hazy and dismissive here on recall it's because our entry into the film establishment was a fruitless nightmare during which a host of overpaid, undertalented dolts took umbrage at the idea of the Rolling Stones taking on their game. The Stones could not be deflected into cardboard cutout Keystone Cop pop-replicas. For one thing, they were known to be 'difficult'.

**Keith Richards**, in *NME*: 'Guess you've heard of the plans for our movie. We're all pretty excited about that, right now. It seems to be all we ever talk about. Mick's been running around seeing every movie he can, trying to pick up some new ideas or something. Mick will play a guy named Ernie, who is kind of a hero, and I am sort of his right-hand buddy. We're trying to get Nicholas Ray to direct.'

**ALO**: Nicholas Ray was flown in from Spain for a meet with a view to his directing *Only Lovers Left Alive* with the Stones. He was put up in a Montagu Square mews house. Mick Jagger and I had been recording at nearby Pye studios off Marble Arch and one evening we bounded up Great Cumberland Place headed for Mr Ray in his mews abode. It was raining and both Mick and I agreed, while dodging shoe-ruining puddles, that the scene would play more optimistically had we been driving on Sunset Strip and turning right into the Beverly Hills Hotel instead of slogging on foot to the tune of an endless grey London drizzle. However, we remained encouraged by the idea that what had been good for Jimmy Dean could be equally good for Mick Jagger.

Ray, according to Ephraim Katz's *The Film Encyclopedia*, was 'the darling of the auteur theory cultists, a dynamic socially conscious director with a keen visual sense and a gift for attaining fluid motion on the screen'. Ray scored his first hit in 1950 with *Knock On Any Door*, followed by *In a Lonely Place*, starring Humphrey Bogart as a Hollywood screenwriter playing out a less than savoury relationship with starlet Gloria Grahame. He struck true gold in 1954 with *Johnny Guitar* and went platinum with 1955's

*Rebel Without a Cause*, which starred James Dean and changed all our lives and diction.

Dean had previously portrayed the troubled Cal Trask in Elia Kazan's *East of Eden*. The layered, incestuous relationship portrayed by Dean with Richard Davalos as his brother and Jo Van Fleet as the madam-mother in *Eden* was a notch above my affinity with such family values. I was taken with the brotherly Cain and Abel pain and the early Armani-esque sand and ochre college hues that Dean wore, a mere shade away from the colours of Eden. One cannot help but wonder if the experience with Dean and Kazan did not toll for the career of Mr Davalos the way *Performance* would for James Fox, following his bout with Jagger and Donald Cammell.

After *Rebel Without a Cause* Ray seemed to disappear into the slopes of Europe and never was at one with the street again. It is said that the moment your artistic meanderings leave the street and relate to room service you'll end up writing a different song from the one the public chooses to whistle. You may get a final run from the penthouse, but the street has a beat of its own. Ray would never direct another motion picture.

It was under those circumstances that I sat in a dark, cruddy mews house in late 1965 and introduced a rising Leo, Mick Jagger, to the fading mane and fellow Leo, the maverick Nick Ray. Tall and lanky, he needed to stoop as he ushered us into the teeny mews living room, or perhaps he stooped anyway. His short hair was grizzly grey, his skin was ruddy and gone with the wind, and his eyes were cobalt and lost somewhere between disinterest and betrayal. He looked like he had spent too much time in his middle 50s, not unlike his *Johnny Guitar* star Sterling Hayden playing Captain McCluskey in *The Godfather*.

The lighting of the room came from lamps set on side tables that added a conquered still to the proceedings. Ray offered us a drink from the decantered silver tray. I think we had whatever he was drinking, and, whatever it was, Mick and I both drank up but didn't really feel it. The director sat himself down and curled his long ruddy hands around the cut glass. He wore the outfit of an American director of the 40s and 50s: *de rigueur* bone-buttoned, staggered-vented, grey herringbone jacket, grey trousers, and shoes buckled and brown.

'Have you been to the United States?' he asked. Mick and I looked at each other and realised that the director was according us the lowest level of interest. No homework and even less bullshit. We told him, yes, we had in fact been to the United States and had just got back from our third visit. Ray cleared his throat. It was obvious he didn't care if we'd just got back from the moon. He was beyond surprise and looked upon Mick as a pup sent to amuse him. If drink or whim infused him he might throw a few scraps of cv Mick's way – otherwise . . .

His neck looked scorched, like worn-out bagpipes. It heaved and retreated with every breath. Was he smoking? I can't recall, but he inhaled with a smoker's wheeze as he searched for his words. On closer examination he took on the aspect of a man who had inherited Red Ridingwood's hand-me-downs from F. Scott Fitzgerald's *The Last Tycoon*. Suddenly Eric Easton, by comparison, looked dapper. Ray embarked on a long and clearly well-worn monologue on the art of James Dean and how he'd found it. He seemed to study Mick's patience, watching to see how much of this he would take.

The one thing we shared in common was the inability to voice enthusiasm about working together on *Only Lovers Left Alive*. The brunt of his Jimmy Dean oration seemed to be that the actor was an unruly, undisciplined pussy who had only been worth Nicholas Ray's trouble because he could act out Ray's vision. The question seemed to be whether Jagger felt he was any of the above. Mick deferred on the pussy angle and gave Ray a feeble, 'So what do you think of the book then?' Ray rejoined with a perfunctory, 'It needs a lot of work.'

Ray scratched his neck and examined his glass, stooped up and asked us if we'd join him in a refill. We both said no and knew that the meeting was over as it had never really begun. Ray tugged at the kerchief tied around his withering neck. I have always mistrusted this affectation in America's cinemafolk. On the English it's merely an affected mistake. On an American, it screams for attention with the fey import of 'I direct.' Nick Ray was pathetic, and perhaps it was the idea of the real Stones in a real movie that was pathetic too, but nobody was putting that card to the front of the deck. The idea of Hollywood was enticing but the reality of the Stones' being as stiff as a Cliff Richard in *Summer Holiday* was there as well. I just hoped Mr Ray had used the free travel to visit a tailor.

The rain had not stopped, but that did not stop us from leaving. The sound of our heels slapping smack on the wet mews cobblestones grew louder with the echo of the dull night. The ricocheting disappointment left our brainset as we turned on to Upper Berkeley Street. Mick was joining Chrissie Shrimpton for a quiet supper in Chelsea; I was going home to Sheila in Primrose Hill. I allowed him the first taxi and having hailed it closed the cab door on him, but not before Mick broke the silence that had dogged us in our walk from the mews. 'Andrew, don't ever put me through that again.' I promised I would not and we parted in mood and lighting reminiscent of Trevor Howard and Celia Johnson in *Brief Encounter*. I walked off in search of another cab but stopped off at a pub for a drink instead.

**Bryan Forbes**, actor/writer/director, *A Divided Life*: Tom Wolfe called it the age of the Kandy-Kolored Tangerine-Flake Streamline Baby, those mad 60s when the grouse-shooting son of a crofter told us we had never had it so good and Beatlemania and the Stones splattered the eardrums of most teenagers. I did have one close encounter of the third kind with this new genus of teen when, unannounced, two of the Rolling Stones arrived at Seven Pines one summer afternoon, stepping from a Rolls Phantom dressed, strangely enough, in furs and accompanied by their manager Allen Klein and his sidekick, an erstwhile pop singer, Andrew Oldham. Klein informed me that I had been selected to direct Mick Jagger in *When The Kissing Had To Stop* and that money was no object. It was more a verbal rape than a proposition and every time I attempted to deflect Klein's nauseating conceits, he became increasingly aggressive. How could I possibly turn down such an offer? Didn't I realise I was being given the opportunity to become an overnight millionaire? He was handing me the chance of immortality. 'You get to keep all the loot,' he kept repeating. The serious novel he had chosen somehow did not seem the ideal vehicle for Mick Jagger's screen début. 'How about Jagger?' I asked. 'Does he want to act, and more importantly *can* he act?' 'Who cares whether he can act? That's your problem. I'm talking about making money.' As I recall, the two Stones (Jagger himself was absent) listened to his tirade without comment, and betrayed not the slightest interest in the proceedings. Perhaps they were so conditioned to being manipulated by this fast talking little guy who controlled their destinies that they found nothing strange in his efforts to manipulate a complete stranger – wasn't that the way the world turned? They looked absurdly young – the dissipation was yet to come – sitting on a sofa still swathed in fur while Nanette served them tea. 'You'll do it,' Klein said, walking me in the garden while pressing his rapacious philosophy. 'I've yet to meet somebody doesn't have a price. Don't be bashful, tell me what you want. You name it, I'll provide it. I don't take no for an answer.' I didn't doubt him, but his rancid, devil's advocate voice grated and I distrusted him on sight. Pleading other commitments, I managed to stall him and they all trooped back into the monolithic Rolls with its darkened windows without a word. I was left bewildered by the strange encounter.

**ALO:** What? I do not recall this strange encounter, but if my monolithic, darkened-window Phantom V Rolls-Royce was present I may have been there in the flesh, if not in mind. I can hardly imagine attending a film meeting without Mick, nor can I imagine Klein turning up *chez* Forbes unannounced with two unneeded Stones in tow. Who were they? It doesn't sound like Bill and Charlie – they were never big on fur. Brian might have made it in a furry frame of mind, but I doubt that Keith would have given the meet four bars, let alone a full chorus of his time. However as this book allows for your truth, my truth and the perhaps truth, we must allow every dog his day. Allen Klein can defend his own corner, but the words that Bryan Forbes puts in Klein's mouth sound more like projections on Forbes' part of what Klein meant than words actually said. That aside, Forbes' recall of my sidekicking Allen as manager does somewhat validate the fact that once we'd said hello to Allen Klein, money moved me into the second division with the Stones – and that does not come down on either side of whether Klein planned it, destiny demanded it or I hurried it along – it was just a longer playing version of my previous 'so long, Marianne'. However, there is a truth that a third party must be present, even if unknown, in every quarrel for a conflict to exist.

**Keith Altham**, writer: With Allen Klein it was not so much physical fear as the sense that he was prepared to go into a record company office with an abundant knowledge of contractual law and accountancy and demand to see certain things that nobody had ever asked for. The reason the companies became fearful of him was that they were hiding things, and they were hiding things because it was making them more money. So rather than have Allen Klein come down on them, they'd fork out huge sums. Allen was like one of the Bowery Boys; he just went straight for the jugular. Instead of doing nice English business he would just mentally attack people. I saw him once operating with three guys who came round to the Hilton from ATV Television at the time Andrew was trying to finance *Only Lovers Left Alive*, wanting to do a deal for a Rolling Stones TV spectacular. Klein made them wait downstairs for half an hour while he read a comic book. It was all a game. Then he brought them up, shook hands, ushered them to seats, put his basketball boots up on the table, looked at all three of them and said, 'Messrs Smith, Jones and Barker, which one of you three would like to be spokesman?' He wasn't gonna bother talking to three people at the same time. One of them said 'Oh, I think I can speak on behalf of my colleagues, Mr Klein . . .' 'Fine,' he says, 'I've just got one question to ask you. Can you sign your name on the bottom of a cheque on behalf of ATV?' 'No, I can't,' the guy replied. 'Thank you, gentlemen, the audience is at an end,' said Klein and out they trooped. It might have been crass or considered to be bad mannered but it was actually quite clever business because it cut right to the quick.

**Keith Richards**, *In Their Own Words*: We went down with Andrew to the Hilton to meet him. In walks this little fat American geezer, smoking a pipe, wearing the most diabolical clothes. But we liked him, he made us laugh, at least he was under fifty. Andrew had got Klein in to get us out of the original English scene. There was a new deal with Decca and Andrew told us Klein was a fantastic cat for dealing with those people, which we couldn't do. Andrew knew he didn't know enough about the legal side of it to be able to do it. So we had to get someone who knew how to do it. I said, let's go with someone who can turn everything round or fuck things up once and for all.

**Chris Hutchins**, journalist: Andrew told me that during the meeting between Klein and Decca, Sir Edward Lewis said something about, 'We've got a lot of good people working at this company, Mr Klein.' Klein turned round and said, 'Well, I hope they can sing, because you've lost the Stones.' Andrew loved that; it was a great line.

**Chris Stamp**, co-manager, the Who: Andrew made Allen Klein the Mafia. Allen Klein was a Jewish accountant, for fuck's sake, but Andrew thought it'd be better if he was the Mafia. That was Andrew's imagination.

**Allen Klein**: When I started with the Stones, Andrew liked having me portrayed as this shadowy American who could take care of anything. That was Andrew, he just created it, that I was like a gangster. He said they'll love it in England. No one would ever talk to me about it. That's what the British think of all Americans who might be Italians. There was supposed to be a film, *Only Lovers Left Alive*; we bought it and we owned it. They were just not going to do it. Don't ask me why; I wasn't getting involved with that. I thought it was a good idea. They liked the book; I don't know what happened.

**ALO:** I'll take it as part of our exchange, dear reader, that you'll allow me to discover truths as I write along and share them with you for us all to view. There has been a prevailing climate to this tale that seems to hover over mostly all: it's the ill chill of 'So we're successful – so what?' Not an endearing overview to be conjured up for higher posterity, I admit, but, as always, it is what it is.

As for the offers of gelt and immortality that Forbes ascribes to Klein, methinks director Forbes doth protest too much. The spread at Wentworth hardly gave the impression that Mr Forbes was in need of a few bob. And, minor point that it may be, I must insist there was nothing erstwhile about my having a career as a pop singer.

Dear Bryan, you seemed to acclimatise yourself to a life of pop, Rolls-Royces and furs within short order via your later friendship with neighbour Elton John. I doubt you told Sir Reg to go home, dump the furs and the slingbacks, and dress properly. I also doubt you chided John's manager John Reid for being too bullish and crude about money. But that would have been in the 70s when our bunch of madness was here to pay.

**Bryan Forbes**, *A Divided Life*: Shortly after this Allen Klein meeting, Nanette and I had to make another trip to Hollywood. We were pursued there by Andrew Oldham bearing further blandishments from Klein and so many red roses for Nanette that the bouquet had to be dismantled before it would go through the door of our Beverly Hills Hotel bungalow. He was dressed like the head of the school, I remember, a blazer and tie, polite and deferential. I think he and Klein were genuinely amazed that I resisted; it was something that they had not come up against before and it became a matter of pride for them to try and wear me down. Though I had nothing against Mick Jagger, and indeed admired his phenomenal nerve on stage, they did not succeed in persuading me, and so for the second time in my life I passed up the opportunity of becoming an instant millionaire. Klein later moved in on the Beatles, since all pop groups seem to attract his breed, usually at their cost. I had no further contact with the pop world until Elton John became a near neighbour. This was during the early 70s, a time when my two daughters determined to prevent me from lapsing into middle age. Under their influence I grew my hair longer and hobbled about in cowboy boots which I could never pry loose unaided. Photographs taken at the time confirm that such devotion to filial influence was misguided. In fact I looked like a complete prat.

**ALO:** On this, Forbes and I agree, but with this one small adjustment: I'd backdate the complete prat to eight years earlier. As to this bungalowed meeting in the Beverly Hills Hotel, sure sounds like me, what with the voluminous amount of flowers for the ravishing Mrs Forbes and the fact that I'd meet almost anybody in the Beverly Hills Hotel. In the trenches of 1964–6 I continued to do battle on behalf of the Rolling Stones movie never to be. I do recall one meeting with Forbes that took place in the canteen at Shepperton studios where I was Jaggerless and accompanied by Tony Calder who, with his wife Jenny, was Forbes' Surrey neighbour. Alas the conversation never gained ground on the subject of a Stones movie and at best Forbes remained an also-ran and rehearsal.

At one point during the lunch Forbes enquired whether Elvis Presley was gay. In answer I related a story Peter Noone had told me about his visit with Elvis. Peter and his Herman's Hermits had been taken to Bel-Air to meet the King. Elvis had engaged in his usual childish behaviour at Peter's expense for the amusement of Elvis's Memphis buffoons. Standing on the marble steps of his Bel-Air mansion, he'd positioned one of his bodyguards to kneel behind Peter so that Elvis could shake hands and then push Peter over the living stool. This, amongst tuts and titters, seemed to be interpreted by Forbes as quasi-confirmation of an aberrant sexuality in the King. The British New Wave was stillborn to this sort of inanity.

The reality was that nobody wanted to do a movie with the Rolling Stones. It was presumed – correctly – that the Stones' alpha wolves would not be putty in filmdom's hands. If they had been prepared to turn up, disintegrate into a willing popopera of vaudeville turns, and supply the required amount of soundtrack all might have been different. The rebel image that had worked for them in rock worked against them in film.

There are not many examples of music personalities who have shifted their creative spark over to the silver screen. Rock stars seem for the most part to lose the very essence of their sensual being the moment they hit their mark and attempt to act – they lose the rhythm, they lose the swing and they end up contorted, unsexed and stiff. It would have happened to Jagger in *Performance*, but that film succeeded on the basis of drugorama over content. It was also blessed by a delay in release that gathered it a pathetic market that had had enough of pop upstarts and warmed to a story of a burnt-out rock star unable to produce anything except mental mayhem. Jagger has been praised for his role in *Performance*, but the first time I attempted to watch it towards the end of the 70s, I still had to turn away and turn it off – Mick Jagger was playing my biggest nightmare and James Fox was playing me. *Performance* remains symptomatic of late 60s ennui. Part of its sinister appeal is that it is an ode to excess, drugs, sloth and an inability to produce.

**Marianne Faithfull**, *Faithfull*: In a sense most of the people in *Performance* weren't acting at all. They were exhibiting themselves. Real gangsters, real rock stars, real drug addicts, real sirens. Let's face it, we were

James Fox in *Performance*, 1968

all pretty lightweight, pretty naive compared to Donald Cammell. Donald was older and more devilish. This is why Andee Cohen was afraid for James Fox's immortal soul. She was very wary of Anita Pallenberg, too. Anita was the dark queen under an evil spell, so gorgeous and dangerous. But the sarcastic, sophisticated and decadent Donald was the major Dracula. His method of directing was to set up a vortex. Into this vortex went every disorientating thing you could imagine. God knows what drugs were taken on the set and then add to that all the indiscriminate sex.

James Fox was, of course, very fearful about sex and drugs and rock 'n' roll, but he was even more terrified of his own dark side. From a very proper and respectable theatrical family (his father was the agent Robin Fox), he was suddenly plunged into a den of iniquity filled with drug-snorting, hedonistic rock 'n' rollers and decadent, sexually ambivalent aristos. His sole bearings depended on Mick, someone with whom he already had a problem gauging the genuine from the put-on. He was totally out of his depth and gave the best performance of his acting career in the film and then went nuts. The film was truly our *Picture of Dorian Gray*. An allegory of libertine Chelsea life in the late 60s, with its baronial rock stars, wayward *jeunesse dorée*, drugs, sex and decadence – it preserves the whole era under glass. By some sinister exchange of energies, the film took on a florid and hallucinated life of its own while those involved (and on whom it was based) began to fall apart almost as soon as the film was finished. *Performance* exposed a lot of things and exposed a lot of people to things they had wisely stayed clear of.

**David Thomson**, writer: There are people who will tell you that the movie *Performance* gives you a good deal to think about. I should hope so, because you've got to have something to do while you're sitting through such a load of rubbish . . . What's it about? 'Well,' I always said, 'whatever you wanted it to be about.' Which brings us to the people who made the film. You see, you have to remember that this was 1968. Exhibit No. 1: Donald Cammell, who could have modelled for Pretentious Git, one of Francis Bacon's paintings. No, I'm pulling your leg, but you know what I mean.

Your Donald was a highly educated gent – probably far too educated to be a filmmaker. First of all, he was Scottish, which is a leg up. Then he was from a wealthy family that had lost its money. And he was raised in highly artistic and intellectual circles. Second, he could draw like an Old Master. Third, he never could get enough sex and drugs. Well, it's only natural that that sort of fellow in 1968 is going to start thinking about movies. Of course, it was meant to be Jagger and Brando. Donald did a treatment – I don't believe there was ever what you'd call a script titled *The Liars* – and sent it to Brando. Turned it down, thank God, because James Fox came along and he's flat-out the best thing in the picture. Not that it was easy, mind you. James was a very nice, straight guy, and he had got into bad habits in the film business – ever since *The Servant* (now there's a film for you, and one, I believe, Donald had very much in mind).

Anyway, Donald was a stirrer. He used Anita Pallenberg as one of Turner's women just because she was Keith Richards' girlfriend . . . And in 2001 they brought it back! You have to laugh after critics like John Simon slagged it off. 'The most loathsome film of all,' he called it. It's the stuff in the house that's rotten. Because Mick, bless him, he couldn't act to save his life. Couldn't say a line. He sings once, 'Memo From Turner', but that's so lively, you wonder why this guy is a has-been. Oh, and all the Borges and Persia stuff. It's like Borges written by Anaïs Nin.

**ALO:** As I said, most pop stars, upon opening their mouth in a movie, lose whatever charisma and aplomb they walked on the set with. It happened to Jagger in Tony Richardson's 1970 *Ned Kelly*. It happened to Grace Jones in the 1985 James Bond flic *A View To A Kill*. She was sexy as ever until she opened her mouth; on the other hand Christopher Walken's bad guy Max was the very essence of cool pop sex. It happened on occasion to David Bowie, even though he is credited as being the only poptop to rise above stiffness. I disagree. It worked in *The Man Who Fell to Earth* only because the Nick Roeg flick was another drug-pervaded effort with all the life of Ritalin with an expired shelf date. *The Hunger* succeeded due to the casting, which gave Bowie the opportunity to shine in a *Three Women* ensemble. For this fan, Dame Bowie's best screen turn remains his stellar double performance in the extended video of 'Blue Jean'.

The Rolling Stones' efforts into filmdom were a comedy of errors with no standing witnesses save my own *Charlie Is My Darling* from 1966. You do have Hal Ashby's *Let's Spend the Night Together* and Jean-Luc Goddard's *One Plus One*. The Stones seem to have had an unwitting effect on Goddard. He moved to England to make *One Plus One*, mixing the Stones' recording of 'Sympathy For The Devil' with Black Power tracts to limpish effect. But the exercise seems to have further depressed him. Subsequently he almost died in a Dylan-like motorbike crash and began to retreat from the world. He rejected his old work on 'ideological grounds'. His old audience rejected him and by 1974, unfinanceable in cinemas, he was reduced to video. In effect, he vanished.

And then came the Altamont travesty, the other side of the twisted celluloid coin that traffics in disaster the same way *Performance* trades on perverse indulgence and the fetishism of decadence. Obviously I'm not a warts-and-all Stones fan; therefore, *Rock and Roll Circus* also leaves me cold. The Rolling Stones' most engaging telefilmic outings remain *The T.A.M.I. Show* and various *Top of The Pops* and *Ready Steady Go!* outings. Mick Jagger slow-writhing in sensual motion to 'It's All Over Now' on *Top of the Pops* and his sultry student-of-Jean-Seberg delivery of 'You Better Move On' on *The Arthur Haynes Show* are pop moments captured with optimum reality and magic, as opposed to the later 'who-am-I' tech and mental malaises allowed once the zoo-keepers had turned on and beaded out.

In all, I was happy to have waved *adieu* to my play with celluloid dream merchants, hustlers, hypers and Chelsea Draculas, and to be back at Ivor Court and about real, as opposed to reel, work.

*

However, my fascination with film's transporting, creative world and those that populate it would continue. In 1974 I had tea with Anthony Burgess at the Dorchester. At the time, Nigel Thomas and I were attempting to acquire the rights to Mr Burgess's *The Wanting Seed* as a possible directorial vehicle for Nigel's mate Ridley Scott. Nigel hung out in the best locations life had to offer. I'd visited him above Loma Vista and below Mullholland while he career- and house-sat with Ridley, waiting on David Putnam to fuel *The Duellists* into go.

Nigel was another friend who would move on before his time. He passed on in the early 90s at the tender age of not-yet-forty-four. He remains a friend forever, as does his wife Pauline. This immaculate duo are part of the small coterie of good souls who have gone the distance and put up with me in lives one, two and three.

It was never a bad life with Nigel and if he let you in you shared a good one. His generosity of heart would bring me, one 70s evening, to Mount Kisco, New York, where, in the few years before *Frampton Comes Alive*, dear Peter was struggling to rise above first fame in the Herd, Jonathan King's telegraphed billing and cooing, his short stint in Humble Pie, and his pretty face and body. He had made a couple of decent solo albums but was not being taken seriously in America, while in England he couldn't get a mention. He toured constantly in the States building up the base that would swell with the mythic success of *FCA*, while living on and off again up in Mount Kisco with a tall, blonde, thin Kate Hudson-type wastrel named Penny Brigton, who was married to one of Peter's roadies. Such were the rules on the spoils of rock 'n' roll that Frampton and Penny seized each other for their own, while the husband roadied on. If this reeks of the scenes in Cameron Crowe's *Almost Famous* in which Peter Frampton played a roadie named Reg, you'll have got it in one, and realised that nothing is sacred on the road.

Penny would later be immortalised by name for three into fifteen minutes in a Frampton song. In my mind she was the embodiment of the Penny Lane in the delightful *Almost Famous*, save in real life it was a little more *The Apartment* and a little less *Terms of Endearment*.

Nigel viewed Mr Frampton and Mrs Brigton's spoils-of-war living arrangement as atrociously convenient. He further found it atrociously inconvenient that I had been wilting away in Connecticut not getting laid, and insisted that I wash and shave and trim up and meet him in Manhattan for dinner at the Plaza Hotel. I certainly did need to groom up, my appearance at the time more Don Haggerty than Don Adams, and my girth widened by booze, junk food and a non-stop diet of couch-ridden American TV.

I cleaned up, tweeded up and Volvo'd myself down the Merritt Parkway to New York City. Nigel had arranged about six for dinner and I was seated next to the more-attractive-than-Frampton Penny Brigton. Frampton was elsewhere, somewhere out in the toilets of the Midwest, stoking the fires of fandom and paying for Mount Kisco. Dinner finished, I found Penny engaging; she found me the same. Nigel beamed a 'Here, kids, take my limo, go have fun.' We did.

We clubbed about Manhattan a bit to make sure, then limo'd out to Mount Kisco where we proceeded to pass the rest of the weekend making love in every room of the house. She was very good and I felt very good inside her. Nigel's call had been correct and welcome. I had been spending too much time of late in my head; now I was out of it.

One resounding recall of the weekend with Penny is of being atop her on the floor in one of the bedrooms, elbows hurting nicely as they dug into the pine while I dug further into Penny, when my aplomb was diminished and my seed left wanting by her series of totally inappropriate questions about the rights of the artist, i.e. Peter Frampton, *vis-à-vis* his current contractual arrangements with A&M Records and that the fact that, according to Penny, all Peter's monies went directly to manager Dee Anthony.

My dick, at the mere *déjà vu* of it all, goes a little limp.

The weekend *en total* was a triumphant, glowing call to arms and penis for which I thanked Nigel. I have nothing but appreciation for Penny – her laughter, beauty, sensuality and 'Peter agenda' were a riot. We joked that she should have got Peter to do his own dirty work. Penny remarked she'd like to orchestrate that one, it being an experience that might remove some of the domestic ice and have Frampton come alive.

A few years later down the other end of the 70s I was out to lunch on a withering summer day outside Bergdorf Goodman on the corner of Fifth Avenue and 57th when Penny wilted out to the corner, drugged and overweight, looking like a Midwest blown-out Marianne Faithfull. Her shopping bags were weighed down by matching Great Danes. It could have been an outtake from the Plaza Hotel scenes in the same *Almost Famous*. Penny looked more untogether than I, so I did not say hello. I hope she stopped and came back from the madness, and I do thank her for bringing me back to life all those years ago.

Back at the Dorchester on that 74 day, Anthony Burgess continued to recall for me his 1961 life-defining year of *A Clockwork Orange* as we sipped tea from the thinnest of porcelain cups. Mr Burgess had been hacking away at his scribing life in 61 when a doctor had given him grave news. He had some cancer, growth or intrusion that would render him dead in a year and a half, two at the tops, so Burgess had better get his life and goodbyes in order. He threw himself into a writing frenzy, buoyed and influenced by Scotch, amphetamines and no sleep. This hazy craze of wordulition produced the Russian–Cockney configuration that bound *A Clockwork Orange*, *Inside Mr Enderby* and *The Wanting Seed* so well.

Mid-chapter-and-verse on this perceived last body of work he sold Stanley Kubrick the film and stage rights to the lot. It was rumoured at the time that the sale price for *A Clockwork Orange* was five thousand, although whether pounds or dollars Burgess did not clarify in our tea-time meet, and I did not enquire.

Anthony Burgess was attractive and engaging, with skin dyed Moroccan olive by the Mediterranean sun and Neroesque, forward thrust blond/grey hair. Having flown in from Monte Carlo or Rome to dance with his second wife at the Dorchester, he enjoyed his telling of the story and let me pour the next cup of tea. He was as comfortably upholstered as the settees upon which we sat and generous with his time and recall, but perhaps the master is better served in his own words.

**Anthony Burgess**, *You've Had Your Time*: There had been an attempt, in the middle 60s, to put *A Clockwork Orange* on the screen, with a singing group known as the Rolling Stones playing the violent led by the hero Alex, a role to be given to Mick Jagger. I admired the intelligence, if not the art, of this young man and considered that he looked the quintessence of delinquency. The film rights of the book were sold for very little to a small production company headed by a Californian lawyer.

If the film were to be made at all, it could only be in some economical form leasable to clubs: the times were not ripe for the screening of rape and continual mayhem before good family audiences. When the times did become ripe, the option was sold to Warner Brothers for a very large sum: I saw none of the profit. There had also been attempts to make a film of *The Wanting Seed*, and I had written several scripts for it.

Later I learnt that the American director Stanley Kubrick was to make a film of my *A Clockwork Orange*. I did not altogether believe this and I did not much care; there would be no money in it for me, since the production company that had originally bought the rights for a few hundred dollars did not consider that I had a claim to part of their own profit when they sold those rights to Warner Brothers. That profit was, of course, considerable.

**ALO**: Mr Burgess let me know that he'd want a cool quarter of a million for the right to option *The Wanting Seed* and another hundred thou or so for writing the first screenplay. He quite frankly didn't care if we used a word of it, he stated, so long as he was paid.

Nigel and I decided that Burgess was making up for Kubrick'd time, and so we gave up the chase. We returned to our own killing fields happier and wiser for a day off in someone else's run, dressed for the next last supper, and debated who would be the meal.

ALO and Nigel Thomas, King's Road, London, February 14th 1977

## · CHAPTER 8 ·

**Nik Cohn**, *Awopbopaloobop Awopbamboom*: Phil Spector was the first man to see pop as the new natural refuge of the outsider, the place you could make money and cut yourself off from filth and also express whatever you wanted without having to waste half your lifetime looking for breaks. The way he saw things, America was sick and pop was healthy. It was uncharted territory and its potential was endless. It was teenage property. In all these ways, he was an important signpost for the hippies that followed him. Otherwise, though, he wasn't so much in any dada-beat-hippie tradition as he was a pop bowdlerisation of Oscar Wilde – meaning that he was sharp and bitchy, fastidious and vulnerable, that he was a cultural snob, that he had great style, and that you always felt he was doomed. His most persistent image of himself was paranoid – creative Phil Spector hemmed in by cigar-chewing fatties, beautiful Phil among the uglies, groovy Phil versus hair-tugging America. His records were his best revenge. They were dirty great explosions, guerrilla grenades. They were the loudest records ever made. Spector knew more about the actual mechanics of recording than any other producer before or since. Most producers say what they want and their engineers provide it but Spector ran it all, understood every last insignificant dial or switch in his control box and bossed it. What he did, simply, was to assemble all of the noise in the world and then ride it. He had been the no. 1 pop phenomenon in America and now the Beatles had replaced him. He wasn't the youngest, the newest, the wildest anymore. He was definitely last year's model. Life was drooping. Stung, he made his best throw yet, ' You've Lost That Lovin' Feeling' by the Righteous Brothers, and it was a world monster. It was also endlessly brilliant.

**ALO**: 'You've Lost That Lovin' Feeling' was about to get a UK January release. That same month Bill and Bobby would jump from no. 5 to no. 1 in the North American charts. The record that had blown my life around the previous fall in Phil Spector's New York office was in for a hard road abroad.

Its future in England did not look that promising with the news that Cilla Black had covered the song for British release. Cilla Black was managed by Brian Epstein and was recorded by George Martin. She had just come off a no. 1 with the Burt Bacharach and Hal David-penned, as originally recorded by Dionne Warwick, 'Anyone Who Had A Heart'. The business of popular music was not yet the globally unified beast it would be transported into during the 1970s.

**Dan Daley**, writer, *Mix* magazine: Despite its extreme length, the record was an immediate hit in the US, though it faced early competition in Britain from a cover version by Cilla Black, the former Cavern Club coat-check girl who'd been groomed for stardom by Beatles manager Brian Epstein. However, Spector's many fans in the UK included Rolling Stones manager Andrew Loog Oldham, who placed his own ads in the British music papers to promote the original version. 'Already in the American Top 10, this is Spector's greatest production, the last word in Tomorrow's Sound Today, exposing the overall mediocrity of the Music Industry,' wrote Oldham. And the Righteous Brothers record duly leapfrogged Black's release to the top of the charts.

**ALO**: At the end of January 1965, *Rolling Stones No. 2* entered the album charts at no. 1 and stayed there for a grand thirteen weeks. The cover contained neither the name of the group nor a title, and this time, unlike the first time out, Decca did not object. In America, where I had no cause to be so commercially compulsive, the same work would be titled *The Rolling Stones – 12×5*. The recording had been made in London, Chicago and Hollywood and I was proud of that. It had been engineered by Bill Farley in London, Ron Malo in Chicago and Dave Hassinger in Hollywood.

The zit-grandised orphanesqued cover photo of the group was taken by Mick's new best mate, David Bailey, whom I had not seen since 1960 when I worked for Mary Quant and made deliveries from Quant to *Vogue*. That fashion world of the early 60s was the first pop business the UK enjoyed. Bailey, Donovan and Parkinson flicked the shutters while Jean Shrimpton made the clothes look great, Vidal Sassoon cut the hair and Mary Quant provided the clothes and the flair. Suddenly Britain had something to say and a look to go with it.

Fashion became *the* export – America was not interested in tired re-dos of fodder that had already had its day at home, and basically British pop fell into that category until the Beatles evened the score. So David Bailey knew exactly what this brand of op was all about – he'd been one of the crew who had invented the mould and didn't need any instruction from me. Besides, if I'd turned up at his studio for the shoot he might have reconsidered not sending me the bill. And this was not cheapness on my part – I was a few cars beyond that by this stage – I just thought you couldn't put a price on David Bailey taking your picture unless he chose to name it.

**David Bailey**: Just before one of the Stones shoots Andrew and I went into a restaurant and some guy started wolf-whistling at us. I think they thought we were a couple of gay guys. Andrew went over and stuck his heel in the guy's foot while he was sitting down. Then he grabbed him by the tie and shoved his face down into the food – real fast. All the guy's mates, the whole table completely backed off. Andrew was slight but fast.

I wasn't really involved with rock 'n' roll. I just happened to be friends with Mick; it all stems from that. I'd never take direction from people like Andrew, whether I'm right or wrong. I always do it my way. I was just photographing them. Andrew never chose the shots; I presented them. My attitude was there's no point in using me if you don't want what I give you. The Stones were all great, all unpretentious really, though Brian was a bit pretentious.

The 60s was the time when all the barriers broke down. Nowadays there are no boundaries between artists, photographers, film directors, pop musicians or fashion designers; it's all become part of the same thing, and the 60s was the beginning of that. It all goes back to the Jews getting chucked out of Europe and then influencing American art, which we re-imported. So, apart from the black influence, even though it came from America it was all sort of European.

**ALO:** I had written the sleeve notes for the Stones' second album in the bath for a laugh, seeing how close I could skate to the land of Anthony Burgess. There was no concerted effort to be controversial – I was just doing what came naturally to me at the time – the violent rhetoric I didn't give a second thought to. I was just very busy being me. The result would be surprisingly rewarding in terms of publicity, coverage and outrage.

Questions were being asked in the House of Lords about my sleeve notes, particularly in reference to my recommendation that Stones fans take up mugging blind people to secure the funds to purchase their records! The National Association for the Blind were in a visible uproar and Lord Conesford demanded to know 'what Government action' was planned to remove the offending notes. The Home Office stated that, 'there was no evidence that these words had been published in circumstances constituting a criminal offence'. Even Decca *jefe* Sir Edward Lewis made a rare public statement, 'I am told this inscription was intended to be humorous, but I'm afraid this jargon just does not make sense to me.' I was thrilled by the uproar – but it hadn't really been thought out at all; I was just lucky enough to be standing in the right place in the right mind. The publicity definitely helped draw attention to the second album, which, with the group's next step into casual brilliance, won over another horde of fans.

The Stones looked under the rug where white America had swept the cultural rhinestone of R 'n' B and culled nine passionate anthems. They tipped their hat again at Chuck Berry with 'You Can't Catch Me', leered and laughed their way through Alvin Robinson's 'Down Home Girl', and rounded out the nine with three originals which blended seamlessly with the classic covers.

I was about to celebrate my twenty-first birthday as the Rolling Stones stepped on and off the plane for their first tour of Australia and New Zealand. The journey was long, boring and economic. We cut across Europe, the Near and Far East. I remember waking up as we stopped for fuel in Bombay or Calcutta and being amazed to see the runway, a concrete maze of tufts of garden inhabited by packs of dogs nonplussed at our landing. Twenty-four hours out of London, far from Tulsa, I reached for the schlap, offered it around to a grumpy group of young men and prepared for our landing Down Under. We arrived at Sydney Airport to be met by 3,000 rabid fans and a press conference. Another cut from *No.2/12×5*, the Drifters' opus 'Under The Boardwalk', had been released as a single and greeted us from the no. 1 position.

**Harry M. Miller**, promoter: I had signed the Rolling Stones for the first tour of Australia, but without any large venues in which to play I was going to look rather foolish. In Sydney we checked out several potential sites, including the open air White City tennis stadium, and committed my Pan-Pacific Promotions to spend AUS $40,000 for the conversion of one of the big pavilions at the Sydney Showground into a concert hall. The place needed a lot of work. We had to build a dressing room block, run miles of wire for new sound and lighting systems, construct a high central steel stage and knock a hole in the concrete floor to the storage area underneath to provide a stairway for the artists arriving in the underground car park. The place had a seating capacity of 7,500. Of all the pop and rock 'n' roll concerts I presented none was more exhilarating than that first tour by the Rolling Stones, not just because of the obstacles to be overcome but also because the Rolling Stones were so plainly on a raw surge to the top. We co-starred them with Roy Orbison and the Newbeats, all of this for admission prices of two and a half to three and a half Australian dollars. I signed the Stones for AUS $12,500 a week (a little less than they now command) for which they had to give up to thirteen performances a week, and paid for the accommodations and economy air fares for five Stones and three managers. Over a three-week tour of Australia and New Zealand it added up to an outlay of almost AUS $100,000, but we grossed about AUS $250,000 at the box office. Perhaps I was a little mean when I refused to bring their own amplifiers as excess baggage. They could bring their guitars but that was all I was paying for, is what I told Andrew. 'We've got perfectly good amplifiers in Australia.' 'Christ! Who are we working for – Scrooge?' he shouted at me down the phone. 'We're all working for our bank managers, Andrew,' I told him. 'And if we don't keep a lid on the cost this whole thing is going to blow.'

**ALO:** In just two days the Stones would give five shows in Sydney. The audiences were wild and woolly and the Stones loved it as they searched for their land legs after a day and a half in the air. There were plenty of nubile young offers to help them; even I welcomed such an assist. The Sydney press wrote up that the Stones were a national scandal, shocking and ugly, blatantly sexual both on stage and off. They intimated that the band was up to no good with the nation's minors and virgins and were indulging in all-night orgies of the flesh. 'I wish we were!' was unfortunately the only quote of mine on behalf of the group that made its way back to London. The truth was that, all work and party allowed and aside, the Aussie and New Zealand summer replaced the English winter and provided us with a well-earned holiday.

On the Stones' first gig in a Sydney tin shed, along with wishing that the Opera House had been completed in time for us, my main duty was insisting that, while on the revolving stage, Roy Orbison, the Newbeats and the other acts had to turn 25 per cent between each song and remain stationary during the song. The Stones, on the other hand, were to have the stage revolve slowly all of the time. This was an early example of downsizing the competition. Outside of that I could concentrate on enjoying the Stones by night and getting a sun-tan by day.

The only violence on the tour occurred when a Newbeat all but had his balls bitten off by a could-it-be-hooker during our New Zealand stopover at a hot spring – the result of his requesting some unchivalrous below-the-belt sexual act. Even the retiring Mr Orbison laughed at the thought of the new heights of falsetto that might be reached that night.

**Gordon Spittle**, writer: We stand on the Dunedin Town Hall seats aged fifteen with shoes on and wave and yell / 'What A Nice Way To Turn 15' / It's like the son of a teacher man is out of the room and out for the count / Where the Stones were different was this sense of progression, hope and daring / Something offered beyond our appointed future compartments as freezing workers cutting up sheepmeat / Back at the show Ray and the Invaders wore bankers' suits – albeit purple – and played as sharp as Hank B. Marvin / Mick and the Stones wore T-shirts, striped sailor tops, buttoned shirts with pin collars and no tie / That 'dadadadada-dedadada da-dadedadadyadeda' of 'It's All Over Now' was as easy as sliding two fingers / It sounded so good and smooth, it had such east and west semi-tones I had to read some more Herman Hesse / When the tour arrives in Dunedin, Eddie Chinn on Rattray Street sends an invite round to the Stones at the Town Hall to visit his Sunset Strip Club / With a name lifted from the *77 Sunset Strip* crime series on the new televisions of the time, the Strip has an all-American finger-clicking ambience that suits sailors and scientists getting some 'rest and recreation' leave in Dunedin between weeks on picket duty on Operation Deepfreeze boats / The room capacity is three hundred people / Yank sailors smoke Camels and French Gitanes and play pinball / Waitresses wear canary yellow, serviette-sized skirts to collect glasses and ashtrays in buckets / At the counter there are 'Cokes, Coffee and Snacks' / Under the tables whisky is mixed with Coke / Sailors trade rare cargo during an era of foreign currency controls / T-shirts, jeans and pea-jackets, Lucky Strike ciggies, aftershave, Black Label and an occasional piece of Fender musical equipment from California and the bassline from Wilson Pickett's 'Land of a 1000 Dances'/ When they arrive on Rattray the Strip is packed / Everything stays cool till Eddie pops off his flash camera at Jagger and Andrew Loog Oldham cavorting on the dance floor / *Flash* goes Eddie. One on top of the other. Andrew Loog Oldham is leaping to his feet and screaming, 'No photos, no photos!' Eddie being Eddie is smiling frantically saying, 'Yeth, No Foto, No Foto!' / Oldham extracts the film from Eddie's camera and that's putting it mildly / Within a year the Stones are back but only for shows in the North Island / The Pretty Things have toured south of Cook Strait and Viv Prince has set new phews of pandemonium by wearing a leopard-skin hat to breakfast in an Invercargill hotel / This follows setting fire to the Town Hall curtains in Dunedin / The

Dunedin show is great, all wailing harmonica and twelve-bar jams that could only have been followed by Them and Van Morrison / Viv is eventually held and deported at the airport. Then the British invasion tapers off and the touring shows of twenty-minute brackets fall apart after uncontrollable visits by the Who and Small Faces in 1967 / And that's the way it was.

**ALO**: In Auckland the hotel took one look at us and wouldn't let us in. We got the same deal in Wellington, so had to fly back to Christchurch to a hotel that would have us. In Invercargill the Stones were greeted by a chorus of boos. The audience expected a headline appearance from Roy Orbison and barracked the Stones show with non-stop 'Bring back Roy'. Mick managed to outrage the Southland farming community with post-show comments that had him quoted as saying, 'Invercargill is the arsehole of the earth and the local residents are a mob of sheep-farmers.' I hope Mick's not having to visit Invercargill on his next solo tour.

By the time we played Melbourne everybody was getting used to the lazy summer pace and will-they-or-won't-they let us stay at the inn. In Melbourne, the John Bateman Motor Inn would. It boasted a manageress that would have given Honor Blackman a run for her money. Mick and I took turns ogling and making moves, while other members of the group concentrated on the daughters. We water-ski'd and even Brian relaxed. He left his mental luggage in the room and became a hearty skipper driving the speed boat as we ski'd all day. It was too hot for Mick to come out in the midday sun, so Keith and I concentrated on getting our tans to last till London. We walked and talked the length of the beach and wrote 'I'd Much Rather Be With The Boys'.

**Harry M. Miller**: The Rolling Stones came to me at a time when the knee-jerk adult reaction to them was that they were Neanderthals – an impression they seemed to delight in reinforcing with their aggressive behaviour and shaggy appearance. However, I found them to be remarkably well-behaved young men. They were never late for a show, never missed a plane or a bus and never cost me a cent in the heavy indemnities I had to take out for their hotel accommodations. They were never short of girls but that was their business and I thought they handled it with great discretion. On stage they always gave 100 per cent, even on the nights when the police and security had to disengage rampaging female fans from around their legs, waists and other parts. Andrew gave me the most beautiful grey worsted double-breasted blazer which I wore till the moths ate it to pieces.

**ALO:** The next leg of the tour was an uncertain trip into the Far East. A promoter associate of Harry Miller's named Freddie Yu flew down to check us out. He had to be sure of the group's behaviour, to see if they were suitable in the matter of saving face. The group passed the test and travelled to Japan and Singapore. Keith laughed and wondered quietly as we landed, 'So, Andrew, did they teach you a new way of saying, "Give me the fuckin' money"?'

When we arrived in Hong Kong Freddie Yu limo'd us to his penthouse for an array of food, booze, pornographic movies and hookers. The first bunch of ladies offered were over the hill and out of teeth; none of us wished to partake. The next batch paraded were marginally younger and prettier, full-bodied and full-toothed. They were followed by a final parade of teens and early twenties. We decided that somebody had to do the honours – we were, after all, in the land where nobody should have to lose face. We drew straws; somehow Bill Wyman won and saved the day.

In Singapore the Stones arrived in the middle of the night to play, none of us having any idea where we were. We were whisked from a military airstrip escorted by machine gun-clad jeeps to a circus tent in the middle of an eerie nowhere. It was all scary shades of the later *Apocalypse Now* in which Freddy Yu was Bill Graham and the Stones were fresh Bunnies flown in for the troops. The audience was 6,000 up-and-at-'em actual screaming British soldiers. The show went incredibly well. Bill Wyman made an exception on this occasion and resisted taking a fan back to his room to discuss the finer points of the show.

The next morning saw the group's last Far East appearance. We were guests of honour at the British Embassy for lunch. We figured that news of our reputation was slow to reach these parts; the taxpayers' money was being spent so that the ambassador's kiddies could ask cute, stupid questions and get autographs for themselves and their school mates. We were able to laze this final day away amongst the Gone-With-the-Empire white marble pillars and immaculate forever lawns. On the white linen veranda we took a four-or-more-course luncheon, waited on hand and foot. We were all bowled over by the tour's second pearled and tanned lookalike Honor Blackman winner, in the form and shape of the very sexy ambassador's wife.

We returned to London via Los Angeles, where we recorded the next Stones single, two new Mick and Keith originals, 'The Last Time' and 'Play With Fire'. After changing clothes at the Hotel Nameless and wolfing down hamburgers, fries and beer, the group, Ian Stewart and I headed down Sunset to RCA to rendezvous and grab that magic. In just one year Mick and Keith's songwriting had graduated from soppy ballads to commercial ballads to album material for the Stones and, with the two songs we were about to record, finally cleared that last hurdle – to a real, live single for the Rolling Stones.

**Al Schmitt**, RCA engineer: Studios A and B at RCA were both the same size; they were big rooms. Then there was also studio C, a smaller room. You could mix in any room. The studios had very high ceilings and nice parquet wood floors. One of the things that made them so unique was that we had all those great live echo chambers. Seven of them, I think there were. This was all pre multi-track. There was very little overdubbing done then. The nice thing about doing everything at the same time was that you knew exactly what it was going to sound like. When you started layering things you were never sure. Then a lot of experimenting came in and it took longer and longer to make records and the expenses went up and up, incredibly.

RCA had a great, great microphone collection. Just fabulous. Great Neumann and Telefunken microphones. Great RCA mikes. Plus they had the great, original Neve console. It was just spectacular. The old Neves are so punchy, so warm – still one of the finest consoles ever made. We were using a lot of Scotch recording tape then. Dave Hassinger learnt most of his microphone technique from me – what microphones to use and how to use them – that's the most important thing. There were no isolation booths at that time, none whatsoever. But we had gobos, we would move them around like separators so you could semi-isolate things. We did have some small rugs that we would put down sometimes under the drums and things, but there was not much of that.

I produced a bunch of things with Sam Cooke. I did all those early records: 'Bring It On Home To Me', 'Cupid', 'Another Saturday Night'. I did a lot of work with J.W. Alexander. We did a lot of motion picture scoring there for guys like Alex North and Elmer Bernstein. I worked with Elvis Presley on *G.I. Blues* in 1960, 1961. I worked with Shorty Rogers, who also recorded under the name Boots Brown. I was also the engineer on Henry Mancini, Jesse Belvin, Gogi Grant and Ann-Margret sessions, all recorded at RCA in the 50s and 60s.

The Rolling Stones started a situation where songs weren't done in a standard four-hour session. They booked the studio for weeks to do their albums. That was new. A little later when I was doing the Jefferson Airplane we block-booked and were there for five months doing *After Bathing At Baxter's*.

**ALO**: After an eleven-hour run, we'd finished 'The Last Time'. I was so thrilled and beside myself with the result, the audio layers were just so total, hypnotic and forever, that I called up Phil Spector and asked him to come to the studio to listen to what we'd done. Everybody had really come through; this was the first Rolling Stones totality. Brian and Keith set up a layer of guitars that allowed Mick and Keith to just sit in the sing of it. I knew we finally had that big American hit; I just wanted Phil to tell me how big. Forty-five minutes later, Phil hobbled in off Sunset Strip in his Chelsea boots to listen to our forty-five. We put up 'The Last Time'. Naturally, the little big man asked to hear it much louder. As the fade neverended, Phil chuckled, shook his head, and sighed. 'Number Ten, guys, number ten,' he said. He'd be right.

We still had to cut the 'B' side, 'Play With Fire'. Brian, Bill and Charlie, exhausted from the all-day onslaught to complete 'The Last Time', headed for the Hotel Somewhere to crash. An elderly well-rounded Negro cleaner in matching grey shirt and slacks quietly swept all four corners of the cavernous RCA studio A. As the morning light rose on the Sunset Strip, Mick sat back in his stool and sang it, Keith's acoustic gave him something to sing to, Jack Nitzsche played a worldly harpsichord, Phil Spector gave the lining by playing bass – and 'Play With Fire' was cut. If you listened hard you could hear the sweeping and if you listened inside me you could hear my heart beating – we were home.

· **CHAPTER 9** ·


**ALO:** 'The Last Time' b/w 'Play With Fire' was released on Decca in the UK on 26 February 1965. Its US release would be three weeks later and its European and rest-of-the-world release would be in dribs and drabs over the coming spring into summer months.

Keith and I took a couple of days off in Paris, and Charlie and Shirley Watts joined us for one of them. The highlight was a swoop 'n' shop at our favourite boutique, Pierre Cardin on the rue St Honoré de Fauberg. Keith and I both bought indoor riding boots in a butter glove leather that rippled down around the ankles the way actual butter glove leather does around the wrists. I remember hoping my skin would wrinkle, age and hold as elegantly. Keith must have hoped for the same. He bought black, I brown. The price shocked us both – £46 each! That was an almost disgusting amount of money for anything, let alone a pair of boots that could not be worn in the street except at your own scuff and peril. Later in the day we went Left Bank and practical over in St Germain and picked up more reasonable double-breasted short navy pea-coats with matching braided discreet peaked sailor's caps that had us, on a later Irish tour, mistaken for railway workers and asked for directions for the train going to Cork. I'm sure by now some of you are wishing I'd been born a guitar techno as opposed to a slut for a shop window, but I was not. And when the going gets rich the rich go shopping.

Back in the UK the Stones non-stop work 'n' tour agenda continued as they headed out on 5 March on yet another package tour presented by Eric Easton Ltd. The Stones were joined by the Hollies, Dave Berry & the Cruisers, the Original Checkmates and American all-girl group Goldie & the Gingerbreads, whom Keith and I had first heard at a Bob Crewe Dakota party where the group entertained along with falsetto minstrel Tiny Tim. Goldie and her Gingerbreads had come to London to record with Mickie Most for Decca and try their hand at reversing the Brit Invasion of the Americas. I would later record Goldie with the Goffin/King potboiler 'Going Back'. Dusty Springfield, as it happened, had also recorded the tune. There was no point in entering the ring on that one, so I withdrew my version from release. Goldie would return to the States, revert to Genya Ravan, and become known for her work with Ten Wheel Drive.

The Righteous Brothers had been booked for the tour but single success had caused the duo to split up, not for the first or last time, and they dropped out at the last moment. The two of them had a certified smash with 'Lovin' Feeling', and that's what broke them up. Story goes that, as Bill Medley, the tall one, got to sing the verse and first chorus by himself, little Bobby Hatfield's ego was miffed and he asked Phil Spector – ego and TV appearances in mind – 'What do I do?' (while the tall one sang alone). Phil is supposed to have replied, 'Start counting the money.'

It was the first total *Day Of The Triffids* tour. At last, the Stones played to a neverending drone of madness. There now no longer existed a 'Beatles Only' territory north of Manchester; it was a shared prize, and in the taking of the Mop Tops' home turf we must have come on like crazed angels. No more derision on the division of north and south. No more bottles thrown on the stage, no more jeers, rumbles and menace. We finally stood on the stages of the north and the sound and bleat of the male and female hordes was ours for the asking. The game had been played, sung and now won and, oh, what a feeling!

**Dave Berry**, singer: With the Hollies and the Stones we tore through each British city, with everybody doing very well. The response from the fans was much deeper and darker than anything that had gone before. The stage invasions became a nightly ritual and the Stones were constantly bruised and bloodied. They were now rarely finishing their twenty-five minute twice-nightly set. It just could not happen. What made it all the more brutal and destructive was the fact that the assault was 50 per cent male; the Beatles did not have that element. But it was the maniac female fan brigade that got the Stones bounced from most of the hotels.

**Nik Cohn**, *Awopbopaloobop Awopbamboom*: In Liverpool one time, early 1965. I was sitting in some pub, just next to the Odeon cinema, and I heard a noise like thunder. Finally, after maybe five full minutes, a car came around the corner, a big flash limousine, and it was followed by police cars, by police on foot and police on motor-bikes, and they were followed by several hundred teenage girls. And these girls made a continuous high-pitched screaming sound and their shoes banging down against the stone. They were desperate.

The limousine came up the street towards me and stopped directly outside the Odeon stage door. The police formed cordons. Then the car door opened and the Rolling Stones got out, all five of them and their manager, and none of them were real. They had hair down past their shoulders and they wore clothes of every colour imaginable, and they looked mean, they looked just impossibly evil. In this grey street they shone like sun gods. They didn't seem human, they were like creatures off another planet, impossible to reach or understand but most exotic, most beautiful in their ugliness.

**ALO**: I recorded my sun gods that night in Liverpool for the EP *Got Live If You Want It!* The band sounded magnificent on that night, and they all knew it. 'I tried to get an effect on the record that as you are listening to it, it's as if you are sitting in the cinema watching the Stones.' This, at any rate, is what I told the *Melody Maker* at the time. Naturally I went on to gild the lily and lower the flat data into pomp and overdo. 'The overall effect is a standard I always aim for in every recording, a ball of sound in which none of the ingredients in the record is more important than the other. One must remember that one is not selling, in most cases, a melody that will go down in history, one is selling a ball of sound which attempts to hit the audience on first or second impact, because if it does not you can forget it.'

The waffle I gave the *Melody Maker* on the *Got Live If You Want It!* sessions now gives me cause to cringe and probably gave the Stones cause to do so at the time – even given the excuse of youth, for we were all that and, in our topsy-turvy lord-of-the-flies world, no quarter was given or asked for on this score. Above and beyond the width of lip and dearth of modesty I was allowed in that time by the media, the facts remain simple. My job was to provide the Rolling Stones with the environment in which they could create, and to make sure their efforts had the technical support to guarantee their work was recorded and delivered as given. Anything else was a wall of noise. The press would invite me to high-wire with no net and fuck up and I would often oblige. To quote once more the master of dealing with the exalted, Graham Greene, from his second auto-be, *Ways of Escape*: 'Success is more dangerous than failure, the ripples break over a wider coastline.'

The tour continued through the end of March. The Stones made time for two valuable *Top of the Pops* TV appearances. When the security guard on duty at the Odeon in Rochester, Kent, would not let the Stones into the theatre, Keith, no doubt pissed off at being spurned in his own county, knocked the offending guard to the ground.

In addition to the Liverpool concert recording we taped the Manchester shows. (On the EP sleeve notes I added the Royal Albert Hall in London as the other venue at which we taped, but that was bull – I couldn't get permission to record at the Albert Hall.) The sound you hear is the true call of the north, recorded superbly on this audio reunion by Glyn Johns, the engineer who had been the first to sound the Stones. Glyn still worked at the IBC studios in London and we took their three-track gear north for the recordings. There was one track for the band, one for Mick and one for the audience via a mike dangled over the front of the circle.

The recording done and assembled by Glyn back at the Great Portland Street headquarters of IBC, I was left to deal with a slight matter of fairness *vis-à-vis* publishing royalties. On side one of the EP I'd placed two R 'n' B evergreens from the Atlantic/Stax vaults, 'Everybody Needs Somebody To Love' and 'Pain In My Heart'. I called the UK publishers of these tunes and 'requested' 15 per cent in return for keeping them on the EP. I was refused. I felt abused so I indulged in a loogistic move by claiming the ten-second prosodic audience screaming 'We Want The Stones' as a composition credited to the five Stones via the *nom-de-comp* Nanker Phelge, so that the publishing and compositional equation was broken down between three songs as opposed to two. Money for new hope.

Press opposition to the group reached a new level when on the final night of this tour the Stones became embroiled in what would become known as the 'pissing incident'. I'd like to take credit for engineering this event, but that would not be true – I merely recognised the moment and transferred the credit from the bass line to the lead vocal as piss-artist. Some would call me clairvoyant, some might not be so kind. The Stones, led by Bill, were caught with their flies down addressing the wall of a Romford service station; the actual loo locked and not an offered option. The fellows were reported to the police and arrested for urinating on the service station wall. Fleet Street went ballistic over the story, so I moved Mick into the headline and the band's image as long-haired monsters of the drip was enhanced. I say 'I moved' – it probably involved nothing more than my lying in the affirmative when some optimistic scribe asked whether Mick was in the front line.

**Tony Calder**: It doesn't matter how much you do; it's do you do the right thing at the right time? Andrew would come in and do one thing, make one call, change one person's opinion and make the whole world work for him. The business about, 'Would You Let Your Daughter Go With A Rolling Stone?' – Andrew may not have said it first, but he heard it first and he used it. It was just a part of someone else's conversation. Andrew heard it and turned it into not just a headline, but a byline for life. That was one of the cornerstones of the imaging of the Stones; the other was the pissing in the gas station business. It was Bill Wyman who did the pissing, but Andrew was there to put the act down to Jagger. Andrew knew how to make the incident go national – I don't even think Mick was there.

**ALO:** Amidst all this piss-pop publicity and furore, 'The Last Time' went straight into the charts at no. 8 and to no. 1 in the UK by its second week, becoming the group's second consecutive no. 1 single. We didn't have to be about buying records in the stores anymore. 'The Last Time' had svelte and cunning and a forever underbelly of layers that leaked fresh audio delights unto the listener depending on the room and box it was played from. The group now knew who they were, sounded like it, and were relaxed and unfrenetic in their musical explanation of themselves.

I bought a new car – more than a car, a total celebration of automerit applause for the road so far – priced at a fitting £4,000. A white four-door left-hand drive 64 Lincoln Continental, its bright white sheen resting in a bed of red leather – it looked like a swimming pool on wheels. Reg was thrilled at being let loose on the street in this new toy, and I had him look into the possibility of us 'Boadiceaing-up' and having knives attached to the

Tony Calder, ALO and Reg King, Wells Street Court, London, 1965

wheels, rubber-tipped of course, which at a press of a 007 button on the dash would extend to threaten the legs of the pedestrian enemy. I could not get any car firm to take my money to develop this idea. On a short Irish tour at the start of the year Keith and I had purchased pistols and shoulder holsters in Dublin, the continuing beginance of Keith's love of a good weapon. We were both well pleased with ourselves as we descended the aeroplane steps on our London arrival, smirking at each other, breathing on the weight of our new best friends. 'Anything to declare, lads?' took on a cinematic aspect of its own as we shrugged our shoulders and holsters and replied with a smile.

**James Phelge**, *Phelge's Stones*: One afternoon at the office, the Stones were standing around Andrew's desk as I stood out in the hallway looking up at a poster-sized photograph. The neatly framed portrait showed Andrew, looking dominantly down from behind his green-tinted sunglasses.

Reg King suddenly came running out of his office over to where I was standing and grabbed me by the throat. In his other hand he held a gun, which he placed at my head. 'Right, Phelge, it's all over. We're going outside.' With one hand still at my throat Reg used the hand holding the gun to open the door and dragged me into the hallway, then pressed the elevator button. 'Stop fucking about!' I said as he bundled me into the lift. 'Shut up! We're going up to the roof. I've had enough of you,' roared Reg. 'You open your mouth again, I'll shoot you right here.' The lift reached the top floor and Reg pushed me out in front of him and through the fire-exit door and on to the roof. I guessed he was kidding, but did not have much option other than to go along with him. From the roof you could see over London and it looked a long way down. Not being one for heights and with a gun behind me I did not feel too secure. 'Right, Phelge, goodbye.' Reg pulled the trigger. An enormous bang went off from somewhere behind me and Reg started laughing. I turned around and saw he had been pointing the gun in the air. 'That had you worried,' he said. 'No, I guessed you were kidding,' I said. 'What? What? So you think I was kidding, do you?' said Reg. He grabbed me again and pointed the gun at my head. Then he shouted, 'Bang!' and started laughing once more. Then he fired the gun towards the sky again. 'What if that lands on someone's head? Will it stick in them?' I asked, imagining the bullet hurtling back to earth. 'No', said Reg letting his breath out with a sigh. 'It will just float back to earth. There won't be any impetus left. You want to try it?' He held the gun out and I looked at it. 'No, thanks', I replied. 'Where did it come from?' 'It's Keith's. C'mon, let's go down,' ordered Reg, now happy with his little joke. Once back in the office he informed Keith that his new gun seemed to be working okay.

**ALO:** The Beatles were busy doing airports. In the same March they filmed *Help!* in the Bahamas and changed planes at London Airport to continue on to Salzburg for more filming. They flew back at the end of April for a month's indoor shooting at Twickenham studios, which would wrap up their visual input into their second motion picture.

The Stones continued on their British greytrek. At the Palace Theatre, a Manchester girl fell twenty feet from the circle into the stalls – the luck of hysteric immunity and the fall being broken by the fans below allowed the girl no more than the need to replace her broken teeth. That same night we were not allowed into the hotel dining room because we were not wearing ties. Those first few months of swinging 1965 were rife with acts of attritious inconsistency wherein we could enter the hotel dining room with gun and shoulder holster but not without a tie.

Mick Jagger told the *Daily Mirror*: 'The trouble with a tie is that it could dangle in the soup. It is also something that a fan can hang on to when you are trying to get in and out of a theatre.' 'The trouble with a gun is that it could go off,' he chided Keith and I away from the press. Keith told a northern rag, 'I reckon there are three reasons why American R 'n' B stars don't click with British teenage fans. One, they're old; two, they're black; and three, they're ugly.' Brian Jones told the *Melody Maker*, and thereby the rest of the band, 'I play a lot of lead guitar and I am not really interested in rhythm guitar.'

In the first week of April the Stones joined the Beatles and the rest of Brit Popdom at the *NME* Annual Pollwinners' Concert at the Empire Pool, Wembley. This was the last but one occasion at which both acts appeared, another early goodbye to the hurrah of the 60s. It was a quick gig, a show of hands, a few tunes and a quick hello. The Beatles seemed to be walking backwards, saying it's yours and welcome to it. Reg burned more rubber than called for in his attempts to protect the Stones and my Lincoln from the crazed fans. These serial-fan nutcases were made all the more chaotic and dangerous by a frivolous disregard of security, the benign who-do-you-think-you-are? stupidity from the old bill.

Reg miscalculated his control over reverse and hit a few fans, as in they wouldn't get out of the way. The court case a few months later would result in Reg's losing his driving licence for five years and leave me with deep regret and the need to find another driver, minder and friend. Reg would have to change his position in life and find one in which he could afford a chauffeur. He had taken up with speed in an effort to work my hours and pursue his own. Our rock 'n' pop existence had the dynamic of stress as a daily given. The chuckle was starting to fade and Reg was oft of that too-stressed lot. A great deal of his violence was only held in check by his success in the chicken department, yet my hours did not allow him the ones to pursue that most needed commodity – the young, pretty straight boy who would bend just for him. When the magistrate banned Reg from the road, Mick, Keith and I gifted him with one of the dimmer of the Glimmer Twins' songwriting output thus far, a Costa Del Sol, sun 'n' sugar wrenched ballad, 'Each And Every Day Of The Year', which Reg was able to record with his newly found pretty boy band, Thee, and Decca agreed to release. The song also made it to the B-side of Bobby Jameson's 'All I Want Is My Baby' and ended up on the Stones' mix 'n' match 1973 *Metamorphosis* LP.

I didn't see much of Reg over the next few years. You spend an insanely intense amount of time with people, as Reg did with me and I with the Stones – a time that repels all boarders in which every emotion, ripple and nuance of the day is shared and nothing is hidden. And then that time is gone, it moves on and there is absolutely nothing left to say as you move on to fresh and separate playing fields alone. His life as pop manager did not last long and Reg returned to the relative security of dealing in cars. Years later down in the 80s he met his death in Bangkok, where he holiday'd yearly to fulfil his penchant for young fellas. He had picked two for supper and was riding them home on his motorbike when something must have diverted his attention and he forgot to take a corner. Reg King and two young men on a bike cruised over the cliff and death did them part.

Reg was master of his universe save in the matter of his heart and predilection of his libido, which was aberrated paedophilia. While the age difference was still within the same decade he could pass his choice off as an early call, but as his age stretched to forty and his boy choice did not keep pace, life must have taken on a permanent tension that played a not unkind part in his death. For me he'll be forever young, ticking and flicking his well-bred, well-padded shoulders into gear, tossing his blond mane and batting his sheer blue eyes in pursuit of the straight well-hung lad of today and tomorrow. He attended to me as a grand butch seductress determined to refine my day into pleasure regardless of how I'd arrived to it. Reg, with his love of life, is a constant reminder of the good that have died young.

The band and I flew out for the next North American tour as *The Rolling Stones, Now!* LP was released. Our final single of 1964, 'Heart Of Stone', had failed to follow up on the first real dent made by 'Time Is On My Side'. 'Heart Of Stone' had been stupidly released one week before Xmas and by the time the world had rejoined itself from the holiday break, radio had forgotten us, was working from fresh playlists and 'Heart Of Stone' had stopped breaking at a miserable no. 56. 'The Last Time' and 'Play With Fire' would make Top 10 amends for this imbecilic *faux pas* on the part of London Records.

The Stones were still very much in a holding pattern and in the queue for actual American success on the terms by which America defines it. We were in the wings waiting for God's lighting to pan down on us and klieg that moment when a nation would claim us as its own. At that point of majesty there is no separating Van Cliburn, Andy Warhol or the Rolling Stones. All are clutched to America's tit and invited to partake of its milk and money.

The American Top 10 countdown in May of 65 ran as thus: the Righteous Brothers, Sam the Sham & the Pharaohs, the Beach Boys, Wayne Fontana & the Mindbenders, Petula Clark, Herman's Hermits, the Seekers, the Beatles, Gary Lewis & the Playboys and, at no. 1 (again), Herman's Hermits. Many a month in 65 Herman's Hermits had two or three whacks in the US Top 20, and very much at centre stage stood Peter Noone. Armed with the Midas audio touch of Mickie Most and with his own professionalism, cute good looks and winning personality, Peter would, in a two and a half year stretch, score eleven US Top 10 singles.

We were coming back from Australia via Honolulu Airport when Mick got entrapped in a case of mistaken identity by a half-dozen or so giggling Hawaiian braided and pigtailed schoolgirls. Pigtails were unusual for Mick; he normally got city slickers, next runt of the Sid Vicious litter, or Park Avenue minidamettes. The girls' squeals and jumps of joy immediately *Hawaii Five-O*'d into confused silence when they studied the signature on their autographed pages and realised it spelt 'Mick' as opposed to 'Herman'. The squeals were taken up with equal zeal by Keith, and, hiding managerially behind him, me.

The Stones were with the wrong US agents. GAC just didn't get us. Herman's Hermits and the rest of the already succeeding British Invasion (less the Beatles) were with the bouncy Premier Talent, helmed by ex-GAC man Frank Barcelona. Frank would become and remain the major agent representing the acts for the next two decades through to today. In that year he repped Freddie & the Dreamers and Wayne Fontana & the Mindbenders, plus the stateside action of the Ronettes, the Shangri-Las and Mitch Ryder & the Detroit Wheels.

Frank Barcelona had another English connection. He would marry UK music journalist June Harris, who, with Judith Simons, had been two of the first journalists to 'let me in' in my earlier days as a press agent. I recall standing on the side of the stage of the Granada, Slough, during the few days

I repped the Little Richard/Sam Cooke/Jet Harris Don Arden-promoted tour. I watched in awe and amazement the magic being woven oh so gracefully by Sam Cooke as he took over with his soul the basic ready-to-rip Little Richard teddy boy audience and made them his for his nightly moment in style. In the Cooke-induced trance you kind of left your body and got taken up there for that while.

I looked around and there was the elegant Miss Harris, her petite figure adorned in black could-be evening dress, black pumps and white pearls. Her eyes twinkled opal and we acknowledged we were two of the lucky ones witnessing something wickedly cookin' and fabulous. Perhaps this astral visitation and somewhat earthly removal happens when the giver will not be with you for long. I got it with Eddie Cochran, Lenny Bruce and, of course, with Sam.

**Peter Noone**: For a moment there, yeah, we were bigger than the Beatles. But it was never a big deal. There was an extraordinary kind of camaraderie. Like everything could be just so and the next week the Honeycombs could knock the Beatles off the no. 1 slot, so who could possibly give a shit. We didn't care about who was no. 1, we just cared about who was going to get the *next* no. 1. We were all new; it was us against them, getting rid of the old and being the new.

'Time Is On My Side' had been a hit in America for the Stones. It was all out of tune but it didn't matter. It was their attitude that made it work. But Herman's Hermits sold records in America before we ever toured there. We arrived at the top. We had pop top hits and it helped when we got there that we were sort of cute and English. We did all the cuddly Mop Top shit, because that is who we were. We didn't have to have an act like the Stones and pretend everything was a big deal. When 'I Am Henry The VIII' came out we did *The Ed Sullivan Show* and there were, like, 50,000 kids outside our hotel. I met up with the Stones in New York and they must have been saying to themselves, 'Shit, maybe we should be doing the English thing, because they're already doing the American thing.' You're now in America, they're all American already. It's hard to have an American attitude when everybody's got one.

**Mickie Most**, record producer: Andrew was a big spender. I was with him in LA and he had two limos around the clock. Me, I actually just took a cab. He was kind of more expensive; he had a suite at the Beverly Hills Hotel and I stayed in a motel. I didn't see the sense of spending $100 on a room. But he was selling an act and I wasn't. He had to do that and it worked; that same image is what the Stones are today and there's really nothing like that. Andrew's interpretation has stuck forever. The Rolling Stones were never big sellers; they've never been big recording artistes. They've never done the business of the Beatles or Herman's Hermits. The Hermits had a different life span, like you now had with the Spice Girls. They just hit that market and in every country they were no. 1. Bob Dylan never sold that many records; it's a myth. Frank Sinatra didn't sell that many records either.

Andrew never got up my nose. I understood exactly what was going on; I'd been around the block a few times. I always enjoyed his company. We always were able to have fun, especially in New York. He could appear to be unstable if he wanted to be. Some of the time it was self-induced, some of the time it was almost like a bargaining ploy. He used it to get his own way.

It was very difficult to tune people in to this new way of thinking. You had the fashion, Mary Quant, Carnaby Street, the sexual revolution, the pill . . . a whole different thing. It was actually very hard to try and tune people in who were ten years older. When I first went into the recording business as an artist in the 50s the artist was not allowed into the control room. They might play the recording back to you over the speakers. Andrew was trying to break those kind of rules . . . so you get an upstart, some young kid smoking a bit of dope. They thought he'd never make it, but they were wrong. It was very hard to convince them, so he had to be manipulative and he was.

He smoked dope on the aeroplane with me; he actually tried to open the window at 32,000 feet, another bright idea. You could get away with that in those days. If anybody said anything you just said he was smoking Turkish cigarettes. I never went for a sound, not like Shel Talmy. I tried to make the artist and the sound work. That's why I pulled off such a wonderful deal in the US. They were impressed that I made different sounding records – the Animals, Herman's Hermits, the Nashville Teens. That's why CBS paid me a million dollars. The first artist I gave them was Donovan, then Jeff Beck with *Beck-Ola*, then Lulu with 'To Sir With Love', which spent nine weeks in the American no. 1 spot. Then I gave them the Yardbirds. CBS was very happy with me.

My schedule was to leave London at three o'clock on Sunday afternoon, get into New York 5.30 local time. I did this on TWA flight 701 every other Sunday. I started to work Monday morning and kept going until the last plane left for London on Friday night. I never remembered the plane taking off; I was asleep before the plane hit the runway. That's how hard I worked, all week going to meetings at publishers. I'd meet with Carole King and Gerry

Goffin, Barry Mann and Cynthia Weil, Neil Diamond, Howie Greenfield and Neil Sedaka . . . great times, great people. Andrew was probably one of the first in the run of independent producers, managers, publicists. He was somebody out there right from the beginning. His kind of management and PR style revolutionised the way it all worked. The way he worked, they're working today. They all learnt from him. That's a matter of fact – they are pulling the same strokes today he pulled thirty years ago.

**Fred Frank**: The Rolling Stones weren't even on the fucking map, they hadn't really got their vinyl legs wet yet. I was working promotion for CBS and Epic at the time, and the Dave Clark Five scored big with 'Glad All Over'. My whole focus was to create a no. 1 record.

The Stones were fumbling around the secondary markets and going to these Park Avenue-type Andy Warhol parties, but they weren't *business*. When the little girls saw the early promo pictures of the Dave Clark Five, they just couldn't wait for them to come over. On the DC5's first tour, we flew into a private airport in Memphis, Tennessee. We knew that the show was a sellout, but we had no idea what we were coming into. So, we're flying into Memphis on a chartered Martin 404 with about ten people on board. I couldn't believe what I saw as the plane was landing. They broke through the barrier – there must have been 5, 7, maybe 10,000 kids, heading out towards the plane as it made its approach on the runway. By the time we got to the limos, they were upon us. We were sitting on the seats with our feet up, holding up the roof of the limo so it wouldn't collapse. And I'm looking over on the side, and this one girl takes off her underwear, with her telephone number on it, and bends over and shows me her bottom! As much as we're panicking, we all got a great laugh out of it.

The record was no. 1 in town, and Memphis was Elvis's home base. All the guys wanted to do was to go to Graceland. So I called a good friend of mine who went to school with Elvis, Georgie Klein. I asked him what we could do, and he says, 'Let's take a ride over.' Somehow, we snuck away from the crowd and we went there, and they turned us down. We called CBS to see what they could do. I called Epic; you know, *anything*. We were left standing right outside. The Dave Clark Five no. 1 and refused admission into Graceland. We took some pictures outside.

Dave himself, maybe he wasn't the most talented individual – Mike Smith, the keyboard player, was definitely the music man – but Dave was the businessman. Incredible organiser. Whenever I said to Dave, 'I need this to do this', he said, 'You got it.' And it happened. Working with an independent is a lot easier; you have a lot more flexibility as an independent promotion man. But there's nothing like having a party and nothing like having some of the prettiest dirty little legs in the world coming out. These parties were just so incredible. And the word was out; jocks were talking to jocks and everywhere we went, jocks would say, 'Where's the party? Where do we go?' And the record exploded. We had a great record, and we had a great group, and we had a great concept.

On the way to some show in Alabama, another sellout, we had to make an emergency landing because snow and ice got on the wings. We're on the plane and we're all exhausted; we would party until fifteen minutes before takeoff. We're all sleeping. The Martin 404 doesn't go up that far anyway, and you could feel that we were flying pretty low and that there was a lot of turbulence. It was like that plane scene in *Almost Famous* where they all think they're gonna die. The pilot was a guy we called 'Cowboy'. He had a ten gallon hat and cowboy boots, and he'd be stomping his feet to his country music. I saw him yanking on one of his starters – it was a pull starter – until he could crank one engine up as we were going down. He got the one engine started. He was screaming, 'Mayday! Coming into Tallahassee . . . I have to make an emergency landing!' The airport was all iced up because of the storm, and I'm praying to every god I can think of. You get religion from this shit. A couple of years later, it had become a different game and promotion became a lot of money and a lot of dope.

**David Sinclair Whitaker**, arranger: I'd been working with Shel Talmy and Glyn Johns. Then I met Andrew through a publisher we shared named Freddie Poser. Andrew wanted me to go to Los Angeles to record a local lad called Peter James for Reprise. We stopped off in New York on the way over. We were descending in the lift together in the Essex House when a dragon-faced dame in her 60s remarked to her husband in a loud voice something untoward about Andrew's hair and his looking like a girl. This was the swinging 60s. Without missing a beat Andrew said, 'You, lady, also have problems. You look more like a man than your husband.'

We had been invited to Bob Crewe's Dakota apartment, which was just amazing. I mean, English pop music had just not had this sort of financial reward, this opulence and an environment in which it was okay and safe to flaunt it. The walls were full of incredible art, the floors marble with water lapping in marble pools around the living room. Bob was having a very loud party and the local precinct cops were there, having been invited by Bob to drink themselves stiff. It was very bizarre and sort of early Village People, what with all the whacked-out cops and butch body-building types that seemed to have descended on the place. Everybody seemed blond or uniformed and beautiful.

The next morning, a little less blond, we flew on to Los Angeles. It being a morning flight, we were only allowed two drinks apiece. This was not enough for Andrew so he lit up a joint. The stewardess complained about the stench so I pulled out my Gauloise, which confused and diffused the situation. We stayed at the Hollywood Hawaiian Motel on Sunset Strip and went to various all-night parties and a Frank Sinatra recording session. The whole town seemed to be full of dope.

**Bob Crewe**: Andrew became very involved with Baby Jane Holzer, Tom Wolfe, the Andy Warhol set, the whole chic set. God knows he loved the parties I gave at the Dakota . . . I crossbred everybody and everything. I intermingled everything, you can imagine. There would be so many people from different walks of life at my parties, you had no idea who you might run into, from which world. The Stones bespoke authenticity somehow; there was something nitty gritty, gutsy about the Stones that was very enduring. It was not filtered, it was non-filtered smoking, and they really were smoking. They were hot and sexy and they still are. They are timeless . . . Andrew knew that, he knew what he was doing. None of it was by chance. Everything was deliberate and wonderful.

**Sheila Klein Oldham**: Baby Jane Holzer invited me out diamond shopping to wind Andrew up, to see how much money we could get out of Andrew. Linda Keith and I went over to Warhol's Factory for a big dinner party with Warhol where Andrew laughed and laughed. New York humour was dry and Andrew fit in. We were expecting Warhol to be very flamboyant in terms of great artistes, we were expecting him to be more Andrew than Andrew. He wasn't. Warhol asked me to be in one of his films. Jane Holzer had just done one – chewing gum for ten minutes. He sat me down on this chair, switched the camera on and walked off, saying, 'Whatever you do, don't move.' I laughed so much because in the UK everything's got to be authentic; you have to suffer for your art. Andrew put a stop to it, told Warhol, 'You don't film my wife', and we rushed off pretty quick. Out on the street people spat at Brian Jones; everybody stopped and stared. If he stood out in Hammersmith he stood out a hundred times more in America.

**Dan Crewe**, Bob's brother and business partner: Our offices were on 1841 Broadway, the same building that Atlantic Records was in. We had rather exotic offices in those days; everything was done with great splash and panache. I assume that Andrew was quite impressed with Bob's presentation so to speak, since at that point we were really on top of our form. Until Allen Klein appeared, we were in a publishing venture with Andrew. We published 'Satisfaction' and 'The Last Time' and released the Poets' recordings on DynaVoice. We had developed a pretty slick regional way of dealing with records. The English were not really that tuned in to what was happening and how to get it done in the US, and we were not very focused on what was going on in Britain or the rest of the world. There were very few PR companies, very few TV shows in the US; it was all radio. Bob and I sort of owned Detroit before Motown. We would go into Detroit and take suites of rooms in one of the best hotels, then we would send out invitations and we would get all the radio stations and they would all turn out because we put on such huge and successful parties. We would go in there with four or five records with the Four Seasons as the lead and follow up with the other artistes we were trying to break. That kind of mechanism we were able to show Andrew, how you had to approach getting in there, promoting, getting individual areas to respond. Andrew was fast to learn, but even at the very earliest he was bizarre. Even in the American music business Andrew would strike someone as being different. He was strange in the sense that he could befuddle you. He could create an atmosphere and I think people might have been intimidated by him. London Records was a garbage can label as far as we were concerned. They were not hot pop or rock 'n' roll; it was very unusual for a group like the Stones to be there. They were not very hip; you had to grind through the process. The Stones had suffered from radical lack of promotion in the Midwest. At one show they were forced to share the bill with a performing horse. In places like Pennsylvania and Michigan no one had heard of the Stones and few cared; venues, stadiums, sometimes with 15,000 capacity, remained virtually empty. The group was tired, frustrated and confused by their American touring experience thus far. Arriving back in New York was like stepping back into civilisation. They'd played backwater towns, they'd been treated like freaks, creatures from the black lagoon, by concert promoters. The only time anybody spoke to them was to shout 'Hey fairy' from across the street.

**ALO**: The Stones continued to storm North America, dived and thrived in and out of Canada, freeway'd down to Albany and shummed across the state line to Massachusetts. There were further concerts at the Academy of Music in New York, the Convention Hall, Philadelphia, and another appearance on *The Ed Sullivan Show* to promote 'The Last Time'. We wound down south to Atlanta, Georgia; Birmingham, Alabama; and Clearwater, Florida.

Brian Jones broke two ribs in Jacksonville, Florida. We explained it away as having happened during a karate class being taken poolside – a double-edged press release with a 'fuck with the lad at your peril' subliminal undertone while emphasising his healthiness. It was, in fact, Keith and I who were butching up and having the karate lessons, although that may be placing too noble a tone on our friendly persuasion – our agenda being a basic 'Hold the art, honey . . . a few "kill" positions will do.'

**Al Aronowitz:** I was very tight with Brian. It got to a point where it seemed to me he was just the rhythm guitar player. When I said this to him he used to say, 'No, Al, I was the founder of the Rolling Stones.' Brian was very paranoid. He sat up with me for nights writing this treatise on paranoia in longhand. You started to read it and you could see the way, in his mind, one thing kept impinging on another and on another. It was a vicious circle. The first time they held a recording session without him, boy, was he pissed. They went to LA and recorded something behind his back. He was already paranoid. Andrew was on the other side, helping Mick and Keith take over the band. It's too bad Brian was cast aside, but a lot of it was his own druggy fault.

The Rolling Stones, RCA Hollywood, 1965

I was writing about entertainment personalities – Sinatra, Elizabeth Taylor, Brigitte Bardot, Bobby Darin, Ray Charles. Greenwich Village was my beat. Dylan was the first one to tell me about the Stones; he'd seen them when he was in England. I never knew Andrew too well. He was always after the business side, I was after the artistes. I introduced everybody to everybody, brought Dylan and the Stones together, Dylan and the Beatles together. Brian was the most popular here at first. One time he said he'd fucked sixty-four girls in one month. I didn't believe Wyman was the big cock he says he was. Brian was really a druggy; any kind of pill you gave him he'd swallow it, didn't care what or when, any kind of pill, he didn't even ask what it was. It affected him. He had epilepsy, so I understand if he didn't take his seizure pills he could have died. Marijuana had opened everything up, enabled you to really hear the music and get into it, concentrate on it, a real gateway drug. Hanging out with the Stones was like hanging out at the children's table at a wedding, while hanging out with the Beatles was like sitting at the head table. The Beatles were like conquering emperors; the Stones were like wild kids.

**ALO:** I was in Clearwater, Florida in the late summer of 1999. We stayed at the Tropicana Sky Motel, one block off the beachfront ebbing on to the Gulf of Mexico looking towards Cartagena and the coast of Colombia. You drive into what passes for the centre of beachfront Clearwater, turn right and cross over the bridge towards downtown Clearwater and the causeway and freeway into Tampa. It's all very pleasant and Aryan Andy Garcia. You cross the bridge, wheel left and turn right two blocks later on to Fort Harrison Avenue. On the right, taking up the whole block, is FLAG, the southern East Coast Scientology centre. The Rolling Stones stayed there at the front of the second week of May 65. It was then known as the Fort Harrison Hotel, still is. Keith Richards stayed on the sixth floor overlooking the avenue, and that's where he changed life as we knew it and all our summers by writing the structure to 'Satisfaction'.

**Keith Richards**, *Rolling Stone* magazine: I woke up in the middle of the night, there was a cassette player next to the bed and an acoustic guitar. I pushed record and hit that riff for about a minute and a half, two minutes. Then I fell back to sleep. I left the tape running, and when I woke up the next morning I played it back. Amongst all the snoring I rediscovered and found the lick and the lyrical hook I'd come up with to accompany it.

**Nik Cohn**, *Awopbopaloobop Awopbamboom*: They weren't much on melody, their words were mostly slogans, and a lot of the songs were simply crap. None of this mattered. All that counted was sound – an adapted Spectorsound but less symphonic, less inflated – and the murderous mood it made. All din and mad atmosphere. Really, it was nothing but beat, smashed and crunched and hammered home like some amazing stampede. The words were lost. You were only left with chaos, beautiful anarchy. You drowned in noise. Their best record was probably 'Satisfaction'.

**Mick Jagger**, *Rolling Stone* magazine: The original lyric calls to mind the Chuck Berry song 'Thirty Days' which features the line 'I can't get no satisfaction from the judge'. Keith may have heard it back then, because it's not any way an English person would express it. I'm not saying he purposely nicked anything, but we played those records a lot. I wrote the song's verse by the motel pool the next day.

**ALO:** There is an order to the events that started on the sixth floor of the Fort Harrison Hotel and ended up with the Rolling Stones getting their very first international anthem. The first order remains that they were given the opportunity to record in America. This removed the intimidation and homage factor that belaboured bands chugging out US covers from cold mortuaric studios in West Hampstead and other grey slabs north and south of the Thames. The Stones were allowed to find themselves in America – the landscape was right there in front of them. All they had to do was write it up and embrace it on to tape. Recording in the Chess studios in Chicago and RCA in Los Angeles allowed them to be at one with their original inspiration.

On 9 May the group played the Air Crown Theatre in Chicago. The next day it was back to Chess. We recorded eighteen hours off and on the trot for two days, cutting four or five tracks. One of them was a harmonica-laden version of 'Satisfaction' that just would not do. It was acoustic-driven, wayward, and the hook registered as marginal to nowt. The only thing that rose above the scumline was Brian Jones blubbering like a sitcom outtake in search of a perennial residual. He was too enthusiastic about this version of 'Satisfaction' for it or him to be taken seriously. I'm sorry, dear Brian, if in my books as published by Random Above you think I've been giving you an unfair grilling in absentia, but, truth be told, by now you were becoming a daily liability and hourly pain-in-the-arse.

And so, back to 'Satisfaction'. We were not getting what I wanted or needed. The real deal it was not; rather, it was a step backward in the strides the band had been making with Mick and Keith's material. The track chugged and heaved in quicksand delayed by an echo all of its own. It had nothing to do with anything, let alone us. It sounded as if the Stones had done a version of the 1963 'Walk Right In' by the Rooftop Singers. This version called for striped shirts, Brylcreem, basketball slacks and a time-out. I was not happy; I heard a lot more but was not getting it. I said nothing because in those ol' days you didn't talk it out – you did it.

We flew to Los Angeles and headed straight for RCA. 'Satisfaction' was recorded again and nailed. It was unusual for a song to be allowed longer than thirty minutes to find its way, let alone be given a second chance, but there was something about 'Satisfaction' that had the whole group happy to whack it out once more in Hollywood.

'Satisfaction' is a house of cards in which no one player held the winning hand – the house did. Recording live offers the advantage of audio sensuality that layered-and-divided tech just cannot give you. A stab at the piano will leak over the room and connect with a certain smile of the high-hat or bass. They'll embrace and create a new harmonic, and you'll have that on tape even though no one person played it. It's the voodoo of space and tone.

Keith overdubbed the magical fuzz – his call – the bullets were now in the gun. He then laid down a bed of acoustic guitars in order for Mick to have something to ballad the verses to and avoid falling into the spaces and make opposites attract. He set up the spot for seduction, sleaze and ease. Jack Nitzsche played a stellar non-intrusive piano that glued the elements into that comfortable place. Jagger got it in one take, at his most pro and very best as he laid down one of the verses of the century. The acoustics were put back into their pocket and the group's first national anthem was mixed and ready to wreak havoc on the world. There's no drama to tell of – it snapped into place and got itself done in a day. The Rolling Stones and I belonged together for that wonderwhile, when we could do no wrong, and in that time came perfect recorded moments like these. With 'Satisfaction' maybe the weather helped; maybe Hollywood added that laconic, easy, successful feel.

I've read that Mick and Keith had doubts as to whether 'Satisfaction' should be a single, but I recall no doubt on anybody's part, including none from where we'd expected it – Ian Stewart, who just shook his head in quiet amazement at what his little three-chord wonders had just accomplished.

Everybody breathed a little easier as another sly side of fame was looked at via 'The Under Assistant West Coast Promotion Man', a fitting encore to the power of the day. It's an offhand tip of the hat to George Sherlock, our actual London Records West Coast promo man. George was all tan, B-movie hound's-tooth suits, Dane Clark meets Kramer in *Seinfeld*. He had a lot of questionables (i.e. a promotion man's Rolodex of 'wants and needs' so that he could cut to the chase and please), teased grey hair which we teased him about, and enough nerves to undermine the San Andreas fault-line. Our homage was a good call. The last time the Stones had mocked one up was to me via Mick and Phil Spector's 'Andrew's Blues,' cut out of hysterical relief at having nailed 'Not Fade Away' in London's Regent Sound Denmark Street office in February of 64. This time there were no hysterics. We are what we repeatedly do, and that's what this wonderful game gave us the opportunity to become – art. Excellence, a field in which the Stones were replacing dreams with reality, is not an act, but a habit. My boys were becoming hit-cutting men.

Two days later the group continued on with the West Coast leg of the tour and I flew to New York to master the two sides with Big Dom at Bell Sound. '(I Can't Get No) Satisfaction' b/w 'The Under Assistant West Coast Promotion Man' was released in the US at the end of May and would ripple-release around the rest of the world in the coming summer months. 'Satisfaction' would chart no. 1 in thirty-eight countries. As Anthony De Curtis put it in his 1998 *Rolling Stone* piece, 'The Making Of "(I Can't Get No) Satisfaction" ': 'In the summer of 65 – on the radio, in the streets, in the car, at the beach – it sometimes seemed that there was only one song and that was "Satisfaction".'

We all got a few days off. Mick and Keith drove through Arizona and Civil War buff Charlie went to Gettysburg. Bill and Brian collected their due by remaining in LA as the only Stones in town. With the success of Mick and Keith's songwriting came an inevitable split in the group – and resentments.

**Denny Bruce**, ex-Mothers of Invention: I always heard stories and always assumed that the Stones would have been big grass smokers. By the time I met them – this would be the *Aftermath* sessions – they were introduced to the really good, green stuff. The first night we were all together, Brian and I were at Jack Nitzsche's house. The Stones' US road manager Michael Gruber was there with an attractive girl. Keith was there, too. Michael had on this expensive suit and was trying to impress this model, and Brian made him get down on all fours like a dog. Michael had said, with his New York accent, 'Man, I've been smoking shit since I was eleven'. He takes about two hits and is now on all fours, barking, and those guys are all rolling on the floor, laughing. I looked around for Brian, and he was out in the kitchen making a mustard, ketchup and mayonnaise sandwich and eating it, with it dripping off his chin. Yet he's dressed immaculately, and his hair looks like a Breck shampoo commercial.

Joey Paige was from Philadelphia, where he had been in a band that Dick Clark made famous called Dickey Do & the Don'ts. Somehow, he hooked up with the Everly Brothers, got to go to England, and the Stones played with them. Joey became friends with Bill Wyman. When the Stones came to LA, Bill produced a single for them called 'Cause I'm In Love With You' on the Tollie label. The song was written by Sonny Bono. The 45 began with, 'Hello, I'm Bill Wyman of the Rolling Stones, and I've just produced my good friend Joey Paige, and I hope you like it!'

**ALO**: I'd have killed Joey Paige and Bill Wyman if I'd heard that intro.

On the morning of 24 May I was back in California, and by the afternoon I was on the transatlantic flight to London. Sheila had gone into labour. Reg collected me at London Airport in the Lincoln Continental and braked and raced me to the Haverstock Hill Hospital well over the speed limit and in just under half an hour. I was nervous, tired and excited – mostly nervous. The doctors informed me that all was in order with Sheila and bairn, and that 'nothing much would be happening for an hour or so . . .' I was relieved; this allowed me to repair to the car for a joint. When I ambled calmly back into the hospital my son had been born to share the same birthday as Bob Dylan. In honour of our mate Sean Kenny, our boy would be named Sean.

**Sheila Klein Oldham**: Andrew wasn't a doting father. He was always working. He didn't know what a family was; he was brought up in a series of boarding schools so he had no idea what a family was. He just didn't have a clue. We very rarely ever sat down for a family meal together. If we ever did it just seemed terribly uncomfortable. He'd rather roll in at three o'clock in the morning and have scrambled eggs in the kitchen. There's only so much a person can do. He had those other babies called the Rolling Stones, who yelled louder. He was their mother and father; there wasn't any room for anybody else.

## · CHAPTER 10 ·

**Kurt Vonnegut**: Don't waste your time on jealousy. Sometimes you're ahead, sometimes you're behind. The race is long and, in the end, it's only with yourself.

**Michael Lindsay-Hogg**, writer/director: The Ad Lib was the club of clubs. On any given night (if it was a Friday, they'd probably been on *Ready Steady Go!*, my show of shows) you could see, sitting on the banquette on the right as you came in, a couple of Beatles, a Rolling Stone or two, visiting Americans, Bob Dylan, Nico, Byrds and assorted Animals, Kinks, Yardbirds, Pretty Things. One evening I was there with a date (why not call it a fig or a kumquat, I wondered sometimes) and was engaged in an important conversation when, in the dark, someone tripped over my outstretched Anello & Davide wedge-toed boot. I looked down and, seeing another Anello & Davide wedge-toed boot, knew the person would probably be okay. I looked up, and who was it but ALO? I was delighted to see him because I hadn't for a while, nor any of his chauffeurs or bodyguards or Stones. He explained that they'd been away, in America, recording, and were now back, brimming with their usual confidence and dangerous swagger. We immediately agreed on the Rolling Stones being on *Ready Steady Go!* in two weeks to début the new songs, including one that Andrew was especially hyped about. It was called 'Satisfaction' and, Andrew said, had the first lyric about a girl having her period in the entire history of popular music, as far as he knew, although maybe some sixteenth-century troubadour whose name he couldn't remember had alluded to it. As we stood watching the band rehearse a couple of weeks later, Andrew gave me a sophisticated nod as Mick sang what the girl is saying: 'Baby, better come back maybe next week, can't you see I'm on a losing streak.'

**ALO:** The Beatles recorded their last-ever live radio session for BBC radio for broadcast on 7 June 1965. That same week Buckingham Palace announced the Fab Four were to be honoured with MBEs. Some old medal holders did not approve and returned their medals to Buckingham Palace in disgust.

The contract between the Decca Record Company and Impact Sound had now run its course and the matter could no longer be ignored. While I had been in the US with the Stones Eric Easton had been negotiating with the powers that be at Decca, and on my return he presented the results of his efforts to me as a *fait accompli*. The new deal boasted an advance of £600,000 which, once investigated, turned out to be not an advance but a figure based on an 'if earned' basis. The value of the deal was double whammy'd by the fact that due to the way record companies paid foreign earnings (a year to eighteen months later than the sale date) Decca was only offering up money we had *already* earned. I raided the shortcomings of the deal with Eric in my most diplomatic tone, but managed to infuriate him anyway. He told me to 'stick to the creative side' and leave the business to him.

The Stones took their place in the wings and placed bets on the result of this contest of wills and ego as Eric and I circled each other centre stage. The deal smelt – Eric was pushing for it far too hard. It would turn out to have golden parachute factors in it for him, a capital gain made possible by the fact that he had already moved the rights to the Stones' recordings into Eric Easton Ltd and out of Impact Sound. I now owned nowt of the work I had done and, further, was beholden to Eric for every penny. This was not a partnership – it was an employment contract without the contract. This data is third party information given to me and the group; I did not see either the deal written up, nor sight the assets of Eric Easton Ltd. What I did know first-hand was that Eric was pissed with me and, to him, this deal was his entitlement. He had had enough of me and, deal done, would be saying goodbye to us all. So he was really pushing for broke – and the Stones and I were the ones that would be. I was nervous. This was a game I hadn't played or studied and the Stones watched for some inkling of an outcome. Mick and Keith were natch concerned about my ability to combat Easton on this huge issue; they knew what was and was not the area of my expertise.

Bill Wyman and Brian Jones sided with Eric. They still believed in the man who had worked hard and well for their career, and they regarded him as more for 'the group' as opposed to my being glued to the glimmer brothers. They perceived Eric to be the steady balance required against my media-driven madness, Bill because that had been his experience, and Brian because Eric had no great affection for Mick, Keith or me. As for Charlie, he shrugged his well-tailored shoulders, smiled at Ian Stewart, and then went home to Shirley leaving us to sort the mess out. I attempted to get on with my day-for-night business, unaware that the next day's movie would change the state of our nation and all the rules of play.

I had set a breakfast meet at the London Hilton with J.W. Alexander, who was Sam Cooke's publishing partner in both Kags Music and Cooke's independent record label, SAR. Kags Music published the Bobby Womack-composed 'It's All Over Now,' the Valentinos' song that Murray the K had given us and we had recorded at Chess. It had gone Top 10 in the UK and Top 30 in the States and moved us on up around the rest of the world. Now, though a trifle late, I was looking for a piece of the publishing – never missing an opportunity to polish my craft and seize another Johnny Jackson–Sidney Falco moment, one foot gliding through Soho, t'other steppin' out on Broadway.

I crossed the Hilton lobby shortly before 9 a.m., averting my eyes from the goodies calling my name in the watch and jewellery store to the right of the hotel entrance swing-glass doors. I strode past the reception, enjoying the click of my heels as they slapped on the marble with a gratifying echo, timing my steps. I wore the choco brown Pierre Cardin butter leather boots and a rich brown and dull gold-striped double-breasted suit with inverted pleat, covered buttons, flared sleeve and trouser cuffs with slash pockets on the trews and jacket. This much yellow had me looking like a pink-zitted albino canary who should have stayed in bed. No matter – I went for joke with a roll-collared yellow linen shirt.

I glided towards the lobby's breakfast and coffee shop nestled in the far right-hand corner. I had become a regular here, loved the no-nonsense, no-menu, £7 eggs. There was a pre-Kojak moment of 'Who loves you, baby?' as the actor Telly Savalas held centre court, ordering breakfast with his engaging seductive rasp as his eyes ogled anything and everything and counted, as an actor will, how many sets of eyes were ogling his. He was in London filming his part as one of Robert Aldrich's *The Dirty Dozen*.

In the corner I spied my breakfast date as he casually recognised me and parted the seas with a welcoming wave. J.W. Alexander was a cheerfully robust black gentleman with comfortable crinkly eyes and smile, gospel in his heart and soul, and greyblack hair that seemed to recede into a halo. There's a kind of relaxed that God giveth out and he gave it unto J.W. It's the kind of relaxed I'll never be, even at the height of calm. The man looked like Don King all gone to heaven and all forgiven. He wore a camel hair blazer, brown sports shirt, slacks and loafers. The buckle on his belt emphasised his happy girth and promoted some team or other. Having made my sweeping crane shot entrance into the coffee shop in one Scorsese take, eyed and admired the future Kojak, greeted and been greeted by this large percussive dark angel, I took my bearings.

I paused to ready, sitting down with continuing one-shot aplomb when I realised that J.W. Alexander was not alone. We stood; he paused and turned to the man on his left. 'Andrew,' he smiled, 'say hello to Allen Klein.' Mr Allen Klein got up, we shook hands and we all sat down and, in that five seconds, I'd said hello to another length of my life. For all the toughness I would from this moment on observe Allen displaying on behalf of himself and his clients, he had the most petite soft feminine hands I'd ever skinned with this side of Vivien Leigh. Martin Sheen could play him now, but Allen owns the whole wing, not just the west one. Back then in the day only Allen could play himself as he played you and offered you a world he ruled.

He had cut his teeth on Steve Lawrence & Eydie Gorme, Bobby Darin, Bobby Vinton, Sam Cooke and an earlier foray into the film business. Then he set his sights on the teething British Invasion and honed in first on Mickie Most, then the Stones and me, then Donovan, and finally the Beatles. Along the way he crossed swords – for and with – the Who and the Kinks. He was the modern-day music biz Yank in King Arthur's court; Allen came, saw, conquered and, some would have it, plundered. He definitely raised the stakes of the game. He was in his early thirties, casually dressed in sports shirt and slacks, and I liked him. He was not greasy; he did not have three chins. He did not swear like a trooper or a gangster. He spoke calmly, invitingly and warmly and had eyes that pierced through you like James Caan working the first Tangerine Dream'd twelve minutes in Michael Mann's *Thief*. On meeting Mick Jagger on the towpath outside the Station Hotel in Richmond, I'd felt Jagger's eyes asking me what was I doing with the rest of his life. Allen's search seemed to be asking me: was I in control of any part of my life, or better yet, the life of the Stones?

**Mickie Most**: Between Andrew and me, we pretty much had it covered. We were our own masters. In other words, we owned everything, we recorded it, paid for it, we really did our own thing . . . we were not working for a record company. George Martin worked for EMI; he was an A&R man. We worked for ourselves. Thirty-five years ago working for yourself in the British music business was very rare; we were the first ones. It was a learning curve for the likes of Andrew and me and a whole bunch of people. We were amateurs. We took the creative side away from the record companies, found the artists and made the records ourselves and took the tapes to the record companies and said you like it or you don't like it. Then we went on to form independent record companies and provide the product ourselves – do everything ourselves.

When I came back from South Africa the main reason was to produce records. I produced all my own records in South Africa; I felt I had more to offer as a producer than anybody else. One of the first places I went to as an act with the Rolling Stones on the Everly Brothers tour was Newcastle. I went to a club and saw the Animals. I recorded them and they had all the hits. I next recorded the Nashville Teens because Don Arden introduced me to them. I took them into the studio and made 'Tobacco Road'. It was a big hit and I cut another couple of tracks with them. Then they wanted to go off and do their own thing and that was pretty much the end of my association with Don Arden. Then came Herman's Hermits. I had thirty-five hits with them – ten no. 1s in the US – and sold nearly a hundred million records.

Allen Klein came into my life in 1964, after I'd had three no. 1s on the trot in America by three different artists. I got a phone call in London from this guy named Klein, who told me he was in London to sign the Beatles. I said, 'They're already signed,' he said, 'No, what I really mean is I want to take care of their career in America.' I told him, 'You'll find that very difficult because they're the hottest thing in the world.' He said, 'I know that, but I can make them a million dollars. But if I don't get to sign the Beatles for America, I've still got the million dollars and I'll give it to you.'

That sounded quite attractive to me. Allen called me about a week later from the Savoy and invited me up to say hello. I went up and he said he'd make me a million dollars and he did. Allen was well ahead of the game. I spent my time making records and he made sure that the records made more money for everybody, and the only way you can do that is to make the record companies pay more. Allen Klein's whole thing was, 'We'll renegotiate your deal; you are not getting enough.' He was 101 per cent correct. Royalty rates were a joke – half royalties on overseas sales, so everything outside the UK was cut in half. The major UK labels took tremendous advantage. Allen Klein came along and said, 'Stop, you can't do this. You've got to give these people a fair royalty.' And that's exactly what he did; he actually changed people's royalty rate and he certainly did increase my income. Allen got very obsessed with signing the Beatles. The Stones were much more aggravation than he counted on. He was one of these guys who had that love-the-one-you're-with vibe. First time I met Allen the big thing in his life was Sam Cooke; then it was Bobby Vinton. Then I came along and Bobby Vinton got pushed to the side a bit, then the Beatles came along and the Stones got pushed. That's what seemed to happen.

**Allen Klein**: I never had anything to do with the Animals; I was helping Mickie Most. Mickie Most was good for them. I met Mickie in September 1964, before I met Andrew. He played me three records, all by different artists: the Nashville Teens' 'Tobacco Road', the Animals' 'The House Of The Rising Sun', and Herman's Hermits' 'I'm Into Something Good'. Each one was a song not written by the artist. Mickie had great ears and was a former artist himself. He had three records by three different artists; you gotta be impressed. I told Mickie I'd get him a million dollars and I did. Mickie owned his masters. I bought them from him because he wanted to get a capital gain. Andrew? I bought his because he forced me to, he sued me.

**ALO**: Allen told me of his later being interested in representing Brian Wilson and of the non-surfing savant agreeing to meet with him in the Warwick Hotel in New York. When Allen walked into the room, Brian was sitting down with his feet up on the coffee table. He just raised his arms up in the air and said to Allen, 'Okay, dazzle me.' Allen certainly dazzled me and the Stones, at least in the Mick and Keith department, and that's what was driving the train. He may have been almost the same age as Eric Easton, but America and the streets deemed him younger, more agile, interested and interesting. More us and for us. He appealed to the orphan in you and offered you a home. In short order, we had a killer on our side who would handle Easton and Decca – and the Stones and I could get on with the work. The cost is still being debated by those who care and do not subscribe to there being no victims (only volunteers). This was not the nowadays of CDs and video and two leisurely years between product releasement and tours. In our day we needed a single every twelve weeks. The group was on tour fifty weeks of the year and the business with Easton was making us late at the gate. Had Allen and I not found each other, Easton and Decca would have remained a liability – and would have made me one with the Rolling Stones.

**Sean O'Mahony**: Andrew really didn't want to be bothered with all the business. He wanted to evade it and avoid it. That's when Allen Klein took control. Eric didn't see any other way than to attack Andrew to get what he thought was his due other than by going through the normal legal process. The argument was always with Decca, who were holding all the money, as to how the money should be split. The eventual settlement was that Decca

Allen Klein and ALO, Hilton Hotel, London, 1965

agreed to pay all, or most of it, that was owed to Eric. Management partnerships never work. With the inevitable strains and stresses of managing the Stones, it was inevitable that Andrew and Eric would fall out. When people fall out, it's acrimonious; when big money is involved it's even more acrimonious. Eric often talked to me about the legal dispute. He'd go into the various aspects of the negotiations, who said what, the situation with Decca and Klein and so on. The money with Decca was always delayed; that caused a lot of the tension. Eric handled it like a normal dispute. He obviously was annoyed that he'd been elbowed out.

**Allen Klein**: I administered Sam Cooke's music publishing and the Stones had done the Bobby Womack song 'It's All Over Now'. Sam had just died. Andrew was going to get the song if he could get a cover in England. I saw him and he wanted half the song. I said 'Not a chance. You should pay me double; I'm giving you a hit.' I was surprised; I thought I was going to meet Eric Easton. I'd read that Easton was the only one out there and that Andrew was more like a part of the act. He was young and, y'know, he was a surprise. He and Tony Calder came up to the Hilton Hotel in London. I was there with J.W. Alexander, who was Sam Cooke's partner. We had a meeting, he brought over some agreements. I knew pretty much that he wanted me to check into things. I happened to be pretty busy at the time with a couple of matters, so he came to New York and he signed an agreement with me. I used to tell Andrew that if he had been the same age as I was at the time he would have beaten my arse.

When I met him he was twenty-one, and if I'd been twenty-one he would have beaten me; he was that bright. I got lucky. 'Satisfaction' was done. I made an agreement with Andrew to manage him, that I could represent him on behalf of the Stones. I said, let me speak to Jagger; if they say, 'Do it', I'll do it. I didn't want to get in the middle. And so Andrew and I went down to the CBS Records convention in Miami and Jagger flew down and I asked him, 'Do you want me to do this for Andrew?' He said yes and I went back to England. I flew into London. I think I had copies of the documents, somehow I think Bill Wyman had copies of them, and then I set up this meeting at Decca. I said to the Stones, 'Okay, just don't say a word, just act angry.' That's what happened and we got the deal signed in five days. I never met Eric Easton. I'd said get Eric Easton to come; I said let's get all the liars in one room. Eric wouldn't come. You're going to have one guy who is going to deny this and that's Bill Wyman. Bill Wyman was Eric's guy. I'm sure it disappointed him, getting taken in. It was very fast, five days. The deal was for the world, exclusive of US and Canada. Then we made a deal in America. I didn't make the deal for the US in England; we cut that off. That's when we formed our own company and we were the manufacturer. That's what happened. We made the records, recorded the records, Andrew did all the art. We then put it together and London told us how many they needed and we shipped them. Remember, Andrew owned the masters; he owned them, not the Stones. We got a million dollars for the United States and Canada paid directly to Andrew and the Stones. I got none of that. I told Andrew that he and the Stones should get their money direct from London Records individually. We spread the payments so they didn't have to pay tax on it. What else can you do? You can either sell or you can spread it.

**ALO**: The next artist I discovered and recorded was Vashti. She was introduced to me by my shining granddame-in-armour from my press cutting days, Monte Mackay. Monte lived in Grosvenor House – hallowed ground for me as it also housed Laurence Harvey and James Woolf – and she was chief rooster at the Mount Street Al Parker Agency. Monte was the sophisticated and sexy Lauren Bacall literary agent to James Caan's writer in *Misery*. She had removed some of my misery by letting me into her life and letting me press-rep would-be popster Jess Conrad for a fiver a week back in 1960. I had a huge crush on Miss Mackay; I developed an even bigger one for Vashti.

**Nik Cohn**: Vashti I remember very vividly. She was very much of the Marianne Faithfull school. I found her very provocative; she got my number more than Marianne did. Then she disappeared quite quickly. I remember interviewing her. She kept saying, 'I've been told I must be lively. Does that mean I have to tell jokes?' So I more or less made up the interview for her, doing both her answers and my questions, and I liked that.

**Vashti**: I showed some of my songs to a friend and the friend approached Andrew who was lunching nearby. He arranged to hear me sing. He didn't pretend to be interested and at the end sent me out of the room. It was horrible. Then he said he wanted to record me and gave me a Jagger and Richards song to do.

**ALO**: Alas, Vashti was viewed as an auburn Marianne Faithfull spin-off, which more than dented the trail I had hoped to blaze for her. She was a beautiful original with a body Mick Jagger would have wished on his other self. A continental waif off the top Françoise Hardy shelf, she was so far from the madding crowd and I wanted to stop the day's shooting and take some time out in her world. She had a sensuality and rhythm I wanted into. I wanted to walk with her in the hills of Tuscany, I wanted to dine with her by the sea in Sicily. I wanted to make her an offer she would not refuse. I wanted to wake with her in the morning in a shuttered room listening to the sounds in the Piazza Navona – but I bit my tongue instead of her ear. I did not want to scare her or ask her to touch that remaining part of me that was still and dead. I never believed I had a position that allowed me to indulge in rudeness of the heart, even though I was rude on many another occasion. I also knew I'd turn on the two of us – that was the nature of my lame and game. So I listened to my heart, acknowledged its scream, explained the reality to it of *omerta* and its role in my life, slapped it better and moved into song. The song was Mick and Keith's 'Some Things Just Stick In Your Mind', a fitting song and title for my vinyl excursion of the heart with Vashti. When the record was released she would suffer from the Marianne comparison. I'd thought of keeping her recordings unreleased for my ears only, but in the cold light morning that was unrealistic. I didn't really record her successfully, by which I mean I didn't quite capture her eyes. As you can tell, Vashti put my life in quite a flutter – and I'm glad she did. I needed that flutter as I slipped into park.

I needed that boy-meets-girl reminder; I never asked for the get. Perhaps it was already lonely at the the top – or perhaps I had the advantaged special life I'd fought for, but had no idea of how to live it. Later she came to 138 Ivor Court one day when the record was out and over. It was raining heavily outside and she had a scruffy little dog with her on a lead made out of string. The mutt looked at me very knowingly. It wanted nothing and it didn't sing. Vashti wore an old raincoat French movies are made of. I looked into those eyes I had not quite recorded, said nothing, put my heart back into my pocket and returned to the madness of my day.

The Beat Boom was diversifying in the late summer of 1965 and making room to share its good lot with folk-rock. Bob Dylan, whose art was now bordering on the commercial, had started to make his impact in America. The Byrds had been brought to CBS and produced by Terry Melcher, and their version of Dylan's 'Mr Tambourine Man' was a big hit. America was finding its own voice. Motown still defined the way America danced, but Dylan was starting to speak for it all. He had risen out of the coffee bars and into the trailer parks, out of the Greenwich Village cul-de-sacs and on to Highways 61 and 66. He opened up the space with his awesome Al Kooper-driven 'Like A Rolling Stone'. Dylan had his finger up and on the pulse of America. I reviewed the recording at the time for *Disc and Music Week* and said, 'Whether he likes it or not, this man is so commercial and has his finger on the pulse just that little bit ahead of everybody else, which makes him unique. "Like A Rolling Stone" is the most fantastic thing he has done, a Dylan version of "Twist And Shout" with a little Tamla Motown thrown in.' Lou Adler would perfect folk-rock as a Top 10 art by year's end with his recording of 'Eve Of Destruction' by Barry McGuire.

**Nik Cohn**, *Awopbopaloobop Awopbamboom*: The epicentre of California hip was Lou Adler. He managed Johnny Rivers and Jan & Dean. Johnny Rivers was a small roughneck from Louisiana and he was America's first major discotheque star. Discos were an early 60s development and an improvement on big impersonal concert halls. Discotheque records had to be dancing records, and that's what Rivers turned out. He played Elmer Valentine's Whisky À Go-Go and laid down a solid beat, nothing fancy, four-square all the way. He chalked up hit after hit and never smiled once. He gave me the toughest interview I ever did in my life. Every question I asked, he answered by grunting. High grunt for yes, low grunt for no. And all the time I was there he looked straight past me at Lou Adler and Adler looked back at him, both of them expressionless. This wasn't being moronic, this was being cool. This was image. Adler was a very successful man and a very tough one.

From the whole Californian image race Adler emerged as the runaway winner. I have a photograph of the Adler team in London. They have tried to get into the hotel restaurant and have been told they can't sit down without ties. So they're all sitting around a corner table with assorted flunkies and girls, and Adler and Rivers are wearing T-shirts, flash jackets and so forth, but they're wearing completely incongruous ties, old school models supplied by the restaurant. They look quite ridiculous. But they're not smiling, they're deadpan. They see absolutely nothing funny. And that was California cool.

**Al Aronowitz**: First came Dylan, then came the Beatles and then came the Stones . . . the Stones were no. 3 on my list. The Beatles had conquered the world in a flash, but Dylan had set out to secure a more persuasive hold on the future and felt he'd been more uncompromising than the Beatles in achieving success. Dylan felt his success, if not greater, was purer, and scorned the Beatles as bubble-gum music. Dylan told me he would never cater to screaming teenyboppers by making 45 rpm singles for Top Forty radio. These stations were called Top Forties because they played only the top forty records from the *Billboard* and *Cashbox* charts. If Dylan didn't like Top Forty, the feeling was mutual. Programme directors and disc jockeys considered Bob Dylan the most unlikely artist to come up with a Top Forty hit and yet, with 'Like A Rolling Stone', Bob not only crossed over into Top Forty but demolished another wall by getting a hit with a six-minute single when everybody said you'd never get a record played that was over two forty.

'You've got to be psychically armed' is what Bob used to boast – and he knew he was. He used to taunt me with, 'Why don't you go ask Mick Jagger if he thinks he's psychically armed? Go on, Al, why don't you ask him?' Bob Dylan, that hipper-than-thou player, plays a vicious hardball. He was king at a time when some razor-tongued originals put the dis into disrespect. When he got finished putting you down, you could crawl out of the door through the keyhole. He could also slit your throat and you'd never even bleed.

It'd taken Mick and me years to start to get to know each other. I'd never been too swift. Me, I was the kind of simp who needed eons to figure things out. We'd met back in 1964, the night of the Stones' very first Carnegie Hall concert, when they'd hit shore riding the trough behind the Beatlemania wave. Like when Avis was no. 2, the Stones had to try harder. They'd got themselves barred from some English pop TV show because of their nastiness and they'd kept running through London, drumming up all kinds of headlines to prove their sympathy with the devil. They tried to make the Beatles look like cherubs with pink asses and powdered faces. The Beatles were no angels. The Stones came on punk not only because it was fun to act arrogant but also because they needed to get noticed.

When I opened the auditorium door of Carnegie Hall that night, it was like somebody splashed a bucket of sound in my face. The Stones'd already started playing when I walked in. The sound was so thick I had to push a path through it just to get down the aisle. I'd already been hanging out with the Beatles, nailing them when they'd first stepped off the plane at Idlewild so I could write a cover story for the *Saturday Evening Post*. But the Stones were something else. Not better, but different. Any group that dug Marvin Gaye's 'Can I Get A Witness' enough to put it on their album two times had to be cool. The Marvin Gaye record was a pet of mine and Dylan's, too. He'd stayed up until dawn listening to it over and over again while he wrote 'Mr Tambourine Man' one night. Bob couldn't believe this English rock hype, this Beatlemania bullshit. I kept telling him about the Beatles but he'd just put me down. He thought he was the only thing happening. Then he'd gone to England and had come back raving about this new group he'd caught at a concert in Hyde Park or someplace in London, raving about how free they were. That's the word he kept using, free. They were free, loose, uninhibited, fresh. That was my word for the Stones. Fresh.

On stage at Carnegie Hall, I noticed how Brian Jones, with his orange-gold hair, kept stepping up to the footlights to tease the teenyboppers into defying the cops stationed there, tempting them to jump the stage and grab him. After the show, I walked across Seventh Avenue to the Park Sheraton with my wife and Gloria Stavers, a skyscraper-tall beauty queen type with a Southern accent that'd grown hip on New York's jazz circuit. Gloria amused herself by being the first to score each new young sexy rock star for an interview in her role as editor of *16*, the magazine that was cashing in on the prepubescent void by merchandising pinups of these cutie boys to diaper rashes learning desire.

The Stones were throwing a party at the Park Sheraton, where they'd checked into adjoining rooms. They couldn't afford suites yet. The first thing we saw when we walked in was Mick sitting on a bed surrounded by a flock of elegantly styled chicks fluttering as if they all wanted to rub his body. That's what one of them was doing. Okay. Mick'd discovered room service. Like the ball-carrier, the lead singer always got to be the star. Immediately, Gloria and my wife tried to get into Mick's action. I couldn't hack it. What beaconed me was Brian Jones' Day-Glo-like hair. He was standing in Carnaby Street's last word, up to his neck in Mod, a drink in his hand, hopping with energy as he talked to Bill Wyman. Brian was like a Fourth of July sparkler, spraying excitement. When we plugged into each other, it was as if we had a million things to rap about. We ducked into the adjoining room.

'It's not simple to get those coloured blues records 'n England,' Brian was saying. 'I 'ad t'go searchin' everywhere. But that's all the group does, coloured records. We just give our own feelin' to it . . .'

Suddenly my wife was next to me again. 'Boy, is he conceited!' she said about Mick.

'Whatsamatter?'

'I went up to him and told him I liked the show. And he said, 'Should I be flattered?''

That'd soured me on Mick. He judged books by their covers. I liked my wife. The Stones were babies in those days. They didn't even smoke pot. Eight years later at the St Regis, I watched as Mick hunched over the coffee table with the rolled-up twenty. I always let Mick take the lion's share. I figured he needed it.

At the July 65 Newport Folk Festival Dylan tried to play electric but was booed and heckled off the stage. Some said Bob was in tears. I'd been rooting for him to go electric, which would make his music more accessible. He had something to say and more people should be hearing it. I argued that the purists, the academics, the old guard and the fundamentalists always existed, change being the only thing that is constant in the universe.

**ALO**: I had met Bob Dylan and his manager Albert Grossman at the Cumberland Hotel in London in 1962, when Dylan made his first UK appearance on the BBC American beatnik-style television drama *Madhouse on Castle Street*, written by Jack London. I'd got a fiver to handle Dylan for the week. At the time, Grossman was a very casually dressed, neat, grey-haired guy, nothing like the ponytailed wild man of Woodstock he would become. He looked like a well-to-do lawyer in his weekend clothes. His devotion to Dylan was apparent and this singular devotion impressed and inspired me. I remembered it well when I went to work on the Rolling Stones. They were both very happy together. They acted like they knew something we didn't know yet. Bob Dylan already was.

Listening to the playback of 'Like A Rolling Stone'; sitting L to R, Roy Halee, Tom Wilson, Albert Grossman, Artie Mogul, Sandy Speiser and Al Kooper; standing, Pete Duryea and Bob Dylan. CBS studios, New York, 1965

**Fred Goodman**, *The Mansion on the Hill*: On 1 June 1965, drummer Bobby Gregg's opening snare-drum beat on Bob Dylan's 'Like A Rolling Stone' resounded like a rifle shot from radios across the country and announced a musical revolution. In the three years leading up to that moment, Dylan's songs had already defined the lyric parameters of popular music, demonstrating better than any others that the seemingly simple folk idiom could express the most sophisticated and ambiguous emotions. But this was something else – this was a rock record. It was not a two minute and thirteen second rock 'n' roll single made by Chuck Berry or Little Richard or the Beach Boys or even the Beatles. It wasn't about dancing or driving or teenage love lost and found. This was an electric epic, simple in its music but remarkably complex and ambitious in its scope. Its length, subject matter and performance were totally at odds with what constituted a hit single. 'Like A Rolling Stone' erased every rule of pop music. It was the voice, not of a pop star, but of the bitter truth. 'Like A Rolling Stone' became a huge hit and did more than any other record of its era to direct rock away from the constraints of the singles format. Rock music was capable of far more than almost anyone had imagined. Albert Grossman was right; his client was an artist.

**Chris Hutchins**: We were out on a boat on the Hudson, out on the river all day Sunday, on Allen Klein's yacht. Andrew was there talking to Klein and I interrupted and broke into a conversation in which Andrew and Keith were asking Klein how they could get rid of Brian Jones. I don't mean kill him; they just wanted him out of the group. I thought this would make a great story for the *NME*. I still ran the news desk at the paper, except we just didn't run stories like that. We wrote only good things about rock stars, or nothing at all – that was the way it still was. That night we all sailed, me, Klein, Andrew and Keith, on the boat right into the back of Shea Stadium for the Beatles concert. Back at home the furor would not die down over the Beatles being given MBEs. Four years later John Lennon would return his to Buckingham Palace.

**Peter Noone**: If you think about that moment the Beatles got the MBEs, it was very confusing, because, if for anybody, you'd kind of think of Sir Cliff & the Shadows. Not for the Beatles. We thought they were on the other team. It was a very confusing time – a cultural and political revolution, not just a musical revolution. Like the Beatles smoking a joint in Buckingham Palace because they were so embarrassed that they were getting those MBEs. That's what they said afterwards – that they smoked a joint there – but they probably never did.

**ALO**: At the time of all this hoopla I wrote about it in *Disc and Music Echo* as so:

The Beatles, who have had every word possible, good and bad, said about them in their meteoric rise to stardom. This group, whose talent has made them mean much more as representatives of our country than the shabby government under which we live. The whole world makes a star and the whole world helps to break one. The Beatles go on from success to success and this week release a truly fantastic record 'Help!' from the film of the same name. This record is great and proves beyond doubt that the Beatles are still head and shoulders above the rest of pop music and, far from being finished, are still growing, not only financially, but as artists. It is a very hard task to grow inwardly and mature as an artist in beat music and still remain commercial. This the Beatles have done and I salute them.

Brian Epstein responded to the thoughts of Chairman O with the following: 'Andrew is an incredible person. Whilst the media still plays up rivalry between the world's two top groups, this is an example of the groups' managers and their artists enjoying each other's success.' We were all certainly enjoying our room at the top, with omnipotent largesse and more than a grain of *pro patria*. I was also unwittingly setting myself up for the fall. It's unsettling, as in writing this and walking the beach in Malibu and seeing the ghost of Laurence Harvey past, sitting elegantly in new faded denims looking the twenty-six miles to Catalina Island, nursing a glass of chilled Chardonnay and the increasing pain in his gut.

Laurence Harvey, Malibu, 1972

## · CHAPTER 11 ·

**Keith Richards**: It's no longer funny, it's bigger than money.

**ALO**: In May 1965 'Satisfaction' was recorded and released three weeks later all over the North Americas. It was the first Stones US no. 1 and perhaps England has never forgiven its second greatest hitmakers for treating America to this audiogem first, putting the UK in second place with an autumn 65 release. The single had not been released in the UK due to the Easton/Decca brouhaha and the arrival on the scene of Allen Klein, who'd started to handle our business in June 65. Life with Klein moved us to a new and fatter gradient.

The Stones toured the UK in September and October with the Spencer Davis Group and the Moody Blues and then headed straight for the US and their fourth tour across the North Americas, the first with actual money in their hands. This tour would feature at different east/west locations the Byrds, Patti Labelle & the Bluebelles, the Shangri-Las, the Righteous Brothers, Bo Diddley, We Five and Paul Revere & the Raiders. The group went away on this tour boys, still fresh, enjoying their new toys. They came back men. The non-stop tour continued back Down Under in January 1966, up through Europe, back to the States, back to Europe (stopping to record at every opportunity in Los Angeles) and then, basically, the first golden run was over. The spark was gone, the glimmer was dim and from April 67 till the second run that began in late 69, *sans* yours truly, the Rolling Stones did not step on stage and there were no more tours.

From May 65 to March 67 the Stones received eight US gold singles for the eight singles released and six gold album awards. When they returned to the UK in November 1966 the boys were tired, wondering about the cost of money and fame, and in need of rest.

One part of their souls resided in a bizarre revisitation of Baudelairean nineteenth-century debauch and baroque, the other in a Neanderthal and pretentious, psychedically entitled and tripped-out world. With leisure came drugs and their aftermath, removing the need for watchclocks or moral compasses. Mistakes were made as obviously-out-of-it velvet-clad rock stars tripped out of Rolls-Royces into their King's Road abodes. It was much too near both the copper shop around the bend and the real money lurking around the corner. The Stones were tolerated, even loved from afar, while away and on the road they could be 'confused with earners'. But fame and familiarity bred contempt and, while they may have been able to purchase respectability, they were about to learn they were considered neither worthy nor to the manor born. They'd been allowed to lay waste in the suburbs but they were not welcome to sketch arrogant in the drawing rooms that sought to rule their world. Oh, later Mick was allowed back in when he was harmless and had had his claws removed; but the 'in' had always belonged to Keith, and Keith wasn't interested.

Back on that first 64 tour you'll recall I'd been taken by Sonny Bono to RCA's studio B on Sunset. Jack Nitzsche, with Dave Hassinger at the controls, was producing the vocals for a Spector 'Zip-A-De-Doo-Dah'-type version of 'Yes, Sir, That's My Baby' for Atlantic Records. There was no actual group, just a moniker invented for a group of session singers and friends that Jack and Sonny had pulled together. I watched and marvelled at the laid-back professionalism that pervaded the room, a far cry from the shame attached to the game in Britain of late. This was an original American art form and hustle, and everybody dressed their bodies and minds in their Sunday best and came to work wailing. The chorus consisted of Sonny, Cher, Jackie DeShannon, Gracia Nitzsche and the late Bobby Sheen (aka Bobb B. Soxx of the Blujeans).

Everything felt fine now that I knew I'd found the Stones a new home in which to work. Regent Sound had served its purpose, but it was a Regent's Park rowing boat compared to the oceangoing liner that was RCA's studio A. You could have fitted the Stones and all of Liverpool into the studio and still have found space for most of Manchester. I didn't give out instructions or guidance – well, perhaps suggestions, for we were all learning to bounce off the recording ropes at the same time. Mick and Keith played the tune they'd composed. Sometimes it spoke for itself as to arrangement, or Mick and Keith would have an idea and direction already in mind. Sometimes they didn't and would throw the song over to the rest of the group, no attachment, ego-less, to be kicked around for a while looking for that particular place to go.

There was no reverence, no preciousness allowed – nor mercy. How about a 3/4? A polka, a country swerve? Everything was open roadhouse and anything was possible if it would get the job done. Like what to do with 'What

To Do' or what to do with 'Paint It, Black'. That song was going nowhere, I thought. Another ten minutes and it'll be time to move on, change the energy, flow and song, and perhaps come back to 'Black' another day. We'd only done the second chance thing once before when, after the acoustic attempt in Chicago, we came back fuzzed to 'Satisfaction' in LA.

At the last moment, either Bill Wyman played or was listening to Jack Nitzsche fuck around with the pedals of the Hammond B-3 organ in a piss-take of a gipsy figure. 'That's it!' I thought. I'd heard the sound and movement that we needed, the whimsy that spelt 'radio'. A grey paisley-shirted, brown velvet-trousered, at his most attractive looking Jagger dictated lyrics to Keith like M to Moneypenny.

'Bill . . . Jack, do it again.'

I was not sure whether it was Bill or Jack. We'd finished one track in the past hour, and I'd been out for a joint – we didn't smoke in the control room. I had come back immersed in the texture of my Levi-type bottle-green suede jacket and how it displayed traces of prospected gold under the neon lights of the studio control room. I'd then turned my concentration towards Keith's nigger-brown twin to see if its light held the same gold-rushed imbue. Bill looked over and said, 'Do what again?' Jack looked around and would not commit. 'That thing you and Jack were doing with the pedals.' Bill had been down on his knees playing a bass pattern on the Hammond.

God, don't ask me for definition, or the trap of having to explain. 'Oh, this?' Bill gave his churlish smirk. He knew I held him somewhat in disdain and had doubts I'd ever noted his playing, except for the time I brought it dead centre as the final overdub, hurrah and run out on '19th Nervous Breakdown.'

'I was just doodling; I didn't think anybody was listening'.

He smiled on, too long. 'Do it again before you forget,' I commanded, not interested in the Formica rationale behind the movement.

'Oh,' grinned Bill, insisting on the last serf word, 'I won't forget it. I was doing Eric Easton going gipsy on the Blackpool Tower pier organ'.

Even Charlie looked up at that very Fellini-esque image of thought. The room was starting to get interesting and interested. Laughs all over. Bill carried the day. 'You mean this, don't you, Andrew?' Bill did it, Keith had already got it, had clocked in and was ready to work at it. Mick shrugged, got up from the studio stool as in removing the wrinkles or a run, as if decreeing an, 'Okay, why not? I'm here, doesn't sound too stupid', and everybody got down to work. Every song got about twenty minutes to find its legs. We averaged two to four songs a day and were in that wonderful stride where we didn't seem able to get it wrong. Okay, 'My Girl' may have been wrong, the track may have been Ritalin-stiff, but it was a lot of fun to do.

In the previous December's sessions the Stones were four or so minutes into 'Goin' Home' and to everybody it felt like a great take – *the* take. But as I tapped along and looked through the control room window into the studio I knew something was up as Charlie looked at Keith, who didn't look back, and Bill looked at Charlie as if to say, 'I don't know either.' I turned to Dave Hassinger. 'Dave, they don't know how to end it; they don't have a fuckin' ending.' Dave, as if *he* could help, looked up but said nothing. A quiet Midwest-seeming man, Dave was the epitome of our Brit view of a John Ford-ish Quiet American. In those first hallowed couple of years at the golden trough of the Americas, all of our meetings were just one reel away and a generation away from the movies, as in the American western. Sonny Bono was the town crier, your younger hippy Gabby Hayes; Jack Nitzsche was the pale pacifist who finds his courage in the last reel; Dave Hassinger was Randolph Scott, or David Janssen, minus the saddle, spurs or Excedrin.

**Lou Adler**: When Andrew hit on Hassinger, he hit on somebody sympathetic and he lucked out for himself and the Stones. A lot of the engineers didn't even want to record rock 'n' roll. There was a whole school that thought it was beneath them. They were used to the Frank Sinatras and the Tony Bennetts. Dave Hassinger was a new breed of engineer at RCA.

ALO and Dave Hassinger, RCA Hollywood, 1965

**ALO**: Dave Hassinger was tanned, tall and well-built, with slight side tufts of oncoming grey in the temples letting you know the middle years were but a throw of the horseshoe away. He was clad in simple one-colour, no-nonsense light-toned V-necks, white button-down broadcloth shirts, plainsman black trousers, black solid shoes that spoke of military grounding, haircut atop to match, with a thin gold ID bracelet as the only giveaway that he was about God's business – entertainment and the field of dreams. He would have been equally at home on the range or a rig, chewing tobacco instead of smoking it, a man happily at one with his craft. His wife was Doris Day's stand-in and that just added to the attraction.

By this point the Stones had taken on lives of their own in the fantasies of their fans. Like characters out of literature or the movies, their doppelgängers had escaped and were having imaginary adventures quite independent of them, out there night and day doing outrageous things that the Stones themselves had nothing to do with. Rock 'n' roll delinquents, scourge of bourgeois society, menacing doltish adults, a long-running orgy of weed, women and song. Even the mild-mannered Dave Hassinger wasn't immune from these flights of fantasy.

Back in studio A, Dave turned oh so slowly towards me and shot me a look that said 'there ain't nothing I can do about it'. Now at the five-minute line of 'Goin' Home', the Rolling Stones kept rockin' along. Mick's vocal was over and he crossed his arms without missing a beat. Keith curled into his guitar, playing away any problem, not allowing anybody to catch his eye. As we crossed into six minutes, it was still the one, still the take, but if something didn't happen and somebody take charge and find an ending, we could be derailed. It didn't matter that the take had eclipsed the four-minutes-tops borderline; the track was holding and I wanted the Stones to make every second of this majestic piece releasable. When they had mapped it out they hadn't allowed they'd nail such a great one that fast, and now they were a plane looking for a safe landing. They needed a real ending; this motherfucker just would not work on fade.

Charlie couldn't catch Keith's eye; Keith would only let me have the sly underbelly of his. I locked eye 'n' grimace with Charlie and started to prance up the dance, as in 'keep the motherfucker going'. His snare picked up the order and the level, the band followed suit and matched tone, and for the next four minutes the train stayed on track resolutely 'Goin' Home'. At seven minutes Charlie looked, I waved a circle, meaning just keep it moving. He looked at me for a few seconds, figured it in and nodded his head. Bill heard Charlie step it up and followed him. Brian and Keith now admitted they were playing together, stayed on the money and got on the ride. Stu shrugged, grinned and started to glide. Mick looked for and found the right harp, wrapped his lips around it and sucked his way into our ears forever with a triumphant groan 'n' moan.

Charlie looked in my direction, then made the obvious suggestion by looking down at the floor. The Stones followed suit and allowed themselves to descend to a last *après* skasmic crawl. Eleven minutes-plus on the slopes and spent; thank God we'd had enough tape between reels. The group fell about, as well they should, exhilarated. They laughed, hugged each other and collapsed on the floor. 'Goin' Home' was done and so were we. I had just witnessed a musical moment of the forever, the Rolling Stones having just broken the sound barrier with ease.

When *Aftermath* was released, 'Goin' Home' was praised by fans, critics and peers alike as a standout event on the recording. In 1965 only Dylan and the Stones had defied the three-minute law – and kicked open the doors to the future.

At RCA the band continued that first golden recording roll. Beginning with 'The Last Time' Mick and Keith mastered the art of providing compositional food for the pack. With 'Satisfaction', 'Get Off Of My Cloud' and '19th Nervous Breakdown' they mastered the art of the notional anthem in step with the nation. With 'Mother's Little Helper', 'Out Of Time', 'Play With Fire' and 'Under My Thumb' they came off the street and into the suburban home, opened the diaries, the liquor and medicine cabinets and echoed the shared hypercritical blight that suppressed and splintered American youth.

The Stones' – fuck the other groups – experience of America, and in particular Los Angeles, was limited to wonder, room service, a general sense of affinity (as opposed to hostility) and, overall, a climate and a hospitality that was sunny, grateful and optimistic. One did not have to wait for Robert Towne and *Chinatown* to realise that behind the military/industrial shrubs of Wilshire's country clubs sat the fat bow tied men who hovered over, controlling all. And therefore, down in the valley on Sunset, Hollywood and Vine, the musical watering holes were a magnet for the voice of youth disaffected by trailer park squalour – as white lower-middle-class dads returned from Korea without a bean to find their places in the assembly line taken by eager immigrants – and affected by the very idea of having to die in the inhospitable dykes and crannies of Cambodia and Vietnam, as the arrogant military would have them do.

I say 'fuck the other groups' because, in 65 and 66, the Stones, in their lyrics and attitude, were the only UK import that seemed to be at one with what ailed America. Once they'd got it the Rolling Stones went straight from the airport to the studio, to the radio and to Beverly Hills. Inspired by what they had in fact said and stood for, American hope and fungi started to congregate, compose and rail against the system via music. And this movement was just as middle class, until Hendrix, as the pony Brit R 'n' B movement that first attracted Jagger and Jones.

The confidence of the Rolling Stones grew in this time of recording in America, an experience that was, then, unique in and of itself for a British band. We cocked our guns and guitars and took aim at convention, violated musicians' union petty rules and went for it. The Stones were not intimidated. They got America down in America. The Beatles took over America, but the Stones belonged to it.

Opposite RCA off Sunset stood Martoni's, an Italian eatery where we'd stand behind Frank Sinatra to get in and nobody was refused admission. Dean Martin, Tony Martin and Cyd Charisse were always already seated. Richard Conte drummed his dice hand at the bar. Sonny Bono watched us eat with glee, while the rest of the star-studded ensemble paid us no mind in the way the old guard would have back home. They just figured if we had the good sense to be there – enjoy it. We were in the entertainment capital of the world and we started to create pop entertainment for the world. The Rolling Stones and I were in the midst of our finest recording hours together.

I told *Disc* magazine by phone:

The whole set-up is terrific. We completely insulated ourselves from the outside. The boys recorded for fifteen hours non-stop, from 11 a.m. till 4 a.m. the next morning. Then we spent the next day overdubbing on to the results, Mick and Keith doing the vocals and editing the masters. As their producer I can honestly say these sessions have produced a new Rolling Stones sound and certainly brought out the best of Keith, whose guitar playing has been magnificent. The only outsider is Jack Nitzsche, playing the Nitzschephone. This is actually a child's toy piano, which is projected through two separate amplifiers. Jack is able to make it sound like any instrument you like; on some tracks it even sounds like a trombone.

This was rubbish, as we know. I was just getting more ink on the Stones by summoning up that mythical instrument. As my Sidney Falco rolled on to the page, the British press managed to daub it with the post-Epstein spin of the day – highfalutin' upper-class manager talking down when talking about 'his boys', a damning I hardly qualified for, as I spent so much of my time, perhaps too much of my time, being one of the boys.

Looking back on that *Disc* item and other write-ups and headlines of the day I am amazed at how the very words and sub-headings used to describe me are a blueprint of the ups and downs of the bi-polar depression I constantly strove to keep in check by accomplishment. 'Accomplishment' – i.e. production – required daily, constant travel outside the body and inside the head, a constant movement of ideas and people, time and space. These were the only ways I knew to keep my depression in check.

It always worked in southern California; somehow that lady never let me down. Perhaps we were as shallow as each other, but, if so, we were deliciously so. Perhaps we bonded out of collusion at the fact of both living above the fault-line. It has been said by myself and others that it sometimes does not pay to meet your heroes. Hollywood had been my hero from the moment – at around nine years of age – I'd first been allowed by myself to set foot in that wonderful dream tunnel of London known as the Underground. It took me from the Mother-protected-and-edited life of Hampstead and Swiss Cottage to Piccadilly and Soho, but en route (and on return) the film posters that adorned the curved walls glued me to my calling. The powerful Saul Bass posters that described the Otto Preminger flicks of the 50s – *Carmen Jones*, *Saint Joan*, *The Man with the Golden Arm*, *Bonjour Tristesse*, *Anatomy of a Murder* and *Exodus* – epitomised the world I fell in love with.

On one level I was provided with an escape as the posters took me out of Baker Street and the mundaned Metropolitan Line straphangers too concerned about their daily lot to escape with me to the Hollywood that pulled and beckoned me with every poster, credit and slogan. I allowed myself to be sucked into that teeming world; I could feel the gun in my hand on a slow boat to Israel, the gun in my holster at the OK Corral. On another level I was getting an education as I studied the Woolf Brothers' Romulus Films and Jimmy Woolf's managerial promotion of Laurence Harvey and absorbed the idea that Otto Preminger was a breed apart as one who produced and directed and controlled his canvas. I marvelled at how Mr P allowed designer Saul Bass his head to explain the work in those ground-breaking canvases that separated the Preminger films from the competition sometimes more ably than the films did themselves. I would later apply to the Rolling Stones the myriad flickering poster images that I took in as my Piccadilly Line sped me south into Soho by paralleling that experience, flicking through a rack of records with an eye towards those whose cover images stood out from and above the fray. Message was everything; content came later and was deemed redundant if your carrier pigeon didn't home.

As life became polar with flights from London to LA, mine became more bi-polar and I upped my self-medication to cushion those days when I knew I'd snap and crash as a result of the highs. I tried to clutch those days to my chest and disappear. Sometimes I couldn't, and whomever I was with would catch the black silent swell I became. My mouth would grip my mind in anguish and it was all I could do to mumble in taut pain, betrayed that I had not anticipated the descending wall of darkness and, having done so, given a witty aside and dived behind the descending curtain to the sound of applause.

Sometimes I'd be *The Manchurian Candidate*, others a rabid *Raging Bull*. I saw *The Man with the Golden Arm* again the other night on a Film & Arts channel pumped down to Colombia from Mexico. Frank Sinatra remains amazing (especially on a one-take basis), Eleanor Parker shows that concern is a dangerous lady and Kim Novak moves like heroin itself. She is the translucent horse I saw abound in slo-motion from the hotels Royalton to Algonquin. The Elmer Bernstein score is balletic and almost the edit itself. The withdrawal sequences are, of course, condensed highlights but, given the 1954 occasion, are still quite restimulative to someone who has been there. And sometimes I still think I hear mummy; I look up and it's Angela Lansbury barking orders at Laurence Harvey's Raymond Shaw in front of the *Manchurian* chessboard.

\*

Before I could shake *The Man with the Golden Arm* image from my screen and separate myself from stalking Frank in matching Paul Smith retro dark-grey-flannel suit, I recalled the late 80s in my own downtrodden Manhattan hell when I started to realise that the city now belonged to somebody else and I had better move on. Long before I did I nearly fell off the gay gaudy cocaine railings of the time and developed a near fatal attraction for a leggy Texas blonde who played guitar and heroin.

The manners I adhered to in matters of the heart and hearth had me walk the line. So rather than take the physical fall I did the next logical thing and shot up with it. That was just another one of the days I nearly died. I remember sitting on the toilet hanging on for dear life as it did its damnedest to suck me in and flush me out, with the anxious Farrah-Texan pulling me out of the abyss, smacking the life back into me that I'd nearly smacked out, and walking me around the room, cold-towelling and talking to me until all the different parts of my mind and body made their connection again and informed us all we'd decided to live.

Two blocks south of the East Fifties apartment in which this sordid slagmire occurred was the workplace of Tony Russo, the brilliantly mad and talented commercial editor fuelled by life in all its naughtiness, and the same Tony who had joined me for dinner at Marianne Faithfull's north-of-Canal mewsy abode to set her battering-prone, poor excuse of a boyfriend straight. Tony's enthusiasm for drugs as a *de rigueur* social state was endearing at the time – a time when his career was on hold and burn out. I felt comfortable in his company. Tony and I managed to hoist our now oft-degrading drug dependencies to the level of swashbuckling pirates warding off any invaders of reality. The sun had set on that first line long ago and, like worn-out French Foreign Legionnaires in search of a decent movie, we paraded over the dunes of marching powder in search of the holy grail (the one entwined in our brain cells), always remembering the wonder and hope attached to that very first line.

When I had overshot my manageable daily load and found myself out of sorts, spirits and wherewithal, I would avail myself of Tony's hospitality while I waited a few hours for the excess to wear itself out, exorcising all real and imagined pain and actualities from my system with a couple of hot lemon teas and a soft scrambled egg and mayonnaise sandwich on even softer white bread. I'd then be ready to converse with Uncle Tony, my barometer for a return to the world, and after a to and fro banter to make sure I really was okay, we'd Jack Daniels and Juan Toot ourselves back into the front line of life.

Tony Russo's office topped a brownstone on East 49th Street overlooking Second Avenue. Time could stand still in the view from its bay windows. Tony Russo was Tim Roth before he existed – a small, tight, ponytailed schnauzer of a man, rimmed to the eyeballs in coke and hope, the eye of an eagle, the caustic wit of a dangerous nation under siege, the cut of a priest defrocked. The rubber band that tied his hair was matched by the rubber strap on his 'director's' sports watch. Everything about Russo was ready to snap and made you want to hug him all the more. On his other wrist Tony wore a coloured, braided-fabric hippy bracelet – but Tony was too hip to be hippy – and he used this muse as an asset to communication. His ability to kick at life was belied by a casual demeanour, worn tennis shoes and on-location attire.

Tony and I would make occasional forays into health with visits to an Upper East Side acupuncture guru, the late great Dr Robert Giller, introduced into all our lives by Pete Kameron. Once needled by Dr G, we'd gain a forty-eight-hour spurt that would allow us, in a state of wellbeing and street decorum, to pass as normal and join the throngs at some eatery of the now without a cocaine panic taking over and ruining the splurge into other people's reality. Dr G had another number to glue one to the wall of whatever – a forearm-sized, dildo-shaped syringe that served as an 80s 'homeopathic' sub for whatever Dr Max Jacobson had been about in the 60s.

Once out and about, though, one wrong word, one rude waiter (perceived or real) could end the meal on wheels and we'd be back out on our well-worn pavements, teeth grinding, angry at the world and happy to be so. Once ensconced on a bar stool, coke-fuelled and brandy-fumed, we'd flirt with anybody: Uma Thurman wannabes, David Bowies, Gary Oldmans. Bring out the spiv on a cocaine platter – anybody was fair game, until they presumed. Then we'd pounce, strike and withdraw. You might wonder why communication with an outside world filled with ambitious, self-centred twits, though it might have assuaged our aloneness, was our party of choice. Far from it; we both preferred the days when God had given the gift of the gab to only a chosen few.

Our stop-offs into the Jay McInerney 80s were unsettling. The only amusingness was Tony and me and the way we were and saw all. We'd chat up the barman, star – or his or her loafer or chauffeur. I was sockless and overly influenced that year by Don Johnson in *Miami Vice*. I thought, via 'Heartbeat', that he was Sony's brightest recording star.

I'd sit clad in tight worn 'n' frayed jeans, tasselled woven-weaved beige loafers, a blazer or velvet pile casual evening jacket that draped the waist this good/bad life was giving me, a crisp white shirt to give me colour, and a lot of gold to dim the schlap into *La Cage*-less contour. A bemused and beaming Tony was my Manhattan Peter Meaden, seated next to me enjoying our exchanges with the aliens while letting me have a peek at his accessory – that .357 resting on his hip – the way a girl may let you have a peek between her legs.

It was all good fun as we both saved what was left of the best of us for when we were at home with our respective advantages. My stop-ups at Tony's had wisdom, within their reason. In those hours of overloaded OD'd madness, as I waited to once more become whole, I would take care not to be seen or heard. Outside I might react, not always to what another had said, but to the way I had read it, and risk clocking up another irretrievable error on the trail of manners. Tony's room was a womb that kept me immune from such errors or the pain of being correct while not being so myself. This day I collapsed on the couch at the back of his workspace and Tony asked me if I had any blow.

'You've got to be kidding, Tony,' I said, as in, the state I'm in, you think I've got some blow on me? I managed this from the inside of a locked mouth that would have been a challenge to an anaesthetist.

'Well, I just thought I'd ask. If you had, you certainly wouldn't be needing it, the state you're in. That's all.'

Tony would sit hour after hour re-editing existing commercials copied from the television that he thought left room for improvement. The fact that the commercial was already being aired and had nothing to do with him did not deter him from trying to improve on it. It was this act of devotion to a craft that had temporarily abandoned him that endeared his very soul to me.

An hour or so had passed, Manhattan was nearly home, and so was I. I'd managed the soft egg 'n' bread spread and it sounded like a munitions factory while I chewed. Gone was the taut and noisy silence. The visuals were no longer punctuated by black spots, my ears were no longer ringing or screaming whenever a thought threatened to get out of hand, and the sound effects were in order, normal and not peaking or shrieking.

Then Tony, who'd gone out for a spill at an O'Lunney's on 44th where he could assimilate his Italian into Irish faster than you could pour a leprechaun, returned. He tiptoed into his own space, finger on his lips, as in 'hope I don't disturb', entered his well-appointed bathroom and carefully closed the door. I let it be and allowed myself back to the calm that was at last enveloping me. A few minutes later I was drawn back into the room by the sound of a hoof in a stable. Can't be back to zero, I thought. I wandered off again but was called back by another resonant sound of a hoof. This time I could place its origin – it was the sound of a shoe'd hoof kicking against the panelling of a horse carriage, the type with wood slats on the side that one passes on the motorway or freeway on the road to Newmarket or Saratoga Springs.

I got up and moved to the front of the wood-floored office past the bathroom, having forgotten Tony was there. Night had now fallen and outside East 49th Street was quiet with only occasional crosstown traffic, none of it urgent or loud. I switched on a couple of the lamps and dimmed the overheads. I walked back to the rear of the floor, took a last slug of the deli lemon tea and heard the sound of hoofs kicking again. I tried to focus on where this sound was coming from, as it was becoming increasingly clear it was real and not in my mind.

With no reason for doing so I called out, 'Tony?' While I did that my body was moving ahead of my mind and I strode towards the bathroom door. I gripped it and tried to open it; it was locked.

'Tony, are you in there?' I heard another would-be hoof beat and knew that he was. I have no idea of what providence I was granted that allowed me my next fortunate move. 'Tony,' I barked in my best controlled military fashion, 'I want you to get up. I want you to stand up. I want you to hear me. I want you to focus on the door.'

I listened for more hoofs and only heard the sound of Tony's sighing and my own heart pounding. 'Tony, I want you to slowly put your hand around the door handle.'

The outside knob slowly turned and when I saw that I gave a sigh of relief. 'Tony, I want you to unlock the door.' Nothing. 'Tony, hold the door handle and unlock it. You must do this.'

I could now identify the hoofs-against-trailer sound as that of Tony reeling and falling down again. I then heard him mumble and curse his stumble, work himself slowly to his knees and attempt to stand up again. 'Tony, you must stand up, you must concentrate, you must open the door!'

The door, unlocked, slowly opened and in the crack I saw with horror what had happened to my mate. He had a huge bloody gash on his forehead from falling to the floor. He looked like Herve Villechaise doing the Jack Nicholson 'Here's Johnny!' routine from *The Shining* – and underneath the horror he just looked like a little boy who knew he'd done wrong. I looked over his shoulder and saw blood on the side of the bath where he'd fallen and cracked his head. To his right above the towel rail the wall was smeared with more blood, and over his left shoulder were his shooting works, spoon and syringe footcrushed into the marble floor. Tony started to shock out and fall again. I grabbed him, slapped him, shook his shoulders and started shouting in his ear and marching him wet-towelled around the room. When I ran out of things to say and had got fed up calling him a cunt I just left-left-left-right-lefted him until I felt some life in him. I cursed him for his selfishness and bad manners. I admonished him for having the gall to nearly die on me.

'This is all I fuckin' need, you cunt, if you'd fuckin' died they wouldn't have even mentioned your fuckin' name. It just would have been "Ex-Stones Man Involved In Overdose". You cunt, you fuckin' lame wop fuckin' whore.'

Tony moaned and groaned and then he laughed. I slapped his face with affection, hugged him and marched him around the room again. Just two weeks later Texas would be doing the same for me.

*

Back in the 60s, things were going my way – and it was a disturbing feeling. I recall the pleasure of stepping out of the RCA studios into a glorious Sunset Strip day, into the land of 'What Are You Doing?' as opposed to the London that stated 'How Dare You!' I managed to keep the hounds at bay in Los Angeles, where the sun always gave me a shadow I could talk to.

The endless socialising at parties had started to take its toll on Brian Jones; he was now partying with professionals and this raised his normal plethora of drugarettes to a whole new plateau of madness. Girls in London might sit in awe of the slovenly sexual guru, agog at his ability to consume and transport them physically within him. Some he may have just bashed about. But the American groupine animal led the event, taking no prisoners, and Brian started to get very frayed around the edges. He could still triumph in the hotels of Manhattan, LA and major stopovers, but this cost him concerts and commitments throughout the Midwest and caused Keith to go it alone in Wisconsin, Kentucky, Kansas and Ohio. Mick and Keith didn't even bother to tell me until Brian started to nod out in the studio.

**Linda Leitch** (neé Lawrence): I was very, very close with Brian in those early days, with him all the time. Brian and I were a team, partly because he lived with me at my parents. We were very bonded.

Then I got pregnant after we'd been together a year or so. That was when Andrew first appeared in Reading. We'd been to see the Who, Brian and I; they were playing in Reading. When Andrew came into the picture it all started going very strange for Brian. He was an insecure person. He really wanted his dad to respect him and his music. When we'd go to see his parents in Cheltenham, Brian, who had severe asthma, would get these attacks and he would really need the inhaler. He'd been a bad boy when he was younger and had made some girl pregnant when he was at school, so he was the bad boy of the town. Cheltenham was a very snooty, snobby town, and he felt rejected. There was a lot of emotion attached to going home, and he would get these attacks just before we'd get there.

Brian was very sensitive. When Andrew came into the picture it seemed like everything started to change. At the time Brian was writing songs and trying to integrate his own stuff into the music. He'd be at my parents' house writing songs in the middle of the night when he'd come back from a gig. I'd make him eggs and bacon at three in the morning and he'd be strumming away and writing ideas. Anyway, when Andrew came into the picture it seemed like the focus started going on to Mick and Keith. There were lots of arguments. I'd hear him on the phone with Andrew and there were lots of negative things going back and forth. Brian wasn't too pleased about this Andrew Oldham character coming into the picture and taking over. Mick and Keith kinda got on really well with him. And because I was pregnant,

Andrew and the other Stones didn't really want me around because of the press and people seeing me, but I kept going to all the gigs.

I remember the boys driving around in a Mini while Brian and I drove around in a Humber Hawk, which was a big solid car my father had suggested Brian get instead of a Mini. My father liked a good solid car if I was gonna be out there. We were kinda the squares. Andrew and the boys thought we were kinda unhip being in that family situation, me pregnant and thinking about getting married and all those corny things. I started to feel rejected and pushed out and that I wasn't welcome around the band anymore, and Brian started feeling the pressure. That began our split. So there were terrible feelings for the next six months or so after I had the baby and we drifted apart.

Then he went to America and the feelings were getting harder and tougher for Brian. I could feel his insecurity growing more and more. He'd gone off to America and he sent me postcards saying he loved me and that America was great and it was a wonderful thing to be playing to all these big audiences. Then when he came back he took me to Morocco with Robert Fraser, Deborah Dixon and Donald Cammell and I thought it was because we were going to get back together, but instead it was to kind of introduce me to other people because I knew he loved me and he didn't want to just leave me out there. When we were in Morocco he said, 'Look, I'm gonna have to leave you now. It's for the best. You're too good for me and I'm just gonna be dragging you into this whole thing and it's not gonna be good. It's better to let you know now and I'll give you this little bit of cash if you sign this piece of paper.' I don't know if it was Andrew's idea or the lawyers'. Obviously there was a lot of money coming in at that time and they didn't want me to have any of it. Somebody had convinced Brian of that. I have a feeling that Andrew played a large part in that, or he'd introduced Brian to the lawyers who'd advised him. At that time when you had a child they tried to take it away from you because there was no financial support from the government. They'd always say if you're not married you should have the child adopted. I kept Julian, because when he was born Brian and I were looking for houses and were gonna get married so I was still thinking it was gonna be okay.

Then after the Moroccan thing I was very disillusioned. I realised it was over and I had this £1,000 which didn't even cover the cost of the phone calls Brian had made, the phone bills that were left at my mum's house. So I basically just paid off the bills and didn't have money for myself.

I'd met Anita Pallenberg in Morocco. Brian was very kind to me; he was trying very hard to give me a life. He would say to me, 'I'm just not good enough for you. I'm gonna die before I'm twenty-something.' He seemed to know he wouldn't be alive after a certain age anyway. I thought he was just saying that to get rid of me. I went to Paris and met all these people, did some modelling with Deborah Dixon and Anita Pallenberg and hung out with them for a while. Then Anita ended up going to London and met Brian. I thought I was gonna get a flat with her when I came back to London. Instead, she moved in with Brian. That was devastating for me. Then Brian got deeper and deeper into drugs and I found it more and more and more difficult to communicate with him. But every now and again I would try and make contact with him, take Julian up to say, look, we have this wonderful thing going here and don't block me out. It's all in Marianne Faithfull's book. I don't even get my name mentioned; I was just some girl who came up crying at the door and stuff. Anyway, I went up very often to try and keep in touch with him, but I was pushed out and pushed out and eventually totally rejected by the whole scene up there.

My thing with Andrew was basically I felt that he pushed Brian away from the Stones but also away from me. I've hung out with Andrew in the years since and I don't blame anyone. Brian was a strong person. He had insecurities, but he knew what he wanted. Mick and Keith were young; they didn't quite know, so it was easy to manipulate them, which is what Andrew did. He couldn't do that with Brian. Brian knew what he wanted and Andrew couldn't tell him what to do.

I met Donovan at a *Ready Steady Go!* party and when Brian found out I was going out with him he advised me not to. He didn't think Donovan was good enough. Then when I was seventeen or eighteen I went to America after meeting Alan Pariser, a millionaire groupie of the Stones'. I started doing beach movie stuff in LA and I hooked up with Phil Spector, then with Pete Kameron. Donovan had got some other girl pregnant. He had a place at the Chateau Marmont. He got involved with Gram Parsons, around 'Wild Horses' time, and he got lost in there, the Joshua Tree bit, spiritual mushrooms. Then I was with Bobby Whitlock, it was big Ferraris time, marriage proposal, the Eric Clapton party, the 'Layla' time, heroin; and then I was back to Donovan for good – for life. It was all in the astrological charts.

**Donovan**, singer/songwriter: You could say I met Andrew Oldham's persona when Linda found me a London flat in 1965 at Ivor Court. It had been Andrew's flat and the tapes were still in the cupboards of his office. So I met Andrew's flat, not him in person. I would meet this 'hustler-whizz kid' later on down the rock 'n' roll road. I'd begun dating Linda and she had been up in Ivor Court seeing Charlie and Shirley Watts and sorted out the apartment from there. Of course, soon as I met Linda, Andrew and the Rolling Stones became very much a part of my inner life. I ran into Brian and Mick and Keith now and again, but very rarely. Never did I run into Andrew during the whole 60s. After 64 and 65 when it popped for everybody, you didn't see many people socially. Brian Jones was the first charismatic British rock star, the first white R 'n' B phenomenon of the 60s, as Elvis was in the 50s. It was Brian, before John Lennon remembered his art school background.

Mickie Most had just become my producer. There was a strict studio system – 'three songs in three hours' – before the neverending session that the Beatles invented because they couldn't play live any more, the fans were throwing things at the stage, they couldn't move from hotel to airport. It was just ridiculous; they had to stop. In the 60s most of the bands were playing the night before, so when they arrived in the studio they'd pick up where they left off, and that's why a lot of the records have such a wonderful feel to them. Actually, Ray Davies took forever on singles. He decided that singles needed a lot of attention and would be known to spend three weeks on one song. We made 'Sunshine Superman' in about six days. Mickie Most used John Paul Jones and Jimmy Page in the studio. He would sift through my material until he'd say, 'Right, I'll have that one and that one for singles.' He knew right away. 'Mellow Yellow' was just a song I used at parties for everybody to sing along to. Mickie said 'That's it!' and it went to no. 2. Mickie related the pop form to three gears on the car: pull away in first, go down to second for the first chorus, go into third for the second verse and go back to the chorus again. I met Allen Klein around this time. Allen had his eye on me as soon as I made my first American TV appearance on *The Ed Sullivan Show*. I don't know whether Klein introduced me to Mickie or Mickie saw me on TV and said, 'That's it, I'd like to record that guy.' I was heading for pop anyway; I wanted to fuse pop with bohemian ideal and bohemian music. Allen was a pirate and he eventually boarded the Beatles' ship. The jury is still out in my life over Klein, whether he was the guy who helped or hindered me. Sure it's a mess and I've still got to sort it out, but he took me from a little label and sold me to an American label and presented me. He took me from Pye and put me on Epic/Columbia.

**Linda Leitch:** I would turn up all over the place, and the Stones and Andrew hated it. I wasn't gonna be pushed out like Chrissie Shrimpton and all that lot. I went to the first recording session for 'Come On' which Andrew supposedly produced. He said to the engineer, 'Right, give me the tape', and as we were walking out the guy says, 'Don't you wanna mix it?' Andrew said, 'Mix it? Right, yeah, okay.' He didn't seem to know anything about what he was doing but he was a con man and could talk his way into anything. I had all the old demos they did, like the Rice Krispies commercial. I should have kept them.

Andrew was just a bubbly young red-headed guy who seemed to appear out of nowhere and take over. Then the Stones turned into these really cool, hip people and Brian and I were too normal and too much in love.

Brian was more rootsy and would have preferred to keep the band that way. I love the Stones' every album. Julian and I would buy everything, but we still love the early stuff the best. I do remember the feeling of them playing live in the beginning, just so heartfelt, so deep and moving. As it got on, the music got more anti-women and anti-all kinds of establishment which Brian was anyway, and I was too, but in our own way, the beatnik way rather than the pop way.

They'd been asked to play at this rich Jewish party and I remember this girl, Linda Keith, turned up and started going out with Keith. I got on really well with her and then Keith dumped her and she ended up in LA, totally neurotic and crazy. Her father tried to have her committed; she escaped and came and stayed with me for a while in LA. Keith's first girlfriend, a black girl, was one of my best friends. There was another black girl, Cleo, who was going out with Mick. Andrew recorded her. They would come down to Windsor and we would hang out there and then it was Linda Keith and Chrissie Shrimpton who took over after Cleo. Charlie had Shirley. She was a great comfort to me at that time, when I was pregnant. She helped me when I thought I was gonna get an abortion because everyone was advising me to get rid of the baby.

I was there when the Beatles came down to see the Stones in Richmond and I remember John Lennon had a girlfriend and a wife too who was hidden. I felt a bit like that; we were the two who were told we mustn't be talked about or be seen with the guys. That's how it was then. Brian was the blond beauty, yes he was. I remember Brian and Mick getting on really well, good friends, deep feelings between them about everything. It devastated Brian when Mick took over; it crushed his ego. He'd be looking in the mirror going, 'Oh, God, Linda, do I look okay?' I cut his hair, of course, because I was a hairdresser. I was the one who started that longer hair thing and that falling in the face. I know the Beatles had theirs, but I started it with Brian . . .

Very strange isn't it, my whole thing with them. Even to this day, I still don't understand what it was about me that was so weird that they didn't want to accept me. Usually, when I dream about them, which I do every so often because it was a major part of my life and a big change, I still don't understand it.

Robert Fraser, Deborah Dixon, Linda Lawrence Leitch and Brian Jones, Tangier, September 1965

## · CHAPTER 12 ·

**Tony King**: I was a promo man at Decca. I started at age eighteen, originally at the Albert Embankment building. I went to the Great Marlborough Street office four years later to work with Tony Hall. It was a big place, four offices and a huge reception area where we could stage cocktail parties and receptions for visiting US artists. Tony Hall's wife, Malfalda, chose the building and decorated it. Tony was an old-school jazz fan, and I was his pop ears, turning him on to a lot of pop stuff he might not otherwise have listened to. I first met Andrew through Mark Wynter, at the tail end of Mark's Decca days before he had his hits on Pye. Andrew started dropping by the office to see me. I think he thought of me as a friend, but he also thought I could be helpful to him – not in a cynical, 'I could use this person' way, although Andrew was capable of that. There was a genuine sense of friendship.

I had a very big crush on Andrew for a long time. Then one day he came over with Sheila, who he introduced to me as his girlfriend, and we all went downstairs for coffee. I didn't even know he had a girlfriend; I didn't even know he would have wanted a girlfriend. At the time Andrew was very camp. He had an effeminacy and he liked to retain that sense of sexual ambiguity in the same way that the Sitwells used to. He would delight in having this kind of double life. Publicly he was out on the town, mysterious – 'is he or isn't he gay?' But he was secretly very happy that he had this bourgeois home life, a wife and a son. A lot of the managers at the time were gay – Kit Lambert, whom we called Kitty, Robert Stigwood and Brian Epstein – and I think Andrew wanted to blend in. He pulled it off very well, and I don't know – maybe he did dabble, maybe he experimented, and maybe he was bisexual, but I wasn't convinced.

I left Decca to work for Roy Orbison in Nashville. When Roy and his wife Claudette broke up I went to Spain and worked as a bartender, where I caught hepatitis. I was in a hospital bed when I first heard 'The Last Time', and I thought, they've finally done it, the Stones have finally crossed over. Andrew always said they were going to be as big as the Beatles. They'd finally made a pop record; up until then I'd always thought their records slightly missed the mark. When I was in hospital Andrew sent me a note saying to come and work with him when I was better. I met with him, he played me an acetate of 'Satisfaction' which I knew was going to be the biggest record ever, and he then told me about his plans for an independent record company – that was Immediate. I was appointed Immediate's head of Promotion and worked hard on promoting 'Hang On Sloopy' to radio, pulling in favours. We were not in it for the money; it was just sheer fun. I did all the mailings myself, all the packing of the envelopes, everybody was hands-on. Stephen Inglis was around, always popping in and out. I had a tiny office next to Andrew's and I was just furiously stuffing envelopes full of 45s, sticking on stamps, taking them to the post office and running around town delivering them to the BBC. I loved doing it; I would do it some nights until midnight or two in the morning. Work was fun.

Tony Calder lived in Ivor Court with his girlfriend Josie. Jenny came later; she worked for us and then he married her. I think she'd gone out with Eric Clapton. I'd come into the office some mornings and Keith would be in the spare bed; it was a good bed to stay in when you'd been out or working late. Charlie Watts had a flat on the same floor; he and Shirley lived along the corridor. Tony Calder was Andrew's henchman. It was his job to whip up the troops. He used to piss people off most of the time. Once he was shouting in this southern burr of his, 'I want work!' – Andrew and I fell about laughing and it became the sort of catch phrase around the office.

Tony was important to Andrew but Andrew was dismissive towards him a lot of the time. Tony was hard-edged, hard-nosed in business; he could be Andrew's bad guy. When there was dirty work to be done Tony could do it and Andrew would still look okay. All of what we were up to had never been done before, like the very idea of Andrew and the Stones controlling their own recordings, or the very idea of Immediate Records. None of this had been done before, at least not in jolly old staid England. None of us knew where pop music was going to lead us, so Andrew was just taking every opportunity and would often just make a big mess of everything, but he would learn from the mess and the chaos and maybe that would give him his next idea. The only thing that was predictable about Andrew was how he ended up at the end of the 60s, drugged and crazy.

There was a lot of pot around and I was the official pot holder. I'd go around the corner to these two call girls who always had really good stuff. I'd keep different types of grass in different drawers in the office. Andrew, Sheila, Mick, Chrissie, Donovan and I were going to this film premiere.

Eddie Reed, who'd taken over as Andrew's chauffeur after Reg King's departure, was driving us in Andrew's new Rolls. At the theatre this cop opened the door and this great cloud of marijuana smoke wafted into his face. We rolled out totally stoned on to the pavement, just as the cameras were flashing. I learnt later that the police didn't actually know what pot smelt like; they probably thought we were just smoking foreign cigarettes.

There was this Middle Eastern restaurant on Old Brompton Road where the owner used to let them smoke dope at the table, with a hookah and everything. One night we sat next to a party of CID officers. The owner said, 'It's okay, carry on smoking, they know what goes on here.' We went to Scotland for a Philips sales conference; me, Andrew, Nico and Greg Phillips, smoking dope all the way.

Before Cynthia Stewart arrived at Ivor Court it was chaos, but it was fun. Then Cynthia organised everything, kept everything and everybody in order. I think Andrew rather liked the idea of having a high-powered woman PA who couldn't type. She was quite ferocious and kept all sorts of people out of the office.

**Gregory Phillips**: The next time I met Andrew he was with the Rolling Stones. It was beginning to take off for them. We were both on *Thank Your Lucky Stars*. Once again Andrew and I seemed to click in some unstated way. My father spent a long time talking to him in the screening room. A bit later, my father came back to my dressing room and he was laughing his head off. He told me the story. The singer Craig Douglas, who had a big hit at that time with some ballad, was topping the bill. My father had seen him rush into his dressing room in a fury and slam the door shut behind him. When dad came back past the room again, there was a knot of producers outside the door trying unsuccessfully to persuade Craig Douglas to come out. Craig had been a milkman in his former life and this was well known. It transpired that Mick and Keith had left four empty milk bottles outside his door. Craig had found them and got into a terminal huff, and he was refusing to go on.

We met again at *Thank Your Lucky Stars* when I was promoting 'Angie' and 'Not Fade Away' had stormed the charts. The Stones had pissed in the garage forecourt and Andrew had conned the mainstream press into printing the career-making headline 'Would You Let Your Daughter Marry A Rolling Stone?' Everyone on the management side was really furious with him for the success he had made of these 'dirty yobs' who were rude, disrespectful to their elders, had fleas, lice in their hair and 'did you see the mud on his (Brian Jones's) boots?' I on the other hand thought they were great because they took the piss brilliantly. Above all they were having fun, and Andrew was the funniest of the lot. The recording for that show took place in Birmingham and on the bill were Gerry & the Pacemakers, Freddie & the Dreamers, the Searchers, a French woman who had won Eurovision, the Rolling Stones – and me.

After that, Andrew and I saw each other regularly at promotional shows and we became friendly. Although I was working all the time, I was becoming more and more disillusioned with Pye Records and Delfont. I did not want to be a dork in a dinner jacket any more. The only relief was hanging out and smoking dope with Steve Marriott who'd taken me to see his manager, the notorious Don Arden.

Even if you weren't on the bill at *Ready Steady Go!* you went there anyway for the party after the show. One day, Vicki Wickham, the producer, rang and asked if I would like to go on instead of Chuck Berry, who'd pulled out for some reason. I said sure, and did 'Everybody Knows'. The Ronettes were there and Cathy McGowan asked me to stand behind them in the shot and push them on a three-person swing as they did their song. Steve and the Small Faces were on the session and I remember Mitch Mitchell and his band Riot Squad – a great band. Steve took me to the Four Tops' dressing room and we had a smoke with those guys who are fabulous performers and great people. After the gig, Andrew and Tony Calder came up to me. As he often did, Andrew pricked the lapels of my suit (blue handmade three-piece mohair, if I remember rightly) and said: 'Still wearing suits, are you?' I was very stoned at the time and Andrew had spotted this, but he wasn't quite sure what it was.

Ivor Court was a mansion block off Gloucester Place. Tony Calder had a flat with his wife and children on the floor below the Immediate office. There was no sign for Immediate. The 'office' was a flat with a bedroom, a bathroom, a small outer office and a bigger one for Andrew. They were all dial telephones in those days and the secretary's desk had about six of them on it. Andrew was alone when I arrived. I was stoned on strong grass and I had some methedrine, amphetamine. I am pretty sure that Andrew hadn't had anything like that before. We split a glass ampoule of methedrine and began to talk and smoke joints. We had a wonderful rap. Suddenly Andrew looks at his watch and says, 'Jesus Christ, it's 6 a.m., where's the night gone?' He was in a bit of a panic and said he had to rush off. I didn't realise it at the time, but he was married and that's where he had to go. I was living in the country with my parents and there were no trains that early. He told me to stay there and sleep in the bedroom and he'd ring in the morning. We'd had a fantastic connection. I'm sure that our long and (to this day) close friendship dates from that night. I thought that the Ivor Court flat was Andrew's home, so I went to bed. I couldn't sleep. I decided to have a bath and dozed off in it.

I was woken by a loud scream. Andrew's secretary, Camilla, was standing there, shocked and amazed, with a dog under her arm. 'What are you doing here?' she asked.

I covered myself as best I could and explained. She told me to get dressed. When I was dressed I went out to her office and heard her calling someone and saying rather irately, 'I found one of Andrew's friends in the bath here!'

Later, I realised that she must have been talking to Andrew's wife Sheila, who was a friend of hers. While I was there she opened the top drawer of her desk and took out a rabbit. Bridget the dog paid no attention at all.

I started hanging out at Ivor Court a lot after that night. Andrew signed me to his production company and promised to find me a great song to suit my voice. Because of the initial incident, I had acquired a reputation with Sheila for being a bad influence who took Andrew away from her. But I really hit it off with Andrew and we spent most of our free time in fits of laughter at the craziness of the social and musical revolution that was going on all around us as we stood at the centre of the whirlwind.

**Steve Inglis**, designer: When I was sixteen years old I started working at *Ready Steady Go!* on the graphics. I wouldn't say I was a graphic designer; I'd just had some experience of this, that and the other. If they were in town the Stones and Andrew would come down to *Ready Steady Go!* even if they were not on the show. It was free drinks on Friday. I got to know them and would help them get in and out of the building. By this time there would be hundreds of girls outside the door waiting to fuck them. Lionel Bart and Sean Kenny were Andrew's best friends. Sean would keep his creative juices flowing. Lionel was outrageous, totally crazy, a lovely wonderful person, very showbiz. When he wrote *Oliver!* he was the generation before Pete Townshend and *Tommy*.

Tony Calder and Andrew had a Jekyll and Hyde act. Andrew's up there, everybody loves Andrew, we're all following Andrew. Meanwhile, Tony Calder's saying sign this deal with Andrew, sign that one, sign the lot. They had a very complex way of doing things. Cynthia was like Andrew's Margaret Thatcher – his office mother.

**Cynthia Stewart Dillane:** I was employed as a buffer between Andrew and the public. I came to him from the disc jockey Alan Freeman. Alan, 'Fluff', used to do a column in a pop magazine and he used to have a celebrity over to his flat in Maida Vale every week and he'd interview them. We had an incredible social life. There would be receptions, parties, the whole of the business would meet at Fluff's; it was such fun. The business was very socially orientated and Fluff was a great cook. I met Andrew when he brought Phil Spector straight from the airport to Fluff's flat for dinner and a pop interview. When I went to work for Andrew my value was social. I was never a secretary or anything like that. I couldn't type or do shorthand but I had very good contacts in the business and Andrew needed somebody to block people out.

In all the years I worked for Andrew he never showed me anything other than courtesy. Of course, I saw him being pretty grim to some people but he treated me like the gentleman he really was. He started drinking and he had this globe you would open, full of Kalhua and vodka so he could make his Black Russians. For a while he absolutely adored Black Russians. Part of my job was to pour drinks and things, though Eddie Reed handled most of what you'd actually call *things*. Andrew knew his music and his show business very well.

When I first went to work for him he was twenty-one and so enthusiastic. I think he actually needed his clothes because he was never really that confident. Everybody used to think that he was but he wasn't. I used to wonder why Andrew never took lunch or spent time with Brian Epstein, or never spent time with Kit Lambert unless they were stoned, why none of them socialised or compared notes. The reason is they couldn't; none of them wanted the other to know how scared and alone they were on their own. Andrew was a very young boy doing amazing things. His clothes were his cloak, his armour.

When I joined him the Stones were on tour, so I didn't meet Stu until Glyn Johns introduced us at Ivor Court when they came back from tour. As you know I married Stu later. Andrew had a great influence on the Stones and Stu never liked him. Andrew said Stu's face didn't fit and rode him out. Andrew liked things to be visually pleasing. Andrew was very fond of Sean Kenny, but not many others. He was a funny young man. He was cold to most people, but when he did like you he liked you from his heart.

**Sheila Klein Oldham:** Cynthia was quite a strange character. She was a bit like a big sister to Andrew; she protected him quite a lot. Eddie Reed was another story; Eddie saved Andrew's life many times. He also got our son Sean drunk when he was eight. If I were able to have a wife, Eddie Reed would be it. At Immediate everybody would always agree with Andrew. He was surrounded by 'yes' people. They had to 'yes' him; they were earning and spending his money. It had a very bad effect on him. Andrew was paying for everything, so he had ultimate power. Nobody would ever question him. He used to say all the time, 'You must never believe your own publicity', but, of course, he always did. He could just switch personalities like a change of clothes. He actually thought that was him and he became that.

The whole time Allen Klein was with the Stones he was trying to get the Beatles interested in him. We used to spend days and days and days when Allen would just talk and talk and talk. But somehow it wasn't interesting. It was all the psychological things about, 'Well, if you did this, they would do that and if you did something else . . .' How to get it right. Something to do I suppose with his wanting to manipulate everything. I suppose I classified him as a certain type of character and wrote him off and he was aware of that. He was always trying to make some kind of contact with me so I'd be on his side and he knew that I never was. I was very cautious of him. George Harrison's reaction to Allen Klein – by the way he told it to Patti Boyd – was very interesting. George's response to John Lennon getting horny for Allen Klein was, 'Ah, I don't know, man, I'd rather drive my own car.'

Andrew didn't have a clue, learning as he went, but Allen was a hard-nosed businessman. Andrew was a soft touch at that stage, to say the least, because he was out of his depth. Before that they didn't have any money. The fact that Andrew didn't have more money may have been very helpful. Maybe Andrew was frightened that if he'd had more money he'd have killed himself. Allen took his power away and Andrew always felt very powerless and that was always the worst place for Andrew to be – stuck in some corner somewhere, not knowing how to get out of it. Think about a little stick and how difficult it is to break it. If you're a big stick you need to bend a bit. Klein stuck where he was and didn't change, ever. He didn't have to grow, didn't have to be fair – people don't realise when your heart is closed it turns inward eventually.

**ALO**: At the end of October we flew to New York for the group's fourth North American tour in eighteen months. They would play thirty-five cities in six weeks. At the end of September 'Get Off Of My Cloud' had been released in the States and gone to no. 1 faster than 'Satisfaction'. The work was getting harder. Allen Klein orchestrated everything. This was the first time the group entered the States as stars, as more than workers. We arrived in New York for a fast press conference and headed off in a private plane for the first date in Montreal. Allen Klein announced the tour would gross $1½ million and for the first time the group and I would be returning to the UK from a US tour with some real money.

Allen arranged for GAC to be replaced with the more rock 'n' pop-orientated William Morris Agency. This move from Eric Easton's choice would cost the group $50,000 in an out-of-court settlement, but it would pay dividends as the William Morris Agency, under the drive of Jerry Brandt, whacked up the Stones' touring fees into the big league. Of course, 'Satisfaction' helped.

Launched in 1898 as an agency for vaudevillians, William Morris had booked Charlie Chaplin and Al Jolson and was now the leading booking agency in the world, with offices in all the major playing countries and cities. The agency had forty departments and 150 agents, and derived 60 per cent of its income from the monster growth of television. In 1965, David Geffen and Barry Diller were in the mail room and Jerry Brandt was running the 'new' wing, repping the Beach Boys, Sam Cooke and Sonny & Cher. Jerry Brandt was the American dream. He stepped off the celluloid screen of my mind, landed on the streets of Broadway and survived the leap into reality.

**Tom King**, *David Geffen: The Operator*: Jerry Brandt was not an easy guy to miss. He wore expensive suits and Ebel gold watches, rode around in a limousine and took frequent vacations to Puerto Rico. He had put the Morris music department on the map by signing the Rolling Stones, who had just hit in the United States with their first single, 'Satisfaction'.

Brandt told Geffen that he, too, had begun his career at the Morris office mail room. He had been fired after delivering an envelope two hours late – he had been in Central Park smoking a joint and did not realise that a roomful of executives were waiting for it. He then got a job in the booking department at GAC, where he signed such early rock acts as Danny & the Juniors. But Brandt wound up quitting after clashing with the agency's chief, a stodgy old-timer who thought that rock 'n' roll was just a passing craze.

Brandt told the agency's senior executives that they might get a chance to sign the Animals, one of the hot groups at the core of the so-called British Invasion.

'Animals? William Morris doesn't sign animal acts!' growled Harry Kalcheim's brother Nat, also an agent from the old school. 'We could have had Zippy the Monkey!'

Newcomer David Geffen listened intently as Brandt complained that the dullards at the Morris office would have missed the boat on the rock revolution altogether if not for him. He told Geffen it was a miracle that they had allowed him to sign the Rolling Stones, given that the group's manager, a crafty entrepreneur named Allen Klein, demanded that the agency charge only a 7 per cent commission. The Morris office charged its other clients 10 per cent. Lefkowitz and his lieutenants relented only after Brandt ran the numbers and explained passionately how lucrative the act could be.

By clueing Geffen in on the terms of the deal, Brandt was essentially giving Geffen his first lesson in the nuts and bolts of rock 'n' roll concert booking. For every Stones concert he booked, Brandt told Geffen, the agency pocketed 7 per cent of a $25,000 advance against 60 per cent of the gross receipts. Clients in the agency's nightclub department such as Eartha Kitt and Maurice Chevalier had never earned an advance anywhere near that sum. What's more, the Stones' tour was packed with concerts for ten solid weeks, far longer than the average Las Vegas booking.

**ALO**: At either 7 or 10 per cent Jerry Brandt had a European air to wrap around his American drive bathed and born in Brooklyn of a Jewish /Puerto Rican cage; he was a Sidney Falco mind-like-a-platinum-trap who had travelled and succeeded at getting out of Brooklyn and more. He knew how to buy a pair of shoes in Paris and how to order food in Rome. He was devastatingly good looking, dark, fine-featured and boned; a fine man in the heart department whose eyes could open yours. He was someone who cared and yet he was an agent.

**Jerry Brandt**: The William Morris Agency was a throwback to the showbiz 50s. When I got there, the biggest act they had was Connie Francis. When the agency saw pictures of the Rolling Stones they didn't want to know anything about them; they were frightened to death. They saw the money when they heard 'Satisfaction'. 1965 was amazing. It was probably the best year of my life.

Andrew just wanted insanity; he was a totally insane man, he liked chaos. I planned the tour, although I learnt a lot from Andrew. He was pretty aggressive about how to get things done. I just tried to accommodate his needs. The Stones could average between $25,000 and $50,000 a night for the promoter's guarantee and that was humongous. Frank Sinatra wasn't doing that. Outside of the Beatles this was the biggest tour ever in the world. There was a scene in Rhode Island where the police wanted to keep the kids from barging on stage so they put a hundred kids in wheelchairs up front. Is that sick or what? It didn't stop anybody; the cripples just got trampled. There was a police captain at the front of the stage in Boston, and Mick Jagger took his hat off and started tapping him on the head like a tambourine. That was another riot.

Any time you gave them an excuse they just wanted a riot. All the preventive motions were the creative forces behind the riots; they didn't realise that. We'd keep telling them to put on the show and let it go, just don't antagonise the people and everything will be fine. The promoters who did what they were told were fine and the ones who went the other way had the riots. It was unbelievable. What was so great about that tour was that everybody was an innocent; nobody had been through it before. There were not ten bands who'd done it before, or twenty agents who'd been there before. We were all young, all capable of partying and staying on top of business.

That late 1965 Rolling Stones tour was a defining moment for the US decade of the 60s, but you can't define a decade until its end. We were experiencing things we'd never seen before; we knew that we were doing something that was different. The Stones were brats, too. They'd order four hundred pieces of toast in Hawaii; room service never stopped and nobody ate. I couldn't figure it out. I was pretty clean, pretty straight, so I could not figure out all these trays of food. You'd wake up in the morning and nobody had eaten anything. Anything you can think of – it happened on that tour.

Pete Bennett, Jerry Brandt, local Police Chief, ALO and Keith Richards, Chicago, 1965

We chartered a plane and we were playing cards when the window broke and the plane started dropping. Brian was sitting next to the window and I looked at Keith and Keith said, 'Don't move; let's see what happens to Brian'. . . in other words, if he got sucked out of the plane.

Another night the plane is veering all the way down to the left and all the way down to the right and I said, 'This isn't turbulence, this is fucked up.' So I ran into the cockpit and there was Brian, laughing his arse off, breaking amyl nitrate under the pilot's nose. I said, 'Lord, I'll be good, just make this guy fly us okay.' Brian was a good guy; I liked him a lot. He was an ethereal guy, an okay guy in my book.

The stage collapsed in Montreal; I can never forget that. It was Andrew's fault, although he did not actually make the stage collapse. What happened was he could sense a riot coming and he loved that. You could feel the tension in the air, like a tornado; the air would just change and you'd feel it. The chief of police came backstage and begged Andrew to turn the lights on, so that there wouldn't be a riot. Andrew refused. He didn't refuse because he wanted a riot; he refused for the aesthetic reason. I looked at Andrew and said, 'The riot's going down; it's going to happen.' He said, 'Fuck it, let it happen.' Then the stage started to collapse. I was on stage. I just looked at Mick and we both jumped into the audience; there was no other way out of there. It was a different kind of audience than now, a lot more innocent but a lot more dangerous. They could not contain themselves emotionally. I kept seeing the headline, 'William Morris Agent Found Dead Under The Stage'.

**ALO**: The stage in Montreal was a sandpit and we were the Christians; it was a snake pit and the venom of chaos and death was in the very air. You had the audience in front, at the sides and behind. You just could not contain it. It was not the stage that collapsed, it was the tiers of seats that wrapped around the side and back of the stage that fell on to it and on top of us. One moment we were standing on the side of the stage, the next moment we were lying on the ground with an ever-rising amount of bodies landing and lying on top of us as the whole back and side audience followed the collapse of the seating structure and plummeted down on to the stage. It felt like being underwater, except the water was bodies, and we were fighting to be able to swim to the surface and find air and room to breathe, pinned down by an octopusation of dead weight, panic weight in slow motion of flaying arms, bodies and legs. You'd find a gap and stick your arm up but your body could not follow; a set of arms, a trunk, a chest is atop you and you are five bodies down and you cannot breathe and your chest has had enough of the pressure and the heaving and it wants to rest and go to sleep. You know you cannot give in to it, you must fight and strive and kick or die.

**Jerry Brandt**: We climbed back up on to the stage. We had to, it was the only way out. In some places bodies were five deep around and above us. I saw Andrew punching and kicking his way above the sea of bodies. Finally we seemed to all crawl and gnaw our way off stage to the rotunda and into one of the limousines. We did not know it at the time, but Bill Wyman had locked himself into the basketball locker room and Charlie Watts was in the women's toilets. I said, 'We have to find them; we're not all here.' Andrew said, 'No, they are all right. They're hidden or else we'd have seen them. We have to get the fuck out of here.' The limo driver had to be sixty-five years old and the guy was fucking petrified.

**ALO**: I'd managed to climb above the sea of maddened bodies the only way I could, by pushing another layer of them closer to the floor. I was having somewhat of a confessional in my mind, no actual sins, no actual fact or data. I was too physically busy for the detail, but cleaning the slate was my intent as I worked at and around the bodies.

It's another day of the locusts, the klieg lights scream from writhing hell. One boy lifts his arm for help and I use it to move myself another body up above the swarm. I hold his hand, stand on a chest and I get the room to jump and I'm outta there in the air, in the alley and in the limousine. As I bolt down the alley I catch sight of Bill and Charlie disappearing into doors on my left and right, slamming them shut. The limo is in a tunnel; inside it are Jerry Brandt, Mick, Keith and Brian. We are all accounted for. In another moment we will not be able to move as the fans swarm in from all directions, surrounding the car and getting up on the roof. The roof will not handle it and is starting to buckle and cave in. The limo driver is frozen; he cannot, he will not move. Keith and Brian are in the front. Brian leans over, shoves the limo driver into his door and puts the thing into drive. Keith leans over and shoves his foot on the pedal, and we move, Brian holding the limo driver into the glass. We are moving, just slamming and hurtling kids out of the way, the duelling guitars playing as one again. Finally we are nearly out of the tunnel and the roof is still caving in with the weight of the kids hanging on top of the roof. Brian and Keith stop and start the car in rapid jerks between reverse and forward, the kids fall away, and we are nearly all right.

**Jerry Brandt**: So finally we're out of there, Keith and Brian have done their number on the driver, we're going fast down the highway and there is a girl holding on to the trunk. We pull over and Mick, Keith and I try to get her to let go. Three guys and the girl is hanging on – we just couldn't get her hands off that car. Finally, Andrew just punched her in the face and she let go. She released all that energy, we picked her up and then we just laid her down in the grass on the side of the road and took off. Later, when the concert building had been cleared, we went back for Bill and Charlie who had done the right thing and sat tight behind closed doors. It was very scary until we were on the plane and then we all started laughing because it was over and we were outta there.

Prior to the Stones there were no rock promoters in America. We had to take wrestling promoters and turn them into rock 'n' roll promoters. Maybe there was one in New York, one in Philadelphia, a Bill Graham or something, but it was not the way it is today where every town has its guy. We had to buy the out-of-town newspapers to find out who was promoting boxing or wrestling and make him the rock 'n' roll guy. We worked the phone books; we had to invent these people. The Rolling Stones went where rock 'n' roll had not gone before.

The whole explosion, everything that you want answers to, all came out of 'Satisfaction'. Without that, nobody is a hero. If it hadn't been a hit it would not have mattered who was involved. It was the record that went in the opposite direction of the Beatles. It was perfect; it gave the Stones their wings, permission to fly. It was not a revolution but an evolution going on. All of us, anything we said, everybody stopped to listen. It was one of those you-could-do-no-wrong times. It was quite easy actually; nobody would deny us and nobody would challenge us. And it was still only 1965.

**ALO**: Keith and I took our next day off in the Miami sun. The flight back to New York coincided with the big power failure of 65. We circled New York for what seemed a year, then headed for and landed in Virginia.

**Seymour Stein**: November 65 was the first blackout in New York. The Stones were at the Lincoln Square Motor Inn; now it's the location of the Chinese residence for their UN delegates. That night they had an unbelievable blackout party. Brian Jones was being shot up by Dr Max Jacobson. It made him wild, but it was legal then.

**ALO:** With our Max Jacobson visit Brian had taken me to a new high, one that I would not care to repeat. Brian continued to visit Dr Feelgood, having by now gone a long way down the road the rest of us had not even requested a permit for. With Anita Pallenberg by his side, his I-am-invincible factor went up as he consumed bottles of anything and pills of everything, and although I was no babe in arms I was nevertheless in a slightly slower lane. Brian was becoming daily more unreliable. The bags under his eyes told the full story of his unhappiness and addiction to drugs, booze and sex. The year of 65 had seen a serious debilitation in his contribution to the group. This was not yet a problem on a management level; the Stones kept it hidden and the group kept on going.

The fourth American tour continued down the Pacific coast until the final show on 6 December in the Sports Arena, Los Angeles. Anita joined Brian in LA but not in the studio. The duo would fly to the Virgin Islands for Christmas where Brian would be laid low by a tropical virus. A few days prior, Keith had been knocked unconscious by an electric shock on stage in Sacramento. This was not the first or last time. The group attended a party to celebrate the end of the tour at acid guru Ken Kesey's house. I didn't have time for the party; I wanted to get the group into the recording nest. We entered RCA and in four days recorded the tracks for 'Mother's Little Helper', 'Sittin' On A Fence', 'Take It Or Leave It', 'Think', 'Sad Day', 'Ride On Baby', 'Lookin' Tired', '19th Nervous Breakdown' and 'Goin' Home'.

**Harvey Kubernik**: When the Stones were in town, the world was different and better. You could leave high school with a lunch pass and stay out for the rest of the day. At Pink's on LaBrea hot dogs were a quarter each, down the street from A&M, the site of the Charlie Chaplin studios. The AM airwaves were pumping the real deal. It wasn't talk format. FM radio was lurking around the corner. LA always had a special relationship with the Rolling Stones. A local deejay, Dave Diamond, hosted a 7–10 p.m. Sunday evening shift on long-forgotten KBLA AM radio – 'Stones City'. Air personality and ex-KHJ jock Humble Harve, Harvey Miller, had done an early form of 'Stones City' on KBLA, sometimes calling it 'Stonedex', and Diamond continued the tradition. I did my homework to '2120 South Michigan Avenue', and got ready for a history exam after Diamond spun 'Stoned' and the entire *Aftermath* LP in mono. All this while some girls in high school started joining with the Stones and leaving the Beatles' fan clubs.

The Stones 1964–6 live shows in the LA market integrated acts and bands from my city. In 65, the Byrds opened for the Stones in Long Beach. A second 1965 downtown LA concert at the Sports Arena included the

Vibrations of 'My Girl Sloopy' fame. For the 1966 Hollywood Bowl event Buffalo Springfield were added to the line-up.

Once the quintet camped at RCA and released noise that shaped the world, other rock 'n' roll bands followed them into RCA studios – Jefferson Airplane, Grateful Dead and the Monkees. The basic tracks for Creedence Clearwater's *Bayou Country* were cut in the same room at RCA.

There were half as many people, and everyone drove with their windows down. I was a paper boy for the *Citizen News* and the *Herald Express*. I'd read about the Stones as I sold papers on Beverly and La Cienega. You could catch Keith buying some records or a new Fender guitar at Wallichs' Music City, paying with a roll of hundreds out of his front pocket. Steve McQueen always came to the Whisky and would leave his red Ferrari with a tip, a dollar rolled around a joint.

**Roger McGuinn**, musician: The Byrds did a tour with the Stones. We were the opening act on a stadium tour – places like San Diego, Sacramento, up and down the California coast. We met Andrew at that point, and we hung out with the Stones a little bit. At the San Diego show, the Stones were late. We only knew about ten songs, so we did them all. The Stones hadn't arrived yet; they were stuck in transit or something. The promoter was frantic, and he motioned to us from the wings to keep going. We didn't know any more of our own songs, so we started doing Stones songs like 'Not Fade Away' and a couple more things like that. The Stones arrived while we were doing that, and it kind of cracked them up.

Mick Jagger, Bob Bonis and ALO, backstage, US, 1965

I thought Andrew was cool, and I remember talking to him. I think I might have met him before that, at the Columbia Records convention in Miami. He was talking about keeping the Stones as an opening act to get them well known; he didn't want to put them in situations where they might not draw and so it might be an embarrassment. I remember him saying that, and I thought that was pretty cool. He was a very original thinking guy and very young, too, at the time. I think he was younger than the Stones were.

We hung out with them later in London when we went over there, and they took us out to Stonehenge one time. Keith Richards was driving us in his Bentley and Mick was in another car. Gram (Parsons) was with us, sitting in the back seat and we had a bottle of Johnnie Walker that we were passing around. We went out to Stonehenge, and it was freezing, and the thing I remember was that, aside from passing the whisky around to keep warm, our feet got soaking wet, and Mick, out of compassion, drove us to the next town and bought us all new socks. They kind of seduced Gram to stay and hang out with them in England, and he was happy to do that. Who wouldn't be? It was like the Beatles asking you to hang around or something.

**ALO**: Between Christmas and the New Year Sheila and I moved to Hurlingham Road off Parsons Green to a house rented from the light and sprightly Noel Harrison, the actor son of Rex. Noel and his wife Sara's style of living was in perfect Aquarian mood with our own, and they were off to Los Angeles where Noel would star in *The Girl From U.N.C.L.E.* with Stephanie Powers. The Harrisons' comfortable plush orange settees were joined by our Chinese theatrical masks on the wall, leather rhinos in the hearth, a chair carved into a peacock and a cage in the kitchen that housed Conway Twitty, a yellow canary gifted to us by Marianne Faithfull, who had been bemused and bewildered by the bevy of stuffed hummingbirds encased in a glass dome in the hall. Noel and Sara packed; Sheila and I unpacked.

**Sheila Klein Oldham**: I hated moving. There were just so many clothes for a start, but he'd just say, oh, we're moving in three days, I'll be back and then he was off. He probably thinks he helped move everything, but he'd bugger off with Eddie and be back to supervise the hanging of a painting in the hall. Andrew was always packing; he'd be home for twenty minutes. Lou Adler was a good friend and I think that's where he'd go. England can be pretty dreary and good to get away from. Nico was a neighbour of ours when we lived in Kensington. I once went over to her house. She had a large table and it was completely covered in tiny pieces of screwed up newspaper. She and

Anita were very similar. Very cool, very fashionable.

Anita was gorgeous and mysterious. I said to her one day 'Oh, I love your shoes.' She took them off and gave them to me. Marianne Faithfull was very hard work for me from the very beginning. She was a daddy's girl and if there was a man around, forget it. I got roped into taking her to this meditation centre. She was nodding off all the way there, nodding off all through the meditation. We got back on the train and she just let rip into me, she was absolutely beastly. Another time she invited me over; don't know what she gave me, but I was so sick I had to stay the night.

**ALO**: Tony King arrived with fresh-cut flowers and put the kettle on for tea. David Niven stopped by with a list of Hollywood don't-forgets and must-calls for Noel. Mr Niven was another who seemed to bring his own lighting; he looked and was the most pleasant star – thin, elegant, open white shirt topped by V-neck black cashmere, dark *noir* cuffed flannels and yellow socks and chocolate suede slip-on brogues. He discussed his world, made it ours, and sparkled magnanimously as he held court in the kitchen and asked for a second cup of tea. He asked after Mick as he did after Rex; we were all beholden to the same trough – work. The actor's enjoyment that you were doing well made a cold London evening glow. Niven stood in the kitchen, stretched his toes and ankles and smile-lines as if inspecting his lads in *The Guns of Navarone*, happy at this exchange of residential flurry, the result of employment, movement and good fortune. I thought he was Father Christmas and made my Christmas wish, asking that I could keep this magic moment and repeat it at will. It was so wonderfully normal and special and I wanted some of it on more than just the days around Christmas just as the lump in my throat said, Andrew, you're getting pathetic . . .

**Gregory Phillips**: Mick Jagger and Keith Richards were often at Ivor Court and I was quite friendly with Mick. One day, Andrew announced that he was a dollar millionaire. Mick and Chrissie Shrimpton, his girlfriend, came round in Mick's new Aston Martin DB5. Chrissie was a friend of Camilla Wigan's and in fact had got her the job as Andrew's secretary. I had some strong Afghan dope, so we all had a good smoke and lots of champagne to celebrate. Camilla had always been slightly uptight with me, but now she started to loosen up and dance around with Chrissie, pretending to hug and kiss. Mick sat on my lap and we reduced ourselves and them to hysterics by doing a camp rendition of the Kinks number 'See My Friends' while Andrew crawled around helpless with laughter on the office carpet with a large brass paperweight saying 'Big Deals' in one hand and a small one saying 'Little Deals' in the other. A week later, there was a knock on the door of my flat in Leinster Mews and Mick was there with his DB5 outside.

'Have you any shampoo?' he said.

'Shampoo? What do you mean, shampoo? Yeah, oh well, come in anyway.' I realised that what he wanted was dope. 'You want a joint, don't you?'

'Yeah.'

He came in and we got very stoned. I remember we turned on the TV and watched Donald Campbell on the news killing himself in black and white slow motion in *Bluebird on Lake Conniston*. It was very odd.

Two days later there was a loud purring noise in the mews. I opened the door. It was Andrew with a uniformed chauffeur in an enormous brand new Phantom V Rolls-Royce which took up most of the width of the mews and all but two inches of its narrow entrance. Andrew came in.

'Mick came round last week.'

'You want some shampoo?'

Collapse of both parties.

We had an hilarious two or three hours and then poor Eddie Reed, who turned out to be a loyal and lovely man, had to back the Phantom V out of the mews with Andrew coughing in the back. This session was often repeated. Andrew and Mick played musical chairs at my pad, each of them wanting to know how stoned the other had been.

**ALO**: As the King's Road took back the fashion crown from Carnaby Street with clothes that allowed for the glowing combo of money and tripping, Brian Jones was out there sometimes just shopping for company. Now that we were back at home and there was time to consider, concern became homely. Charlie Watts told me that he had persuaded Brian to see a doctor who had told him that, if he kept on drinking and drugging at the rate he was, he would have not much more than two years to live. Ian Stewart would show no such concern, later telling journalists, 'Brian set out to be as stupid as he could be. As soon as he got any real taste of money or success he just went mad.'

**Stan Blackbourne**, Rolling Stones/ALO accountant: Brian came in one day dressed like the Archbishop of Canterbury; he'd obviously had a good bit of his stuff. Shirley Arnold, their fan club secretary, was shocked to see him come in like this. I said, 'Good afternoon, your grace!' Brian said, 'Oh, you recognised me then, how beautiful; isn't it marvellous!' He'd been to

Bermans, the film and theatre costume people in Leicester Square. He said, 'Stan, I want to thank you for all you've done for me. I want to take you out to tea; I won't take no for an answer. We can walk to that nice place nearby. I've told the chauffeur not to bother waiting, that we'd be back in a while.'

Andrew told me later that Brian was 'emotionally loaded'. At the time I did not know what he meant. I told Brian that he could not walk down the street dressed as the Archbishop of Canterbury and I persuaded him to get in the car. We got to the tea-room and they just could not believe it; the waiters recognised him immediately. We had a nice long chat about things. He was okay and receptive, he'd calmed down, his stuff had levelled off and we had a normal chat.

Brian's mother was wonderful, a lovely woman. She used to ring me up to find out how he was but she just refused to believe that he was on drugs. She'd tell me I was lying. Eventually she believed it, she had to, but it was all so foolish. I had a great deal of regard for the Stones as a whole. I'm not talking about their music; I'm talking about them as a group, as a whole. I never thought their mental capacity was that high apart from Brian's. I always thought Mick Jagger was a buffoon; he had no manners. It's a pity he never took after his parents, because they were wonderful. I used to call Bill Wyman the ghost, all dressed in black, face all white. I knew how old he was, he said you must never tell anybody. You could tell he was much older; it was his whole attitude. Andrew used to float about but his mind was working all the time. He knew exactly what he was after. Some of this floating about was a complete disguise. He used to sit down with me after some particular battle and say, 'Well, Stan, we put that right, didn't we?'

**ALO**: The Scotch of St James had replaced the Ad Lib as the top night spot. The Ad Lib, which had been above the Prince Charles cinema off Leicester Square, had burnt down in 1965. Owner Brian Morris had tried to make a go of it from new premises in Covent Garden but the fickle elite had already moved on to the Scotch. The Scotch was at the end of a cobbled yard off Mason's Yard in the belly of St James, a stone's throw from Buckingham Palace. Gered Mankowitz's studio was around the corner from the club, as would be the Indica Gallery run by Marianne Faithfull's now-husband John Dunbar and Miles.

You'd knock at the door and be auditioned through a peep-hole. Once in you'd travel downstairs via the twisting staircase – the same one upon which Keith Richards extracted payment from Robert Stigwood with a pummelling in lieu of unpaid fees from an earlier Eric Easton arranged and co-promoted tour. The Beatles, the Stones, the Yardbirds, Eric Clapton, Long John Baldry, Keith Moon, the Searchers all starred in the main room on their nights off. Vicki Wickham would arrive fresh from *Ready Steady Go!* accompanied by the latest American group passing through town.

Tom Jones was often centre stage, a little out of place or ignored by rock royalty, making a spectacle of his recent success. Sonny & Cher would share fame with the Hollies while Lennon and McCartney, Jagger and Richards and I and our ladies would sit back in a dark corner and smoke and gloat. Brian Epstein was beginning to withdraw and remove himself from the window of fun. He still worked just as passionately from behind the scenes but was not yet outing his private hours, whereas the rest of the gang rocked on with nothing to hide.

The ubiquitous Jonathan King would be there still celebrating his no. 1 'Everyone's Gone To The Moon', and Eric Burdon celebrated anything. It was a nightly theatrical event, a celebration of being part of what was happening in the most exciting business in the world, a place to celebrate and rest your status amongst your peers and flaunt it above those you perceived as the also-rans. Entrances and exits were perfectly timed, every word counted and measured, every glide across the dance floor posed and lighted. It was the swinging 60s leisure hour . . . who could ask for anything more?

**Tony King**: There were a lot of problems with Sheila. I went round to Hurlingham Road one evening and she was just lying there in the dark. Andrew was off somewhere and things had not been going well between them; it was the beginning of a long and protracted break-up. Sheila was very ethereal, very other-worldly. I think that was one of the problems between her and Andrew; he was very methodical and she was very vague, like you'd go around for dinner at eight o'clock and she'd come down at midnight and say, 'Oh, you came for dinner? I'm sorry, all we have is fishfingers.' At the same time she had that attraction for him. Andrew could never have married someone who was not special. Sheila had impeccable taste. I think a lot of Andrew's style was added to by Sheila. She added to what he had to offer, she embellished what he had and tried to be, and was an influence on Andrew and everybody she knew. Charlie and Shirley Watts would say that Sheila was the most stylish person on the whole scene.

**John Douglas**, school friend: Andrew had got into the drug scene pretty hard. I was very straight. I remember going to see him and Sheila when Sean was only a toddler. They pilled me up and had what seemed like the most enormous joint and I was well out of it. He came in with a knife that was covered in blood and said that he'd just killed Sheila; then she came in roaring with laughter. I think the magic was going, including his marriage; the success was just taking him to giddy heights. I think he often reinvented himself by becoming a fan again, flying over to New York to see Dion at the Bitter End, just to keep himself going.

When he heard a track he loved, like the Mamas and the Papas or *Pet Sounds*, he was able to become a fan. I noted in him what could only be described as panic attacks and a little bit of fear creeping in. By then, even though we were old school friends, I think he felt I was out of touch with his life and he couldn't really confide in me. He wanted to show off the glitz of it all but not the heartache. The huge superstructure that he'd built around his own ego inevitably meant that people were only interested in that, they just wanted the show, and so like some old club comedian he would just turn it on and act outrageous.

**ALO**: Sheila was getting on my fucking nerves, starting to act as if she'd invented me and now wanted to redesign my mind and change my clothes. Tony Calder would join her in this illusion, and later I'd be gone and they'd have each other. The advent of drugs in the streets and minds of the public was a reality that could no longer be ignored, and brewed as one bitch of a potential nightmare. The protection of a private club would soon be gone, its members' privileges rendered obsolete and its uniqueness grounded. I saw no advantage in the public's turning on, except on the occasion it assisted getting laid. I was wrong, of course. It would be the bonanza that transformed 45 vinyl into 33 long play big pay. The record companies now had a manacle on middle-class income, and the product of the day would be an acid-faced reflection that I could not relate to. One of my lives was gone. With this knowledge I upped my drug intake in an effort to stop myself from getting stoned.

'As Tears Go By' had been released in the US as the Stones' Christmas single, something I would not attempt in the pull-the-other-one land of England, where it became the B-side to the February 66 release and no. 1, '19th Nervous Breakdown'. The American release was B-sided with 'Sad Day', and it was another bright day on the farm as the platter went American no. 1. I had no idea that this would be nearly the last no. 1 in my run and the beginning of the end of it all.

1966 would bring many changes in the lives of the two biggest bands in the land. The Beatles would give up concert performances forever. They just couldn't stand doing them any longer; there was no more need for Pierre Cardin-inspired, Dougie Millings-tailored monkey suits. For the Beatles, the war was over and the charade came to an end.

Maureen Cleave of the *Evening Standard*, who had been so instrumental in getting me next to Phil Spector in my press agent days and been so good to the Stones first time out, had stopped looking at pop through the glasses we'd prescribed and was now much more into putting pop into its place. She would give me a nervous breakdown – and the desire to break her legs, had she been a 'Monty' Cleave – when she took the shine off our no. 1 glow with the following revealing column printed on the day of the British release of '19th Nervous Breakdown'.

For some unaccountable reason Mick Jagger is considered the most fashionable, modish man in London, the voice of today. Cecil Beaton paints him and says he reminds him of Nijinsky. Mick is also reported to be a friend of Princess Margaret. He has said nothing – apart from a few words on the new single – to suggest he is of today, yesterday or any other day. He remains uncommunicative, unforthcoming, uncooperative. He is twenty-two, lives in a three-bedroom rented flat near Baker Street. As a boy he appeared regularly with his PE teacher father on a television programme called *Seeing Sport*, often seen canoeing, rock climbing, or camping in a tent. He has seven 'O' levels, two 'A' levels and left the London School of Economics after two years of training to be an accountant. He hasn't many close friends, naming David Bailey (for whom he was best man in August 1965), Andrew and Keith amongst them. His favourite song is 'Satisfaction'.

Maureen Cleave, *Evening Standard*

I got two O levels, no As, my favourite tune at the time was also 'Satisfaction', and hell hath no fury like a journalist on the rag. When I read this Cleave savaging of my client I called Mick to ask him what on earth he had done, what had happened to set this woman against him this much, and against the day-in-the-sun control we enjoyed. The bitch was foaming at the nib, enjoying the idea of sticking pins in every part left of him, the very idea of Jagger.

I hoped Mick *had been* rude, spilt tea or champagne down Miss Cleave's front or on her lap. I hoped he'd been a sexist pig; I hoped he'd been *that* Mick. I hoped he'd tried to pull her, corblimy'd, ogled her tits and tugged at his dick. He assured me he'd done none of the above; he'd been on his cucumber-sandwich best. This just made matters worse. Clearly the worm had started to turn, the vicious quill had drilled a hole in our wall. Perhaps Miss Cleave just thought, how dare you, you little classless bastard. I know the *barrio* you bled in and I weaned you off the back page into an acceptable feature and now you are trying to pass yourself off as art as opposed to something that your father's gym slipped in. I have no idea why she called the truth marker in so damn early. Maybe Mick just forgot she knew him when, and she decided to remind us. It's probably some of that, and he probably tried to pull her as well. Hope the mutt succeeded. I would very shortly be reaching out again to press maestro Leslie Perrin for assist – this time, to attend to our uncovered flanks and run damage control over our daily lives. Leslie would continue this task after I departed.

In the meanwhile we got away from the rising cold winter of discontent by repairing Down Under for another bout of Australia and New Zealand.

**Mark Wynter**: I bumped into Andrew in Sydney. Andrew had become much more bohemian in his guise, much more flamboyant and theatrical, and a lot more on edge. He was wearing the shades all day and night, he had the scarves around the neck and waist, the big frilled shirts and velvet jacket with fur piping and military buttons, all of this with an old tattered faded pair of jeans. I got the impression he might have lost his focus a bit. He was having some terrific conflict with Mick Jagger. It was almost like Professor Higgins and Eliza Doolittle. There comes a time when the pupil thinks they know as much as the master and all of a sudden they don't want to listen to the master anymore. I ran into them again outside Brisbane at some fancy Elizabeth Bay mansion. Mick was sulking in a corner and Andrew was holding court and showing off with all the locals who would listen.

**ALO**: Running into Mark Wynter Down Under was like running into the ghost of hope and ambition abused. A lot of us were crawling along that ledge. On that second tour of Australia I remember the Searchers' drummer Chris Curtis being escorted by the military police off the navy dockyards and mess quarter area. Childless Chris lived behind Harrods in London and was renowned for having a voluptuous *au pair* girl who freely serviced those in need. He'd gone out at night after a show, a Gladstone doctor's bag in hand, trying to pass himself off as a doctor to all the young conscripts. On medical advice he was flown back to the UK and a substitute drummer flown in. I was also getting more than a little out of hand on one too many occasions. I was escorted by police and ambulance back to the John Bateman Motor Inn in Melbourne upon getting catatonic and violently weepy after being greedy with absinthe and having a quasi-breakdown at the house of a local poet. Australia was getting 'don't-take-care packages' – self-mailed drugs from Vietnam – and I was later told the poet had added acid to the absinthe. That remains no excuse for cracking up on the job. The cost of ambition would soon have me cashing in some of my chips, upping the ante, and raising the level and voltage – via the insanity of ECT – of my game.

## · CHAPTER 13 ·

**Pete Townshend**: The Beatles were very remote as people. They were already huge cumbersome stars. I used to think the Beatles were very old fashioned, even when they were new. I remember someone saying to me, 'Don't you like the new Beatles album?' I said, 'It's full of those fucking Italian love songs.' That's how it seemed. Because the Stones built the wall they couldn't see it as clearly as we would, the Who or the Small Faces. I think that the Stones also could not see that they'd built it and the Beatles hadn't. The rules were laid down: you do not sing about fucking love, you don't do it, you don't sing soppy love songs. There are songs about I Can't Reach You, You're Beyond My Reach . . . I Exhort You, I'm Gonna Fuck You, but, We Are In Love is a No . . We Are In Love . . . that was just ruled out. Kit Lambert and Chris Stamp knew nothing about the music business, but they learnt quickly, and some of the lessons were quite hard. The tape lease deal with Shel Talmy fucked up the Who for a long time. We're still paying Shel to this day for records he had nothing to do with. We had a 2½ per cent deal at the time. The Who did not make any money until at least post-*Tommy* and most of it was earned on the road. Kit and Chris, it would be wrong to call them crooks, but they charged us 40 per cent commission and I think, looking back, this was utterly corrupt. What was different about Kit and Chris was that they came in, not as managers, but as equal partners. Their tenet was that they had as much talent as we did.

Shel did absolutely nothing. Actually that's not true; on 'I Can't Explain' he actually did a lot, but nothing that we approved of. Kit was preproducing the songs at the Marquee from rehearsals and delivering them to Shel who literally just sat there while Glyn Johns recorded them. Shel then applied his post-production technique and his sound machine to it, which was brilliant. Shel was a bit of a collector and he stumbled into something quite rich at the time: both the Who and the Kinks had something special about them. With 'I Can't Explain' he brought in a session guitar player, a session drummer and the fucking Ivy League to sing girly backing vocals. I don't think I ever had one conversation with Shel about what I was doing.

On 'Anyway, Anywhere, Anyhow' and 'My Generation' I had to force my way into the control room to hear the playbacks and the only reason I got in was because Glyn Johns was the engineer and a friend of mine. Glyn had been singing in a band called the Presidents. I managed to get him to let me in, and Shel was blind, and I was sitting there and Glyn says, 'Shel, Pete wants to sit and listen', and Shel says, 'Well, I suppose that's okay.' The other guys in the band come in and Glyn says to them, 'Out, you lot!' Shel had allowed me in there because I was the composer. Kit wanted to come in and listen and Shel just wouldn't let him in the control room. He was making these records with us but we had no real idea of what was going on; there was certainly no dialogue. We were fucking anarchists. By that time we were already sort of out of control, there was no politeness about anything we did. Roger rarely sang – he just sat up there and growled. I rarely played; I just made fucking noises. What Shel brought to those early Who recordings was a method, which was brilliant because when Kit took over our productions, our records sounded like shit for a long time. All of them nicely recorded but none of them had the fire that Shel managed to capture. With Shel we could go and take our live act into the studio, but when we started to work with Kit we found we couldn't, because Kit needed to control things that Shel didn't. But we enjoyed it more with Kit because he would involve us in the recording process.

**Richard Barnes**, *Maximum R 'n' B*: Kit and Chris were brilliant – serious ducking and diving with class. The mixture of Chris's East End suss, living on the streets, the son of a tugboat man, working hard, and Kit's aristocratic bearing and his family's connection wasn't a combination you'd want to mess with. Kit turned up at the Railway Hotel in Wealdstone, where I was promoting the High Numbers. I was shit scared of him, because he looked so straight. He was around thirty years old and was wearing a really expensive Savile Row suit. He looked trouble.

**Pat Gilbert**, *Mojo*: The son of Constant Lambert, the classical composer, Kit was an alumnus of Lancing College and an Oxford graduate whose sense of adventure was wonderfully irrepressible. Having freely experimented with drink and drugs at university, he had served as an army officer before joining an expedition to Brazil in 1961 to chart the course of the Iriri River. When his travelling companion was speared to death by a remote tribe of Indians,

Kit had to fight his way out of the jungle alone. This harrowing experience seemed only to have exaggerated his fearlessness. Kit's partner in New Action was Chris Stamp, the younger brother of actor Terence. Stamp and Lambert had met when they were working as director's assistants on *The L-Shaped Room*. New Action began working out of Stamp and Lambert's flat at 113 Ivor Court, off Baker Street, in the autumn of 1964. Andrew Loog Oldham maintained two offices in the same block at 138 and 147. Stamp was usually conspicuous by his absence, working abroad on films like *The Heroes of Telemark*, from which he'd send back his wages in a struggle to keep the group afloat.

**Richard Barnes**: Because of Kit's upper-class background and upper-class voice he could walk into virtually any bank in London and open a bank account, then demand an overdraft. They had the Royal Bank of Scotland in Knightsbridge and the Midland in Sloane Square . . . we'd be borrowing money from anyone and anywhere.

**Pat Gilbert**: Following the release of 'I Can't Explain' in early 1965, after a run-in with the bailiffs (soon to become a regular thing), New Action moved to Eaton Place, Belgravia, where Kit installed Pete Townshend in the flat above the offices, along with a couple of Revox tape machines. Lambert had recognised an important fact: an R 'n' B covers band, albeit one that cooked up a glorious noise, had a limited shelf life; a band sustained by a repertoire of songs as great as 'I Can't Explain' could last for years. The Beatles had done it, the Kinks were doing it, now even the Stones were making a career from releasing their own compositions. Why not the Who?

**Roger Daltrey**: Kit seemed completely out of place, really flamboyant. He had this upper-class accent that was so out of kilter with everybody else's. He said, 'Hi, I'm a film producer.' He wanted to make a film about the West London Mods. He was sharp, he had ideas. You couldn't help being impressed. Chris was like this East End barrow boy, a really amazing looking, hip guy. Better looking even than his brother. They made an odd pair but they effervesced enthusiasm.

**Nick O'Teene,** president, Aweful Records: After you've been in the music business for while, you realise there's nothing really new. Except for the hype. Hype springs eternal. Back in 64 I was reading this story in the trades about Kit Lambert's big plans for the Who. The story came about as close to the truth as music papers usually come – about as close as parsley is to pussy. It was a clever write-up. It tossed about the notion that these boys were geniuses and that these geniuses had just made a big breakthrough. It wasn't just a big breakthrough in popular music they'd got planned. It was gonna change the world as we know it. It made your head spin. And it was all this guy Kit Lambert's idea. Sort of. Kit was the manager of the Who, along with a barrow boy name of Chris Stamp. Together they were a diabolical pair. Kit was a brilliant nut case. He had plans. Big plans. He was straight out of grand opera. He loved disasters. In Kit's book the whole point of building something up was to watch it all crash down later on.

Big news of the day – For Immediate Release – Kit Lambert, Esq., was gonna get his lad Pete Townshend to write actual songs. I had to set down my tea cup for this one. No more R 'n' B covers for the Who, it said. None of that. Pete was gonna write 'em all from now on. All by hisself. The way it was written up you'd've thought he'd invented a cure for bad rugs. Never mind that the Stones had done it, the John Lennon–Paul McCartney bit, a while back – this was news. The Big New Fing. It wasn't all that big and it wasn't new at all, but in the land of hype, that doesn't matter. As long as you yell it loud and long enough people are gonna swallow it. And not only that, this Kit Lambert was gonna produce those mini operas himself, the very ones written by his own art-school dropout Puccini–Rossini – Pete Townshend. It was a bloody renaissance, he was telling us, happening before our very eyes. Where, you might ask, did maestro Kit get these grandiose notions? From that other nutter, Andrew, of course. 'Andrew seems to be getting away with it' is what the quote said.

He didn't have that far to go to find it, neither. Two floors above him were the offices of Lord Loog Whimsy and his own personal Igor, Tony Calder. All these lunatics, see, inhabited the same building: Ivor Court, a royal house of freaks, it was. In the basement you had some Euro-dyke who did press for some nearly something record company. On the fifth floor was the very grand, very gay Roy Moseley, dropping names like ninepins – 'As Larry Olivier said to me when I was pinning up Judy Garland's gown on our way to Lord Delfont's . . .' Going up! Eleventh floor: poncey poofs and bolshy barrow boys (the offices of Kit Lambert and Chris Stamp). Twelfth floor: Charlie and Shirley Watts. Thirteenth and fourteenth floors: outré fashion and mad schemes. In other words, the offices of Oldham & Calder, teeming with assorted maniacs, rogues, Rolling Stones, press flacks, rock molls, cheeky buggers and, to top it off with a bang, the psychopathic Reg the Butcher. All you needed were bars on the windows and men in white coats and you coulda started your own asylum.

The whole city was in turmoil, for that matter. That was London in the 60s – they were here with a vengeance, but as soon as you tested them they evaporated. It was like a benign virus spreading south from Liverpool and, in London, north-west from Ivor Court. It was an unlikely revolution. Leading this army of freaks, fret-wizards and talented layabouts were: two highfalutin pooftahs, Brian Epstein and Kit Lambert; a butch East End yob (Chris Stamp); and one Mad Hatter from Hampstead, a wide boy with public school weapons – Sir Fuckin' Andrew. Hendrix was managed by a gangster and a bass player, poor guy; one of the Kinks' managers had originally been the group's lead singer, fer chrissake; and Dylan was *hondled*, as they say in Yiddish, by a splenetic, ponytailed ex-hardware store owner. Pity the poor muso with that lot to lead 'em.

Folly is contagious, and once the wild thing hit the streets everyone wanted to be quite mad. They held festivals of madness and everybody came. After you'd had the three Mad Hatter's balls – Monterey, Woodstock and Altamont – the days of the high-flying, eccentric managers were gone – and some of them along with it. One way or another they all exploded or imploded. That's the way it is with crazies – they burn out. In the mid-60s the flamboyant (and flaming) manager gave an act street cred. By decade's end that was all done and on came the Zen bruisers, actual bouncers and focused percenters – Elliott Roberts, Peter Grant and Shep Gordon – doing the absurd balancing act of accounting, GBH and artistry.

You had managers who managed the managers – Allen Klein (Andrew) and Pete Kameron (Kit Lambert and Chris Stamp). Off stage the Who were outrageous, violent and on the ledge. They brought all that fury on stage – just like the Stones usta do. But fame quenches anger. By 1966 the Stones were no longer street punks. They were gentry, buying manor houses in the country and cottages in the suburbs. Their songs were lyric-driven. They were playing for the man and the money. They had found the Hollywood Hills and were resting. The Who, Hendrix, the Doors, Janis Joplin and the whole San Francisco scene were outside the gate, ready to kick the door in and don the mantle until the Stones woke up twice and got back to the street for the Stones Mach II.

**Pete Townshend**: When Shel Talmy started to make a lot of money from us and the Kinks he started to go a bit crazy. Plus his eyesight was getting worse and worse. Recording with him, we were also blind. We never knew what we were doing; we did it so incredibly quickly and we felt just like paid and instructed session players. Kit was very impressed with Andrew Oldham and he only wanted to produce records because Andrew was doing it with the Stones. After I'd written 'I Can't Explain' we played it a few times at our shows at the Goldhawk. The recording was very rough but Kit got all the kids from the Goldhawk club to come to the *Ready Steady Go!* show to support us. He managed to get one hundred tickets, so when we débuted on *RSG!* our audience went fucking berserk. Kit would tell me this was like being Purcell in the court of Charles II. Chris would say this is what rock 'n' roll is going to become; we speak for the kids, rock 'n' roll is about the street.

**Chris Stamp**: Totally up yer arse, up yer cunt, down with the motherfuckers. We wanted to destroy what existed, we wanted to tear down the establishment that had kept us all in prison. When I said things to my father, my father didn't approve of all this, because the minds of working-class English people had been so conditioned they thought it was good they'd been given some shitty job and they were grateful they'd been allowed to pick up the shit. It was anger against all of this because our minds had this sort of low esteem built in because of our birthright. We were very clear-cut about the Who's manifesto; it was all very clear amongst all of us. We weren't there to sing silly love songs. The Who were great musicians but it wasn't just about the music. There was this whole other thing going on that was just as important as the music, if not more. We never went along with the blues thing either. In actual fact we could have sung the blues and been a much bigger band much quicker, but everybody was doing that; that was too fucking easy. We religiously stuck with what Pete Townshend would come up with rather than go getting some blues riff and adding a few fucking lyrics. We totally understood what everyone was up to from day one; all the other wankers were doing was let's go and find a few black riffs that may be in the public domain and add a few Chelsea-type lyrics to them. We recorded this 'I Can't Explain' song as a demo. We knew we had to get the Who a record contract; that was the vital need. We knew there was Decca, Pye, Philips and EMI . . . and that's all there was. Our secretary had a girlfriend who was married to Shel Talmy, so Shel heard us and thought that we were great. We met him and he seemed okay and he'd just produced the first hit for the Kinks.

**Shel Talmy**: The Kinks were the first act I took into Pye. I had taken Georgie Fame and Manfred Mann to Decca and been turned down on both of them. I thought that as an independent producer I had better start getting independent. So I went to Pye and started making a deal with them. I spent a lot of time working out how to get guitar sounds. I didn't just drop out of the sky and say this is the way I think I'm going to do it; I really had worked out a lot of this stuff. A lot of it was very technical – reverb, compression, echo. I spent a lot of time working with the primitive equipment that was available. There were no magic units around in that time. I worked it all out from the existing units, pushing them to parameters they were not created for in the first place, and found new ways to enhance the sounds I was working on. Jimmy Page was the best session guitarist around at the time, simple as that. I did not use Jimmy as a lead guitarist with either the Kinks or the Who, at any time. I did initially use him with the Kinks on rhythm guitar because Ray Davies wanted to concentrate on his singing. I saw Andrew once or twice socially; I'd see Mickie Most every now and again. I suppose we were all rivals to some degree so nobody got incredibly friendly with anyone else. I thought that most English records were incredibly wimpy and not many bands played with any balls, so I liked the Who immediately. They were one of the first bands I heard who could get out there and put on a performance. I was strictly a producer; I never had Andrew's gift for promotion. He did a super job for the Stones and himself. I went in and spent my own money on the Who's recordings. I took them to British Decca who turned them down. I then got to American Decca. (Decca used Decca in the UK and the name London in the States while Brunswick, who had taken over the American Decca, used that name in the States and Brunswick in the UK.) Brunswick were extremely nice. They realised that they were out of the loop in terms of rock 'n' roll but were willing to go along with us and, in fact, they broke the record. I never saw Chris Stamp, I never told him not to come to the studio. He just never came around. Kit Lambert was around and I did tell him I didn't want him around the studio. What I did and what I do as a producer is work with the band on the songs and the arrangements. I don't just record anything that comes in and say, 'Oh, yeah that's great.' That would be nonsense. No producer I know, who would call himself a producer, would do it that way. What's the point; you may as well be an assistant janitor for all the input you'd have. It was considered good to be fast in the studio, because if you weren't you were thought of as a shitty band, a totally different attitude to what it is now.

**Chris Stamp**: Kit and I made the 'I Can't Explain' demo. We produced it but we didn't know it was called 'producing'. We hadn't worked that one out. Andrew had, because he was much closer to the scene than we were. Shel offered us this deal and we signed with him. It was a mistake; we realised it literally from day one. He had a pretty good sound. He didn't get too stroppy in the studio because Kit and I were there, and we were very insistent on certain things. Shel didn't really want to use the Who; he wanted to use Jimmy Page and some drummer but we said no fucking way. It wasn't about the sound, it was about personal growth. We couldn't leave that in the hands of this guy.

**ALO**: At the end of July and beginning of August 1965 the Stones played some UK concert dates with the Moody Blues, the Fourmost, Steam Packet and Julie Grant. Also on the bill were the next greatest thing since sliced bread – from California, following the P.J. Proby trail to united kingdom come: Scott Engel, John Maus and Gary Leeds – the Walker Brothers. They had arrived in London with a Mercury-via-Philips release produced by Jack Nitzsche, 'Love Her'. Love them the UK did and a version of the Bacharach–David warbler 'Make It Easy On Yourself' set them up for the big one.

**Bob Crewe**: The American and English music business was closely interwoven by that time; there was a synergistic thing that was happening. There was a big love affair going on in America with all things British, which was ironic because so many of the brilliant English writers and bands found themselves out of their fascination with American music. It was almost like a harmony, one against the other, but intertwined musically. Things would happen like the Walker Brothers would cover my record of Frankie Valli's 'The Sun Ain't Gonna Shine Anymore' and have a no. 1 with it. I gave the Valli record to Johnny Franz at Philips because Mercury were doing nothing with it; it had not become a hit in the States. I said, 'John, you'll love this song. Why don't you take it and see what you can do with it?' He took it and produced it with the Walker Brothers.

**Tony King**: Andrew loved 'The Sun Ain't Gonna Shine Anymore' and he loved Scott Walker and his whole drama-queen image, the tragic poet with the booming voice. He'd say, 'Oh, God, just listen to that.' He loved the Frankie Valli record and all the Four Seasons records. He'd go crazy about 'Walk Like A Man' and a Frankie Valli solo record, 'You're Gonna Hurt Yourself'. He loved all the back-up vocals. Andrew loved records that had a bit of camp to them, all the girl vocal things, like the Shangri-Las. 'I Can Never Go Home Anymore' was a favourite. Of course he'd make Mick and Keith listen to all of his favourite songs as well. Whenever Andrew liked something the whole world had to hear about it.

**Mike Watkinson and Peter Anderson**, *Scott Walker: A Deep Shade of Blue*: With the Vietnam war escalating, the fear of the draft helped convince Scott and John that now was an appropriate time to leave, following a final excursion into RCA studios with their new drummer. According to Gary, it was he who suggested the Walkers record the Barry Mann/Cynthia Weil song 'Love Her', although Scott has asserted it was the choice of arranger Jack Nitzsche.

Formerly an Everly Brothers B-side, 'Love Her' introduced the distinctive Walker Brothers sound – heavy orchestral backing over which Scott would emote, with John providing high supporting harmonies. In a 1973 interview, Scott said that the disc's Spectoresque feel, achieved by the presence of a thirty-eight-piece orchestra, was the brainchild of Nitzsche. 'What he was tryin' to do was achieve something similar to the Righteous Brothers – only a little more refined, because he felt they were getting to be a bit of a drag.'

But having worked out the orchestration, Nick Venet and Nitzsche ran into difficulties over the vocal track. Clearly a much fuller, deeper voice than John's ethereal tones was required. Venet and Nitzsche huddled in earnest consultation for a moment before the former broke off to stride over to the Walkers and enquire: 'which one of you guys sings the lowest?'

John hesitated fractionally before replying, 'Well . . . Engel does.' Much to his mother's disappointment, Scott had rarely sung since the Eddie Fisher debacle two and a half years earlier, and only then when John's throat was hoarse. 'We need someone who can sing bass,' Venet smiled encouragingly. 'Come on, let's do it!'

So, more through luck than judgement, it was Scott who stepped tentatively into the vocal booth while John remained on the sidelines. One of the greatest voices in popular music was discovered that day. 'Scott got stuck with lead because his voice handled it better,' confirms Gary. 'There was no jealousy on John's part, that was just the way it worked.'

Nitzsche, the man who erected the great Wall of Sound, which was later rebuilt around all the Walker Brothers hits, is best remembered for his arrangements on Ike & Tina Turner's 'River Deep, Mountain High', and a string of other Phil Spector-produced classics. Nitzsche's recollections of the session which spawned 'Love Her' were surprising, especially in view of the record's historic significance. 'It was no big deal,' he said.

'River Deep, Mountain High'! Now that was a song that mattered to me because it was *very* special. I cannot compare 'Love Her' to that because it was so average. I guess it sold about two copies in the States and you cannot

Jack Nitzsche, Darlene Love and Phil Spector. Gold Star Studios,
Los Angeles, 1963

put it in the same category as 'River Deep'. As we were recording 'Love Her',
the studio door opened and in walked Mick, Keith and Charlie, makin'
everyone feel about an inch tall, I guess. When it was over, Venet came out
of the control box, jivin'. He was sayin': 'That's your greatest ever
arrangement, Jack!' – or some crap like that.

And how did Nitzsche remember Scott? As a fine bassist with latent
songwriting talent or a charismatic vocal performer perhaps? 'I remember
Scott,' he said thoughtfully, 'as bein' a great hairdresser. That's right! A
hairdresser! He was foolin' around in the studio and started rubbin' this gel
into my hair. It was called Dep and it wasn't as heavy as lacquer. After he'd
rubbed it in, dried it and backcombed it, I ended up looking like I had more
hair than when he started! He must have done it three times that day and he
was pretty good. I knew nothing of the Walker Brothers before we went into
the studio. These small labels used to complete four tracks in each session
so it was pretty much another job for me.'

According to Nitzsche, 'Love Her' was originally meant to be recorded by
the Righteous Brothers, but the song became available following a
disagreement between Spector and Mann. Nitzsche also claims that the actual
demo, by a singer called Freddie Scott, was far superior to the Walkers'
release. While he remembered Engel as 'a sweet and lovable guy', Nitzsche
did not particularly rate his voice and was astounded to learn of Scott Walker's
'god-like' reputation on the other side of the Atlantic almost thirty years later.

**Kim Fowley**: Scott Walker was nothing special; he was just a guy. I define
him like this: somebody stood up at Gary Cooper's funeral and said, 'Gary

Cooper was an empty canvas on which the world paints its masterpiece.' And if you look at Scott or John, they were as empty as that. They had a great sound and a great look and Scott never spoke to anybody about anything, so naturally he became an icon. Sometimes when you have a still life watercolour of a person, you don't do anything. That's it, that's all Scott was, just empty and ready for the Proby formula to be recycled. I had done production work for Maurice King in 1964 for Piccadilly Records, who had an act called the Hellions, featuring pre-Traffic Jim Capaldi and Dave Mason, and that's where Gary Walker met Maurice King, so he knew to take the Walker Brothers to Maurice King when he got to England. Gary Leeds had been in England earlier and he'd stayed with us and studied the Proby formula, which is, 'You're American, you come to England, you do the hustle and everybody buys it.' So he went home a little before I did, found two blond guys who looked a little like the Everly Brothers and they went back as a trio and did that whole thing. Scott Engel became Scott Walker. John Walker was John Maus.

Out of all this comes the Walker Brothers. Scott was just this guy who wanted to be a crooner. He adapted like everybody else to Brit pop, and became this moody, Jacques Brel guy. I'm sure that Lionel Bart and everybody said, 'Oh, my, isn't *he* a pretty one!' and whatever. I know Jonathan King did. But the mastermind of the Walker Brothers was Gary Walker, born Gary Leeds, who had understudied me and Proby, who had done the formula.

**Tony Calder**: We had Scott Walker – he agreed, he was on board. He was going to record solo for us. His manager Maurice King tried to put injunctions on me and Andrew but in the end he gave up. Scott was there ready to record; I negotiated the deal. I mean, what a fucking star, but I couldn't deal with him. Even Andrew couldn't cope with him. Scott Walker was the only artist Andrew shut up for. Scott was talking about Brel, we were talking about Mort Shuman. He was talking about I-don't-know-what, something about philosophy. I thought, 'What's this all about?' My idea of philosophy is a no. 1 hit record.

**ALO**: Scott Walker was attractive, but I made sure I never really spoke to him because I knew, up close and personal, he'd bore me. He was Neurotic Boy Blue one sigh away from being a wanker. The idea of him was better than the reality. Jonathan King told me I'd like him and encouraged me to get together with him and Scott 'for a chat', told me how much we'd have in common and that scared me, for starters. I didn't like the place from which Jonathan King looked at pop music – down on it – and I feared Walker no. 1 was the same. As Elia Kazan I was concerned that Scott was really Richard Davalos and that John Walker would turn out to be James Dean. Scott had great pipes, emoted great, but I didn't need another social Brian Jones drain in my life. Besides, like Brian, he didn't write. He's safer hiding, which is the best career move he could have made. I couldn't have done anything for him; we'd have got on each other's nerves. Jonathan called me and Tony once and said, 'You must get up to Regent's Park. Scott is having a breakdown; he's snapped, he's talking to the hedges.' I thought, 'Yeah, all on half a bottle of Mateus.' Gered Mankowitz and I went around to Scott's banging on the door, shouted through his mailbox and told him to stop acting like an old poof and do the decent thing and put his head in the oven.

Amongst the better kind of snaps forever facsimilied into my mind-smile is the look of amazement and utter disbelief on Paul McCartney's face as he sat in Sheila's favourite peacock chair and watched Mick, Keith and myself alternate between the Supremes and the Four Tops as Tony King pumped up the lead volume and we mimed it out to the very best of Motown. McCartney's expression was not unlike that of the straight Bill Hunter character in *Priscilla, Queen of the Desert* the first time he lays eyes on Terence Stamp. Total disbelief. I mean, you know he wasn't going around to Brian Epstein's where Brian and the Nems gang were getting up in drag and miming to Cilla Black. The few London clubs that were worth going to – the Ad Lib, the Cromwellian and the Scotch of St James – all closed at two o'clock. So on evenings when night was not done with I would open up at home, and such was the night Tony King, the Glimmer Twins and I provided the cabaret.

**Tony King**: The famous one was my impersonation of Diana Ross. I studied her on *Ready Steady Go!* and copied what she did with her arms, mouth and eyes. We did the Supremes and the Four Tops. I'd do the lead vocal and Mick, Keith and Andrew would do the backing. Andrew got Paul McCartney to come all the way back to Hurlingham Road and we got high and I got up and did 'Stop! In The Name Of Love' and 'Nothing But Heartaches'. I loved doing it; I'm a show-off. Andrew had this incredible green art deco chair that was made to look like plumage and Paul McCartney sat there looking at us going, 'I don't believe this'.

**George Gallacher**: Tony King was a ponce. He was like someone who had knocked on the wrong door, discovered there was a party and decided to stay.

I never did find out what he did but we thought he was a clown. Guys like him appeared at the Apple headquarters years later, when I was up there around White Trash time, basically useless bastards who somehow gained entry to the scene and convinced themselves and others that they were an indispensable part of the creative forces of the times. They gained importance by association. Always in a suit, all King contributed to the office was empty-headed comments on how we all dressed, childish gibberish really; basically a fucking half-wit. So the Poets had cracked the Top 20 with their first single, but not much else. Our second single only got into the Top 50. We weren't dancing in the street, we were dancing having peaked. We were pretty demoralised towards the end at our failure to break through, the lack of promotion of our singles, living on Tony Calder's pathetic handouts, just drifting. But there was no brutality on Andrew's or Tony's part, no 'right, you've failed, that's it, get the fuck outta here'. No, it was nothing like that! It was in contrast to the image of the pair as the ultimate bastards of bastards in a business where to be a bastard was a prerequisite for entry. We never gave them credit for their faith in us.

The first time I met Jagger was the first time I was in the office meeting the Stones, the Shrimptons and Marianne. I'd gone into what I thought was a toilet to find a room with Mick in front of a full-length mirror rehearsing all those James Brown movements. He looked ridiculous and he knew it. He looked just like one of those grotesque caricatures portrayed by those crap 60s comedians who, when their lack of talent failed to get them laughs, fell on equally crap impersonations of Dylan and Jagger to save them. Nor did he stop for me. He just said 'hi' and continued like a stick insect in some weird mating dance. Lennon would have cringed. I made my apologies and left. And there had been naive me thinking that all his moves were impromptu responses to the music. Oh, well!

**Gregory Phillips**: Tony Calder began to resent us in general and me in particular for introducing dope (i.e. fun) to Ivor Court, and because I became close to Andrew. I got the impression that Calder and Sheila Oldham had it in for me and were always criticising me behind my back. I went to Andrew's marital home only twice and all I heard was Sheila bawling him out for playing 'Sea Cruise' and 'California Girls' too loud and too often. They were his most favourite songs. Sadly, he and Sheila were destined to split up.

By this time I was beginning to wonder when, if ever, I would make a recording with Andrew. Jimmy Page was around a lot at Ivor Court, a lovely, smiley young guy who always wore a navy donkey jacket. He was working on

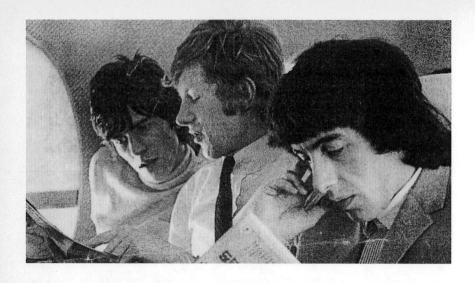

Keith Richards, ALO and Bill Wyman, October 1964

a lot of sessions for Andrew. One day I got a call from Andrew to say that he had found my track. It was a song called 'Down In The Boondocks' which was a hit for Billy Joe Royal in the USA. Billy Joe Royal's management had decided not to release his version of it in the UK. I listened and liked it a lot. I met up with Jimmy, who was working on the backing tracks for it at Regent Sound in Denmark Street, a studio where many great records were made. Jimmy told me that it was going well. When they were finished Andrew asked me to go down and record the vocal. Andrew and Jimmy were in the control room. They played me the backing track and Andrew said, 'Sing it and then we'll do the vocal harmony.' I got it right on the second take and then did the same with the vocal harmony. They were amazed as they had thought it would take all night, and Andrew teased me a lot for being 'One-Take Phillips' and so on. A day or two later, the master of my 'Down In The Boondocks' arrived back at Ivor Court and I went round to listen to it. Everyone liked it. Marianne Faithfull and Nico were there on that day. Marianne's relationship with Mick Jagger was starting to go strong by this time. Chrissie Shrimpton was desperate and Camilla persuaded me to bring her together with Steve Marriott. They got it on, but it turned out to be a disastrous relationship for both of them. They got busted for dope when Chrissie was off her head and still infatuated with Mick. Then there were plenty of mad moments with Reggie King, such as the time he had to forcibly put me on a plane back from Ibiza where I'd gone for a holiday with a bunch of his gay friends, only to fall for a hippie girl who I met on the beach.

At about this time I became friendly with Keith Moon. Moon was a wonderful companion – almost as mad as Reggie King, who would walk down hotel corridors picking up fire extinguishers and dustbins to throw out of the window – madness, really. I met Long John Baldry, who was the campest person ever. He had Steam Packet, a great, great band with Elton John, Brian Auger and Rod Stewart. I met Long John somewhere and he said, 'So, you're the lovie who likes to smoke pot!' and invited me back to his flat. There he got out a Stratocaster, rather than his dick as I had feared, and played and sang incredible blues all night. Nico became a friend and I did a promotional tour with her miming to our records. On a flight to Manchester, Andrew told the stewardess that Nico and I had got married, so we got rat-arsed on free champagne. That sort of thing happened all the time when Andrew was around. Nico was living in Augustus John's old flat in Chelsea which she'd rented from Talitha Pol, who was one of the artist's granddaughters, I think. Nico was fantastic – so beautiful, with a great deep voice. I became friendly with Anita Pallenberg and Marianne when Marianne and Jagger were living in Chelsea. Those women had so much electricity and spirit; to be honest, I thought that they were the soul of the Rolling Stones. They had far more spark than Mick and Keith, who would just sit around rather glumly and say, 'All right, you can buy that' as Marianne and Anita brought beautiful things into their lives. As for 'Down In The Boondocks', not much came of it, because Billy Joe Royal did indeed release his version when mine began to take off, and Royal had the airplay and the hit. On top of that, Calder had his own record out by the Fifth Avenue, and I think he preferred to work on that as opposed to what I'd done with Andrew. It was all like that; you didn't have to be gay to be a bitch. Still, my version of 'Boondocks' is hailed as a classic to this day. It's been released quite a few times in the past years.

**ALO:** The road was fun. Back in 64 I was on the north-west leg of a Stones ballroom tour when I decided to head over to Liverpool for a busman's holiday with John Lennon and Paul McCartney, shortly after Liverpool welcomed back its Fab Four from their first full-length US tour. After the wall-to-wall screamatic sound-drowned concert at the Empire Theatre I joined John and Paul for an M6 to M1 cruise back to London in John's amazing new black-windowed Rolls-Royce Phantom V. As you know, I fell in love with the car and wanted one of my own. I had acquired my new man Eddie Reed after meeting him driving Freddy Bienstock's grey Silver Shadow, trainspotting Allen Klein around London. Eddie was a good-looking

Fulham lad who loved a pleated skirt as much as Reg had loved the charge of the short-trouser brigade. He and I spent more time with each other over the next five years than we did at our respective homes. We got on very well and were very good for and to each other. When I eventually got my own Roller I had Eddie in constant touch with John Lennon's driver over the details in John's, wanting the exact extra embellishments that he had, as it all worked so well. I kept insisting on the same two sets of windows, one black and the other clear. After a lengthy conference the two chauffeurs worked out the problem. There was only one set of windows on the Lennon Phantom V; I had been sufficiently stoned not to realise that the second 'clear' set were just 'open'. On the first day of Eddie's employ he had to drive me to court where I was fined £20 for driving without due care and for having no current driving licence. I had already failed my driving test; it was a demoralising little moment I had no wish to repeat. I think it was the botched three-point turn, the accompanying expletive and some crunching through the gearbox that did it. An acquaintance of Eddie's, whom I'll name Paul, was hired to take my driving test in a remote village in Gloucester, it being the time of no picture requirement for driving licences. I passed my test – I'm told my three-point turn was immaculate – and for a short while our friend had a busy little sideline, reputedly taking tests for the likes of Keith Richards, Steve Marriott and many other too-busy-to-steer pop 'n' rollers. Paul finished this little detour in his career by taking and passing, for a bet and a dare, his wife's test in drag.

Eddie Reed, ALO, Phantom V, Cynthia Stewart and Lou Adler,
London, 1965

The black Phantom V was immaculate. It had blacked-out windows, beige interior and a completely impractical telephone system at £1.37 per minute, per call. It boasted two stereo systems; one high-end and true, the other 'spatial' or, as we dubbed it, 'sound-in-stonederama'. A bar hidden under an office desk rounded out the extras which priced the immaculate glider at £19,000 as opposed to the in-the-shop tag of a mere twelve.

Back on the Stones roll, I was on the last legs of being eager to get any Stones film made as soon as possible. I arranged for a film crew to shoot a documentary during a short Irish tour of Dublin, Cork and Belfast at the start of September. In Dublin forty or so young men got on the stage and a riot ensued. They swarmed all over the stage, pushing Mick Jagger to the floor, grabbing his microphone, taking turns at yelping and playing Mick. Brian Jones was attacked and punched by half a dozen of this out-of-their-heads, would-be band on the run. Oh, mother, if you give a name to it, it surely will appear. Bill Wyman was forced to hide behind Ian Stewart and the grand piano on stage, Keith managed to make a run for it, and Charlie Watts just kept on playing. *Charlie Is My Darling* was to be a sort of trial run, get-your-celluloid-legs together for any forthcoming feature film and an effort on my part to keep the Stones interested in the idea of film. It would be titled *Charlie Is My Darling* based on the fact that he was, and it would be photographed, edited and directed by Peter Whitehead.

**Peter Whitehead**, director: Andrew was completely responsible for *Charlie*; it was his idea. He gave me complete freedom and was very generous of spirit. It's thanks to him that *Charlie* exists as a document. I had just done a film, *Holy Communion*, at the famous poets convention at the Royal Albert Hall. I'd filmed it on my own, using a hand-held camera in the new avant-garde style. Andrew must have got wind of this crazy guy living in a little flat in Soho, using these new filming techniques. When I got to his office for the meeting, he just said, 'How much?' I said £2,000. He said, 'Right, Cynthia, get a cheque made out for two grand. We'll pick you up at eight o'clock Friday morning.' Andrew said nothing about direction – he just said do what you want and that was wonderful. You come along, you make a film, you do what you want. I think one time there was a press conference and he said, 'Do you want to film the press conference, then continue filming on the train from Dublin to Belfast?' I said, 'I can film anywhere.'

With the realism of *Charlie* I tried to show they were just the lads next door. It was just a socio-realistic *cinéma vérité* film. I was really trying to portray these guys as ordinary blokes to whom something amazing had happened, who loved their music and were doing what they wanted to do. Andrew was ruthless; anyone with any common sense who met Andrew would know exactly who he was and what he was. He was a powerful guy, captain of a big ship that could sink at any time. There were no guarantees. He had no guarantee, I had no guarantee, and neither did the Stones. There was no guarantee the Stones would last even a year longer. For me it was an amazing experience and *Charlie Is My Darling* caught that mania. I realised that to these kids Mick Jagger was a god. The kids were ecstatic, just insane for thirty minutes. Mick needed to push it all just that teeny bit further and they would have got on stage and killed and devoured him, the entire theatre, two thousand people, just jumping up and down in one huge mass that became fused to the music into one colossal being. For me it was a revelation that pop music was so important and powerful, that it was such a deeply archetypal experience for teenagers. I was completely detached, observing it as someone who was interested in the Stones as a social phenomenon. It was obvious I was a little aloof, not like some guy fawning over them. Andrew must have sensed that was probably quite useful, or he just didn't care. He just wanted to see what they looked like anyway – to hell with Peter Whitehead. I was the guy there on Monday morning and he wanted to film by Friday. Okay, go do it, fuck it, if it comes out fine, if not, okay, it's a few grand down the drain, what the fuck. That was the feeling.

It was very moving for me because of everything Brian talks about in the film. He obviously has a total premonition about his own death. I would say for a young guy like that, a total narcissist, for him death was the trip anyway. He was in his prime, yet even then he was talking about the indeterminacy of everything, everything coming to an end. He could sense this rejection, this fall, this failure, this sinking into oblivion. It was all there already; he was being stalked.

Mick had enormous resources to deal with it. He was a very together guy, always has been, you could tell then. Plus he was aware of his power; he was totally luxuriating in it. Brian was incredibly jealous because it was Mick who had the power. Brian was jumping up and down strumming his guitar, looking pretty with his blond hair bouncing off his shoulders. Mick was right out there at the front just rubbing up against every single person in the audience, just touching them up, just masturbating them. The boys as well, that was what was so extraordinary. Andrew was very aware of this. It was the boys as well, don't think it was just the girls. The boys were standing at the front weeping! '*Miiiick!*' They wanted to be Mick Jagger; to be Mick Jagger they either had to fuck him or kill him.

It's not *A Hard Day's Night*; it's weird, this film. Andrew used *Charlie Is My Darling* as a trailer to show people, because at the time he was trying to get together a feature film on the Stones; they were trying to raise a million pounds to do *Only Lovers Left Alive*. I began to realise that nothing was going to happen when Allen Klein said shelve it, you don't want that fucking *Charlie* film coming out. He was going to get a million dollars, get them all loads of loot from soundtrack deals; they were all going to get rich. They never made a fucking film again. If they had made a film it would have been awful. I think Andrew saw the writing on the wall and just let it go. He probably saw it was something that he could not control, and if young Andrew could not control something, he very quickly lost interest.

# · CHAPTER 14 ·

**Bertolt Brecht**: Life is short and so is money.

**ALO**: I had the pick of the litter with the Rolling Stones. My life was not complicated by having to manage over-entitled dykes in distress or gutter scum-line inbred, ungrateful midgets, although the Small Faces would come under my vomit-watch a while down the Immediate line. I say vomit-watch as Ian McLagan and Ronnie Lane made my Small Faces experience much ado about all-or-nothing, while the calm and manners of Kenny Jones and the loving madness of Steve Marriott made the journey worthwhile. My Immediate adventures and those with its artists, the wonderful and the wankers, are best left for another set of pages, of which time, passion and circumstances will determine the need.

The Rolling Stones and I were still having fun getting it done and the shit to come was holding its breath. Within a year I would be unable to distinguish whether I was driving the plane or a passenger who has lost control of the ride. You'll recall I had not learnt my job. I had no actual management skills; that was not what had attracted the Stones to me and vice versa. I was the front man, the shill, the barker, and therefore, regardless of any third-party agenda, day-to-day just had to be run and I was a travelling Stone with a free pass for a remaining while.

**Nona Hendryx**, Patti Labelle & the Bluebells: Hmmm . . . the road. Going on the road at that time meant the Chitlin' Circuit, so-called for the low budget, bus riding, station wagon, fried fish, chicken in a box, sardine and soda cracker eating, rooming house-type hotel staying, mostly southern route taking, playing mostly clubs on the wrong side of the tracks. Maybe you'll get paid or maybe you won't, or maybe you'll be cancelled without notice. In the South in the early 60s during the civil rights movement, things were escalating. Desegregation, bussing, early black militancy, the murder of JFK, Malcolm X, Dr King, Medgar Evers and those four little girls killed by a bomb in the 16th Street Baptist Church. We were on the Chitlin' Circuit, so our encounters with white southerners were far less destructive. We were met with No Room in the Inn (if you were a certain colour), white and coloured bathrooms and drinking fountains. So we stayed in coloured hotels or rooming houses and coloured-friendly motels when we could. Being refused service at a rest stop restaurant was common and sometimes it ended with a threat to send us to our maker.

Keith Richards, Mick Jagger and Nona Hendryx, backstage, US, 1965

So, being asked to open for the Rolling Stones on their tour of North America was welcome news. We were with the William Morris Agency where Jerry Brandt and Wally Amos (Famous Amos Cookies creator) were our agents. We were told the Stones asked for us. Jerry and Wally, two good-looking, smooth-talking New York City dudes, made it happen. Indeed Jerry was a hotie . . . tall, dark and handsome with bedroom eyes and an appreciation for sisters of colour. I don't know if he was a great agent or not but he was cute! Wally Amos was a good-looking, long-tall-drink, short Afro, clean-as-a-whistle brother. They made a very dynamic duo and more welcomed eye candy for us girls. The Stones could've asked for us because we were known in England and the British Isles from touring and TV, especially *Ready Steady Go!*, the cool, hip, hit music programme. Roy Tempest was the promoter in England and maybe he promoted shows for the

Stones and suggested the Bluebells. Our name changed to Patti Labelle & the Bluebells during one of our trips to England. There was a famous dance troupe *à la* Rockettes with the same name. Previously, we toured with James Brown, Otis Redding, Joe Tex, Sam Cooke, the Staple Singers and Curtis Mayfield & the Impressions, and thought we knew what touring was and wasn't about, what to expect.

Boy, were we wrong!

Sex, Drugs, Rock & Roll & Shop 'Til U Drop. The biggest places, the loudest screaming crowds of girls and the absolute hysteria – I'd only seen this stuff on television. That was for the Beatles and Elvis and on TV, not in pot-induced, psychedelic-stereo-living colour. The first show was in Montreal, Canada, in a huge (at the time) arena. We arrived by car; we travelled in a station wagon or a mobile home most of the time, the one so conveniently placed on the back of our first album. Hal B. Robinson, owner of Newtown Records, our record label, also owned a car dealership! Early use of two-for-one advertising! We were so naive, we thought how nice that he would give us this brand new mobile home to travel in! *Très* stupid! He got us to promote the record, advertise his car business and charged us for the privilege. We made monthly payments towards buying the mobile home, which seemed to be ongoing!! No wool was pulled over our eyes! Baaaaaaaaaaa! I digress. We got on so well with the Stones that we were invited to fly on their chartered aeroplane for the rest of the tour. The Big Time! The Stones not only had a manager but a road manager. There was catered food back stage, separate dressing rooms, cars to take us to and from the aeroplane, flight attendants, hotels with real names. There were celebrity guests arriving back stage or in the audience, mostly other famous music artists but also artists from other fields, i.e. Warhol, Truman Capote, Jane Fonda, Liz Taylor, etc. The Stones had been on most of the major television shows including *The Ed Sullivan Show*. They had roadies, a sound man, a light man, and their own equipment (unheard of for us), plus . . . the newly dubbed and henceforth and forevermore joined at the hip, if you don't have at least one then you're doomed to obscurity band aid . . . groupies! Ninety-nine per cent female fans who would rock to their music and rock their world later at the hotel were waiting in every town. Some innocent, some well-worn merchandise hopping from tour to tour, band member to band member or their entourage. We didn't even have our own band; we were backed by the same band as the Vibrations, if memory serves. They were also from Philadelphia, so it's highly likely. This was post doo-wop days and only artists like James Brown, Otis Redding, Sam Cooke, Joe Tex, Little Richard,

Bo Diddley, B.B. King and other big stars had their own bands. When we played the Uptown Theatre in Philly, the Apollo in NYC, the Howard in Washington, DC, the Regal in Baltimore, the Royal in Chicago, the Brooklyn Fox in you-know-where, the Fox in Detroit or the Peachtree nightclub in Atlanta, it was with the house band. We had charts – musical arrangements – and would rehearse with the band the day before if we were lucky or the afternoon before the show at night. In our case it was usually anywhere between two or four shows so you couldn't depend on your hit or semi-hit; you had to have a deep musical well to draw from and for most of those places you had to be really good. Theatre gigs were welcomed because it meant we were in one city, one hotel for a week to ten days. Moving from city to city doing one-nighters was an exhausting way of life even for teenagers.

Stonehenge? No, Stones Unhinged was more the experience. We saw shopping on another level. Even though we were still on a weekly salary we lived vicariously through the Stones. It seemed as if they had money to burn. The English pound (money) was about $3.60 or $3.75 to the dollar then. This made everything really inexpensive for the guys and shopping almost as much of a high as Sex & Drugs & Music. Shopping has to be elevated to the now famous acronym. This was our first encounter with major after-show parties thrown by the Stones. It was also my first teenage love affair with a mop-topped rock star.

Worlds colliding in more than one way is putting it mildly! Colour, Culture, Music, Money, Politics, Sexual Mores, the lot. Other than some of the same musical influences and being relatively the same age, there wasn't much we shared in common. Adding to this the civil rights movement and the early stirrings of the Black Panthers made this travelling musical circus even more incongruous, if not impossible. The Stones' audience was 99 per cent screaming girls who didn't even register that we were there. So there weren't any racial difficulties because to them we were invisible, not there, didn't matter! They screamed, 'Mick, Brian, Keith, Bill, Charlie!!' throughout our performance. Some girls were carried out on stretchers while we were singing and long before the Stones had even entered the arena. The dolls, the scarves, the cakes covered with images of the Stones were sometimes passed on to us. I remember sharing one really gigantic cake with the guys, which turned into a food fight. I know some of you will say 'how juvenile', but we were teenagers, remember. It was hysterical – all of us with the exception of Charlie, I think, joining in. The room was a mess and became messier as beer, wine and champagne were added to the mix. Somewhere vaguely lurching in my memory is the image of the dressing-room toilet and cake everywhere. I would imagine a plumber was needed the next day!

**Christine Ohlman**, singer/writer: I was mad for the Stones from the first time I heard them. My mother, who was cool, would have preferred I stick with the Beatles as the safer choice, but at least I was allowed to have Stones LPs in the house. Most of my girlfriends had to sneak the records and hide them from their parents. This, of course, just added to the fun. I can remember listening to *England's Newest Hitmakers* with my friend Linda, the record player muted under stacks of pillows in her bedroom. That was how much her mother hated the Stones.

It was the summer of 1966 and the second time the group had come to Connecticut. I'd been there in 1965 at New Haven Arena, nearly breaking my neck with two girlfriends when we tried to crawl out on a metal grating to knock on what we thought was the dressing-room window. (We had good reason to be doing this – a purple, six-foot stuffed furry snake we wanted to present to the group.) By 1965, I'd seen a few Brit Invasion shows – notably the Dave Clark Five's at the same venue – but the Stones had a level of coolness that devastated the competition. I remember Mick wore a button-down shirt open at the neck and a blazer and Keith might have been sporting his famous striped jacket. Even in 1965 we Stones fans prided ourselves on being more on-the-edge; we knew that at least some of their repertoire had been nicked from blues artists and we dug that. You'd never find Herman's Hermits or Freddie & the Dreamers covering Jimmy Reed. And we dug the Beatles – loved them – but there was no *danger* there.

The difference between 65 and 66 was monumental. In 65, we still weren't sure what we were seeing – we just knew that we liked it, and we liked it a lot. By 1966, we'd figured it out, and so had the Stones. It came down to three things: flamboyance (with Brian leading the way, stage dress had evolved to frills and paisley – and we'd gotten bolder, too – our skirts were mini *mini*, eyes were black-rimmed and lips white); sex (the danger element again); and an absolute disregard for authority, which Vietnam only fuelled.

1966 was the summer of 'Paint It, Black', and I hitched a ride with a school friend and her father (who kindly dropped us off and waited outside) to the early evening outdoor show at Hartford's Dillon Stadium, a minor league ballpark that served as a concert site by the addition of folding stage and chairs. The opening act called themselves the North Atlantic Invasion Force (NAIF), and they'd been burning up the local club scene with a pretty decent rendition of 'Paint It, Black'.

The show got started with NAIF doing their best to bear up under the general moaning and screaming of about 4,500 teenage girls who wanted the Stones and only the Stones, but then the band made the fateful decision to trot out their club-pleasing cover of 'Paint It, Black' as their set-closer. Just as the set had been completed and the band began exiting the stage, a man I knew to be the Stones' manager – there was no mistaking the sharp-cut suit, the fabulous haircut and those sensational skinny shades – hurled himself, the veins in his neck fairly popping, at the group's hapless lead singer, George Morgio, in full view of the entire crowd and began a heated physical and verbal exchange over NAIF's having the brass to usurp the star attraction's current charted single. Morgio himself has said, 'He was screaming, "I'll make sure you never make it in the music business!" And, you know, we never did.' Events culminated in a microphone stand being picked up and Roger Daltrey'd by Mr Oldham, who aimed it at Morgio's neck.

What could be better? We were thrilled. Everyone knew who Andrew was. We read all the fan mags, and prided ourselves in making the musician/manager connection. Beatles = Brian. Stones = Andrew. From those mags, we knew how tight the managers were with their charges, and here was ample evidence – he'd risk physical harm for them!!! Right then, he won our hearts. Who did that opening band think they were, anyway??? This was the essence of all things rebellious, all things cool. And besides, Andrew was undoubtedly the best-dressed man there, or anywhere else, for that matter.

I saw back-to-back shows that summer. The same friend's father drove us to Forest Hills Tennis Stadium in Queens, New York, the following evening, while the radio blasted 'Love Is Like An Itching In My Heart', 'Sloop John B', 'Bus Stop', 'I Saw Her Again', and 'Sunshine Superman'. There, we caught the Stones plus the Ike & Tina Turner Review. Tina Turner was a revelation that night – a sequinned, spangled whirling dervish, alternately screaming into and fondling the microphone – but it's Brian Jones's image that burns in my brain. I can still remember him, attired in a funky, frilly shirt and vintage-looking, tight-fitting jacket, sitting off to the side of the stage strumming an autoharp during 'Lady Jane'. I'd never seen anything like him at a rock 'n' roll show (not 'rock concert' – these shows were still relatively small-time, held at hockey arenas and tennis stadiums and small-time ballparks, the Beatles' Shea Stadium appearance notwithstanding).

By all accounts, and in retrospect, this should have been the beginning of the end for Brian; he was becoming more 'wasted', they said. Let me tell you something. Brian Jones was the most beautiful man that we little girls had ever laid eyes on. Forget Mick Jagger. We wouldn't have known 'wasted' if it had jumped up and bitten us. But we knew beautiful when we saw it.

The Rolling Stones, Chicago, 1965

**ALO:** The fifth American tour took place in a land deeply divided by the Vietnam war and disturbed by the first run of the drug culture. The unrest in America seemed to permeate everything. For this and many reasons, it was the most harrowing of tours. The bounce was still there but a lot of the slap was flat. Even with a slew of hits, the lilt was wilting under the pressure of life getting posed and jaded – never mind the Doors, Joplins and underbelly of American music waiting in the wings. Down the Delta road, Brian was an increasing problem. He disliked having to play Jagger/Richards songs on principle, the principle being that he'd been unable to come up with the goods and write commercial art himself, as opposed to miming to it or mocking the song that fed us. He told friends that 'The Last Time' and 'It's All Over Now' (although not a Mick and Keith-ette) were probably about him and that on occasion, no doubt dependent on the match of drug and paranoia, Mick, when singing the pivotal words in the chorus, would turn to Brian and sing 'because I used to love you, but it's all over now' and 'this could be the last time'. Brian was now more often hospitalised and started to miss a number of live dates. I was not aware of this at the time. The Stones ran a very tight ship and were not prone to moaning; they just punched in and got on with the gig. Fortunately, these Brian-less occasions took place in the sticks – Brian was still *inamorata* with the big city and would not 'get ill' in a major market.

**Pete Bennett**, US promotion man: I worked for Allen Klein. I got the Stones on the radio. We were somewhere in the South-west in limousines going from one town to another for another show. We liked to keep moving; we didn't make many stops. The locals thought that limos were just for the governor or major movie stars going to a Hollywood opening, so we kept moving. The South was still kind of backward and rough.

We found a quiet-looking diner on an interstate lay-off and decided to stop and eat. Everybody got out of the cars except Brian. He wasn't hungry; he was going to stay in the car. We all came back to the limos and no Brian; he'd changed his mind and gone off to eat. Andrew was annoyed. We didn't like hanging around in the open and we were running late. We turned and saw Brian inside the diner at a table against a far wall; he waved at us.

Andrew said, 'Pete, go in and get him now,' I did. I did everything Andrew told me.

I went into the restaurant and picked him up by the neck and dragged him out to the car. All of the other Stones and Andrew were falling over laughing. Brian got in the back of the car as white as a sheet.

Andrew and Keith said to me, 'Hey, Pete, you should have let him finish eating.' I said, 'But, boss, you told me to get him now.'

**ALO**: A date in the North-east was stopped after just one minute when fans broke through the inadequate barriers and police and invaded the stage. The police used tear gas to break up the riot, thus blurring the line between a Rolling Stones concert and student unrest, but the cops didn't care – they were into rehearsal. This was all starting to get less than show business. We had similar experiences of ineptitude and violence in Connecticut, Pennsylvania and Washington – the authorities seemed to be using us as a dry run for the-times-they-don't-want-changing.

While the Stones played around upstate New York and the eastern seaboard I dealt with the world from the more pristine confines of the Drake Hotel. My tailor, Roland Meledandri, was located opposite the Drake. He was a miracle worker, able to combine the tradition of yesterday with the breath and flair of the day and a sense of fabric that was sensual. Roland cut a fine suit for many, including the dapper threads Steve McQueen touted in the original *The Thomas Crown Affair*.

ALO, Drake Hotel, New York, 1966

Sheila was in England minding Sean. Linda Keith, who was still seeing Keith, called me up and told me to take her to dinner. I was wary of Linda because I found her attractive, very attractive. Back when Sheila had been frumpy, uncomfortable with herself and pregnant, I had fairly lusted after Linda's bones when I perceived them as offered over the Christmas break. My mind was prevented from the physical by the fact that Linda's parents were in the next room, which rather dimmed the view of a hard-on, and by the fact that I was sure that Linda was the type of gal who would give and tell.

After dinner Linda hauled me out to Steve Paul's club, the Scene, which sat under the 59th Street Bridge. In its previous incarnation, this had been the jazz club location where, in *The Sweet Smell of Success,* Tony Curtis as my man Sidney Falco planted pot on jazzman Martin Milner on the orders of Burt Lancaster's J.J. Hunsecker. I'm not sure if I recalled that at the time, but I did feel I was about to be busted.

Linda said she wanted me to meet her latest discovery, Jimi Hendrix. Actually, she was dating him, and I was being used as the beard. One of you bright young things may wonder why *this* bright young thing did not change the course of history, make a beeline for Jimi Hendrix and attempt to make him mine. Panic wove the threads of the evening. I knew Linda was trouble, but could not work out what part would be mine. I could hardly refuse to take Keith's lady out to eat (she might complain to my lead guitarist) and my mind had no time to zone in and notice Jimi Hendrix as it was in a wee bit of a tizzy and domestic haze. On getting back to my rooms in the Drake, having left Linda entwined with the thin black duke, I received a message that confirmed I had every reason to be on my domestic para-toes. Sheila had called from London to say . . . that Linda had called from New York to say . . . that I had asked her out and was it all right with Sheila for her to go out with me for a meal? The message ended with a request that I call home, which I did, to a blazing transatlantic row. Ah! Girls on the road.

**Sheila Klein Oldham**: Linda Keith discovered Jimi Hendrix on the Bowery. She got involved with him, then her parents flipped and carted her off to a nuthouse. I think she ended up having shock treatment, too. She told me she took Andrew to see Jimi and hoped Andrew would manage him, but that Andrew was just not interested. She took Seymour Stein to see him, too. Her parents were very Jewish and straight; that's why she didn't stay with Jimi for long. She was out of control. While still with Keith, Linda had moved on to Brian Jones, and she was always coming around to our house for secret dates with Jimi Hendrix. Thank God Andrew was always out.

Keith was a very nice ordinary boy. He was mad for Linda and she really wasn't interested. She was smoking a lot of grass and he was completely straight, Keith. So I said to him, maybe if you smoked a bit you might be able to be on the same wavelength. At that time Keith had not the slightest interest in drugs, but he thought Linda the bee's knees.

**Philip Townsend**: Andrew and I fell out over this Linda Keith business. Andrew was being very loyal to the Stones and I'd sold a picture of Linda Keith overdosing to the newspapers. Linda's father was Alan Keith, who'd had the longest running programme on Radio 2 – 'Your Hundred Best Tunes', or something like that. Andrew was like that, especially towards Keith; that's why he didn't want pictures of Linda blowing it all over the papers. It wasn't about the Stones or their image; it was all about Keith. There was this code between them that I don't think was in any contract, like the time he and the Butcher went up and smashed a journalist's hands because he'd written something about Keith's complexion.

**ALO**: Other freeze-frames from 1966: In LA the Stones are booked to play their biggest concert yet at the Hollywood Bowl, with 17,500 tickets sold within a few hours. But even in the freewheeling atmosphere of Hollywood the mood is sour. The *Los Angeles Times* announces by headline that the Stones are a 'Long-Haired Nightmare'. Suddenly the jibes of the UK press seem quaint. There's a feeling of being in the beginning of a real war. Sunset Strip will turn into the battleground. A 10 p.m. curfew is put in place and rigorously enforced; the police use optimum force to indiscriminately drive kids off the streets. The prevalent mood all over America is disturbing. The 60s are about to change owners and the stage will be passing its crown to the crowd. The quote John Lennon had allowed Maureen Cleave in March about the Beatles being more popular than Jesus gets America wired as the Beatles start their last-ever Americas tour in August. Beatles records are burnt and destroyed throughout the Bible-and-Elvis Belt. Lenny Bruce dies in horrific circumstances hounded by his own drugged demons, aided and abetted by the law. This brings Phil Spector to a new low. Lenny Bruce was a mate and idol, and Bruce's passing, coupled with the US lack of success and/or recognition for his 'River Deep, Mountain High', causes Spector to announce his retirement. The fact that the Ike & Tina Turner outing is lauded by all and goes to no. 2 in the UK is of no consolation to the master, and he hangs up his cloak and shades and calls it a night. I try to reach him but he's taking no calls. The King of Teen Anthems is in Beverly Hills seclusion.

**Robin Guild**, interior designer: Andrew was living opposite the Hurlingham Club and he used to have this amazing wardrobe at home, all the clothes arranged by colour, jackets and suits starting with white and ending up in black – just an immaculate guy, right? But he was also spending a lot of time at the Mayfair Hotel while the offices in New Oxford Street were being finished. One day Calder said to me, 'Is he ever going to finish this damn office? When can we get in? He has this suite at the Mayfair – that doesn't bother me. The fact that he only uses it during the day – that doesn't bother me. The fortune he's spending on telephone calls – that doesn't bother me. The fact that he's spending £100 a week on cherry cake doesn't bother me . . .' I said, 'Hold on, £100 a week on cherry cake, that doesn't bother you?' Calder says, 'No, what bothers me is that they eat the cherries and leave the cake – that's what bothers me.'

I thought he was joking but I went up to see Andrew one afternoon in the Mayfair. He's got some young guy called Steve working for him, and whenever you saw Steve sitting in a room he always had his hands covered with a tea cloth, the reason being he was always rolling joints. If it was cool, the tea cloth came off and it was back to rolling. After a while he ordered some tea, and room service came in with a trolly with six cherry cakes on it, all sliced up. It was true they ate the cherries and left the cake.

**Cynthia Stewart Dillane**: While we were working out of the Mayfair and Mick and Marianne first got together, Marianne was performing at the Olympia in Paris. Andrew was meant to be managing her again to keep Mick happy, but he really wasn't interested and couldn't get it together. So he said, 'Darling, you go to Paris and take the sheet music with you.' I hated to fly and refused all foreign trips so I went on the ferry, stayed a while and went with Marianne to see Edith Piaf in concert.

**ALO**: The American evangelist Billy Graham arrived in London to play Earl's Court. Cliff Richard would be appearing with Mr Graham, so this was a must-see. Cliff had survived the Beatles, the Stones, a lot of slagging and much gossip about his sleeping with more than the Lord. He was already the grand survivor of the pop game, a master of behaviour, and the thought of Cliff in celestial volumic surroundings had me fly back from Stockholm to catch the last night of the Graham event.

Eddie and I got off the plane at London Airport, picked up the black Mini-Cooper we'd left in the parking lot, and headed for Hurlingham Road. Sheila was out or away. Eddie rolled a joint and made a cup of tea. I was

291

hungry. There was a bag of biscuits on the kitchen table with a card pinned to the top stating, 'Try these!' We were late for our date with the Lord so I grabbed the biscuits, we headed for the car and I started trying them. We arrived at Earl's Court and joined the flock entering the Exhibition Hall. My only experience of crowds in the recent years had been of only sheer bedlam, panic and pandemonium, but this crowd was orderly, at ease and friendly. I felt the same way and nibbled on another biscuit. Eddie and I found our seats and waited for Cliff. It was a long wait, so we had a cup of tea and I had another biscuit. The arena started to come and go in waves, the crowd's reaction to whatever was happening on the stage went out of sync, and the laughter and applause went on forever. The hands were clapping out of time with the sound of the same hands clapping behind the sound I was about to hear. Eddie saw me reach for another cookie and asked me for the bag. He nibbled at a corner, mulled on it, played with it in his mouth and saliva, took another little bite, confirmed the whatever, cleared his throat, and spoke.

'How many have you eaten of these biscuits, Andrew?'

I was annoyed at this invasion of my concentration, as I was sure the moment was nearly Cliff. I answered and heard a tired voice follow my answer three beats after the words mine had just spoken.

'Five or six, Eddie, I don't know. Why?' I sighed, hearing the totality of the breath echo inside and outside through the whole hall. I was surprised that nobody else heard.

'They're hash cookies, Andrew, that's why,' said Eddie. He studied me, then asked, 'How are you feeling?' I didn't answer. 'Perhaps we ought to take you home,' said Eddie, getting us both up and out of our chairs.

I didn't see Cliff but I certainly saw God. Well, I saw Cliff, but from a hashish-in-surround point of view. I saw him through a telescope in reverse and heard him from the sinking flotsam that was me, my brain and I. I saw him sing but all my brain fed through was the sound of trampled gargling.

I take it Eddie took me home. I remember a lot of 'excuse mes' as we shuffled past and stepped on the toes of a row of young Ena Sharples and assorted *Rosemary's Baby*-types. The faces I passed morphed chillingly into what they would become. The movie wasn't even out, but I could see their future and they could see me now. I don't remember my body leaving, but my mind recalls a *Hiroshima Mon Amour* fairly reckless, legless evening saved by the bell that was Eddie.

My next memory is of sitting up in bed at about ten o'clock the following morning feeling as if a sledgehammer had whacked my brain, a steamroller had rolled over my body – a body my mind could not find. There were plenty of parched men in my head, panicked eunuchs trying to find a way out and into my body, which was still buried beneath the sands. Cynthia sat at the edge of the bed, a concerned look on her face as I came to.

'What the fuck happened?' was all I could muster. I was still in pre-rigor mortis.

'The cookies, dear, absolutely loaded with hash, my dear. Do you have any idea of how many you had?'

That's our Cyn, I mused, the caring dart, straight to the heart of the matter, fuck the shorthand – the lady has wavelength, and has mine. I managed a wry smile at her, which she took as meaning I was probably about to lie to her.

'Half a dozen . . .'

'What, before you went out, or after you went out?'

'Probably a dozen . . .'

'That's more like it.'

I was getting some body feeling back. I looked around to be sure of my bearings and noted I was still in bed. I attempted to raise my arms; I did so but they were very sluggish as if carrying invisible weights. I don't remember eating; I was still very parched out. It was either by that evening or the following one that I could get up and get back into life. Eddie reappeared in my bedroom and flung £40 in old-fashioned white fivers on to the bed.

'What's that for?' I asked.

'That's the money you put into the collection plate that I thought it better to take back,' he smiled, as he got up off the bed and took himself and an empty tea cup downstairs for another cuppa.

Towards the end of the summer of 66 I rented a house in the South of France with theatrical agent Donald Langdon and his most recent wife. Donald, a comfortable soul, slightly portly and slightly bearded, represented comedians John Bird, Dudley Moore and Peter Cook. I was flying in from Los Angeles to Nice to meet up with Sheila and son Sean who had been ensconced on the French Riviera all summer long while I'd toured, recorded and officed on behalf of the Stones. I had not indulged in LSD on the same front-line level as had the Stones, having neither the time nor the inclination. I was too busy working, and, regardless of what you may have read elsewhere on these pages, was attempting to keep a roof over my head and my mind intact with a reasonable lid on the madness. By the end of 1966, the Stones, however, had fame, money and some time off – an incrementally dangerous amount.

**Philip Townsend**: Mick, Brian and, to a lesser extent, Keith could now achieve their need to mix with the nobs. Up to now old money had kept themselves to themselves, but now they were bored and needed entertaining and the new rock stars could provide all they needed – and the drugs as well. The main go-between was a rich, stupid, gay and untalented twit called Robert Fraser. He was an art and drug dealer with an address book full of the same kind of people as him. He soon became the Beatles' and the Stones' best friend. While he was the son of a self-made banker he had wormed his way into the old money crowd.

The first time I met Robert was in Ireland when he was chaperoning Mick, Keith, Marianne Faithfull and Anita Pallenberg at Desmond Guinness's superb Georgian castle, Leixlip, near Dublin. Mick and Marianne were lording around the grounds like the old money Mick was not. It was amazing how quickly he laundered himself from a terraced house in Dartford to a very large castle in Ireland. It had taken the Guinnesses a hundred and fifty years to achieve the same transformation. It took Mick fifteen months.

The Duke of Marlborough and Mick Jagger, Blenheim Palace, 1973

**ALO**: I indulged myself on the near fifteen-hour flight from LA to Nice by taking acid. I bought the first two seats in the front row of first class, ordered vegetarian food, loaded myself up with Mickey Mouse colouring books, crayons and the little gadget that rotated Disney slides, and let the acid take over. Donald Langdon picked me up at Nice Airport in his Jaguar and when told of my flying *modus operandi* asked me if I had not been scared, as in 'freaked out, man'. The opposite, I was able to tell Donald. I was at one with the sky, felt I'd touched and walked on God's circle and would forever remember the feel of the clouds – besides, I added, I didn't know how to fly a plane. I arrived in Nice very tired from the acid and the summer workload. I collapsed and rested, then threw myself into the visiting celebrity agenda that was part of summer holidaying *chez* Langdon as Donald ran his office overlooking the Mediterranean. And so I disappointed myself, Sheila and no doubt Sean, as there was no real rest and no real family time.

**Sheila Klein Oldham**: By now we were breaking up every year. This allowed me to go off and recuperate. Then, just when I was about to get my life back together, Andrew would find some wonderful way of coming back into it. Generally he did it musically; he'd come in and play some beautiful heartrending record. He'd play it again and again and again and it worked. Because he was such a powerful being I'd be doing what I could do to keep him happy. I found myself waiting on him hand and foot but he didn't want that. I remember Andrew saying he'd been with John Lennon who had been in a rage because his wife asked him what he wanted for supper. The mentality behind that being his wife should know what he wanted for supper – Andrew was the same.

There was an electricity when Andrew and Lennon were in the same room, a combination of art and brute force. Lennon could look at Andrew and see everything Epstein wasn't. Andrew would be looking at Lennon and seeing everything Jagger wasn't. There was a mutual fascination between the two men. Andrew was killing himself for the Stones; he and Mick were fighting a lot. Do the fuck what I say! I'm the manager! Andrew was full of angry self-righteousness. Allen Klein was very persuasive and he was as obsessed as Andrew. Allen would think nothing of spending twenty-four hours non-stop trying to convince you, to work it out; it was like a chess game . . . 'If I say this, they'll think that.' They were at it day in, day out. In the beginning Andrew was very impressed; Allen Klein was full on.

By now I was on Valium. Maintaining the level he and the Stones were on was much more difficult than getting there. Brian – at that time you couldn't have a conversation with him; he was just not there. By that time everybody was so busy posing. I think Andrew really did understand what the chemistry of success was. Andrew, from studying his heroes, knew it could be manufactured.

**Roy Moseley**: I guess you could say I was there for the beginning and end of Andrew's life with the Stones. Andrew was appearing on some BBC show. I don't know what he was doing there, but Mick Jagger was there with him. I was there with John Gielgud; I now had my own agency and was doing things for Alfred Hitchcock. Sir John was doing a George Bernard Shaw play for the BBC. He called me to come up to his dressing room, said there was an awful din going on in the dressing room next door and could I do something about it. There were Andrew and Mick screaming at each other in the corridor. Johnny G came out of his room and nearly got knocked down by the door. He told them both to stop it and said he knew who Mick was and thought he should be a little more professional in public. Sir John told them both off, gave them both a good talking to. Andrew was very upset; you could see that was the beginning of the end of them.

**Gered Mankowitz**: One of the things that has changed so drastically in record production is that the knob-twiddlers, the engineers, they became producers as well. But in those early days, in my experience, there was an engineer who was often a permanent fixture of a particular studio or was assigned to you. I'm sure that once you knew who were the available engineers at places like Decca in West Hampstead, you could ask for somebody specific. However, you sort of got an engineer and you got a tape boy, an assistant who changed the tapes and fetched the tea. The producer did not necessarily touch the board. I mean, in Andrew's case he absolutely pretty much went out of his way to avoid touching the board. And the whole thing was very simple, technically, compared to how it became.

The technological changes and possibilities that came towards the end of the 60s were astounding, but I think one of the things that I've always found and noticed was that people who are interested in the 60s, different aspects of the 60s, have no real concept of what the 60s were like technologically, where we were coming from, the links that we had with the 50s and the 40s. Every age, every decade owes so much to the previous one. But now in the last twenty-five, thirty years, technological advances have been so extraordinary that everybody who is interested in music has a sort of technological concept that seems to have taken root in the 70s and not in the 60s.

**ALO:** I never had the honour of singing on a Rolling Stones record, although Mick was kind enough to sing 'Da Doo Ron Ron' on one of mine. But I did get the pleasure, at RCA in Hollywood during the first weeks of September 1966, of joining Mick and Keith as the 'singing guitars' needed to choral the start-me-up to 'Have You Seen Your Mother, Baby, Standing In The Shadows?' Brian and Bill had flown back to England, Brian nursing a broken left wrist he gained after another set-to with himself or Anita. Charlie had stuck around to shop and be on hand to lend his percussive hand as Mick, Keith and I mopped up with Dave Hassinger. The tracks were complete. We'd already bounced the four-track recording to another reel, opening up two tracks to allow us to overdub Keith and Mick and complete what we all felt had the hum of being our next single. There was a degree of urgency to the proceedings as we were due in New York in a little over a week to make another Ed Sullivan TV show appearance, where the Stones were to mime to their last platter, 'Paint It, Black', and their next, the soon-to-be-finished 'Have You Seen Your Mother?' We were mixing down to mono and Dave ran the four-track down to us another time. Each time we heard it the intro sounded just that little bit lamer.

Bill Wyman and ALO, RCA Hollywood, 1966

'There's just no balls on the front.' I said to everyone in particular. 'Right up to the brass and guitar figure, it just dies.'

'Bring up the guitars,' said Keith.

'I can't,' said Dave. 'It'll just bring up the room noise. Listen, I can't give you enough of the guitars without the room. I don't think it'll work.' He thought right.

'Then try doubling the guitars,' Keith offered, guitars having worked out most of his life.

'Won't work,' sighed Dave. 'All in the same frequency.'

In other words, we had fucked up recording the guitars, under-recorded them and could not bring up the level without giving you a room full of noise and air-distort.

'You could try a harmony, do something up the octave,' said Dave.

'Yeah and sound like the fuckin' Byrds,' snarled Mick.

'On speed,' I added.

'Yeah,' grunted Mick, not thinking much of my contribution.

'Well, I don't know,' said Keith. 'We can't leave it like this. The front sucks.'

Mick and Keith wandered out into the hall and back again. Charlie and I wandered around each other. We were all stumped. Then I had an idea, a mad one, but nonetheless an idea.

'Why don't we try it with voices?'

'What the fuck are you on about?' chided Mick. 'You want me to call Phil Spector and ask for his fuckin' choir?'

Fuck you, too. 'No dear, I mean like this.' I squeezed my nose with my thumb and finger. 'Why can't we go na-na-nanana-nana with our voices, throat up, no body, noses on hold, in unison with the guitars?'

The room went quiet, everybody waiting for everybody else to say something, hear it or lose it. Finally Dave, his eyes on his shoes, his shoes on the console, broke the silence.

'It could work.'

Keith agreed. 'Who's going to do it, Andrew?'

'You, me and Mick – and Charlie can tell us how it feels.' We went into the studio. Dave cued the track up for himself, found some noise cue; there was no count-off. Mick and Keith practised sounding ridiculous. I already had that down.

'Listen for the guitar clicking on – that's your cue.' Dave ran the tape and we pulled it together in two. We looked at each other, then towards the control room.

Charlie shook his head, then looked up with a grin. 'I dunno, you guys. You're all mad, but it works.'

'Have You Seen Your Mother, Baby, Standing In The Shadows?' was released simultaneously stateside and in the UK. It was our last single release of 1966. While we were in New York for *The Ed Sullivan Show*, Jerry Shatzberg took the classic Stones-in-military-drag photos that confirm the English propensity for 'any excuse and it's into drag'. I found time to attend a Cilla Black cabaret opening at the Plaza Hotel with Brian Epstein and his US attorney Nat Weiss; it's one of the few social occasions I remember ever taking with Brian. 'Have You Seen Your Mother?' peaked at no. 2 in the UK and no. 8 in the US. Keith did a Richard the First and aired our laundry in the *New York Times*, protesting that I'd used the wrong mix on the single and that the original was 'fat and fantastic'. Quite possible, dear, and, if so, it's the horns that did it. The single was perhaps too spiked and hippy for our core base fans, and the single sleeve with the group in World War II military drag came off a little frivolous in those frowning American times – to the emerging and opinionated underground movement it was the Stones in commercial gear and not a real deal. The resultant shaving of our potential sales base earned us our first non-no. 1 in a long while.

**Lou Adler**: The Stones, unlike the Beatles, never actually exploded in Los Angeles; they had a very gradual build-up. But it definitely was not like the Beatles – that all-at-once thing, that explosion. It took the Rolling Stones two years to go from nine-hundred seaters to two thousand for a run, and finally to twenty thousand. With songs like 'Paint It, Black' and '19th Nervous Breakdown' the Stones were definitely in sync with what was starting to go on in the streets. You know they recorded it all on Sunset; the sounds just came out of the studios and into the riots. There was this definite movement coming on and Buffalo Springfield captured it with 'For What It's Worth'.

**ALO:** The Stones both captured the street and missed it. In 1966, while Buffalo Springfield gave voice to a generation gripped by the horrible certainty that was Vietnam, the Doors rose from the pavement's disaffected blue jean squalor and really spoke for the times, led, almost predictably, by a military brat, Jim Morrison. And in LA, while the riots festered and burnt, shadows took up our space on the street, unbeknownst to us, and new life was born.

**Richard Meltzer**, writer: In the 50s, maybe you knew the names of both of the Everly Brothers, maybe you didn't. The Beatles were the first band where everybody had identity. I was gripped by the fact of rock 'n' roll again, and by each of these bands. I mean, for ten seconds the Dave Clark Five were the band that followed the Beatles. The Rolling Stones weren't really played in the US for at least six months, and I remember hearing the single – I think 'Not Fade Away' was the first thing I heard by them – and then they weren't played again for months. But by somewhere in 65 when you had the Beatles, the Stones and Dylan and five or six other bands, but not really that many overall – the Zombies, the Kinks, the Yardbirds, the Byrds – suddenly it was like a torch held high in the world, bright enough to light the galaxy. It was somewhat astounding; it was, like, where did this come from? It was suddenly immense.

When I started writing for *Crawdaddy*, the Doors had a residency at this club in Manhattan called Ondine. They were there for three or four months, and they played three or four sets a night. And we'd go down and see them, for free, and I saw them I'd say forty times, and they were just – I went there with three people from the paper, the first night they played, and I just knew – I heard their first album and it didn't make much of an impression on me, and when I heard 'The End', I thought, 'Oh, how theatrical', and then I saw them *live*, and the four of us looked at each other and said, 'Is this the greatest thing ever, or is this the greatest thing ever?!' There was something just mesmerising about it; they were like – they seemed to us to be something beyond the Stones.

Maybe that's what they'd come out of, we couldn't really tell. But there was something about Jim Morrison. Before he had leather, he had jeans and a surfer shirt, and it was just really . . . something about the night. And the Beatles – let's say that the Beatles were not the Stones, but the Stones were a band that, six months after every Beatles album, did their version of the same thing. The Beatles were the band that showed the world how to strip-mine an idea; every album they did was a concept album. They're the only band that ever was that; from the moment they were the biggest thing in the world, they only got better. There's no other band that's ever been the biggest thing in the world that ever did anything but get worse from that point on. And they just had an astounding run, from 64 to, let's say, somewhere in 68.

One of the things that was so important about the Beatles also was that it was perceived that they were friends, that there was some actual existential relationship between these people. That never seemed to be there with the Stones. I remember reading an early interview with, like, Mick or somebody, 'How often do you socialise with Charlie?' 'Never,' That kind of thing. I mean, the Beatles, when they made their two movies, there was something just so . . . They were films that did get the energy of – I mean, just to see little scenes there where you see John talking to Ringo and there was something that felt urgently real about it. Elvis was the same thing, Elvis was just a unit – a single atom – but in 1956, 1957, it really felt like there was something about anything he did; it mattered. Any news item about him, any photo of his latest haircut. And the Beatles was the same thing. And to some extent, many of the British Invasion bands, too. It mattered what Ray Davies did. And then when you added drugs to the whole thing – drugs were not part of the initial buzz of the British Invasion, and once you could come up with your own alternate world, using this stuff as the soundtrack, as the backdrop, as the cue, it really was rather liberating.

As for Phil Spector . . . he was somewhat overrated. I mean, you could stand to listen to that stuff on the radio but it just wasn't – there was nothing awesome about it; it was just well-wrought tunes. And if anything, my favourite Phil Spector-produced single was one that didn't even have the Spector sound. It was 'Pretty Little Angel Eyes' by Curtis Lee, just a silly song. And I always thought later, in longer retrospect, that 'Have You Seen Your Mother, Baby?' just leaves Spector in the dust.

**ALO**: We had enjoyed three years of mutually-agreed-upon mayhem, as presented to the public in tandem with our willing partners, the press. But you could sense the change and chaos on the horizon. There was a backlash coming. The Stones spending more time at home – framed by the perception of wealth with a non-stop life of chauffeurs, loafers, Rolls-Royces, Aston-Martins, shopping, clubs, clothes, mates, hangers-on and dolly birds – was going to get on the proverbial English tit, and it would only be a matter of deadlines before the UK press would suss the mood of a nation and reflect it. I could not put myself out front in an effort to quell the rising storm because I was perceived as one of the gang and another nouveau riche yobbo in need of a day of reckoning. So I went back to Fleet Street and asked the grand major-domo of the press corps, the honourable Leslie Perrin, to step back into our life and become our Dr No, and this time out, instead of saying 'yes' and getting us into the press, to be his wily taciturn goodself and deal out an acceptable roadblock of 'no'.

Leslie Perrin's first gig was our 'thank you' tour, which featured the Stones, the Ike & Tina Turner Review, Long John Baldry and the Yardbirds. This brought 1966's concerts to around sixty, down from 1965's 150-plus. In the upcoming year the Stones would play a lot, but only fifteen times on stage. The grand 'thank you' was a way of saying, 'Please don't get down on us because we are enjoying the fruits of four years hard work. This is a talent-packed tour on which we are losing bread in order to say thanks and bring you the very best' – as in, it's costing us our money to entertain you. I was attempting to turn off the up-gushing resentment faucet.

The auntie of the blues, Long John Baldry, signed on as a well-paid and very camp compère. The Yardbirds were squeezed in between the Stones and the Turner Review. Mick, Keith and I had decided they were cocky little upstarts, had had one more hit than they deserved, and this sandwiching between the headliners should put pay to their career.

As the Stones wound down and touring became a local social pastime I found time to circulate on the town. Keith and I greeted Bobby Darin at the Dorchester and saw Jimi Hendrix at the Speakeasy. Jimi had arrived in England and Linda Keith had fixed him up with Chas Chandler, the Animals' bass player, as a manager. This was a great move save for the fact that Chas came saddled with his manager, a scumbag and a rogue, Mike Jeffries. We marvelled at Mr Stand-By-Me, Ben E. King, at the jumping and humping Scotch Club. London was now fulfilling *Time* magazine's proclamation as being the number one city of the 60s. San Francisco would have to wait its turn before it could blot its copybook.

The Stones and I, John Lennon, George Harrison, Eric Burdon and Donovan tripily attended the opening of Brian Epstein's new pride and joy, the newly renovated in rock 'n' pop splendour Saville Theatre, to catch the wonders of Motown via the Four Tops. Sheila was able to get out and about and busy herself in her social scene made up, in the main, of George Harrison's wife, Patti Boyd, the designer Ossie Clark and his partner Celia Birtwell, and the always-present Tony King. In terms of my estrangement from the inquisitive and the caring, my mother was now firmly on the list of people I avoided seeing. It seemed much easier, and the polite thing to do at the time, to walk away than appear a mess in front of my mother.

**Chris Hutchins**: We had good reason to believe Andrew was crazy. He was the first person ever in pop to go into detoxes – of course, we would not call it that at the time. He told me that it was a sleep cure, that he'd been put to sleep for three or four days in France, whereas it turned out to be Highgate. He thought it was wonderful because he'd come around detoxed. We didn't know that then; he'd just got all of the stuff out of his system. He wanted to be a bigger star than any of the Stones but he knew that he didn't have what it takes to make girls scream in theatres. He was always hopping on planes to go to America; I was just in awe of his spending power. At the time nobody would have shed any tears to see the Stones walk out on Andrew, or Andrew walk out on the Stones – everybody had had enough of them. But artists loved him because he was the first manager to be a part of the band.

Elton John would turn out to be very much like Andrew. Andrew was destructive, and the person he destroyed more than anybody was himself. You could almost see bits of Andrew flying off when he got into one of his rages but he would not conform, he would not give in. He had to come out on top, he had to have the last word. It was all right to do this with Sir Edward Lewis, maybe, but it was not okay to do this with your act. I saw him arguing with Jagger a lot. There was a lot of aggro between him and Jagger; they were like a couple breaking up. There was another whole relationship way under the surface between him and Jagger that none of us know anything about. From those very early stages Andrew had made it clear that he was the boss. I saw him battling with Jagger, with the whole band. I saw shouting and screaming, which you never saw with the Beatles and Brian Epstein. He lived life very dangerously; he took enormous chances and enormous quantities of drugs. I would have thought he'd have been one of the first people to take cocaine as well – Benzedrine was as bad as the rest of us got. He took the piss out of everybody and everything. Even Kit Lambert didn't dare pull some of the strokes Andrew did. But there was always humour behind it – always humour, laughter and tears. I always thought that Andrew would be the first to go.

## · CHAPTER 15 ·

**Keith Richards**: I'd rather the Mafia than Decca.

**L. Ron Hubbard**: You can blame your whole confusion on the fact you bought illusion.

**John Lennon**: Nothing happened in the 60s except that we all dressed up.

**Lord Goodman**, chairman of the Arts Council, 1966: The pop groups are winning the battle against those who would promote the arts as a means of teaching people what are the worthwhile things in life.

**Nik Cohn**, *Pop from the Beginning*: I have a memory of two fat years, 1964 and 1965, when you did nothing but run loose and waste time, buy new clothes and overeat and gab, when you thought you'd never have to work again in your life. It was futile, of course, pop has always been futile, but it seemed elegant, it was easy living, and English pop was better than it had ever been, than it's ever likely to be.

**Robert Hewison**, *Too Much – Art & Society in the Sixties*: Sex and rock 'n' roll could be tolerated, but drugs could not.

**Tony King**: We sat up all night with Peter Whitehead in an editing suite on Wardour Street cutting *Charlie Is My Darling* – Andrew, Georgie Fame and his girlfriend Carmen and I. We'd already been up for four days smoking dope and Andrew taking whatever. He was back off to America the next morning to rejoin the Stones. He'd only been back in England for four days and he'd not slept at all. Then Andrew went to the airport and called Cynthia to see if I was at my desk at 9 a.m. like a good boy.

Andrew put conditions on TV people that were unheard of. They were suddenly dealing with this tricky manager who demanded that his band be on top of the bill, that they have this and that. He was especially hard on *Ready Steady Go!* when Michael Lindsay-Hogg was involved. Andrew was very conscious of how he wanted the band to look and how he wanted the show shot. He kept on flexing his muscles, making sure the Stones always got the best. He actually told them how to shoot the band, which camera angles to use.

It was all about Andrew's idea of what he wanted. The *Ready Steady Go!* scenes where the crowd is rioting a bit, that was all orchestrated by Andrew. Epstein was a benign manager compared to Andrew. Epstein did what the Beatles wanted, whereas Andrew was much more actively involved in creating the whole aura and image of the Rolling Stones.

I left Andrew after about a year. It was getting too much and I went to work for George Martin and Air London. I just couldn't get along with Cynthia Stewart; she started organising everything, putting everything in order and it was no longer fun. She used to arrange Andrew's sleep cures with Dr Mac, and that caused a lot of friction between her and Sheila. After I left I met Andrew one lunch time and he asked me what I was doing for the afternoon. I said, 'Not much.' He said, 'Come on, we're off to the south of France.' He phoned Cynthia to arrange it, and that afternoon turned into four days getting stoned on the beach, a suntan and a new wardrobe. We'd go out for dinner, Andrew, Sheila, Mick, Marianne and me; we'd be out of our heads. Just doing silly things like ordering dessert first, if we had a craving for sweets. I think I'll have the apple pie to start with. Sometimes it was quite normal. I was one of their son Sean's godfathers and we'd do normal things like walking in the park and lazing around on Sunday watching movies and reading newspapers.

**ALO**: We gave parts of *Charlie Is My Darling* to TV companies to use to promote our singles – a little pre-video-age action in production – we had to. The fame had made it impossible for the Stones to whip around and do quite so much in a twenty-four-hour day. Now we had logistics, security, hired help. You couldn't just say, 'Okay, boys, meet you at the BBC at eleven o'clock in Bond Street' anymore; chauffeurs wanted to know which car to bring. High passion was getting sublimated to suburban detail. Immediately after finishing the Irish tour and the basic filming of *Charlie* we were off to RCA in Los Angeles to nail another single. You still needed a new single every twelve weeks. Success in the 60s did not take the pressure away from product requirement; it just re-emphasised it. The Stones stood up to it very well and rose to the challenge in sound and song, though none of us realised how exhausting it was at the time. We were strong, we were invincible, and they delivered.

**Keith Richards**, *The Rolling Stones: In Their Own Words*: It's difficult to realise what pressure we were under to keep on turning out the hits. Each single in those days had to be better and do better. If the next one didn't do as well as the last one, everyone told you you were sliding out. After 'Satisfaction' we all thought, 'Wow, lucky us, now for a good rest', and then in comes Andrew saying, 'Right, where's the next one?'

**ALO**: They were raised on the responsibility of having to come up with a single every three months. Once Mick and Keith had got the writing groove down, eliminating that masochistic search for someone else's song to fit the bill, we just got on with the first golden run. The song business would have killed us if Mick and Keith had not pulled it off. You cannot rely on 'It's All Over Now' or 'Time Is On My Side' falling into your lap each time out; it is just not going to happen. Had my dimmer twins not got it right, it could have been a life of searching the bin for records not covered by the Searchers or the Swinging Blue Jeans. For me a final bell had tolled one summer of 63 day when Freddie & the Dreamers released their cover of James Ray's 'If You Gotta Make A Fool Of Somebody'. Mick, Keith and I all liked the James Ray original – I more than liked it; I thought it was royalty, an amazing recording and song. Full marks to Freddie or his A&R man John Burgess for unearthing this gem, but for me it meant Mick and Keith had better get a-writin'. Even the rare gems were being unearthed and moved to the high street. Nobody gave me any moody about pressure; they were workers. Brian was still a different story, the tormented peninsula cutting himself off from the main land mass. Fortunately I could ignore Brian because the band were already doing just that.

At the end of September it was back on the UK road for a three-week trek. The Beatles had the month off. At the Odeon, Manchester, the fans smashed three rows of seats trying to get to the stage and the police had to form a human barricade to stop the fans from trampling those in wheelchairs sitting on top of the orchestra pit. Keith was hit in the face by a flying missile and knocked out, and another thrown object hit and cut Jagger above the eye – the fans were no longer just calling their name. In Berlin, I suggested to Mick that it might be a good idea to goose-step a little around the stage to 'Satisfaction', for the fans and as a good laugh for me and Keith. Mick took the suggestion one goose-step *Führer* and *zieg-heil*ed his way around the stage to the kick and riff of 'Satisfaction'. The stadium erupted in celebratory memoric violence. Forty-three rows of seats were trampled and destroyed and 123 cars were smashed and wrecked outside.

Mick remains a moving effigy, but the effigy he was mocking – the goose-stepping *Führer* – was getting taken at face value by the young German audiences. His put-on, instead of being seen as a kind of Nazi camp like 'Springtime For Hitler', turned inadvertently into an impromptu Nazi rally, more like the embodiment of Hitler (in *Jaggersprechen – The Picture of Dorian Gray*). He was turning on the German audiences but on a terrifyingly comedic –- and real – level. Once all of *die Halbstarken* got out of the tin-shed stadium and away from the police the violence really began – first the nearby parked cars fell victim to the violence stirred, then they wrecked every train taking them back to the sticks.

'Get Off Of My Cloud', the result of our most recent recording trip to LA, entered the US charts in the second week of October. It would stay there for twelve weeks.

The *Evening Standard* reported that the Rolling Stones have a new agent, Tito Burns, who also represents Bob Dylan in the UK; that they have a new co-manager, Allen Klein; and that they have signed a new five-year contract with Decca. Judith Simons reported in the *Daily Express* that the Stones will stay with London Records in the States. I was quoted by her as saying, 'Under the terms of the deal concluded with our American business manager, Mr Allen Klein, the Stones are guaranteed $3 million over the next five years.' Miss Simons continued, 'Expenses are high. Each guitarist owns about eight instruments, and the total cost of the present equipment is about £4,000. When the Stones are on tour, hotel bills are about £700 a week. Salaries for secretarial and other staff account for £200 a week.' Brian Jones announced it is not true the group are moving to the States and says, 'I think this got started because I've just bought a house in Los Angeles. It's purely a business investment and neither I nor any of the others have plans to settle out there.' This was desperate bullshit. I felt sick. Judith Simons recalls the story being leaked to her by 'someone in the Stones' office'.

The *Daily Express* piece was a story about money and how we'd given up the ghost and finally the Stones were in show business. This was a puff article worthy of Colonel Parker, reeking of American 'doing well' nonsense, out of place while at the same time an ironic hint of the future life Mick would step up to all on his ownsome without any assist from Allen Klein. At that time, however, you didn't originate a story on how well you had done out of the working man while he was on the job. I found it counterproductive and rude to tell a public who had forked out hard-earned dosh for vinyl and shows just how much money we were earning – or worth. It's okay if the press originates such a speculation, but from the horse's mouth it's just not on. For the Beatles, okay – the whole world wanted to see them do well. But for the Stones? I don't think so. The jury was out on them until they got busted – which was just around the corner. It's not a dissimilar situation to the Krays. The public may have admired them from a distance but if the Kray twins had taken to poncing around Mayfair in Rolls-Royces with personalised number plates, the tide of public tolerance would have surely turned. And that's press rules according to Loog.

I said nothing about Allen Klein taking the press reins on my turf, but my territory had been invaded by him and the Stones knew it. My days were getting done in a third-party scenario where Allen was Andrew, Andrew was Stu and the Stones remained the same.

Our new agent Tito Burns had also once managed Cliff Richard & the Shadows and was the UK agent for Dusty Springfield, the Searchers, Peter, Paul & Mary, Otis Redding and the Lovin' Spoonful. He's one of the great old showbiz *menschs*.

**Tito Burns**, agent: Actually, I go back with Andrew way before he was in show business. I was on holiday with my family in Juan-les-Pins and we used to go to a place called Butler's Tea Rooms, a little place for lunch or tea, because it was owned by this Englishman. This was about 1960. We'd have eggs on toast, my two little girls would have beans on toast. One day old man Butler said, 'I've got this new little waiter starting today; he's going to work the season', and then this little slight blond boy comes along to serve us. That's when I first met Andrew. I didn't see him again until I was asked to become the Rolling Stones' agent. I was picked by Andrew and appointed by Allen. When I was Cliff Richard's manager and mentor we were doing this thing for the BBC and Cliff was topping the bill. They had this little group of tearaways on the same radio show. Everybody looked at them and said, 'Oh, my God, look at that lot.' But when they came off, when they'd done their thing, I said, 'Hey, wait a minute, I like what you did. My name's Tito Burns, I hope you have a lot of success.' And that was the Rolling Stones.

When I became their agent, after the first UK tour I fixed them up in Europe. After Amsterdam there was a two-day break and they were going to disappear and get it together again in Rome. I said, 'Hey, fellas, you're on at eight o'clock sharp in Rome on Thursday, y'know, be there.' Then they all disappeared out of the door. I'm in Rome, standing there at twenty past seven in the dressing room saying to myself, 'Oh, Christ, where are they?' Then at seven-thirty they come in one by one saying, 'Hi Pops!' I've never seen such discipline in all my life from a group that is supposed to be a bunch of tearaways. Andrew didn't arrange tours; he didn't know about tours and such things. We just had this respect for each other. I respected his modern outlook and I guess he had respect for my agency situation. As Andrew once said, 'Y'know, Tito, everybody has their function and everybody must know their job.' I said, 'Andrew, that's a very cold-blooded way of looking at show business', and we both laughed.

**ALO**: *Out Of Our Heads* was released and became the Stones' first no. 1 US album. It entered the UK charts at no. 3 and stayed in the Top 10 for eighteen weeks. The photo for the English cover was shot by Gered Mankowitz, whose main qualifications were some nice snaps of Marianne Faithfull, being a nice guy, and being the son of Wolf Mankowitz. David Bailey was globe-trotting for *Vogue* and Gered became our man.

**Gered Mankowitz**: I was born in 1946. My dad was Wolf Mankowitz; he wrote *Expresso Bongo* and *A Kid for Two Farthings*. Andrew liked him. He was a big part of the post-war creative boom that took art out of the upper-class drawing rooms and into the middle-class stalls. He took our family for a winter vacation in Barbados in 1960, and since he wouldn't let me alone in London (I was 15), I went and started taking photos professionally in Barbados. Back in the UK I met a young actor, Jeremy Clyde, who sang with Chad Stewart part-time as Chad & Jeremy. They recorded for Ember Records, produced by Shel Talmy. Shel was quite a happening producer at that time. I was best friends with Jeremy, and Ember Records realised a young photographer of the same age as upcoming Chad & Jeremy was an interesting idea.

Photography wasn't a trendy profession; it was a journalistic profession. It was still really related to news photography. The only real fashion outlets were a very few magazines like *Harper's Bazaar* and *Vogue*. David Bailey, Terence Donovan and Brian Duffy were beginning to emerge as the new wave of British fashion photography. But fashion was always a world of its own; it was an upper-class world, models were debs. Bailey, Donovan & Duffy brought in a working-class spirit and sexuality and energy and excitement to all of this and turned it upside down and started producing quite vivid work.

Journalistic newspaper photographers like Harry Hammond and Dezo Hoffman were Fleet Street/Tin Pan Alley-trained. Most of their photos were taken live on stage or back stage, gimmicky poses in order to get the artist into the papers. They were old men as far as a seventeen-year-old youth was concerned. Ember Records recognised in the sort of pictures I was doing of Chad & Jeremy a difference that basically came from inexperience, naivete, youthful exuberance and confidence. This allowed me to do things because nobody knew any better. Chad & Jeremy had hits and I went with them to do a *Thank Your Lucky Stars* up in Birmingham. On the same show was Marianne Faithfull plugging 'As Tears Go By'. We met and got on like a house on fire. I did some photos of Marianne and everybody loved them. Then Andrew Oldham and Tony Calder asked if I'd like to photograph the Stones. This was early 1965. I didn't meet Andrew until I'd established a working relationship with Marianne; I think I dealt more with Tony at first. Andrew was working out of Ivor Court with Tony King next door to keep him amused, or, as Tony Calder once said, 'to make sure Andrew looks straight', which I found an interesting remark for one partner to be making about the other.

Andrew was flash, extremely smooth, funny, incredibly energetic, eccentric, seemed to be talking in riddles a lot of the time, which one became tuned in to after a while. I was very aware of the Stones. They appealed to me more than the Beatles; I liked their naughtiness, their two-fingers-up-to-the-establishment approach, their eccentric clothes, the way Mick wiggled his arse. They were funny, outrageous. I liked the music and I liked the image. The most important thing for me was that Andrew seemed to like my work. He'd already worked with Bailey; the previous Stones sessions had been with Bailey.

This first session I felt was really important. There was always a destructive air about Andrew; you always felt that he was on a bit of a knife-edge. But he focuses that and he's a very inspiring person. I'm not sure how he did it or how he does it but that first session with the Stones was so productive. He was such an integral part of that. We got an album cover (the Brit *Out Of Our Heads/December's Children*), the tour programme cover, masses of promotional pictures and the American tour programme cover. It was an extremely positive session. I believe the band enjoyed it. Andrew enjoyed it, liked the atmosphere in my little studio. It was fun, but most important there was an awful lot of material that could be used.

The band felt comfortable with me. I was precocious for my age, independent, the eldest of four boys, and I always got on with adults. I was very attuned to what was going on. The one problem for me was I wasn't mature, sophisticated, experienced or skilful enough really to take advantage of the situation I found myself in. However, I think that slightly naive approach to things held me in good stead. I wasn't in any sense a threat. I don't think Andrew manipulated me any more or less than he would anyone else, but I responded extremely well to his direction and thoughts. He and I began to click quite quickly. Ideas seemed to emerge. The basic approach to any session in those days, as far as I was concerned, was do two or three rolls inside and two or three outside – this was how work was done. We had to work creating pictures as fast as they had to work in the recording studio. I was conscious that if I was going to succeed I had to take pictures that were useable – we were doing photographs to try and promote an image.

Then they asked me to go on the American tour in the summer of 65. I think that was because Andrew made a list and decided nobody had taken their own photographer on tour so that's what he decided to do with me. I was another first for Andrew. The actual day-to-day running of the tour was done by Jerry Brandt, Bob Bonis and Stu, and the Klein office. The band had their own private aircraft for the whole tour, which seemed incredible but it was bit of a beaten-up old plane. It was a propeller job that was so slow that when we went from Phoenix to Vancouver they all went on a regular airline; it was faster. But they had their private plane and I guess that was the main point. It was all great fun, but by late 65 I had moved to a much more formal relationship with Andrew. Once he had me doing what he wanted I guess he moved on to his next mission. He became very formal for a while, almost establishment. I had a much better relationship with Glyn Johns, for instance, and my consolidated relationship with the band on tour. There was a bit of oddness between me and Brian but then there was oddness between Brian and everybody at some point.

The film I was shooting was being sent back to London, processed and shown to Andrew. My jealous colleague started telling Andrew he had to pay in advance for the cost of proofing everything. This upset him terribly, because I was being treated like one of the band, first class everywhere, there was no holding back. Andrew got very indignant. He got on the phone when we were somewhere down south and he was really upset, angry, told me to get the next plane back to London. I spoke to Klein about it; I was upset because I couldn't understand what I had done wrong. Klein seemed to sort it out and I stayed on the tour.

In general Andrew wanted the photographs to promote the Stones as sullen, moody, dark and mysterious. He'd stand in the background telling me he wanted everything stark and gritty. Andrew was a very influential catalyst. He brought two elements together and somehow pointed you in the right direction and then let you spark, and something would happen. That was a great talent. He had a clear concept of what the Stones should be and conceptually the Stones were Andrew's. Mick, Keith and Brian caught on to the conceptual idea very quickly but at first did not take it over from Andrew; they were at first extensions of his ideas. Then they began to come up with ideas of their own that more than fitted in with Andrew's concept. In the beginning I was dealing with Andrew's wants and needs. My job was to try and promote and further an image he had in his mind. Andrew was interested in promoting an image, that was all, and we clicked on that.

**Pete Townshend**: Andrew played me '19th Nervous Breakdown'. Great sound – I remember being very inspired by this, going home and recording a song of my own that evoked something of the spirit I'd heard. 'Substitute' was what I went home and recorded. Andrew found out that Kit Lambert and Chris Stamp were losing control of the Who and he stepped in and suggested he pay for me to fly to meet Allen Klein in New York. I went and came back a few days later and it was all around that time I was having trouble with Kit and Chris. Then Guy Stevens stepped in and got me to have another meeting with Chris Blackwell at Island, which came to nothing. During a meeting at my house Kit Lambert arrived and sat down and wept and wept and wept; he just couldn't believe I was going to dump him. I told him, 'Listen, if you can get the band back in shape again everything will be fine.' Because there was an internal struggle in the Who and Keith Moon and John Entwistle wanted to leave and form another band. They'd had enough of Roger, who had started to beat Keith up because of his drug use. Somehow Kit managed to pull it back together and for a while the way he managed it was by sussing Allen Klein and Oldham and not exactly learning from them but in some way encountering them. From that time on Kit and Chris's friendship with Andrew sizzled. They blamed Andrew for driving me to walk away, but in actual fact I felt that Kit and Chris did not know how to take the Who to the next level. It was Andrew who set it up, riding in his big Rolls-Royce with Eddie in charge up Park Lane. He had one of the first car phones and I remember him talking to Allen Klein on the car phone and arranging for me to go over. Eddie organised it all, took me to the airport, and I ended up in New York on my own and went to see Allen Klein on a yacht on the Hudson River.

There was certainly something visionary about Andrew, no question of it. He was truly ingenious and unaware of any character defects that have become politically incorrect. He enjoyed being who he was, enjoyed the industry and brought a lot of life and colour to it. I remember saying to him, 'What's the Phantom V like?' and he said, 'It's just great, it's a great car. We shot up to Blackpool the other day, made a few calls, sat in the back and listened to sounds. It's great; you should get one.' You got no sense of what one would have expected not to happen from him, that he would fall prey to grandiosity and snobbery. He was not like that. He was brash but he was never grandiose.

**Chris Stamp**: It was never that close between us and Andrew anyway. We got stoned a couple of times, that's all. We were downstairs in Ivor Court; it was chaos in our place. It was all strategic planning. We'd given the Who

313

lights, so a little band gets up in a little local club and they've got a fucking light show. We were never that great financially. We had tons of money going out on these ideas. The Who sort of made it alongside the Stones. They had a couple of big singles before us, and by the time they had their third big single we'd had a big one as well. One became aware of Andrew in those early days in Ivor Court. It was all incredible fun and it was obviously the same for Andrew. There was this sense of us, y'know – Andrew, Epstein and us. We had this vague notion that we were on this sort of trip. It got very limitless, that massive things can really happen. This is not show business – this is society, this is a phenomenon, a totally different level to what has gone before. It's all upheaval and radical change. Kit and I, in our philosophies, we were very concerned with left-wing politics. Andrew, he was just caught up with his Laurence Harvey material thing.

Terence and Chris Stamp, London, 1966

**Jerry Brandt**: For sure there was method behind Andrew's madness; I accommodated that without even being told to by anyone. I understood the game. As far as Allen was concerned, he was the businessman. I was more interested in pleasing Andrew than Allen. Allen was a great sponge of a person, meaning he would spend hours with anything or anybody that had something he wanted and just sponge it all in. I remember spending almost two years of five times a day on the phone on him.

I perceived Andrew and the Stones all as equals. That's how I perceived them; how it actually was one never knows. I never got the feeling, oh shit, here's Andrew, you know what I mean? Oh, we all had a great amount of

314

attention in America. Anyone over thirty, you didn't talk to them – remember that shit? So we all played on that. I never missed one date on the road, because I was responsible for it. I had to be there because they were my dates and my promoters and my so forth and anytime there was a problem I was there to take care of it.

I stayed at William Morris until 1967, then I struck out on my own. That's when psychedelia hit, that's when it all changed. I started the Electric Circus Club. I removed myself from groups and the agency game, although the relationships I had survived with everyone I'd known except Allen Klein. That's how I was able to come back and do the Ritz. I just didn't like him anymore. For me, dealing with Allen was like selling your soul to the devil for a Coney Island hot dog.

Andrew was the most flamboyant of them all, there was no question about it. Him and the Mamas and the Papas. I remember guys saying I wish I could be like them, but they couldn't be. I remember them coming out of clubs in LA just decked to the gills. I just thought they were from another planet. A nice planet, but another planet. Andrew stood out above everybody. He also somehow got caught up in the whole fame shit and probably didn't take care of business as he should have for himself. With drugs you can't stay on top of your game. The rot will set in. When you are that successful, it leaves room for a lot of mistakes. Showbizness is the only business that allows you to make mistakes and still come out ahead. Somehow every other business doesn't allow you that privilege. Andrew developed and delivered the best band in the history of the music business. Period. You don't have to do much more than that.

**Allen Klein**: Andrew, me and the Stones were on a boat, my boat, in the Hudson. We had this meeting. I was doing it for Andrew; I wanted him to be the producer. Maybe at the time the Who were trying to get rid of Shel Talmy, I don't remember. It didn't work out. Years later Townshend and I got back together again at the opening of *Tommy* at a party held down in the subways of New York. I could tell he wasn't happy. David Platz told me there was a big fight because Lambert and Stamp controlled the companies. I went in and got him his rights back with no lawsuit and no problem. That was in 1978 and 1979. Pete really slagged me off; when Kit Lambert died he said that I had caused it. Pete Townshend never has to speak to me or see me; I get my money direct and he gets his direct.

**Chris Stamp**: Andrew had Allen Klein and suddenly Andrew saw himself as the rogue baron of rock 'n' roll. He saw the Who and sort of thought they'd fucked up with Shel Talmy and perhaps he could steal them away from Kit and me and put them together with Allen Klein and it'd all be a quick deal, but it didn't happen. We told Talmy we were breaking our contract using the underage thing; all of the group were minors when they signed. He started to fight back. We put out 'Substitute' on Robert Stigwood's label Reaction and Shel Talmy got an injunction on the record. Shel said he would be willing to renegotiate our deal whereby he would leave us alone to do the producing and that he would back off if the deal was done by Allen Klein. We said okay. This is where Andrew went off with Allen Klein, leaving the communality of us, so to speak, and going into the area that for us was like the enemy. We were against the big business structure; we were for the freedom of this whole idea. This is a philosophical point.

Allen Klein and Andrew flew us all out there – Kit, Pete, me. We get to New York and we're going to meet Allen Klein on this yacht down on the 77th Street pier. Now Kit and I are from the movies, we know you can hire these things by the day. We're not impressed at all. Andrew was on the yacht but he didn't come round much, he was on the other side sunbathing. Then Allen Klein shows up, all charming, working on one riff basically. He's going to get you a lot of money, that's what he's gonna do and that's what he always says to the band. At the time most of these bands were like teenagers, and here is this American telling you you're gonna get a million dollars. He's impressed you all the way.

So we have dinner and Klein is sort of charming but he doesn't have much to talk about if he's not offering you a lot of money. We are going to get a million dollars. We think it's going to be with MGM but we're not absolutely sure about it. The idea for them, Klein and Andrew, was to get Lambert and Stamp out and Andrew in as producer. We were trying to make a deal with Allen that would get us free of Shel Talmy, but he didn't come through. We sort of won; we renegotiated with US Decca whereby Kit and I would be the producers. We got a lot more money and they allowed us to do the promotion. Andrew was a fantastic producer but he never had the right sort of partner for us with Allen Klein. Then Andrew went off and started to do things like Twice As Much and the Andrew Oldham Orchestra, a waste of time and effort.

**Shel Talmy**, producer: My drug of choice was ladies and I pursued that drug a lot. I was also very fast in the studio and very pleased to have that reputation. I'd learnt to be quick when I was an engineer. Anyway, why waste time when you know what is happening in the first place? Certainly I always rehearsed the band before we went in. Certainly Townshend had a tape set-up in his house where he would do his own personal demos and I would hear them and we'd discuss how we were going to rearrange them. That was a necessity. I had no knowledge of Kit and Chris and I did not have a lot of communication with them. Business hassles are always just that – a hassle, especially in the entertainment business. It seems to be part of the deal. There are just so many things, so many elements. The Who, for example; I never made anything but hits with them. Kit Lambert was jealous of the fact that I allegedly had influence over his band and he tried to get rid of me, which he did not succeed in doing. I kept collecting, still do. Unfortunately I didn't get to continue recording the band, which I've always regretted and resented. What can I say; that's show business.

**ALO**: I never intended to become the actual producer of the Who; it would have been an unrealistic scenario. First, from the point of view of the Stones it was okay to have a record company but a bit much to have another actual band. I had to think how they might feel about it and the incredibly all-consuming timetable and agenda we maintained already. The second reason was that I was not qualified, and I knew it at the time. I liked the idea of the Who. I particularly liked Pete and Keith Moon and the wham-bam-thank-you-ma'am management combo of Chris and Kit Lambert – Chris being the wham-bam and Kit the very grand thank-you-ma'am.

Daltrey and John Entwistle were to me the Who's version of Brian Jones and Bill Wyman – very essential parts of the engine but not a part of the passionate roar off stage that propelled and created momentum the way I could with Mick and Keith, as Kit and Chris so obviously did with Mr T. I liked the whole idea and end result of the Who – the manifestos and the potential for international anthems – but I didn't have a passion for the spare parts, the detail or the ingredients that manufactured the fury. Therefore, I would not qualify to hold the producing reins.

I was at one with my own amiable laconic louts, with their trivial pursuit of fame, wealth and position. It is only because this newly arrived sense of and/or actual wealth was driving a certain coldness into matters and manners of the Stones' day that I decided that, perhaps, I'd better get involved with something that was just business, something to which my heart was not attached and thus a moving target that could bleed. My Who agenda was very simple. Pick up the mantra of fuck Shel Talmy, for whom, from my snob-driven lack of an ethical position, I had no feelings one way or the other.

Insert Lambert and Stamp as producers, myself as Executive Producer on the art and hustle, and Allen as the financial manager over the whole lot of us. I knew it was not going to happen on Allen's yacht with Chris, so I stayed away and concentrated on my tan. Kit and Chris could not accept my intentions as not including wishing to be rid of them. If anybody had that revolving tortured intention at the time it was Pete Townshend, and Chris was just picking up the right vibe from the wrong party. Lambert and Stamp, it was apparent, would never take to Allen. They had Pete Kameron and nobody counted that factor in at the time. So it all just ended up as a nice try on a nice boat, whosoever's it was.

*

Allen Klein told me I had ended *Stoned* in the spring of 1964 because I had not worked out how to handle *him*. That's pretty arrogant, an understandable call from Allen, and the natural entitlement of a barracuda keeping the shine on his ivory tower. The history of an art form can never be kind to the Allen Kleins of this world. And I say 'of this world' even though Allen is a unique artist in his own world – the art of making money and taking control. My life is very simple when viewed on this movie screen, whereas on that of another morality play, say the world of Gordon Gekko in *Wall Street*, I'd be out of here by the end of the first reel. Not so Allen, who'd be riding off into the sunset in the back of a limo in a ticker-tape parade with dollar bills raining from every Wall Street window. My life is simpler in this scenario because I created. I was able to take somebody else's vision of themselves, a group of people who had an idea and love of a music form and a way of life that might go with that music, and I was able to work that concept into making sense for the artist and communicate it to the music business and a greater section of the public.

Allen is an acrimonist. An acrimonist is only required when something is wrong, or something can be perceived or presented as wrong, and by that standard he's a required part of the chain. Almost famous doesn't enter that equation; you have to be actually famous for a Klein to brew – he is only able to play mummy and daddy when the art is in question, in decline or in chaos and the kids are fighting over the toy of fame. Allen comes in when your harvest is not as plentiful as your expectations on the sow, and part of the price is that he gets the farm. The next thing you know, you are causing havoc wherever you go because for some inexplicable reason life doesn't add up to any more than it did before.

The irony is that the 60s are not over and may never be. It's a fruit with so many peels of wrath, and one of those skins involves the what-are-we-worth call. It's part of life's agenda, and I wish you your Allen Klein in that time of your climb. Gross is the number and nature of the artbeast, the skin on the bone. Allen didn't change the game; he enjoyed it. There was a price to be paid for being made to feel you were as big as you were, and in Mick and Keith's case that price was their songs.

*

The Beatles made only one UK appearance in 1966, a fleeting fifteen-minute set at the 1 May *NME* Annual Pollwinners' Concert. There was some disagreement over the joint appearance of the Beatles and the Stones.

**Derek Johnson**: John Lennon came into the *NME* to see me in disguise. He'd got a false beard and he was dressed in the most ragged clothes you've ever seen. He said, 'I don't want to be recognised by anybody. Let's go and have a cup of tea.' We went to Julie's and sat talking about the concert. After a while another café door opened and another altogether disreputable figure with ragged trousers, beard and lanky, dirty hair shambled up to the counter to pick up a cup of tea. As he passed our table he said, 'Hello, John,' and John said, 'Hello, George.' The next week there was one hell of a battle back stage between Oldham and Epstein about who was going to close the show and finally it was worked out that the Beatles would close it. But in fact they didn't. We had the awards and then the Beatles did their act. They'd insisted on one of the lesser acts playing after them to finish the show so that they could nip off in their limos before the audience came streaming around the stage door and trapped them.

**Maurice Kinn**, founder, *New Musical Express*: The Beatles had agreed in writing that they would close the concert after the presentation of the awards. The Stones weren't due to play that year. About ten days before the show I got a call from Andrew who said the Stones would like to appear at the Poll concert but that they wanted to be a complete surprise, they did not want any announcement made in the papers. They just wanted to walk up on stage and that would be that, the first anybody knew about it. The Stones didn't want any money, but even the Beatles only got £70; it was a prestige show. Andrew made one stipulation on behalf of the Stones – that they would not appear immediately before the Beatles. I said, no problem, they'll close the show after the awards. The Stones walked on and the place erupted; their appearance totally unexpected, what an extra bloody bonus, one of the major attractions in the world, what an unexpected surprise. They'd done a couple of numbers and then John and the Beatles appeared at the bottom of the stage. I said to Lennon, 'John, you're much too early; the Stones have got another ten minutes, then it's the awards. Go away, you're not on for another thirty minutes.' He said, 'We're not waiting. We're going on now.' I got hold of Brian Epstein and, he said, 'Maurice, I can't do anything with them. John's insisting they go on now and that's it, that or nothing.' I've got a contract with the Stones, so what am I going to do?

I took my life into my hands and said to Brian, 'Let me tell you the position. The Beatles are not going on next. I'm going to tell Jimmy Savile to tell the audience that the Beatles are here but they refuse to appear. There will be a riot, this place will be smashed up, and not only will you, Brian, be responsible for the thousands of pounds worth of damage, but you'll be sued by the *NME* for the irreparable harm you've done to the reputation of my paper.' Epstein gave me a balling out: 'We'll never appear here again as long as we live. You can't do this to us.' I said, 'I don't care if it's the King and Jesus Christ together. I can't change it. I gave it in writing to Andrew; that's it.' So the Beatles waited. It was a brilliant move of Andrew for his boys. Outside of that incident I never had much contact with Andrew but I had loads with Brian Epstein. I can't say that I was ever a particularly big fan of the Stones. Perhaps they were too wild for me, if you know what I mean. We went out to dinner once with Andrew, and Keith Richards was at the table and he was just bloody rude. That's how they were.

**ALO**: You could say that Brian Epstein was losing his grip. I'd prefer to think it was just I who'd had a better day and perhaps confirmed for Brian that the decision to stop playing the Beatles was correct. The decision had to be both logical and not so. After all, you got to the top to have the world in your hand, and then your answered prayers bit it. The price was being unable to continue with the very joy that propelled your mission in the first place. You had no barometer save perhaps Hitler or Jesus. Stop touring, stop invading, stop preaching. Same choice. That's a lot of adjusting to do.

**Cynthia Stewart Dillane**: The Terrazza Trattoria in Soho – we used to have lunch there every day. It was so exciting; it was the in-place – Laurence Harvey, Frank Sinatra when he was in town. Everybody used to eat there. We had wonderful lunches; lots of people used to come by and talk with each other, Andrew used to love going there. It was a very friendly wish-each-other-well time, almost the last of them, I might add. It was just off Old Compton Street, north of Shaftesbury Avenue. It was very avant-garde, the first place I can remember with Spanish-type tiling on the floor. Andrew was very proud that if he'd had a heavy night with Sean Kenny or somebody he could get from the table on the basement floor to the bathroom on the second floor and only throw up when he got there. He couldn't fathom people who were unhygienic, dirty people. We had a lad at Ivor Court and Andrew said, 'Darling, that boy smells. Tell him to use a deodorant or he's fired.' You could fire people in those days. Andrew was always immaculately clean and, if for any reason he was not, he hated it. He was almost neurotic about cleanliness. When he had his tailored suits on and his hair cut he was devastating.

**ALO**: The Terrazza Trattoria was like a shrine to me, a sign that I'd arrived and that I enjoyed. It was the favoured eating place of the celluloid aristocracy and favoured by me, as opposed to Alvaro's in the King's Road. It reverberated work and action rather than the oncoming Chelsea sloth. When Nik Cohn arrived to interview me at the Trat I was very taken back and shocked when, after our meal, he passed on espresso and took out a bag of cocaine and offered me some.

Eddie arrived at the Terrazza with the Phantom V and I offered to drive Nik to his evening appointment. The Phantom now sported an orange light on the roof top, replicating Her Majesty's blue light placed on top of her matching Phantom V (although I know hers was without the dark windows and will presume it did not have the telephone or record player). I'd decided en route to give King Cohn a rock 'n' roll shock for his highness and nerve at bringing out a mound of off-white powder on to the Terrazza table. I discussed with Eddie what I wanted in rapid-code on the Soho pavement as I girls-and-Nik-first'd us into the back of the car.

The Phantom V did a smart right on to Pall Mall, headed for Buckingham Palace. We approached the gates and kept on going. Cohn was in disbelief about what was obviously about to happen; he jumped off the back seat on to all fours on the floor, having forgotten that the dark windows rendered this move redundant, let alone cowardly. The policeman on duty at the gates saluted and waved us through, and we drove towards the Palace, through the arches, and circled the inside at a leisurely pace. This was all possible in the days before the pursuit of me-ism had driven the populace to a position of aberrated entitlement that would allow a gent to appear in ma'am's bedroom in the wee small hours of the morning. The later pursuit of drugs and terrorism by the populace in general would call for security in all the monied homes of the land.

We then exited the Palace. As we did so, Cohn screamed bejesus and

Eddie nonchalantly electric'd his window down and informed the saluting bimbo on the gates that we had forgotten something over at Princess Margaret's and would be back. I was pleased to squawk at Cohn about how we'd pulled that off without the need of MBEs and instructed Eddie to carry on the drive and take Nik to Kit Lambert's where he'd be meeting with Kit, Chris, Pete Kameron and Pete's cousin Burt. I was invited to lull for the evening but fortunately refused, as that might have involved dropping Nik off home at the end of the night. When Cohn did exit a few hours later he was so visibly the better and worse for wear and tear he was detained by Her Majesty's finest, a fitting end to a royal evening.

**Nik Cohn**: Andrew was the genuine young meteor in terms of the impact he made and then in how quickly that peak was passed. But there was something genuinely meteoric about him, there was this thing about him, a vividness. Andrew wasn't off or on stage, he was all the time, that is what made him unique. I've always been fascinated by self-inventors and here was a guy who wasn't dazzling looking, and as for his background, that changed every time he told you a story; it would seem each time to be from a different previous life. Why was Andrew great? Because he said he was great. That was very attractive to me and in retrospect still is; I like that. As far as I'm aware he never backed down from that, certainly not during his first incarnation. He had an understanding and respect for the pop tradition at a time when it was very fashionable to sneer at anything that didn't come from the black Motown, Atlantic, Stax, Chess tradition and all that sort of blues thing, all that one was meant to like about American music. One was not really meant to like pop, not teen dream pop, but he did and I did. I suppose we were unusual in that way and that was why there was a certain mutual connection. Andrew really understood teen dream pop when what was normally found attractive was suffering black men. I always found this a rather patronising thing and anyhow hopeless, because Howlin' Wolf was so good at being Howlin' Wolf there wasn't much point in a boy from Pinner trying to imitate it. I still think that Billy Fury was the most talented English pop artist ever, much more talented than all the Beatles put together. So, what was seen as a golden period – we've got rid of all those people like Billy Fury and replaced them with the Beatles – was not, as far as I'm concerned, an improvement.

**Pete Townshend**: I can remember asking Nik about cocaine – what does it do? He told me that cocaine is just the best drug that there ever has been;

the only trouble is it doesn't work for very long. He said for about a year you are going to be as good as you are ever going to be. The terrible thing is that you realise from there on it's not going to work in quite the same way again and that you'll be in permanent decline from there on in. I thought, well, I'm not gonna use that again. But I watched them all using cocaine, and for a while they were a pretty dynamic bunch – Kit, Chris, Nik, they were fantastic. After a year it did start to happen; they started to come apart. When Nik was stamping around London kind of saying Billy Fury pisses all over the Beatles, Billy Fury brought out some single, 'I've Gotta Horse', from a movie of the same name. Nik never mentioned Billy Fury's name again.

**ALO**: Nik was the first to get it and write it up. He had an Elmore Leonard dissolute on-the-street understanding of us all – all warts and haloes allowed and counted on. He got pop's purity of purpose, celebrated it for and with us, and left it before the needle slipped off the vinyl and into the arm. There are not many of us self-inventors inventive enough to cover more than one decade with aplomb – and young King Cohn did just that when he met and created Tony Manero and left us with the best quick-take on the 70s, *Saturday Night Fever*. In the mid-80s I had occasion to run into him on Broadway and he joined me in a trot up to Allen Klein's office where I was about yet another advance to handle my drug-addled ways. We entered Allen's office and I got surprised when we ran into Tony Calder. I went into a combine of kill minus will – the shakes, a familiar drug tone. I was too high too much of the time to have anything but sickened mixed emotions about my former partner's having been a most recent partner of my first wife. I was glad when Nik took me by the arm, led me away and out to the fire escape landing where I was able to enjoy a good whack of smack. The idea of Tony didn't look quite so frightening when Nik and I nodded back into the room, and I had enough narco-composure reinstalled to recall the fact that it still takes two of you to do it – and a third party to start a war.

The Who had come a long way. We'd all come a long way from our lives as told in *Stoned*, when my mate and our founding father, Peter Meaden, showed me what could become of that life and his with a group he called the High Numbers. And it's still just six years since I spied Philip Townsend in the shade of Monte Carlo. By the early 80s Peter had had enough and he toppled down the stairs living back at mum and dad's and died. This was within a week or two of Keith Moon's overdosing on the very pill that was designed to stop one's boozing.

**Philip Townsend**: After nice but dopey Peter Meaden split up his and Andrew's business partnership at the 44 Maddox Street office, Peter came and worked with me at my studio and office at 59 Brompton Road. Then suddenly one day he disappeared. The next time I saw him he was managing an eight-piece West Indian combo called Jimmy James & the Vagabonds. They specialised in playing at society dances and universities. It was at a summer ball at some Cambridge college that Penny and I had been invited to. Peter was in his element surrounded by adoring undergraduates and their partners while he fed them stories of exactly what it was like being a 'rock mogul'. The only trouble was he lost face when he had to hump the equipment off the stage after 'his boys'' set. This was something you'd never have seen Andrew do. He may have admired Charlie Watts' drum casing, but he'd never have humped it.

I didn't see Peter for a few more months and then he turned up at a Peter Evans eating house in Fleet Street. By then he was managing the Who and having the 60s version of the power lunch with Pete Townshend and Roger Daltrey. Shortly afterwards Pete and Rog decided Meaden was not up for the job, after having been the High Numbers long enough to get a Meaden written and produced Mod-anthem single out on Fontana. They replaced him with Kit Lambert and Chris Stamp and pensioned him off for a year. Then he disappeared from the scene never really to be seen again. While it was true he was not as clever as Andrew or some of the other swingers around at the time, it was Peter who created the Who in his image as a band of Mods. If it had not been for Peter they may have remained just one of the thousands of mediocre bands around at the time. But then, in the flower power 60s, people with the upper hand thought even less of sticking the knife in than they do now.

**Pete Townshend**: *Aftermath* is still my favourite Stones album and that was Andrew's album. It was not about bossy autocratic individuals taking control. It was about negotiation, creativity by committee, absorbing a lot of delicate egos, their agenda with regard to the way they wanted and needed to represent themselves to the public, the Stones with Mick, Keith and Brian all emerging as very, very powerful and ambitious people requiring somebody like Andrew to consolidate them. He facilitated them and he empowered them. You could sense the power struggle – Brian on the one hand, trying to keep the band in the original greener pastures, and Mick and Keith, who were far more interested in the engine of the band, keeping the band rocking, playing genuine rock 'n' roll. Brian and I used to sit and talk about music in a way that I don't talk about music with many people – its spiritual side.

**ALO:** On the same day, *Aftermath* was released and 'Paint It, Black' zoomed to no. 1 in the US and the UK. Appallingly late – this was, after all, 1966 – *Time* magazine gets the picture and heralds London as the world's most happening city. It decrees a decade dominated by youth and tells of London's having burst into bloom. London swings – it is the scene. The London summer is as never before, London is switched on. *Time* just foams at the nib as to the city being alive with Mini cars and skirts, Beatles and telly stars, and how, in a once sedate world of faded splendour, everything new, uninhibited and kinky is blooming at the top of London life. With this *Time* issue began the continuing cycle of announcements and issues devoted to telling us what had already passed and averaged out.

The Rolling Stones didn't really get a mention, their lack of uniform and loutish reputation preventing them from joining the rest of the swinging 60s into *Time*-speak. Just as *Time* was promoting London, the British Invasion of America was waning and stalled on the beach. England had dominated the stateside charts for almost three years and now America was back with a vengeance. The *Billboard* Top 10 had been retaken by the Mamas and the Papas, the Lovin' Spoonful, Bob Dylan, the Young Rascals, the Beach Boys, Paul Revere & the Raiders, a lot of Motown, and Percy Sledge. By the end of 1966 Top 20 one-offs and inroads were being enjoyed by the Mindbenders, Dusty Springfield, Donovan, Crispian St Peters and the invincible Petula Clark, but only the Beatles, Herman's Hermits and the Rolling Stones managed to really hold their own.

Some of our 60s are over, while for a whole world it's only just begun.

## · CHAPTER 16 ·

**Nick O'Teene**: I met Oldham in the 80s. He was not in competition with me or anyone by that time – except himself – so he had the time for me. I don't mean bad on him by that, but in the 60s everybody was too busy to socialise unless there was something in it . . . you know, social was work. Epstein didn't hang around with Oldham; Andrew didn't hang around with Lambert and Stamp, 'cept to get high. Oh, there was rivalry all right, but maybe they were all so fuckin' scared – not knowing how they'd got it, they didn't want to give the game away. So I spent some time with Andrew in New York in the 80s, I met Chris Stamp with him. He lived there too. Nicest couple of guys you couldn't wish to meet. They only came out when they could handle life, if you get my drift. Difficult time for them both. You know, in the 60s they were kings of the hill. In the 70s, it's what have they done lately . . . not much, save scorin' enough drugs to keep the wolves at bay. In the 80s it's 'where are they now?' by which time they didn't even know.

They'd have been just another item in the tabloid boneyard – 'Rolling Stones Manager ODs in Mid-Town Hotel Room' – if it hadn't been for the great ladies they both had. They were the saving grace; they held the fort and saved the day from really dying. Shows you somewhat the upshot of being a total poof, I suppose. Epstein and Lambert didn't make it. Peter Grant, although no poof, once Zeppelin died so did he, even tho' he was in recovery. A lot of them went on the mend. At least Tony Secunda died with his boots on, hustle in hand. Recovery is a strange fuckin' mistress, and those two boyos, Stamp and Andrew, are two of the luckiest fellas alive. Chris Stamp was your basic narco, he'd admit to that. Oldham lived on the wheel of pain. It's hard to understand how his kidneys or liver did not give out, when you allow what his day-to-day routine was for many years. I was with them in the bar of the Sherry Netherland. Oldham was filming some lame-o group out in Brooklyn, God knows why or for who. Mick Rock was helping him discern between regular pot and angel dust and Chris Stamp was minding Andrew's back; I guess a fella just has to have something to do.

He was by now employable only in his own mind. I'm minding my Ps & Qs with ginger ale, Oldham's at the grappa and doing coke under the grid line every time the barman turns his back. They've just scored some Vicodan from a Paki pharmacist on the corner of Sixth and Central Park, so they are all feeling very, uh, creative. You should have heard these two guys rapping about pills, just amazing, two walking editions of pharmacopoeia. It's the middle of fuckin' winter, and they are buzzed. Stamp is all done up in a great Russian fur hat and overcoat, looks like a Brit spy gone mad. It was the gang that couldn't toot straight, keeping each other warm in the cold straits till they came through. Stamp got his act together way ahead of Oldham. I met Andrew again in London in 94 in an Italian restaurant off Sloane Square. Andrew was eating grappa, staying at the Draycott hoping Gary Oldman was as nuts as he was and might buy into Ouspensky's *The Strange Life of Ivan Osakin*; Oldman's in the same hotel and by all accounts having his own troubles with the life. It was Andrew's brain that was going. His body had sort of held up but it was his brain that was finally collapsing.

**ALO**: I sat in the everyday thunder of the late 80s and early 90s while fifty-fifty narco-generic combos stopped any four daze becoming a total rain-stopped play. It was hardly cricket. One slip of the hand and the body follows, one mistake in the memory of what's been took and the next taking could be the last. I was devolving into a never-ending hyperactive narcoleptic downshift into the very brake pads of my mind. And I couldn't even cry over spilt milk – for that's all it was. If it had been more, had it had some absolut spirit to it, I'd have lapped it up and poured it over my cornflakes.

The body was willing but the engine was shot. Pads so low that when my scuffed shoes hit the high road of my mind, the heels would smoulder to a stop, screaming, 'Don't leave me on this alien standby!' Awful, just awful. I'd fuck with my body, fool it with some food; it would roar back with the sound of life but it was just not game anymore. A Chapter 11 body should stay at home, not run the gauntlet against younger cars without thought or overdraft and with a whole reserve of real staying power. Confirmation that I was truly whacked would come when booze didn't do it, coke cut right through it and Percodan was just making me sicker. You've reached the stage when the Percs have stopped working and it's time to go flirting with brown sugar again. Then I'd feel the quicksand in my temples dissolve into liquid glass and I knew I'd be okay for the next few . . .

**Michael Lindsay-Hogg**: Andrew and drugs. I never had any real sense of the two being connected. He always seemed to contain within himself enough personal intoxicants, elements of self-discipline and lunacy, denial and excess, so I never thought drugs, in the big sense, were anything he really needed. Except for a marijuana experience in 1965 and then in 1966, after I'd returned from a trip to Italy and was rehearsing a television play, we'd never had drugs together. On that morning, we'd had breakfast at the Hyde Park Hotel, or somewhere equally grand, and after his juice and coffee and my scrambled eggs, he shook some powder on the back of his hand, snorted it, put some more on the back of his hand, with its fine reddish-blond hairs, and put it under my nose, as the Italian (and still some English) waiters glided on the thick carpet, silently picking up the empty porridge plates. Snort, sniff. He dropped me in a limousine at my rehearsal, showing me, on the way, his articulated ring of a couple fornicating. The coke made me impatient and cross and so, on that day, I was not a joy to work with and I felt guilty towards the actors. Then, over the next decade or so, we'd meet only occasionally in the street – Old Compton in London, or Broadway in New York. Our lives were moving in different directions. Although, in 1979, we had been in a room together. I'd flown from London to see Mick Jagger in his apartment in the Carlyle Hotel in New York, to talk about the videos we were going to do for 'Miss You' – that album. This was a time when MPJ seemed to be drinking his body weight in Heinekens every day, but I'm not sure if he ever really was drunk. I used to think he was only pretending so he didn't have to deal with things which bored or irritated him. When I came into the living room, I saw two men from the back, sitting on cushions, looking as the sun set across the reservoir. As Mick and I were discussing what we wanted to do, Andrew and Lou Adler raised themselves off the floor, and with perfunctory, at best, goodbyes, left the apartment.

Then in Los Angeles in the early 1990s I was at the Dome restaurant having dinner with someone when there was this sense of a loose presence in the room, near the maitre d's desk. Over my shoulder, I couldn't tell if the person had just arrived or was leaving. I looked around to see Andrew, or a version of him. It's hard to describe accurately what was up, but he definitely was. His body moved as though the puppeteer had dropped the strings. I got up to say hello, and he talked gibberish. I'm not even sure if his words were in what we'd call any common language. He spoke emphatically but made no sense, as though his mind was as loose as his body, disconnected, unreliable and subject to collapse.

What had begun in 1963 with the first Chateau Beatles and continued through to the glorious vintage of 1965 from the great Lafite-Rolling Stones and Who vineyards, but not forgetting memorable and delicious pressings from the Animals, Kinks, Dusty Springfield, Them, P.J. Proby, Hollies, Marianne Faithfull, Donovan, Yardbirds, et al. was, by 1966, starting to turn a little sour. Bands were breaking up, lead singers going solo, star guitarists going from a band where they only played lead to a band they led. Drugs were starting to have an effect. The Beatles stopped touring. And *Ready Steady Go!* went off the air at the end of the year. From 1964 through 1966, *RSG!* was the Koh-i-nor diamond of televised popular music and then, because of schedule changes, new time slots, whatever, it was as if ash and soot settled over it rather then stardust. The last show was a joyless affair. Mick and Keith had their frightening, set-up drug arrest, from which they barely avoided serious jail time. And everyone wondered who was going to be the first to end up like the ex-heavyweight champ – a paid greeter, eking out a living pressing the flesh, mumbling of old triumphs at midnight in a Las Vegas hotel.

**Dan Bourgoise**, publisher: I'd come out with Del Shannon to California from Michigan. I moved out with his family in 1965, where we hoped for the first time that he'd be on a major label. Del looked at this as a very liberating thing, to come out, move to the West Coast and sign with a major label. The odd thing about Del's career is that he'd transcended the whole British Invasion, and was one of the very few from the early 60s who had.

When he signed with Liberty Records they had a formula. They had Gary Lewis and the Playboys, Bobby Vee and a number of artists. The way they'd put out albums was that they'd go and look at the charts, and everything that had a bullet and was moving up the charts that wasn't theirs, they'd point their finger at it and say, 'Go cut those.' That didn't quite work for Del, doing cover versions of other people's hits. In 1966 I had been working with him for about six months when he realised that his Liberty records had totally tanked, nothing was happening, and they were going to pay him a large guarantee, a royalty advance, which he had never had before. So he looked at it like, 'I'm getting so much a month, I don't have any hits, I love it here in California, I'm not going to tour, I'm not going on the road, I'm just gonna kick back.' We got out here, and there was a revolution going on. The Byrds were at Ciro's, suddenly there's a new pop flowing everywhere, all brand new, completely different. There was a culture shock going on, and things tended to be a bit confusing in terms of the record side of things. He had three kids and he put them through school.

It was a great time, but I was really disappointed when the plan didn't materialise – moving to California to work for Del Shannon with two records in the Top 5. We'd been out for six months and came back from a tour. The latest record had flopped. Del's bouts with depression were tied in with successes and failures. He came out of being a farm boy, living in Michigan with a wife and three kids, playing at night in a local bar, and working by day in a carpet factory to support his family. Then he comes up with 'Runaway' with his keyboard player Max Crook, who had the Musitron organ. And it's heard by a local disc jockey, who calls a guy he knows in Detroit, who comes down to see him, who rushes him to New York, and who records it and ten minutes later he's sold four million records and he's a rock star. And he's no longer Chuck Westover, age twenty-six, married with three kids. His name has been changed to Del Shannon, he's now unmarried, and he's twenty-one years old. And if that's not schizophrenia, I don't know what is. I don't know how any of us would have fared, given this whole new identity. Instead of being a schlub at the carpet factory, he's on stage with Dion & the Belmonts at the Brooklyn Paramount.

He was listening to Bob Dylan but he could not move on from the perception of being a teen idol. Del loved the Stones. He recorded a version of 'Under My Thumb' that kind of snuck into the charts, because the Stones never released that as a single. So we went to London. There was a lot of press in London, and they were happy to have him back. This is 1967, Del hadn't had a hit there since 1965, so it had been two years of nothing after non-stop hits. It was a very successful tour. It really punched him up a little bit, and he was in really good spirits after doing all of the interviews and talking to the press and seeing things in *Melody Maker*, *Record Mirror* and the *NME*. He was doing a live morning show on the BBC. After Del finished his interview, this person stepped out and said, 'Del, my name is Andrew Loog Oldham', and of course Del knew who he was, and it was like 'What's he doing here?!' and he said, 'I'm a big fan of yours. I love all of your records.' Then he said, ' I have the new Beatles single in the car. Would you like to come out and hear it?' So it was like, 'Oh, new Beatles single? This trip's getting better and better.' You know, to hear a new Beatles single before anyone else, this is something you gotta write home about. We went out to his car, which turned out to be this Phantom V Rolls-Royce, a great old car. And in the front was Eddie, his driver, and the window comes down and Andrew says, 'Eddie, do you have a joint?' and out comes this big joint.

So we sat out and Andrew proceeded to play the Beatles single, which was 'Penny Lane' and 'Strawberry Fields'. Andrew said, 'Would you like to come by the office? We're nearby, do you wanna stop in?' Then he said to Del that he'd really like to record some things together, and would Del consider it? At that point Del had no direction, no plans as far as his career was concerned, and he'd really been striking out on anything he'd tried for two years. And now he's sitting with the man who'd produced some of his favourite records by one of his favourite groups – and this guy's a fan of his. This is good fortune. Then Andrew plays some songs by some of his staff writers in his publishing stable.

We walked out of there just totally inspired. He had Eddie take us home in the car. I look over at Del and all of a sudden I could see he was feeling himself again, feeling respectable again and this was something that had totally eluded Del since the move to Liberty Records.

None of Andrew's problems were evident. He came off very self-assured, very confident. I was terribly impressed; I had no idea that there had been any turmoil in his life. There was never any discussion of his lot with the Stones. The whatever of that was totally hidden. The sessions were all done with the orchestra playing there live, so it wasn't a case of overdubbing this or that. Del sang live, and would have gone back and put on additional vocals, as needed. The secret as to why Del transcended the British Invasion was because he in fact went in and made those records with a band called the Royaltones. He would rehearse them, get the band hot, and then take them to New York and record them as a band. Nobody really was doing that from his era; they never really thought to do that. They were still recording with arrangers and orchestrators. Del had so much trust with Andrew and his vision and ideas that this was part of the fun, like, 'Go ahead. You've got the vision.'

We recorded at Olympic in Barnes. We'd go down there every day. Mick Jagger was producing some cuts for Marianne Faithfull there at the same time. Andrew had the studio booked around the clock for himself and Mick.

We recorded half the album, came back in May or June after a break, and completed the project. When we went back in June, it was the Summer of Love in London. John Lennon would be driving around in that psychedelically painted Rolls-Royce. Del did a show with Chuck Berry at the Saville Theatre, Brian Epstein's theatre. Del and I flew over with the Four Tops, who Brian was bringing over to tour as well. That night there were two boxes at the Saville, the opera boxes that sit way up high where the Queen would sit. In one box were the Beatles and in the other were the Rolling Stones. I got to sit up with Andrew in the Stones' box across from the Beatles'

ALO, John Paul Jones (background) and Del Shannon,
Olympic Studios, 1967

box. Can you imagine that? It was a wonderful, wonderful time. Andrew then took time out and went to Monterey. He left us with Eddie and the car, which was a lot of fun.

Andrew comes back, the record's finished, everybody's feeling very enthused about it, and we get back to LA in late June. Monterey has happened. The record company people have changed overnight. Hair is no longer greased and slicked back; it's now dry and forward, styled by Jay Sebring. The ties are gone, they've all got Nehru jackets on, everybody is wearing beads! And we're all excited and we play the record, and it's a great pop record, and that was its undoing. The Liberty people said, 'Del, this is pop stuff, it's not, ahhh, you gotta be psychedelic. Del, baby, pop is not happening anymore.' They'd all been to Monterey, they'd all seen Jimi Hendrix, Janis Joplin, the Grateful Dead, and Clive Davis was there signing everybody. We were disheartened and kind of shuffled off to one side. They put out a couple of singles we'd done, but nobody worked them, we were not about to have that hit.

Del felt he had let Andrew down. He felt very bad about it. We both did. Here, we come back, Andrew's produced this great album, and the record company says, 'It's not happening.' We really felt we had let Andrew down. At that point I think that they viewed Del's being on the label as a liability, and they had to go and sign new people. They went and signed Canned Heat, and now as a label they're hip & groovy and they want to have hip and groovy things to show that they had been at Monterey and Liberty Records had got the message.

I don't know how much communication there was with Andrew after that, or whether Andrew ever got a call from Del and they discussed it, or whether Andrew just figured out what had happened over at Liberty. Andrew's always been an inspiration in my life since then. Knowing him helped me to define what I'd become in the music business. He was such an inspiring and creative person.

I stayed in touch with Del till the end. I spoke to him the day before he died. He was in a deep depression, and I tried to pull him out as best I could. I never knew that he was considering suicide; he never really told me that. At the time he was about to record with Jeff Lynne, Mike Campbell, Tom Petty and George Harrison. He was going to replace Roy Orbison and become a part of the Traveling Wilburys. I was managing him and we had a whole new shot. Del wasn't saying, 'Dan, by the way, while you're out there working for me, I'm thinking of killing myself.'

I think about him every day. I miss him terribly.

**Art Linson**, film producer: I went to the University of California at Berkeley in 1960, finishing up at UCLA, and then I went to UCLA law school. In 1967 I was employed by John Phillips and Lou Adler with the intention of helping them get a foothold in the movie industry, which I knew nothing about. The vast success of the Mamas and the Papas was fading, and they were looking for new conquests. What was interesting from a movie-producing perspective was that in that time rock 'n' roll royalty were the stars of the neighbourhood. They had that heat the movie and television minions were chasing. On any night the cast of characters circling the Whisky and Sunset Strip was a microcosm of bizarre Hollywood hopefuls, from agents and publicists dressed in tie-dyed shirts and beads, to young Midwestern girls just off the bus, looking for Jim Morrison. If you threw a party and John Lennon or Bob Dylan or Mick Jagger was going to show up, everybody in town clamoured for an invitation. Actors wished they could play the guitar. For a brief moment in time, movie stars were in second position.

It was a zany life, with Phillips and his wife Michelle living like royalty in Bel-Air up at 783 Bel-Air Road. There were a couple of plumed peacocks roaming across the front lawn between four Rolls-Royces haphazardly parked near the entrance. It was a large Tudor-style home perched on a hill overlooking the ocean. What had once been occupied by 30s movie star Jeanette MacDonald was now a home to 60s rockers. There were people dropping acid, naked women – I just couldn't believe what I was seeing. I'd arranged a meeting for them with Ned Tanen at Universal Pictures. We get into an old four-door Rolls, John wearing a psychedelic robe and Russian fur hat and Michelle in a thin Indian robe and sandals. If you could have cut off the top of the car we'd have looked like a bad Easter parade. We're up on the fifteenth floor of the Universal Black Tower. Michelle is spread out on Ned's couch. She looks pissed off, she's got a toothache. She keeps saying over and over, 'When is the Darvon going to kick in?' As the entourage had proceeded down the hall, every employee on the floor was prepped for our arrival. They all stood up to get a glimpse of the famous rock stars. You could almost hear them humming 'California Dreamin'' when the procession passed their desks. I'm just thinking, 'This is fantastic! This is show business!'

**Sheila Klein Oldham**: We were staying in this house in Monterey with the Mamas and the Papas, and Nico and Brian Jones came to stay. The maid had thrown all the grass out in the rubbish along with the scrambled eggs. I remember Nico picking tiny bits of grass out of the scrambled eggs. It was freezing. I thought it was going to be normal California and warm. Jimi Hendrix was there; he looked pretty freaked out as well.

Before Monterey we visited John and Michelle in Bel-Air. They had this dinky Rolls-Royce with blue windows. They'd just be wearing pyjamas, nighties and wearing slippers. They never got dressed, none of that uptight English bullshit. It was wonderful.

While we were staying with Lou Adler in Bel-Air, we hadn't taken any acid and when we did we were given some really bad stuff. Only did it once. David Crosby said, 'Oh, there's this wonderful stuff that's really organic and it's a really gentle ride.' And blah blah blah – I shared half with John Phillips and Andrew shared half with Michelle. And they immediately started throwing up and it was getting stronger and stronger and then we got this call saying, 'Ooops, we made a mistake; it's one of a batch that Owsley made, fifty of which is STP.' Some people had actually died from it. Then they said you had better take some caps of Doriden – that didn't help, that just made it worse, it went on for days and days. That was a really mean thing to do. The Who and Jimi Hendrix had been given the same stuff.

**ALO**: Sheila and I drove the hallowed half-mile from Lou Adler's Stone

Canyon Road abode down to the mock Tudor on the intersection that had housed Tony Curtis, now housed Sonny & Cher, and would later house *Hustler* publisher Larry Flynt. We turned left, up Bellagio Road's twists and turns, and headed for Mama and Papa John and Michelle Phillips' 783 Bel-Air Road tinseltown Tudor mansion and lair. The Phillips *deux* lived the highest of high lives, all you could smoke, snort, eat and drink. Another guest, the said David Crosby, kept offering me this pill. He looked like this schlocked-down Sunset Strip suedette imitation of Robin Hood, ready to raid the pill cabinets of the world to feed the poor in choice.

'It's fine, Andrew. I wouldn't put you wrong. You'll just groove for a few hours, then go to sleep,' Crosby slurred like too many young rascals. I didn't trust him, or myself.

'Yeah, but David,' I slurred back, 'tell me exactly what it is. I like to know where I'm going and if I want to go there . . .'

'It's nothing, man, mild . . . sort of like an English Mandrax. No side trips. You'll just groove for a while . . . then sleep.'

I looked around the Phillips living area at a lot of people grooving for the while, a lot of far-outs, a lot of smiles that belied scars and agendas, a lot of talent believing all this was really so, safe in the garden of Papa John and Michelle opiated foliage where the living was easy. If life was a karma-devoid kaleidoscope in these lofty top-ten heights, then even given the glow there were already a couple of colours missing, some full wattage on the primaries dulled. Or was it bulbs and brain cells? I remember the warning but did not let it do more than register. Perhaps one just put on a brighter coloured paisley scarf to make up for the contradictory signals that dulled and glowed in the same fountain. We may have been eight miles high, twittering like all-knowing metamorphic birds in the canyon, while Crosby had the lair of the song never fading. I knew that two miles down on the Strip the lights and the life were true and screeching, but on the eve of this Summer of Love Sheila looked happy and blissful, away from the strains of suburban bust-driven Britain, happy in our choice of Thea Porter ruffles, silk and un-drycleanable bell-bottomed velvets. So I let it be and joined the waft and boffo top-tenned wisdom of the exalted tunesmiths, *meisterstück* musical gland-gliders of the mind of this odd Hollywood lot. Joints were the uniting factor passed from musos to road crew to Dominick Dunne and Lana Wood. The brocades and fabric of the time were contrasted by the odd TV'd pinstripe, your David Janssen, R.J. Wagner or George Hamilton coming to suss out the soon-to-be-leftovers and be sure they had not missed a photo op. The same three amigos could be found in most decades hovering around the pool of fresh blood. Ten years later Janssen wore the same suit, Wagner the same all-knowing look and Hamilton the same tan when the new Hollywood had changed from its hippy hues into dressing like curtains. John Phillips to Elton John through to John Candy – for a certain Hollywood-surviving bloodhound everybody else was merely a backdrop to being seen. This glittering group ignored the baying from the Strip and the valley. That same summer Lou Adler had taken Sheila and I to sup 'n' toke atop Cielo Drive, hidden on a bluff off Benedict Canyon, with Terry Melcher and Candice Bergen, both young/old second-gen Hollywood royalty. Terry Melcher was a record producer at CBS, and responsible for the Byrds and Paul Revere & the Raiders. He was also the son of my favourite, Doris Day. Miss Bergen was the daughter of Edgar, who had found his incredible fame by putting his arm in the back of a wooden dummy named Charlie, working the drill as a ventriloquist on radio and into the hearts of America.

In less romantic times in another valley at what would become known as the Ranch, Melcher and Beach Boy Dennis Wilson had entertained Charles Manson's notion that he should be recorded and given his shot alongside the Beatles at the top of the holy pop grail. Perhaps, in keeping with the times, Terry Melcher was just being careless and no doubt good-intentioned whilst he and/or Dennis didn't mind listening to a stray tune while running down stray pussy. Charles Manson would not forget or forgive that his moment did not pan out, deprived of his place with the fools on the hill, nor would he forget where his deciders resided. Two years later his clan trooped up the hills and slaughtered actress Sharon Tate, the wife of director Roman Polanski, as well as their child-to-be and assorted houseguests that included a Folger's coffee heiress and hairdresser Jay Sebring. Manson had not checked who was in residence, or whether Melcher was still there. He really didn't care; whoever was at home qualified to receive his wrath.

I remember, from the night we visited the Melchers, how the horrific and unspeakable could happen, how the twists and turns of the canyons and ridges can soundproof the bloodiest of curlish screams. I also remember the slate stone walls of the canyon abode and the rafters. They were silent and surly and already reflecting the night. As the sexual musical chairs swung through the Hollywood Hills and collided with the swinging 60s, an early version of six degrees of separation came into play during the days following these savage killings.

Given the times, Mr Polanski had reason, based on his own tryst with

Michelle Phillips, to believe Papa John Phillips might be the potential murderer. Detective work, thought through the emergence of the Manson family, would wipe this idea from the Polanski screen. I'm glad I was not in the area at the time or I, too, may have turned up on a short list, Polanski having enjoyed a London dalliance with Sheila and Michelle Phillips one English tea-time that I spied from across the street from the director's mews abode simply just by being there. I may have loved to have served hot cross buns to Mama Michelle, but perhaps I preferred to stay in my head as opposed to a friend's bed. Not to say I did not stray – you've read as much – but the times they were estranging.

Back atop Bel-Air, no thought was given to the mad minds and criminals this drug promoting summer would unleash as we happily fiddled with roaches, goblets and each other and let our anthems light a fire down below. Like a fool I decided to believe Dr Crosby and allowed myself to fiddle with fate. I accepted the off-white tablet, but thank God was only half a fool – I only took half. Half an hour later I was not feeling so funny, nor groovy, nor well. I looked for Sheila, found her, took her hand and told her we were leaving.

So much for drugs having made the species equal.

'What's wrong, Andrew?' Sheila's concern shone through her beauty.

'That's no fuckin' Mandrax and I'm not staying here so that cunt Crosby can watch it work . . .'

Sheila agreed, we performed a few tight-lipped smiles as we backed out of the house, and in a minute we had made it to our car. I reversed, in spite of valet parking and John Phillips' coterie of Rolls-Royces, Jeeps and wandering peacocks, and out of the gates of this Kenneth-Angered, drug-façaded, Nelson-Eddy-&-Jeannette-MacDonald slightmare we sped. I felt a whole lot better and allowed myself a moment of relief and let it breathe. We were quiet for a few. We had not been having too many good evenings together. Sheila was content away from the madness that had dis-embowelled our swinging London; I, however, only occasionally landed. I was torn between the wish to have the strength to go and stand up next to the Stones in their legal ordeal and knowing the reality that this was wishful thinking. The electric shock treatments and accompanying psych-drugs had burnt and frayed my nerves and most of my endings. I was so confused I could not discern if Allen Klein was taking over the escalation of my former duties because someone had to, or was following his own plan. Sheila would often have it that I never got over leaving the Stones. Until I did she was right, but she had the wrong leaving. It was not the public leaving; so much of that could be swathed in ego and heady protective pronouncements about 'going our different ways' and 'musical differences'. That was an exercise in dumb-speak anyway – it had always been Willie Dixon meets the Ronettes; the musical differences were what had held us together. It was the leaving itself that had broken the bough, not the later parting with the Rolling Stones. It was this particular bottle going that had caused me to flee the UK in panic over the idea of, one, being busted myself, and, two, not having the wherewithal to stand by the Stones and function on their behalf. And thus I ended up on this long, spiked and winding road, attempting to bathe my wounds in the dressings and bandages of Bel-Air. Life was no longer eternal and for quite some while I was no longer happy at my job. Of course much later I would realise that that very moment occurred when I stopped taking drugs and they started taking me. That is when I lost the plot.

My abrupt reversal of mood and hurried departure had put the brakes on the lofty Bel-Air evening. Snaking down the hill, I started to get this disorientative lock set into my ability to drive and control the vehicle. Maybe it's my imagination, I hoped, while my mind weighed up the reality of the alternatives. We slowly continued the drive back to *chez* Lou. In time we reached the halfway point, the Tony Curtis Tudor manse, where we had to turn right. I did so and as we drove on up towards the Bel-Air Hotel the two-way Stone Canyon Road split itself and divided into at least half a dozen choices of road. I didn't know which one to steer on, so I told Sheila to shut up as I tried to steer on them all. The leaves and shrubbery on the left and right of me were no longer brown and the sky was black, not grey. I felt like I was driving through the maze in *The Shining*. The leaves spoke, thrust and threatened like wet tongues of a rat inviting me to collide with their night. The six-lane highway of choice that had replaced the sedate paved Bel-Air Drive echo'd as a jump-cut fast-forward in time and likened itself to the famed 90s San Francisco Golden Gate disappearing Bridge earthquake scene. In hopscotch fashion the road rose and fell, inviting me to swerve, stumble or fall. Trip did not come into the equation; I knew I was already there.

'This is a fuckin' nightmare,' I screamed into the night. 'I'll kill that cunt.' Peace and love were not around my corner. Sheila looked as if she didn't dare care; that just made me want to kill her. Insurmountable odds and layers of unspoken abhorrence towards your mate will do that as time removes the basic ingredient of survival – decency towards another and, therefore, self. After a couple of lifetimes, we managed to get home to 800 Stone Canyon.

I made straight for the bathroom and threw up more than an acre. For an hour I kept vomiting, then I crawled into bed. Inside the blankets I tripped beyond reason. I felt I was in a cylinder circling the earth, out of control, the horrors never ending, a roller coaster tearing my body and mind apart. Then I made another mistake. After another acre of vomiting, I took a couple of sleeping pills to try and slow down the hellish journey and somehow return to earth. The sleepers started to shake hands with the foreigners occupying my space, and this meeting only served to make matters worse, accelerating the tunnel of no-love I could not climb out of. I screamed, cursed and froze in fetal position encased in this rotating grey coffin cylinder, going faster, getting giddy, going slower, thrown sideways and into reverse. I alternately threw up and continued on this journey until, sometime around dawn, body spent, I managed to find some sleep in Sheila's arms. Sheila was wonderful; she always was when I needed her – a doyenne of support. Naturally on my recovery I interpreted that as meaning she could only handle me helpless. When I awoke everything was better and I gently tripped the next twenty-four hours. But what wouldn't have seemed better after that vomit-ridden nightmare in the aphasic abyss?

I found out later that what I'd been given by byrd-brained Crosby was STP, a powerful hallucinogenic that had driven more than a few good men out of their minds. If I was going to get fucked up, which I would continue to do, it would have to be by my own choosing. I could not afford to accept candy from strangers; they were laced, spiked and full of untruths.

A couple of years later I stood in New York's Kennedy TWA terminal, in line behind a demented David Crosby who, with a sedately demented ex-Hollie Graham Nash, had been allowed to teach our children well (the lame leading the blind, or fame leading the lame?). He and Graham had left their passports and their marbles in LA. Crosby was outraged as to why 'they' would need them to fly the next leg to London, when by appearance and disposition the only thing they didn't need was a plane. I still say, 'Fuck you, David Crosby', though I'm glad you finally got your new liver. There are no accidents and I have to put you down as part of my experience. But I would have been the first one to laugh if the liver you got had been one Keith Richards had thrown away . . .

**Pete Townshend**: I didn't take any STP until we'd done Monterey and left. Owsley had invented this new form of acid called STP; my wife and I took some on a plane coming back from Monterey. I'm surprised I ever touched any kind of substance afterwards. It was just spectacular – spectacularly awful. It was like a normal acid trip but stretched over about three or four days. The hump, the bit where you don't know what's going on, when your sense pathways are mixed up, feeling what you're hearing, smelling what you're seeing, something about how it scrambles up the neuron pathways – that lasted for at least thirty-six hours. By the time you came out of it, you were physically, mentally and spiritually devastated. You felt like a blubbering child. You probably hadn't been able to get to the lavatory, so you might have pissed yourself, shot yourself or anything could have happened. After that, then what you got was an equally long and exaggerated glide out of the acid trip, through a long period when everything around you looked illuminated, social, different and new. Then slowly but surely, and painfully, you're dumped back in the grey fucking world that you really have to inhabit for the rest of your life.

**ALO:** For the most part, I did enjoy the lack of pressure and the exciting time that was LA that spring and summer. Lou Adler and John Phillips took over the organisation of the Monterey Pop Festival which, with the later Woodstock, defined the future of popular music. BMW = Beatles, Monterey, Woodstock. The festival was planned for 16, 17 and 18 June. Lou and John formed a board of directors to advise on talent and policy and to explore the possible beneficiaries of the money gained by this non-profit event. I was invited on the board to head 'International Affairs'. Derek Taylor handled PR and D.A. Pennebaker took the film, which was recorded by Wally Heider Mobile, board manned by Heider and Bones Howe.

**Lou Adler:** The first generation raised on TV and rock 'n' roll came of age that summer and there was much for them to be negative about. When I think back on that 1967 Summer of Love, it's amazing it was ever called that. John F. Kennedy had been assassinated only three and a half years before, a huge US military buildup was underway in Vietnam, the anti-war movement was roaring. Martin Luther King Jr urged massive civil disobedience and Stokeley Carmichael called for a black revolution. Race riots erupted in eight US cities. The Summer of Love obviously got its name from something else.

In early 1967, promoters Alan Pariser and Ben Shapiro proposed a two-day rock event at the Monterey County Fairgrounds, home of the Monterey Jazz Festival. They booked Ravi Shankar and approached John and Michelle Phillips of the Mamas and the Papas. Because I was the group's manager and producer, John Phillips came to me. It brought to mind a recent conversation we'd had with Paul McCartney at Mama Cass Elliot's house about how rock music, for all its growing sophistication and creativity, was still not regarded as an art form like jazz. John realised two things: one, the festival ought to have an international bill of pop performers from every genre; and two, no one could afford to pay them. The answer was to have all the participants donate all their performance fees to charity. Shapiro was not interested in a non-profit event, so John and I, Paul Simon, Johnny Rivers and Terry Melcher bought him out.

To validate what we were doing we put together a board that included Paul Simon, Paul McCartney, Brian Wilson, Donovan, Mick Jagger, Smokey Robinson and Andrew. Although it never met, the board served its purpose. We wanted not only to present the most amazing rock show the audience had ever seen, but to have the best of everything for the performers as well. We started by contacting artists in our own backyard on Sunset Strip. In late 66 you could hear innovative LA bands on the Strip at nightclubs like the Whisky À Go-Go, the Trip and London Fog. From LA we enlisted Buffalo Springfield as well as the Byrds. Simon & Garfunkel and Otis Redding came aboard. Andrew and Paul McCartney brought us the Who and an unknown act called the Jimi Hendrix Experience. John and I knew that in order to have a successful as well as meaningful festival we needed groundbreaking San Francisco groups like Jefferson Airplane and Big Brother & the Holding Company. The scene in San Francisco carried the mark of the colourful LSD commune of Ken Kesey and the Merry Pranksters. San Francisco's bands had learnt their trade at psychedelic street festivals and at concerts at the Fillmore Auditorium and Avalon Ballroom. They were suspicious of anything from LA, and it didn't help that John and I had recently produced Scott McKenzie's hit 'San Francisco'. With just six weeks to go we flew to San Francisco to meet with representatives of the groups. They besieged us with what we considered counterproductive demands and threats of an 'anti-festival'. We respected that they knew things about the area and lifestyle that we didn't, so we listened and learnt. Although obstacles remained, Ralph Gleason (the first member of the San Francisco *Daily Press* to report on pop music) and promoter/Fillmore owner Bill Graham finally surrendered enough approval that we were able to sign the San Francisco groups.

**Rock Scully and David Dalton**, *Living With the Dead*: Poor old Haight-Ashbury. Being exploited like crazy by the media *and* the bus companies!

Everybody jumped on it like a big piece of cheesecake. But of all the shifty schemes and scaly exploitations of the hour, the Monterey Pop Festival is the most nefarious. We know from the outset that it's going to be a rip off, but it's galling to get ripped off by guys making millions of dollars doing 'California Dreamin''. We're the ones doing the dreaming, they're the ones making the bread!

We already know from friends in the Airplane and others that the principals of the festival, Lou Adler and Papa John Phillips of the Mamas and the Papas, have something up their sleeves. It starts with John and Michelle Phillips coming to see us, representing themselves as fellow musicians who have also taken acid or *maybe* taken acid. But whatever they've taken, they aren't anywhere near as crazy as we are. Or as naive. Phillips is a musician whose group we respect, but why, we wonder, is he talking like that? The hip malapropisms, the music-biz clichés, the fake sincerity. We are soon to discover that once you get beyond the fur hat and the beads he is just like a goddamn LA slicko. We all get the same vibe from him: he's here to exploit the San Francisco hippie/love phenomenon by building a festival around us and Janis and Country Joe and Big Brother and Quicksilver and the Airplane.

The meeting is over on Fulton at the Airplane's palace. In spite of our misgivings we are led on because we aren't big yet, we don't have a hit record and the Mamas and the Papas are huge. We never even hope to achieve the kind of success that the Mamas and the Papas have on AM radio.

Phillips has no idea what we're about, and he doesn't much want to find out. For one thing, we're asking too many embarrassing questions. 'Hey, brother,' he's saying, 'what are you guys so paranoid about? You've got us all wrong. You're gonna dig this trip if you give it half a chance. You're really going to flip when you hear who we're bringing in: Jimi Hendrix, Otis Redding and the Who, for starters. And we're working on getting the Stones. Isn't that right, Andrew?' They've brought the Stones' manager with them, the infamous Andrew Loog Oldham. Sir Fucking Andrew himself! We're impressed, all right. 'Out the door and around the back, man, innit?' Oldham remarks dryly and proceeds to embark on an extravagant automotive metaphor.

'It's a bit like a car, a festival. D'y'know what I mean? Well, unless or even if your engine is frozen up like a Swanson's TV dinner, if you got the right ingredients it will still roll over. See what I mean, darling? Only problem with a gig like this, that's got its own momentum, is will it *overheat*? Y'know?'

As beguiling as it is being shone on by John and Michelle Phillips, cajoled by super promoter Lou Adler and, uh, *talked* to by the redoubtable Andrew Loog Oldham, Danny Rifkin and I have to blow them off, which we do by saying we'll think about it.

Time for Andrew and Lou Adler to drive back up the coast. They drive down and Andrew is still going on about it. 'Lovely drive,' offers Sir Andrew. 'Although the fuckin' waves were a bit overdone, didn't you think?' So just to make their trip back even *more* scenic . . . we dose 'em.

ALO, Tom Wilkes (back to camera), John Phillips and Lou Adler, Monterey Pop offices, Sunset Strip, 1967

**ALO:** Offices were taken on Sunset, opposite the Hyatt Riot House. Last time I drove past, the office space boosted a tattoo parlour. I remember having a natter about management of Buffalo Springfield with Stephen Stills. Lou Adler and I flew up to San Francisco to meet with the journo patron saint of the West Coast movement, Ralph Gleason, and explain the festival's intentions to hopefully return to LA with Gleason's approval. This would make life easier and make it possible to deal with the very necessary San Francisco Bay Area groups. Mr Gleason approved. We left his home in the waiting limo and on the way to the airport I asked Lou if he'd think me crazy for wondering whether the writer had spiked our afternoon tea.

'Feels the same way to me,' said Lou, a few correct words being one of his many qualities.

'How is it?'

'Not bad, Andrew.'

'Not bad for me too, Lou.'

My appointment to the Monterey gang was a busman's holiday blessing in the sky with diamonds. Lou was familiar with my reasons for being in limbo in LA and my wish to have no prearranged arrests by the London police. Mick and Keith had been busted at Keith's Redlands home on 27 February. Waiting on whether Mick and Keith would be detained at Her Majesty's pleasure did not provide a very productive mind-set to work and I would be found lacking as a friend in a court of my own peers, or did it really make any difference with what had worked out as the Stones' next course? None of the Stones could deal with recording and time booked at Olympic in late spring was wasted. Only at the 'We Love You' session in late July, when the apparitional John and Paul appeared again as one live one, did anything get done.

You have to know this about the twin Mop Tops. They never let love and peace bring or slow them down. A feast of velvet, silks, hustle and speed hovered into Olympic like knights of the real table. Genghis can and do. Prior to their arrival the atmosphere in the studio had been akin to a bunch of relatives waiting graveside for a priest to do the honours and give living death some order and shine. The two Beatles didn't listen to the 'We Love You' track for much longer than they'd spent running down 'I Wanna Be Your Man' to my songless Stones just two and one half years before. They picked up the cans and sniffed each other out like two dogs in heat for the right part. Harmonic results from the Stones were, for the most part, either 'interesting' or the result of hard work. John and Paul just glided in and changed a runway into an aeroplane with wings. Their voices locked and smiled like brothers, creating the signposts to give the disarray, the fractured parts and rhythms something to belong and cling to. Everybody, my gobsmacked Stones as well, straightened up as vision became reality. We'd just had another major lesson from the guv'nors as to what this recording thing was all about. In plain English, I'd just seen and heard a fuckin' miracle.

Back at the Summer of Love I asked Lou Adler and John Phillips, 'So what do I have to do?'

'Just don't get busted,' cracked John – a friendly way of saying take care. 'Don't go back to England, just call. Let Allen Krime go,' he Shirley Ellis'd and grinned.

Monterey Pop was moving fast and Lou was talking slowly.

'We've got Derek Taylor here, Paul McCartney there, you here. All we need to know is which acts do we need from England.'

Only in America. I smiled. 'Easy. The Who and Jimi Hendrix.'

Lou to John, 'That's exactly what McCartney said.' And to me, 'Who do we call?'

'I'll do the Who, Kit and Chris.'

I picked up the phone. 'Kit, Andrew – remember that America that didn't want you? It's changed its mind. I'm calling from the Monterey Pop Festival offices and we want the Who.'

JUNE 16 · 17 · 18 · 1967

**Chris Stamp:** Monterey was fabulous. Andrew was the one who suggested the Who and Hendrix because he knew they were the great thing happening at the moment and that they should be on the bill. It certainly changed my life, and the Who's. We were taking on the might and music of the USA. They invented all this and we were coming over, puny white kids against their protein-fed kids. No one knew who the fuck we were. Jimi Hendrix didn't even have a record deal in America; he only had his UK deal with us at Track. Monterey was the beginning of me being out of it; we all discovered acid, right? We thought we had the secret of the universe, for a moment.

Strangely enough, in terms of what we were doing, acid was so sorta right because it made it all the more so sort of, like, divine. All the things we'd been going towards musically and as a phenomenon, acid really enforced all those principles. Love and communication and all that shit . . . But one of the very obvious things was the Who's market in the US was gonna be very much defined almost the same as it was in England, by this basically white working-class, white-trashy type of audience, places like Michigan, Detroit, those hard industrial centres. It appealed to the same Mod mentality.

**Al Kooper**: I had a nervous breakdown in 1967 in New York City. I'd quit the Blues Project, and my wife at the time, Joan, took me to her makeshift rehab in Oakland, California. After living on a bloodstained mattress in the attic of a former Chambers Brothers manager's communal crash pad, I felt that perhaps the rehab would be better in southern California, and, after fanning my little black book, we were accepted at David Anderle's home in Laurel Canyon. David sized up my mental miasma and diagnosed me into the planning offices for the Monterey Pop Festival, then six weeks from fruition. It was filled with the camaraderie I needed. I worked the Monterey phone from the moment I walked in the door each day until sundown, charming businessmen and managers. Anderle had almost cured me. The rest of my therapy was advanced by Derek Taylor, the specialist in dilated humour. He really helped me smile a great deal and became a close friend from that time until his untimely death in the late 90s. I had additional fun

Brian Jones, Nico and Dennis Hopper, Monterey Pop Festival, June 1967

flying from LAX to Monterey on my first LearJet sitting next to the only one of the Stones to attend Monterey, Brian Jones, who appeared to be convening on Jupiter.

**ALO**: I had trouble raising more than a few days' enthusiasm for the new San Francisco acts – all it meant to me was another reason to buy a new wardrobe. As the San Francisco Sound took off on a trip, the once-again-late *Time* magazine called the city 'a caldron of creative activity', hipper even than London. I didn't like the bands; to me they weren't stars. They were dirtier-than-thou, unoriginal and totally fuelled by drugs and liquor. Although via Monterey, and especially via Clive Davis, these new bands seized back for America a large part of the pop 'n' rock mantle from Britain, I couldn't understand the attraction. I like my stars to behave like stars.

**Pete Townshend**: Haight-Ashbury was like a fucking tourist dive. We came back with psychedelic posters and beads. It was just empty, it was stupid. What was going on in London at the time seemed to be much more interesting. I was surprised at how shallow it all seemed. The bands at Monterey were really pretty bad. I couldn't get Janis Joplin, I just didn't get it. She was just an ugly, hard-drinking, screaming woman who to me didn't evoke Ike & Tina Turner or any of the other people whom she was compared to. She just seemed to be a hollering woman. Her band, the Holding Company, were just about the worst fucking band I'd heard. Country Joe & the Fish were on; Country Joe was interesting as a kind of political balladeer but the band he put together around himself, they were all geeks . . . When Otis Redding walked on with Booker T & the MGs, complimented by the Memphis Horns, I started to think this means something. But I thought, even Otis Redding is gonna get blown away when the Who and Hendrix walk on stage. That's what happened; we blew 'em all away.

**Lou Adler**: We had to deal with Monterey itself; the police chief was alarmed by rumours of thousands of Hell's Angels invading his city. He alerted the National Guard of Fort Ord to be ready for trouble. We did our best song and dance show for the town's fathers (and mothers) to convince them it was a cultural event. John Phillips also thoroughly charmed Mayor Minnie Coyle, and they let the show go on. Although we were bombarded by many last-minute crises – e.g. the renegade chemist Augustus Stanley Owsley III distributed free Monterey Purple LSD – things seemed to work out. It must have been meant to happen, because on Friday, 16 June 1967, when the Association hit the first chord of 'Along Comes Mary', the festival was underway. Thirty-three music attractions performed, and talents like Hendrix, Joplin and the Who were catapulted to international fame. The Festival signalled the pre-eminence of every performer involved. Record companies mined the San Francisco acts for new signings. It was a melting pot of musical influences. At last there was talk about rock as a serious art form. Monterey helped ignite the rapid expansion of rock music into today's multi-billion dollar industry. A phenomenal 1,100 media people – managed by Derek Taylor – guaranteed the lasting impact of the festival. Our media barrier was broken. Instead of the police chief's nightmare, it was a peaceful hippie dream. For three days, it was a perfect world. By the end the policeman had flowers in their hair and the national guardsman had painted flowers on their shaved heads. For one weekend the harsh realities of Vietnam, student unrest, the Cold War, racism and urban riots were suspended and even transcended. More than a rock festival, Monterey kicked off a musical and cultural explosion that still affects society today. The Foundation has to date donated hundreds of thousands of dollars in the name and spirit of those who performed. It was a generation's coming out party, more than two years before Woodstock. It couldn't last and it didn't, but the music remains – and what we did forever captured the energy, optimism and aspirations of a generation.

The Sunset Boulevard Riots, 1967

## CHAPTER 17

**Philip Townsend**: By the end of 1966 it was all falling apart. In early 1967, Mick, Keith, Brian and Robert Fraser got arrested for drugs. Brian was continuously stoned but still drove his one-headlight Rolls up and down the King's Road. What people who were around in the 60s know but tend to forget is that very few of the movers and shakers were in it for the Flower Power. They didn't believe in love and peace; they were bread heads who believed in dosh and very little else. They had a talent for making money and, having made it, used it for their own self-glorification. Brian Jones spent a lot of time at Granny Takes A Trip and Hung On You. The latter was run by Michael Rainey, who was very well connected and was in the South of France in 1960 when Andrew and I were there. The clothes were great. Hendrix, the Stones, the Beatles and the rest were his customers, but not Andrew; he still liked his bespoke. The Flower Power scene had collapsed by the end of 1967 and Rainey's stuff was no longer the image. He and the rest of psychedelia were soon out of business. Recently one of the Granny Takes A Trip/Hung On You-type jackets designed for Jimi Hendrix went for sixteen thou at Bonhams. Probably not much consolation for Michael Rainey, who was last heard of driving a taxi in Australia.

**Adrian Millar**, musician/entrepreneur: Only a brash flash young git could have pulled it off . . . an older more experienced git wouldn't have wasted his 'valuable' time . . . couldn't have dredged up sufficient energy, chutzpah or belief, not in his artist . . . but in himself . . . to get away with what Paul Newman's character in *The Sting* described as 'the big game.' Anyway, back in those days, banks still contained cash and it was much easier to do a bank job than to promote three ugly sods plus two *really* ugly geezers who couldn't write a song between them. And it makes me sick to see those cunts speak of Andrew as if he were just some fucking press agent they hired who was 'good at his job'. Just ask history, and she'll tell you that conclusion is always reached from the outside, because from inside it's only a dream or a fantasy and much too distant to grasp as a reality. How would the Rolling Stones have fared as six with Ian Stewart, or with Brian Jones, Giorgio Gomelsky or just Eric Easton as their manager?

The Stones without Andrew is a far more complex conundrum. Without him they would not have been dragged to Oldham's altar of pop and been forced to write songs. And remember that, early on, Mick Jagger wasn't even Mick Jagger. Andrew Oldham was a star and that, of course, was the eventual problem. Think about it . . . this was a nineteen-year-old kid. These days a nineteen-year-old kid has to be in bed by midnight and on his way to college just to get a job as a doorstop, but this one was already out there and creating the most enduring music package of the late twentieth century . . . and making easy work of it.

**Nik Cohn**: By 67 London had livened up – it livened up quickly, in a rather pseudo and trashy way. In career terms Andrew made a big mistake, *big* mistake, by not dying. From the moment that he got the Stones to the moment the Stones were no longer enthralled by him . . . it was over very quick; you had to be there. There was something quite pathetic about Brian Jones towards the end. I would never have described Andrew as pathetic. He, like myself, like most of the people who survived that period, had times when we were very much on the ropes. He was damaged but he was able to use his damage productively most of the time. Brian's damage was paralysing, it was deadly. The last time I saw Brian Jones he really did look as though he'd be better off dead. He was a very weak sister indeed. I liked him but he couldn't take a punch. Andrew took quite a few punches.

**ALO**: The first Stones single of 1967, 'Let's Spend The Night Together', was released simultaneously in the UK and US on 13 January. Although the lyric was as fervently sexual as you could hope for from the Stones, the sound was a real departure – no more of that over-the-edge sonic onslaught, nothing spiky, just a real heavily blended, perfectly balanced mix of piano and guitar, with Charlie's drums leading the charge and Bill's rumbling bass covering flank and tone. Even the backing vocals were reasonably smooth.

The Stones flew to New York to promote the single on *The Ed Sullivan Show*. Controversy flared over the sexual demands laid down in the lyrics and the show's producers were insistent that the chorus line of 'Let's Spend The Night Together' be deleted, even though the Stones had previously sung 'I Just Wanna Make Love To You' to the Sullivan show. Now, though, they were inviting the world to spend the night together from a much higher profile and would suffer the consequences. Eighteen months earlier we would have told Ed to go fuck himself and walked off the show. But now it's showbizness and in this moment we're at the top, and we all have something to lose. A decision had to be made on the spot – in public. I asked the band, 'Do you wanna stay or walk?' The next thing I knew, Mick was rolling his eyes and singing, 'Let's spend some *time* together'. Years later Jagger would claim he didn't do it, that he'd mumbled his way through the line, but it's clear from the tape that he sang the alterations.

To promote both the single and the album in the UK, I agreed that for the first time the Stones would appear on *Sunday Night at the London Palladium* just one week later. Previously I had noisily and publicly refused to allow the Stones to appear on the show (even though the Beatles were regulars), considering this bastion of all-round entertainment, televised to ten million viewers, too 'family-orientated and showbizzy'.

The UK papers picked up the Ed Sullivan story – the Stones had backed down and toed the line with authority and the establishment who ruled the American TV networks. Now Mick was a rebel with a pause. And so, just one week later, methinks perhaps having lost face in front of himself and being perceived to have done the same in front of the rest of the Stones, Mick finds himself reminded of the events of the week before. Nobody gives him the op to grab his land back by objecting to 'Let's Spend' or the dealer-homaged and

Glyn Johns, MPJ and ALO; *Sunday Night at the London palladium*, January, 1967

drug-addled 'Connection' that the group is going to perform on the show so, in another huff and puff, he blindly looks around for another house to blow down and decides he's not going on any bleedin' *Palladium* roundabout to wave to the nation that put him and the Stones there in the first place. Then again, that's all subjective hindsight; it's just as likely to have been part of a plan to test me where I would hurt, with the kill to come later.

Anyway, rockopera lovers, you still don't shit where you eat, and this childish gesture – 'I'll sing but I refuse to wave' – translated into 'Who Do You Think You Are, Mick Jagger?' As much as any drug bust, this cast the mould for the triangle between Mick, the press and the public that exists today.

At the end of January 67 I was about to turn twenty-three. Just twenty-one days later Mick and Keith were busted, the honeymoon was over and Mick, who three weeks before would not wave to a nation, was holding back the tears and waving, albeit handcuffed, to the nation in a replaintiff call for support from the back of a well-bobbied Black Maria.

The first major drug bust of the era happened – where else – at a Stones party. Keith was to be the designated rock outlaw, so it was appropriate that it happened at Keith's house on 11 February. Tipped off by the *News of the World*, his Redlands country retreat in West Wittering was swooped upon by the Sussex police, who found Mick, Marianne Faithfull, Robert Fraser, Michael Cooper and 'acid king' David Schneiderman all present. Amongst the drugs found was a quantity of heroin, amphetamine and marijuana. Mick, Keith and Robert Fraser were arrested and charged, with a court date set for 10 May. 'Drug Squad Raids Pop Stars' Party' sang the *News of the World* merrily. I went missing in California as soon as I heard the news, a block above the exclusive Bel-Air Hotel on Stone Canyon Road, enjoying Lou Adler's hospitality.

On the same day, 10 May, that Mick, Keith and Fraser – supported by Allen Klein and Les Perrin – were remanded on a £100 bail for a 22 June trial, Brian Jones got his. At 4 p.m. Brian and Prince Stanislaus Klossowski de Rowla were taken from Brian's Courtfield Road flat to Chelsea Police Station and charged with possession of hashish. Detective Sargeant Norman Pilcher, the pop-pot buster, ordered a large amount of property to be held for analysis. After being released, the pair headed straight for Allen Klein at the Hilton while the night before, after his appearance in court, Keith Richards had left in his Bentley for Paris with Anita Pallenberg. The next day, 11 May, Brian and the Prince, known as 'Stash' to his intimates, were remanded on £250 bail at the Magistrates Court on Marlborough Street for a 2 June trial.

The following day, Brian would be spotted on a shopping spree at the Chelsea Antique Market.

After a while I returned to England quietly and remained silent over the bust. On the one hand I was terrified I would be busted myself, and on the other I felt that the Stones had asked for it by their behaviour both on and off stage in the past few months. Allen Klein flew into London with none of the trepidation I felt. He told the *Daily Mirror*, 'Their problems are mine. I'm working my ass off to get them the best lawyers and will be in the front row of the trial every day.' To escape the media glare that the drug bust had brought upon their lifestyle, Mick, Keith and Brian were also keen to get out of the country. They fled to Morocco. Stigmatised by the drug bust and uncertain as to whether they were facing prison sentences, the Stones were still forced to uphold contractual agreements. On 24 March they'd set off on a European tour, their last live gigs for the 'foreseeable future'. I stayed behind, in the nursing home or in LA (I can't remember which – they were both home).

Customs officials at every airport they flew through took great delight in haranguing the 'drug group', methodically searching every last piece of luggage. The group stormed Sweden, Germany, Austria, Italy and France, continuing on to Poland and Russia, where shortage of tickets led to huge riots and police with machine guns and tear gas were brought in to disperse the crowds. The Stones provoked worsening displays of mass vandalism in Switzerland, Holland and Greece. The group were relieved when the tour was finally complete, Mick informing the press he was 'done with touring and would never tour America again'.

I continued to find ways to kill the pain and escape the hell that seemed to be around every corner. Electroconvulsive therapy (ECT) was considered effective treatment for severe and clinical depression through the 60s. The side effects include devastating brain damage, in which memory, personality, intellect, ambition, persistence in life and vigour can all be impaired. For a while the treatment seems to work, but only because the brain is so injured the patient is too confused to know or remember what was troubling him. When the brain begins to recover, the problems usually return and ECT is more likely to destroy a person than cure him. The patient may become 'docile and quiet' – manageable – but the treatment does not address the source or cause of problems. For the next near-three decades, I would display classic after effects of ECT. Along with the brain mutilating psychosurgery, Dr Mac had me hooked on the equally dangerous path of pharmaceutical psychosurgery. I'd spent many nights at Dr Mac's house surrounded by antique tables loaded with psychotropic pills, the latest drugs on the market (and there seemed a new one every week) – antidepressants, tranqs and mood elevators. I had come to rely on McLoughlin. If the pills did not knock me out and there was nothing on TV, Eddie would arrive in the Phantom V and drive doctor and patient up the M1 to some northern 'fish & chip' nightclub to see comics like Bob Monkhouse and Frankie Howerd. Rumours about my mental condition spread fast, but in my mind I had nowhere to go save Dr Mac's for peace and quiet, and Messrs. Monkhouse and Howerd for a good laugh.

**Tony Calder**: The only sound coming out of Olympic was a death knell. I remember the Stones came in one night when they were out on bail. They were doing 'We Love You' and it was a dog. Lennon and McCartney came in and Lennon said, 'Set the mike up' and they went in and put the falsetto voices on. I had tears in my eyes; it was magic, that, absolute magic. It rescued the record – no, it made the record. It was phenomenal. The single was scheduled for release after Mick and Keith had been sentenced. Everybody was hoping they'd get off the drug charges but if they didn't . . . Andrew had prison doors clanking shut simulated and prerecorded into the beginning and end of 'We Love You' and a video filmed by Peter Whitehead just in case Jagger and Richards ended up behind bars. It was shot in a church in Essex and featured Marianne Faithfull, Keith, Brian and Mick acting out the trial of Oscar Wilde.

**ALO**: It was now the beginning of the satanic majestised winds and weeks of forever change. Calder and I had finished an early supper at the Terrazza. Eddie had arrived about 8.30, called Olympic from the reception of the Trat, and come downstairs to give me word that no Stones were expected at Olympic before ten o'clock. We stood on the pavement outside the Terrazza Trattoria as Eddie cruised my Phantom V around and Tony's new driver Brian followed suit with Tony's brand new six-door chocolate brown Mercedes, waiting on two pop tycoons who had no particular place to go. In a few years Tony's Merc would end up *chez* Pete Townshend and my Phantom V would first go to Lou Adler and was last seen with Sammy Davis Jr. Perhaps we should have bought the film rights and remade *The Yellow Rolls Royce*. Brian was a pal of Eddie's and had joined Tony on a temp basis, not having completely left his all-over-the-globe boss . . . Laurence Harvey.

'Brian sez that Harvey's filming nights in Chalk Farm and would love for us to hop by. How 'bout it?' sez Eddie.

How about it? The confused existence I was prescribing to and the presumed station I was chunting through had my surface blasé, no visible reaction at the night's invite, but inside I was churning and excited at the very idea of meeting the man who had been my hero and propeller into all things pop. I knew that all was not well in my world and just hoped it wouldn't show.

'Tony, how about it?' said I.

'Sounds good to me. At least somebody's working,' said a not-in-the-least-bit bitter Calder.

'Okay, lads, back to show business.' I managed a smile, we got into our cars and convoyed off to Chalk Farm and Mr Harvey.

Our man was starring with Mia (Mrs Frank Sinatra) Farrow in the spy thriller *A Dandy in Aspic* as directed by Anthony Mann, and the yards behind the Chalk Farm Roundhouse were doubling for Berlin at night. Our cars passed Checkpoint Camden and cruised on to the set. Suddenly I felt a whole lot better. Action was in the very air. Lights, trailers, wind machines, crew, cameras, a few old Mercs with left-hand drives and German plates: all the emery of production and work but no Laurence Harvey. I'd been Laurence Harvey and would be again – from *Expresso Bongo* to life and *Room At The Top*, *The Manchurian Candidate*, the bleached and bearded Buster Crabbe in *The Silent Enemy* – but I'd never met my influence and alma mater, so I was nervous . . . very nervous.

Brian filled us in on what was going down on the set.

'Anthony Mann is not at all well and it's rumoured that Mr H may take over. He's already directed some scenes when Mann was too sick to turn up for work.' (Anthony Mann died a week later in Berlin and Laurence Harvey picked up the directing reins and completed the picture.)

Half an hour later Brian led Tony and myself into Harvey's trailer. Brian's knock at the door was answered by the man himself. David Bowie once said that it is disappointing to meet one's idols, for they are always smaller in real life. Not this one. He was not taller than I thought, but as tall as he should be. His black shiny hair was long and elegantly dishevelled and fell into his face as he beckoned us into his trailer. His bright green eyes pulled you into his life. He wore a thin beige rollneck, dark brown jean-style drainpipe uncuffed trousers, matching brown suede Chelsea boots, and a gold wafer-thin watch, perhaps Audemars Piguet. A heavy gold ID bracelet hung from a thin wrist as we shook hands and sat down.

'Welcome to a quiet mess. I do wish it were more organised here and there was something for you to see, but at the moment we won't be doing a thing until eleven. How about a little wine? Some Pouilly-Fuissé Louis Latour perhaps? Brian, you know where everything is.'

Brian did, and we poured up and wished each other a nervous cheers as Larry Harvey picked up the flow.

'And all that trouble you've been having with the police . . . it's all a bit Oscar Wilde revisited to me. I've never had a problem with the police or drugs. I'm my own drug, dear hearts . . .'

I was right. Laurence Harvey was Britain's first pop star. He smiled and segued into. 'So you've got a Phantom V? Just be careful how you use it. Too much parading up and down with dolly birds and jolly old Britain will soon stop wishing you well. I should know; I had my first Roller in 54. Couldn't afford it, but that's half the pleasure, isn't it?'

I laughed so hard, Harvey laughed back. He laughed so well at himself.

'You mean you can't afford yours either? Good for you. Back when I got mine everybody said that nobody under sixty should have a Rolls, so I just had to have one. Now I'm running around in a Mini-Cooper and working nights.' He checked his watch and sighed, 'Brian, please go out and find out what's going on.'

'Andrew, you come with me for a minute.' He got up and addressed himself to Eddie and Tony. 'Have some more wine. I'm just going to show Andrew my new toy.'

With that Harvey patted me on the shoulder and guided me out of the trailer. He wasn't all Mini-Coopers yet. He led me to a gleaming grey Roller, Ward-Mulliner model as I recall, opened the back door and we got in. He'd brought an opened bottle of Pouilly-Fuissé and two glasses emerged as magic from his brown corduroy trench coat. He poured, lit a cigarette and placed it in a holder, and continued from where he thought we'd left off.

'Andrew, I'm never one for putting my opinion where it might not be wanted, except with an audience, of course. But I do know a little about you and I do know that if there's something you might admire about me it's mostly my dear departed Jimmy Woolf. An actor doesn't usually give credit where it's due; in fact he usually tries to disown it and claim he was responsible for himself. Brian has told me of your interest and knowledge about Jimmy, and I'm happy to tell you that everything you could have thought about him is true. The man opened up his life to me and taught me everything I know, and were he still alive I can assure you he would not put up with me being stuck out here in Chalk Farm waiting to work. He showed me what I could be and how to accomplish being exactly that.'

He paused and looked away and let the rain sliding down the window in lighted drops catch their breath and his meaning. 'He gave me all this unselfishly and unsparingly, more than any woman could or has, because his love for what I could be was above all barriers. Jimmy died; he left me, which sort of makes my life simpler and harder at the very same time. I have his box of tricks, I know how to use them and I'll never have the curse of thinking I can do without him. It sounds by all accounts as if you have given some of the same to your Mr Jagger and his Rolling Stones.'

I stumbled and muttered in the dark, 'Yes, of course you are right. I gave . . .'

I was losing it. Mr Harvey did not mind.

'Of course you did. If you don't mind me saying so the boy couldn't have learnt to be that camp on his own.'

We laughed. Christ, the man did not fuck about. His voice was warm and honed.

'Look, Jimmy loved control, he loved the game and not much more. You'll get hurt. You can't fight a witch-hunt. Sean Kenny has told me what's going on and I've read the papers. Your lads are turning from boys into men; they're leaving home and there's nothing you'll be able to do about it. It's the nature of the beast. The artist has to rise and shine and dismiss his maker – it's as true as Adam and Eve . . .'

We talked on for quite a while. I can't remember what I said. I think for a change I mostly listened. Finally, I'd got to the end of *Expresso Bongo* and had it delivered by the master in real.

We got into our cars outside the set. Tony and I made plans for tomorrow as I prepared to go to Olympic.

'What did you two talk about?' Tony asked.

'I didn't talk too much, Tony. I listened.'

Tony looked surprised.

'He gave me a message from Jimmy Woolf,' I added.

'I hope it helped. See you tomorrow.' And with that we were gone.

The nightly Olympic sessions were running true to form, and they were not recording sessions as I had known them. Charlie, Bill, Stu and Glyn Johns would be the first stream to arrive and when Brian, Mick and Keith *avec* entourage eventually arrived and then eventually deigned to play, they didn't sound so much like a group as a waste of life. Something had gotten hold of their hearts and it wasn't me – Andrew's rallying cry to volume and commerce was not inviting anymore. The camaraderie of the road and of making it had been replaced by a jaded been-there-done-that air of henchmen plotting to usurp the throne. For that while the life had gone out

Glyn Johns, Keith Richards, ALO, Charlie Watts, Brian Jones and Bill
Wyman, Olympic Studios, 1967

of them and they communicated in ways I did not comprehend. Everybody
was very clever, laughing at every laugh and nuance of left-unsaid
conversation. Sentences seemed to be unnecessary – everybody was very
cool, uncalm and hardly collected, very detached and, with the exception of
Stu, Bill and Charlie, stoned. Brian was now showing the abuse and terror
nightly; Charles Laughton could have donned a blond wig and played him in
drag. The costumes had got out of hand and, on any street he walked or
stumbled, removed the need for a Belisha beacon, traffic light or zebra. Keith
was bringing up the rear waiting for something to happen on Mick's front and
Mick was all front, stoned as a matter of convenience and in control of the
game and the ball. Whether they were playing everything badly, or just blues
badly, it was all Ravi Shankar to me. When they experimented with
mellotrons and keyboards and astounded themselves, I listened for and
longed for your actual beefy, solid track. I listened for riffs and figures and
got none. I don't even know if they knew they were torturing me by not
coming up with any songs. We were young and invincible and it was my turn
as they became beyond songs.

Occasionally they merged and got it together, but it would invariably
fade into a false alarm. They appeared to be rejecting everything they had
become masters at, making recordings out of songs. They wanted, it would
turn out, to be masters of their own art, but we were not masters of
communication. The drug busts, the nights in jail, the near misses, the every
night of watching for the law – this was some welcome home to England.

Checking your cars and houses to make sure you were clean must have been a hardship when you were not. The press had turned on them since the Palladium fiasco in January, the busts had tripled in a few weeks: the world had turned on the Stones for making it and daring to come home for some time off. Fleet Street smiled that smile and raised its sodden elbows – 'You've Had Your Time, Boys, Now Read Us And Weep'. Mick Jagger, Keith Richards, Brian Jones and the Rolling Stones were spelt the same, took the same headlines, but as of 67 we had no control over the cop,y and that, regardless of who's been driving their car, has remained the same, with press reaction to Mick's recent solo and sexual escapades as present-time proof. In 1967 the Metropolitan Police took over our PR and Fleet Street lapped it up and pounced on the big beat in verbatim, just as only a year before they had lapped up our PR whims and outrages. The Rolling Stones, and to a lesser extent the busted of the Beatles, were being taught a lesson in public – you can't get away with it anymore; we've decided who you are and the public agrees.

Mick Jagger, Keith Richards, Tony Calder, Phantom V and ALO, Piccadilly, 1967

One night Mick told me that Michael Cooper was doing the next album sleeve, which meant Gered Mankowitz was not. That meant Mick was not listening to me anymore, as in a final blow. But the final blow for me was a different one. We'd recorded nothing in three weeks. The studio bill was £18,000 and here we were discussing the fucking sleeve. Cooper stood on one foot, hand on the other hip, watching Mick bring his pictures into the picture. I knew that Keith loved Michael Cooper and I knew that Mick needed him. Michael Cooper was not an extraordinary photographer. He was just around for an extraordinary time with extraordinary subject matter, the Stones, as they started to look the part of their second run.

The youth run was over. Soon they would be street fightin' men. Brian hovered behind the Hammond organ, a blond wigged-out acid junkie version of Marlon Brando in *Apocalypse Now* – a bizarre pale grey deformity of candy-striped Granny Takes A Trip box-jacketed, double-breasted suit and off-white shirt. He picked his cold cobalt marble eyes off the ivory Hammond keyboard and seemed to marvel that it was my turn, too. Stu shrugged, buried his head in his arms at the grand, and let his little three-chord wonder start to nip at the heels of kill. Bill chatted with an embarrassed Charlie and pretended neither he nor I was there. Keith studied his guitar, his gnawed fingers and ignored me in that order. Michael Cooper felt like an angel of death, a smackstenched gargoyle of doom hovering with Jagger over my moribund state, not daring to go for the kill or the body but eager for a wing to chew on. Cooper was Mick's weapon of choice – he was his Uzi. Talent had nowt to do with it; he wielded the photographer like a gun. Gered bit his lip and got paler by the exchange. Even with all this going down I had time to notice Mick's attempt at middle-class fey hippiedom trying to pass for the real thing, all sixes and sevens in a mismatch of pale blues and greys that just made him paler as he envenomed. And here we were, nothing actually recorded, discussing the fucking sleeve.

After Redlands, Keith started to get noticed. Before that it had been all Mick and Brian. Keith's turn started in the witness box. That rebel yell, that defiance, that's what started the folk hero . . . the legend. And Keith was no dummy; he got the picture fast and liked it. It gave him that first real sense of self. He turned the drawbacks of the busts to his own advantage. The demonic bit, the knocking at death's door charade – in the end he actually became all that for us, fortunately nearly always knowing how to keep something back for himself.

The police wanted me as well, of course. I was petrified of getting busted and basically stayed out of the country until it was all over, which in the end was what became the unmendable break between me and the Stones. Mick and Keith felt I'd abandoned them and decided I had.

We were three weeks into *Satanic Majesties*. It had been a nonproductive party, one that I had not organised, did not want to go to and was getting disinvited from. I felt redundant. '2000 Light Years From Home' and 'She's A Rainbow' would be all that would emerge from this psychedelic effort in trying to top the Beatles. The Stones may have got the clothes to go with the material but they did not have the material itself. I looked at Glyn Johns sitting at the console saying nothing. Whether they played something or not, it didn't matter to Glyn – he was still getting his fifteen quid per hour. Glyn's clock was ticking, so he didn't mind. I did. They stayed away from the studio for five days on the trot. Later I found out Mick and Keith had flown to New York to see Allen Klein, to get his okay on what they had in mind for me.

Mick Jagger, Allen Klein and Keith Richards, New York, 1967

**Allen Klein**: Andrew is an incredible character but he doesn't want to accept the limitations that he has. He can't be perfect in everything – that's really what it comes down to. I believe that Andrew had no idea what was happening.

I think that Andrew always had a problem because he was so insecure he didn't want it to appear that he was not the whole thing, and he used to be jealous. He wanted 'Let's Spend The Night Together' and I wanted 'Ruby Tuesday', and we made a deal because he wanted to get out of New York and get to Ireland. I told him to let me have 'Ruby Tuesday' as the A-side and he could leave. There was no difference in money; it was just personal. 'Ruby Tuesday' went to no. 1. Andrew has the best ears I know, musical ears, he really does. He's better at picking out hits than anyone I know. He has great taste.

The Stones learned well. It's easy to look at someone who has had one or two successes and say they're lucky. They'd been through a lot. *Let It Bleed* was a great album. So was *Sticky Fingers*, which was really an album done in 69. It was mine; I settled and gave it to them.

Andrew got his money. I wouldn't allow him to get hurt. He would get his royalty forever. But he was sort of paranoid – this was on *Satanic Majesties*. There was a lot of money in the artwork and the session costs. He was concerned that it was going to come out of his end. He was the producer; he had to deliver it. He was afraid of that, and it's a theoretical possibility. But I don't think so – that they would just waste the money so that Andrew wouldn't get anything. I know that's what Andrew thought. It was a possibility that the Stones would do that. There was no deliberate reason for them to do it – they wouldn't benefit any. Andrew owned the masters. It wasn't a producer royalty – he was the owner. He got half; they got half. That's the half I bought, his half. Then I had to buy out Eric Easton because he'd taken Andrew to court, suing Andrew for his piece of it. So I bought Easton out.

The only people who know why things happen are the people who were doing them. Most of the books say that I was the cause of the split. Not a chance – you ask them. Ask Andrew. The only reason I was involved was because Andrew was there to take care of the things he did. I don't do that. I was never angry with Andrew; I didn't want him to leave. He was in court with Easton. I remember it pretty well – it was Yom Kippur. I told him I don't work on that day, and for every day I work it's going to cost you a thousand pounds an hour. That's when Andrew said, 'Listen, I'd like to sell.'

The thing that affected the Stones and Jagger was the fact that during the trial Andrew wasn't there and I was. He was very scared, and I was there. I had to be there; Andrew wasn't up to it. I believe that is a potential reason for their split. Everything else is on the side. You get creative people together and they disagree. You know how kids are; they leave home. They don't listen to their father and mother all the time, and that's what you had. It didn't matter that they were all the same age or that Andrew was younger. It was just 'you don't need a father anymore'. I recognised that. It's not a total rejection, but it was tough for Andrew.

On the publishing Mick and Keith get the writer's share. I get the publisher's share and Andrew gets his percentage of what the Stones make. I made him take it. He wanted to sell – he'll tell you. I was at my office and Tony Calder was there, and it was getting to be dawn and the sun was coming up. I said to Andrew, 'Don't sell; take less, but don't sell your songwriter's interest'. Calder wanted him to sell it so he could get a piece. Andrew didn't sell and he still gets his. He asked me, 'Allen, why are you doing this?' I said, 'Andrew, if you ever blow all this money, I'll have to support you.' And he did spend all the money I'd given him when I bought all the recordings. I got sued by the Stones because I bought Andrew; that's why the Stones sued me. Truth be told, and keep this one to yourself, because I don't want to get into verbal diarrhoea with Jagger, the Stones were offered the right to purchase the master recordings, but they were advised by their accountants that it would cost them too much. You must remember in those times the tax on regular income was 90 per cent. It would have cost them a fortune to buy it. It wasn't that they didn't want to buy it – someone told them it's too much because of the taxes.

**Marianne Faithfull**, *Faithfull*: After Andrew abandoned ship, the next logical step was the Beatles. Mick called up John Lennon and told him, 'You know who you should get to manage you, man? Al-len Klein.' And John, who was susceptible to Utopian joint projects such as alliances between the Beatles and the Stones, said, 'Yeah, what a fuckin' brilliant idea.' It was a bit of a dirty trick, but once Mick had distracted Klein's attention by giving him bigger fish to fry, Mick could begin unravelling the Stones' ties to him. It was just a matter of time before the relationship was severed.

**Ian Stewart**, *Melody Maker*: There must have been some sort of bust-up with Andrew because all of a sudden they really wanted to get rid of him. Before they started *Satanic Majesties* a lot of time had been booked at Olympic. Andrew was supposed to be there as a producer. And he was there only in a literal sense. We went in and played a lot of blues just as badly as we could. Andrew just walked out. At the time I didn't understand what was going on.

**George Chiantz**, Olympic engineer: They had just finished *Between The Buttons* when I joined Olympic; I missed that one. They were working on what would become *Their Satanic Majesties*, 'We Love You' and 'Dandelion'. The studios had recently moved from Carton Street down to Barnes into what was originally a French reform church and had been a synagogue. There was great excitement that the Stones were in. I think the Stones had come to the conclusion that they'd probably got most of the ideas that they were going to get out of Andrew and wanted to go a different way. Andrew used to practically walk around with a mobile chemist shop, uppers and downers; psychedelics were not his scene. The Stones hadn't even begun to finish the songs. The vocals hadn't been written; the tracks were being done with no idea of what the vocals were even likely to be. The tracks were largely composed in the studio and there was an enormous amount of time-wasting. The studio staff thought Andrew was being pushed out by the Stones who saw Andrew's world as something they really didn't want to relate to – too cramped for them to expand into. They were hanging around with Lennon and downing psychedelics like there was no tomorrow or going to Maharishi classes – though I doubt whether it was quite as effective. It's a well-known syndrome. Andrew was out of the club suddenly and they didn't want to work with him. Plus they believed *Between The Buttons* had got panned and hadn't sold particularly well. The Stones looked towards breaking their contract with Andrew and they found they couldn't. But they did find that he was responsible for the studio bills. They were certainly careless with money; the *Satanic Majesties* sessions went on for several months – perhaps more than six – and quite often the Stones used both studios. They suddenly found a reason for saying that the portable four-track wasn't as good as the other four-track in studio two. It was all done on Ampex four-track and we did four-to-four transfers. The pressure to keep the bills under control was definitely not present and the Stones could have worked tighter than they did, but they chose not to. One day Mick came in and said, 'Right, Andrew's out of the way, Glyn. You're doing it.' The Stones were trying to break free and they went back to Glyn, who was now freelance. They never really trusted Glyn, but they'd always come back to him, the old faithful. Then Olympic became the nightclub that was open after all the other ones closed. We got the bloody lot, the whole scene, all the hangers-on, sometimes fifty people. Olympic lost an inordinate amount of headphones and property.

**John Paul Jones**: I did one session for Andrew and the Stones for *Satanic Majesties*, the arrangement for 'She's A Rainbow'. I just remember waiting for them forever. I just thought they were unprofessional and boring.

**Bill Wyman**, *Stone Alone*: Andrew had got fed up. He didn't think Mick and Keith were writing very good songs anymore and they started to contradict Andrew. His ideas were not as interesting as they thought theirs were. The band was more aware of what we wanted to do musically. Andrew disagreed. As the days went on more ideas and suggestions from Andrew were thrown out.

**Mick Jagger**, *Rolling Stone*: I think we were just taking too much acid. The whole thing, we were on acid. We were on acid doing the cover picture. It was really silly but we enjoyed doing it. Also we did it to piss Andrew off, because he was such a pain in the neck. Because he didn't understand it. We wanted to unload him, we decided to go on this path to alienate him. Without actually doing it legally, we forced him out. I mean, he wanted out anyway. We were so out of our minds.

The Rolling Stones, London, 1967

**ALO**: Vinny Fusco said it best, 'The ultimate destiny of the manager who breaks the act is to get blown off; it's almost irrevocable. Unless the artist is going to continue to grow and needs a grower, now anyone can do the job for a lot less money. Get a fucking bookkeeper.' Mick Jagger remains one of the greatest performers of this century and has also proven himself to be more than a great bookkeeper. I don't think in that time, in that situation, that it could have been handled any *nicer*.

I left the studio one night, another night of nothing recorded, just a lot of drugfoolery and clever asides. I walked out of Olympic's front door. Nobody noticed, nobody said goodbye. I got into the Rolls and Eddie drove me away into the night. We stopped. Suddenly I had had it, and I got out of the car to make a call. What was I doing? It was as clear as day. I felt finally that I did not belong and was not wanted. I dialled Olympic and asked for Mick.

'Yes, Andrew.'

'Mick, I'm not coming back. I think it's time we called it a day.'

'Well, Andrew, if that is how you feel . . .'

There, I thought, that didn't take long. 'Yes, Mick, that is how I feel,' I said, feeling like that and shit.

'Well, Andrew.' Was that Andrew to me? No, it was thrown by a pro to the control room stalls. 'If you've made up your mind.'

'Yes, I have. We don't need to do our laundry in public, so if you agree . . .'

'I agree.'

'We can sort it out between ourselves and Allen. Hopefully, Allen can work it out.'

'Sounds good to me', said Mick. 'So that's it then?'

'Yep, that's it, Mick.'

'Okay, Andrew, goodnight.'

'Goodbye, Mick, have a good life.'

I left the phone booth. I somehow felt better when it seemed things couldn't be worse. The silence had stopped and I heard the creak and sigh of relief from the phone booth door's hinges. I cringed, shrugged a don't know why, sort of sighed and got back in the car.

Les Perrin would deliver the official statement:

The Stones have parted from their recording manager because the band have taken over more and more of the production of their own music. Andrew Oldham no longer has any connection whatsoever with the Rolling Stones.

Mick Jagger added this in the *NME*:

I felt we were doing practically everything ourselves anyway. And we just didn't think along the same lines. But I don't want to have a go at Andrew. Allen Klein is just a financial scene. We'll really be managing ourselves. We'll be producing our own records too.

In what was the most agonising moment of my life to date, I tried to appear strong and fair. I told the *NME*:

Everything the Stones have done has been natural. They were not puppets, they were people. Whatever else is said about them they were as close to professional as any five artists can get. We split because we had no need of each other anymore. As people we went in different directions. There was no definite decision. It was just over. We just weren't on the same wavelength anymore. We'd gone as far as we could together. It was time to move on.

Eddie was looking very good. He was intoxicating, life-saving company. 'Where to, Andrew?'

'I don't know, Eddie . . . just drive around.'

'What happened in there, if you don't mind me asking?' Eddie enquired as he squired the Rolls towards the Hammersmith Bridge.

'Is it over?' He helped me along.

'Yes, Eddie, it's over.'

'Well, it may not feel so at this very moment, but in my opinion it's for the best.'

'Yes, Eddie.'

'C'mon, Andrew, you're better out of that mess.'

We drove across the bridge around Hammersmith and back over, down past Olympic and headed for Barnes. The roads were eerily quiet, still and all-knowing in the space they allowed us. When we came off the M4, turned left, and passed the Station Hotel in Richmond, even I had to laugh as we flew by the past. Eddie heard me.

'That's better, Andrew . . . so what happens now?'

'How do you mean?' I replied and allowed myself a slight cry inside.

'You know, you and the Stones . . .'

'I told Mick I'd ask Allen to sort it out.'

'Well, he'll be happy. He's been waiting for that from the start.'

'We don't know that, Eddie, maybe, maybe not. It doesn't matter now, it's easier for me if Allen sorts it out.'

We rounded Richmond, cruised the M4 for a while, then repeated the procedure.

'You ready to go home, Andrew?' asked Eddie, as in he was.

'Not really, but it's close to three and I really have no place else to go.'

'What are you going to tell Sheila?'

'That's the problem – I don't know, maybe nothing.'

'You've got to let her know.'

'I wouldn't know what to tell her. "Hello, dear! I'm home and, oh, by the way, I just left the Stones – how was your day?"'

'Yeah, I see what you mean,' concurred Eddie as he twisted the wheel another degree closer to home.

Eddie had been taking on a shining light in my life. I could disappear into his world and obtain a peace and privacy I didn't get at home. I sank in the back of the limo surrounded in beige and mahogany, feeling cursed in a hearse.

*

**Pete Townshend**: If you spoke to someone liked Keith Richards about the fact that 'Don't you think that when you listen to a pop record there's a possibility that it could have something kind of spiritual?' he wouldn't know what the fuck you were talking about. Kit understood that, although he moderated me by slinging me in the other direction. But he understood it and so did Andrew. I think when he left the Stones you were left with a bunch of people, estimable though they were – Jimmy Miller was a great producer, Allen Klein is a brilliant businessman, Glyn Johns continued to engineer for the Stones and got them a wonderful sound – but they're all journeyman, they're just journeyman. I always believed the Stones were one of those bands that could ascend the spiritual heights if they wanted to, but they didn't seem to want to. Certainly they never attempted to do so since the early days.

We'd just recorded *Tommy* when we did the *Rock And Roll Circus*. We did two takes in the afternoon but the Stones didn't go on until 4 a.m. I think the only people in the audience left by then were me and my mates. Mick kept sending the Remy Martin and I kept drinking it. But what was really going on was much more . . . I believe that Brian was dying. I think he'd already decided to leave the band; certainly I knew he wasn't going to be in the band anymore. Anita Pallenberg, who, with Brian, I'd hung out with in places like Paris (and I'd always seen as Brian's girlfriend) was suddenly

368

with Keith. Brian was just a wreck; he was terrible, he couldn't play. I'd always loved Brian. He'd always been incredibly nice to me, much nicer than anybody else in the Stones, and they kept wheeling him out and in the end he had to sit down and play . . . then they'd take him off again, he'd come back a bit perky because he'd had a cortisone injection or something. He was in very bad shape; he shouldn't really have been there. Mick was spectacular; everything he did was spectacular. If you watch the video he never loses concentration for a second. He's playing to the camera all the time but the band were not very good compared to what they could normally do. You could see Brian Jones was gonna die and you could feel that the Stones were gonna let it happen somehow. I know that's a terrible thing to say; I know it's not what actually happened but that's how it felt to me at the time. Brian was one of the first people I felt responsible for; he'd been my friend.

**Sheila Klein Oldham**: Brian came around to the house towards the end, shortly before he died. He was trying to smoke a cigarette and couldn't find his face. I think Allen had sent him round hoping that Andrew could find some way of helping him but we didn't know what to do with him. What he needed was good professional care. I think it all comes down to the fact that we don't have rites of passage and don't know how to have relationships and didn't know then. Interventions and clinics were unknown then. There weren't that many people taking drugs in those days that were in the public eye. The Stones were losing Brian, as they would rid themselves of Allen Klein. Brian, of course, did a good job of eliminating himself. Allen Klein would prove a little trickier.

When Andrew came back after the split with the Stones, he injured himself. There was blood all over the house. He'd go into these psychotic rages where he'd try and kill me – he tried to kill me about twenty times with hammers and all kinds of things – but I was strong enough to get away from him. He was manic depressive. It's a chemical malfunction and what his doctor was doing with the shock treatment at the time was the worst thing possible. He'd be very up and then very down. This was the worst episode.

I could see the Rolls parked outside. I saw him get into the car and then get out of it again – I could see he had a towel wrapped round one of his arms. Then he jumped on a bus. Why, I don't know. I drove around all over the place looking for him, but I couldn't find him. Where he'd gone was this nursing home in Highgate manned by nuns. Took a couple of days to pry it out of Eddie where he was. The manic depression was a regular occurrence

ALO and Eddie Reed, The Old House, Richmond, 1967

and sometimes it would last a very long time. Sometimes it was triggered by going from recording and touring to doing nothing and he'd sink into depressions very quickly. A lot of it was exhaustion and not eating properly. If he'd had some proper help then he wouldn't have suffered that much.

People were idolising him and his ego got out of equilibrium. Not enough support and too much adulation. Idolatry has a specific karma. There's a price to pay for it. It's fashion – you're either in or you're out and it's hard when you're not the flavour of the month.

Andrew's problem was that you can't be on the stage all the time with that particular character he'd created, and I think it got harder and harder for him to switch it on and switch it off. Because the *off* bit was probably the real him. Andrew can be quite sentimental and that was a very private part of him, the vulnerable tender part, and that frightened him. When you get really hurt – that might've been – I mean how he and Mick must've wounded each other is terrible – they probably really, really hurt each other. To have all those relationships going on at once and then falling apart at the same time. Karmically nobody escapes.

**ALO**: In the Judy Garland–James Mason *A Star Is Born* (1954), when the end comes for Norman Vane (James Mason) he wades with style and dignity (or his double does) into the Pacific Ocean and the next life. Mason's exit is much better than Kris Kristofferson's pathetic rock 'n' pop cry for attention in *A Star Is Born* (1977), the Barbra Streisand soapadelic retread. James Mason, with the frugality of the 50s, merely wastes a pair of swimming trunks, whereas our boy Kris shows the excess of the time and, in putting himself away, wipes out a perfectly decent Maserati.

Brian Jones' death was dignified, a private affair attended by only 'a few close friends'. He just wastes a life, maybe. It depends on your point of view about completed cycles, the inevitable, and succeeding at your death wish. Shortly before midnight on a humid, balmy Wednesday night, 2 July 1969, Brian, slightly or quite affected by the evening's heat and his intake of drink and downs, got fed up with watching telly and went for a swim in the heated pool of his Cotchford Farm in the plural belt of Sussex.

Less than one month before, Brian and Mick Jagger announced to the world, via Leslie Perrin, in a non-combative united address, that the paths of Brian and the Stones had separated and that Brian Jones had left the Stones. In perfect Brian-speak he 'no longer saw eye-to-eye with the others over the discs we [the Stones] are cutting. The work of Mick and Keith has progressed at a tangent at least to my way of thinking.' Mick added, 'Brian wants to play music that is more his own rather than always playing ours. We have parted on the best of terms.' Twenty-one-year-old Mick Taylor had already passed his audition and would be Brian's replacement in the Stones, making his public début when the Stones held their free London Hyde Park concert on 7 July, five days after Brian's death. Taylor came from solid muso stock, having just served time with approval in John Mayall's Bluesbreakers, and came highly recommended to the Stones from all of England's board of blues chiefs.

In the last days of May the Stones, with Glyn Johns and Jimmy Miller and minus Brian, were recording at Olympic studios and invited Mick Taylor in to see if he fitted. He did, and the track he sat in with would be the Stones' second national anthem of their second golden run. The hybrid, intoxicating 'Honky Tonk Woman' would take them back to no. 1 in the US two and a half years from the last chart-topper, 'Ruby Tuesday', in January 1967.

Mick Taylor had more in common with Brian Jones than guitar

excellence and a unique style of playing their first love – the blues. Just as the before-bloated-by-excess-and-pain Brian had been to so very many, Mick Taylor was very pretty – ash-brown long hair, shy and pale. The Stones had another double-header handled for the next five years in sound and image. Tall and thin, he fitted right into the triple-threat front line backended by gaunt muscle, and the movement continued at anthem with the times. Still fresh from the club circuits, Mick Taylor's face showed him unused or using, wide-eyed, unabused and eager, with no particular devils in his dance of life so far. He and I would work together only once, in the early '90s, when he gifted my Argentinian Ratones Paranoicos production with his guitar. We toasted ourselves on being the only two to leave the Stones of our more-or-less free will and live to tell the tale. Others would not be so lucky.

Brian had seemed to handle his break from the Stones in a remarkably sober and practical manner, at least on the surface, and I had admired this newfound aplomb from my distance. I hoped that the surface had some substance and that Brian intended to use the split for positive change and not abuse himself, or others, any further. Certainly, he did choose wise counsel with whom to discuss his future, the caring blues guitarist Alexis Korner. He was supposed to have been positively feeling out forming a new band, fascinated with and using as his example and role-model the American-based pop 'n' blues band Creedence Clearwater Revival, John Fogerty's West Coast combo who'd hit big that summer of 69 with 'Proud Mary' and 'Bad Moon Rising' and who seemed to have struck the right balance between their musical integrity and the selling of it. It was quite easy to understand Brian's finding inspiration in CCR, for there were parallels between him and John Fogerty that he could openly connect with and formulate a solid game plan around.

For Brian Jones, there was no going back to the past of clubs, pubs and the blues circuits of the world; in that year of 1969 a return to your roots would have been synonymous with failure. Creedence Clearwater Revival were a good model, both in the reality of Brian's fame and his situation (i.e. his standard of living and breathing needs). Whether Brian realised it fully or subliminally, he and Fogerty shared not only musical but physical similarities in what they did and how they portrayed themselves. Brian could adopt the front man persona, without competition from a lead singer's dapper diva danceability, to get back to where he'd felt best and wanted to feel again and do it for the growing festivalistic audience who thought of him as a hero and icon. Brian could also have felt he was entitled to find his voice, the one

I'd buried in 63 on 'Walkin' The Dog', and, further, was entitled to write his own music and dismiss my opinion that you can't write down to the public – well, not knowingly anyway.

On that warm July 1969 summer evening in Sussex, Brian's immediate plans were to go swimming. Nobody wanted to join him, so he went alone. A while later he was joined by his girlfriend, Anna Wohlin, and the builder who was living in Brian's house while he carried out renovations. The builder's girlfriend, a nurse also staying *chez* Jones, came out of the house to check that Brian was doing okay, given his evening's alcohol and chemical intake. She found him to be all right and returned to the house, followed by Brian's girlfriend. On their arrival back in the house the nurse realised that Brian had been left alone. She went out again and found him lifeless at the bottom of the swimming pool. What happened next, and whether Brian was alive and for how long after the builder and the girlfriend had joined the nurse and got him out of the pool, becomes and remains a matter of confusion and conflicting opinions, chiefly as to whether Brian was alive when the ambulance and medics arrived and as to the diligence of those who might have sought to revive him. We do know that the police duly arrived, followed by a local doctor who examined Brian and pronounced him dead.

Brian may well have been having a mental revival of sorts that helped buoy him up against the trauma of 'deciding to leave the Stones', but a physical revival had been out of the question for a long time. At the coroner's inquest, his asthmatic condition, the possibility of an epileptic fit and his drug and alcohol intake were examined as to the part they played in his death. The pathologist would announce that Brian had pleurisy, an enlarged heart, and a diseased, excessively enlarged liver. The coroner recorded a verdict of death by misadventure, drowning under the influence of drugs and alcohol.

The swimming pool was an incidental, thrown in for Brian's closing night, for Brian had, for a fatal length of time, been drowning under the influence of life. It is one of the sad ironies of entertainment and life in the public eye that only a minute percentage of those in the field of artistic endeavour rise above the odds to find themselves embraced (so often for no self-sustaining, accountable reason) and held in high esteem by the public. So many enter this camel race and attempt to fit through the eye of that needle that so attracts, already suffering from and cripplingly bereft of any reasonable self-esteem. For if the moment of the actual 'doing' is not the moment of truth and is not self-sufficient and apparent, and if you find yourself waiting for the applause and approval to confirm the moment you missed in the first place, then you are fucked from page one. Brian was such an excessive arse licker in his attempts to satisfy his excessive need of everything and everybody that his tongue had to have collapsed along with his liver and other life-giving parts. Brian had no business, except the business of trying to buy approval, of making Ian Stewart the empty promise that 'he would be taken care of' when Stu was told I didn't want him in the Rolling Stones, and that the group were not going to do anything to deny me my wish and my reality about their future. That is, unless Brian had convened Eric Easton, myself and the Stones to have us all agree that Ian Stewart was to be treated as an equal financial partner in the group. No such meeting was called and Brian's move on Stu could only be seen by him as the pathetic empty promise it was.

Brian's death had no heartfelt effect on me at all. It was the first death I found useless and the first funeral that I did not attend, finding its honour role of inbreds and supporting queens completely pathetic and fake. In the flesh, Brian was one of the first people I'd met who was truly dead on this earth. I can recall his eyes for you – they were searching for something I wish upon nobody, something not even Anne Rice has figured out, but David Mamet understood from the off and Truman Capote got scared to death by

374

because it was around his every next corner and thought. There was no point in trying to have empathy for the dear monster-child; he'd only use it against you. It was as if, having been granted, like a cat, nine lives, Brian had been sent back mistakenly for number 10.

In the Stone-by-Stone interviews Peter Whitehead conducted in the September 1965 Irish filming of *Charlie Is My Darling*, Charlie Watts was my darling, entitled as such when it became apparent upon viewing the footage at Whitehead's Soho cutting room that Charlie, and Charlie alone, was the only member of the group who managed to be natural on camera, and, in that reality-vérité mode, reasonably unselfconscious and true. Bill Wyman came in second, much to the surprise of my effete elitism, with Mick, Keith and Brian tying and dying in last place. Although I said nowt about it at the time, not having the skills to confront this reality without leaving blood on the floor, I remember the cold grim black and white morning I left Whitehead's and walked around Soho Square knowing that the Stones were not to the celluloid manor born. I probably headed for my office and spewed out a hundred film progress announcements to cover my tracks.

In *Charlie*, Brian was in full intellectual overmode, spinning his claim to be not only the vision but the brains behind the Stones. You have to remember that it did not matter to me about what might have been; I had been in the business of what was. Brian didn't communicate with his interviewer, nor did he listen. He just talked a collection of revisionistic wishful-thinking meanderings, a collection of words, not even sentences, that had Peter Whitehead and I falling about rewinding and playing bits to make sure that Brian had indeed spewed out this nonsense.

'Listen, Peter,' I'd said. 'It's just words; he's not actually saying anything.'

'Yes,' said Peter, 'while the rest beg off from being asked to take themselves seriously that's all poor Brian does.'

It was a style I saw years later developed into a multi-syllable similarity by producer/Atlantic Records *honcho* Jerry Wexler while revising his career into the art it already was. When Brian did say something, it was to tell of movies he was writing, although it was clear they never passed his daydream agenda. This was easy for me to suss, being an early graduate from the school of 'films-in-my-head'. The saddest part was Brian's premonition that he did not envisage himself living longer than twenty-seven years.

Be careful what you wish for and just as mindful of what others wish for you – for sadly, on the screen at age twenty-three, Brian was on the road to being right.

In the middle of the 80s I was preparing a Christmas greetings radio spot for Allen Klein to promote the CD issue of the originally released in 1966 *Big Hits (High Tide And Green Grass)* and the rest of the Abkco/Stones catalogue. I was using as the basic material an actual Radio London Christmas greeting spot the Stones had done in 1966, making this new spot not from the used portions of the original but from the unused outtakes. They were funny, off-the-cuff, 'real', natural and happy – the Stones laughing at their own mistakes and their inability to read one line without cracking up. Charlie would mispronounce the album title and Bill would forget to mention he was with the Rolling Stones – Mick and Keith were just giggly Christmas titters. Brian's voice was totally scary and gave me the real chills. It came from a dark and different frequencied, disconnected place and shared none of the joy and mirth of the rest of the group. Brian had his own sound, underground, that I could not edit into Mick, Keith, Charlie and Bill.

It didn't belong . . .

**Keith Richards**, *The Early Stones*: Andrew learned record producing at the same time we did. The only reason he was sitting there was because we were on the other side playing the stuff. I mean, Andrew knew nothing about recording except what he thought he wanted to hear, which may be the purest form of producing because he is not going to turn to the engineer and say, 'Wait a minute. I want more bla-bla-bla.' It must be maddening when somebody does that. But in those days it didn't matter because it was all in bloody mono. It was like you were going for a certain sound and a lot of the time Andrew was right. I mean, he was trying to make records that *he* wanted to listen to and so were we, and most of the time he was right with all his enthusiasm and so on. And he was quick to learn. I mean, when he found out something that worked with the Stones, he didn't forget it. He was very resourceful.

But we started to learn more than Andrew did, and all of a sudden Mick and I figured that possibly we had more of an idea what this band could do than Andrew did. Andrew just wanted hit records; we wanted great ones. But Andrew should get a lot of credit. He was very smart. He got us one of the best engineers around, Glyn Johns. And Jack Nitzsche, for instance, would come in and help us get just the sound we wanted.

Actually, it was Glyn Johns who recorded our very first session even before Andrew was involved with us, and Andrew, as I say, was no dummy, and he would always make sure that he had the best people around him.

## · CHAPTER 18 ·

**ALO**: In 1973, things got back to the normal rock 'n' roll madness and pressure when I agreed to work with my old mates Humble Pie again.

Paul Mozian told me about an A&M Records Humble Pie offer, and it didn't make much sense. After being forewarned by me of my Immediate Records going under, Humble Pie had jumped boats before mine sank and signed with A&M in 1970, knuckled down on the American road and by 1972 had journeyed right to the hard rock top. Their records were heavy, their life was heavy and they had managed to put that big fat stage sound on disc, a feat I was not well known for. 'Dee (as in Anthony, the Pie's manager) sez the boys really want you,' Paul told me. Paul had worked for Allen Klein when Allen ran Apple, looking after the whims and needs of the Beatles and Phil Spector, and had taken care of a few odd jobs for me on the side until one day Allen announced, 'If you like him that much you can have him full time.' Paul did work for me full time, attending to my whims and needs on a lesser budget than that provided by his previous clients. He was in his thirties and bearded, droll and full of humour. Paul sat astride his Mediterranean heritage and mean streets triborough upbringing and turned a cynical eye to the world. He was well engaged in his home life and could raise a meiotic glass with the best of us.

'Okay, Paul, ask for a lot of money, something in the Todd Rundgren flavour-of-the-month range,' I replied on the phone from my second-floor East 51st Street maisonette. Life was reasonably grand since I'd vacated Wilton, Connecticut, and moved back to Manhattan. I was engaging life a tad more, had cut back on the wooded recluse image and was getting out and about in reasonable shape and for the most part enjoying people. I had just finished the Arica programme, a grand fruit cocktail of proven methods at pulling up your bootstraps and getting into shape. I was pretty fit and just smoking myself silly as opposed to drinking myself mad – as in, I was reasonable company for reasonable people. Arica was created by Chilean Oscar Ichazo, who hailed from the small pueblo of Arica and named his non-profit business of enlightenment after his home. I got my money's worth on the programme's forty-day smorgasbord of salient improvement. I may even have, not for the last time, saved my life. I was definitely given the tools to go out and reconfront the world, but I was not given the tools to confront myself. It may have been no more than a credible makeover, but it would certainly do for the moment.

Paul asked for the lot of money, and lo and behold he got it, no problem. All was fine with Jerry Moss and Abe Somer at A&M. Dee and Humble Pie were supposed to be pleased, the contracts were drawn and signed, I was partially paid and Alan O'Duffy was booked as engineer and Olympic studios as location.

ALO, Sheila Klein Oldham and Sean Oldham, Connecticut, 1972

I called Eddie Reed. Luckily he was available. He booked an apartment for me at 3 King's Yard, a cobblestone across from the back of the Connaught Hotel, and, alas, the last residence for dear Mama Cass when she said goodbye at a speed and age of only thirty-three. Decent wheels would be a requisite, so I shipped my white 450 Merc by boat from New London, Connecticut, to Southampton, England; it would be nice to have a left-hand drive in London again.

Although legally separated since 1972, Sheila and I had been seeing each other on occasion, the main occasion being our son Sean, who had left my Connecticut home when I got the roam urge back and had moved full-time to England and his mother. I had enjoyed an idyllic and, in the main, peaceful time with him.

Though on occasion it was not that peaceful. Recalling the piano lessons I had had at an early age and mindful of their help in coming up with the occasional keyboard part, I arranged for the then-nigh seven-year-old Sean to take piano and reading lessons with a teacher/jazz musician in nearby Westport. I'd drag Sean kicking and screaming there. He would curse at me and yell for his mother, but to the class he went. I also enrolled myself, being already of the mind that my days of just whistling or humming out my wants and needs to an arranger were probably over. It was a new day, and should Sean ever decide he wanted to play in the game of music, he'd need to be hands-on in both the areas of engineering and musical arrangement. My good intentions just turned into pleasant Bloody Mary mornings as both John (the professor also played jazz nightly at the bar across the street to Westport Station that greeted all the Jack Lemmon/New York daily commuting nine-to-five bar divers) and I rose above Sean's disinterest and refusal to cooperate by raising our glasses to a musical discourse that encompassed the merits and origins of the MOR anthems of the day, John not being up for Lennon or something Sly. Thus Paul Simon, James Taylor and general soft 'n' slushy rock would all get their church of origin located, discountenanced or applauded as we Bloody Mary'd onward. After many a lesson as I walked off John's porch, the mid-morning sun would hit me in the same spot the booze had and, feeling Sean's hand in mine, I would note my condition and responsibility and observe the speed limit and get us both safely home, even if it meant a harsh 'shutttuupp-cant-chu-see-i-am-fuckin-drivin!' to a relieved Sean happily done with the piano man and full of nervous natter, pleased to be on his way. Many years later he asked me about this time and I told him a version of the above. By then he regretted not earning some basic musical chops and was belatedly taking guitar lessons and getting to grips with four-track recording.

'You should have made me take the piano lessons, Dad,' he said. 'Had I done any more making, Sean, I'd have been put in jail for child abuse, in addition to driving under the influence of alcohol and/or drugs,' was my reply.

He had been a spunky free-willed seven-year-old and did not recall the kicking and screaming he had engaged in twice weekly as I attempted to tune his life up into the future. I can still recall the breeze and the spurning heat as I father-knows-bested the boy and passed that summer of love with my son. He'd sit pretty and withdrawn in the passenger seat of the Heineken-green Camaro as we zoomed down Route 7 to and from Westport, his long mousy hair waving in the breeze and his annoyed freckled face bent on the road ahead without so much as a by-your-leave in my direction as I sucked black coffee through a straw and on a joint in the morning wind. I never had that totality with him again once he 'knew all about me', the unfortunate result of parents fighting with each other over the child. When Sheila and I bound our legal separation into the long goodbye via divorce, I moved away from both her and Sean with a cold finality when faced with the demands and intrusions of the legal system, for I was not about to reveal that I had needs and feelings that could be lobbied around the courtroom as barter or bait.

Right now I was needed for my Humble Pie work in London. Sheila was pleased at my 'after-Arica' countenance and agreed to move in with me while I recorded the Pie. I did not ask whence or from whom she was moving. I just hoped it would work. Sheila, in fact, was more than pleased with this new me; she was downright amazed. I appeared non-violent, shards of bitterness gone, depression thrown over my shoulder and left in a heap on a past corner as I bounded smiling into London – long-haired, bearded, second to none and bejesused, so very full of hope for a new and calmed life around the bend.

The Arica Foundation was going to be holding its first London sessions, north of Trafalgar Square towards Covent Garden and near the dance centre on Floral Street. Sheila signed up for the course, eager for some of the same that had produced such a change in me. I had really acted up, pushed and amplified the new-me-ism as part of my wish to make Sheila and I work.

I got down to Olympic for the first night's recording nervous as I always should be, buoyed and hot to trot. I'd instructed Alan O'Duffy in advance to prepare the sessions by building the amps, speakers, drums and general ensemble just as if it were a stage. This was in order to deflect the group from worrying about being there to record and let them just get down and play. On arrival, as usual, things were not as they had appeared. It would become apparent that there was a reason that my price had been agreed to without a moment's pause, though I had not had an actual hit since the Stones in 1967 with my dual-*adieu* 'We Love You' and 'Dandelion'. Six years is a very long time in any game, but a lifetime in popular music – in fact, a death knell if you have not kept having hits. I'd attempted a few well-intentioned signings, aborted sessions and mismatched castings as my upward spiral into disarray rendered it impossible for me to stand and deliver a valid finished product. My time at Arica had shaken out some of the malfeasant dysfunction. The recently produced *Essence To Essence* with Donovan, though patchy in its totality, had proven my ability to once more start and finish a project without looking for war with my own side.

Meanwhile, I discovered that the reason A&M Records had agreed to my fee – with all expenses, travel and even Eddie allowed as par for the slate – was that everybody had forgotten to tell me that the group was no longer. Humble Pie had broken up!

The first two nights, only two Piemen showed, drummer Jerry Shirley and bassist Greg Ridley. The third night guitarist Dave 'Clem' Clempson, who had replaced Peter Frampton, arrived, but we were still in no-go without Mr Marriott.

'Steve's having problems,' explained Greg.

Mr Greg Ridley looked like a wild plainsman, a rocked-up younger William Tell version of James Arness in *Gunsmoke*. Tight, frayed jeans and well-worn suede cowboy boots, tall, well-built, healthily gaunt, blond-along curly haired, yer William Katt betwixt *The Greatest American Hero* and '*Carrie*-on-acid' with a smile that could kill. When he pulled his Jim Bowie knife out of his boots or britches, offered you a line off its blade and told you he'd kill for you, you were inclined to believe him.

'I think he'll come to the sessions if first you'd go out to his house in Essex for a talk.'

Greg was a man of few words, so Jerry Shirley had finished the thought for him.

So to Essex Eddie and I went. Steve was ranting and raving. He'd had it up to here with A&M Records, up to there with Dee Anthony. He'd worked four straight . . . well, four years on the trot and was tired and broke. The taxman was after him, wifey was after him, and Steve had just learned that the real estate, a compound named 'Rock's Rest' that he thought he owned with the rest of the group somewhere in the Bahamas, wasn't his at all.

It all sounded oh so familiar. I'd heard this longplay so many times before – same song, different track.

'But Steve, we've got an album to do,' I lamented. I could have added how peeved and threatened I felt by the irony of having reported for work in my most *compos mentis* state since Stonegate and RCA and how the lion I was being paid to tame and display was mangy, bad-tempered and in no mood to show 'n' strut his stuff for the man . . . but I didn't. This was all about and just about Steve.

I cannot recall why and how logic prevailed, but Steve agreed to come and work on the album, which, with what seemed a wry nod to their Bahamian-less being, would be titled *Street Rats*. He'd come to town and grind out the album if I'd come out to his home studio and make a solo Steve and Greg effort on the side, then take it to New York, mix it and guard it till it was deemed releasable. I said yes, Steve said yes, and thus the last Humble Pie album got under way.

Basically I had not been hired as a producer. I'd been hired as a friend, perhaps the only one who could get out of them one last Humble Pie elpee, get them down on tape while they were breaking up, breaking down and going around the bend. Now, once I found out this was the situation, why didn't I walk and say 'it can't be done'? Because in that time I was an obstinate fuck, and perhaps A&M were relying on that and knew that I'd dig my heels in, attempt to meet this stupid challenge and do my best to complete the job. Anyway, I believed in me and I loved Steve Marriott and wanted to see the right thing done for this talented unforgiven. I'd been called back into their lives and found such a sad state of affairs. I wanted the opportunity to help them find that one last great song . . . that final triumph. I knew from experience that the game does not play out like that, but I also knew that the search can be life-saving.

The studio was booked around the clock and we were supposed to clock in at 7 p.m. each evening. By nine o'clock Humble Pie would start to drift in from their Essex marginal rock 'n' roll manors, but nothing would really get started until they had ordered and received some terrible coke. This was madness. Their attention span was non-existent. Steve would get bored on the run-throughs, a wired cocker cockney spaniel in retreat, so the woodsman – Greg Ridley – would take over the singing chores, which would end up as his end-run duty on 40 per cent of the final record, while Steve wished himself out of there and the deal he'd made with his devil via me. Steve was at an all-time self-destructive paranoid high. We cut basic tracks that were note-for-note rave-ups of well-known Beatles songs: 'Paperback Writer', 'Rain', a couple of others, and 'We Can Work It Out'. Basically, Steve wanted to rip off John and Paul and come up with a sufficient variance on the melody, welded with some James Brown cockney patois verbiage, to be able to call the song his own.

I let him change 'Paperback Writer' into his own 'Street Rats', but drew the line at letting him plagiarise 'Drive My Car', 'We Can Work It Out' and 'Rain'. It was just too obvious and grim; they would have to remain Beatles songs. Constructive, unconscious, even applied plagiarism is a given in our trade, something to be allowed for and divined upon. John Lennon said there are only five songs, and we know there are only twelve notes to each key.

Steve didn't care. The insidious madness grew and seemed to glow in the dark of us all. His mind was badly coked and frazzled, his human resources undernourished and scarily thin. He wrote average lacklustre songs and took it all as a sick payback joke, which it would be – on himself. Then he did a couple of breathtaking vocals, incredible I'll-show-you-don't-count-me-out performances, each of them delivered in one tasty take.

This just served to frustrate yours truly, mind in pride and a lump in the throat, and the on-looking Piemen, ears boggling, at two takes of reminder as to how great our cunt could be. There was nothing to be done, nowt with shouting or praising. Our Stevie's heart was not there. It was broken, embarrassed and nothing mattered to him anymore.

Things on the New Age marital front were not, it would turn out, running any smoother. I had Humble Pie by night, slept thru the day. Sheila was out attending Arica or seeing Sean, who was staying at her mother's, so there weren't enough hours on our clock in which to make things work. I wanted it to work. We both had Sean in mind; he was eight and hadn't planned all this. Day by day Sheila was *chez* Arica and getting 'centred', night by night I was returning to rock 'n' roll and hour by hour we were coming apart.

In spite of knowing it was over, I refused to give up and fooled myself into thinking I could buy it back together. I told Sheila to go out and buy us a new house.

She had one in mind, a mews house in Pimlico, 77 Ecclestone Square Mews to be exact. Before Eddie drove me back out to Steve's in Essex I half-heartedly saw and approved it, said I loved it and put in motion a plan to buy it.

I then went out to Essex and stayed there a good week.

The sounds Steve had come up with for Steve and Greg's now titled *Joint Effort* were fresher, had a great vital groove and were much better than anything we'd produced at Olympic for Humble Pie. Steve and Greg had opted for Ian Wallace on drums, Tim Hinkley on piano and Mel Collins on an assortment of horns. Alan O'Duffy ran the board with zest and vigour. It was like Steve's little big mod jazz funk James Brown East End review. Actually, that labelling doesn't do it justice – it was an up instant groove, clever, new money from an old mint, and Steve and Greg wailed along slipping vocals happily inside, around, duelling like kids playing musical chairs with each other. In that week, Steve, who'd spiked O'Duffy's tea with acid in a misguided effort to get Alan to get the good thing, took over the board, added all the right stuff and was very much a-groovin' and in control. The long face of London pushing his body under was gone. Blue skies were here again and liked what they heard. Steve was boppin' and happy, at one with himself and all at once young again. We finished on Tuesday and on Friday Steve would come down to London and Olympic to dub his voice over the remaining three Humble Pie songs he'd promised he'd sing.

I felt there was something I didn't want to know about what was going on with Sheila. We'd dropped into separate lives too smoothly and too soon, and I didn't want to avoid what it was or roll over it and pretend it was nothing. I knew I was up for a verse of 'There Goes My Everything', and I hated that song. I wanted to get it all out on the table and faced. As for the mews house, she and Sean could have it, but as far as Sheila and me, I knew I hadn't fallen in love again and refused to go back to living out the big error. I told Eddie to call her – I didn't want her to hear the sound of my voice and its distant pain – and tell her we'd be back around lunchtime on Thursday.

About two o'clock on Wednesday morning we had a last cup of tea and a spliff for the road with Steve, said goodbye, confirmed with that dual Aquarian look that we'd see each other on Friday at Olympic, and Eddie headed the Merc towards town. Paul Mozian had been in England a week and had been with us out in Essex the past three days.

Unbeknownst to Eddie, who would not have approved, I'd asked Paul Mozian to draw up a financial agreement between Sheila and me to 'amend' our legal separation agreement. None of what follows is a condemnation of Sheila or her life; it's just a fact tracking of mine. It was me who had jumped back into her life so 'enlightened', who'd said let's get back together through my new shine and glow, me who'd dangled houses as bait, trying to make the already impossible work, for my new gloss and glow was merely an overcoat trying to overcome the me I had not really addressed or confronted.

And so at 5.30 a.m on Wednesday morning Eddie pulled the Merc into 3 King's Yard. The stereo wasn't playing Simon & Garfunkel . . . the turntable in my head was silently screaming wah-wah, and bleeding isn't it a pity, and how all things must pass.

I quietly opened the front door to the right-hand side of the redbricked archway. Just as quietly I climbed the stairs to the first-floor apartment that overlooked the cobbled mews.

Having left Eddie and Paul downstairs in the Merc, I let myself in the flat door and carefully took the two steps down into the mini-kitchen. From the kitchen I opened the combo living and bedroom door, holding it firmly so as to avoid any squeak of its hinges. On my left the fire in the fireplace was still burning, and so was I when I heard, from the far end of the room, two people breathing as one. I went into my *Kung Fu* TV-Zen mode and edged my way parallel with the brocaded screen that served to separate the living and sleeping area. I looked over to the bed where Sheila had company and scanned a young man and Sheila sleeping side by side.

I'd found what I'd known I'd find, wanted to find in order to get this charade I'd ordered in out of my life. The hypocritical me watched and allowed my outrage to simmer up to a boil, as this time the only thing I was fucking around with was Humble Pie. I gave the prearranged sign of curtain movement to Eddie and Paul on the other side of the mews.

'Hello, folks, sorry I arrived home earlier than expected. Don't let me get in the way or disturb you; I'm not staying.'

'Andrew,' said a stirring Sheila.

Her sleeping partner woke up with a start and sat up. His first reaction, quite rightly, had his hands leap in defence of his sex.

'Andrew, don't do anything silly,' said Sheila. 'Why didn't you call and say you'd be here? You could have avoided all this,' she added, a tad addled.

'I didn't want to avoid all this,' I leered back, nearly not finding my voice, locating my hand, waving it and feigning disgust at the physical viewing.

'Now, look, man,' said penny lover, pulling his pants and jeans on, 'just take it easy.'

Perhaps he'd heard about me, perhaps he was reading me, whichever. Half-dressed, he started to get brave. 'Now look here, man, if you can't handle this it's your karma – not ours, yours.'

'My karma,' I shouted as Paul and Eddie came through the kitchen door. This guy had to be from fuckin' Arica, I thought – Sheila's bringing the help home. My mind jumped back to the New York training as I recalled that the students I'd avoided were mainly bent on fucking their karma away. My mind did another loop in time and recalled the young man of a wedding gift Sheila had offered me that, no-thankyou'd, she'd taken for herself.

I looked at her enlightened lover and noticed that one foot up to the knee was swathed in plaster, broken foot or ankle. 'Needs a partner,' I thought.

'My karma,' I shouted again. 'Let's deal with my fuckin' karma.'

I grabbed him, shoving him on his one good leg in the direction of Eddie and Paul. I'm not exactly proud of what happened next, but it goes without saying it just happened, and what happened, as said, was less about Sheila and more about me.

I asked Paul to help me keep a grip on the runt as I started to shove his good foot, toes exposed through the slightly grimy plaster, into the fire. Sheila was pleading with me to be reasonable, so I was and yanked him and the foot away from the fire. With two good legs he could have held his own, but that's not the way he came to dinner. I pushed penny lover back across the room towards the sturdy front door, as he didn't have enough control of his balance to follow his own directional wish. I held his right arm with my left hand against the open frame, my folded right arm pinned across his neck. My left leg was sloped backwards and straight enough to support both legs and my body weight, and my right leg crossed left into his groin – ergo, the little runt could not move. I let his right arm go and with my freed hand crashed the door against his forearm. He yelled, Sheila screamed, Paul Mozian and Eddie looked on in disbelief, and I heaved a sigh of relief.

'Andrew, stop it,' pleaded Sheila. 'Stop it! What is it you want?'

I shoved the creep Arican back to the fireplace. His body was now in shock, and I didn't have to hold him. Although a sturdy guy, he was hanging on to the wall, so I leaned down and shoved his leg once more into the fire. He held on to the mantelpiece for support and in an effort to resist, but this time I was more about the drama than the pain and it was really more show than glow.

'What I want,' I delivered in my most workmanlike way to Sheila, as I went about having it look as if I were only about shoving one bad foot back into the fire, 'is for you to take that pen and paper from Mr Mozian, make sure you are under no duress and are of sound and balanced mind, and just sign the fuckin' piece of fuckin' paper.'

To cut a long disgraceful story short, once I'd let Hopalong Cassidy Jr go, she did.

I told Eddie and Paul to leave and take Hopalong with them, and, thoroughly disenchanted with life and myself, poured a large tumbler of Scotch from the decanter on the tray on the table by the settee, sat down, ignored the shaken Sheila and stirred the Scotch with my index finger, exhausted and empty. I drained the glass and, drained by the lot I'd got, fell into sleep.

When I awoke a few hours later, I was alone and Sheila had gone.

I felt disgusted, not with myself, of course, but with the cards life had dealt me, my appraisal of them and the hand I had played. I'd abused and blackened what I'd got from Arica, though in truth ethics were never part of their play. Nonetheless I'd used it to try and fool Sheila into a new life when we hadn't even worked through the first. The bitter irony of that moment was that not only had my game plan not worked, she had bypassed me and gone for the source.

The hand I'd waved as mine was not mine to wave, so it just turned around and gouged my heart. And reminded me I had to stop playing God – and the writer/director of my own life.

I sat on the settee and watched the smoke wind its way to the ceiling and the subtitles have their say. You couldn't stop being you and be the way I planned you. I'd written you a great part in my life as long as you didn't dig too deeply, and furthermore I gave you a happy ending, but you wouldn't stay in my character. I knew something was wrong when I saw the daily rushes in my head. That's when I knew the movie could not work, so I let you breach your contract and then I closed the picture down.

I went back to the studio, Olympic Sound Studios, to finish *Street Rats* – the last Humble Pie movie. Steve Marriott turned up as promised on Friday and sang his three songs for me, then went home slugging me out of the side of his mouth that wasn't smiling, saying, 'That's all you're fuckin' getting, Andrew, so don't come back asking for any more.'

I did ask for more and I got it. It was the second week of recording at Olympic though the clock was already down three, and I still had an album to fill. I had the band just playing grooves, anything they felt like. We were still working on the sound, having broken it all down for the Essex sojourn, so another good reason for letting the group groove around was that inspiration might strike and unearth another much-needed song.

Out of nowhere they hit a figure that was pure Steve Marriott, evoking his life's musical structure from 'All Or Nothing' through Stax and back to 'Lazy Sunday'. It strutted, walked and talked good, he knew it and he felt it, it was right there in the pocket. The little cockneymeister shook his head and pranced up to the mike in his brown velvet flared-bottom trews. He began to sing and I felt my part of the earth move as Steve started in on Chris Montez's 'Let's Dance'.

In the control room I couldn't believe it. This was the hit moment I'd been waiting for, and as it gained ground as Stevie wailed on, I could already smell hit, hear it on the radio – I liked it. The tape was rolling. They got thru the first time round, they didn't fuck up, it stayed on the money, hit the second verse, just as simple . . . it worked! Oh, for God's sake, I don't ask for much, just let 'em finish it is all I ask. You'll have your own weapon, you'll have yer own dance. I was here, there and everywhere in that moment. I was past, present and future – that's how it feels when you hear the whole nine yards. Steve turned to me in the control room, saw me getting off, smiling, praying he'd continue and finish the whole deal, chapter and verse.

Suddenly he shouted 'Hold it!' like a sergeant major, and Greg, Jerry and Clem did, and with that went this magic sound.

'Got you that time, didn't I, Oldham? You think I'd do that fuckin' song?' Alan O'Duffy, sitting next to me – my gentle giant in charge of the sound – gasped an 'Oh, no', and looked fit for tears. I pressed the talk-back button.

'You got me, Steve, you really got me . . .'

I let the talk-back button go and looked up into the control room lights, trying to stick my incoming tears to the ceiling. Steve and I had said we'd never lie to each other. He was born on 30 January, me the day before, so it really was a most practical agreement for two Aquarian souls. He'd got me going, then, in my view, pulled the plug on both of us. He needed a hit, I needed a hit. Enough of this next-to-last tycoon shit; I was twenty-five years away from having gone the distance, and poor Steve would not live to claim the grade. He had to show me the commercial cunt in him and pull it all away. He'd had 'fuck you' music in his hands, the gun against every little big hurt. You couldn't fuckin' handle it, you coked-up whore and worse, what's so scary about a simple hit? I asked the room and cried.

Steve then let me know that the scene wasn't over and read the lines he knew by heart.

'Hey, Andrew, what would you like us to do next for ya, "Sha La La La Lee"?'

Schoolboy titters and nervous giggles in the studio; shivers, sighs and the quiet sound of dying in the control room.

'It depends on how you do it, dear. We do know the song's a fuckin' hit.' That was all I could manage, though I remember noting it was the second time in a week I'd had trouble locating my voice.

'Oh, fuckin' leave me bleedin' alone.'

With that Steve threw down his guitar. The feedback felt like an award of applause, and before you could say they're coming to take me away ha-ha he jumped off the stand dead centre in the studio and walked out of the studio door.

Jerry Shirley and Greg Ridley tried to make it better. The lines of coke did help isolate and numb the pain and the brandy lit a fire of adieu to the hollowness and the shame. Of what? Of having wanted it, of having heard it, having heard that hit between my ears, of having wanted that magic that grabs that third ear between your legs, that golden thing that makes you alive again.

'Well,' said Jerry. 'That's one boy who is not coming back tonight.'

'I didn't ask him to do it, he started doing it himself'.

'He's just scared about what he's good at,' said Greg.

'You wait, he'll hear on the radio. Grand Funk Railroad have just done "The Locomotion", and it'll be a number one.'

'That's only going to make life worse,' said Greg, whether for the world or Steve Marriott I didn't ask, just agreed with my nose to house the rail of marching powder asking for a home on the end of his Jim Bowie.

'And the cunt . . . shfmmmm . . . knew just when to stop, another . . . schmmmm . . . minute and I'd have had enough to edit the fuck together.'

'Don't think Steve didn't know that going in, Andrew,' said Jerry.

'Yeah, that's the hurt, the curse.'

Maybe Steve was right, for himself. He sure played 'Let's Dance' like a fuckin' hit but he could not stand the idea of standing up, getting fucked over and hurt again. The drugs and lifestyle rendered the mite just too damn vulnerable and lacking the tools that made him mighty. He already knew he could not handle fame again. It was enough to grin and bear the pain; it was enough just to live.

In 1998 I wrote (for a rerelease of my Nico recordings) about that grand dame, Keith Richards and Steve: 'At the time I knew her she had that gift that advances any work you do with talent. She was with you in the minute, you just thought, she got it before you spoke, you didn't have to translate, edit or change, all of which led to a truth-only encounter. I had the same thing with Keith Richards, still do. I had the same thing with Steve Marriott, would do . . .'

The next time I saw Steve was six or so years later in the 79 of New York, a year by which, unbeknownst to a lot of us, she and that other lady in our lives, the white one, were starting to exact every ounce left in us – the creative and the physical ebbing away of the last grand reserve.

He had a deal for a version of Humble Pie at Atlantic, and, as if to appeal to my commercial military nature, he called to tell me that he had everything under control. Atlantic was paying him $120,000 for a finished product, and Steve assured me he could bring it in for a fast forty-five grand. I always seem to bring out that end of the street in people, without there being any intent. I remember around those years taking a Fifth Avenue stroll with Ronnie Wood, who was not doing as well as he could at the Jaggerhaus. He let me know he'd just copped one hundred and fifty grand from Epic; I patted his back and sent him to the top of his class. At the time Steve looked like he could bring the gig in. He wasn't that out of it and seemed to be looking forward to the money as opposed to waste. I was happy for him and hoped he'd bring it home. Next thing I heard was that, as usual, America, or at least Steve's vision of it, had driven the old boy off the deep end again. He'd got his $120,000 all right, but had spent north of a hundred and sixty bringing it home.

The last time I saw Steve Marriott before he died in a senseless fire in 1993, ignited by his nodding off alone in a house huffing on a lit and farewell fag, was circa 1988. Alan O'Duffy was pleased to take Esther, six-year-old Max and me to see Steve, who was supposed, according to the ever-optimistic O'Duffy, to be in a happy and tranquil state, with a new missus taking damn good care of him. We drove from our rented Redcliffe Square apartment to the Dingwalls club at the back of the Camden Lock to see a Stevie gig with his band, A Packet of Three. In the main, I wanted Esther to meet Steve. She was slowly getting to meet all the men in my life – all the bright lights that had meant a lot. Steve wasn't trying to play stadiums. He had gone done with the ruse of a star, had settled down comfortably to club and pub gigs, and didn't want another shot. He knew it could kill him. He'd put on weight, lost some hair and had found time to stop, breathe and care. When I embraced him I felt the man heave breath and flesh, a much healthier state than the wired-up little coke bottle he'd felt like so often when still pretending to be in the race. He could still play and sing with the gift God gave him, and he did so without the pain and the cost.

Whatever took him to Los Angeles and Peter Frampton the month before he died to try again, to go for that shot, that useless title, I really have no idea.

When I heard the news I was with Lou Adler in his office atop of Malibu. We both looked at the twenty-six miles to Catalina and somewhere in time I heard 'Endless Sleep'. We spoke quietly on the phone to the Hollywood Hills with Elmer Valentine, a man who had loved Stevie too.

'He knew he couldn't handle America. Why didn't he stay at home?' Elmer quietly fumed.

Wherever Stevie is in that nightclub in the sky, I imagine him stopping off at Judy Garland's table, as they recognise the trouper in each other and the burns from the spotlight of pain. Steve'll force a chorus of 'Somewhere Over The Rainbow', but he'll stop her before they reach the very last line.

Instead Steve will tell her, 'We don't have to anymore . . . now come on, darlin', drink up, you old slag.'

· **CHAPTER 19** ·

**Alan McGhee**, head of Creation: If all Mr Oldham had ever done in his life was discover and bring to stardom the Rolling Stones, that would be enough in itself to merit an award of some kind. But in reality we are looking at someone who did nothing less than originate the pop life as we live it . . . emerging in an era when managing a 'pop performer' was all about getting them on the Billy Cotton Bandshow, and how many summer seasons can we get them when the hits dry up (okay, it still goes on . . .). Oldham, just nineteen years old at the time, saw another route and created the conditions where being a pop star was not just a stepping stone to becoming a light entertainment fixture and family favourite, but an end in itself. Andrew Loog Oldham brought to the table the idea, which still resonates, that personal obsessions can fuel everything, and his obsessions, from Jet Harris to Phil Spector, from *Expresso Bongo* to *A Clockwork Orange*, from the cutthroat world of American PR to the mercurial world of fashion design, from East End gangsterism to West End theatre design, still seem cool thirty-odd years later . . . the first pop figure to not be obsessed with the sordid details of small-time showbiz, but to insist that band photos looked like stills from French New Wave films, his attitude seems shockingly modern to us. As a publicist for Mary Quant, Joe Meek, the Beatles, Phil Spector and a host of others, he moved his job description from fawning to the entertainment press to the far more interesting one of blazing a trail for them to follow. As a manager he changed the game from father figures counting the pennies to outrageous gang leader setting the pace. As a producer he was among the first to chance a feel for the now and a grasp of pop past and present as a qualification for the role, hitherto held by snoring ex-big band arrangers and major label staffers . . . knowing what is cool and what is a hit being of course far more important than working the equipment or being able to read the sheet music . . . and we haven't even yet got to Immediate Records, the first UK independent label in the modern sense. You know, when we started Creation, we didn't want to be like the nice nice brown rice indies of the early

80s . . . we wanted to be like Immediate . . . innovation, mavericks by the truckload, an absolutely disgraceful lifestyle and real pop hits. I think we took that particular ball and ran with it. So, Andrew Loog Oldham . . . king chancer, trailblazer, role model (for sure, even if only to me and Malcolm McLaren). Not many people fundamentally changed the rules of the world they work in. Here's to one of the few who did.

**Tony Boland**, friend: I was seventeen when I left Dublin. I came to England because Ireland was a completely dark place with no opportunities and very stifling. London was the Mecca. For me the fantastic thing about London was meeting other young people like myself. I managed to get my job at the *Irish Independent* by lying my way into their London office and writing a pop column – which is how I first came in contact with Andrew. Andrew was hustling a story to the *Independent* on ex-Shadow Tony Meehan because Tony was from Ireland. One of the most remarkable things I remember about my first encounter with Andrew was when I called up and I got this voice on the end of the line saying, 'Oldham House', doing this whole number of rattling the phone and putting you through. This is what you got when you rang the phone, you know? It wasn't until I actually had to go over to see him that I discovered that there was no Oldham House, no secretary – in fact, all he had was a desk in this tiny little one-roomed office in a music publisher's place on Maddox Street. I thought this was fantastic, the fact that somebody would bother doing this, and then look at you with, 'Oh, so!' nothing to apologise for, for being caught out. Absolutely. And you knew if you said anything, you'd be the one who'd be wrong then! Andrew in those days was always immaculately dressed as though he'd walked out of a fashion plate, looked like a male model. He out-pop-starred the look of most of the people he was publicising.

After his life escalated with his involvement with the Stones and Marianne Faithfull and such, Andrew started coming to Ireland a lot. Most of those trips are complete blanks to him! He knows he spent a lot of time in Ireland, he could tell you a lot of the places he spent time in in Ireland, but the details of what happened there . . . elude him somewhat. He loved the time he used to come and spend here. He didn't have to pretend to be anybody. In London and LA and New York I think he felt he had to be on his guard all the time. He'd read books – I won't say he went for long walks and things, that would be a slight exaggeration . . . generally he took it easy. He used to come just to hang out. I lived in the country then. If we weren't having a traditional roast on Sunday, Andrew would always insist on going on the bike to buy a roast from the butcher because he believed that when you're in Europe you should have a roast on a Sunday.

At one stage there was a literary historical society in Trinity College and, up until then, they'd always had people like famous authors or lawyers or people like that who'd come and give them lectures, and some bright spark came up with the idea that they'd like somebody from the new generation, so they rang me because they knew of my association and asked me could I organise Andrew, and I did. So Andrew came across . . . absolutely out of his tree, completely. Got up on the stage and held forth in the manner of Oscar Wilde for a good hour and a half, and they listened raptly. The funniest thing of the lot was to see him in from of these completely starched Trinitians, all nodding faithfully while he held forth as only Andrew could on anything and everything under the sun – pop music, fashion, *A Clockwork Orange*, change in society, Phil Spector, the quality of light in LA and on and on – some of it absolutely brilliant. But he made no sense whatsoever. And he was, what – all of nineteen at the time? I don't think they had a clue what he was talking about. I know *he* didn't. That was a wild weekend. He stayed in a hotel and let's just say I don't think he went to sleep the whole time he was there.

I saw him again when they came to make that Stones film, *Charlie Is My Darling*. I don't know if it's in the film or not, but he gave an impromptu lecture on stage in the Adelphi Theatre where the group was due to appear that night, about the art of rock 'n' roll and God knows what else. Fascinating nonsense, you know.

Over the years we became on a personal basis quite friendly, and then when he broke up with the Stones and he was a bit footloose and fancy free he used to come here from the States for a couple of weeks at a time. One time when Andrew came over he rented a car from a guy who used to hire out American cars. We were coming back from the television studios to my house in the country. Andrew was driving, and it was about two o'clock in the morning, and he got a puncture. We were about twenty miles from the house, in the countryside, and I said, 'Well, Andrew, we better stop and do the changing.' He said, 'No, I'm not stopping.' He was out of his tree, you know. And we went on twenty miles like that on the flat tyre at sixty miles an hour, at night, and absolutely flattened out the hub of the tyre completely into a tunnel thing. It made sparks as we roared along, and Andrew was fascinated by this. It made a groove in the road all the way home. Lucky we bumped into nobody. I was absolutely terrified. Nightmare trip. He couldn't be stopped and you couldn't talk to him at that stage. And then the next day he came up and said, 'What happened to the car?' Could not remember. Honestly could not remember. Whether he could or not I'm not absolutely sure but he certainly professed not to be able to remember.

I remember once when he came I'd gone out to pick him up at Dublin Airport; I think it was about 74. Right then a bomb blast went off in the airport. Everybody had to take cover – we were lying on the ground for an hour or so. Andrew couldn't believe it. There and then he swore he was going to give up the drugs immediately – the effect they were having on him was getting too much!

He'd come to Dublin and bring his own inimitable style of living at the time. He really was lost at that stage, it's fair to say. He came here once with a character called Brett Smiley, one of his reincarnations. A young pop star in the 70s of ambivalent sexuality – it was very much the time of David Bowie, the glitter and glam. He was promoting this protégé of his quite heavily, arranging interviews for him and so on. One woman I remember who interviewed him suggested that Andrew was in fact taking advantage of this young man and the rest of it, and in good Andrew fashion he absolutely *blistered* the skin on the back of her neck!

My recollection of Andrew through all that period was that here was this man with this incredible talent, like a firecracker – he had had such success at such an early age. I can't understand how he would keep going – to have produced the biggest rock 'n' roll band in the world, to have this adulation, to have this power that all of that brought, both here and in America and all over the world, really. What are you going to do for an encore? Where do you go next? You have to be afraid. You don't take the risks you would have taken before because you can't be sure. I used to feel at that stage that, in all honesty, this was the jockey that rode his back. The amount of anger that he had after all of that was unbelievable. Recovering from that is, I think, what took him all those years. It has in a sense become his second career. I'm certain that whole drug thing wasn't just about being involved with drugs; it was that he literally hadn't a clue where to go, what to do. Well, what is real and what isn't real, when you get to that stage? And, you know, back then I don't think Andrew would have had any time for therapy or anything like that. In fact I know damn well he wouldn't. So drink and drugs were for him the only way of getting the picture back into focus.

I actually think the fact that Andrew's survived and come through what he's come through is one of the most amazing stories of the music business and of all the people who came through the 60s. London in the early 60s was a wonderful, exhilarating time and Andrew was right there at the white-hot centre of it all. After 67 it actually became boring, but in the beginning it really was a whole side of young people discovering for the first time that they didn't have to be held down, that opportunities were infinite. To meet people like Andrew and be a part of something like that was a dream.

**ALO:** In 1972 I had co-opted, with Nigel Thomas, a lofty apartment on West 64th Street overlooking Central Park. I'd done so to accommodate my rare sojourns into the bright lights from Connecticut. I sat in the high corner window of the West 64th Street Lincoln Towers and looked south down Broadway to number 1700 at 53rd. I focused my eyesight so as to gauge what floor of this shiny black building I was viewing, calculated and counted my way up to the forty-first floor. James Fox had played me in *Performance*, and now I was doing brother Edward in Fred Zinnemann's *The Day of the Jackal*. I stiffened my shoulders into a lock, moved two notches to my right and focused on the corner suite of Allen Klein's 1700 Broadway office. Through the sights of the telescope atop the rifle I hugged into my shoulder I beaded in on body movement. I could track and follow the physical blurs that bobbed and gesticulated to the left and right of the steel-bricked Broadway cornering eleven blocks south. I held the image in my sights, tensed my body into combat, held my breath and allowed my forefinger to hug into the trigger and Zen at the ready. I wondered if it was Allen I held in my sights, and hoped it wasn't John or Yoko. I savoured the long hallowed tranquil view to the kill. I breathed in the idea, the energy was water to my vine, jackal scraps to my table. I let my breath go and in perfect slo-mo sighed nicely inside myself a 'not today, maybe we'll look at this again tomorrow', let the rifle go, looked down at Columbus Circle, lit a cigarette, poured another glass of wine and made plans for another paregoric night.

When I met Allen Klein I started my long goodbye to the Rolling Stones. I am not going to perk off the boil about whether Allen screwed the Stones. Suffice it to say he started out representing us and ended up owning us. This is something Mick, and maybe Keith and Bill, have never got over. For nigh on thirty-five years I served my own love-hate Stockholm-syndrome relationship with Allen, brought on by what I then considered unavoidable circumstances – my later drug and alcohol loop and the truth itself.

Allen told me later, and in doing so only added more fuel to my Stockholm pariah, that the only reason he hadn't relieved me of every per cent was that he'd then have had the task of supporting me. This thought didn't do much for my independence and sense of self. I was running scared and hurt. The Stones were out there crowing about their wonderful collaboration with Jimmy Miller, and with good productive reason. Mr Miller had replaced me after the group's own self-produced *Satanic Majesties* adventure. This Miller alliance would reap a score of hits and classic songs that would chorus out the Stones' second run and entitle them to their self-invoked mantra as the world's greatest rock 'n' roll band.

'Honky Tonk Women', 'Brown Sugar', 'It's Only Rock 'n' Roll', the hits just kept on tumbling down. I sat in the shadows of the early 70s dwelling on whether my fifteen minutes were done, as Mick and Keith dismissed my very existence by lauding Miller as the first record producer they'd ever had.

About the same time – mid-80s – I'd been staying at Allen's and used the occasion to make an effort to clean up. Allen proudly told his associates and friends what I was up to, which just put the capper on things that my sense of order had already done. 'Cleaning up' meant I wouldn't buy cocaine, nor get my own Percodan triple-scripts – I'd just visit those who had both. I got a gram of heroin a week to ward off the jitters, smoked a spliff twice a day and had a Friday fill of grappa to stay on course. And for a month I managed to make no purchase nor get my own perco-scripts. Now, before you wonder what's the big deal, this is not bad for a man who once had a bumper sticker made that read 'I Brake For Percodan'. Anyway, on another smack-elevated night I got back to Allen's having bought one of every pastry at a nearby cake shop, and when Allen and I were alone in his den I braved this scenario.

'Allen, we're alone. A lot of time has gone by, we're friends for life – well . . . we're friends, anyway. Can I ask you something, and can I have an honest answer?'

Naturally Allen looked at me a little quizzically, he kinda underwater smiled at me and said, 'Sure, go ahead.'

'Allen, the Nanker Phelge thing, everything Bill talks about. Did you do it? I don't mind, it's long gone now (and so am I, I could have added). I just think if you did, it's the greatest scam ever. It was so simple, it was brilliant.'

What I was referring to was the held-by-more-than-a-few-Stones contention that in 1965 Allen had formed a company in New York called Nanker Phelge Music Ltd and, in line with the same-named UK publishing company owned by myself and the five Rolling Stones, told us we'd all own it and it would own the rights to our North American recordings, we should sign our rights to it over to ourselves and wouldn't it be nice. The shares were never issued to the Rolling Stones and myself. Allen had issued them to himself and we'd signed with Allen Klein, who'd just made the move from business manager to owner of the Rolling Stones' recording rights in North America.

'No, no', Allen said. 'You don't understand. You couldn't own it, you couldn't get the tax break, you couldn't get the capital gain. We went to tax council in England; they said you couldn't own it.'

Suddenly the shine had rubbed off the high. Allen was as believable as ever, but I'd heard this answer before and it just didn't, nor will it ever, ring through. I was as tired of it as I was of the rote answers Mick gives on how young and irreverent I was and what a good publicist I was, and Keith on how well I could scam the press, and Allen on how, if he hadn't been thirteen years older than me, he would not have been able to get the better of me. Maybe Bill's age had something to do with his doubt, although, for my part, Allen never stole anything from me that I was able to own.

**Paul Mozian**: When I was working for Allen Klein my job title was Assistant to the President, so I was Allen's personal assistant. The way Allen treated it was that I represented him with his clients, whether it was the three Beatles, Andrew, Phil Spector, whoever. I was like an executive babysitter – go to the airport to pick them up, make hotel reservations, keep people awake, call up people, make sure people showed up on time. I first met Andrew around 66, when I'd just started working for Allen. I was nineteen and just a messenger then. The Stones were doing *The Ed Sullivan Show* and I had to go to the Drake Hotel, where they were staying, to pick up some medication. Andrew came up to me in this lovely suit and he told me specifically where the prescription was, in which dresser, inside which pair of socks. He was really pompous – and kinda nasty actually, but I knew the guy had talent because he did what he did and he was the customer and the customer's always right. That's how I got on in those days. I worked for Allen for eight years and throughout those years he was very supportive of Andrew. He served a function; whatever deal they made, they made. Allen lived up to his end and Andrew lived up to his end. Allen is very grateful to people who moved him along in life and Andrew certainly helped Allen attain what he has attained. He is of the ilk that likes to give back. I've heard people say some horrendous things about Allen but I've only had honourable things to say and thoughts about him. He was the nicest person to work for; he was thankful and extremely generous. The bad rap he's got over the years is totally unwarranted. I was assigned to Spector when he was producing the Beatles stuff. The thing he and Andrew had in common was that they both liked their music loud in the control room when they were listening to playbacks. I think Phil might have topped Andrew because you could actually have blood dripping from your ears by the time you left with Phil. Actually there were times when I could confuse the two, because the mannerisms were the same, especially after so many drinks. Philip was far and away more paranoid than Andrew, who always seemed to have a pretty good grip on reality. Phil always thought somebody was doing him. One minute he thought I was very faithful, next minute he'd say, 'Oh, you work for Allen.' All of a sudden you were 'a spy' and 'sneak'.

I left Allen Klein in June of 74 and worked for a guy named Sid Maurer. At the same time I started doing stuff for Andrew, and then I worked solely for Andrew for a year or so. He was wild, heavy into drinking and snorting . . . he would never do it in front of you. He was a good coke-head; he would go into another room for the most part. He always seemed to function, sometimes worse than others, but if he had something to do he would keep himself together and do it. An addictive personality but still ambulatory, he could get the job done if there was a job to do. I guess some people viewed him as difficult. By this point, he's classified as a producer, and, y'know, producers are as hot as their last hit. A friend of mine at the time, Fred Halsey, an attorney, had done some legal work for Andrew; he's since been disbarred. His wife managed Jimmy Cliff. Somehow there was a conversation, and somehow Andrew got a gig producing a live concert album for Jimmy Cliff, which was a very good album. It was fun doing it. Andrew was drinking, doing coke and smoking reefers every once in a while. When he was knackered he was an abusive person, but he always showed up on time. His cleverness in the studio, what he could do, far exceeded whatever he didn't do.

**Sheila Klein Oldham**: In 1967 we spent quite a spectacular evening at Edna O'Brien's. We were invited over after dinner. She was having dinner with Princess Margaret, who should have left by then, so it was a bit of a put-down being asked to turn up after dinner. But Margaret was still there. Sean Kenny was very close with Andrew at the time, an amazing Irishman who'd actually kissed the Blarney Stone, very inventive, wonderful mind, very funny, very anti-authority. He'd known Edna for a long time and Andrew had said to me beforehand, whatever you do, don't have an Irish coffee; she's going to spike it with poteen. So we get there and it's all very nice. Sean Connery was there with his wife and quite a few people. It's quiet and we're sitting around and Edna said, 'It's time for Irish coffee now, anybody want one?' Everybody said yes, and she said, 'And you, Sheila?' And I said, 'Not for me, thank you very much.' And she said, 'Oh, you make it very difficult; I'm offering you my best Irish coffee and how ungracious of you to refuse.' So I said, 'Yes,' and thought, 'I won't drink it.' So she came over to me and whispered in my ear, 'You cow!' I was a young thing not expecting that stuff. The Irish coffee comes and everybody drinks it and I think I'm going to be left out, I might as well. I got terribly wigged out and went and hid in the bathroom for hours. Several years later I saw this film that she'd written, *X,Y & Z*. It had Elizabeth Taylor in it and Susannah York and I thought that's a bit familiar, there's Edna being played by Elizabeth Taylor and I'm the Susannah York character. How women are with each other is incredible.

Poteen is called firewater; it's made from potatoes. You only need the tiniest little bit and then if you drink water afterwards it brings it all back again, makes it stronger. Not recommended in that situation at all. It's an ancient thing. Goes back centuries. Sean Connery sat there and talked quietly with his wife, probably couldn't move actually. For most people it would be quite an internal experience but Andrew would react externally with it. He would take it with Sean Kenny and the two of them would be up on Parliament Hill ten sharp on a Sunday morning in ten inches of snow wondering why they were the only two that had turned up for a game of football. It was when we were living in Hurlingham Road. That was a very good period, actually; it was a very nice house we had rented from Noel Harrison. I used to make cakes, and Tony King would come round. Cook the cake, take it out of the oven, put it on the table, turn around and it would've been eaten. Dirk Bogarde came over one time, which must've impressed Andrew enormously, and he was absolutely charming, wonderful manners, came with a wonderful French pâté, lots of theatrical charm and glamour. Telling us theatrical stories. Very light.

**ALO**: Princess Margaret was there. I don't think she could move either. Perhaps she'd had one of Edna O'Brien's Very Irish Coffees during dinner. I did not like Edna O'Brien; she was very vicious and predatory towards all incoming mates. She was another bag determined to spite and spike her way through the new 60s that had capped her run at the top of the hill. The room was all brocade, smoke and Pinteresque verbal flying saucers spinning around the room in paingain. This end of their 60s was very swinging, full of darts aimed at the hearts of any innocent stupid enough to have stopped by. All was fair game in the quest for a synopsis or fresh line of dialogue sucked from fresh or dead blood to support the coveted lifestyle and desperation that sets in when one has become manacled to the famegame. Sean Kenny told me she had a navvy cum artist waiting abed in case the evening produced nothing more celebratorial. I sighted Princess Margaret across the room. Ma'am was upright, embalmed and glued to a chair wearing a huge fur coat and way past bedtime or 'honoured to meet you ma'am'. Sean Connery I approached with some childish critique on a movie he'd just made. He looked to be getting up to me so I shut down. I could not see what Sean Kenny enjoyed about Edna O'Brien; the whole wrecking crew looked like a stillborn Bacon painting stepped out of the frame and into the room gasping on the breath of the newborn and hung.

**Sid Maurer**: I first met Andrew back in 67 when I went to London to hang out with Donovan. I went to two very wild parties and Andrew was at both of them. We didn't really get to say more than a hello and didn't really hang till the end of the 70s. The first party was at the writer Edna O'Brien's place. This Andrew sidled up to me and said, 'You look new here, so let me give you a warning. Don't drink the Irish coffees; they are spiked with poteen'. That was some kind of Irish acid. I thought it was nice of this guy to warn me, but I probably tried it anyway. It was a star-studded affair – Princess Margaret, Sean Connery, Sean Kenny. Andrew got into some to-do with Sean Connery about some film. Sean Connery stood up – Andrew sat down. Everybody was pretty loaded.

Then in 1980 I was managing Phyllis Hyman and she lived in a high-rise across the street from my studio on Broadway. Andrew, of course, was a frequent visitor. He'd come up all the time and we'd hang out and chit chat. He'd come in with Mick Rock, a wundernutzo called Tony Russo, a couple of Colombians whose names I never quite caught, and Chris Stamp. Some days those two looked just this side of green.

**Mick Rock**, photographer: I met Andrew in New York in 1977. He was still in his New York love affair phrase. I started off in West London in the early 70s taking pictures of girlfriends on the ceiling. The camera didn't have any film in it. Oh that's nice, you took pictures of my girlfriend, take a couple of pictures of my band, here's 20 quid. The late 60s, early 70s was not an elitist time. I shot Syd Barrett when I was sharing an apartment with Syd. We moved his apartment, he painted the floors and I went over there that day and they were the pictures for *The Madcap Laughs* LP. Before that I'd been doing the Pretty Things and other bands on the scene. Then I met David Bowie just before everybody started to get interested in that Ziggy Stardust thing; then David was off and rolling. Syd Barrett was much more meaningful than David Bowie. Bowie was vaguely known in England because he'd had the *Space Oddity* hit; he was like a pop singer, came and went in 69. I met him in February 1972; he'd got his hair cut and was off on his Ziggy Stardust trip. Then I moved to New York.

In the space of one week, two different people introduced Andrew to me. One was a young journalist called Jon Tiven, guitar player for Jim Carroll for a while. He said you've gotta see this band the Werewolves at Max's Kansas City. Then a few days later I got a call from this guy, Jon Podell, big-time booking agent. I'd met him thru Lou Reed, who for a while he was managing. At this time he was booking Alice Cooper and Blondie for Shep Gordon. Andrew Oldham had been introduced to him and there was the Werewolves – this was the act that didn't happen. It was all Andrew, more Andrew than the band. Everybody was talking about Andrew and no one cared about the band. When I first met him it was like, whooooaaaa. It was like the first time I met Lou Reed. Andrew was like a magician, an alchemist, a pure artist. With the Stones, he dreamed, created, showed them how to steal shit to write songs, the publicity was all Andrew. Andrew in his infinite street criminal madness – nick this, nick that, do that, get on with it. I did the first ever pictures of the Sex Pistols. What Malcolm McLaren did was very interesting; the Pistols were still another variation on how to be naughty and upset everybody. Essentially it was Do You Want Your Daughter To Marry A Sex Pistol? Malcolm was very smart but in the end a bit smug. Andrew is never smug. You have to catch him singing his own praises. Andrew was so much fun. Malcolm's not that much fun because Malcolm's a bit too self-important. Andrew is not; he's a lot of things and he's upset a lot of people over the years, but one thing he's not is self-important – even in all states and beings. One day Andrew called up and I was doing a session with Iggy Pop. Yeah, y'know, come on over. Iggy was totally intrigued as well. There's a certain innate shyness to Iggy. How he learned to overcome his shyness in life early on was when he found his Stooges persona. As a person Iggy's essentially a very sweet guy but when he took his shirt off, that's when he really became this animal, his physique. Andrew never liked the Dolls or the Stooges, none of that shit – he didn't even like Jimi Hendrix. Andrew was a genius; the Stones were the original anarchic force. The Stooges took one element and went out on a jag on that one, but without the early Stones, that richness and reference. I learned a lot from Lou and David. Lou is deep, although he still doesn't quite get who this Lou Reed guy is – he's aware that Lou Reed is him but he's also another guy. Without the Rolling Stones I'm not sure about the Velvet Underground. Musicians can't help but be ultimately more interested in themselves than they are in anybody else. Andrew, as much as he is very absorbed in himself, is absorbed by other people, his contemplation of other people. I was in a privileged position as a friend, observer, with the Werewolves. I worked with him as a pure project on both LPs. I was flying when I met Andrew; I was hotter than he was and I continued to be until 1982. I spent a lot of time with Andrew. It never stopped until he moved out of New York and decided he was safer residing in Colombia. In a sense he was, but in another sense, how could he possibly be? Under those circumstances. We didn't sleep in those years, a lot of people didn't, especially in New York. New York did not sleep in those years. They were the years of Studio 54, the Mudd Club. As wild as London ever got, New York 77–82; there was never another place like it. I had the studio on Madison Avenue; that was the wildest photographer's studio that ever was. Then there were my own years of the blow-out but through those years it never stopped with Andrew. It didn't matter what state I was in; he helped me emotionally, psychologically. Finally he helped me physically when he got word I was at death's door, in hospital in late November 1997. He got on the phone with Allen Klein and Allen got me out of those hospitals and put me in a new medical centre and got me the best treatment.

**Brian Papageorge**, writer/singer, the Werewolves: We had a certain amount of money to do our second album so Andrew, out of fun and frustration, decided we should do it on two yachts in the Florida Keys. He hired two sixty-five-foot beauties. We lived on one and for the other one we had Bearsville studio from upstate New York send their engineers and equipment down and convert it into a recording studio. It was the best ten days I ever spent. No idea was too wild for Andrew. If it seemed impossible to do that was the incentive to do it all the more; that's the way he was. We sailed around the Florida Keys getting high, recording and waterskiing. When it was over we came back to Bearsville to do the vocal overdubs. One night I was doing a song that Andrew wanted me to sing with an attitude I wasn't quite getting. We'd been in the studio for a couple of hours and he was having a hard time conveying the attitude he wanted. Right in the middle of trying to explain it to me for the umpteenth time he suddenly called a halt to the session and took me out to see *Saturday Night Fever* with John Travolta. All through the movie he was leaning over, nudging me, telling me that's the attitude, that's the attitude. We got back to the studio about midnight and I did the song in one take.

**Phil Chapman**, engineer/producer: I started out at Olympic studios in 1968 as Glyn Johns' tape operator. Glyn did a lot of work for Andrew – he was the same generation, making it in the same field but also wanting to make it with exactly the same product. Glyn recorded them, so he wanted to be the producer of the Stones. He couldn't hack the fact Andrew got to be the producer of the Stones by virtue of the fact that he managed them. By the time Glyn was back with them and Andrew was out and it came to things like 'Honky Tonk Women', I could recognise it was Glyn's sound. He had a particular way of recording the drums, so in Glyn's mind he produced that. That was the time when engineers were beginning to feel they were producers; that's how it started. The recording techniques became as important as the song and the act. When I first started at Olympic I used to go through the masters down in the basement. There was loads of Andrew's stuff and I used to study it. I found that on some of the cover versions he produced, one track of the four-track recording was the original record; they'd obviously played to it. Andrew used to make two kinds of records: little symphonic, complete fantasy productions like Twice As Much and Marianne Faithfull and then other things like the Stones, which were absolute reality. In a way he was irresponsible but you just couldn't stop him. He just loved making records; he was not at all influenced by what people said about him nor what they did to try and stop him. He would just keep going on as if studio time didn't matter – it was irrelevant to him. All he wanted was the end result as he'd pictured it in his mind. As a producer Andrew's personality was one of his greatest attributes. Like Berry Gordy and Phil Spector he was real Machiavellian in the studio; he controlled absolutely everything. A lot of people say he diluted the Stones' sound by trying to over-orchestrate it, but when you look back it's all integral. I pestered him to go through a lot of the Stones songs. He was very influential in their writing without ever getting credit. He would tell them which records to listen to, nick this line, put it together with that; he was very good at that. Under my nagging he'd pointed out several Motown records. Just listen to the brass line on this and now think of this tune. With all the big hits he was able to point out the influence that they actually borrowed to write those songs. Anna Oxa was half done in Olympic; it was a standard pop album, not political or trendy. She was a current singer/songwriter in Italy and I think they wanted a British touch to it. In Italy the *Anna Oxa* LP went Top 10 in 1979, as did a single of the same name. The men at RCA Italia quickly booked Andrew for a month in September to produce Francesco De Gregori.

**David Sinclair Whittaker:** The seaside near Rome. A beach house once lived in by Orson Welles. His crowd were waiting for a chum to arrive with the dope from New York. Andrew said he carried it in his boots and he almost tore them off he was so desperate. I shared out my 'hemmies' while they were waiting, these awful yellow bombs which actually stun the central nervous system of the brain. They're meant to stop you drinking – in fact they just get you high enough to think you can handle drink. Then we would eat at the RCA 'grease palace', which seemed full of Mafia-style men with greying sideburns in expensive sports jackets and grey flannels. More terrifyingly, Andrew was driving from Rome on a couple of occasions when he was high. Inwardly I was furious but too weak and desperate for a drink to complain. Andrew's gang bought flick knives, which they smuggled back to New York taped to the inside of speaker boxes and the drum kits. RCA studios were in a self-contained compound just outside Rome, like a 60s film studio. They had their own factories, banks, studios, restaurants, bars, offices and football pitches. The acts had to turn up every day for lunch to stay in favour with the executives, and were told what they were recording and with whom. It was like a Mafia set-up and it worked. And it worked for Andrew; he was having hits again.

**Phil Chapman**: When we arrived in Italy, Andrew played me Bob Dylan's *Slow Train Coming* when we started the Francesco LP. This was my first experience of someone playing me another album and saying I want it to sound like this. He didn't say it in as many words but you knew that's what he meant. I remember thinking, all right, things are hard left and hard right and the drums are very dry. That's what he wanted and the template had been put on; I was there. I had the blueprint and I knew what to do. Up until then people were always striving for something new. He wasn't. He was serving the act and he was quite happy with what existed. If he liked it, he just said, 'Let's have a bit more of this, please.' All I was interested in was the sound and he used to give me free rein to do whatever I liked. His idea of production was just to bung all the right elements together and let them get on with it. He would keep an overview on it and keep everything rolling. When I worked with Shel Talmy he would tell me exactly what he wanted, 3 DBK, etc. He knew the board; he told you exactly what frequency he wanted. Andrew would let me do whatever I wanted on the board because I never threatened his position as a producer. I was happy with that because it gave me a lot of chances to try out things that I didn't have to take the responsibility for, pile on loads of acoustic guitars or naff string lines. I knew I wouldn't have to answer for that; he would. Andrew was closer to Shadow Morton than Phil Spector. He might have used the Phil Spector techniques but he was much closer to Shadow, who could actually create a complete drama out of a very small idea. Shadow Morton did the Shangri-Las stuff, another nutter, churning out these little soap opera things that were really sensitively produced and have lasted. This is what would happen with Andrew . . . a simple thing like we're going to record an album in Italy would suddenly turn into convoluted layers of social interaction. He was able to make a drama out of most situations. Towards the end of the album, he got a bit over-enthusiastic about things, often in black moods. He got so fed up with the straight-laced attitude of the studio that he punched the monitors off the control desk. He was into knives and guns. I went into his bedroom and he suddenly pulled a gun. Everybody else ran a mile but I just started laughing because he was a bit of a showman. Two of the musicians went home. They wouldn't stay on that album; they couldn't cope, especially with the guns. That was it. Another one went home because he couldn't find any Quaaludes in Italy. They were all terrified of him, except Jerry Shirley and a guitarist who was doubling on dealing. Then there was Esther, who was very classy, very calm about all these things.

Esther Farfan Oldham, New York, 1980

## CHAPTER 20

**Tony King:** Last time I saw Andrew was in 94 in Buenos Aires. I'd seen him at the start of the Stones tour in New York. He hadn't been on his best behaviour – actually, he'd been on his worst behaviour. I was very disappointed. He got me into a row with the Stones; I'm their PA still. He was a bit out of line and people knew I'd been responsible for his tickets and access. In Buenos Aires I said, 'Please don't put me in the shit again.' And that time he was taking care of his Ratones Paranoicos and he was very clever about keeping it away from me. The Ratones were an Argentinian band Andrew had been having some success with.

The Ratones Paranoicos, their manager La Rata and ALO, Buenos Aires, 1994

I don't think Andrew ever recovered from the break with the Stones. I think that was such a great loss to him. It must be very hard over the years to watch the progress of the Stones, to see what's gone on since and not be affected by it. That's a pretty hard pill to swallow, isn't it? The doctor who used to put him to sleep for days on end completely fucked Andrew up. He needed therapy, somebody to talk to; he didn't need to be made a zombie. Your problems are still there when you wake up – maybe more so, because a lot would have happened in those few days when you were out. He was confused at the time. The busts didn't help. We all heard Andrew was next. Brian had been done . . . Andrew was pretty flamboyant about going out and being stoned, fucking great joints in the car . . . Andrew's closeness with the Stones helped him come unstuck. In any artist/manager relationship you must be careful you don't start getting too much on the artists' territory because they'll turn on you. I think Andrew's biggest mistake was when he ultimately sold them to Klein for a chunk of money. That, if anything, has been the reason for the sour relationship between him and the Rolling Stones. Andrew and Mick's relationship was always very volatile. Somewhere along the line something didn't go right and it's not something that's ever been mended. I don't think it ever will be; it's too deep an issue to ever get resolved. Maybe they'll both get older and calmer, bump into each other at an airport one day and sit down and be able to have a good laugh about it all. Artists will always survive. The ones that stay at the top are tough; there's a lot of bodies littered along the way of their success. That's why they are where they are. Mick, Elton, Barbra Streisand, Diana Ross . . . they move right along. If you look at the managers of that period – Epstein died, Kit Lambert would die, Peter Grant died, Robert Stigwood would end up a recluse on the Isle of Wight. They were all sensitive guys who had enormous success that they found very hard to cope with and flipped out. I wish Andrew would find the peace he's been looking for all his life.

**Pete Townshend**: Andrew had a huge fucking ego, that's why he and Tony Calder can get away with writing a book on Abba. 'S.O.S' is such a record; I'd die for one of those records. Produced by a bunch of nameless Swedes from up in the sky somewhere, then when it comes on the radio every bone in my body shivers. I forget myself. It's a spiritual experience. I can't work it out, it's got something to do with the blood running through my veins. Andrew is of that ilk. Andrew lost it; he has lost everything. He is really a nonentity. In 93, when *Tommy* was on in New York and we met up, it was quite painful because he was still who he used to be, he still had that vigour, enthusiasm and brilliance and I just thought, 'What's happened to this guy?' Basically he'd run away. Chris Stamp has run away too; in a sense they're both from the same mould. Anyway, I was pleasantly surprised when I met Andrew in 93. He was still the Andrew I remembered. He's got enthusiasm for pop. Basically rock music has become so discredited and is so valueless I don't use it any more.

The reason people don't find it easy to honour Andrew is he's not here. A book might help a lot to actually bring him back into focus. He's got to have the courage to reappear. I've said this a lot to Chris Stamp, who's happy to show up at Who gigs and be seen around a bit in New York but doesn't take the risks that he used to take. What happens is, because they were so important, they pass into a kind of mythology. What's awful about that mythology is that when you wheel fucking Phil Spector out on the stage to honour him at the Rock and Roll Hall of Fame, you can see that the guy is dead – physically, emotionally and spiritually dead. There's a tragedy involved in that. When Chris and Andrew were not doing that well physically the last thing you wanted to do was confront them in the street or confront them when you've got a hit show or a hit album or you're just about to get an award. You don't want a deadbeat on the top table. I think if Andrew continues to keep himself together . . . because to honour somebody they've got to be fit enough to honour, otherwise one has to wait until they're dead – then you can memorialise them. But I think Andrew deserves to be honoured in his own lifetime and I think he will be, and deservedly so.

Quite simply, I personally feel that the Rolling Stones are the world's best rock 'n' roll band. My speech when I inducted them into the Rock and Roll Hall of Fame in 1989 had been edited by Jann Wenner, who I think had shown it to Mick. I had the sense that Jann Wenner was only looking at my speech so that he could make a quick copy and fax it off to Mick, wherever he was staying, so that Mick would know what it was, so that he'd have Mick's approval. Mick wants to do new things. He would much prefer to be David Bowie than have to work with Keith Richards because when he makes a record now he has to deal with the fact that Keith Richards wants to be like Muddy Waters and grow old and die playing the blues.

Even back then, there were those difficulties. This sense that for Mick the big picture was that he was going to have a good life, he was a normal guy, I suppose I was middle class. At that Hall of Fame I think what I mentioned was, I said, Blah blah blah . . . 'and Andrew Oldham. I don't know if he's here tonight but thanks.' Chris Stamp came up afterwards, saying he sat with Andrew who'd been pleased that I'd said what I said. At the Rock and Roll Hall of Fame another thing going on, I'm afraid, is the Jewishness of the American music business, and of course in the UK it's the Germanness of the music business.

**Chris Stamp**: He sat and he watched Mick & Co. deliver an acceptance speech which studiously thanked everyone who had played a part in making the Stones story such a success: Jimmy Miller, Brian Jones, Mick Taylor, Ian Stewart . . . But the manager who played such an incisive role in creating the Rolling Stones' unique persona? Who packaged and hustled them to international prominence? Designed and produced their biggest records? Who had forced Jagger and Richards into songwriting? No thanks. He's always had charisma, right. There's periods you understand him and then there was a long period where you didn't understand very much he said. I went up to the studio once, end of the 70s, when he was producing the Werewolves on Broadway. I said, 'Hey man, how ya doing?' He said, 'Oh, I've given up smoking.' I said, 'Great.' He had these things clipped into his ear that he had to press when he fancied a cigarette. We were in the studio for about an hour listening to the Werewolves and when I left I remember looking at Andrew and his ears were bleeding from pulling those fucking things. That was round the time I retired from producing; the last record I produced was 'Born To Lose/Chinese Rocks' by Johnny Thunders & the Heartbreakers. Andrew and I hung around together quite a lot in the early 80s in New York. We were disillusioned; we were cynical. All these kids we thought we'd given birth to were yuppies. It was all yuppies and we couldn't believe it. So we were cynics and there was a sort of oldness in our hearts. In the end it was something very deeply personal. What had been more important was that journey, rather than the commerce. We'd all been under thirty, man. We didn't want to become the railway, so when it looked like that's what was happening one just backed off. You can look at it and think what could have been, but it was what it was. The music industry is like shit; all that fighting and struggling we did and what have you got? They're all just like fucking puppets. Now it's exactly like what we fought against in the first place. I've been straight for a long time now.

**ALO:** In 1992 Allen Klein invited me up from Bogotá to New York for the Rock and Roll Hall of Fame induction. I met and again embraced Keith Richards, who was also there for a good time and to induct guitar innovator Leo Fender. I joined Keith and his wife, the beautiful Patti, and son Marlon at their table. We were being reasonably naughty and having a good share of laughs when Billy Joel came over and sat down. Billy and Keith knew each other from the Central Park trot and Keith introduced us. I told Mr Joel I was pleased to meet him, and indeed I was. I love songs and hits and Billy Joel has given the world a lot of both. My favourite songline of 83 had been the first line, second verse of Joel's 'Pressure' when he strode, 'You used to call me paranoid – pressure!' At Les Trois Couronnes Clinic in Vevey, Switzerland, recuperating from the rejuvenation I so needed in that same 83, Esther and I lay abed watching Joel in concert from Wembley, London. I got that old pop-lump in my throat, tears from my eyes to my pillow as Billy brought on the twenty-odd Vietnam vets he'd flown into London to join him on the four-hankie tear-jerking choruses of 'Goodnight Vietnam'. My popheart heaved and sighed as the vets locked arms, shoulders and chorus'd, 'And we will all go down together.' A great pop moment when you've just completed an afternoon shopping spree of quasi and actual morphine derivatives. Straight, I might have said get the fuck out of here.

I was pleased to meet Joel for another reason. He writes alone – a hard task and one I've always marvelled at, the craft of the seemingly impossible mission. Which wall do you bounce off when you are writing alone? When one writes in twos or threes you've always got that other wall to bounce on, that other opinion to bring you back to earth when you reach that moment of not knowing any more, that restraining element when you are about to go over the top and out of public range that pulls you back into the theatre of simplicity. When A and B write together B is worth his weight in gold – as in half the proceeds – if he knows when to tell A to pack it in, close down for the day and go on home. To create alone, from start to finish, is a different kind of special gift. It is one that has always intrigued me. Does it require a dance with madness or is the requisite that there's nobody home? I'd once tried to find out more on this from Bruce Springsteen. We walked one late 70s autumn eve up Central Park South from my pad on the corner of Sixth to his Hotel Navarro; I was agog at his rock John Garfield and his audiomovies that spoke to the troubled backroads, songs that confronted his country's post-60s Vietnam depression and ethical malaise. I got no more than a wink, smile and shrug from this taciturn man. It was still a fair exchange and he asked for and I gave him a copy of Phil Spector and Jagger singing 'Andrew's Blues'.

I was not getting the same exchange from Billy Joel. I told him about 'Pressure', I reflected on his Wembley gig viewed from the clinic in Switzerland, and talked of the ability to write alone. I was, in my opinion, pleasantly and socially stoned, and thought I'd mastered the rotational loop

411

for the night and cracked 777 as opposed to the dreaded 666. Perhaps I was not being as clear as my recall. Maybe Billy, as was his right, didn't want to hear unnecessary data again. I searched for clearer words to get him to name that tune. Futile 'C'mon, Billy, you're American, you remember those old Cary Grant and Grace Kelly movies . . . the Rock Hudson/Doris Day movies . . . they had that American dream, now you've replaced it, people like you are writing it . . . you are the new Ross Hunter . . . this year's Universal-International.'

Keith saw me grasping for straws and his look told me this was going nowhere – and worse – that it was boring.

'You must have got it . . . the writing . . . when you were a kid . . . I got it when I first saw Audrey Hepburn in *Sabrina* – that's when I knew what business I wanted to be in, but you write the fucking things, that must just feel terrific . . .'

Nothing . . . Maybe I wasn't blond enough. Keith sighed and leaned between us.

'In other words, Billy,' said Keith. 'Fuck off!'

'Nuff said. Billy did.

Sometimes the secret of magic is the fact that nobody's really home. The problem with being a way of life begins when life has no meaning. The minute your theoretical meanderings have no meaning in your soul, it's going to reflect it.

**Steve Rosenthal**, engineer: I first met Andrew when he came to a studio called Opal Recordings where I was working on 54th Street in New York. He was hanging out with this macho drug dealer who was going to buy the studio. Then late in 1985 we did some work on the Stones records, early reissues for CD. We did *Got Live If You Want It!* from scratch because the original was so fucked up, audience on one side, band on the other. Remastering the Stones albums was amazing, just the way those old records were balanced – very, very different to the way you balance a modern record. The vocals on a normal record are at a certain volume but if you put Mick's voice at that level it doesn't sound right. There's a level with his voice that Andrew knows; Andrew puts Mick's voice inside the track and all of a sudden it becomes a Stones record. That's something he knows instinctively how to do.

Andrew knows so much about how it actually works, not just the hype or the bullshit. You could say his viewpoint is cynical or vitriolic but it's actually because he was there at the beginning of it. When they made those records they thought they'd be lucky if they'd last another three weeks; they didn't know if they were gonna last thirty-five years or a hundred. They had a very different attitude about the music business. That irreverent attitude he has about the business is still there.

I did Compania Ilimitada, Colombian group, late 80s. One track, a single, 'Siloè', went to no. 1 in Colombia and Venezuela. Andrew flew me down there and we recorded it in this beautiful studio on the outskirts of Bogotá that was designed by the people that did Bearsville. There were some odd problems with it – the electricity would go out a bunch of times a day. I started to lose it, but nobody else could give a shit; it was a natural local occurrence. Andrew would stay up for days, four or five on the trot. The way he communicates in the studio is very different to the way other people do it. In order to understand him you have to have a real deep record collection and knowledge of different kinds of music. He might say, 'I want the drums to be like a combination of Gene Pitney takes Phil Spector out to dinner . . .' but if you didn't know that stuff you'd have no idea he was talking 'Every Breath You Take'; you'd think he was mad as a hatter. It was rather terrifying in Colombia. Armed guards out in front of the studio, guys with machine guns waiting for the revolutionaries to come over the hills. None of this seemed to freak Andrew out; he was very mellow. At night we'd come back from the studio, running all the red lights. Andrew had been up for a while and he was driving. I really didn't think we were gonna get out of this one – he was going about 120. But he was very cool; he seemed to be in control. The rest of us, however, were totally terrified. We got stopped by the military police, and they spent hours going through my vitamins while we stood with our hands spread on the car bonnets. All they would say was, 'Drugs, drugs, guns . . .' Finally they let us go. It didn't faze Andrew one little bit. I decided I wouldn't go back there again. It was like the movie *Missing* – they would have had to send Jack Lemmon down to find me.

**Pauline Thomas**, friend: My husband Nigel Thomas and I met Andrew in Connecticut during the time of Mad Dogs and Englishman. Nigel had started as a manager at eighteen, managing Alexis Korner, Steampacket with Long John Baldry and Rod Stewart, and the Grease band. Then after the Grease band split he started managing Joe Cocker – he was managing Joe and handling Leon Russell for Europe. Denny Cordell took us over to meet Andrew when they were rehearsing for the 'Mad Dogs' tour in Westport. Andrew had this stuff called Cool & Creamy, a dessert by Birds Eye. He had these two huge American fridges in his kitchen – it was a wonderful house – and he'd say 'Oh, this is fantastic . . . you've got to have this Cool & Creamy.

Chocolate or vanilla?' He opened the fridge and all it had was Cool & Creamy in it. I had some and then I started to feel peculiar and had to go lie down for a while. The next week they removed all of the Cool & Creamy from the local supermarkets – there was obviously something in it. There were some very dark days with Andrew in Connecticut. He adored Sheila but she played with him. The whole relationship was forever breaking up and then going back to each other. You can't blame her because half the time he was a little nuts, but the next day she would literally be with someone else. That's not possible unless you've got that relationship going already. Sheila was horrid, but in a way you can't blame her – she was nuts as well. So the two of them together was just a disaster area. From an old-fashioned point of view, she should have been there to support Andrew. But she broke his heart a million times. Sheila was in one of her leavings, when she'd go off with someone else. Andrew got so upset that he finally thought, I'm going to be the big guy here and I'm going to confront this guy and take my wife home, so he went to her place where she was living with this guy and kicked the door down. He went straight through it and broke his leg. Sheila comes out, saying, 'Oh Andrew, darling, poor dear', and off they went together. It had to end.

The first time I met Esther we had dinner at Morton's. Sometimes I found it a struggle to have dinner with Andrew, although now that he's straight he's quite blustery and forthcoming. He went through this terrible stage of whispering. I used to say, 'Sorry, Andrew, I can't understand what you're saying.' Then he'd go tell me all his troubles . . . We came out of Morton's and he proceeded to pee all over the front of a car. We went back to our flat in Albert Court, behind the Albert Hall, where we had some friends, an American Jew and his German wife. Andrew said something like, 'Oh, you fucking Jew, are you going to make it in the oven tonight . . .' He asked them if they were Necronazis. It was just so ghastly; he could be so embarrassing. Nigel was very fond of Andrew but as Nigel got older he got much more correct, very public school, very eccentric in the way he lived. Protocol meant a lot to him. He would never go anywhere in the wrong clothes, whereas Andrew got more and more rock 'n' roll as he got older, and out of control. Nigel didn't; he reverted more to type. He wasn't wild at all. He was so sad about it. He'd say, 'Why can't Andrew just be himself? Why does he have to do all this "I've now got to be Andrew Loog Oldham" stuff?' It amused him but he was very sad about it. He'd be thrilled with the way Andrew is now.

When Nigel died, Andrew was in New York. He flew over straight away. Esther flew in from Colombia. He came with Tony Calder and I was so stunned. I said, 'Andrew, what are you doing with him?' He said, 'Darling, it's so marvellous, we're back in business together.' I said, 'Andrew, are you sure?' He said, 'Oh yes, darling . . .' Of course it was an utter disaster. About a week after the funeral in 93, we made a date. He was staying at the Draycott Hotel off Sloane Square. We made a date and I arrived and had to wait and wait and wait . . . He was completely gone. He was so drunk it was beyond belief; so drunk. The maids hadn't been able to get into the room for days. The paraphernalia in the room was completely bizarre; it was as though he'd taken his old life back again and he was going to be Andrew Loog Oldham. I said, 'Andrew, what on earth are you doing?' It was dreadful. He couldn't speak properly. Eddie Reed arrived. I said, 'What are we going to do?' Eddie was very upset. I said, 'Andrew, if you want to go join your friend Nigel, you are seriously going the right way about it.' I tried to calm him down, said this Tony Calder thing was nonsense and 'You're never going to have any business in the condition you're in.' Then a week later I went to see him again but he was even worse; he was throwing up everywhere, dribbling everywhere, crying. He's a lovely guy but he's manipulated by people. Tony was just using him. Andrew's a very shy man, and he probably thinks to himself he can't believe he actually did that and so he almost has to recreate it to prove to himself, 'Yes, I did do it.'

**David Dalton**: It was the summer of 1994. I was in London interviewing people for Marianne Faithfull's book. Poncy antique dealers, thuggish ex-managers, liars, weasels, pompous asses, and Andrew. He was coming to London too for some sort of business. The Mad Hatter of Pop was then at his maddest – at least in my experience of him. He'd stood Marianne and me up several times (the best way to catch a plane is to miss the one before it), and Ms Faithfull had hied it back to Ireland.

'You deal with the sacred monster, darling,' she instructed me and hopped in a cab. I was exhausted from a week with little sleep. At dinner at Pamela Mayall's house the night I got to London Marianne had blithely announced that she'd spent all the money for my hotel on 'an exquisite little bauble I couldn't resist'. I had no choice but to stay with my aunt near Hastings – a two-hour railway trip both ways – and borrow the money from her pension fund to pay for the train tickets.

My last night in London Sir Fuckin' Andrew agreed to see me. He was staying at the Draycott, a chic little designer hotel tucked in just behind Sloane Square and 'A Stone's Throw From Harrods' and a short walk from Dirk's. A discreet inn favoured by the rich and famous who crave anonymity.

And edgy movie stars. The afternoon I arrived, movie stars were crawling out of the wallpaper.

As I crossed in front of Peter Jones department store, the evening paper was ablaze with the latest ALO shocker: 'Mick Jagger Says He Hasn't Had A Homosexual Experience Since He Was In School. "When Did Mick Jagger Leave School?" Asks Andrew Oldham.'

As I got to the hotel, out slunk Christopher Walken, immaculate and sinister, cloaked in Abel Ferrara gloom and mistrust. I watched as he, like a mobster in a coke opera, slid into his limo. He did it in one take.

Behind the front desk was a grey (and gay) bespectacled old gent – a camp double for the British comedian Ronnie Barker. I asked for Andrew Oldham. 'You're in luck, love,' says he, giving me a nod in the direction of a guest standing at the other end of the front desk.

'Do we *know* you?' a loutish – and very drunk – Gary Oldman asked.

'No, man, I'm looking for Andrew Oldham,' I said as meekly as possibly.

'Are we, *darling*?' he asked. He'd obviously run into Sir Andrew during his stay.

'Room 102, top of the stairs, dear,' the man at the desk informed me. 'The party is expecting you.'

I slipped past the obstreperous Gary and I was making my way up the thick red-carpeted stairs when a door flew open and out popped Andrew like a jack-in-the-box in full nutter armour – a loud plaid suit, made more alarming by the frenetic energy of the demon wearing it. It was his mad pelt.

'David, how-nice-of-you-to-come,' he said in mock Eliza Doolittle. 'You're just in time for, um, tea.' Except that he didn't exactly say 'um'. He sort of clacked his teeth together in a terrifying manner.

He was glad to see me, it seemed. A bit too glad, I thought – the way Brer Fox is always glad to happen upon Brer Rabbit. Except I weren't no Brer Rabbit. He was seriously dusted and light years ahead of me. I felt as if I were moving in slow motion as he regarded me with a curious gaze – the way salmon, who see at sixty-four frames per second, look at humans. As it is, on a normal day – the post-powders and potions Andrew – I have a hard time grasping what he's saying, what with all the allusions, lines of dialogue and various forms of hipster/camp/cockney patois all clipped and delivered with a droogish nasal insinuation.

He was now at warp-speed. He was talking so fast and about so many things at once that he seemed to be double-tracking himself with a little dash of Spectorish echo. I felt like running down the stairs, but this would be a mistake. In the tastefully dim hallway he was a terrifying apparition. Uh-oh,

I thought, I'm in *Batman III* and for some reason nobody has informed me. My role is of the hapless journalist who ends up getting hurled from the Joker's 40th floor office just on a whim.

The suite was filled with people. There was Tony Calder with some hipsterish leering Kraut whom Tony informs us later is a nasty little Eurotrash scam-artist known for his record company stock market swindles. Tony is probably a very nice gent when you get to know him, the kind who likes children and dogs. *Not!* He's always looked to me like a junior league Kray with the in-yer-face-mate East London mayhem. Forgive me if I digress for a minute on Tony Calder. What does he look like? Well, he resembles De Vito on steroids and stilts and on an off day, Harvey Keitel in *Bugsy*. His eyes operate like rearranged slot machine windows on payday and, in his Zen-gangster simplicity, he looks permanently deranged. Tony isn't actually from the East End. *Wishes* he were from the East End – he got to work there when he was a deejay. He's from Southampton; in fact, you'll be familiar with that anal burr of southern England. Southampton faces the Isle of Wight, which apart from one dismal pop festival, prisons and people doing Her Majesty's bidding, is supposed to rear the best bodyguards in the kingdom. Southampton is a port, which must have had something to do with Calder's ferocious knack for music.

ALO and Tony Calder, Draycott Hotel, London, 1994

It was a den of thieves and journalists, I tell you. Aside from Keith Altham. Keith, who used to write for the *NME*, was there, too. On a sainted mission – he was writing the life of one of the forgotten soldiers of rock, Ian Stewart (Andrew must have *loved* being interviewed about *that*). But for some reason Keith was exempt (or immune from) the Loogish hazing.

The manic Loog walked around me in an insolent 360-degree stroll. For the occasion I was wearing a foolish checked woollen jacket that my sister had bought for me in an attempt to make me appear a little modish.

'Where'd you pick that up?' he asked sneeringly. 'Some fag boutique on Melrose?'

Before I was able to stutter out an answer, he'd marched over to the desk drawer, yanked it open. 'I think you need to get up to speed, darling,' he announced, like a hip Dr Jacobson. He had just the medicine. Several large lines of cocaine sparkled on a plate. I demurred. I had given up drugs and drinking seven years earlier, thinking they wouldn't exactly induce the patience needed in bringing up a child. This, of course, brought on another torrent of scorn. His flack of demons roared in derision.

Next he grabbed my duffel bag and dumped the entire contents on the floor. It was some sort of fiendish show-and-tell. He began picking up various articles from the pile and riffing on them with diabolic scorn. It was a sadistic piece of performance art.

Item one, an Aero bar: 'Oooh, look what we have here – a fuckin' Mars bar. Seeing Miss Marianne later, are we?' A sweater. 'Marks & Sparks?' he said with incredulous disgust and threw it down as if he'd been sullied. I felt unworthy. Presents I'd bought for friends and family – the finest Brit kitsch admittedly – a piggy bank in the shape of a thatched cottage, a clock in the shape of Big Ben, a coffee cup with one of Prince Charles's ears as a handle – came in for merciless ridicule.

It was like being grilled by a demented customs officer.

Finally Tony Calder, bless him, got on the phone to Marianne in Ireland and had her speak to Andrew. I imagine she told him, in her best Major Faithfull manner, 'to straighten up and fly right'.

'The blind leading the blind,' Andrew said as he got off the phone.

Things improved *marginally* after that. He barrelled on in his manic mode. He carried on several conversations at once. 'He's gone over the fuckin' Chinese line this time!' he said, railing on about some unknown persecutor. Then, like some extraterrestrial data-scanning satellite that collects random voice samples from earthly media, he mimicked dialogue from *Blue Velvet* and *Hawaii Five-0*. Everything was blurring into everything else. He did a hilarious impression of Brian Jones trying to write a song. Brought his usual cool pragmatic eye to bear on all things Stonesian. Why had their song-writing style changed in 66, I asked.

'Why wouldn't it? They all had cars and girlfriends and houses. They had nothing to be angry *about*.'

Vicious, lightning, razor-blade put-downs were liberally sprinkled throughout the conversation. Ronnie Wood: 'This season's Sylvia Miles, darling.' Mick: 'Linda Hunt will be able to play her soon.'

As I left the hyena's den, I saw Gary Oldman at the bottom of the stairs, still railing on at the concierge about an outrage he'd suffered on some airline. And the gay old thing, not really listening, telling him, 'It's criminal, dear, really it is.' I snuck by Gary but he'd seen me: 'How's *Loooog*, then?' he asked.

'Oh, he's fine,' I said. 'Still mad as a March hare.'

## · CHAPTER 21 ·

**ALO:** The fifteen-storey white opaque-flanked horse had done its work and delivered its message that 5.15 a.m. Manhattan May 95 morning, striding in slo-mo out of the Hotel Royalton as I de-cabbed on the corner of Fifth Avenue and 44th Street. I got my bearings, steadied up from my loaded mind down to my loaded feet and assumed the fuck-with-me-atcha-peril position against real or imagined muggettes. The tall horse of gauze hoofed in perfect Tommy Tune harmony, at one and alone with the battalion marching down the powdered keg that was my head and at two with the empty echo of the perfect street. The horse stepped up on to the curb and into the Algonquin Hotel to trough with the Indians and report that we'd met and that the rest was up to me. The image of the horse transferring itself into grey liquid as its white woven chassis melted itself into the north side of 44th Street remains a special effects award winner with me forever in my vision, even now. Thirty years in the making, no expense spared in the unmaking of my mind as I finally made it up. I knew I must yell 'Cut!' if I was to go on living.

The gauze bespoke see-through horse, all fifteen storeys of Trojan flank and limb, devoid of internal actuals but a sum of magnificent total, had read unto me its warning just by its appearance into my life. The smack, grappa, booze, cocained pillorama and antidepressant cycle had now converged onto one worn-out rusty rim of tired tread, attempting in vain and pain to hold together this spineless spent bird of the 60s. I was way past the days of wine and poses, the daze of letting the body advise that it was getting its needed nutrition through drugs and boozing, a line and a gulp, a resultant flush, sweat and dick dripping, a burst of dying flame amidst a sequence of mixed, fucked-up signals of doom and gloomed warning.

The horse with my name had winked its warning at my thirty-year-old game. Even you must appreciate the ironic calling card that spake as the horse hoofed in matrix two-step into the dividing bricks and clay between the Algonquin and Iroquois hotels; was it the call to register in the hotels or happy hunting grounds? I barely had the credit, but I had the card – an hour or so before I'd been using it to grind up another line of grey. I knew the game was up. I caught no breath and wheezed for it anyway, causing the remains of my last piss-attempt to drip uncomfortably down the left hand side of my inner leg. My left hand dry-cleaned it into the linen fabric and the resultant sting wheezed of a little life.

I'd straddled the game of recent youth-gotten fame with reasonable aplomb in the 70s, armed and charmed mainly – or only – with a line in one hand and Percodan in t'other, no booze for the most part, and just the odd dab of Cadbury's Smack whenever my car overran the yellow Endo lights or slightly shot its brake linings and brain pads.

It was the advent of the compact disc that did me in. In 1987 I'd been called up by Allen Klein to remaster all the early Stones elpees for CD. I just couldn't handle this direct confront with my early masters – the sound was too true. I managed to stay on track and deliver the job, but then cracked through the ice that had protected my blades and dived into a final madness that lasted till the spring of 95. For nigh on twenty years I had been able to handle the game of my fame as third-partied and written up by others. But I came up very short when stuck in the cold museum of time alone with my original paintings, and threw my carefully controlled, manipulated rotation of excess to the wind and buried my head in the sands of time running out. Now I knew I had to yell 'Cut!' and knew I could stop . . . because I had to.

The horse gone, its searing reality branded indelibly into the every scared fart of me, I slid my way back through the lobby of the Iroquois and into the elevator without having to eye or be known to another. The lift doors opened onto the orange urine grey wading fumes of my possessed ninth Jimmy Dean floor. I flayed through the weight of the madness I'd created, found the key to the door, let myself in, checked myself out in the mirror above the fireplace to make sure it was me and that I was there, saw it was so and collapsed my sack of breathlessness onto the settee, at last able to somewhat breathe.

I thought about help and got dizzy, queasy and short of breath at the mere idea; not at the idea of help itself, but at the exhaustion of attempting to explain the route to now. I got up off the couch and picked up the Yellow Pages, fumbled the move and watched the book fall. As it did I spied again under the front door, and knew from the swish 'n' swill still movement that the animals were baying and crawling back in the hall. The book of Yellow Pages also had habits. It had opened on the floor at the section for escorts and whores. Another of me wondered if I might find my name there. We grimaced at the idea and moved on to the pages that yelled help.

I called Tom Steinberg and asked if he'd mind stopping by. Well, that was the quiet external attempt while the inside screamed *get over here, now*. I was scared to eat without assistance or witness; I was scared of how far this had actually gone even now. I was scared I could choke on over to the other side and leave that disgusting legacy that would savage my family and cause many to gloat in that *schadenfreude* fuel for their survival. I wolfed down a couple of bananas, two small cartons of milk and a beer under the arrived Tommy's concerned eye. I wore looser clothes these days, and on this one I tried to feel the remaining touch of comfort in a combo of linens and silk – a double-breasted off-the-shoulder silk navy blue jacket, loose linen beige flecked shirt and trousers and raffle-weaved Italian golden-beige loafers – but it wasn't working. The double-breasted was a bloated physical must and the shoes were worn without socks, not in homage to Don Johnson and *Miami Vice* – though I'd done plenty of that – but because on intake of anything, be it food, booze, pills or drugs, I'd balloon up, swell in my middle and my feet, and waddle somewhere on the light side of Orson Welles.

Steinberg had worked for me till a couple of years ago. A lovely, crazed pit-bull worrier, he'd taken the opportunity to straighten up after more than half of every decade in the employ of first Mick Rock and then yours truly. Our madnesses collided and gave out in the Frank Sinatra suite in the Fontainebleau in Miami when, attempting to get some rest from the Ratones Paranoicos madness, we made the mistake of trying to spend a weekend without coke. During that time I needed Tommy to watch over me while I slept, or better put, when I slept.

I had spent some time in God's Country in the early 90s, up in the mountains in bear country one hundred miles from the nearest phone misbehaving like a good ol' boy, shooting and tooting and living the finger lickin' life. I was in Little Rock, near-home to many a landing strip of Colombian export and launching pad of El Clintoneze. I was there ostensibly to check out a local band that had caught the eye of a good friend, Jefferson Fletcher. His father was a gentleman-farmer heart surgeon, so it seemed the right time to avail myself of my host's hospitality and check myself in to a Little Rock hospital to get to the bottom of my sleep apnea, sometimes known on the legal circuit as narcolepsia. The results had been quite alarming. I was ceasing to breathe for up to a minute at a time, many times per hour, during what passed for a night's sleep. Alas I was in the wrong county, wrong climate to be told that had I not been alcoholic, I would not have gained the weight that on my slight frame had caused the apnea. A man could go mad in Hot Springs and Little Rock; I nearly did and got on a plane for Houston and Bogotá in the nick of time on that shoot 'em up-*At Close Range* Christopher Walken puffed daddy gangster loop I'd cast myself into against the young Fletcher's Sean Penn. Life in the 90s had a disturbing factor, not present in the innocent 50s and 60s – I did not make my movies alone in my head anymore. Thus I was able to cast real madness into my dangerously living reels and found it wasn't that hard to enlist equally mad players into my shooting schedule.

Back in Manhattan I still had the weight as I fast-snacked, fast-gulped and upped a wee line of marching powder to settle me down and take my mind off the bulbous Buddha that was me. It banged angrily from the inside to the outside of my stomach walls. And so I dived and delved further into the Yellow Pages for help. I got nowhere as I spoke to quite a few people who sounded worse than me – and they were the zoo keepers. All they really wanted to know was whether I was game to be committed, locked up, analysed, represcribed, and whether I had the insurance to handle any and every event. This fool was looking for insurance from them, but none would give me any data until I'd let them lock me up. I reached out to a multi-addiction establishment in Tucson that the tabloids boasted had enjoyed the company of Michael Douglas and Robert Downey Jr. I was still looking for the kid-glove celebrity handling, but did not feel sufficiently celebriac to place the Betty Ford clinic on my for-whom-the-bell toll call. The Sierra Tucson clinic just wanted to send me forms, brochures and videos. I don't think I could have told the difference between that and a Mario Perrillo & Sons 'come-a-to-Ital-ie' cruise commercial. I may have asked the voice from Tucson if they were offering two-fers so that I could take the man in my head along.

Some two weeks before, as you may have gleaned from the preface of *Stoned*, I'd breakfasted on brandy and beer in Connecticut with my good friend Thomas 'Doc' Cavalier. While he ate, I drank and gulped through the silence he gave me as I somewhat settled up a debt from the 70s. Doc recalls my cry as I hugged him and stumbled into the New York-bound limo. The stumble can be blamed in part on the brown lizard-toe-tipped black leather cowboy boots, and the rest billed to me. Atop the boots I wore a double-breasted grey and beige-flecked Prince of Wales checked suit and black-studded cowboy shirt with a turquoise and mother of pearl-inlaid 'country' tie thong. Below it all I sweated. I'd played out my Al Pacino in *Godfather III* at the end of an Oslo game, too criminal and abysmal to detour into here; I was now channelling Dennis Hopper in *Blue Velvet* crossed with Michael Caine in *Dirty Rotten Scoundrels*, and it was a very hard role to pull off. My pal Rafi Ameer had given me a video copy of a bald, black-suited, clear-eyed Dennis Hopper lecturing in the Actors Studio series. I viewed Mr Hopper in the limo; he was erudite and handsomely sub-manic, but of no use as a continuing role for me. He was straight and sober. This recent physical nearness to the all-seeing Doc Cavalier allowed me to crash through that misplaced English-bred pride as a choice against survival. Back in New York not even one day (and barely a night) I knew the horse had me at the end of the final run. I picked up the Hotel Iroquois phone and dialled nine-one-two-oh-three and Doc's number. He came to the phone and in quiet panic I got my thoughts off of the floor and into my brain, down into my mouth and formed seven life-determining words.

'Doc, I'm in trouble. I need help.'

ALO and Iggy Pop, New York, 1980

At that slow-moment my body screamed to a halt in silence like the roadrunner on the edge of the cliff. The remains of me thanked me for confronting the weight and the reality. I was at the beginning of free. Eighteen hours later I was packing my last roustabout into my suitcases. Doc had called back and given me the name and directions for a Fred Ulan, a nutritionist in upstate New York. Drug zombies were not his lot and I'd find out if they were 5 per cent of his practice I was that 5 per cent. I'd called a limo to deliver me unto Fred, lodged twenty minutes north of Saratoga

Springs and an hour north of the NY state capitol, Albany. I didn't ask Doc for other details on Fred. I knew Doc knew, and I just wanted to get on with it. I made an attempt at an early supper at the kindly Un, Deux, Trois down the block on 44th near Sixth Avenue. I might have managed had the liver been as pureed as the mashed spuds, but as it was I couldn't handle solids for fear of choking amidst disorientating panic attacks. I clung on to the edge of the table, rammed my toes so I could feel them in the front of my shoes to trick myself into not disappearing into the smoke I was blowing. You'll understand I was very nervous and in a totally anticipatory state, still in roadrunner mode, looking down and checking my feet, almost whimsical about how close to the cliff's edge I'd come. I played it safe and ordered the soup of the day, a beer and a grappa. I could handle the bread when dunked in the bean soup. I could handle the beans when squashed with a spoon. I could handle it all with one sensible spoon of coke. I knew enough not to attempt more than one task at a time – it was either eat, chew and swallow, or ask the waiter for another glass of water, but not both. My mind and body were inflated, deflated and out of order and I feared that any shift in concentration might put me in the tabloid land where, it is presumed, Mama Cass ate her world goodbye. I somehow had enough sense of decorum, flushed by ego, to monitor that ghastly potential legacy. My mind rue'd on how many had lost life in recovery and my body told me, 'Although I applaud your intention, don't be foolish and put me in shock as we might not get through it and we definitely won't if you dare overdo it.' Now is not the time, those days are done. I implore you, just maintain me, lull me in that limo upstate and let me grab hold of the rest of a life. Back at the Iroquois I held a breathless farewell in the reception. The lady manager looked at our worn-out celebratory gathering with concern and care. My comings and goings and altered states had not gone unnoticed by the staff, and they had made a concerted effort to care for me when I was not capable of caring for myself. I had given them cause for alarm when they viewed some of the drug malaise and traffic I had let into my life and on to their property by night, and most of the mornings I'd brown-bagged my way into the day.

It was the cream to my coffee that gathered to bid me a safe journey into the new unknown. The first hug and embrace was from Rafi Ameer, the Middle Eastern filmmaker to whom I had lent the deep vowels from my smack-driven voice to grace his searing documentaries on war-torn Afghanistan and other points of civilisation teetering in turmoil. The diplomatic Rafi had also doubled as the aviator-lensed 'Palestinian terrorist' I'd hired when surveying – as in stalking – the Westport abode of A.E.

425

Hotchner around the time he barfed up *Blown Away*, his travel guide to the Rolling Stones. I had thought about blowing him away, but he beat me to the paddy wagon by tracing some calls to my 'UN located' Manhattan hotel, and I found myself being asked by cops to explain the .357 Magnum I kept in the room. (A.E. Hotchner was the unpleasant turd who'd been brought in to salvage my non-starter mid-80s million dollar book deal with Simon & Schuster by Kevin Eggers and Pete Kameron. Hotchner's eventual own tome ended up bitterly savaging the very idea of the 60s, never rising above the shrill quill of an outsider looking in. In my successful attempt to dump all and sundry and be gone from this malaise I behaved very badly in front of Hotchner and he behaved badly in front of himself.)

Next in line and with one was Miguel Zapata – not his real name, but a real dealer who hailed from Colombia and lived in Queens. Miguel had passed by earlier and embraced me with the couple of grams I'd decided would be prudent for the journey. This might seem imprudent, even hypocritical and dumb, given the azureness and resolve I had given myself (and you) over the matter of the recent equestrian intervention, but it would seem that way only to those unfamiliar with drug turf and unaddicted and unaddled by its war. The logic that prevailed and had me call upon a two-fer from Señor Zapata was the feeling that if I were unmanned or ungrammed, the junkie in me might use it as an excuse to throw in the towel halfway up the New York Throughway and turn back to town for some coke. In the fragile but committed condition I was in, you have no idea how comforting it was to touch that little silver foil of no-hope.

The next embrace came from my Colombian soulmate Kiko Camancho. On more than one occasion his friendship and good counsel had stood me in good stealth and on many others his wife's home cooking had rescued my body and being from its own bad seed. In the early 80s I'd been on a plane from Panama to Miami en route to New York when a drunken, loaded Indian collapsed in the seat next to me.

'Eenngleesh, buy me drink,' was his opening salvo.

I decided against the obvious comment that he was what he was ordering and placed it with the stewardess, who correctly decided against asking my new companion what ticket stub allowed him to jump class. My loaded Indian, reeking and well under the influence, proceeded to educate me up on the plight of the red man and the sins and soon-to-come day of reckoning for the pink man.

'Cocaine is for the preservation and protection of the Indian and revenge on the pink man,' my lacklustre, black-toothed Eli Wallach-ish Nada Zapata leered, punching my arm to make sure I'd got it. These uncanny fucks always picked on a pink cocaine fiend 30,000 feet away from a dealer to deliver their litany on their hope for dope on all niggers, pink and white folk. I didn't have time to ask for a refill; to do so would have meant interrupting this Aztec visionary, and in his condition I would have seemed disrespectful, in or anal-attentive and rude. 'We're killing you all with the cocaine, you know.' His voice got all singsong, less macho, plain happy and gay at the thought. 'Plus all the niggers . . . we got them, of course. Fuckeen' no good crack heads, we sure got 'em with the curse. Tryin' to get all them lower middle-class jobs you fuckeen pinks allowed the black motherfuckers to have. Huh! Well, we killed out a whole fuckeen nigger generation with crack, man. Let the brothers, the Indians get the fuckeen jobs. You just watch, Eeengleesh, twennny year from now, we goonna unite with our northern Indian brother and take the fuckeen land back from you fuckeen pink Europeans that you stole. Drugs and gambling, brother, that'll be the new machete, the key. You watch, you listen, you learn.'

I did, but at the time my concern was not for the plight of the black man, drugs or gambling and when a week later we coffee'd on the Upper East Side of Manhattan I asked Kiko the following:

'Kiko, you know the bit about cocaine being for the preservation and protection of the Indian and revenge on the white man?'

'Yes, Andrew?' The wily Indian did not insist on pink; suffice to say he knew I coked.

'Well,' I shrugged, 'is there something to it? What do you think?'

He looked at me with his aquiline Mesquito-shot eyes, found the wisdom, sorted out my real question, smiled and replied. 'Don't worry, Andrew, you are Colombian.'

Yeah, but not Indian, I thought. I shrugged again and decided being Colombian would have to do. I excused myself and headed for the bathroom.

The embraces in the Iroquois Hotel lobby were long and strong, the good wishes genuine and heartfelt. The limo ride from the Iroquois was restful, restless and eventful. I found myself taking on Edward G. Robinson's adieu to his body of work and the body itself in *Soylent Green* when encapsulated in the life-recalling casket. As I sat aback of my Cadillac casket humming into the upstate night, my mind and vision wandered over my own playing fields, my stately manors and fall from grace, and that England's green and pleasant I had left or lost so long ago. I moved from the freeway to the motorway and recalled the joy of it all as in the spring of 64 I had sat aback John Lennon's Phantom V on the jump seat sharing a tab of life with John and Paul McCartney on the M6 run back to town after their triumphant return to Liverpool following their first American in-person triumph, the same triumph that shaped our pop music forever by allowing us an America. We had laughed at life and people and John and Paul had laughed at the enough of it all as they imagined the windows of the Phantom V smashing, sharding and disfiguring their beaming visages to such an extent that the Beatles would have to call it a day and mop up in monkey suits in order to face their world crowd.

I felt a shudder and a fist-size emotional lump in my throat as I recalled the end of that innocence some thirty-one years down the motorway. I turned my face into the reflection and turnpike swish of the near window as this memory called my name. The camera caught my very thought and Giorgio Moroder scored the unedited take. Next I felt like a fuckin' beautifully sad Farley Granger, a stranger on the train watching it sidetracked and derailed in time – his in the 50s; mine, I suppose, in the 60s. I thought of Mick Jagger and the *Angel Heart* of us both. Fuck 'Memo From Turner'. In my flick I was Harry Angel and Mick was Lisa Bonet. I remembered all the wondering about and feelings spilt in ink, these spent emotions turning out to be the only dialogue between MPJ and me. I smiled at the Louis Cypher, Allen Klein and Keith Richards of it all, wondered if Louis C was a Sag, too, knew it didn't matter and still couldn't tell the difference.

I remembered the moments that mattered and the moments that I had allowed to hurt. How the 1989 Stones induction into the Rock and Roll Hall of Fame had only had my part in their game whispered as an aside by a knowing Pete Townshend. That had hurt, but I was a victim at the time – and about being hurt. I mused on others' trains and boats and planes and how my finest hours were contained in clothes and planes and limos reflected in my own vinyl screen. One afternoon in 67 in need of another high I called for an E-Type Jag. I got my high by being too busy to traipse or troll from New Oxford Street to Berkeley Square to pick one out; I had the showroom drive every colour round, which I viewed from my Immediate window and after one, two, due consideration, like the petulant overwrought fake child I'd become, I stuck my finger towards the fire engine red Jag and pouted, 'I'll have that one.' I recalled a Michael Caine book and video *Acting in Film*, which I'd absorbed with the same panic as I'd absorbed David Mamet's *On Directing Film* because I by now needed tools in this merciless task of directing myself. Although Mr Caine's book 'n' video had some useful hints about listening that I was not able to take in at the time, they also caused me trauma via his statement that fame was a better friend when it came late in life and how its early arrival was hard to survive. This very thought gave me a lot of worry but at the same time an edge of insane resolve to prove him wrong. I longed for the Zen and threads of Laurence Harvey. I didn't have the texture – both in what I wore and the within from whence I wore it.

The angel of getting all you wished for had ripped apart my heart and now I could only pathetically mime to 'I Who Have Nothing'. Cocaine has a song-resonance all of its own, a nasal echo-chamber that has one sounding quite good to oneself, although I'm sure to my driver I sounded more like a throttled parrot. I had the foundations and support but had to claim myself back before I could return and be at one with wife, son and home. I had called Esther from New York the night of the translucent hoofed warning. I'd told her I was not coming home, did not know where I was going but would call her when I got there. I remembered the call, her bewilderment glued to trust, the resolve of her joined-to-my-hip sigh. I looked into the camera that tracked the limo shot, allowed myself a heave of bereft gratitude to that lady of grace – my advantage. My midnight express changed highways north of Albany and I woke up and thought it all looked like train crossings in and out of Stuttgart. It got a little hairy when my driver overshot our exit. I cursed him, Faye Dunaway-regaled him, had him stop at a 711 for a six-pack, and while he fetched it calmed myself down with a toot and a hit from the hip flask.

We finally then entered the hallowed land of Dorothy Malone and all things *Peyton Place* as the limo crawled into the town square of Glens Falls. I looked at the white picketed bandstand, the library, the green, shook hands in my mind and took hope. I felt this patch of earth would become familiar, well-worn turf in my life and recovery and I wanted to make friends with this hope. Over the next few days I would see the ghosts of Barbara Perkins and Ryan O'Neal falling in and out of love reflecting that black, white and clear world of *Peyton Place*, its time and simplicity lost to my complex world of expressed mood elevation, liquid diet and a triturate mind.

The Queensbury Hotel dominated the surrounding green. We parked in the forecourt and I strode shakily in. The reception and lobby were quite magnificent and three storeys tall. I whimsically looked up the walls imagining horses; the painting over the fireplace displayed hounds. I paid off the limo driver, sort of apologised again with a tip, checked into my room, left my bags at the door and collapsed on to the bed and started the wait. I can still get pale and mouth-watered at the thought of how absolutely weak I felt in that moment. I had an appointment with Fred Ulan at the Natural Health Improvement Center at 2 p.m. the next day. I lay still and hoped I'd not checked into the Overlook Inn. I was already in my own version of *The Shining* and wanted desperately to check out. I could only look at the ceiling and begin one of the longest nights of my life.

I'd ordered a dinner of fish, rice, mixed veg, three iced teas, a couple of fruit salads, two milks and a couple of glasses of white wine. I wolfed down the main grub, played with the house salad and looked at the wine. It didn't look inviting; it looked like aged syrup that had turned. I leaned over and had a sip. The sip was like time travelling back into the poison which rushed in my very veins. At that point I had a short line to kill the poison and at the same time said goodbye to the wine. That tipple of fate had me once more exhausted and I recollapsed on the bed and resumed the wait. I wondered what the Natural Health Improvement Center would be like and, based on the already-sighted brick, green and trees, imagined a Hampstead Flask Walk, leaf-covered, one-up two-down town house, the air of briar pipes, shrinks in suede patch tweed jackets, pseudo-stomach Jews dressed up in mauve socialist hues, mutton dressed as ham, hush puppies, lots of silent torturous moments as one looked for the real we as the crow and fifty minutes fly.

I'd be wrong on all accounts. I thought of ringing Doc but decided not to show fear and bad faith 'n' taste. I was in the understandable midst of wishful thinking and *delirium tremens*, knew it, and might as well get on with it. I channel boogied my way through to a 1.30 a.m. ex-70s ABC TV Movie of the Week with Stuart Whitman as a Malibu-based, driven private dick. When Dorothy Malone made a guest appearance on the terrace, I breathed a sigh for mother and gauze and managed to get an hour of kip and a little peace as Mr Whitman displayed that Rockford/Malibu Percodan gait of pain when pursuing the baddies – a specific run brought about by too many blows to the body. I had empathy – my stunts had been limited to blows to the head. I got through the night in fits and bursts, finally getting my best sleep shortly after *Good Morning America* greeted us into the day. Around eleven I breakfasted and managed to shower. From then until 1 p.m. remains a daze as the wallpaper tried to remind me of a sepia Victorian homage to the cover of *Satanic Majesties*. In other words, the walls were still moving. I thought about walking, did so to the lobby, thought better of continuing, and ordered a cab.

Five minutes later I was in the reception of 15 West Notre Dame Street and filling out a form on the drug history of my life. I'd been wrong about the set and location. There were a lot of leaves but they were on the trees. My house on Carroll Street was austere, grey-stoned and bare of façade. I remember feeling quite put out that I managed to get all of my decline and fall on to three pages. Nonetheless I wrote up the cocaine, the alcohol, the heroin, the mood elevators as in Zoloft and Ritalin-tin-tin. I segued into the tranquillisers, Valium and Librium on down to the sleepers; the Halcyon into the morphine-driven and derivated Percodan, Percocet, Vicodan, Dilaudid and DF 118s; the pot and the hash; the opium and the recall of all the brand names whose names I dare to forget. Endo was my Cartier and triple script be thy name. I wrote up the numbers, the volume, the curse. I recalled the also-rans, the low end of the volume totem pole – the LSD, the mushrooms and the STP. I didn't write up the asking of how I would survive being straight, or whether I *could* survive being straight.

I didn't write up the question of whether I would ever have another brilliant commercial idea. I'd later find I could embrace a good idea more than once every day as I followed a regimen of eating, sleeping and a discipline of good health. I discerned between the idea and its being commercial and allowed it to remain in and of itself – in the future I'd let it determine its own commerce, volume and art. As I lay in the trough of madness I mentioned quietly to myself that I hadn't had one idea that could fly. I could count the non-starters oozing out of every pore. Every germ of an idea remained a germ as I reached the depth of a mocking survival . . . a cardinal sin to be recognised as part of the long goodbye.

Nary an idea to cling to, not a murmur of *mañana* worth jumpstarting into gear. If I'd had one bright thought I certainly did not have the wherewithal to bring it into being. None of this I wrote on the page; I just shaved the grazes and scabs from my skin and pulled them into mind and vision and wished the jaded game away. The death thread I'd spent years weaving no longer had any meaning, support or hope – it had become a sarco-transporter as weary, worn and brittle as sackcloth. I suddenly had the wherewithal to expunge the saphrophyte member I had let fester and breed inside me – the enemy that has to turn on you, the enemy you called friend. Somehow through all this shudder-letting I had the beginning of my grasp at survival. I'd purposely confused an attraction for talent with a physical attraction but had always stopped short of letting the kettle boil off the whistle. I had recently watched this ghost attempt to re-enter the garden of discontent and offer up another paradise in hell when twenty years later Tony Calder had received a call from me saying, 'Why don't we form Immediate III?' That was another fool on the hill proposal that begot a well-timed and well-received book on Abba but a mute run at a musical hurrah with Tony taking advantage of only that which my condition allowed.

We'd sat down in London with Bill Wyman and in Santa Monica with Brian Wilson but even these two would not let us drive their car, and quite rightly. Immediate III ended in the spring of 95 and I nearly joined it as I made three false starts for London Airport not sure if I was loaded enough to go. How could the lost fail to moth to the light of a book that offers you the chance to live your life again? But it couldn't, not if you were about the business of dying. I wrote up the cycles like a mathematical graph depicting the rotation and the out-of-control time. I studied my face in the mirror and saw the dead clay mounds of flesh that passed for life around my eyes and nose; I looked at my eyes and their vision was even grimmer. There was no light, no sign of life. Only I knew that there was somebody at home. I wrote up the apnea. I wrote of the cessation of breathing, the fear and the sweats in the night. I wrote up the pains on the insides of my forearms that I'd kept quiet about out of fear and because they yelled stroke. I pulled for some breath and continued to write, moving on to the pain in my chest, burning liver, the cramping in my temples, left leg and foot, left hand and small of my back. I wrote up my oft inability to walk without charting the every single left-right-left of my left and right feet. I wrote up, or confronted – because that was what this was coming down to, this cleansing straight to the page. I wrote of my nigh-on-inability to stand focused in the shower and how I had to look down with my eyes very carefully and slowly to make sure of and believe I had feet. This meant my motor had broken down and there was no registration of circulation being transmitted to my brain from either foot. I had spent an inordinate amount of bathing time avoiding injuring myself. What was between was Death Valley, and that's where I lived and got high.

I wrote up my *sinus delecti*, the holes so deep in their valley that I often whistled while I talked. I wrote of how I could not walk for any distance without pain, spasms and exhaustion, and of my now total inability to work. I wrote up my dripping dickette, the shot circulation, the inability to control my bodily functions, my affinity with the June Allyson commercials and how when I held my dick in my hand I held a withered widow, immune to any touch, way past sailing with cocaine on its masthead – definitely more dead, less wed, than alive. This was true of the rest of me, for of late it was as if I wore a mask like the phantom, and on the occasion the collision of drugs found some life in me, it didn't go deeper than the mask. There had been no deep relief, no reason to propel this addiction as I finally – daily, hourly, every ten minutes – searched in vein, literally and with shame, for the bejesus relief of that Madonna – that very first high.

I wrote of my life's co-star, that dame called depression, who pulled every good moment into distress and disarray. I wrote up the 1967 to 1970 electric shock treatments – the electroconvulsive therapy to which I had submitted myself in an effort to remove the pain and memory and trauma of what I perceived as my dregs of a personal life. I wrote how my good doctor had injected me in order to get me to speak the truth. And how I used to fake breakdowns to get to the doctor's, to get jabbed again into telling the truth. How I was there for the high of counting backwards from ten and nodding out. To get to this high I put up with the rubber shoved inside my mouth to stop me from biting or swallowing my tongue. I put up with the zombie I felt like when awoken; I degraded myself and invited all this to quell the perception of pain, dark and hurt.

The last question I had to answer was to explain what had brought me here. I stated that I did not know whether I would live or die but had decided that I wanted to live.

Fred Ulan read my chart and writings and surveyed the tattered Susan Hayward doll before him as I brushed imagined bangs from my brow. He sighed; I raised my eyes in agreement. He put down my writings and started to muscle-test me. From that moment on we never actually, save where it was medically needed data, spent or wasted any time discussing booze, depression, the lust for self-medication or drugs and my experience in all. I had made the decision to stop all and now we were about a nutritional programme to assist me in that, repair the damage and have me grow back into being. The muscle testing located the volume of deficiency and located the main ingredients of danger: my adrenal glands and heart. I started taking nutritional supplements for all those near-destroyed and depleted parts. I swallowed hard at the idea of how bad I had got, and how close to the final ride. I mouthed a thank-you for that fifteen-storey intervention, tried to swallow but could not locate my tongue. My throat was so confused and swollen I could not tell the difference between it and my tongue. I held the chair to hold the panic, felt the body parts discern and explain themselves to me. I breathed and then I laughed. That night it felt as if the whole town was quiet for me, breathed for me and lulled me through the dark.

I saw Fred again the next day at two, and by three was back in the Queensbury Hotel. At seven I called Fred, got a machine, and he called me back rapido. I explained that I knew we had an appointment on the morrow, but I really felt so damn weak, tired and close to dying that I needed to be sure that if I went to sleep I'd wake up and would indeed be making the morrow's appointment with him and not with a morgue. He reassured me, gave me a layman's version of how I was dramatising, and suggested I should calm down and rest. I did so, but first I called home. I had spoken with Esther on the night I left Manhattan and I hadn't told her very much. Now I called

433

her and told her I was not coming home until I knew I was, and would stay, well.

I put two and two together and got life. I mulled to myself that Doc Cavalier was a Scientologist and he'd got clear and well. I recalled Fred and his partner Lester's office and that inviting feeling of being very well. On one wall was a photo of Fred and his wife Dana; I almost envied that very healthy glow in the know, and wanted it. On another wall, amidst the nutrition samples, were sayings of L. Ron Hubbard as they related to being a professional, a survivor equipped to get on with life. Without further ado I blurted out to Esther that there was not much detail I could impart, but I gave her the address of the Scientology centre in Bogotá, and advised her to call them for information. I had a feeling Dianetics would be at the end of the first run of this start. It was.

I got better in daily increments, in a reverse parallel to the way I got unwell. At the end of the first week I had a minor trauma in the form of some vascular collapse. It took some of the returning colour out of my day and gave me a brash return to the grey and the spectre of dying. Fred Ulan answered my emergency call, came by the hotel, dispensed some clear cheer, extra Vasculin, Cardio Plus, Minchex, Mintran, Cataplex E2 and a warning. He knew on day two in Glens Falls I'd done my last line of coke and had then thrown away the remaining powder and the crutches of maintenance and non-survival, embraced the routine, the discipline and got down to the survival run.

'Whatever you do, Andrew,' implored Fred, 'you've given up the ghost, the coke, given it all up. Just don't even attempt to give up smoking cigarettes. It's probably the only thing that's been giving any stimulation to your heart, and if you try to give it up now you'll go into shock.'

I had tried just that, and so for the next few years I continued smoking.

Over the next five weeks colour came back, with the miracle of food and a sense of smell. I was able to walk around the block and by week three walk around the local mall without being attacked by the people, traffic, signs, shop displays and 'how can I help youse' sounds of shoppers. When I'd arrived at the Queensbury Hotel I thought the square floor corridors were a Kubrickesque replica set reconstruction of *The Shining* – now they were just a part of getting to and from my room. I looked out on to the Queensbury village green and found Peyton Place in present time, Christopher Walken no longer Armani white-suited, Venetian, a dis-*Comfort of Strangers*; he was hoofer Ronny once more shuffling in *Pennies From Heaven* galore. Dante's Inferno resolved itself into my health and I welcomed back Dante and the Evergreens.

Within a very short time the pains began to fade and my breathing improved as Fred jostled with the remaining screams and complaints from my body and I literally started to come back to life and tested second gear. We fine-tuned these callings, four-walled the nutritional needs and made daily adjustments, and I felt slow but definite improvement. During week four Allen Klein's son Jody journeyed the two hours north to take me out to lunch. It was the first time I'd partaken socially and dined with anything other than the TV, and by the end of lunch Jody understood I was well but still very tired. By the end of five weeks I could handle such outings with relative ease, and have enjoyed many more meals with Jody that are no longer blemished by my need to be excused by a nose on wheels. I spent the next two weeks of my ten-week total learning how to adjust myself and my day with the nutritional supplements. The next week I started to go shopping and knew that soon I'd be ready to leave. I'd been calling home every day, and Esther later told me that for the first time in nigh on twenty years I had a voice, was swearing less and laughing more.

That was the spring of 1995 when I took back the summer of my life and began clearing my universe, my body and mind. In present time I have made a life again and every day is a day I work at and in which I am once again at one with the world and we both know it.

## CHAPTER 22

**Gruff**, lead vocalist, Super Furry Animals: The Super Furry interest in the Loog comes not only from the great music he's been involved in. He is also one of rock 'n' roll's original scamsters, and we have his gob looking down at us from our SCAM blackboard along with Howard Marks and the KLF.

In fact we were brought together by scam. Given a bigger-than-usual budget of £30,000 by our ever-understanding record company, Creation, to make a video for our song 'Demons', the obvious thing to do was to take the money and treat ourselves to a well-earned holiday in Colombia.

Gruff and ALO, Bogotá, 1997

Wigan's own Brian Cannon – co-conspirator and sleeve designer to Oasis and the Verve – was enlisted as director. He ran into one of Oldham's former drug buddies in a London pub, was given the Loog's Colombian e-mail address and Oldham met Wigan in a beautiful union in cyberspace.

All is arranged. The Loog turns out to be a keen accomplice and is awarded the title of producer. Arriving in darkness at Bogotá Airport (after a brief encounter with Miami) we are met by a confident middle-aged dude in a straw hat and the latest NY gangsta gear – the Loog. Bogotá, at 8,000 feet above sea level, can cause an altitude sickness in pale, unfit Celts, so he piles us into the back of two pick-up trucks loaded with crates of Club Colombia beer and sound systems blaring out a salsa radio station at Jurassic volume.

We bounce our way through deregulated traffic, past Bogotá's toxic rim and down from the high plane to a valley of 5,000 feet (according to my G-shock watch that tells you how high you are) as the deejay keeps reminding us we are in *COOOLOMBIAAA!* and everything is fucking *FAFFAAABBTTTASSSSTTTTICCCCOOOO!*

A couple of hours later we are in the village of Santandercito, sitting in the jungle at a mansion-like blue hotel run by a confident Englishman called Simon. He gives us a warm welcome and we spend the night sitting outside round a candlelit table bearing a small mound of local produce, sipping on Colombiana's. (For similar effect mix one-third Iron Bru, one-third Latin-American beer, one-sixth white rum and one-sixth lemon juice. Also used as a very effective hangover cure in Colombia.)

I contentedly watch the hotel's armed guard patrol the gardens until the early hours. I look out of the window in the morning only to find myself in heaven. My room, located above a wide central staircase that leads directly down into a garden which is encircled by a tropical colourful jungle, sits above a wide lush valley surrounded by a high wall of purple-blue mountains.

'Fuck me,' I think to myself, 'I'm in Fleetwood Mac.'

Over breakfast Andrew and his wife, Esther, launch into a bag full of pills of assorted shapes, colours and sizes. Noticing my alarmed look of curiosity they explain the pills are part of their two-year-old clean-living diet; they've quit rock 'n' roll excess.

Apparently we are the first Welsh band he's worked with since he released 'If Paradise Is Half As Nice' by Amen Corner. I inform him that a shell-suited Andy Fairweather-Low can be seen walking his dog in suburban Cardiff. My host replies that he can't, come to think of it, remember any Welsh acts he got on with except Shirley Bassey!

Back in the pick-ups we head along a dirt track towards the village of Tena, which is about to begin a five-day fiesta to celebrate the 60th anniversary of the murder of the shady local landowner. Our local guide, Sheppy, apologises for the sunny, cloudless weather, explaining the valley is usually much greener and damp! He blames El Niño. I don't know what he's on about but in the course of the next few months it comes up again and again on the news in the form of Indonesian smog, Australian firestorms, Mexican blizzards and European floods.

Sheppy then explains that Tena has a Marxist guerrilla presence but he talks fondly of them; they fix roads, educate and occasionally storm into the churches to advise local men (at gunpoint) not to mistreat the women of the village. Since the collapse of the USSR they have no outside funding and are forced into cocaine production and bank robbery. Unlike the fascist drug cartels of the north and west, they do not sell their product to their own kind and can justify its manufacture – safe in the knowledge that it's all exported to the US to kill the ever-evil imperial Yankees (we are mistaken for North Americans on a dodgy Bogotá street a few days later and have stones and rocks pelted at us).

Anyway, we are very welcome in this area and spend the next three days darting around the valleys, stopping occasionally at roadside, while-u-wait discos, food stalls and bars, then retreating at night to our hotel in Santandercito. It is to this very village that world-famous footballer Faustino Asprilla retreats while mysteriously absent from pre-season training at various big European clubs such as Newcastle United and Parma. His usual excuse is that old chestnut: civil war. In reality, however, playboy Asprilla is to be seen looking particularly unburdened, terrorising the tiny village with his skilful handling of a giant Harley-Davidson fanny magnet.

On our last night in the valley the mayor of Tena invites us back to the village fiesta which is still going strong. In the centre of the village on a rickety stage the mayor gives us an official welcome as a smartly dressed salsa band in straw cowboy hats rock out. Most villagers dance in couples to the loud music. We meanwhile join the shy and lazy under a canopy and drink a frozen spirit called Nectar, watched from the distance by a rifle-wielding soldier we rented for $12. After a heavy night's fiesta, now fully acclimatised to the altitude, it is time to return to Bogotá and its 8,000 feet.

We stay around the corner from Andrew's penthouse, where he picks us up in a customised Mini-Cooper to go out for the night. As can be expected of a modern city of seven million, Bogotá can give you a good night out a world away from the previous night's entertainment and at another extreme of Colombian society. The Loog takes us to a booming UV-lit club playing the latest European and American techno. He seems refreshingly free from romanticised nostalgia when discussing his past. Here we are then in a bullshit-free zone in downtown Bogotá having the time of our lives in the bar with our guitarist Bunf, celebrating the news just in of Princess Diana's death with tequila slammers.

Mr and Mrs Loog are beside us sipping mineral water with cool indifference. No one here gives a fuck! The next day we are taken by the whole Oldham family to the Estadio El Campin for a local football derby, Santa Fé De Bogotá vs the Millionarios. Before we depart, Esther gives us gifts of Colombian jewellery and Andrew devises a Super Furry scam to break America from the south, starting in the Welsh-speaking areas of Patagonia.

Andrew and Esther had been close friends with Simon Humber, the transplanted English hotelier whose Hotel Palo De La Alto based our group and thirteen-man video crew. They called us six months later to tell us Simon had died there, in typically tragic, panoramic and dramatic *Under the Volcano* style.

**ALO**: These days I wake up around 5 a.m. and go down to my second-floor office and check into the computer and the day's e-mail. The computer sits above an oak floor covered with two *mola*-inspired, artisan-thick, indigenous Colombian carpets in blazing blacks and reds. The furniture is likewise, blazing red and black art deco leather from Jazz on Melrose in LA. The walls are home to a panorama of books, videos and music. One of the benefits of my years of being 2Stoned is that, as a result of my fear that books would disappear in the form we hold them, I bought doubles of all my favourites. Now my walls feel like Graham Greene in need of 3-D glasses. Bogotá runs and lazes for miles across a sun-drenched, drizzly green mountain plateau. The northern hills of this 8,000-foot-high Colombian capital are grenaded with shantytowns occupied by more than four decades of the displaced who have slowly transformed their lot into vibrant scuzzy new towns with running water and mayors. The view from my den faces south, down on to the city as Bogotá is hugged and surrounded by more green mountains clasped and redbricked by apartment blocks and houses, winding fast-lane highways, universities – and further south, the dense industrial and steepled downtown.

On a quiet, very early Sunday morning I take our beagle, Ruby, for a long walk around our blockage. It is amazing to behold the variety of architectural eras fighting for space in an area that used to be residential, but that now, alongside the few apartment houses such as the one we live atop, encompasses mock Tudor façade'd office buildings that neighbour white Irish-style thatched farm houses, all knee-deep in lush green vegetation and coarse, solid palm trees. The only pavement traffic is a stream of rucksacked day-for-night porters changing shifts. Our block hugs the corner of our own Hendon Way which, on a Sunday, has its northern route made available to Bogotá's multitude of cyclists and walkers. By seven I've had a breakfast steak and coffee, and half an hour later I'm singing this song for you. Tomorrow it's back to *trancon*, Bogotá's own rush-hour madness, and it's down to going out in my heavy metallic grey 1994 Lancia Thema Turbo. We don't go out much during the week, and hardly out of town at all anymore. There, it's cowboys and Indians, Saturday morning pictures in cold blood, killings and kidnappings as the various guerrilla narcofinanced factions rule 40 per cent of our fair country and kill and maim for more. So our excursions are not carefree and are mainly to the supermarkets, the fruit and veg street markets, our various 'clear body, clear mind' centres, a few restaurants and coffee shops, or the airport. 'I was born in the heart of the city' ran the first line of 'The Shrine On The Second Floor' as warbled by Cliff Richard in my life-forming *Expresso Bongo*. I now live in the heart of this city, and it's wonderful to be at one with it and at home.

Last night I had a dream about Mick Jagger, something I have not had for a very long time. It was dry and quite touching. I've shared with you my deflowered 60s with all their behavioural warts, weeds, sublime shopping and sonic haloes, so why pull up short and hang on to a dream? Dreams are oft prompted by a daily event. Perhaps this, and the cheeses I eat in the evening with spinach soup, rice and herring, is what did it.

I sit and watch. I know this is a dream; it's the only time I don't know what I'm wearing. We are talking, we are on unstable bench-like seats, but it's not just the seats that are unstable. At first I presume we are on a plane, but it's not a luxury John Travolta/Warner appointed affair. Everything is freshly painted white, corrugated and loud. From the rockin' I deduce it's not a plane. We're on a boat, perhaps the *African Queen*. 'Oh, I hope so,' whispers the ghost of Sir John. No, this is bigger and butcher, a lot more freight – more like John Wayne's *The Sea Chase*, or is it the Duke and Lauren Bacall in the same year's *Blood Alley*? We're not on deck – we're down below and Mick is playful, earnest and cheering. It's the first night of his solo tour and we're sailing to Providence, Rhode Island. We don't talk about the past; perhaps it hasn't happened yet. If we're in present time, time has been kind

– photographers and Joan Rivers have not. The dream is timeless – nothing flawed, wrinkled or war'd. It isn't so much a conversation as me listening, and isn't that how this all began? Mick wears linen, beige trousers, white shirt and a decent watch. He's giving me tour logistics, battle plans, venues, the unknown and excitement to come. Prince Rupert is in a wheelchair or a golf-cart, somewhere between Sebastian Cabot and Michael Dunn. He assures me he's losing money on this tour – I decide to believe him. He explains to me life as Mick Jagger and I get it. It's all very easy to be got. Perhaps this is the meet Tony King hoped for. I doubt it. I'm not death in Venice. Mick gets up and excuses himself with an old smile; he has to get ready for work. We are still below deck. I walk around, I stop and chat with writer Keith Altham. Keith is in a Take 6 three-button jacket and he still has his hair. So does Mick, as a matter of fact.

Who is directing this dream. Buñuel? Abel Ferrara? Personally I'd settle for Gary Oldman or Cameron Crowe. The noise of the engine room is joined and overtaken by the sound of musicians tuning up, warming up to 'Drift Away'. Perhaps they'll do 'You Better Move On'. Ah, we're on stage. We have not left the ship; this is the tour that docks. Now I figure I must be on the *Love Boat* – can't be – the boat's too raunchy. World War II steamer and *big*. You can smell the grease, you can hear the crowd. I look around for the ghosts of Oscar Werner and Vivian Leigh; perhaps this is the *Ship Of Fools*. Or more likely *The Damned* – the scene where the Aryan youth is all hung over, bloated and white. Now I'm at the Captain's table. I'm surrounded by yelping Texas up north; there's lots of freckled tits, sun-burnt yippe-eye-oh's in halters and not much else. The band starts up – this is a review. The stage is narrow, the band is wide. Aren't you glad I hung on to this dream?

Mick is still in linen; he don't need no back-up to help him coast through the 80s tonight. Mick is not in marching 'Are yer all right?' strut and panic; he's smooth, stands nearly still, save for the dance in his feet. Mick moves in memory to his early James Brown, stirs in a little Marvin Gaye and plays Ikette with the girls. The lights come down on a little boy blue for 'The Spider And The Fly' and 'Lookin' Tired', clockwork orange up for 'Mustang Sally', and the set finishes with a nod to Captain Who and 'Who Are You?' through a down-and-dirty 'Bony Moronie' and a horn-clad 'The Last Time'; then it's 'She Said Yeah' and goodnight. I leave the Captain's table to take in the smile of the night on deck. I didn't hear every song, but I heard the sound, got up and wrote it down for you before this dream done gone.

I'm awake, in pyjamas and dressing gown. I'm cold. I go upstairs and put on a sweater, Mephisto shoes and jogging trews. Our star has left the building and there's a morning chill drifting in. I look at my decent watch. Today is Esther's and America's birthday. Yesterday's the day Brian Jones and Morrison died. The moon is full and loony. I walk Ruby again. She walks like I shop – that's why we're so George Jones and Tammy Wynette. I look up at my house and I'm so glad the lights are on.

Let's go back a bit, to the beginning of the particular journey that brought us both to these pages. It's the Bogotá summer of 2000 and I'm thinking about my next book. I'm on time in a town where it's never late and everything is going well and yet not going well. I'm writing basic tracks for the second part of an auto-triography I have been working on for some time. I view the events of my life with a new clarity, but the price of accurate restimulation is often a temporary nervous shock to the system. The first volume, *Stoned*, has just been published to maximum reviews and credible sales. In it, I'd decided to enjoy and celebrate the boy I was in the late 50s and early 60s, and to leave much of the Rolling Stones story to be told in this book. In *Stoned* we war babies shake off the malaise of a decade of rationing and flame into being: before I turn nineteen, as a press agent, I work the Beatles, Mary Quant, Phil Spector and Bob Dylan. *Stoned* is about the wonder of youth, the defining of one's own holy grail and the search for it. I'd always liked the kid I had been; I'd enjoyed recreating my age of innocence and *Stoned* generated a nice hash-infused Buena Vista glow. While 'realistic' films about American life at the top like *Sweet Smell of Success* thrilled me as a teenager, I hadn't yet stopped to think what I might do were J.J. Hunsecker out to get me.

But mapping out *2Stoned* had me relating to the Michael Corleone of *Godfather III*. As Michael and I both learned, there comes a time when one goes from choosing to being chosen. It's not easy living on your own and I was interiorising emotions that my wife and son could live happily without sharing with me on a daily basis. I noticed myself handling homely conversations with my family as if I were frustrated that questions had not been submitted in advance. Please pass the mustard. Behind every request for a condiment was the haunting refrain that set me off to begin with, thirty-five years ago – 'So, we're successful . . . so what?' – and it was stilting my progress on *2Stoned*. I was working the method again, and I didn't like the distance I was bringing to the family table.

Now, as I gaze out of my home office window, high above a mile-high city, waiting for words to fly, Luz Marina, our maid, hands me the phone. 'Don Andrew . . . un engleesh,' she smiles, leaving my caller's identity a mystery to both of us. Across continents, a cultivated voice asks tentatively,

'Andrew?' I answer surely, 'Yes, it is.' It certainly is engleesh, and it's not broken – it's Marianne Faithfull. I must have had no more than a dozen phone comms with Marianne in my life; any more have been wiped away by shock treatment. I find the artist gives great phone, as she has given some great records. Marianne thanks me for the way I've recalled our discovery of each other and the making of each other and our 'As Tears Go By' in *Stoned*. She compliments me on the overall tone of the work. To let me know she's read more than her bits, she mentions catching an analogy wherein I deftly compare Mick Jagger objectively to my pet beagle, Ruby. Marianne tells me she is to be in concert in New York in the first week of September. We decide it has been far too long and I tell her I'll see her there. Refreshed by our conversation, I returned to action at the front.

A few days later Luz Marina steps into my office again with another 'Don Andrew . . . Eengleesh', and this time it's Lou Adler calling from Malibu. I point out that Lou is of the Americas, like us, not an engleesh like Marianne, but I fear the distinction is lost on Luz as she returns to the kitchen. Lou reports that Beach Boys icon Brian Wilson is going to perform *Pet Sounds* in its entirety at the Hollywood Bowl in late September. Would I join him? I tell him I'll be there – it's just a matter of luggage.

What had I mocked up here? I had been writing the aftermath of my Marianne Faithfull adventure and thirty-six years on the lady calls. I'd been recalling my meetings with Brian Wilson back when our causes and effects raced each other to express themselves in our music, and now Lou offers another dip in the hot tub of Brian's genius. Thirty-four years earlier in London Paul McCartney and I had enjoyed tea and smoke at my Hurlingham Road abode and awaited Lou's arrival from the city of angels to ours of the near-permanent grey. My Phantom V had whisked Adler from London Airport to my home. He was bringing his good self and an acetate of *Pet Sounds*, which neither Paul nor I could keep, since this was a time when personal tape recordings were not on or done, and the odd Grundig not oft hooked up to the home record player. That afternoon settled for us that the LP was inevitable, as we settled into more tea, lots of smiles, more smoke and no doubt some munchies, and a long, long listen and a lot of wonder from Paul and I. The remembering of it all settles my travel plans of the now.

Soon I am down in the garage matching luggage, clothes and travelling library. My 'so what?' gives way to 'why not?' – I now have a mission I can pack my bags around. As safe and warm as I'd been at home, I'll be the same in LA. I am certain *2Stoned* will benefit from the duo-coastal change of climate and altitude. My family celebrate my journey with joy and sadness and wish my altitude well.

First the fly-by to catch Marianne Faithfull. I arrive in Manhattan and take lunch with Allen Klein. We are still somewhat joined at the hip – it's the worked-at affection of time. Whether I like it or not, the data that remains at the end of the day is that I have spent thirty-five years in reaction to Allen's actions, and that's what happened to my iconette sprint around the throne. The spleneticness and anger is gone. We order the chicken and smile at each other as we both stay away from the sweets. Being with Allen is reasonably comfortable; he's no longer embarrassed by my not being able to. Being stoned did not go with the job description I had and lost. I recall this for one last time in order to reach the reader who has the same opportunity in any walk of life and is tempted to play with the band. I bid *adios* to Allen and Iris and whistle my way to Fifth accompanied by my orchestra. It's a perfect Manhattan September day, sunny and breezy. I almost expect Cary Grant to glide out of the Plaza and head *North By Northwest*. I shop and window the afternoon away. Recreation for the eye is a New York-splendoured thing; reconnaissance is invigorating and the resulting purchases good for the soul and not bad on the pocket.

Marianne's rare Manhattan appearance is at the Danny Kaye Theater within Hunter College's mid-town campus. I have asked my friend and occasional Watson, Ron Ross, to join me, so I know that I'll be able to conduct the concert post-mortem immediately. Ron is attired for the premiere of a movie yet to be cast. Tonight he looks like Ronnie Kray attending a Jazz Singles mixer held in the Glitter Gulch Jewish Community Centre. For Ron it's probably a Sammy Davis thing, but since he is rather tall and Caucasian, I recast him mentally as the Efrem Zimbalist Jr private dick from the late-50s TV series *77 Sunset Strip*. Pearl-grey gabardine trews underneath a salt-and-pepper silk sports jacket and black silk Sulka shirt drape down to black suede half-brogues. Let the audience wear Gap and Kenneth Cole; Ron will defy convention and wear an Alfred Dunhill tie. Every night is Date Night for Ron. I'm in a midnight blue homage to John Travolta in *Broken Arrow*: navy two-button linen sweater piped in black; midnight blue silk and denim LAX combat jacket with black-vinyl trim; string-drawn midnight blue/black slacks and black Mephisto dusters. My spectacles are titanium and my mind is a steel trap. The pre-concert crowd failing to impress, we opt for the street and a rapid espresso. We are in the middle of Lexington Avenue when a familiar scream calls my attention – 'It's Andrew, Andrew!' It certainly is. I turn and see my caller across the street.

It's Uncle J's favourite nephew, Tony Russo. We hug, he tells me how well I look and how he's seeing a psych three times a week to get in touch with his anger all in a very first breath. Inspired by a fond recall of our drug-buddy follies I suddenly feel like hugging him back and I do so. Tony's advantage, Sally, beams from the sidewalk on seeing two naughties together and well. Straight becomes Tony – I am moved at seeing my 80's dance partner making the grade. We hold the hug – we need to. He's not wearing Magnum – that tells me everybody's back on the farm. I'm so very happy, moved and glad. I'd always been able to balance my love of what I had been about with the nudging knowingness that the field of play was so often counterfeit. Nothing about Tony Russo was counterfeit – and that could only be said about a few. In addition, he served as part of the search one makes when one is fatherless, even if on most days we both played the son.

We enter the theatre where Marianne is late, and half an hour in straight-and-present time is half an hour too long. When the questionable female couples start to boo in their disconcerting alto voices, she eventually meanders on stage. The half-hour we have waited is clearly much longer to us than the thirty minutes during which Marianne had procrastinated was to her. She had not wanted to give us anything but her best, she confides hoarsely, and having given her all and more to whomever bought a ticket the previous night, she might not be able to give us anything but love. Just before she offers to return our money, she remembers herself and gives us 'Broken English' for our trouble. One now has opportunity to study her outfit. Her gently worn Manolo Blahnik thrift-store pumps have a certain charm. Her black-jeaned legs remind us Mick Taylor had once been blond and well-bunned. Marianne's red and black top might be a Dale Evans look by way of Vivienne Westwood with a knowing nod to Trigger. Thus Marianne's tits take centre stage and hold the spotlight. Her hair is a hot white shade and she runs her hands through it all night to let us know it. She speaks for worldly women of a certain age – attractive and glowing – and makes you one.

She is a bit silly but that is part of her charm. I find her stunning – as potentially wonderful as she was when I knew her as the youngest girl. The socks on the jaw the girl has taken in life have replaced the ankle socks of her 64 beat. Her war wounds are worn like medals and survival shines in her eyes. She aerobicises Leonard Cohen, soothes us with Roger Waters and, sharing her toy chest with us, pulls out a Harry Nilsson nevergreen. The audience responds enthusiastically to the best of her late 70s triumphant-return-from-the-abyss. We get 'Why D'Ya Do It' and 'The Ballad Of Lucy Jordan'. Marianne now casually smokes Marlboros during the solos, her sore

445

throat apparently no longer an impediment to air pollution. While she's at it, the roadie brings her a spot of tea and she beams at him as if he were a dealer giving samples. Marianne retains four endearing stage looks: Panic, More Panic, 'God, I'm Getting Away With It!' – and finally, 'I *am* good, aren't I?' Sometimes her idiosyncratic sense of rhythm makes walking across stage an act in need of a safety net; other times she moves like a woman one would enjoy dancing with, if that sort of thing were done. She sits smartly on her summer of 65 hit, 'Come And Stay With Me', and stomps it along, causing one to want to remove the pumps, reshoe her and command 'Boots – Start Walkin'!' Marianne gives me the moment I came for as she sails into 'As Tears Go By' in a way that would not be lost in Branston. I get that feeling I came for and allow myself that tear.

Marianne Faithfull on stage, 1990

I remember how in January of 98 a technical glitch had temporarily halted Mick's spew of testosterone at Madison Square Garden and, being Jagger, he thought he'd take that opportunity to sneer at the audience, 'What do you want me to do? "As Tears Go By"?' No, Sir Mick, don't bother, until you do Bing Crosby in a Christmas special with Dame Bowie. The song belongs to Marianne. That same night in 98 held memories of a concert for which I'd had tickets thrust on me that I didn't want, then Barnum'd my family into believing they'd be witnessing the 70s-era Stones when what we got was a mass of America trying to claim a night back it had not been entitled to in the first place. Beer-propelled fiftyites – what's left of hair combed forward into the night, arms wrapped around what I hoped were secretaries and not daughters – let you know why there could be no sequel to *Easy Rider*; it had already been done and named *Waterworld.* The Stones were not that good in Manhattan; they were far and away better in the sticks of actual America or shining like Evita in Buenos Aires. The next night I'd joined one of my original New York 1964 hostesses, Linda Stein. We took in each other and Bob Dylan on an eight-night run at the Paramount, the little theatre inside the same Garden. The walls were adorned with posters of Julio Iglesias, as they should be, a timely reminder of what's been and what's done. Bob Dylan was tight and superb, a better example of preparing yerself for sixty than had been the last night, too-tight Stones.

Back at the faithful, I discreetly turn my attention to the audience and spot designer Calvin Klein, columnist Fran Lebowitz, and actress/comedienne Sandra Bernhard sharing what appear to be two seats, but I am sure I imagined that. There is more than one odd trio of ma, pa and sullen youth enjoying a night of retro-groove from our lady of 'El Rockero'. The parents' regret and neglect is reflected in eyes wired by Ritalin and single scripts and cheeks creased in doubt and acne. They remind me of dealers I'm glad I've never known.The demonstrative element in Marianne's audience share a distressing taste in sensible walking shoes. Marianne helps these 'girls' believe that good can come of suicide attempts and that pharmaceutical-grade drugs are a fitting substitute for many everyday relationships. They seem to think she wrote 'Working Class Hero' just because she sings it well.

I cannot help but think of Marianne's mum negotiating her recording contract with the newest of my companies in 1964. Eva had nothing against work, but required the aura of the manor to be maintained long after the manor itself was gone, regardless of the kind of work one actually did. It was a sort of *noblesse oblige* she expected even new-to-the-manor rock 'n' roll entrepreneurs to uphold. My reverie is interrupted by a fresh burst of applause accompanying the entrance of a young man my faithful companion Ron thinks we're supposed to recognise.

World's Forgotten Boy, Evan Dando of the Lemonheads, has joined Marianne on stage for 'As Tears Go By' and then 'Sister Morphine'. As the role of Gram Parsons is taken by Evan and Marianne hits a vein as Keith, I am transfixed and appalled by how fully I am taken in by this old trick, whereby Marianne gets to play muse and muso. God forbid she next do a

Mick and strap a guitar on herself. The audience is happy to experience this actual re-creation of a near-death experience; many a Ma squeezes Pa Kettle's hand as Sonny nods off and the sensible walking shoe brigade heave ecstatically as identities are fused before them. It's a great trick, the splicing of vaudevillian chicanery mesced with opiated recall for the stalls. If this is what she's leaving us with, I can tell that backstage is going to be fun.

Backstage Calvin Klein looks unopiated, wrought, stretched and ironed. Fran Lebowitz looks like Oscar Wilde as a runway model showing the best new Burberry reinvent yourself clobber. Sandra Bernhard, we later learn, is one of those single mothers. She makes me uncomfortable in the same way as Mickey Rourke when he knew his nine-and-a-half weeks were up. Come back, Robby Benson, all is forgiven. You were right to play a true soul. As I slip backstage in happy anonymity Ron and I lose each other, and when he finds his way to us, I am pleased to introduce him to Keith and Anita's son, Marlon. Ron is as charmed with Marlon's togetherness as I have been. For above any bias I have for his dad, the son holds up. Ron wonders how much Marlon's friend paid for his flare-trousered, nipped waist, high double-vented denim suit in today's dollars and I suggest he get a life. I look at Marianne over the wall of smoke and shoulders. I wait my turn and reflect: for those on the left side of fifty she is certainly more an artifact than a star, having had her way with most of the Rolling Stones, misbehaved repeatedly on powdered drugs, attempted suicide at the worst possible moment (from Mick's pov), and even been accused, undeservedly, of serving nothing but Mars bars at drug-crazed orgies. The fact is that between August of 1964 and the autumn of 1965, a year before she settled into a domesticity with 'child-bearing lips' so deadly that drugorama was soon required, our girl had four Top 10 singles and was grafting up there with all the lads where she belonged.

It's my turn; we embrace. I play Harrison Ford to her Meryl Streep and Ron plays Sydney Pollack at a discreet distance with the steadicam. I tell her off about handing her health and control to the audience and she promises she won't repeat this tack. In the backstage flurry Marianne needs to be reminded who Tony Russo is. I tell her, 'Just a guy who saved your life.' Backstage is just that, so we leave after a close up and long shot and promise to do it again away from the spotlight – and we must. Ron and I head out of the stage door taking a right towards a nearly silent Park Avenue, enjoying what few 'round midnight sounds there are. Before we make off, a carrier-bagged fan with Son of Sam eyes asks Ron imploringly, 'Didn't I meet you with the Grateful Dead?' Then he asks what is really on his mind, 'Has

Marianne left the building yet?' I smile at Marianne's faithful serial killer and say, 'No, Sam. She's only recently moved in.'

*

I met him at the candy store, he turned around, you get the picture? He was RJ and I met him in Glens Falls, where I was spending a few post-Faithfull days getting my nutritional reading from Fred Ulan and Lester Bryman. Once RJ had assured himself I was not about *Gods and Monsters* and not asking him to be Brendan Fraser to Sir Ian McKellan's James Wale he sat down at my table and gave of himself. Actually, he was blunter than my filmic descriptive mode of retelling. RJ just came right out with, 'You're not a fag, are you?' and assured me he was not gay. After all this time, this is an allowed – my zoning in on quality goods. I do have an eye and vocation for a depth-of-field-attractive out-flow. It is a calling. If I had not found Mick Jagger, Marianne Faithfull and sundry others attractive the public may not have been given the same opportunity. Mick and Marianne still share the fact that one was and the other remains a twat, and that one has made a life and recovered from the fact that I found them and saw 'it', and the other has not. But – buyer beware – they remain artists. I did inherit this gift from those I idolised: I was careful about what I wanted and I got it and made it work. I idolised on cue. I savoured their gifts from the distance. Diaghilev, Jimmy Woolf, Johnny Jackson – I sensed I came from the same genetic code. I look in the mirror now and am glad I am at one with myself. Mick Jagger should be happy for the same. The gift does not leave you; if you are lucky it even smiles with time. RJ is RJ reincarnate fifty years down the game, except with the saving grace that he's never heard of Robert Wagner and just barely of Natalie Wood. He wears eyeglasses that belie the toughness and he has yet to leave New York State, but, boy, does he have dreams and vision. I clean my window fames and listen to this 21st Century hip-hop fox. He could have been a criminal except that Jim Morrison came into his life and rendered him unto the manner born. He had 'Tutti Frutti' rearin' parents, backbone/backdrop to beauty getting a beat.

I'd always had a loathing for groups that relied on sustained organ and keyboards, and thought it worse when they were featured as the star. I viewed the Doors with hostility and dismissal for different reasons – my fierce loyalty to the very and every idea of the Stones and the fact that I could smell the competition and all-powerful brain-fodder licking itself into street readiness around the corner in the being of Jim Morrison and crew. It was a sign that America was recovering from our invasion and from here on in the game was anybody's and we'd better be on our guard. It's a different time now. I can let my guard down and get edutained to a whole new way of life. Jim Morrison can still change a life in a way that Jagger, McCartney and even Lennon can barely do . . . unless you are an airport. The machine is the instrument of expression and we sit in my rented Jimmy and listen to RJ's poems and music. I feel like I've been touched by and am in the presence of a star, and I like it on your behalf – that is the nature of my game. Now, whether RJ becomes a household world in his near-future depends, in this day and age, not so much on finding an Andrew Loog Oldham, but on being one. That is the new state of the game.

I get to the West Coast and I drive. I lunch with Bob Crewe. I've now been cleared up long enough for us both to be able to laugh at it all and at ourselves and remain amazed about the power of the art. I put calls east to David Dalton and Nik Cohn; we talk about everything and nowt. I put down the phone and realise I've just been trying to suck some osmotic into being out of another writer. They both seemed to know it, so just how much has really changed? I drive along the Pacific Coast Highway in tune with right-wing radio and radio'd *Dragnet*. I am getting from this writing journey that which I did not expect. My first tome *Stoned* as catharsis? Bollocks. The pleasure is of once again being able to produce work and result. *2Stoned*, I'd have to say yes. I thought I knew what was to be on these pages, but I missed a lot of it by a mile. If *Stoned* was *Little Women*, *2Stoned* would be *In Cold Blood*. Those extra new layers of truth, happenence and possibility surfaced and demanded to be worded up. Thus far I had written up my overts against myself and humanity but not those committed against art, and that proved to be the hardest part. I talked to and gave thanks to the elegant ghost of Laurence Harvey as I walked and talked Malibu. I looked out for newly Malibu-inplanted Gary Oldman and found instead a beaming Starsky of *Starsky & Hutch*. I read manager Bernie Brillstein's autobiography *Where Did I Go Right?* about his thoughts on the unnatural act of being an act and how he did the gig for the emotional exchange. Both Larry and I agree, as Bernie sez, 'People who put on make-up for a living exist on mood, whim, impulse, and who knows what else? That's their great gift and their great weakness.'

*

I sit back in the black Explorer with Lou and Page Adler and watch our driver merge us with an endless convoy of similarly armoured SUVs with privacy-protection windows, an image that recalls the parade of bodyguards and jeeps outside my son's Bogotá school in the morning. A sea of cell-phoned lane-changing Outbacks, Jimmys, Wagoneers and Laredos, almost all either black or white, make the occasional powder-opaque lane-clad Charlie's Angel in a Mercedes SLK a welcome respite. In the main, the views from a California freeway resemble those passing through, say, Dallas or Sacramento; it would require the romantic vision of a Bacharach/David ditty to distinguish between the landscape of one 'San' city and another. Los Angeles is different. Its headlights are brighter and more driven, smoother and more ambitious – the better to get on with the night. I recall the lights of Bel-Air, and silently bless Lou for that last heartfelt embrace I'd shared with an ailing John Phillips, true Captain of American song, on the steps of the Waldorf one New York Hall of Fame eve in 1998.

Lou sits up front next to our Argentinian driver. He's wearing a zoot suit felt titfer atop his neat grey coif. Everything about Lou is neat. His weathered, grey-bearded face is handsome, the result of climate and control. He wears a lightweight raglan-sleeved brown plaid raincoat Ms Lebowitz would die for over a rich cable-knit grey/brown sweater, loose red boating trews, and red and white tennis shoes. I sit aback with Page. She wears beautifully – if she smoked I'd catch fire. Bogey's Bacall is alive and re-living in Malibu. I'm still in midnight-blue *Broken Arrow* mode with black Mephisto dusters, save I've exchanged the silk denim jacket for a zip-up Dacor navy-and-maroon-piped after-diving jacket. I pack more books than shoes when I travel now.

Tonight is the *raison d'être* of my American journey: we're off to see the three-minute wizard, Brian Wilson. Whether Brian has left Oz or is inviting us in is moot. I'm nervous. When *Pet Sounds* changed my musical road map in 1966, I was twenty-one years old and enjoying my second year at the top of the pop heap. The droogie tycoon who lived *A Clockwork Orange* by day needed the virtual sunshine of the Beach Boys in his room by night as audio solace for my fragmented, neglected personal life. The Beach Boys' response to being deposed by the British Invasion was breathtaking, and for an important while they kept those of us who were searching the hit horizon for new ground on our toes. Drugs and resentment of friends' success had not yet curdled creativity, and Brian Wilson in many ways set the sonic pace once Phil Spector had started dancing in space. *Rubber Soul* raised the bar in 1965 and the Beach Boys didn't even graze it as they soared ahead with *Pet Sounds*. Paul and John's experience with it spurred them to produce *Sergeant Pepper*. I manoeuvred the road movie from London to Hollywood that culminated in *Aftermath*. *Aftermath* – and that most English of Stones albums, *Between The Buttons* – were the first two to be written entirely by Mick and Keith, another indirect result of the shifts in power taking place between those who wrote the material and those who recorded it. In a sense, my mission with them had been accomplished, and so it was logical, if wrenching, that 1967 would signal the end of my run and the beginning of the Glimmer Twins' second. *Pet Sounds* changed my life for the better. It enhanced the drugs I was taking and made life eloquent and bearable during those times I set down in London and realised that I was barely on speaking terms with those who lived in my home and understood them even less when they spoke – that's when Brian Wilson spoke for me. My internal weather had been made better for the cost of just two sides of vinyl.

As you know, I met Brian Wilson for the first time in late 1965 at RCA studios on Sunset. The Stones and I were recording in studio A. Puissant marijuana may have enhanced Brian's inner dialogue but his communication skills that day could only be said to be impaired. He told me then that he would one day write songs that people would pray to. As far as I was concerned he was preaching to the choir; I already considered Brian to be a leading hymnist of our generation. He had by that time stopped touring with the Beach Boys and would soon fall off the edge of his flat planet into a valley of fear and suffering, hauling a pharaoh's stash of drugs and unwholesome food behind him into a Bel-Air cave and throwing away the key to now. With Brian out of town, the brothers Wilson did not fare well. The lively and addicted Dennis survived a brush with Charles Manson but drowned in 1983. Finally, brother Carl fell to cancer in 1998. The irony that he had survived his brothers, against all odds and most bets, could not have escaped Brian. This left Mike Love to helm the Beach Boys by default. An oafish entertainer even in his prime, Mike in middle age, bereft of hair and manners, was a disturbing sight, a power-mad maitre d' who exploited the contrived camaraderie of arena singalongs to bring back that long-gone lovin' feeling of endless summer and fun. Brian started the long trek back to reality via the controversial and expensive methods of Dr Eugene Landy. Say what you will – and everybody did – he got Brian up from his deathbed and worked him down from obscene obesity to a publicly presentable figure. I met Brian again in 1993 during Landy-time at a restaurant in Santa Monica for a sitdown arranged by Andy Paley. At the time I was suffering from my own bout of dementia, trying to regroup while a few fries short of a happy meal.

Brian arrived with two 'health bodyguards' who allowed him out of the restaurant every half-hour for a Marlboro. I was not yet into survival so I used the interval to sniff a line of my favourite digestive in the loo. Brian was getting up from the mat but was still behind the count; he had not got all his ball-bearings back, although he was looking strong and once more like a Beach Boy. We chatted about London as if I still lived there and Brian remembered it. There was no point in me having him connect the state of my nose with my adopted nation of Colombia; it would have been a disservice to my country and disturbed the warmth of our chat. We talked about Dennis, of whom I was very fond, and a lawyer we had all shared, of whom we were not. We talked about music and long-lost recordings – it was clear that whatever he had at that moment Dr Landy was treating it. At the end of the meal Brian asked for the bill and struggled with it as if trying to work out how to sign it. I asked him if he'd like me to sign it for him. For the first time Brian answered in present time and not on a ten-second delay.

'No, too many people have done that for me in my life.'

In the parking lot his attendants whisked him into a black Mercedes and back towards Malibu. An attractive Beverly Hills matron with a freckle-chested pearl-bedecked resemblance to Grace Kelly's mother (as acted by Jesse Royce Landis) in *To Catch a Thief* squeezed my arm and asked if that had not been Brian Wilson the Beach Boy.

'Yes, Ma'am,' I Elvis'd.

'Well,' Jesse Royce gasped. 'How nice to see him out for dinner and looking so very well.'

Back in the present States, the sixty-piece orchestra tunes up on the Hollywood Bowl stage as Lou, Page and I slip into our booth a split second before showtime and order coffee. Longtime collaborator and fellow loon Van Dyke Parks waltzes on stage to conduct a twenty-minute suite of Beach Boys classics by way of an overture. His white dinner jacket over leather jeans brings the Buddy Ebsen of *Beverly Hillbillies* to mind. Clearly I need to choose my expectations, and fashion is not a choice this evening. Our waitress enjoys telling us we'll have to wait 'til intermission for our coffee a bit too much; I put away my Zen-or-otherwise baseball bat and let it be while thinking, 'Fuck you!'

Could it be that Mr Parks has forgotten that 'God Only Knows' and 'Nights In White Satin' are not interchangeable? The music is tired and awful and reminds me of a handful of 60s *Sound of Music* nightmares that caused me to retch and leave the London stalls. I feel Julie Andrews winking at me from somewhere over a Hollywood rainbow of evening sky-blues, green palms and golden tans and I catch her patting her Aryan skirt into place and mouthing, 'Fuck you, too.'

The well-to-do bloated and embalmed season ticket holders appear to swallow Van Dyke's shtick whole, happy to relate to their adolescence via this schlock muzak rendition. There is not much reaction from the reasonably priced seats. Just as I'm having second thoughts about splicing this night into my dailies, Brian Wilson saunters on to the stage, waves and grins sheepishly at us. Then he sits himself down behind an electric piano that he never once plays. A guitarist/vocalist is on hand as a sort of EMT nurse to double for Brian in case he falls out and forgets . . .

The first half of the show, the fifty-eight-year-old Brian is backed by a ten-piece ensemble of which Los Angeles pop band the Wondermints form the core. The music is competent but not much more. Wilson is sluggish and displays idiosyncratic mannerisms that are uncomfortably a tweedly-dee away from the cuckoo's nest. On occasion he watches his feet swing as if above the fabled sandbox he sat in for much of the 70s. Is dementia always so very close to our daily reality, I wonder, or is it just brother to recovery? We try to assimilate the realisation that Brian has always been both very, very young and very, very old, and to succeed with that as a core identity in middle age would have required him to transform himself into Robin Williams at some point twenty years ago.

A hit is always a hit unless we stop believing, 'Wendy', so we surrender to Peter Pan when he gives us 12,000 visitors to the Emerald Kingdom. 'Darlin'' rocks with gait, stride and venom, the band happy to get it on. They nail it and we all cheer and offer up the other wrist in search of another bleedin' rocked-up song. I had been wondering if my epiphany for the evening would be an insight into how hard it is to write a gold record on a theme of 'Rhonda' until the strident 'Darlin'' came on stomping and strong. It also occurred to me that in an odd way all the young dudes had made a kind of martyr of brother Brian years ago. He was the universal wuzz who filled a void left by Pat Boone and Bing Crosby. He also happened to write some of the most achingly poignant poems about the hearts of very young people.

We get our coffee, do our own version of some air-kissing with the neighbours, and pretty soon Brian slips back on stage like he's hoping we won't notice he's back yet. He's in one of those very expensive pyjama suits older R 'n' B stars wear to awards shows. I'm still nervous – I am not the kind of guy who enjoys videos of the vandalisation of *Guernica* – and soon *Pet Sounds* itself will be at the mercy of the mad genius who birthed it. Brian is alarmingly pallid, tense and sweaty. I have no idea what his medication regimen might or might not be but it occurs to me that I am watching a body so used to being propped up in various places by potentially toxic prescriptions that he could have been clean for years and yet on the verge of a stroke. Fortunately for us, Brian is more at one with his art than his body, and rises to the level of his greatest achievement. Before the evening is over we will have remembered that one of the hardest virtues for a teen to express is compassion, and we'll be grateful once more to St Brian for taking up the cross, speaking for us, abiding our sufferings, and allowing the rest of us the illusion that we were tough. His voice is mostly on and magnificent, catching nearly every nuance and slide of the original inspired performance. When Brian announces 'side two-cut one' we are back in a world before random access and fibre optics, when science fiction was a gallon of gas that cost a dollar and guys and girls had crashing waves and cool convertibles to help them handle their hormones. We all inwardly swear allegiance to analog if not to mono, and remember how much bigger the music always was than the

Brian Wilson we saw on TV or on stage. The dynamics of orchestra and rock band are heavenly and sure; I'm not sure what is going on in Bogotá or on the Gaza strip, but in Hollywood it's a perfect night. Lou Adler reminds me that Brian is doing the vinyl version. This is where we all came in. Brian Wilson was the voice in the teenage dark when we got laid for the first time, fell in love, got confused and hurt. Brian Wilson gave us space to repair ourselves and grow from boys to men. This is an awesome task for an artist. It crippled Brian and prevented him from growing into himself. The burden of speaking for so many drove him out of the sun he shared so generously and into the dark. I'm glad he finally got so lonely in his shallow grave that he had to work his way back to the surface. It was a pleasure to attend a faith gathering with him after all this time in the shade.

Two days later I hire a white flatbed truck from Malibu Budget Rental and point it down the Pacific Coast Highway to San Diego. I am driven to discover how well Brian does in back-to-back games, but, ever the optimist, I look for a reprise of the Hollywood Bowl love-in. It is the last stop of his summer tour and I want it to be mine as well. I've packed up my laptop, said goodbye to the *Last Tycoon* suite Lou Adler lent me.

I settle on to the Long Beach Freeway and put the truck on cruise control.

I look back towards LA and out at the Pacific Ocean.

I put a Beach Boys CD into the player and my forearm into the sun. I am driving towards San Diego in search of one more vibrantly hopeful chorus of 'God Only Knows'. As my Chevy passes John Wayne Airport in Orange County, I salute like a Yankee Doodle Dandy. I titter to myself and remember reading that Anthony Hopkins enjoys rental car anonymity when he drives alone, off-duty. I bless Esther for showing me how I could be. I smile – I more than laugh – at having been able to go full circle and be back where this journey began – with America, the dream and the music. My amusement raises the image of Hopkins' Hannibal Lecter, still insatiable as the credits roll at the end of *Silence of the Lambs*, Panama-hatted and off in search of the next meal, as am I, though I merely require my meal to be sung.

'Only in America,' says I, and sing along to 'The Warmth Of The Sun'.

# · ACKNOWLEDGEMENTS ·

In order for there to be a continuum from my first book, *Stoned*, there may be some familiarity with the material for those who have read it. Both my books, but especially *2Stoned*, allowed me an intense retrospection that had me get back in true contact with my work, to receive pleasure from my work, and bring closure to the time and my work. Thanks to Steve Martin I'm able to repeat the phrase 'my work' three times in one sentence. I owe a big productive debt to Stuart Williams at Secker & Warburg for saying 'yes' to the work and providing an overview to the process that divined art and craft and all their second meanings. The state of play was akin to the primocadaver of the work the book attempts to describe, therefore there can be no higher praise. Smoke and goo is due David Milner who was my editor at Secker & Warburg for *Stoned* where he opened the doors to my writing efforts. By *2Stoned* he'd left Random House and become an agent – mine and a score of other pageburners'. I'm a tad concerned about completing my triography in case that prompts David to become a lawyer.

The sixties I write of, and my own particular aftermath, were both a shared and isolationary time. There remain three sides to every story: yours, mine, and the truth, and I thank the following for lending their voices and/or written words to give shine and truth to the time and story: Lou Adler / Herb Alpert / Keith Altham / Pete Anderson / Al Aronowitz / David Bailey / Richard Barnes / Toni Basil / Pete Bennett / Dave Berry / Stan Blackbourne / Tony Boland / Dan Bourgoise / Jerry Brandt / Denny Bruce / Anthony Burgess / Tito Burns / Tony Calder / Phil Chapman / George Chiantz / Nik Cohn / Bob Crewe / Dan Crewe / Dan Daley / David Dalton / Cynthia Stewart Dillane / Donovan / John Douglas / Marianne Faithfull / Bryan Forbes / Kim Fowley / Fred Frank / George Gallacher / Pat Gilbert / Roberta Goldstein / Fred Goodman / Gruff / Robin Guild / Nona Hendryx / Chris Hutchins / Steve Inglis / Derek Johnson / John Paul Jones / Pete Kameron / Tom King / Tony King / Maurice Kinn / Allen Klein / Al Kooper / Harvey Kubernik / Linda Lawrence Leitch / Michael Lindsay-Hogg / Art Linson / Gered Mankowitz / Sid Maurer / Alan McGhee / Roger McGuinn / Richard Meltzer / Ken Mewis / Adrian Millar / Harry M. Miller / Roy Moseley / Mickie Most / Paul Mozian / Peter Noone / Christine Ohlman / Sheila Klein Oldham / Sean O'Mahony / Nick O'Teene / Brian Papageorge / James Phelge / Cynthia Plaster Caster / Tim Rice / Mick Rock / Steve Rosenthal / Al

Schmitt / Rock Scully / Gordon Spittle / Chris Stamp / Seymour Stein / Shel Talmy / Pauline Thomas / David Thomson / Philip Townsend / Pete Townshend / Gregory Phillips / Vashti / Brian Wilson / Mike Watkinson / David Sinclair Whitaker / Peter Whitehead / Bill Wyman and Mark Wynter.

Simon Spence conducted the interviews and gathered the research upon which both *Stoned* and *2Stoned* were founded. Simon made my life and times his agenda whilst I was losing the first and pissing on the second and for that I say thank you. Many books influenced the process and provided data. I have to single out *Stone Alone* by Bill Wyman with Ray Coleman as being the guvnor on where and when. Additional interviews were conducted by or adapted from existing work by David Dalton, Mathew Greenwald, Dave Thompson, Pat Gilbert, Richard Barnes, Scott Woods, Ron Ross, Martin Wilkinson and Harvey Kubernik and finally I had something to mix. In countless books and essays David Dalton is a pioneer on the wording of our music and the lengths we all went to to get it. He charmed me into examining my life to an extent that was more than I'd been prepared for and in doing so helped me take you there in whatever way I have. His first edit billowed of his love of the times and the players and embraced me further into the true. For many years I have admired Christine Ohlman as a writer and singer and the recorded results of her work with Doc Cavalier. I got the opportunity to enjoy the foundation of that work when Christine came on board to do the final edit. We became both bounty and hunter with edit or die our daily biscuit. She was as lethal as we had to be and together we dragged the book out of the studio and on to the radio. I thank her for her knowledge, skill, affinity and guillotine. Further thanks go to Lou Adler and Doc Cavalier to whom I sent fledgling pages and stranded versions in the hope of getting that injection of forward motion they both so professionally and caringly gave.

Finally this work is dedicated to Laurence Harvey, Eddie Cochran, Jack Good, Johnny Otis, Phil Spector and the Rolling Stones. Mr. Harvey for that first intoxicating prepubescent rub and shine against the wonderful world I would embrace and belong to; Eddie Cochran and Jack Good for the sound, vision and hope on a teenage Saturday night; Johnny Otis for the first time I remember hearing *it* on the radio; Mr Phil Spector for changing the rules of our game and developing it to a level I could play in – and Mick, Keith, Brian, Bill and Charlie, the Rolling Stones, for providing the game and way of life.

The author and publishers are grateful to the following for permission to reproduce illustrative material which appears on the pages indicated. Photographs on pages other than those listed below are from the Andrew Loog Oldham Collection or are of unknown origin. Information regarding copyright holders or copyright material will be gratefully received by the publishers, and any errors rectified in future editions.

348, Dennis Hopper; 95, 149, 196, 210, 221, 246, 251, 281, 286, 297, 332, 370, Gered Mankowitz; 343, *New Musical Express*; 312, Neal Preston / Corbis; 453, Neal Preston; 170, Eddie Reed; 446, Ebet Roberts / Redferns Music Picture Library; 417, 424, Mick Rock; 104, Tom Smith / Camera Press Ltd; 46, Harriet Wasser

Grateful acknowledgement is made to those listed below for permission to reproduce text from the following publications:
*You've Had Your Time* by Anthony Burgess, reproduced by permission of The Random House Group; *Awopbopaloobop Awopbamboom* by Nik Cohn, reproduced by permission of Grove Press; *Pop From The Beginning* by Nik Cohn, reproduced by permission of Weidenfeld & Nicolson; *Faithfull* by Marianne Faithfull with David Dalton, 1994, reproduced by permission of Penguin Press Ltd; *A Divided Life* by Bryan Forbes, 1992, reproduced with permission of Curtis Brown Ltd, London, on behalf of Bryan Forbes, copyright © Bryan Forbes; *The Mansion on the Hill* by Fred Goodman, published by Jonathan Cape, reprinted by permission of the Random House Group Ltd; *David Geffen: the Operator* by Tom King, reproduced by permission of Broadway Books; *Phelge's Stones* by James Phelge, reproduced by permission of Buncha Asshole Books; *The Early Stones* by Perry Richardson and Michael Cooper, reproduced by permission of Hyperion; *Living With The Dead* by Rock Scully and David Dalton, reproduced by permission of Cooper Square Publishers; *Scott Walker: A Deep Shade of Blue* © Mike Watkinson and Pete Anderson, 1993, Virgin Publishing Ltd; *Wouldn't It Be Nice* by Brian Wilson, with Todd Gold, 1992, Bloomsbury Publishing Plc; *Stone Alone* by Bill Wyman, reproduced by permission of Penguin Putnam Inc.

# · INDEX ·

Figures in **bold** type are 'voices'; figures in *italics* refer to illustrations

**463**